DEITIES AND DOLPHINS

The story of the Nabataeans

DEITIES AND DOLPHINS

by Nelson Glueck

Hebrew Union College-Jewish Institute of Religion

NEW YORK *Farrar, Straus and Giroux*

FRONTISPIECE: *Head of a broken Nabataean pottery figurine from Petra, with right hand touching beard. It is similar to some stone sculptures in high relief from Nabataean Khirbet Tannur, which reveal strong Orientalizing influences. (See Pls. 42, 129, 127, 128, and pp. 195, 197, 183)*

Courtesy Paul Gotch, Director British Council, Shiraz, Iran. Photographer, F. vanHouten Raymond

CONTENTS

LIST OF MAPS

Introduction

A stone sculpture in high relief of the bust of a goddess with a tiara of two dolphins on her head was found among the ruins of the Nabataean hilltop temple of Khirbet Tannur. The site is located on the south slope of the great canyon of the Wadi Hesa (Biblical River Zered), whose perennial stream empties into the southeast end of the Dead Sea. Uncovered in the excavations of the temple were nearly all the members of the pantheon of deities once worshiped there. The explanation of the appearance of dolphins in stone on dry land at the edge of the Arabian desert and of the role played by the Atargatis they adorned and of the company she kept in the sacred precincts of a most unusual sanctuary has been attempted in this book. *Deities and Dolphins* seems thus to us to be a fitting and accurate title.

The subtitle, *The Story of the Nabataeans,* indicates that the objects, decorations, plan and place of Khirbet Tannur cannot be discussed even in relative depth without dealing with the history, economy, art, architecture, languages and religion of the Nabataeans and their relationship to Arabia and the Fertile Crescent on the one hand and the Mediterranean littoral on the other. The rapid rise and precipitate fall of the Nabataeans were largely determined by geopolitical factors beyond their control. The forces that affected the prior development and then the destruction of Israel, Judah, Edom and Moab, among others, in the center of the heartland of the world were essentially the same ones conditioning the burgeoning fortunes and the final ignominious fate of Nabataea.

Romantically considered especially since the nineteenth century of our era because of the rediscovery then of their extraordinarily beautiful former capital of Petra in southern Transjordan, the Nabataeans are beginning more realistically to be known because of the nature and extent of their kingdom, the uniqueness of their pottery, the international ramifications of their widespread commerce, the high excellence of their agriculture, soil conservation and water engineering and the Hellenistic-Semitic character of their art, architecture, religion and general culture.

This long overdue account is based primarily on the results of the excavations of Khirbet Tannur by the joint expedition of the American School of Oriental Research, Jerusalem, and the Department of Antiquities, Palestine, in March, April and December, 1937, under my direction. It incorporates also the conclusions reached from the discovery of some half a thousand and more hitherto unknown Nabataean sites in southern Transjordan, the Wadi Arabah, the Negev and parts of Sinai in my archaeological surveys during 1932-47 and 1952-63 of over fifteen hundred sites. The related explorations and excavations by others in these areas as well as in the Arabian and Syrian parts of Nabataea have naturally also been studied in this effort to reconstruct the nature, color and spirit of the Nabataean past. Exact references to these as well as to other relevant materials from many sources will be found in the *Notes*.

In order to reduce the number of the *Notes,* the contents of various articles and books of mine dealing with the subject matter have been incorporated in one form or another in this volume usually without specific references to the publications in which they are contained. They include articles in the *Bulletin of the American Schools of Oriental Research, The Biblical Archaeologist,* the *American Journal of Archaeology,* the *Hebrew Union College Annual,* the *Journal of the American Oriental Society, The Illustrated London News, The National Geographic;* sections in *Explorations in Eastern Palestine* I-IV, published between 1934 and 1951 in volumes XIV, XV, XVIII-XIX, XXV-XXVIII of the *Annual of the American Schools of Oriental Research,* and chapters in *The Other Side of the Jordan* (1940), *The River Jordan* (1946), *Rivers in the Desert* (1959).

One half of the archaeological objects secured from the excavations of Khirbet Tannur are stored in The Jordan Archaeological Museum of the Hashemite Kingdom of Jordan in Amman. The American share of the division of the finds is on display in the Cincinnati Art Museum. Photographs of most of them are published in this book, as well as many others from various sources. I am grateful to many individuals and institutions for making them available, as well as for the permission, when necessary, to publish them. Specific acknowledgements are made in the *List of Plates.* The assistance of members of the staff of Farrar, Straus and Giroux, Inc. is deeply appreciated.

I am grateful to Sir Gerald Lankester Harding, formerly Director of the Department of Antiquities of the Hashemite Kingdom of Jordan, for the token grant to our expedition, which his Department co-sponsored, and particularly for his deep interest and active participation in the excavations whenever his official duties permitted, as well as for the help rendered by his assistant, Hasan Awad. I am especially indebted to him for sending me in 1951 photographs by Richmond Brown of Khirbet Tannur sculptures found in private possession, removed from the site before our excavations there began. My deepest thanks to Sir Alexander Kirkbride, then the British Resident in Transjordan, for his unfailing helpfulness and encouragement in all of my archaeological work in Transjordan, and also to Brigadier John Bagot Glubb (el-Farik Glubb Pasha), then Officer Commanding the Arab Legion, for his personal interest as well as for the assistance rendered by the Arab Legion. The very generous support of the late Messrs. Louis Rabinowitz and David W. Klau made possible my archaeological exploration of the Negev, resulting in much new light being cast upon the westward extension of the Nabataean kingdom.

Mrs. E. Philip Vogel, my Archaeological Assistant, has rendered invaluable aid in the preparation of this book. She has also prepared the Indices, done the basic work on the maps, and, together with Mr. Brooks Holtzclaw and several other Hebrew Union College graduate students, helped to check references. Mesdames Leon Alex, Lionel Staples and Edwin Grusd have rendered valuable assistance in typing the manuscript. The encouragement and support of my great teacher and mentor, Professor William F. Albright, then President of the American Schools of Oriental Research, and of the officers and members of its Board of Trustees, and of beloved Professor Julian Morgenstern, then President of the Hebrew Union College, and of its Board of Governors, who gave me long leaves-of-absence to serve as Director of the American School of Oriental Research, Jerusalem, during three different periods of years when much of my archaeological work dealt with in this book was accomplished, cannot be too warmly acknowledged. I am grateful to Mrs. Herman Shapiro for her drawings of the el-Bared murals Pls. 203b, 204b, and to Mr. Lawrence Kushner for his sketches Pls. 5b, 155b, 156b. Mr. F. van Houten Raymond has given countless hours to photographic work in reproducing and enlarging illustrations for study and publication. Mr. Alfred Bernheim is responsible for the coin photographs on Pls. 58-62.

The devotion of the members of the field staff during the periods of excavation of Khirbet Tannur, under difficult physical conditions, made the work possible. I mention with profound gratitude Messrs. Carl Pape, draughtsman, S. J. Schweig, photographer, who is responsible for all the photographs unless otherwise indicated, L. H. Wood, then a fellow of the ASOR, Jerusalem, and above all the late Dr. Clarence S. Fisher, then Professor of Archaeology at the American School of Oriental Research, Jerusalem, who served as the architect. His untimely death prevented him from writing the chapter on the architecture of Khirbet Tannur that would have been incorporated in this book. The plans and reconstructions published in it are completely his. I have had the benefit of some of his notes and of countless conversations with him during and after the excavations of Khirbet Tannur.

Professor Fisher was a great archaeological architect and archaeologist and all who came into contact with him learned much from him. His Opus Magnum, the *Corpus of Palestinian Pottery,* never completed because of his death, was a rich source of instruction to those permitted to study his plates of pottery drawings and to listen to him expounding on his work in progress. His contributions to Palestinian archaeology are of profound importance. He was an inspiring teacher to those eager to learn, a sensitive, modest, gifted scholar, generous to a fault, the fatherly friend of orphans and the underprivileged. I dedicate this book to his memory.

NELSON GLUECK

Hebrew Union College Biblical and Archaeological School,
Jerusalem, Israel, March 26, 1964

DEITIES AND DOLPHINS

I. THEY BEGAN AS BEDOUINS

1. *They Began as Bedouins*

1. FIRST APPEARANCE

The mystery that once shrouded the past of the Nabataeans has been much modified in modern times by numerous and rich archaeological discoveries. Arabia seems to have been the cradle of their beginnings, and its transit trade an enduring factor in their ephemeral success. Impelled by the hunger driving all nomads and seminomads to engulf lands less lean than their own whenever possible, they infiltrated and settled in Biblical Edom and Moab, which had been conquered by Babylonia and stripped of the power making their desert borders bedouin-tight. The newcomers also seized control of other regions from southern Syria to western Sinai, where too they made themselves very much at home. The disturbances attendant upon the downfall of Babylonia and the emergence of Persia as the supreme power of the ancient Near East did their cause no harm. Indeed, they took brilliant advantage of the resulting shock waves of change and chance till they themselves crashed on the rock of Roman imperium.

The Nabataeans were long considered to be little more than nomads, who dominated travel-routes and caravan traffic between Arabia and Parthia and the countries bordering the eastern Mediterranean. It appears now, however, that they were one of the most gifted peoples of history. They quickly achieved a highly advanced civilization based on agriculture and commerce, as scintillating as it was brief. Their rise to high estate from nomadic and seminomadic origins was fairly fast, but their eclipse as a separate people was precipitate. Weaknesses arising from upheavals of empires afforded them opportunities of development which they were quick to exploit and expand. The growth of their kingdom was limited only by mighty Rome. Nabataea was finally erased practically by Roman decree.

The earliest backgrounds of the Nabataeans are still obscure, but it is clear that they progressed rapidly from the severe abstinence and puritanism of desert necessity and ideals to the gladsome appreciation of wine and to the widespread use of sculptured forms of gods and men and beasts and fruits of all kinds.

It would seem that the origins of the Nabataeans may be traced back to southern Arabia. Some of them and perhaps many of them must have been familiar with its advanced art, architecture and agriculture, highly developed for centuries before their appearance above the horizon of the unknown. They learned much from the Edomites and the Moabites whom they were to displace or absorb, but their previous background cannot be accounted as a *tabula rasa*, even though extant literature assigns it to the simplest nomadic estate. During their entire period of upsurge, their very active trade in incense and spices must have kept them in close contact with the sophisticated South Arabian civilization.[1]

Even when Greek crowded Aramaic in their speech and letters and "Philhellene" became a designation and characteristic of some of their kings, and excursions to Rome a frequent occurrence, nomads and seminomads continued to be included among their number. The Nabayot of the Bible (Genesis 25:13; 28:9; 36:3), who were connected with Esau (Edom) may not, however, properly be equated with the Nabataeans, despite the superficial similarity of names. Nor, for that matter, can the Nabaiataeans of Arabia, against whom the Assyrian king, Ashurbanipal (668-633) waged ruthless war, be considered their early predecessors.[2]

It is from the Greek historian, Diodorus Siculus, who traveled in Egypt during 60-57 B.C. and also lived in Rome for several years, that we get our first, definitive information about the Nabataeans.[3] He pictures them as nomads who already then trafficked in the exotic products of Arabia and Africa and India, but who at first did not engage at all in agriculture. On the contrary, in the beginning, according to him, they seem to have abhorred the cultivation of the soil and the use of wine and to have made a virtue of living in tents and not constructing permanent houses of stone. In this regard they could have been the physical descendants of the abstemious Rechabites, whose entire way of life and religious orientation may have exercised a direct and profound effect upon the philosophy of the Essenes. The thinking of the Essenes has with reason been connected with the contents of some of the Dead Sea Scrolls.

At the beginning of the Christian era, however, the Greek geographer, Strabo, was able correctly to describe the Nabataeans not only as being devoted to trade, but also as dwelling in stone houses and engaging intensively in agriculture throughout their entire kingdom. Archaeological evidence indicates furthermore that the earlier ban on wine was not only ignored by them, but that wine had assumed a significant role in their religious ritual. The grape and vine motif became one of the most commonly employed in Nabataean sculpture and painting. During the approximately four hundred years of their finest period, between the second century B.C. and the second century A.D., the Nabataeans developed into tillers of the soil without peer among their contemporaries or predecessors. Their equals in agricultural skills and in some respects their superiors existed later on only among the Byzantines, into whose ranks they were ultimately to be assimilated. Although their singularity became effaced and their paganism blotted out, their influence survived their disappearance.

2. A RECORD OF ACCOMPLISHMENT

The Nabataeans made much out of little in the lands of their origin and adoption. Theirs was a record of remarkable accomplishment, extending from commerce to agriculture and from engineering to architecture and art. They carved entire cities out of mountains when necessary and performed prodigious feats of imaginative farming. In the course of bending even deserts to their fruitful use, they learned to improve greatly upon the techniques of soil-and-water conservation acquired from inhabitants of territories they overran. Nabataeanized Edomites and Moabites in southern Transjordan, as well as descendants of Kenites and Rechabites who never forsook the Negev, and perhaps also natives of southern Syria, contributed to their knowledge. South Arabian agricultural techniques, with which many of them must have been familiar, also stood them in good stead.

Only an immensely able people could look at blistering wastelands, such as occur in the Wadi Arabah and the Negev of southern Israel, for instance, and envision in them productive farms and burgeoning flocks and flourishing villages connected by thronged roads, and then perform the miracle of translating such dreams into living reality, as the Nabataeans did. They sought out the scarce rainwater of the brief rainy seasons with the diligence of gold hunters, diverting it from barren hillsides, forcing it to percolate and remain in suspension in the wayward earth held firmly in position behind innumerable stone terraces, storing it in countless cisterns and reservoirs and behind occasional dams and leading it at times over long aqueducts to points of convenience (Pls. 210-214, 215b).

Quick to learn and eager for advancement, the Nabataeans readily assimilated in new environments whatever might promote their well-being. Many and diverse cultural influences were reflected in altered form through the prism of their genius. The unmistakable imprint of their handiwork can, however, be discerned in almost all of their works. Appreciative of the blessings of nature, they were sensitive to beauty and strove to incorporate it in their buildings and pottery. They loved bright hues. Painting their stuccoed houses (Pls. 202-205) and temples particularly with flashing reds and blues and gleaming whites, their villages must have stood out as patches of brilliant color even among the drabbest surroundings. The high good humor of the Nabataeans and their zest for life are revealed in such excellent, naturalistic murals as those at el-Bared near Petra. Robustly portrayed in them are arrow shooting, flute playing, goose clasping, winged figures of ancient mythology, set in intricate bowers of flowering vines, among which flit or rest birds of bright plumage (Pls. 203, 204).

3. THE ELOQUENCE OF POTTERY

Much about the nature and extent of the Nabataean kingdom can be learned from the character and spread of the absolutely unique Nabataean pottery. Only a deeply rooted, permanently settled people of advanced cultural and economic attainments could have produced it. Much of this wheel-turned, kiln-baked ware was almost unbelievably thin, requiring high skills in its manufacture. It was beautifully decorated with sophisticated designs mainly of branches and leaves and fruits. Delicate rouletting was also a common form of ornamentation, and sigillata of Pergamene type was manufactured too. Lamps adorned with heads of deities and figurines (Pl. 81)[3a] of many kinds were formed in molds before being fired together with wheel-turned vessels in numerous kilns (Pls. 66-68, 74-80). One of these kilns has been found at Abda in the Negev [3b] and another is probably located at Bir Madhkur in the Wadi Arabah, and others undoubtedly will be discovered elsewhere. At such potteries, carefully selected and levigated clays were shaped and fired into enduring vessels, bearing the stamp of Nabataean artistry. The finest and thinnest of Nabataean painted pottery was found underneath the paved floor of the central altar-shrine of Khirbet Tannur and would seem therefore to have to be dated to no later than the end of the first century B.C.

I have found at literally hundreds of sites eloquent fragments of these fragile wares that have retained their unmistakable identity over twenty centuries of turbulent history. They occur among ruins extending from desert stations bordering Arabia to those of villages, urban centers and individual homesteads in the southern Transjordan, Wadi Arabah, Negev and Sinai parts of the Nabataean kingdom. They might be found in Arabia too if archaeological exploration could be carried out there in appropriate areas.

Not so, however, in the Jebel Druze region of southern Syria and northernmost Transjordan, even though they too were under Nabataean rule, as evidenced particularly by remains of temples, sculptures and inscriptions. The Nabataeans seemed to have occupied this part of their kingdom in insufficient numbers to warrant manufacturing or even importing their strikingly unique and beautiful pottery, and made use of local wares. They functioned there, it seems, more as colonial overlords than as permanent settlers in completely homogeneous communities, and apparently did not form the decisive majority of the native population.

Expressive bronzes indicate their metallurgical skills. They probably exploited the ancient copper mines in the Wadi Arabah, following the example of Solomon and some of his successors there, and others before his time going back at least as early as the Chalcolithic period in the fourth millennium B.C. The small bronze leopard (?) from Nabataean Abda has the same posture with uplifted paw as that of the griffin on the tiny dolphin altar there (Pl. 8a), of the griffins on Nabataean plaques at Petra (Pl. 167a, b) and of the feline of Araq el-Emir (Pl. 168).[3c] The diminutive bronze figure from Abda with the wings and claws of an eagle and the torso and head of a woman represents a siren,[3b] whose origins hail back to much earlier antiquity. A bronze Assyrian bird with a human female bust and head furnishes a striking analogy, for example.[3d] The hairdress and facial features of the Abda siren are like those of Nabataean goddesses at Khirbet Tannur and elsewhere.

4. NABATAEAN, ARAMAIC AND GREEK

Among the main ties binding the Nabataeans to other peoples in the vast cultural sphere extending westward from Parthia to the eastern shores of the Mediterranean and reaching from Asia Minor in the north to Egypt in the southwest was the widespread, strong and long lasting one of a common language. It was Aramaic. Current in several slightly differing dialects, it prevailed not only in all of this region but penetrated to distant places beyond it too. Some of the Book of Daniel and other parts of Sacred Scripture were composed in it, and much Aramaic is contained in the text of the Jerusalem and Babylonian versions of the Talmud. Jesus and all his fellow Jews spoke it from earliest childhood on, being even more familiar with it than Hebrew, which, however, they also mastered. Aramaic seems to have become the language of the Nabataeans by the time history became conscious of them as a separate people, shortly after the middle of the first millennium B.C. It replaced the proto-Arabic of their earliest years and was written in a script peculiarly their own.

Hundreds of their funerary and religious inscriptions have been found, most of them incised on rock (Pls. 194-199a, 207-209). One of them (Pl. 209b) reads: ". . . *lt* the son of *whbu*, peace." [3e] However, nothing is yet known of the Nabataean historical accounts and royal records, even if they may possibly have been lacking in the speculative or hortatory treatises contained in the contemporary religious documents of their Judaean neighbors. Nevertheless, the possibility exists that someone someday will stumble across a Nabataean library. This does not seem to be too far fetched in view of the discovery, for example, of a Nabataean business document not far from Qumran of the Dead Sea Scrolls fame, among the hills overlooking the northwest end of the Dead Sea. In one of the caves of the nearby Wadi Murabba'at was found a beautifully inscribed Nabataean papyrus of the first century A.D. It dealt with a land transaction between two Judaeans, who for some reason had summoned a professional Nabataean scribe to record it in the distinctive, cursive lettering of his native tongue.[4]

The hope of securing numerous additional Nabataean writings of economic, historical, diplomatic or even theological character has been heightened by the discovery somewhat farther north in the same deeply fissured, hardly habitable area, of a number of invaluable documents in Hebrew, Aramaic, Nabataean and Greek, contemporary with some of the Dead Sea Scrolls. They were found in one of the cliffside caves in the canyon of the Nahal Hever, located in the tattered crazyquilt of hills above Ain Gedi,[5] overlooking the middle of the west side of the Dead Sea.

Some Nabataean, Aramaic and Greek papyri, ranging in date from A.D. 93/94 to A.D. 132, were preserved there, together with fragments of the Book of Numbers and of the Psalms in Hebrew and a series of dispatches in Hebrew, Aramaic and Greek signed by Bar Kosibah (Bar Kochba).[6] He was the indomitable leader of the incredible Judaean revolt, A.D. 132-135, against the immense might of Rome. It was David against Goliath, but this time Goliath won. Three years were required, however, for the heavy handed legions of the Roman imperium to put out the fierce flames of rebellion. The Judaean revolutionaries holed up in their inaccessible aeries, to which entrance could be gained only by swaying rope-ladders, and they never yielded till death overcame their suicidal intransigence.

Among the Nahal Hever documents were some attesting to ownership of property in Nabataea by various Judaeans and particularly by a Judaean woman, Babata, and to claims for legal redress of various kinds filed by her in Nabataean courts. The Nahal Hever cave she fled to from Ain Gedi, sometime after the outbreak of the rebellion, became her sepulchre. The fragile papyri she carried with her, certifying her possession of property in Nabataea and authenticating the legal rights she hoped to preserve for herself and her son in a happier future, served to memorialize her name more enduringly than any monument might possibly have done.

The Nahal Hever documents in Nabataean, Aramaic and Greek, with the latter sometimes bearing summaries in Nabataean, Aramaic or both,[7] reveal the intimacy of commercial and cultural relationships enjoyed by the Judaeans and the Nabataeans in the period between the two hapless insurrections against Rome, the one that ended in A.D. 70 and the other that commenced in A.D. 132. In that interval of over half a century, Judaeans, particularly from Ain Gedi, prospered in Nabataea. They continued to own impressive properties there even after the Nabataean kingdom became incorporated into the Provincia Arabia in A.D. 106. Some of their lands were located at Zoar and Mezra'ah on the southeast side of the Dead Sea. One of the Nabataean papyri from the Nahal Hever, number 2, dated to the equivalent of November 19, A.D. 99, mentions the ownership by a Judaean named Shimon of a date palm grove in the vicinity of Zoar, bounded by a series of Nabataean owned gardens. One of these belonged to none other than the last of the Nabataean kings, Rabbel II (A.D. 70/71-106).[8]

Another of the Nahal Hever documents, number 19, dated to the equivalent of September 11, A.D. 130, deals with the sale of dates from apparently the same date palm grove, which had subsequently come into Babata's possession through inheritance, to a Judaean, named Shimon ben-Yeshu. Written in Greek by a third Judaean with the fascinating name of Germanus ben-Yehudah, it concluded with a summary in Nabataean, attested by Babata's representative, a Judaean with the name of Yohanon.[9] A Greek record from the Nahal Hever, number 27, written by the same Germanus ben-Yehudah, and dated to the equivalent of August 19, A.D. 132. shortly before the catastrophic rebellion began, had an Aramaic summary by a Judaean named Babli ben-Menahem. It confirms the receipt of a quarterly payment of rentals to the widowed Babata on behalf of her son.[10]

It is significant for the cultural interrelationship between Nabataeans and Judaeans to note that in the Greek document, number 14, from the Nahal Hever, dated to the equivalent of December 2, A.D. 127, Babata attests to the correctness of a listing of her land properties handed in to the eparch of Rabbath-Moab (modern er-Rabbah in East Jordan) in accordance with the requirements of a land census that had been ordered, by taking an oath in the name of the Tyché of the "Lord Caesar." [11]

The Roman conquest of Nabataea in A.D. 106 seems to have brought no change whatsoever, thus, in the relationship between Judaeans and Nabataeans and for a considerable period thereafter no perceptible deterioration in the Nabataean economy. To be sure, a Roman legate replaced the Nabataean king at Petra, but the Nabataean language, in addition to Greek and Aramaic, continued to be officially recognized and frequently employed for legal and administrative purposes. Many Judaeans were obviously completely conversant with the Nabataean language and script, which is not to be wondered at in view of its closeness to their own Aramaic. Both Nabataeans and Judaeans were familiar to a considerable degree with Greek and to some extent also with Latin.

Not only were numerous Judaeans very much at home in Nabataea both before and after it was made a part of the Roman Provincia Arabia in A.D. 106, but many Nabataeans must have been equally at home in Judaea and may well have owned property there, too. It would seem certain, for instance, that Jericho was frequented by Nabataeans, as must have been Ain Gedi,[12] among other sites. The perfume factories that existed at Ain Gedi in the times of the Judaean kings,[13] may have flourished there also in the Hasmonean, Herodian, Roman, Nabataean period. The Nabataeans must also have traded and many of them probably owned property and lived in nearby Judaean Peraea, through which Jesus journeyed, on the east side of the Jordan. Its southernmost hill fortress of Machaerus commanded the approaches to its southern border and the northern tip of the Nabataean territory beyond it, that touched the east side of the Dead Sea. There was also close contact obviously between the Nabataean Negev in southern Palestine and Herodian Judaea, directly north of it, with Nabataeanized and Judaized Idumaeans of Edomite origin living on both sides of the border and trafficking in the goods that passed through their territories on the roads to and from Egypt.

In this general connection it is worth noting that a whole series of Nabataean coins, minted during the reigns of some successive Nabataean kings, from Aretas IV to Rabbel II, spanning the years from 9 B.C. to A.D. 106, and covering much of the history of Khirbet Tannur, were found together with other coins, in the Wadi Murabba'at,[14] near Qumran. These coins bear no relationship however, to the various documents found in the Wadi Murabba'at, most of which, like many from the Nahal Hever cave, deal with the Second Judaean Revolt, A.D. 132-135.

Like the rest of their Aramaic speaking and writing contemporaries, the Nabataeans also made much use of Greek and to a lesser degree of Latin, representing respectively some of the forces by which they were at first enriched and then erased. The irresistible Hellenism of their era affected all the forms of their self-expression and was modified in turn by their own enduring Orientalism. Most of the gods and goddesses of their maturity seem at first glance to have been modeled completely after those of Greece, but closer examination reveals fundamental characteristics that are unquestionably Semitic.

The Nabataeans never ceased worshiping Hadad, the age-old thunder god of their background, even though he came gradually to be represented in the guise of Zeus. The very title of "Philhellene" which the Nabataean king, Aretas III, favored for himself gives eloquent evidence of the intensity of Hellenistic influence in his court and among his people. More popular and permanent, however, was the Semitic appellation of Nabataean rulers, *rahem ammu,* meaning "the loving protector of his people."

This latter title applied to Aretas I, who was called *hrtt mlk rhm amh,* "Haretat the King, Who loves His People." His second queen, frequently portrayed with him in twin profile jugate, was called *sqylt mlkt nbtw,* "Shaqilat, the Queen of the Nabataeans." The king after him, Malichus II, A.D. 40-70, was known as *mlkw mlk, mlk nbtw,* "Malichus the

King, King of the Nabataeans," and his queen, Shaqilat II, was called *sqylt 'hth, mlkt nbtw*, "Shaqilat, his Sister, Queen of the Nabataeans."

And so it went with their successors, whose titles, as long as their kingdom lasted, were stamped in Nabataean characters on their coins. The son of Malichus, Rabbel II, ruled for five years, from A.D. 70/71-75 in a co-regency with his mother, Shaqilat II. Their profiles appear together, and her name is emblazoned as *sqylt amh, mlkt nbtw*, "Shaqilat, His Mother, Queen of the Nabataeans." When she died or was removed, and he married, a new issue of coins appeared, bearing the likenesses of both king and queen, who ruled from (A.D. 75-106). His queen was known as *gmlt 'hth, mlkt nbtw*, "Gamilat, His Sister, Queen of the Nabataeans." He apparently had at one time another "sister," because in an inscription from Petra there is reference to a "Hageru, His Sister."

The equal "billing" commonly given to kings and queens on Nabataean coins would seem to indicate the high position of women, at least among the members of the Nabataean royalty. Even when the pair of heads of the king and queen and their names in Nabataean script are absent in some instances and the portrait of the king alone occurs, identifiable only by the use of the first letter of his name in Nabataean script, his queen was seemingly never forgotten. Her existence was called to public attention by placing somewhere on the coin the first letter also of her name in Nabataean script. This can be seen on one of the few, legible Nabataean coins found at Khirbet Tannur (Pl. 57a, b).[15]

On the obverse side of this particular coin is the diademed head of the king, Aretas IV (9 B.C.-A.D. 40), wearing his hair long, as on other coins of his reign. The head is contained within the frame of an imperfectly struck raised circle. On the reverse side are two crossed cornucopias, also enclosed within a somewhat better stamped, raised circle. This coin is smaller than the others minted during the reign of this ruler. I have, however, gotten ahead of my story, because on neither side of the coin is there any complete or partially complete inscription to identify it.

Two letters on each of the faces of the coin are all that one can go by, because the portrait itself is insufficiently determinative. In both instances, on the right side of the coin is the Nabataean letter, whose English equivalent is "H," standing for the full name of Haretat (Aretas) and on the left side is the Nabataean letter, whose equivalent is "SH," signifying his queen, Shaqilat, who succeeded his first queen, Huldu.[16] The latter consonant is clearer on the reverse side than on the obverse. The two names indicated seem in all probability to be those of Aretas IV and Shaqilat I. This coin cannot be dated earlier, because, apparently the use of crossed cornucopias on Nabataean coins started with this king, and he is the only Aretas whose queen was named Shaqilat.

This interpretation of the Khirbet Tannur coin in question was suggested to me by the late Stella Ben Dor. Some of the Aretas IV-Shaqilat I coins bear either the "SH" or the "H" letters, but no others carry both, so far as I know. However, the fact also has to be borne in mind that the "H" letter occurs also on coins of Obodas II, together with another sign, and it may be that such single signs or letters represent mint marks and not always abbreviations of names.[17]

The discovery of broken Greek pottery at Petra and at Abda,[18] datable to about 300 B.C., is also indicative of the exchange then of physical articles and intangible ideas and influence between Mediterranean lands and Arabia. This was demonstrated also by our discovery at Tell el-Kheleifeh (Ezion-geber:Elath) of earlier, black glazed Attic sherds of the fifth century B.C.

Further evidence of the influence of Hellenistic Asia-Minor and Syria upon areas which were to become main parts of the Nabataean kingdom is furnished by the discovery of two late third century B.C. coins at Abda and Khirbet Tannur. Both of them must have remained in circulation for centuries. The one found at Abda in Nabataean surface debris, and dating to about 220 B.C. (Pl. 62), was minted in far off Bactria, which encompassed parts of Persia and India. It was a silver coin of Demetrius, surnamed King of India, who was the son and successor of Euthydemus I, King of Bactria. On the obverse side is a portrait of Demetrius wearing an elephant's scalp on his head, and on the reverse side is the figure of Herakles, crowning himself with an ivy-wreath in his right hand and holding a club and a lion's skin in his left hand. On his left side in Greek characters is *basileos,* and on his right side *demetrioy.*[19]

After having been a satrapy of the Persian empire, Bactria was conquered by Alexander the Great, and then came under Seleucid control, till it achieved semi-independence under Euthydemus and Demetrius. The latter began the conquest of eastern Iran and the Indus valley and gave new impetus to the Greek culture and the numerous Greek settlers transplanted and strongly rooted there from the time of Alexander the Great on. The currents of culture and of trade from India and eastern Iran to Nabataean emporia in the Negev of Palestine are mirrored in this late third century B.C. coin of Demetrius, King of India, found at Nabataean Abda.

The other coin (Pl. 57e, f), found in the excavations of Khirbet Tannur, was struck in Antioch on the Orontes and belongs to the period of Antiochus III, circa 223-213 B.C. On the observe side is the head of Apollo, and on the reverse side the figure of Apollo, with left leg bent, is holding an arrow in his right hand and leaning on a bow with his left elbow. On either side of him, in Greek letters, is the incomplete legend, reading *basile(os) (ant)ioxoy.*[20] A worn coin of Antiochus IV (Antiochus Epiphanes) was also found at Khirbet Tannur.

By the latter part of the fourth century B.C., the Nabataeans had made

Pl. 1   Dolphin Goddess (p. 315) |_____|
                                                     5 cms

13

a

b

c

Pl. 2   Dolphin Goddess ⊢————⊣
5 cms

a. Right profile (p. 319)   b. Left profile (p. 319)   c. Top side, with grooves for curved binding pins (p. 122)

Pl. 3

a. Unfinished Dolphin Goddess
   (p. 510)
b. Unfinished male bust in relief
   (p. 510)

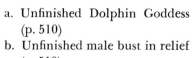

a

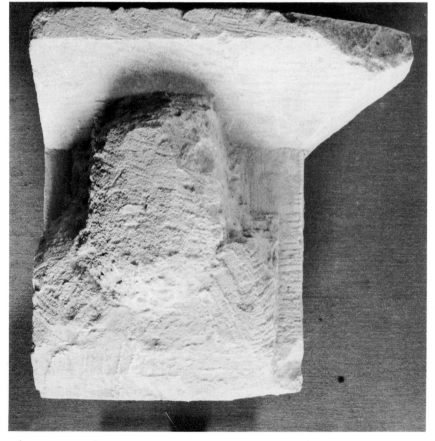

b

a

5 cms

b

Pl. 4

a. Dolphin heads on end horns of a Nabataean capital, Khirbet Brak (p. 60)
b. Enlargement of the more intact of the dolphin heads of "a" (p. 60)

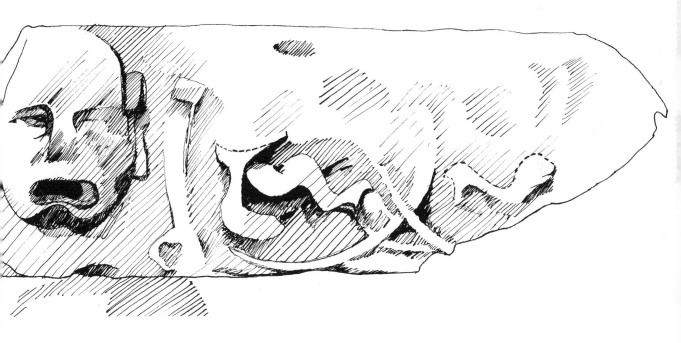

Pl. 5

a. Relief of tragic mask and dolphins, Petra (p. 243)
b. Drawing of mask and dolphins, Petra (p. 243)

Pl. 6   Tragic mask, Petra (p. 243)

Pl. 7 Syrian tragic mask (p. 243)

a

b

Pl. 8

a. Griffin and mask on Abda altar (p. 7)
b. Wadi Ramm, dolphin tail (p. 243)

Pl. 9   Dead boy on a dolphin, prov. unknown (p. 359)

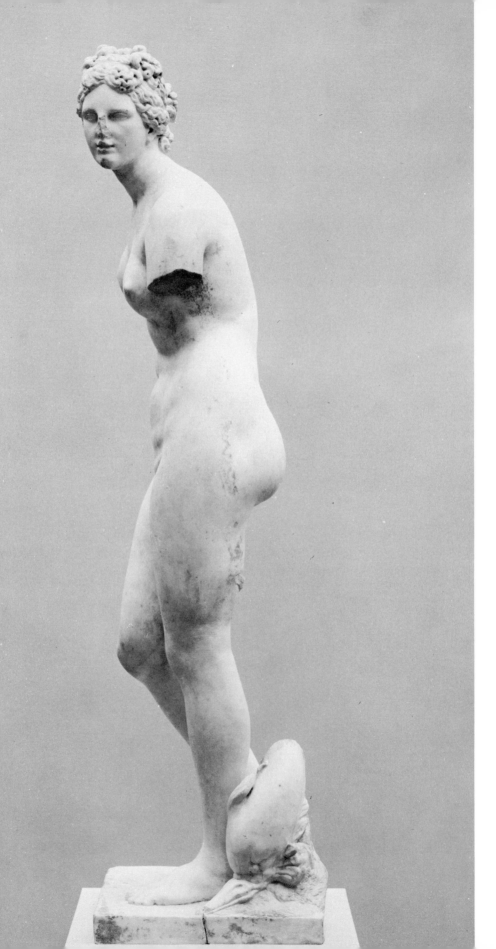

Pl. 9B   Dionysos Cup with dolphins by Exekias (p. 360)

Pl. 9A (*opposite*)   Metropolitan Aphrodite with dolphin (p. 360)

a

Pl. 10

a. Cerberos and Atargatis on dolphin-based throne, Hatra (p. 144)
b. Enlargement of enthroned Atargatis (p. 144)

b

Pl. 11   Dolphin Goddess, Aphrodisias (p. 336)

a

b

5 cms   Pl. 12   a, b. Ornamented architraves with busts in relief (p. 146)

Pl. 13 God of Aquileia with dolphin, crabclaw and leaf attributes (p. 346)

Pl. 14   God of Puteoli (p. 347)

a

Pl. 15

a. God of Lixus (p. 348)
b. Oceanos, Mildenhall, England
   (p. 335)

b

Pl. 16

a. Goddess from Ostia (p. 353)
b. Dolphin mosaic, Delos (p. 353)

Pl. 17   a. Punic figure with caduceus above a dolphin, Carthage (p. 351)
            b. Eros on a dolphin, Egypt (p. 351)

Pl. 19 Cupid astride a dolphin on a first-century A.D. *trapezophoros,* Pompeii (p. 535)

Pl. 18 (*opposite*)   Winged Eros on a dolphin, S. Russia(?) (p. 351)

a

b

Pl. 20

a. Eros on a dolphin, Greece
   (p. 332)
b. Winged Eros with trident
   on a dolphin, Greece
   (p. 332)

a

b

Pl. 21

a. Ino and Melicertes on a
   sea creature, Greece
   (p. 332)
b. Winged Eros on a sea
   creature, Greece (p. 332)

Pl. 22   Thetis on a sea centaur, Israel (p. 331)

a

b

Pl. 23

a. Ahprodite on a dolphin, Tunis (p. 351)
b. Aphrodite astride a fish-tailed Capricornus, Aphrodisias (p. 331)

37

a

b

Pl. 24

a. Dolphins and winged Medusa head, Sidon
   (p. 242)
b. Sarcophagus with dolphins, Beth She'arim
   (p. 243)

such progress in wealth and power that, as will be explained in more detail below, they were able to withstand the attack against their capital city of Petra by a Syrian expedition directed by one of the generals who sought to succeed Alexander the Great after his death.

The scope of their influence and the extent of their domain grew steadily, if fitfully. It flickered like advancing and retreating streamers of Northern Lights over a horizon that stretched at its greatest extent from northern Arabia to southern Syria and from the easternmost reaches of Edom and Moab as far westward as the border of the Land of Goshen in Egypt—with the Arabah rift, the Negev and Sinai in between.

In their familiar use of widely divergent languages, the Nabataeans demonstrated the remarkable skill with which they bound the Orient and the Occident together. They fused the cultural elements of both into a new entity, possessed of qualities and characteristics that were, however, in the final analysis, emphatically and recognizably their own. Like a shooting star, their colorful civilization flashed brilliantly across the skies of human history, to be extinguished then all too quickly.

5. CONCORD AND CONFLICT

The Nabataeans and the Judaeans had much more in common than the same basically Aramaic language they shared in addition to Hebrew, which was not the ordinary idiom even of Judaea in that period. They were both contained in the same general economy, exchanging goods and services constantly. Intermarriage seems to have occurred particularly among the higher economic and social classes. The ruling dynasties of both were often on the best of terms despite the recurring antagonisms that frequently set them against each other. They vigorously espoused the same Hellenism, vied with each other in public works of great magnitude and suffered tremulously from the same dependence upon the favor of Rome.

Of all their neighbors, the closest contacts of the Nabataeans seem to have been with the Hasmoneans and subsequently with the Herodians of Judaea. The Nabataeans were allied with the Hasmoneans in their struggles against the Seleucids who, together with the Ptolemies, divided between them the Syrian and Egyptian parts of the Greek empire of Alexander the Great after his death in 323 B.C. The Hasmoneans finally succeeded in winning for themselves a tenuous freedom from Syrian overlordship.

With independence of sorts attained, the new rulers of Judaea and the Nabataeans turned against each other. They fought intermittently for mastery of the Jebel Druze and Damascus and of central and northern Transjordan and to a lesser degree for control of the Negev. The fortunes of war kept on fluctuating between them in East Jordan. In the Negev, however, the victory went decisively to the Nabataeans, who dominated it almost completely, except for the loss of the northernmost part to the Judaeans for a brief period. The Nabataeans subsequently regained the cities of Kurnub, Abda and Khalasa in the Negev that they lost to the Maccabean ruler, Alexander Jannaeus, 103-76 B.C.[21] They also seized power in southern Syria, and about 85 B.C. took over Damascus, which they were to lose and regain several times before their chapter of history was terminated.

The southern part of the Nabataean kingdom reached from Arabia to the border of Egypt, including between them the territories of southern Transjordan, the Wadi Arabah, the Negev and at least that part of Sinai bounded on the west by the River of Egypt (the Wadi el-Arish), which bisects it from north to south. The Palestinian Negev formed one of the most important parts of the kingdom of the Nabataeans. The natural, northern boundary of the Negev lies below the foothills of the Mountains of Hebron, and is furrowed by the extension of the Wadi el-Arad, which under various names crosses west from below Tell el-Arad to the Mediterranean, with Beersheba on its north bank.

The Nabataeans and the Judaeans befriended or fought each other for several centuries with high-strung irregularity. This fitful state of affairs existed during the period of the Hasmonean dynasty of the Maccabees and continued when the Herodians replaced them as the governing family of Judaea. Political, economic, geographic and personal factors affected the connections between the two peoples, who were in many ways and at varying times either closely joined or sharply inimical to one another. The marriage of a Judaean prince to a Nabataean princess was, naturally enough, the equivalent of a treaty of friendship between their nations. By the same token, the dissolution of such a union sounded the tocsin of war.

This complex and highly personalized state of affairs can best be illustrated by referring to the life and loves of Herod Antipas, perhaps the ablest and ultimately the most unfortunate of the sons of Herod the Great. Succeeding to part of his father's domain, he ruled firmly and sometimes foolishly over the tetrarchy of Galilee and east Jordanian Peraea from 4 B.C. to A.D. 39. His name is remembered less for praise than pity. Ambition was his goad, self-indulgence his weakness, a woman's guile and greed the cause of his political oblivion.

His passion for his niece, Herodias, which she reciprocated, proved to be his undoing. She seemed to have a penchant for marrying her uncles. Her new love was the half brother of her first husband, an exceptionally unambitious Herodian, called Herod Philip, who lived in Rome (Mark 6:17; Matthew 14:3). He is to be distinguished from another half brother of the same name, who ruled over the tetrarchy of Batanea and Trachonitis and rebuilt there the cities of Caesarea Philippi and Julia (Bethsaida), located alongside of some of the beginnings and upper reaches of the River

Jordan. Herodias shed her Rome-domiciled Herod Philip, with no known protest on his part. He seems to have been the quietest and perhaps most normal of his clan, shunning their wild jealousies and murderous intrigues, and he may have been pleased to be quit of her. History shows that it was good riddance.

To marry her, Herod Antipas had first of all to dispose of his existing wife, the princess royal of the neighboring Nabataean kingdom. She was the daughter of the brilliant and powerful Nabataean king, Aretas IV, who ruled from 9 B.C. to A.D. 40, and whose kingdom on several fronts touched that of Judaea. Apprised of what was happening, she fled in good time to escape the probability of being drowned, choked or kicked to death, in accordance with familiar Herodian custom, as established with unbelievable ferocity by her former father-in-law, Herod the Great. So frequent and fierce were the suspicions and rages of this enormously able tyrant, impelling him to murder even his nearest of kin, that, according to the Roman emperor, Augustus, it was considered preferable to be his pig than his son.

It was not difficult for Herod Antipas' Nabataean wife to escape. She made her way first of all to the fortress of Machaerus at the southern edge of his Peraean territory in Transjordan. From there it was but a very short distance southward to the safety of her father's domain, which included most of the east side of the Dead Sea. It is not surprising to learn that shortly thereafter the army of the outraged Aretas IV engaged the forces of Herod Antipas in battle and soundly defeated them.

Roman troops dispatched against the Nabataeans by Tiberius, the proponent of Herod Antipas, had been recalled because of the emperor's death.[22] Nevertheless, the very threat of massive, Roman interference against the Nabataeans apparently sufficed to prevent Aretas from attempting to press his advantage and occupy at least the Peraean part of the domain of his former son-in-law. Roman imperial policy was directed to ensure that no one of the small Near Eastern states became too strong. "Divide and rule" is an old technique. It was through these lands on the east side of the Jordan that Jesus journeyed, before turning westward again. Recrossing the Jordan, he was baptized in its waters by John the Baptist before reaching Jericho and ascending to Jerusalem to celebrate the Passover. There, together with other fellow Jews of his period, he suffered the agony of crucifixion.

The wedlock of uncle and niece, while her first husband, who was also her uncle, was yet alive, flouted one of the Biblical laws of purity: "Thou shalt not uncover the nakedness of thy brother's wife . . ." (Leviticus 18:16). It resulted in human tragedy and political disaster. The unholy marriage aroused the fearless, public protest of Rabbi Johanon, better known as John the Baptist, who said to Herod Antipas: ". . . It is not lawful for thee to have thy brother's wife. And Herodias set herself against him, and desired to kill him; and she could not, for Herod feared John, knowing that he was a righteous and holy man, and kept him safe" (Mark 6:18-20). Herod imprisoned John, however, in one of the dungeons of Machaerus. Finally, however, Herodias had her way. In a probably drunken moment, Herod Antipas had promised to accede to any request of hers, if she would permit her obviously voluptuous daughter to do a veil dance before him and his jaded and sodden company at a banquet held at Machaerus. By this device, adamant in her insistence upon the fulfillment of his word, she secured the beheading of the Rabbi who had dared denounce her nuptial indecency.[23]

Neither the taboos of consanguinity nor the vows of marriage seemed to matter much to her. With unbridled lust and insatiable ambition she reared the edifice of her life to discover in the end that neither political intrigue nor savage spite could make it secure and give her the position and power she hungered for. They eluded her despite her fierce drive, brilliance and seductive beauty.

The murder at Machaerus that history has never forgotten or forgiven was overshadowed for Herod Antipas and Herodias by the political disaster which befell them. Spurred on by his wife's consuming jealousy of the title of king granted by the Roman emperor Caligula to Herod Agrippa I, who was her brother and his nephew, Herod Antipas journeyed to Rome to petition for a similar elevation in rank. Informed of his purpose and minded to prevent it, the ungrateful blood relative and brother-in-law whom he had materially aided in earlier days outsped him there to harden Caligula's heart against him through false accusation of treachery. Despite all protestations of loyalty, Herod Antipas was permanently banished to Lyons in distant Gaul. Herodias joined him there, probably perforce, in lasting exile.

Herod Antipas' tetrarchy of Galilee and Peraea was added to that of Batanea and Trachonitis, which his traducer had inherited from another uncle, whose name was Herod Philip. The latter's name is reflected in that of the city of Caesarea Philippi, which he rebuilt and which is located by one of the sources of the Jordan. It is to be distinguished from the Caesarea Maritima, which Herod the Great had built earlier as a seaport on the Mediterranean coast of Palestine. Herod Antipas had been better advised to have remained faithful to his Nabataean wife and to have maintained good relations with her father, Aretas IV, and Herodias might have realized more of her consuming passion for power had she been faithful to her first spouse and plucked the lush flowers of opportunity that flourished in Rome.

6. THE POLITICS OF INCENSE

The first Temple of Tannur may already have been in existence early in the second century B.C. Long before this, the Nabataeans had emerged as a small but effective power, with its capital city and chief bastion at Petra in southern Transjordan. The firm peg upon which the beginning of history's awareness of their existence can be hung is referred to by the first century B.C. Greek historian, Diodorus Siculus. He tells how Antigonus Cyclops (382-301 B.C.) who had been made governor of Greater Phrygia in 333 B.C. by Alexander the Great and who sought, after the latter's death a decade later, to become the master of all Asia, dispatched an army under his friend, Athanaeus, "to the region of the Arabs who are called Nabataei." He describes how this Syrian expedition reached and, under cover of darkness and during the chance absence of its menfolk, attacked and looted the "Rock."

This particular event took place in 312 B.C. That is the first firmly datable year of Nabataean history. According to Diodorus, the Nabataeans then wrote a protest note "in Syriac letters," probably in Aramaic or proto-Nabataean script, to Antigonus, who hastened to assure them, with diplomatic guile, that the attack had been the result of a misunderstanding. At the same time, however, he made preparations for another assault against the Nabataean citadel. Fortunately, not being lulled into a feeling of false security, the Nabataeans had remained alert and were able to defeat the second attack led by Antigonus' son, Demetrius.[24]

The "Rock" referred to as *"Sela"* in Hebrew (II Chron. 25:11-12; II Kings 14:7) and *"Petra"* in Greek, is undoubtedly the high, almost sheer, flattish-topped hill of Umm el-Biyarah (Pl. 200a) at Petra, which the Horsfields and I discovered to have been originally an Edomite stronghold before it was taken over by the Nabataeans. The name of Petra became attached to the entirety of the Nabataean capital city, in which the Rock (Umm el-Biyarah) is located.[25]

One more fact, clear from Diodorus' report about the Nabataeans of Petra in the fourth century B.C., is that they were literate. We know that they sent a politic message written "in Syriac letters" to Antigonus, receiving from him in return a blandly dishonest note assuring them that the attack by Athanaeus had occurred "contrary to the orders given him." It is obvious that the native tongue of the Nabataeans at this time was Aramaic, which already then, as we have seen, was widespread throughout the ancient Near East. It was the common cultural possession of Syrians, Judaeans and Nabataeans, and can be called the *lingua franca* that long prevailed in their part of the world. Referred to by Heichelheim is a very early Nabataean(?) record dating, according to him, to 264/263 B.C. It is supposed to be inscribed on a sarcophagus found in Egypt, and mentions business transactions and the name of a Nabataean(?) trader engaged in the Red Sea incense commerce as an agent of the god, Serapis, in Ptolemaic Egypt.[26]

The significance of these first recorded Nabataean victories is manifold. It underscores the Nabataeans' emergence as a political force to be reckoned with. It also demonstrates that Petra already in the fourth century B.C. was an important Nabataean trade center for the immensely profitable traffic in the spices, incense and gold of southern Arabia. Diodorus mentions that the Syrians in their first surprise attack on the Rock seized much frankincense and myrrh and about 500 talents of silver—all of which the Nabataeans were able to recover when they pursued, overtook and defeated the invaders. The fact remains that already then the Nabataeans were heavily engaged in the carrier trade of precious goods from Arabia northward and that they were waxing wealthy in the process. It is clear, too, that they traveled the Petra-Gaza-Sinai route to Egypt, trafficking also in the bitumen of the Dead Sea that was so necessary for the Egyptian embalming processes.[27] One of the reasons for the attack on them at the command of Antigonus, by his son, Demetrius, was to choke off or perhaps secure for himself this lucrative trade with Egypt and also to prevent Egypt from using this inner land route to Petra and northward to Syria or southward to Arabia.[28]

The existence of the spice and incense trade between Arabia and Syria and Egypt long before the time of the Nabataeans is indicated by the account of the journey of the Queen of Sheba to Jerusalem for her apparently successful summit meeting there with King Solomon. The trade agreement between these two monarchs must have dealt with the copper of the Arabah and the grain, wine and oil of Judah and Israel in exchange for the incense and myrrh and spices of Arabia and for the exotic goods imported there from Somaliland and India.[20] Our discovery of eighth-century B.C. South Arabic pottery with Minaean inscriptions at Tell el-Kheleifeh (Ezion-geber: Elath) furnished proof of early trade between Israel and Arabia.

For all their deployment across strategic trade routes between Arabia and the Fertile Crescent, the Nabataeans might never have gone beyond their seminomadic estate and their carrier trade were it not for a chain of political events and circumstances that catapulted them into prominence and afforded them opportunities they were quick to exploit and expand.

It was the swiftly changing parade of conquerors becoming the conquered that gave the Nabataeans a period of grace lasting for several centuries, as we shall see in more detail later on. Seizing and settling themselves firmly as farmers as well as tradesmen in easily accessible lands that had been shorn of their defenses through political upheavals, the Nabataeans fashioned in short time a unique kingdom and culture of flashing distinction.

Gone were the dikes of restraint that had been reared to hold them and other desert dwellers like them in check. None could hinder them as they flooded in from the sere reaches of Arabia to fatten their flocks and fortunes in greener pastures and on more abundant fare than had been their previous lot. They pitched their tents where Edomites had ruled and on ruins of cities as far as the Fields of Moab. They seized the springs and cisterns and farms and fortresses of the Judaean Negev south of Beersheba and in most of Sinai, too. The regions they had traversed through sufferance as carriers of precious goods from Arabia to Ascalon, Gaza and Raphia on the Mediterranean coast en route to Egypt became part of their expanding state. The crest of the tide of their advance was to carry them as far north as the lush oasis and trading center of Damascus, which they held intermittently with fluctuating fortune. By virtue of their long control of the Syrian Hauran and Jebel Druze they became in effect a minor colonial power.

Taking advantage of endless gladiatorial contests of continental scope among world powers for absolute mastery of the lands of the Nile and of the Tigris and Euphrates Rivers, the Nabataeans found scope for settlement and expansion of brief duration. Located in the southeastern outskirts of the main areas of interest and engagement of antipodal forces of gigantic strength, the Nabataeans enjoyed a quick prosperity of feverish quality. It was based on maintaining a balance between an unceasing succession of mutual and unappeasable opponents, whose names and home bases changed but whose driving aims were always the same.

Forced to choose sides, the Nabataeans appeased or fought or allied themselves with one or the other of the major combatants, as seemed to suit their best advantage. The friends of one day were the enemies of the morrow. They helped the Syrians against the Ptolemies,[29a] the Hasmoneans against the Seleucids, the Parthians against the Romans, the Romans against the Arabians and the Judaeans, and factions of the latter against each other. There were times when they were on the best of terms with the Hasmoneans or the Herodians,[30] but these were outweighed by longer periods of bitter enmity.[31]

The inevitable end came at the beginning of the second century A.D. when Rome swallowed the Nabataean kingdom like a tasty morsel in its insatiable appetite for incontestable power. The momentum of their past and their continuing participation in trade from Arabia to Syria via Petra held the Nabataeans together for many more years, till gradually their individual distinctiveness ebbed away. We shall deal with this subject at greater length in a subsequent chapter. With the flowering of Byzantium and the return of throbbing prosperity to their former territories, their cultural uniqueness and pagan attachments were obliterated by the burgeoning forces of Byzantine Christianity. Only the Jews retained their identity. The Nabataeans disappeared. The nature of their achievements was forgotten, the character of their society and civilization obscured, the brilliance and beauty of their works buried in the debris of the past. It was our good fortune to be able to bring to light many of the amazing facts and fascinating artifacts and help to delineate the high quality of their fleeting historical appearance.

II. SANCTUARIES WITHOUT NUMBER

II. *Sanctuaries Without Number*

1. IN FORMER EDOM AND MOAB

The name of Nabatene or Nabataea, as we prefer to render it, was applied by Josephus to the entire area extending from the Euphrates to the Red Sea,[32] despite the fact that the Nabataean political hegemony was never that great. It is known, to put it more correctly, that the authority of the Nabataeans extended northward from Meda'in Saleh (Hejrah) in northern Arabia to Damascus and Coele-Syria,[33] and westward from their chief base in the former territories of Edom and Moab, across the Arabah rift and the Negev of southern Israel at least to the north-south geographical dividing line of the River of Egypt (Wadi el-Arish), which bisects the center of the length of Sinai. Their effective control probably reached to the borders of Egypt.[34]

In the course of our square mile by square mile archaeological exploration of all of Eastern Palestine or Transjordan, we discovered in southern Transjordan alone, in addition to many others, hundreds of Nabataean sites. All of them were marked on the surface, among other remains, by fragments of the unmistakable, sophisticated and enchanting Nabataean pottery. As a result, our entire concept of the Nabataean civilization underwent a radical change. The Nabataeans had by no means remained merely a group of semi-Bedouin caravaneers during all of their history. They had become a people of highly advanced order particularly during the first two centuries B.C. and A.D., engaging in far-flung and most lucrative commerce from Parthia and Arabia to Italy and Africa and practicing the most intensive kind of agriculture.

Among the conclusions forced upon us was that they worshiped in many distinctive temples of their own. Almost every Nabataean village and town of some consequence seems to have had a sanctuary. Aside from the temple of Khirbet Tannur (an exception to this rule in that it is not connected with any particular settlement and stands completely by itself), we came across, particularly in southern Transjordan, numerous Nabataean temples. Some of them deserve especial mention before we consider Khirbet Tannur itself.

a. Khirbet edh-Dherih

About four miles to the south, southwest of Khirbet Tannur, on the way up along the east side of the Wadi el-Aban toward the top of the Edomite plateau, we came across the ruins of what appears to have been an attractive Nabataean temple. It had obviously once been the central and dominating structure of a large agricultural village, whose remains are now called Khirbet edh-Dherih.[35] A strong spring, good soil, plentiful grazing area and an excellent location on the road paralleling much of the course of the Wadi el-Aban, made it natural for a settlement to be built there. There was evidence of habitation both before and after Nabataean times, but the dominant note struck by the jumble of damaged foundations and fallen building blocks and scattered pieces of pottery was distinctly Nabataean.

Acanthus leaves and tendrils of grapevines, rosettes and pomegranates, triglyphs and metopes, egg and dart and thunderbolt designs were among the decorative themes chiseled into many of the stones (Pls. 176b-178d) that had once been part of the walls of this temple, which we have named Qasr edh-Dherih. Gazing vacantly over this open grave of fragments belonging to the eclectic Nabataean civilization which flourished some two thousand years ago was a carving in relief of the head of a lion ornamenting the face of a massive, pilaster capital (Pl. 163a). Buried in the debris underneath it are undoubtedly other sculptures, including those of gods and goddesses, consigned to darkness and deprived of the loving attention they once enjoyed. Their probable likenesses, however, are fortunately familiar to us from the discoveries in the excavations of Khirbet Tannur.

The surface ruins of the Nabataean temple of Qasr edh-Dherih seem to be contemporary with those of Khirbet Tannur whose main period belongs, as we shall attempt to show later on, to the first part of the second century A.D. The lives of the inhabitants of Khirbet edh-Dherih had obviously revolved around their attractive place of worship. It would have been a heavy and perhaps intolerable burden for them in the course of their daily existence to have had to journey to the temple of Khirbet Tannur, even though only a comparatively few miles away, in order to bring frequent offerings of entreaty or thanksgiving to their favorite gods.

b. Dhat Ras

Another center of Nabataean worship within a limited radius of Khirbet Tannur was located at Dhat Ras,[36] located less than four miles in a straight

Pl. 25   Grain Goddess (p. 315) |———————|
                                       5 cms

a

5 cms

b

5 cms

c

Pl. 26

a. Relief of Grain Goddess on attached pilaster and quarter column (p. 123)
b. Right profile (p. 473)
c. Left profile (p. 473)

Pl. 27 Damaged reliefs of
Dolphin and Grain
Goddesses (p. 122)

5 cms

Pl. 28a, b. Damaged reliefs of Dolphin or Grain Goddesses (p. 122)

5 cms

Pl. 29 a, b, c (*opposite*)

Parts of quarter columns of Altar Pediment III corner pilasters, originally bearing Grain and Dolphin Goddess busts in relief (p. 122)

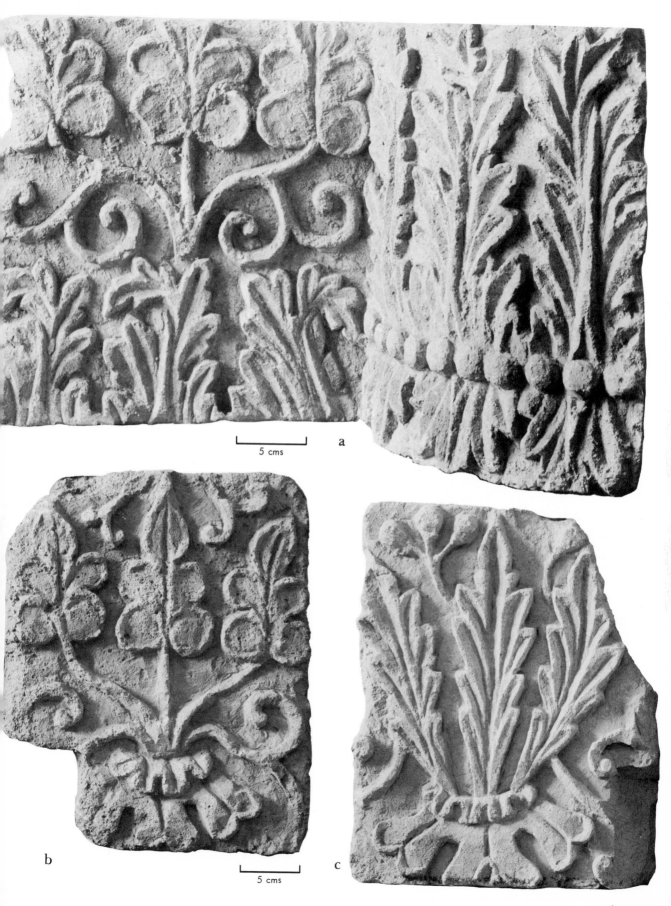

a

5 cms

b

c

5 cms

53

a

5 cms

b

5 cms

line northeast of it. It stands on a low but prominent rise in the center of a fertile farming area on the north side of the top of the Wadi Hesa, where the rich agricultural and grazing lands of the Moabite plateau commence. Representing what must originally have been one of the largest Nabataean towns in this district, it was graced at its highest point by three handsome temples, renovated in the Roman period, and now in a state of pitiful and progressive ruin. They must have attracted worshipers from near and far, whose gifts were sufficiently numerous and rich to maintain them and their attendants properly.

The great trunk highway (Pls. 88-90) that traverses the center of the length of East Jordan passes the base of the eminence of Dhat Ras. It connects it to a whole row of important Nabataean communities to the north of it and also to others on and beyond the south side of the Wadi Hesa, such as the temple of Khirbet edh-Dherih, to which we have already referred. Zig-zagging down the north slope of the Wadi Hesa, this royal road passes the small village of modern Aineh, whose two strong springs, from which it derives its name, may well have provided sufficient reason for a Nabataean sanctuary there. It is directly across the way from Khirbet Tannur, with the width of the canyon of the Wadi Hesa in between. Its nondescript ruins probably conceal the remnants of settlements of widely separated periods reaching back to earliest antiquity. Long experience has taught us that wherever there are springs or wells of sweet water in this semi-arid part of the world, human beings have invariably built permanent places of dwelling, political conditions permitting.

In many instances, Nabataean settlements were established on top or by the side of earlier ones, and in most instances they in turn were superseded by Byzantine ones. There is evidence that at the height of the Byzantine renaissance, the site of Dhat Ras was marked by a magnificent church of monumental proportions, and there may well have been several others, too.[37] The continuous quarrying operations going on among the ancient ruins, which supply the modern villagers of Dhat Ras with ready-made building stones for their rude houses, make it inevitable that the remnants of the three temple ruins there will soon be razed completely to the ground, robbed even of their foundation supports. As at Qasr edh-Dherih, most of the recognizably Nabataean remains of Dhat Ras may be assigned at the latest to sometime early in the second quarter of the second century A.D., contemporary with what will be designated as Period III of Khirbet Tannur.

The latter part of the name of Dhat Ras, meaning in effect something belonging to an elevated position, may reflect its topographical distinctiveness. The land slopes away from it in all directions, so that the site forms a landmark in the southern part of the Moabite plateau. While the "Ras" feature of the name refers perhaps to its physical prominence, it may also well allude to its chief guardian deity. In this instance, the components of

Pl. 30 (*opposite*) a, b. Acanthus, grape leaf, vine and grape motifs (pp. 58, 247)

Dhat Ras could be rendered as the Goddess of the Mountain and would represent a localized form of one of the feminine members of the Nabataean pantheon,[38] perhaps Atargatis or Allat.

A leading member of the male contingent of Nabataean deities was known by the related name of Dhu Shara (Dushara, Dusares, Dionysus), which can be translated as the God of Shara. The latter part, namely, that "of Shara," may possibly have been determined by his relationship to the mountain range of the southern part of the high, broken plateau of Edom in southern Transjordan, known as the Jebel Shara (Shera). Dhu Shara (Dusares) would then be the Mountain God of Shara. In the names of Dhat Ras and Dhu Shara, *dhat* is the feminine equivalent of *dhu*. Dhu Shara would be a particular form of the multifaceted deity, whom we have named Zeus-Hadad.[39]

c. *Qasr Rabbah*

The examination of Khirbet edh-Dherih and Dhat Ras, with the remains of their Nabataean temples, located within a few miles to the south and north of Khirbet Tannur, underscored the likelihood of the existence of a Nabataean temple in nearly every one of the hundreds of Nabataean settlements we discovered in southern Transjordan and in the Negev. In the latter area, with the exception of the evidence of Nabataean worship in such large centers as Abda, Isbeita, Nitsana, Ruheiba, Khalasa and Kurnub, most of the other Nabataean sites have been swept bare of all surface vestiges of the temples that adorned them. Not so in the southern Transjordan part of the Nabataean kingdom. Almost wherever we turned, there seemed to be abundant proof that each Nabataean town or village possessed its own place of worship.

What must have been one of the most attractive and impressive of these Nabataean temples can be discerned in the bedraggled ruins of Qasr Rabbah, some twenty-two miles northeast of Dhat Ras, situated in the center of a fertile agricultural district of the Moabite plateau. A modern village has grown up around the ruins of the temple, with the walls of many of its drab houses incorporating beautiful sculptures purloined from it. Other Nabataean building stones and sculptures can be seen half buried in the courtyards of these houses, and there is little doubt that additional ones are completely covered over by debris in various parts of the village.

To judge from similarities of architectural and sculptural features of various kinds, the visible ruins of the Nabataean temple of Qasr Rabbah are to be dated to early in the second century A.D., contemporary with the last period of the Nabataean temple of Khirbet Tannur. This, as we shall see, seems to have been the period of the most elaborate development of Nabataean temple architecture and ornamentation. Excavations might well reveal earlier periods of occupation at Qasr Rabbah, as was proved in the instance of Khirbet Tannur. The likelihood of their existence is heightened by a clear Aretas IV-Shaqilath coin, which I purchased at Qasr Rabbah from one of its inhabitants, who claimed to have found it there. Aretas IV, ruling from 9 B.C. to A.D. 40, was the famous contemporary and for a time the father-in-law of Herod Antipas.

The rectangular, tetrastyle temple of Qasr Rabbah seems to have been oriented due east, so that the sun's rays could penetrate to its innermost altar on solstice occasions—a feature it had in common with numerous Nabataean and other temples of the ancient Near East in contemporary and preceding periods. Its walls on the west and north sides were still preserved at the time of our visit from eight to nine courses high. A frieze of sculptures may have embellished the upper part of the east façade and run around the side walls, too, as at Khirbet Tannur. In front of the recessed east side, with its main entrance and adjacent smaller door, there can be seen on the ground some of the drums and Corinthian capitals belonging to four enormous columns. They paralleled originally the outer faces of the two corner towers on this east side, matched by slight offsets at the other corners.

In the walls of the modern police post of Qasr Rabbah are several sections of large architraves decorated with floral, leaf, egg and dart designs (Pl. 177a), that could be Roman as well as Nabataean. One of them may have rested over the main entrance to the temple. Nearby was a crude water trough formed out of a section of a similarly decorated architectural piece (Pl. 176a), that could be Roman as well as Nabataean. A tremendous stone with a lion gargoyle, through whose mouth water may once have gushed, had also been stuck, upside down, into the wall of the police post (Pl. 164b). There are several other sculptures of lions of similar type built into the walls of various houses in the village (Pl. 163b). One of them is high up in a wall, together with other Nabataean building stones (Pl. 163c), tooled at a 45-degree angle, typical of Nabataean stone masonry.[40] The tooling served the practical purpose of holding fast the stucco employed so commonly in Nabataean construction (Pl. 205a). The Nabataeans may well have been strongly influenced by the Parthians in their use of painted and incised stucco work.[41]

Above the doorway of one of the houses, set among other decorated building stones of Nabataean origin, is a defaced winged Eros (Pl. 167c), closely related in style to one depicted in a handsome and unique Nabataean mural at el-Bared near Petra. Among the most striking of all the Nabataean sculptures built into walls of the houses of the village is one contained in a frame of stylized leaves of the forebody of a beautifully depicted gazelle with head turned sharply backward (Pl. 169a). It is strikingly similar in style of execution to a fine, unfinished bronze plaque with a recumbent ibex found in the "Persian level" at Sardis.[42] Another equally dramatic sculpture in high relief is that of a panther set in a similar type of bower (Pl. 169b) or inhabited scroll.[43]

At the base of a foundation arch inside one of the houses is a decorated block with a well-fashioned lion's head (Pl. 164a), while at the opposite end of the arch is a bust of a defaced Helios-Apollo in high relief, set against a background of radiating sun's rays (Pl. 137a).[44] Built into a second foundation arch of this same building is another bust in relief, so painstakingly disfigured, however, as to make it completely unidentifiable. In the courtyard in front of this building is a large cornice stone (Pl. 177c), with still other architectural pieces strewn about in more or less damaged state.

The main features of Qasr Rabbah, including its art, architecture and orientation are to be found in parallel or closely related form in every Nabataean temple that has been discovered in Syria, Transjordan and the Negev.[45] There were, of course, differences in details and individual peculiarities conditioned by unchangeable physical circumstances, but almost all of them, certainly at the height of the final development of the Nabataean kingdom, seem to conform in general to a common pattern, which indeed prevailed throughout all of the Hellenistic-Semitic lands of the ancient Near East.[46] The Parthian influence on Nabataean temple architecture seems to have been an especially strong one.

The fertility character of the Nabataean cult as evidenced at Qasr Rabbah and elsewhere is indicated, among other things, by the frequency of the grape and vine motif in architectural and pottery decoration. A national emblem of the Nabataean kingdom could have been represented by a thick cluster of grapes such as was found in sculptured relief at Khirbet Tannur (Pl. 30a). The memory of intensive viticulture at Qasr Rabbah persists in the name of Beit el-Karm (the House of the Vineyard), by which it is also known. Traces of ancient, terraced vineyards can still be seen in the vicinity of the site.

The discoveries at Qasr Rabbah and other Nabataean temples thus far dealt with illustrate well the advanced nature of the brilliant Nabataean civilization. Its Hellenistic-Semitic fertility gods were widely worshiped in probably scores, if not hundreds, of shrines and temples in all parts of the Nabataean kingdom. This was true also of foreign places as distant as Greece and Italy, frequented by Nabataean tradesmen. Aside from the gem-like temple of Khirbet Tannur, the range of Nabataean temples and related tombs extended from the wondrous ones at the Nabataean capital of metropolitan Petra,[47] and those of the magnificent suburb of el-Bared nearby, with its beautiful murals,[48] to the small temple on the important caravan route that led through the Wadi Ramm [49] in southernmost Transjordan to Arabia, and the simple shrine of Allat at the spring of Ain Shellaleh close to it.[50] There must have been a magnificent Nabataean temple at Abda in the Negev, to judge from foundation remains on the acropolis, a Nabataean inscription telling Zeus of Oboda (Abda), a tiny Nabataean altar and Nabataean architectural stones built into the North Church of the Byzantine period that replaced the temple.[51]

d. Khirbet el-Mesheirfeh

Wherever we went in southern Transjordan, we came across remains of Nabataean temples and sculptures. Embedded in a ruined wall of fairly recent origin at Khirbet el-Mesheirfeh,[52] located about nine and a half miles northwest of Dhat Ras and about three and a half miles southeast of Kerak, is a damaged bust in high relief (Pl. 139). I am certain that it is a representation of a Nabataean deity. It was probably one of a group of Nabataean gods that graced a temple there during the Nabataean phase of its history. Made headless by vandals, it is otherwise fairly intact. With the front end of the chlamys folded and thrown over the left shoulder, and a rosette-like clasp fastening it at the right shoulder, the figure was very similar to the Helios[53] bust of Qasr Rabbah and particularly so to the one found at Khirbet Tannur (Pl. 136), which will be discussed below.

e. Kerak

A memorial sculpture, closely related in style, of a Nabataean cavalryman (Pl. 155a, b) appears in one of the walls of the Crusader castle of Kerak,[54] about three and a half miles northwest of Khirbet el-Mesheirfeh. This Crusader castle has obviously replaced the ruins of a Nabataean town and temple, which, in turn, had been built over the wreckage of the Moabite fortress of Kir (Qir-hareshet).[55] I have picked out fragments of Nabataean pottery from the lime between the building blocks of the Crusader castle. The Nabataean deities at Kerak replaced its earlier Moabite gods, particularly Chemosh, to whom, according to Biblical record, the Moabite crown prince was once sacrificed in a desperate and apparently successful attempt to withstand an Israelite siege.[56] We shall deal in more detail with this sculpture later on.[57]

f. Mahaiy

Another Nabataean Helios or possibly Mercury figure was found years ago by Brünnow at Mahaiy,[58] a great, originally Moabite hilltop site about five and a half miles east-southeast of Dhat Ras. The sculpture was discovered at the entrance of the ruins of a temple, since then dismantled, which he considered similar in plan to Qasr Rabbah.[59] There is no question in our mind that this Mahaiy temple was Nabataean, too, although the state of knowledge in Brünnow's time was insufficient for him to recognize it or Qasr Rabbah as such. Moabite and later Nabataean potsherds confirm the existence of settlements of these periods at Mahaiy, during which gods of fertility in various guises were worshiped at local sanctuaries there.

g. *Maʻin*

The existence of yet another Nabataean temple is indicated by some ornamental building blocks set into a rude, modern wall at Maʻin,[60] on the road leading southwest from Madeba down toward the north end of the east side of the Dead Sea. Among them is a Corinthianized, Nabataean pilaster capital with two end horns and a small, now-damaged sculpture of a head in the place of the center horn (Pl. 132c). This type of a Nabataean capital occurs, for example, at the Nabataean temples of Siʻa, Soueïda and Qanawat in the Hauran in Syria.[61] It is also strikingly similar to the capitals of the podium altar of the final Period III at Khirbet Tannur (Pls. 133, 134), which, as we shall see, is to be dated to the second century A.D.

h. *Khirbet Brak*

As we discovered one Nabataean site after another in southern Transjordan, the Wadi Arabah and the Negev, it became possible to fill in the general outlines of the complex mosaic of the Nabataean civilization. Single stones, however battered by the elements and men, oftentimes told us volumes about the glory and the gods of the Nabataeans. Among the scattered building blocks belonging to the ruins of what must have been a Nabataean temple at Khirbet Brak in the hills above Petra was a distinctive Nabataean pilaster capital, under each of whose two end horns was a broken dolphin's head and fins (Pl. 4); alongside it, we found a stone door-jamb with stylized leaf and flower decoration, a pilaster block with the design of a shield or axe in relief on it, which we were to find again at Khirbet Tannur (Pls. 114c, 173a, b, 174c), and also fairly numerous pillar drums and bases. A goddess with a mask of leaves was found there, and another at Petra, with both of them very closely related to the similarly distinguished Fertility or Vegetation Goddess of Khirbet Tannur.

Our discovery at Khirbet Brak of these dolphin sculptures aroused considerable wonderment at the time. Since the unearthing, however, at the Nabataean temple of Khirbet Tannur of intact and damaged busts in relief of Atargatis with two dolphins over her head, portraying thus the "dolphin-goddess," it is no longer surprising to find this marine symbol so far inland.

The dolphin symbol could, however, have been familiar to the Nabataeans long before their commercial enterprises and diplomatic requirements led them on frequent sea voyages to Mediterranean lands. Tyrian coins of the fourth century B.C., emblazoned with dolphins, have been discovered together with some remarkable Palaeo-Hebraic papyri and inscribed seals or bullae dating between 375-335 B.C. in the cave of Mugharet Abu Shinjeh in the Wadi Daliyeh, as Frank M. Cross, Jr., has brilliantly shown.[62] The cave is located in the deeply scarred and broken hill country overlooking the Jordan Valley, at a point somewhat less than nine miles north of ancient

Jericho (Tell es-Sultan). They had been brought there by refugees from Samaria fleeing from the Macedonian forces of Alexander the Great. Tracked down and massacred in their hideaway, they left behind the easily portable possessions they had brought with them, including dolphin-emblazoned Tyrian coins minted before Alexander appeared in the Near East.[63]

Such coins, with their dolphin symbols (Pl. 64a), could have remained in circulation for centuries and have been known to the Nabataeans of the first centuries B.C. and A.D. The Nabataeans could also have become familiar with the fourth-century B.C. Sinope coins, upon which also the dolphin symbol was clearly impressed (Pl. 65). For centuries after they were first struck they remained in use in Asia Minor, among other places, whose seaports the Nabataeans visited regularly in the course of their seafaring trade.[64] Both types of coins could have penetrated the trade marts of Nabataea very early. The connections for good and ill between Asia Minor and Syria in the fourth century B.C. are indicated by the report of Diodorus [65] that Petra was attacked in 312 B.C. by the forces of Antigonus, ruler of Phrygia, one of the generals who seized part of the empire of Alexander when it disintegrated after his death.

It is also necessary to remember that one of the most important Nabataean trade routes led from Petra across the Wadi Arabah and the Negev to the Mediterranean, bringing the Nabataeans into contact with the "fish-goddess" Atargatis of Ascalon and especially with the dolphin deities of the Mediterranean world. The two types have, however, little in common. Atargatis of Ascalon was portrayed apparently in mermaid form, with the fish characteristic of fecundity making the greatest impression upon those who beheld her and besought her blessing of fertility. It is noteworthy in this connection, that among surface fragments of Pergamene-type sigillata of the Nabataean period picked up at Abda in the Negev, located on this Petra-Ascalon trade route, both fish and dolphin reliefs have been found. The transition from the abstemious beginnings of the Nabataeans, whose chief deity was represented at first in the form of a featureless block of stone (Pl. 215a), to the final stage of their history when Graeco-Semitic gods with stylized features of mortal beings became the objects of their constant and ubiquitous devotion, represents a fascinating process of change and adaptation, of rapid development and brilliant flowering of all too brief duration.

i. Dhiban and Other Sites

The various Nabataean temples thus far listed by no means exhaust the number of those that must have existed in Transjordan alone, not to speak of other parts of the Nabataean kingdom. Every time a new excavation is undertaken, as at Dhiban,[66] evidence is obtained of the presence of yet another sanctuary, where Nabataeans worshiped their gods. There also simply had to be a Nabataean temple at the large port city of Aila, or however it was known in Nabataean times, on the northeast shore of the Gulf of Aqabah,[67] and at the Nabataean port of Leuce Come farther south on the east side of the Red Sea, even as it may be taken for granted that there were Nabataean temples elsewhere in Transjordan at such places as Ader,[68] Balu'ah,[69] Khirbet el-Moreighah,[70] Ma'an,[71] el-Lehun,[72] Nakhl,[73] er-Rabbah,[74] and Umm el-Walid,[75] to mention only a few picked at random, in addition of course to the sanctuaries of Petra itself,[76] the Nabataean temple in the Wadi Ramm [77] and the Nabataean sanctuary of Allat at the nearby Ain Shellaleh.[78] It is impossible, furthermore, to conceive of the absence of Nabataean temples in such places in or alongside the Wadi Arabah as et-Telah,[79] Bir Madhkur,[80] Feinan,[81] Ain Hosb [82] and Moa [83] and in large numbers of Nabataean sites in the Negev and Sinai. The discoveries at the major Nabataean emporia in the Negev, including the one at Abda underscoring the existence of the great Nabataean temple there [84] devoted to the memory of one of the Nabataean kings, named Obodas, add further emphasis to our belief that the number of temples in the Nabataean kingdom was literally legion.[85]

2. PETRA, CAPITAL AND EMPORIUM

a. At the Crossroads

The indestructible excellence of Petra's natural position made it inevitable for important settlements to be established there in many periods of the past. The outstanding factors that made Petra a magnet of settlement and commerce and worship from times immemorial are: the presence near its entrance of the powerful spring of Ain Musa (the Spring of Moses), whose perennial flow, supplemented greatly by water caught in many cisterns, sufficed for a large population; the convergence there of age-old routes of travel; the adjacent, fertile and intensively cultivated plateau lands yielding crops in abundance and providing excellent grazing for great flocks and herds of domesticated animals; the ease with which it could be defended; and the atmosphere of holiness anciently and enduringly attached to particular parts of it.

b. An Edomite Citadel

On the top of the steep hill of Umm el-Biyarah there, we found the remains of an Edomite fortress and pottery, contemporary with the period of the kingdom of Judah, terminating early in the sixth century B.C. I believe that this isolated fortress is to be identified with the Biblical site [86] of Sela, that is, the Rock. Its Greek equivalent is Petra, as it has been called from Hellenistic times on (Pl. 200a).

Comparatively late tradition, that may have no basis whatsoever in fact,

locates the spring that issued forth in abundance when Moses smote the
rock at God's behest as being at Ain Musa, above the eastern entrance to
Petra. It also identifies Mount Hor, on the top of which Aaron died, with
the high mountain of Jebel Harun, a place of special Moslem veneration,[87]
overlooking Petra from the west. Whether or not these latter-day identifica-
tions are correct, the fact remains that the recurring importance of Sela-
Petra cannot be separated from the enduring sanctity of its Zibb Atuf
High Place.[88] What was thought to be a smaller one nearby, employed
by the Nabataeans when they were still nomads, and which had become
known as the Conway High Place,[89] has been claimed as a result of excavations, to be a circular corner bastion of a town wall of the Roman
period.[90]

c. The Great High Place

Of all the Nabataean sanctuaries in the entire Nabataean kingdom, that
of the Great High Place of Zibb Atuf at Petra (Pl. 92), the capital of the
Nabataean kingdom, was probably the most sacred and most frequented,
and thus, all in all, the most important. It is built on a hilltop, or, more correctly put, is carved out of it. It would be strange if the sanctity of this hill
did not reach back to early antiquity when, as it is known, Petra was already
inhabited.[91] I have seen modern-day Arabs bring offerings to gods or spirits
they could not name, at places which their tradition held to be sacred, although they knew not why.[92] It seems likely that a shrine existed on the
top of the hill of Zibb Atuf long before the Nabataeans transformed Petra
into a capital city and commercial center of unparalleled size and significance
in southern Transjordan.

The Great High Place of Zibb Atuf in particular seems to have played
the same role with regard to other temples and shrines in the area of metropolitan Petra as Khirbet Tannur did in relationship to those in other communities located near or far beyond it. Commandingly located, anciently
hallowed, nationally prominent, both Petra and Khirbet Tannur loomed
large over the religious landscape of the Nabataean kingdom. The one at
Petra crowned the metropolis of its location; that of Khirbet Tannur transcended the separateness and isolation of its eminence.[93]

The entire plan of the Temple of Tannur and that of the Great High
Place of Zibb Atuf have much in common. One recalls in this connection
that the Temple of Tannur is (1) situated on a hilltop; (2) its sunken forecourt, as well as its raised, inner temple area with its pylon façade are open
to the skies and skillfully sloped so as to provide drainage for the rainwater;
(3) it contains an altar in the forecourt, a main altar on an ornate pedestal
in the raised, inner temple area and a small altar below its west side; (4)
a flight of steps leads from the forecourt to the elevated, inner temple court
with its sacrosanct shrine; (5) it is oriented almost due east.

The bare description of the Great High Place of Zibb Atuf repeats practically in all essentials that of the Temple of Tannur (though perhaps it should be put the other way around), except that the former is smaller and completely hewn out of the living rock. The Great High Place of Zibb Atuf is (1) built on a hilltop; (2) its sunken forecourt, whose side benches form a large triclinium, is carefully sloped to drain off the rainwater; (3) there is an altar base in the forecourt; (4) steps lead up to the elevated altar block, which is obviously considered the holy of holies; [94] and (5) it is oriented east.[95] These similarities are too striking to be accidental. The general plan conforms to a significant, purposed and time-honored arrangement that prevailed also far beyond the boundaries of the Nabataean kingdom.

It is interesting in this connection to read the description of the Syrian temple at Hierapolis-Bambyke in Lucian's *De Dea Syria:* [96] "As for the temple, *it looks to the rising sun.* In appearance and in workmanship, it is like the temples which they build in Ionia; *the foundation rises from the earth to the space of two fathoms, and on this rests the temple.* The ascent to the temple is built of wood and not particularly wide; as you mount, even the great hall exhibits a wonderful spectacle and it is ornamented with golden doors. . . . But the temple within is not uniform. *A special sacred shrine is reared within it; the ascent to this likewise is not steep* nor is it fitted with doors, but is entirely open as you approach it. *The great temple is open to all; the sacred shrine to the priests alone* and not to all even of these, but only to those who are deemed nearest to the gods and who have charge of the entire administration of the sacred rites. *In this shrine are placed the statues, one of which is Hera, the other Zeus,* though they call him by another name. Both of these are golden, *both are sitting; Hera is supported by lions, Zeus is sitting on bulls. . . .*" (italics mine). We shall see how closely this description corresponds to the discoveries at Khirbet Tannur, even as far as its paramount god and goddess with their attendant animals are concerned.

3. THE PENDULUM OF FORTUNE

a. International Trade

The nature and number of Nabataean temples bear a direct relationship to the prosperity enjoyed by the Nabataean kingdom, particularly from the second century B.C. to the second century A.D. In this period of time, its mounting well-being can be traced in the gradually increasing sumptuousness of its religious structures and in the radically altered appearance of its guardian gods. With its access to the Mediterranean and the Red Sea and with its overland routes to Arabia and Syria and beyond, the Nabataean kingdom was exposed to powerful cultural influences both from the Occident

Pl. 31   Atargatis as Vegetation Goddess (p. 143)

15 cms

Pl. 32   Stone horns and eagle finial over Vegetation Goddess (p. 445)

18 cms

Pl. 33

a. Vegetation Goddess relief
   (p. 144)

b. Doweled base of back of Vegetation Goddess sculpture (p. 144)

5 cms

a

b

a

Pl. 34

a. Eagle finial (p. 144)
b. Stone horn on top of Vegetation
   Goddess panel (p. 144)

b

5 cms

and the Orient. These forces vaulted over intervening political boundaries as if they were nonexistent.

Much of the merchandise of the Orient passed through the hands of the Nabataeans, bringing them great revenue. It was brought in part by caravan across the emptiness of Arabia from the port of Gerrha on the west side of the Persian Gulf to the Arabian or Nabataean port of Leuce Come on the east side of the Gulf of Aqabah, which is the eastern arm of the Red Sea. From there it was shipped by boat or sent overland by caravan northward to Nabataean Aila on the northeastern rim of the gulf. The next leg of the journey was the much-traveled route to the great distribution center of Petra, to which also a direct overland route led from the important Nabataean center of Meda'in Saleh in Arabia. From Petra, in turn, the precious goods flowed to Syria, Palestine, Egypt and Europe, carried by beast or boat as the case might be.

The trans-Arabian traffic made use of the bases of Hail, Jauf, Teima, Tebuk, Khaiber and Dedan, in addition to Meda'in Saleh. And one of the main caravan routes from Petra led across the Negev and Sinai "to Rhinocolura . . . and thence to other nations . . . ," according to the Greek geographer, Strabo, who wrote about the Nabataeans at the beginning of the first century A.D.[97] Ships laden with Nabataean merchandise set forth then from the port of Rhinocolura, modern el-Arish on the Mediterranean coast of Sinai, or from Gaza or Ascalon in Palestine, to ply the eastern Mediterranean and touch North African or European ports. A Graeco-Nabataean inscription has been discovered on the island of Rhodes, and a Nabataean sanctuary probably existed at one of the chief ports of call in Italy, namely, at Puteoli, a few miles west of Naples.

Caravan stations developed into flourishing towns as a result of the progressive improvement of the Nabataean economy, with each of them becoming graced, in the course of time, with a temple of its own. The press of population growth that accompanied increasing prosperity forced the Nabataeans intensively to occupy even such marginal lands as the Negev and Sinai, in addition to the fertile areas of former Edom and Moab. It required unremitting effort and infinite ingenuity for them to secure the necessary water and food supplies for the amazingly large number of their desert settlements. Their achievements surpassed the efforts of any of their predecessors. They found it possible to restore and considerably to enlarge the possibilities of settlement in the semi-arid Negev by improving the methods and intensifying the conservation measures that the Judaeans had employed there before them. Whatever the Nabataeans touched, from Arabia to Syria and Sinai, seemed to flourish under their vigorous and enlightened direction.

The brilliant civilization they fashioned through much commerce, some industry and intensive agriculture and animal husbandry, commands admiration even when seen in its ruins. So powerful was the momentum of their creativity, that some of their finest buildings were erected after the structure of their state had collapsed. Indeed, the impact of its conquest by Trajan in A.D. 106/107 [97a] and its incorporation into the Provincia Arabia of Roman rule was hardly noticed at first. Gradually, however, the strength of the Nabataean economy ebbed as the result of changes initiated by the new masters.

b. *Roman Interlude*

When the Romans finally succeeded in diverting the immensely profitable caravan traffic of the East away from Nabataean control, the fairly long interval of Nabataean glory came gradually to an apparently unnoticed and unlamented end. The Nabataean capital city of Petra in southern Transjordan was displaced at first by Palmyra and then by Bosra in northern Syria, but continued to play an active role also in the Roman period. Much of the urban population of trade centers like Abda in the Negev drifted away elsewhere in search of livelihoods. They had been dependent to a major degree upon the steady flow of commercial goods along the east-west Petra-Gaza-Ascalon highway. The dislocation and then for a while the practical cessation of that traffic resulted in the crippling impoverishment of these centers. It was hastened by the fresh arrival of Bedouin infiltrators, less hindered than formerly by regional and local authority. The Romans henceforth made much more use of transportation by sea from Africa to Egypt, no longer deterred by forays against their shipping in the Red Sea by Nabataean pirates.[98]

Only those Nabataeans stayed who were self-sufficient by reason of the cultivation of their fields and the yield of their flocks and herds. It must not be imagined that the Nabataeans disappeared off the face of the earth as a result of the change in the palace guard. Many of them remained in their places, absorbing in part new waves of nomadic invaders. The Romans were interested in the peaceful behavior of their conquered peoples and in fitting them into the mosaic of their empire, but never in their physical annihilation. They could be harsh and cruel, but genocide was never a feature of their imperial policy.

The loss of Nabataean political independence gradually brought increasing economic difficulties in its wake and undoubtedly a decline in population, but the Nabataeans themselves, by and large, remained physically unharmed. The extent of their resistance to the Roman conquest of their kingdom is unknown, but seems on the whole to have brought little destruction to their cities. Such limited damage as Abda, for instance, suffered, seems to have stemmed not from Roman attack but rather from Bedouin raids.[99]

Quick defeat seems generally to have spared the Nabataeans the horrors and wreckage of extended war. Those who could shift for themselves were able to survive, and there is no question that most of them did. It took several long generations before their deteriorating economy made it progressively impossible either to continue, complete or initiate elaborate building programs, among which places of worship figured prominently, or even properly to maintain the costly temples of their former affluence. Lack of care was probably as disastrous to some of them as earthquakes were to others. The final blow came from the indifference and antipathy of newcomers.

c. The Impact of Byzantium

The new rulers were the Byzantines. During the spread and efflorescence of the eastern Roman empire, they halted and reversed the economic decline of the former Nabataean territories. The descendants of the remaining Nabataeans were absorbed and Christianized and their enduring skills put to good use. Wherever the Nabataeans had procured water and engaged in agriculture, the Byzantines followed suit with equal or increased intensity. They also initiated many new undertakings. Their villages and towns rose phoenix-like from the wreckage of former settlements. Once again, the waste places of the Negev, like other areas of the Nabataean kingdom of old, blossomed with new life under stable conditions of widespread peace. It was like the miraculous greening of the desert after the first spring rains, with carpets of flowers springing up overnight to cover the grim, gray earth with heart-warming beauty.

Some Nabataean villages and temples were bypassed in this renaissance, remaining subject only to the self-multiplying ills of abandonment or natural disaster. As a result, they were left more or less inviolate to disintegrate in their ruins, unmourned and untended. Among them were places such as the temple of Khirbet Tannur, unoccupied except briefly by some squatters (Pl. 110a), and till recently completely unknown. Nearly all of the sites were reoccupied and rebuilt, usually with new structures rising on old foundations, while still others were established anew on virgin soil. Abda, Isbeita, Khalasah, Ruheibeh, Nitsanah and hundreds of former Nabataean sites in the Negev and elsewhere flourished once again in different form. Very many, if not most, of their inhabitants were of Nabataean stock who had been converted to Christianity. Their civilian governors and spiritual preceptors were usually one and the same. Together, then, with their brethren and bishops in the new faith, which was so radically different from their fathers' religion, they replaced almost everywhere the resplendent temples of their former deities with magnificent churches (Pl. 216a) devoted to their new god. The *Alpha* and the *Omega* of the new faith, with its hallowed symbol of the cross, encountered the totality of their lives (Pl. 217a, b).

III. THE STORY OF A TEMPLE

III. *The Story of a Temple*

1. THE ONLY ONE OF ITS KIND

We came across the isolated sanctuary of Khirbet (The Ruin of) Tannur on the pinnacle of Jebel (hill of) Tannur in our archaeological exploration of Eastern Palestine, as Conder and Kitchener called it, or Transjordan, as it is geographically known today. Our first examination revealed it to be a gem of a small Nabataean temple in utter ruin on the pinnacle of the massive and almost completely isolated hill of Jebel Tannur. Shattered by earthquakes and scarred by vandals, there still clung to it at the time of our visit nearly two millennia after its destruction the aura of its initial beauty.[100] Concealing the lines of its walls which encompassed the very limited confines of the hilltop was a wildly disordered profusion of architectural pieces, almost all of them of limestone.

Belonging to several periods, they consisted of decorated architraves, molded arches (Pl. 86b), lintels, cornices, capitals, bases, pillar drums and other building blocks, some intact and others more or less damaged by accident and time or on purpose. Among them also were numerous sculptures in relief of Nabataean gods and goddesses, which had been wantonly beheaded or cruelly defaced by latter-day opponents of imagery. And strewn about were masses of distinctive Nabataean potsherds, including delicate, painted, plain and rouletted wares and pieces of Pergamene-type sigillata.[101]

The surface remains of this singular temple of Khirbet Tannur, as it is known to the Arabs of today, alone sufficed to reveal its high importance for further knowledge of the Nabataean civilization. The results of thoroughgoing excavations there compounded the value of our initial finds. An entire family of Nabataean deities was discovered in it, in addition to the altars upon which offerings were brought to elicit their favors and the dining halls where sacred meals were eaten in their honor. The location and orientation of Khirbet Tannur afforded it unusual sanctity and set it apart as a place of special pilgrimage. Its general plan was in harmony with the one prevailing in related structures from Syria to Arabia and to the borders of Egypt. Its architecture reflected the influences of the contemporary cultural world, as they filtered through the prism of the Nabataean genius.

The starkly upthrust hill of Jebel Tannur (Pl. 83), rudely pyramidal in shape, was marked for distinction from the beginning. Once having attained its summit, the visitor can understand that it was as natural for the ancients to grace it with an altar or temple as it was for them to adorn the likeness of a deity with a crown. Commanding attention from near and far, it looms like a mighty tower above the confluence of two canyons, even though its top is still far below that of the high plateaus through which they carve their courses.

The greater of these canyons, the Wadi Hesa (the River Zered of the Bible), starts out in the distant desert to the east. Striking westward, it hews into the crust of the earth a changeably widening but ever deepening wedge, till the small perennial stream at the bottom of it completes its run and perishes in the turbid waters of the Dead Sea. The Wadi Hesa forms a natural boundary between the fabled countries of Biblical Edom and Moab, whose creased and wrinkled plateaus extend to the south and north beyond its tortuous rims. The lesser canyon, the Wadi La'aban (el-Aban),[102] a name redolent of rich-bodied antiquity, pitches down northward from near the top of the outer edge of the Edomite plateau and skirts around most of the south and west sides of the base of Jebel Tannur before reaching the Wadi el-Hesa below it.

Flying in a small plane between the abrupt walls of this great rift, but still considerably above the top of Jebel Tannur with its matting of ruins (Pls. 85, 86a), one can see clearly how this singularly located hill juts almost like an island from the south canyon wall to which its base is anchored (Pls. 84, 85). A narrow ridge, descending steeply from near the top of its southeast side, binds the soaring hilltop to a curving saddle of a bench of the broken mainland below. The mainland, connecting ridge and hilltop, give the illusion of a prehistoric dinosaur, whose sharply angular, crested spine forms the bridge between the creature's bulky, downward-sloping hindquarters and its comparatively distant head.

The banking of the ancient path along the top of the ridge that forms the only reasonably negotiable approach to the temple ruins can still be made out in part; and near the very top, the pathway was cut through solid rock. The likelihood is that the uppermost and steepest part of the ascent was facilitated by a staircase (Pl. 84). Once the summit is attained, the visitor must be prepared to brace himself against the winds that blow sometimes with gale force through the canyon-trough of the Wadi Hesa and over the top of the temple hill.

Standing on top of it, I have on occasion during the sometimes violent winter and spring rains watched the boulder-churning masses of sudden freshets, broad-hooded and upthrust like belligerent cobras, leap with furious speed through the canyon bed below. And I have wondered each time whether the distant rumble and mounting roar heralding the approach of their awesome flood could ever have been considered by the Nabataeans as an utterance of the thunder god of Khirbet Tannur.

The dramatic position of Jebel Tannur on the lower slope of the south side of the Wadi Hesa could not alone have induced the Nabataeans to level off its top and erect on it the temple of Khirbet Tannur. Some special significance must have been attached to it or it simply would not have been selected for a sanctuary site. There was no spring beside it to slake the thirst of man or beast, no adjacent fields for peasants to till, no town where people could dwell, no market where goods could be bought and sold, no crossroads where wayfarers could meet. It was not easy of access. What then were the reasons motivating the construction of a temple there and its repeated reconstruction and enlargement?

Khirbet Tannur was about a mile to the west of the great north-south highway (Pl. 89) leading from Damascus in Syria to Aila on the eastern arm of the Red Sea. The flow of people and baggage along this ancient avenue of commerce and conflict has repeatedly affected for good and also for ill the communities it connects and the countries it traverses. The Kings of the East ran wild along its length in the era of Abraham, irretrievably wrecking from Syria to Sinai and back the handiwork of civilized centuries. Known as the "King's Highway" to the Israelites of the Exodus and renamed in honor of Trajan in Roman times—the paving of the Roman period is still intact in places—it is called the "Sultan's Road" (Tariq es-Sultani) today. Its direction is determined by unchanging topography and has remained almost undeviatingly the same in all periods of history. But Khirbet Tannur was well off the beaten track, isolated from its daily bustle and occasional alarums.

I have followed the zigzag route of this road in its Roman form up and down the steep sides of the Wadi Hesa, as well as the less sharply engineered bends of its modern successor. From numerous vantage points there are fine views of Jebel Tannur. The gleaming white limestone temple on top of it must have been the cynosure of all travelers' eyes as they negotiated the canyon crossing. The shining sight must have whetted their desire or firmed their resolve to visit it. It still, however, could not have served as a natural halting place for transients, where food and lodging and other amenities were available and business affairs could be transacted. It possessed no facilities whatsoever to take care of visitors overnight, and there was no provision for them anywhere in the immediate vicinity.

All of this presupposed the existence of flourishing towns and villages, located either on the great, central, north-south highway, or on well-traveled side-roads, such as the Roman one still visible from the air, which leads down from the Crusader and modern town of Kerak (Qir of Moab) to the eastern side of the Dead Sea. A ford led to its counterpart on the west side, which tied in with the road system of Palestine.

The stream of normal traffic, however, as we have mentioned, completely bypassed the Temple of Khirbet Tannur, some distance removed from its path. It was connected with no through-road whatsoever, and would have been visited only by those who made a special effort and turned aside from the ordinary routine and rhythm of their activities to do so. The fact that it was visible to those crossing the Wadi Hesa did not guarantee their coming to its precincts. Nevertheless, Khirbet Tannur had obviously not been built like a sand-castle on the seashore by idle hands careless of its fate, but as a special assembly place, however much set apart it may have been for Nabataeans and their gods.

The problem of its location was not lessened by the knowledge that there were two closely related Nabataean sanctuaries in nearby settlements, which were situated on the main highway. Their inhabitants and visitors need therefore not have ventured beyond the respective limits of the towns of their sojourn to pay wonted homage to familiar gods. The most rigorous requirements of Nabataean religious observance could have been fulfilled in the local temples, without anyone having to make a special trip to Khirbet Tannur for that purpose, involving as it did many hours of travel out of the way and considerable effort and even discomfort to reach it and return.

Furthermore, I am inclined to believe, as I have already indicated, that there was not a single Nabataean community or way-station in the entire Nabataean realm without an altar or temple of its own, dedicated to one or more of the throng of Nabataean deities, and that could not, therefore, under comfortable circumstances, cater to the needs of local or visiting worshipers. There is already evidence, as we have seen, of the existence of many such sanctuaries, and numerous others are bound to be discovered in the course of time. In view of these facts, the function of Khirbet Tannur seemed at first to defy understanding.

2. A QUESTION OF CHOICE

The Temple of Khirbet Tannur escaped by chance and perhaps by peculiarity of location from being rebuilt and converted into a Byzantine church or having one erected over its foundations. It seems to have been one of the few, if not the only one of its kind in its day, that retained its identity in the absoluteness of its eclipse. We have seen that the uniqueness of Khirbet Tannur becomes all the more accentuated when compared with the numerous Nabataean temples, large and small, which are known to have existed throughout the length and breadth of the Nabataean kingdom. There is, furthermore, no question that the ones thus far recorded represent but a small fraction of the number that once existed. Others must have been located abroad, at foreign trading centers and seaports where Nabataean merchants foregathered in connection with their international commercial ventures. Ships laden with their goods sailed from eastern Mediterranean ports to Alexandria, the Aegean Islands and Italy. A Nabataean-type god found at the seaport of Puteoli (Pozzuoli), southwest of Naples, may have come from a Nabataean temple there, although not of Nabataean manufacture. It is now in the Vatican Museum. He wore a mask of leaves, even as the chief Nabataean goddess of Khirbet Tannur did. And the Graeco-Nabataean inscription found at Rhodes may reflect the existence of a Nabataean community at this crossroads of sea-traffic, which would in all probability have had a temple of its own.

All of the Nabataean temples, save the one of Khirbet Tannur, were located in permanent settlements in the midst of rich farm areas or at commercial centers where trade routes converged, or by sources of water supplying numerous caravans on far-flung desert trails. The one known exception to this general rule is the Nabataean Temple of Khirbet Tannur. As we have seen, it was the religious center of no particular town or village, the chapel of no crossroads, the shrine of no gushing spring. It was isolated, withdrawn from the hurly-burly of everyday life, some miles removed from the nearest highway and easier to avoid than to visit. It must have represented something singularly precious and extraordinarily sacred. Surrounded in widening circles of distance by sanctuaries without number, each serving a separate community, it could not have been the sole place of worship of any one of them but rather a particular holy of holies for all of them. Its importance and appeal must have been at least regional, if not national in character.

Khirbet Tannur must have been regarded therefore as a sacred bourn for the general public, as a high place of pilgrimage for the population at large. It belonged thus to no community in particular but rather to the kingdom as a whole. It may indeed have been built and sustained by funds from the royal coffers, aside from gifts in money or in kind from those attracted to it. Thus far no other Nabataean sanctuary quite like it has been discovered, separate, aloof, alone. Only the Great High Place of Zibb Atuf at Petra may be compared to it. Both, as has already been mentioned, are located on hilltops of timeless human veneration, and both share striking similarities in architectural layout to each other and to the one at Hierapolis in Syria.

Khirbet Tannur differs, however, even from the rock-bound shrine of Petra in that it stands completely by itself, as we have seen, with no adjacent or even nearby buildings of any kind whatsoever in which human beings might dwell or even tarry. It had no permanent inhabitants, except perhaps a resident priest or two. On special holidays and particular festivals, such as marked, for instance, the spring and fall equinoxes, multitudes from all corners of the kingdom must have made pilgrimages to Jebel Tannur to ascend it and bring offerings to the gods ensconced in its temple. It stood in solitary splendor on top of its holy hill, a fitting abode for the images of divinity.

It hardly seems likely that the Nabataeans were the first ones to regard Jebel Tannur as being sacred, although there is no archaeological evidence to bear this out. The tradition of its holiness could have been preserved by some of the people of the land who remained after the downfall of the Edomite and Moabite kingdoms and who were absorbed by the Nabataean population that flooded their former territories. Many deep-rooted historical memories, as well as manners of worship and modes of life, must have been transmitted to the main body of Nabataean infiltrators and settlers by Nabataeanized Edomites and Nabataeanized Moabites. The excellent position of Khirbet Tannur on a striking height with a fine view of much of the east-west course of the great canyon of the Wadi Hesa, whose slopes lead above it to the edges of the Edomite and Moabite plateaus on its south and north sides, could not alone have sufficed to determine its location there.

The built-up area of the Temple of Khirbet Tannur occupied practically every inch of space available on the fairly flat top of the summit of Jebel Tannur (Pl. 85). It is oriented east-northeast by west-northwest and measures roughly 70 by 45 meters. No space whatsoever was left outside the temple limits for dwellings of any kind, as has been mentioned. The slopes beneath them were far too steep to afford footholds for ordinary foundations. The mountain top of Jebel Tannur might conceivably have been selected for the construction of a stout fortress in the preceding period of discord and danger, its difficulties of approach becoming then a virtue instead of a fault. That was the age when Moabites, Edomites, Judaeans and Syrians attacked or assisted each other in changing configurations of friends and foes, with all of them suffering sporadically from nomadic incursions and succumbing finally, with strength spent in internecine discord, to the long-threatening Babylonian conquest.

Defensive qualifications were, however, far from being essential criteria for most places in the Nabataean kingdom during the centuries of its felicitous development. It long enjoyed the well-being of a strong and dynamic central government and shared in the unearned blessing of the pervasive peace of the Pax Romana. Its autonomy, however, was always a tenuous one, and was snapped off like a loose thread when Rome really exerted its power against it. It must be added, too, that a fortress of any

Pl. 35 (*opposite*)

a. Male Medusa, Hatra (p. 335)
b. Male Medusa, Rome (p. 350)

a

b

a

Pl. 36

a. Winged male Medusa, Bath, England (p. 335)

b. Winged male Medusa, Dorchester, England (p. 335)

b

80

a

5 cms

Pl. 37

a. Winged male Medusa, London (p. 350)
b. Winged Medusa, Petra (p. 353)

b

5 cms

a   5 cms

b

Pl. 38

a. Medusa (p. 353)
b. Medusa heads on Lion Triclinium, Petra (p. 353)

Pl. 39 Medusa on cuirass (p. 353) |——————————|
5 cms

Pl. 40   Medusa head, Petra (p. 354)

period on top of Jebel Tannur would have served little purpose, with no fields to guard, no spring or well to protect, no crossroads to command, no dependent population to flee to it for sanctuary behind its gates in times of alarum.

It may very well be that originally a simple Edomite altar adorned the summit of Jebel Tannur before the arrival of the Nabataeans. Whether or not they made use of it at first is debatable. It became clear from our excavations that sometime no later than the first century B.C., they leveled off the highest part of the hilltop and erected, on heavy foundations, an altar of their own. These building operations alone, aside from all subsequent constructions and reconstructions in the entire temple area, would completely have obliterated all pre-Nabataean remains. The architectural requirements of the Hellenistic-Roman period often resulted in the complete effacement of earlier structures in order to erect in their places comparatively large or monumental buildings requiring deep and heavy foundations to support their weight.

The absence of evidence of Edomite or earlier occupation of any kind on top of Jebel Tannur cannot thus gainsay our belief that it was considered to be the seat of divinity from time immemorial. If that is correct, then the construction of an altar and temple there by the Nabataeans must have been an almost inevitable undertaking. It is hard to believe that the Nabataeans selected the summit of Jebel Tannur completely anew, without any reference to its previous history. We believe—and it can never go beyond belief—that the sanctity of the site never lost its appeal and impact. Otherwise it would have made no sense for the Nabataeans to have erected a shrine there, unconnected with local tradition, attendance and support and away from the beaten track of travel. It remains, nevertheless, strange that of all the Nabataean sites reoccupied and rebuilt by the Byzantines, the temple of Khirbet Tannur was one of the few completely bypassed by them. It may have been partly because of the especially powerful spirit of paganism attached to it, but more simply and probably more correctly because its location did not fit in either with Byzantine economic or religious needs or interests which were usually inseparable anyway.

In view of what we consider the age-old, abiding appeal of this imposing and isolated mountain, it could be said that it was not the Nabataeans who selected Jebel Tannur, but rather Jebel Tannur that chose the Nabataeans. No more hallowed site for a sanctuary could have been obtained by the Nabataeans than that of Khirbet Tannur for their fervently worshiped gods of heavenly and earthly abodes and appetites. However variegated the names of these deities may have been, there was, nevertheless, a general commingling of widely divergent cultural characteristics in their forms and features, which could make the Hellene feel at home and the Semite at ease with them. Above all, their appearance and appeal were sufficiently attractive and forceful to Hellenized Semites in general and to Hellenized Nabataeans in particular to inspire eager homage under all circumstances.

The fact that mountain tops have frequently been favored for sacred sites from early antiquity helps explain the deep patina of holiness, which in the course of millennia became attached to the rock surface of Jebel Tannur, as also to the lofty eminence of the Great High Place of Zibb 'Atûf at Petra. The Bible recounts the manifestations of the God of Abraham and Moses at Sinai. Elsewhere, the ancient Semitic storm god, Hadad, is described as reigning supreme among other gods on a lofty mountain in the far northern heavens; sometimes he is addressed as "Lord of Heaven" (Ba'al-shamin), other times as "the great mountain." He was known also as "Ba'al-Zaphon" (the God of the North) and later on as "Zeus Casius." Still another was the "God of Mount Carmel" [102a] with the variation occurring of "Heliopolitan Zeus [God of] Carmel." That particular mountain top, near Haifa in Israel, to judge from Scriptural testimony, had long been frequented by deities.

The sanctity of Jebel Tannur may also have been heightened by its closeness to a dark basalt outcrop of volcanic origin almost directly opposite it on the far north side of the Wadi Hesa, standing out all the more prominently because of the limestone formations surrounding it (Pl. 87). Its presence may possibly have served to emphasize the importance of the thunderbolt worn by the chief of the male deities of Khirbet Tannur. We have called him Zeus-Hadad, because in his appearance is reflected the union of Western and Eastern cultural influences, to which the Nabataeans gave such unique expression. Volcanic eruptions, convulsive earthquakes and the formidable play of lightning and thunder, with their occasional accompaniment of rainstorms and floods, have ever been regarded as manifestations of divine power and sometimes displeasure. The mountain god who reigned of old over Jebel Tannur would seem to have been a particularly well-chosen one for the Nabataeans to revere and propitiate, together with the others of his entourage, in a temple dedicated on top of it to him and his powerful consort Atargatis.

The very first Dhu-Shara (Dushara, Dusares, Dionysus) worshiped by the Nabataeans on Jebel Tannur could have been fashioned by them out of a piece of rock quarried from the basalt outcrop across the way from it. It is apparently this kind of stone of volcanic origin, which is built into the eastern corner of the supremely sacred Ka'aba shrine in Moslem Mecca, and venerated there by millions of pilgrims. There may dimly be reflected in such objects the background of the Sinaitic type of tablets of stone, upon two of which, according to the Biblical narrative, the Ten Commandments were incised. One recalls the Egyptianized stele at Balua'ah in ancient Moab, whose shape is repeated roughly in the rectangular Dhu-Shara (Dushara) blocks at Petra and other Nabataean sites.[103] The anonymity of featurelessness which the Israelites and Nabataeans associated with their gods in the periods of their desert sojourn led the former to the acceptance of (the Word of) God who could not be seen and the rejection of all gods with mortal features fashioned by human hands.

3. SOMETHING OLD AND SOMETHING NEW

a. Reading Backward

The attachment of the Nabataeans to the Temple of Tannur was a long drawn-out love affair that lasted for centuries. Whatever was once constructed was retained as long as possible. Something had to fall almost to pieces before it was repaired or replaced. And when deterioration or disaster made change unavoidable, as much as possible of the old was incorporated into the new.[104]

This applied with special emphasis to the succession of altars and their supporting bases or pedestals erected in what became the holy of holies of the elevated court of the inner temple. The very first of the altar-bases, with foundations sunk into a rubble platform, and marking the beginning of recognizable Nabataean construction on the site, was composed of dressed and coursed limestone blocks. When one of them in the bottom row of its north wall got broken somehow or other, its fragments were meticulously stuck together with a thick, lime plaster.

Generations passed and this innermost altar-base of Period I began to suffer the infirmities of advanced age and proved inadequate to meet the larger needs of the growing community of worshipers. A fine pavement of well-cut flagstones, touching its bottom sides, had been laid over the hitherto unpaved platform supporting it, indicative of the increased wealth of the mountain shrine. The altar-base itself, however, had remained inviolable in its progressive decline. The top of it may have served as the actual altar, although it is clear that in each of the next two periods a special altar was placed on top of an ornate pedestal or base. In the natural order of things, the altar or altar-base of Period I would have been torn down to make way for its long overdue successor. That, however, did not occur. It was preserved in all of its shabbiness and state of impending collapse by being enclosed and covered over on all except the east face by the walls of the larger and more ornate altar of Period II.

The altar of Period II was designed, as was probably that of Period I, to be placed on top of a pedestal or box-like podium, with a staircase mounting its west side. Subsequently, the much larger and more elaborate podium altar of Period III was built over and around it on three sides, preserving its by then broken staircase and impaired walls, and framing within the highly ornate entablature on its east façade the earlier faces of the two preceding altars (Pls. 111a, b, 112a, b).

The procedure had been like fitting a small box inside of a larger, three-sided one and both of them inside a bigger one still, with none of them depending upon the others for structural support. We found that a fairly thin layer of debris separated them from each other, like icing between layers of cake. There is no telling how long this particular tradition of boxing one altar inside of another might have continued had not one or more earthquakes of catastrophic severity destroyed the entire Temple of Tannur so completely that it never rose again. Neither the fervor nor the means sufficed thereafter to erect a new sanctuary in its stead. The enervating weakness of increasing poverty which followed the Roman conquest of the Nabataeans helped gradually reduce their temples and cities into sepulchers of departed glory. Gone were the religious tradition and drive to build yet another podium-altar which would encase all the preceding ones. Together with the rest of the temple, it was buried under heavy masses of scattered architectural debris, with the fallen reliefs of gods and goddesses forming the headstones of the mass grave.

The story of the three altars unfolded itself for us, of course, in reverse fashion. It was like reading a book backward, progressing from the end to the beginning, not only with no diminution of interest but with increasing excitement along the way. It is normal in archaeology for the last to be first and for the first to be last, particularly in places where the entire unfolding scene and progressive span of history remain attached to the same spot. We did not know, of course, when we began excavating Khirbet Tannur that it had three main periods of history, which in some parts of its jumbled ruins required considerable disentangling and in other parts became quickly apparent.

In the instance of the altars built on top of and around each other and over an original altar core, the process of determining their physical and historical sequence was relatively as easy as plucking over-lapping leaves of an artichoke until its heart is reached. We are reversing the actual order of excavation in this review to correspond with the forward motion of time, and employing the designations of Periods I, II and III, which apply naturally also to the history of the entire temple. Period III represents the latest period and Period I the earliest one, going back to the first altar found beneath the double blanket of the walls of the later periods.

It was more difficult to clarify the architectural history of the rest of Khirbet Tannur. The excavations revealed that in the walls and floors of the last phase of its existence in Period III there were incorporated important remains of those of the preceding period. The plan of Khirbet Tannur, first completely executed in Period II, was preserved in enlarged and more elaborate fashion in Period III. It seems, however, to have been carried out in essential outline and in rude form already in Period I.

b. *Repetition in Change*

The story of Khirbet Tannur from beginning to end lasted for several hundred years. I can see the first hardy band of Nabataean pioneers, charged with the task of erecting an altar on Jebel Tannur, ascending the steep path up its southeast side to survey its summit. It will never be known whether or not they found or were already aware of the existence of a pre-Nabataean altar there. At that particular moment, probably near the end of the second or early in the first century B.C., their task was to bring into being a more formal sanctuary for organized religious services.

It was probably axiomatic already then that the position of any Nabataean altar and temple enclosure had more or less to be a lofty one, overlooking a lower forecourt, and that their orientation, if at all possible, had to be to the east. In some instances, a natural elevation, such as that of the Great High Place of Zibb Atuf (Pl. 92) at Petra, met the requirements. In others, an artificial one became necessary. Sometimes both were combined, as at Khirbet Tannur, where the provision of nature was changed or literally heightened by the artistry of man.

First of all, accordingly, a solid rubble platform was erected over much of the west half of the hilltop of Jebel Tannur, into which the foundations of the newly built altar were sunk. The innermost sacred area thus formed was delimited by a low rubble wall, a bare trace of which remained under the south side of the altar courtyard, replaced in Periods II-III (Plan E: Section S-N). The dimensions of this elevated, inner area, measuring 10.38 by 9.72 m. from east to west, remained constant throughout the rest of its history.

The surface of this raised platform sloped slightly but measurably from west to east, thus reversing the direction of the natural slope of the summit of the hill from east to west. The careful retention of this artificial slope in the subsequent periods, providing for the runoff of rainwater to the east forecourt and thence to the steep slope below it, was one of the main reasons animating our subsequent conclusion that the altar-court or inner temple-court was never roofed over.

Steps led down from this elevated, temple enclosure to a large, 15.6 m. square forecourt on its east side, that took in almost all of the rest of the summit of Jebel Tannur. It, too, may have been enclosed originally in Period I by a rough wall of unhewn field stones, suggested by the rough, rubble foundations below parts of the walls of the later rooms 8-11 on its north side (Plan A). Rows of chambers for ritual banquets and other purposes may possibly already have been built in this first period, paralleling the north and south sides of the eastern forecourt and of the outermost extensions of the elevated area to the west. However much some of these features may have existed in Period I, they were first fully developed in Period II and retained and reëmphasized in Period III.

The note of repetition in change, which the sacrosanct podium and altar of the elevated temple-court struck in the course of its history, characterized all of Khirbet Tannur from simple beginnings to crashing finale. The forms of the gods worshipped there in its final expansion would doubtlessly have confused the early Nabataeans who approached its primitive altar with free-will offerings to featureless Dusharas, but they could have found their way about blindfolded in the essential sameness of the architectural plan that prevailed from the very start.

The first altar or altar-base erected on the platform of the inner temple-court and sunk into its rubble foundation, had the form of a small, plain, empty box, measuring 1.45 by 1.38 m. from north to south and was originally about 1.75 m. high. Its walls of worked limestone blocks, revealing already then lines of tooling at a 45° angle generally recognized as being typical of Nabataean masonry drafting,[105] were laid in regular courses. The plaster between the building stones was of a reddish tinged type, formed of lime and crushed pottery, which remained in use also during the succeeding periods. There was evidence of a simple, beveled plinth at the base on all sides except the north, and probably an equally simple molding at the top, although no traces of it were recovered (Plan E: Section S-N). A low ledge or step extended beyond the base of the east side of the altar, and was retained and remained exposed in the period of Altar-Base II.

We found that its entire east façade had been destroyed, with the exception of part of the east side of the molded angle block at the southeast corner and of a few building stones above it. Inside the altar-base was a conglomerate fill of rubble, containing charred remains of burnt offerings apparently of grain and disintegrated bones of small animals. Two levels could be distinguished in this mass, because 1.3 m. above the bottom of the debris that extended lower than the base of the plinth was a distinct stratum of hard-packed earth and lime, above which rose another layer of similar debris to the height of the standing walls.

The remains of the burnt offerings may have been dropped into the inside of the altar-base through an aperture in its roof, with the top layer of ashes and dirt and rubble formed after the east face of the altar had been destroyed, perhaps by an earthquake, but with the altar base still continuing to be used for some time thereafter. It seems probable, as we have already mentioned, that this rectangular, upended, box-like structure, may merely have been the base or pedestal for a smaller altar on top of it, that could be reached by hand. We shall see that in each of the next two periods a separate base or podium was constructed for the altar proper on top of it, requiring in each instance, however, because of the increased height, an outside staircase to reach it.

c. Orientation Eastward

Altar I was oriented almost but not quite due east, being 1°30' S. of E. Since we thought that the orientation should have been due east, in accordance with common practice in the ancient Near East, a letter was addressed at the time of our excavations to the then Director of the Observatory of the American University at Beirut, the late Prof. S. A. Brown, who replied as follows:

". . . concerning the magnetic declination between Tafileh and Kerak (in which area Khirbet Tannur is situated), I have a report from M. Chevrier of our faculty . . . he says that without rather detailed knowledge of the region, and especially of the presence of volcanic rock (basalt), it would be unsafe to assume an extrapolated value, except as a very rough approximation. Such a guess would lead him to expect a declination of 1° or 2° East."

As a matter of fact, as we have already pointed out, there is a very large basalt outcrop on the north side of the Wadi Hesa almost directly opposite Jebel Tannur, and there are numerous other basalt deposits in the vicinity. We have previously suggested that one of the reasons contributing from earliest historical times on to the aura of holiness attending the site of the temple of Khirbet Tannur, stems from its nearness to the great black basalt patch fixed by the fury of a volcanic eruption upon the north canyon slope across the way from it (Pl. 87). It was the kind of site the Ba'al-shamin, the god of the heavens, who could cleave the skies and rend the earth with the thunderbolt of his power, would choose to dwell in and where he could be accessible for appeal and propitiation. And so it was that in the course of many years Nabataean pilgrims by the thousands must have prostrated themselves at his shrine, before the likeness of his being and the symbols of his authority, as they did also before his consort and their fellow-gods, bringing offerings of the yields of their fields and flocks in gladsome acknowledgement of the blessings of fertility or in prayerful hope for their continuation.

Whether the seeming error in orientation of the temple of Khirbet Tannur was caused by human factors or was actually no error at all is not particularly important. The clear intention was to have it face due east, so that the rays of the rising sun, especially on sacred, calendrical occasions, might most brilliantly illuminate the embodiment of the divinity or divinities enthroned in front of the altar in the inner temple-court. It seems certain that in Period I, the gods were represented by rough hewn slabs of stone, and in changing form in Period II, but by Period III in the second century A.D., their humanized figures could be seen sculptured in relief in considerable number at Khirbet Tannur. Variations of featureless Dushara forms may well have continued, however, also in Period III (Pls. 196-198).

One recalls the orientation of the Temple of Solomon in Jerusalem, which was so built, that on the days of the spring and fall equinoxes the first rays of the rising sun, heralding the advent of the Glory of God, could enter through its eastern gate and penetrate into the Holy of Holies. These two occasions, reflecting the annual celebration of two New Year occasions,[106] were observed also by the Nabataeans, to judge as we shall see, from the clockwise and counterclockwise halves of the twelve divisions of the zodiac panel encircling the Period III relief at Khirbet Tannur of Tyché as the Goddess of Fortune and Fate.

The Nabataeans of Khirbet Tannur and elsewhere were thus following age old precedents when they turned their temples eastward, whenever possible, with a remarkable degree of mathematical exactitude. The Syrian Greek, Lucian, writing sometime in the latter part of the second century A.D., about the great temple of Atargatis at Hierapolis in northern Syria, might also have been describing almost any Nabataean temple when he said in his *De Dea Syria:* "As for the temple, it looks to the rising sun."

d. *Progress by Pavement*

Up to approximately the third quarter of the first century B.C., Altar I or Altar-Base I continued in use. Then it became necessary either to rebuild it because of its having been damaged severely, probably by an earthquake, to the extent of its east face being almost completely destroyed and its north side leaning dangerously outward, or to build a completely new shrine around and over it. The latter was actually done. None of the building stones of Altar-Base I was ever reused, nor, with the exception of its east façade, was any part of its remaining walls altered in any way, mainly, we believe, because of the reverence in which it was held.

It is impossible to say exactly when, but sometime before the inverted, box-like base of the altar of Period II was constructed, a fine, limestone pavement was laid over the inner temple-court and around Altar-Base I. It is, however, correct to say that there is a closer relationship between this pavement and Altar-Base or Pedestal II than there is between it and that of Period I. The size and workmanship of the pavement blocks are completely unlike the materials employed in the first period, but closely related to those used in the following one. Indeed, at first, we had every reason to believe that this pavement was contemporary with Altar-Base II. It became apparent, however, when we finally removed the north wall of Altar-Base II, that the pavement went under it up to the beveled plinth of the base of the Altar-Base of the first period.

Had the builders of the altar and supporting base or pedestal of Period II not already had the pavement to cope with, they would most probably have sunk its walls considerably below the pavement level. As it was, the paving blocks under the pilaster bases of the east and west corners of the north side of Altar-Base II were depressed below their proper levels by

Pl. 41 (*opposite*)   Zeus-Hadad (p. 195)

5 cms

5 cms

a

b

Pl. 43

a. Zeus Serapis, Gerasa (p. 312)
b. Parthian-type dress (p. 250)

5 cms

Pl. 42 (*opposite*)   Enthroned Zeus-Hadad (p. 195)

Pl. 44   Atargatis with lions' torque (p. 207)   5 cms

Pl. 45

a. Tyché with semeion and lions' torque (p. 207)
b. Damaged Tyché (p. 399)

5 cms

b

a

reason of the weight above them (Plans A, E: Section S-N). Had we removed its south wall, we would undoubtedly have encountered a repetition of this phenomenon. We refrained from doing so, however, in order to preserve intact as much as possible of the ancient structure.

It would appear, therefore, that the hard packed rubble surface of the temple-court of Period I remained unpaved in all or most of Period I. At any rate, no paving stones of any kind were found that we could connect with it. The theoretical possibility exists that they could have been removed when the fine pavement that preceded the building of the second Altar-Base over the first one was laid. This is doubtful, because, as we have already seen, the overriding tendency of the builders of Khirbet Tannur in all of its history was to preserve what had previously existed, either by building over and around the old or by integrating it into the new construction.

Wherever we removed blocks from the pavement of the inner temple-court, which we were to learn remained in use in Periods II-III,—and that was done by us in three separate places (Plans D: Section E-W; E: Section S-N)—no remains whatsoever of an earlier pavement came to light. Instead, there seemed to be everywhere underneath it a layer of ashes of burnt offerings, extending from around the base of Altar I. There were, incidentally, no similar ashes under the paving stones which covered the lower, eastern forecourt in Periods II-III—a fact which speaks for itself. The outer, east forecourt was designed and used primarily as a place of assembly, and gifts to the gods were tendered especially on the altar in the inner elevated temple-court.

e. Underground Deposit Boxes

Still further changes in the pavement of the inner temple-court were effected in Period III, when three small offering chambers or receptacles were inserted into the floor, with specially cut paving slabs serving as their covers or lids. This required the removal of some of the original paving blocks and changing and rearranging those that were placed back again. It is doubtful if that would have been done in Period II, which seems to have followed very soon after Period Sub-II, to which the original pavement belongs.

There were two of these small, semisecret, offering receptacles or sacred deposit boxes beyond the east side of the altar-base and one, of slightly dissimilar measurements, beyond the west side. We do not know why they were located in their particular positions. The rectangular lid of the one near the northeast corner of the altar-base was still in place when we cleaned the inner court pavement. It was in no wise distinguishable from the rest of the paving slabs except for a hole at its southeast corner into which a finger or hook could be inserted to lift it up (Pls. 106, 107a). There was a hole at approximately the outer center of each long side of this cover, which may possibly also have been used for the same purpose.

The paving slab used for a lid over the sunken offering chamber near the southeast corner of the altar-base had disappeared some time after the destruction of Period III, being plugged up by a fallen stone when we uncovered it (Pl. 107b), even as in the case of the one on its west side (Pl. 108). In the latter instance, however, the enclosing paving blocks themselves were rabbeted to hold the receptacle lid, while in the case of the first two on the east side, the lid rested directly on top of the sides of the stone receptacles which had been sunk into the debris underneath the pavement. The contents of these concealed deposit boxes consisted of some small, charred animal bones, ashes and burned grains of wheat. It may be that they were ashes and remnants of the burnt offerings placed upon the shrine-altar. It is of course possible that these subterranean, stone receptacles contained remnants of foundation offerings.[107] Otherwise, these concealed, underground boxes must have been cleaned out from time to time and periodically filled with parts of new burnt offerings, which had some special significance.

IV. ARCHITECTURAL ORTHODOXY

1. The First Two Centuries
   a. *The Basic Plan*
   b. *Evidence of Advancement: The Architecture of Period II*
2. Enrichment and Renewal
   a. *The Factor of Prestige*
   b. *Change According to Tradition*
   c. *Deities in Effigy*
   d. *The Altar Proper*
3. Open to the Sky
   a. *Pylon Character*
   b. *Significance of Sloping Pavements*
   c. *Sloping Pavements*
   d. *Periods of Construction*
   e. *Earliest Pottery Evidence*
   f. *Squatters' Houses*
   g. *Inviolate Area*
   h. *East Façade*
      1) *Atargatis Panel*   2) *Eagle Finial*   3) *Architraves with Busts in Relief*   4) *Gateway*   5) *Earlier Form of Façade*
   i. *Outer, West Altar*
4. Place of Assembly: East Forecourt
   a. *Dimensions*
   b. *Forecourt Altar*
   c. *East Façade*
   d. *Main and Side Entrances*
5. Antecedents

IV. *Architectural Orthodoxy*

1. THE FIRST TWO CENTURIES

a. The Basic Plan

The altar of Period I on its box-like base in the center of the raised rubble platform of the inner court must have been used for about a hundred years, more or less, commencing probably in the latter part of the second century B.C. and continuing till about the third quarter of the first century B.C. It may have replaced a more primitive altar used by the Nabataeans when they first came to Jebel Tannur. The beginning of Period II at Khirbet Tannur can be fixed approximately by a dedicatory Nabataean inscription found there, dated to the equivalent of 8/7 B.C. (Pl. 194c).[108] The fine pavement over the raised inner temple-court was, as has been noted, followed in style by the masonry of Altar-Base II, and must have preceded it by at least a decade. This pavement could be assigned to a period of its own, designated IA or perhaps better, Sub-II. It had been laid against the plinth of the walls of Altar-Base I (Pl. 112a). The walls of Altar-Base II rested on the pavement and their weight depressed the paving blocks beneath them (Pl. 111a, b).

The fact that the finest Nabataean pottery fragments encountered in the excavations were discovered among the debris and ashes beneath this stone pavement of the inner temple-court, which in effect separated Period I from Period II, indicates that Period I was a fairly long one and that Altar-Base I could have been in use for a long stretch of time indeed. Furthermore, wherever else in the rest of the excavations of Khirbet Tannur we came across pieces of the most advanced types of delicate and frequently painted Nabataean pottery in separable levels, it was almost always in places below the clear level of Period II. This does not mean that excellent kinds of Nabataean ceramic wares were not extensively employed in Period II and Period III at Khirbet Tannur, well into the second century A.D., but

101

it does mean that Nabataean pottery had already attained a very high stage of development before the end of Period I, that is, well before the close of the first century B.C. The manufacture of such pottery presupposes considerable development of potters' skills for generations, that in this instance could well have involved a hundred years.

The large increase in wealth and cultural attainments exemplified in Altar-Base II, with its beautiful east façade, seems to have been accompanied by a parallel excellence in pottery. It achieved a most distinctive quality before the end of Period I and certainly before the pavement of Period Sub-II was laid against the base of the pedestal of Altar I and over the raised, inner court of the Temple of Tannur. For all of these reasons, therefore, involving a) the physical separability of building periods, b) a clear cut, datable inscription and c) the evidence of pottery in an undisturbed level, it seems possible to correlate the history of the first period of Khirbet Tannur with the hundred years, approximately, extending between the last part of the second and the last part of the first centuries B.C.

b. *Evidence of Advancement: The Architecture of Period II*

The temple of Khirbet Tannur took on pronounced and elegant shape during the next phase of its history, which has been designated as Period II. Its enlarged size and attractiveness coincided apparently with the increasing wealth of the Nabataean kingdom. What had existed at Khirbet Tannur in simplest form took on the full and finished aspect of rounded out and shining maturity. The Nabataeans had come far since they first installed the plainest kind of pedestal and altar on a raised rubble foundation sometime in the second century B.C. or perhaps as late as the beginning of the first century B.C. The transition to a sedentary agricultural civilization had advanced materially before the usefulness of this altar came to an end. The caravan trade which the Nabataeans had controlled for well over three centuries continued to be a source of enrichment and to provide them with goods and contacts that changed the shape of their lives, but it now represented only one feature—a major one, to be sure—of their entire economy.

When, therefore, it became inescapably necessary, probably during the last ten or twenty years of the first century B.C., to renovate and expand the outworn and perhaps earthquake shattered facilities of the temple marking the first stage of their radically changing civilization, they did it with a finesse of sophisticated art and beautiful simplicity that placed them among the forefront of the cultured peoples of their era. Their good taste kept pace with their increasing wealth, and both were evidenced in the shining new temple they erected on the summit of the Tannur hill. It must have cost them a pretty penny and may well have represented a regional or even national effort. It showed the Nabataeans at their best in the middle of their phenomenal upswing from seminomads to sophisticated and firmly entrenched masters of an extensive domain.

A comprehensive plan must have been worked out in advance before the building of the Temple of Tannur of Period II was undertaken. It evidenced itself in the ensuing harmony of execution of the architectural whole. In the center of the stage stood the elegant podium or altar-base, whose dimensions of 2.1 by 2.0 m. from north to south and height of 2.61 m. above the pavement were considerably larger than those of the Period I altar-pedestal it enclosed. Its new walls of finely dressed, white limestone blocks completely encased those of Period I on all sides except the east one, which was retained like a picture inside the frame of what had been transformed into a beautifully decorated, east façade. Whether or not the east front of the Altar-Base of Period I was repaired and plastered over in each of the two succeeding periods which left it exposed, cannot be established, although this is what probably happened.

After we had found and placed into position again most of the pieces of the upper part of the east façade of the base or pedestal of Altar II, it became obvious that it could not have served as an altar proper but rather as a base for an altar proper on top of it. This was conclusively demonstrated, furthermore, when we cleared the west wall of the pedestal of Altar II and found remnants of a staircase tied into its outer side and rising from the bottom of its south corner. Two of the steps are still in place (Plan D, Section E-W; Pl. 113a,c). Without such a flight of stairs, it would have been difficult to reach the small altar placed on top of it. All traces of such an altar have disappeared, unless, as seems likely, parts of it were incorporated into the elaborate one built in its stead in Period III.

The architectural excellence of the pedestal or base of the altar of Period II demonstrates the cultural progress that the Nabataeans had made by that time. Its four corners were marked by pilasters. Those on the west side had simple, beveled bases, related moldings at the top, and plain pilaster faces between them. The pilasters on the east façade, however, were beautifully decorated. Their strongly molded bases (Plan C:25) rested on a deep plinth (Pls. 101a,b, 103, 104). The first three divisions of the faces of the pilaster shafts above them were unadorned. After that, the width of the pilasters narrowed slightly from the outer edges inward, creating a very small offset. The rest of the east face of each pilaster was ornamented with a floriated, sunken panel contained within a plain, molded border (Plan C:45).

Above a wavy, molded pattern at the bottom of the recessed panel on the south pilaster of the east façade were three acanthus leaves, from which sprang a continuous acanthus scroll enclosing eight rosettes of eight petals or leaves each (Pls. 103, 104).[109] This theme was repeated on the north pilaster, too, except that the fifth and sixth acanthus-enclosed rosettes were replaced by a niche, meant possibly for a small lamp (Plan C). The concave surface of the half-shell at the top of the niche was grooved with lines spreading diagonally from the top of a central orb, like sunrays fanning out from a setting sun.

It must not be imagined that we found these decorated pilasters in this comparatively intact position. The fine Attic bases of both were in place, as were the lower blocks of the south pilaster up to the beginning of the recessed panel, showing one acanthus-encircled rosette. The other parts of this east Altar-Base façade of Period II were scattered about, particularly among the debris of the ruins in front of it, and an immense amount of labor and study was required before most of the pieces belonging to it were located and placed into position either physically or through Professor Clarence S. Fisher's architectural drawings. Some obviously missing pieces were never recovered, but we were fortunate enough to assemble almost all of the ornate entablature (Plan C) which had once risen above the east pilasters of this façade.

When we first visited Khirbet Tannur in the course of our archaeological survey of all of Transjordan, we were wonderstruck by the sight of a group of extraordinary architectural pieces piled on top of each other (Pl. 86b). They had probably been assembled by residents of the area who had begun to become conscious of their market value as *antikas* and who had already carried off some invaluable sculptures, most of which, however, have since then been repossessed by the proper governmental authorities and photographs of which have most kindly been made available for this volume.

Among them were the two halves of a large slab of limestone, skillfully cut to join together and form an arch, with a molding extending around the curve. Below it was the central section of a beautiful lintel, one of whose end caps we were to discover later on in the excavations. And at the bottom of the heap was the central section of a still larger and most handsomely decorated architrave. All three, it turned out, could be fitted into their architectural places, the first two to the façade of the Altar-Base of Period II and the last to its Period II entablature (Plan C:24b; Pl. 178b).

The two sections of the arch, when joined together, fitted between the two pilasters and rested on top of the uppermost of their deeply recessed side extensions. Near the top of the faces of these pilaster wings was the continuation of the lines of molding which coincide exactly with those around the curve of the arch. This can be seen clearly on the fifth block from the bottom of the south pilaster; its parallel piece on the north pilaster is missing (Pl. 104a,b).

Over the entire length of the top of this arch was a horizontal, ten centimeter wide recess (Pl. 104c; Plan C:29), similar to a differently positioned recess or groove on the underside of the lintel or architrave above it (Plan C:25b). The space between the two, as Professor Fisher was able to determine later, approximated the height of the lintel. It must have been occupied by an ornamented stone beam (with allowances for the slightly greater height of the lintel's end caps) with matching recesses, into which iron bars were set to tie the arch and the architrave together and thus strengthen the position of the entire entablature of the east façade of the Altar-Base. The only other vertical support of the arch came, as we have seen, from the pilaster jambs or wings which upheld it. The back of the arch was rough, as was that of the lintel or architrave, with both being plastered into the upper east side of Altar-Base II, above the east face of that of Period I. The rabbeted stone beam, itself, stretching between the arch and the architrave to the capitals that fitted on top of the north and south pilasters of the east façade, was never found.

On each side of the spring of the arch is a bracket with a broken flint dowel, which, when intact, once held some small ornamental object or other. A bit of the face of the stone behind each of them had been gouged out to accommodate it. At the top of the curve of the arch is a small, horizontal aperture for a lead-fill to help bind the two halves of the arch together. It is contained in a unit, projecting from both halves, which may have served as the base of a relief sculptured on the front center of the missing, rabbeted beam, that originally was above it (Pl. 104c).

I have just mentioned the capitals on top of the north and south pilasters of the east façade of Altar-Base II, between which the lost crossbeam with its top and bottom grooves extended. Only one damaged, foliate capital was found, twenty centimeters high, suitable for the top of the south pilaster (Plan C:45 and 9; Pl. 174a,b), as determined by Professor Clarence S. Fisher's measurements and reconstruction. I am not sure, however, that it has been put in the proper place, inasmuch as it has not the same rosettes as the pilaster panels and the crowning architrave or lintel. In fact, I think it may belong somewhere in Period III.

Above these foliate capitals and their connecting crossbeam was the crowning entablature, composed of two finely molded and decorated end caps and between them a similarly molded lintel, bearing the main decorative theme. The lintel was one of the architectural features we had seen in the surface debris of Khirbet Tannur. It was decorated with a deeply cut, central half shell, on either side of which was a horizontal, sunken panel, containing a continuous acanthus scroll enclosing four rosettes. The continuation of this panel ended with one more rosette on each recessed wing of the south and north caps, whose main shafts bore in separate, horizontal, sunken panels, bounded by molded borders, the representations of a double arrowed, foliate thunderbolt (Plan C:25b; Pls. 103, 104, 105b). The complete decoration consisted then of a thunderbolt panel at each end of ten divisions of acanthus leaf framed rosettes, five on each side of a central half shell niche.

The relationship of this crowning entablature to the north and south pilasters of the east façade of Altar-Base II, with the common motif particularly of sunken panels, marked by raised borders, acanthus-enclosed rosettes and the carved out shell with its spreading petals, is obvious. Yet it could not have rested on top of the molded arch and the north and south pilasters, because of the difference in height between the lintel and its end caps and because the horizontal groove or recess at the bottom of the lintel or architrave, in which fragments of plaster and iron remained, did not match the related ten centimeter wide, horizontal recess in the top of the arch slab. Even if the thunderbolt caps had been placed on top of the pilasters, as indeed they could have, there would still have remained a space of several centimeters between the lintel and the arch, without enough room for rabbeting bars to be inserted into their dissimilarly placed horizontal grooves and connected with anything above or below them. The solution, worked out by Professor Fisher, as previously pointed out, was to insert the foliate capitals between the tops of the pilasters and the bottoms of the thunderbolt caps, of which, to be sure, only the south one could be located (Pls. 104a, 105b), and place between them a properly rabbeted stone beam which would fit into the unmatchingly positioned, horizontal recesses on the top of the arch and at the bottom of the lintel.

Such is the architecture of the east façade of the Altar-Base of Period II. Between its arch and supporting pilasters and crowning entablature, with their acanthus leaf, rosette, thunderbolt and half shell decorations, was framed the east face of the pedestal of Shrine I. What was contained inside that frame? Did there stand there, plastered into position against the east façade of Altar-Base I, a featureless Dushara representation or, less probably, humanized reliefs of the presiding god and goddess of Khirbet Tannur? Those enthroned there in Period III, when the podium-altar was enlarged once again without covering up the exposed face of that of the first period, have survived in whole or in part. Were they newly fashioned then, or had they outlasted the Period II changes, to receive as of old the ever new obeisance of passing generations? We believe that the sculptures in relief of deities in the likeness of humans were first fashioned in the third and last period of Khirbet Tannur.

2. ENRICHMENT AND RENEWAL

a. The Factor of Prestige

As in the case of Altar-Base I, earthquake tremors or age or both may have brought about the collapse of the one of Period II. It had proven aesthetically attractive but architecturally weak. We have previously pointed out that its walls rested over the Sub-II pavement which had been laid up to the edge of the plinth of the walls of Altar-Base I (Plan A:S-N; D, Section E-W; E, Section S-N; Pl. 112a). When the removal of most of the north wall of Altar-Base III revealed the face of the north wall of Altar-Base II (Pl. 111 a, b), we saw that the inner face of the bottom stone at its northeast corner had been cut to fit over the beveled corner base of Altar-Base I and over the plinth beneath it. The fit over the beveled base had not been very good, making it necessary for the gap to be filled with a stone plug set in plaster (Pl. 111a). The inner, bottom sides of the rest of the lowest row of stones of this north wall of Altar-Base II were rudely cut to rest partly on the Sub-II pavement and upon approximately half of the width of the plinth of Altar-Base I, leaving a space between their north walls which was filled with stones and plaster (Pl. 111b).

We were shocked to find that the masonry of Altar-Base II, which was so well dressed on the outside was so poorly cut on the inside. This applied particularly to its bottom foundation stones. The stonemason or contractor evidently figured that no one would ever examine his work, but history has caught up with him. There was a lot of this shoddy kind of performance, as we learned from the examination of the rest of the bottom stones of the north wall of Altar-Base II. The space of from six to thirteen centimeters between its rough, inner face and the smooth, outer surface of the north wall of Altar-Base I, was filled with a solid mass of lime and pebbles. In all fairness, however, it must be said that whoever was responsible for the walls of Altar-Base II was inhibited from sinking its foundations into the rubble platform below Altar-Base I, because of the prevailing prejudice against destroying any previous construction. Otherwise, we like to think that he would have torn up part of the Sub-II pavement and reared the walls of Altar-Base II on a firmer basis than was possible under the circumstances.

Be that as it may, it was inevitable in due course of time for Altar-Base II to give way to something bigger and grander. The change was necessitated in all probability by a combination of factors. These consisted of the constant repairs that about a century of use must have made inevitable, the increasing popularity of this shrine ultimately necessitating its complete renovation, the steady accrual in wealth and power of the Nabataean kingdom reflected in a rash of new or rebuilt and enlarged temples and shrines throughout its expanded domain, and, finally, the expansive spirit of the times in general.

Westward from Italy to Gaul and England, southward to North Africa and eastward to Asia Minor, Syria, greater Palestine, Arabia and India, the might and influence of imperial Rome were translated into vast and ponderous undertakings that materially changed the architectural appearance of entire countries. Temples, theatres and hippodromes, bathhouses, dams and cisterns, harbors and milestone-marked highways sprang up

Pl. 46   Zodiac Tyché (p. 284)

Pl. 47 (*opposite*)   Winged Niké upholding fragment of zodiac (p. 431)

5 cms

Pl. 48   Niké-supported Zodiac Tyché
(p. 395)

Pl. 49

a. Atlas-supported Zodiac Jupiter, Rome (p. 433)
b. Atlas-supported Tyché, Ascalon (p. 434)

Pl. 50   Zodiac Mithras, London (p. 413)

Pl. 51   Tyché of Amman (p. 409)

b

a

Pl. 52

a. Tyché of Antioch (p. 164)
b. Tyché of Palmyra (p. 395)
c. Tyché fragment, Wadi Ramm (p. 164)

c

Pl. 53 *(opposite)*

a. Tyché on corner stone (p. 396)
b. Dionysos with cornucopia on adjacent
   side (p. 410)

114

a

b

5 cms

Pl. 54

a. ed-Deir reliefs, Petra
   (pp. 411-412)
b. Enlargement, ed-Deir
   reliefs, Petra (pp. 411-412)

a

b

Pl. 55   Tyché with cornucopia (p. 411)   5 cms

Pl. 56   Damaged Jupiter sculpture (p. 411)

like magic. Glamorous cities appeared suddenly on the landscape like irises bursting overnight into full bloom to gladden desert wastes with their beauty. Philadelphia, Gerasa, Pella and Gadara in Transjordan, Ba'albek, Hierapolis and Antioch in Syria, Dura, Hatra, Palmyra in Parthia, Caesarea Maritima, Caesarea Philippi, Scythopolis and Sebastieh in Palestine, to mention only a few among many, spell out in part the power and impact of the Roman art of government and of the pervasive Hellenic spirit that preceded, accompanied and long outlasted the rule of the capital on the Tiber.

The Hellenization of the ancient Near East continued unabated long after the death of Alexander the Great in 323 B.C. and the disintegration of his empire. Both the Ptolemies of Egypt and the Seleucids of Syria who inherited part of his domain and fought bitterly and protractedly with each other for the possession of Palestine, were united in their espousal of Greek culture. Its appeal was not dampened among the general populace of Judaea even after the bungling attempt of the Seleucid king, Antiochus IV (Antiochus Epiphanes), to force the worship of Olympian Zeus in their Temple at Jerusalem. That only succeeded in setting ablaze the Maccabean rebellion in 168 B.C. and bringing into being the shaky independence of Judaea first under the Hasmoneans and then the Herodians for somewhat over a century. The attractiveness of Hellenism proved to be irresistible to multitudes in many lands, regardless of political boundaries, economic interests, native languages or racial origins. It was mirrored in their clothes and games, their literature and speech, and, with the exception of the Jews, in the features of their gods. This is fully apparent in the sculptures of the Nabataean deities.

The rise of Rome to mastery of much of the civilized world helped rather than hindered the process of Hellenization. It served the rulers on the Tiber well as a unifying cultural factor amidst the diversity of their far ranging dominion. The artistic spirit of the Greeks was wedded to the driving power of the Romans, and the results obtained were often as magnificent in scope and massive in size as they were handsome in form and beneficent in fact. There ensued a rage for building and beautifying that was contagious in character. Roman emperors and subject kings seemed to vie with one another in the number and range of their public works. Even the few states that for various reasons were able or were permitted to maintain a precarious independence for comparatively brief periods, such as that of the Nabataeans, could not escape following suit.

Both the Herodians and the neighboring Nabataeans were caught up by this frenzy of construction, in which, I believe, their condition of subservience and insecurity was sublimated. The personal pride and private fears of their kings additionally motivated their passion for erecting striking and extensive public monuments and seemingly impregnable fortresses.

Herod Antipas, Herod Philip and their father, Herod the Great, before them, built or rebuilt a series of cities, whose fame and ruins have endured. Among them are Tiberias on the Lake of Galilee, Caesarea (Philippi) on the Jordan and Caesarea (Maritima) on the Mediterranean. Their brilliant contemporary, Aretas IV (9 B.C.-A.D. 40), was also restlessly active in this respect in his own land, as were his predecessors and successors on the Nabataean throne. It is against the background of this entire age and in the context of the swift paced, economic upswing of the Nabataean kingdom, that we must place the establishing and, periodically, elaborate rebuilding of a host of Nabataean cities and shrines, including that of Khirbet Tannur.

b. Change According to Tradition

Altar-Base III of Khirbet Tannur was built completely anew. It assumed again the form of an open end box placed over the pedestal of Altar II, enclosing it on all sides except the east front. A flight of steps, starting this time on the outer south side instead of on the outer west side as in the case of its predecessor, led to its flat top. That is where the altar proper, wth an ornate east face of its own, was placed. The east façade of the Altar-Base of Period III consisted of an elaborate framework. It enclosed and left thus exposed all of the east façade of Altar-Base II, which in turn framed the entire east face of Altar-Base I. It was as if a bare canvas, that of the east face of Altar-Base I, had been put into a fine frame, then placed within a still larger and even more elaborate one. There are traces of stucco in the sunken, vertical panels of the east pilasters of Altar-Base II, with their sunken panels of acanthus-enclosed rosettes. It is conceivable that these attached pilasters and the entablature above them with its decorated lintel and anta caps may have been plastered over in the next period so as not to interfere with the decorative scheme of the east façade of Shrine III.

The dimensions of the podium or pedestal base of the altar of Period III were naturally larger than those of the preceding one, and measured 3.65 by 3.40 m. from west to east and 3.20 m. in height. The height was computed after enough of the scattered pieces of its east façade had been recovered, making it possible temporarily to put most of it back into place and enable Professor Fisher to restore it completely on his drawing board. The existing walls of Altar-Base III, resting on the unchanged Sub-II pavement of the inner temple-court, were sufficiently intact to furnish us its outer measurements.

The north and south corner pilasters of its west wall (Pl. 110b) duplicated the scheme of those of the west wall of Altar-Base II. The corner pilasters on the east side, however, were marked by the addition of engaged quarter columns (Pls. 101a, b, 111a), which, as we were to learn, formed one of the chief, distinguishing characteristics of Period III of Khirbet Tannur. Their Attic bases, resting directly on the pavement of Sub-II, were lower than those of the adjacent bases of the corner pilasters of Altar-Base II, which rested on a ledge retained from Period I. The moldings of the Period III bases, however, were mounted above those of the adjacent ones of Period II, leaving an awkward space between them. The dilemma was solved by fitting a contoured piece of masonry over the moldings of the Attic bases of Period II, filling out thus the intervening space (Pl. 112b; Plan C:24, 25 and bottom). The rest of the height of the face of Altar-Base III between its engaged quarter columns and the outer sides of the north and south pilasters of Altar-Base II was occupied by the side-extensions or jambs of the engaged quarter columns.

The outer face of the rear west wall of Altar-Base III was 1.3 m. removed from that of the rear, west wall of Altar-Base II. It had a thickness of 55 centimeters, leaving thus a space of 75 centimeters that we could not account for at first. Digging down very carefully, we found that a tiny chamber of this width had been left between the two walls, with a poorly built door at its north end. In this compartment, we found two steps of the broken flight of steps bonded into the outer west wall of Altar-Base II, that led originally to its top (Plan D, Section E-W; Pl. 113a). Professor Fisher believed that the width of this rear wall of Period II did not admit more than half the number of steps required, and that therefore their flight must have doubled back on itself inside the face of the masonry. These steps were replaced in the following period, as has been noted, by others on the south wall of Altar-Base III (Plan E, Section S-N; Pls. 101b, 102a, b) for the same purpose and could, therefore, only have been retained in this tiny west chamber, which ultimately became filled with debris, because of a characteristic reluctance to remove anything of an older date. The rough, inner face of the west wall of Altar-Base III was originally plastered, so it is evident that this tiny chamber was used for some time.

The flight of steps on the south wall of Altar-Base III,[110] starting at its east end, had either to double back on itself inside the face of the masonry or had to turn at right angles to the north to reach its top. This would have required their being carried over the top of the tiny chamber, (which became filled with dirt and stones), along the upper, inner face of the west wall, through an opening in the south wall. The original purpose of the tiny chamber, whose inner west wall was plastered early in Period III, becomes all the more enigmatic in this case. One can envisage a late change in the plans of the architect, who thought first to enclose and utilize the steps on the west side, but then decided, before the south wall of Altar-Base III was built to erect steps and bond them in on that side. The very small chamber would have been created anyway through the construction of the west wall of the nearly exact square box of Altar-Base III. There was a small fill of debris between its south and north walls and the corresponding walls of its predecessor.

We found six of the steps of the staircase on the south wall of Altar-Base III, with the socket for a seventh. The violent earthquake that undoubtedly destroyed the entire Temple of Tannur in Period III, caused what was left of the south wall of Altar-Base III to bulge out and made its steps sag. At a much later time, perhaps near or even before the end of the Byzantine period, squatters bolstered up the remains of the staircase by shoving underneath it a large building block and two drums of columns taken from the then collapsed colonnades on the sides of the enclosure of the inner temple-court (Plan E, Section S-N; Pl. 102a). They used the bolstered staircase to cover part of a rude shelter for themselves and perhaps also to ascend to a rude room they may have pieced together on top of Altar-Base III. They were probably the same squatters who assembled a curving row of fallen column-drums and other building blocks across the southwest corner of the enclosure of the inner temple-court. The comparatively small number of coarse Byzantine sherds we found may come from the pottery they used.

c. Deities in Effigy

A most striking innovation in Altar-Base III were the busts in relief of goddesses, rising from the front of the corner pilasters of its east façade, to which, as we have seen, engaged quarter columns had been added. The two panels of goddesses were turned slightly towards each other. Only two of the sculptures were intact, the one of a grain goddess, with ears of wheat above and beside her head, being on the left or south panel and the other of a dolphin goddess, with two dolphins above her head, on the right or north panel. Placed next to or physically attached to the individual pilaster blocks bearing these sculptures were related parts of foliated quarter columns and side-extensions or jambs, which reached to the outer edges of the vertical sides of the pilasters and entablature of Altar-Base II (Plan C:22; Pls. 1, 2, 25, 26).

The dolphin goddess pilaster block stood by itself, not physically connected with the section of the quarter column and jamb that fitted immediately next to it on its left or south side. These were carved out of a single block of stone, each decorated with three stylized leaves and vines of several different kinds (Pls. 27-29). The block with the grain goddess, however, was sculptured together with less than a third of the engaged quarter column. The rest of the quarter column and its side extension were hewn out of another stone. The foliate decorations were the same on both of these two east façade pilasters.

In three other instances, the supervising sculptor used yet another way of dividing the masonry for these particular columns. Out of one stone block he caused to be fashioned the beginning of the jamb, the entire section of the engaged quarter column and the pilaster block with its goddess relief. Separate pieces then were used to complete the side extensions (Pls. 26a, 29).[111] The sculptor also chose a varying form of decoration for the engaged quarter column sections of these three—namely, that of a stylized grapevine with leaves and a cluster of grapes (Pl. 28a, b), as compared with that of the block with the intact grain goddess. The reliefs of the goddesses on these three sections belonged obviously on the south pilaster. To judge from the dentilated decorations on top of the bodices of two of them (Pls. 27, 28a), they could, before their heads were knocked off by vandals, have been representations of the dolphin goddess, unless there was no absolute uniformity of decoration. That particular decoration appears on the one, intact sculpture of the dolphin goddess and is absent from that of the bodice with beautiful folds of the grain goddess.

To judge from the raised borders enclosing them on three sides, both of the intact grain and dolphin goddesses belonged at the bottom of their respective panels. One of the mutilated sculptures (Pl. 27a), of the total of six that we recovered, had been sculptured on a separate pilaster block, as was the dolphin goddess, and, to judge from the one panel line on its right side, belonged on the north pilaster. The shoulder coverings in this particular instance resemble overlapping fish or serpent scales. Inasmuch as there does not seem to have been uniformity of garment or foliate decoration on these sculptures, it is possible that the north pilaster of Altar-Base III carried reliefs of the dolphin goddess, while the south pilaster was devoted to the grain goddesses. Otherwise, as seems less likely, the panels of goddesses must be envisaged as alternating with each other on each pilaster, with a grain goddess beginning at the bottom and a dolphin goddess at the top of the panel on the south pilaster and the reverse order on the north pilaster. There is reason to believe that there were twelve sculptures altogether on the north and south pilasters on the east façade of Altar-Base III, with six on each side.

There are several reasons for this assumption. The excavations showed that the bases for the north and south pilasters and engaged quarter columns of the east façade of Altar-Base III were in place, as was the plain pilaster block with engaged quarter column above the north base (Plan C:24; Pls. 101a, b, 111a). Additional finds indicated that two such undecorated pilaster blocks, one above the other, formed the bottom fourth of each pilaster shaft. Their height paralleled that of the plain part of the Altar-Base II pilasters, above which the sunken panels of rosette divisions began. It was seen then that the intact grain and dolphin goddess blocks, commencing above these two unadorned pilaster blocks, marked the beginning of the decorated panels of the north and south pilasters of Altar-Base III. It was obvious that these pilasters had to reach not only as high as, but beyond the pilasters and entablature of Altar-Base II, in order to support the entablature of Period III over it. It could then be figured out that six blocks, decorated with reliefs of the goddesses, were required on each side in order to produce the necessary height of the north and south pilasters of the east façade, over whose superimposed capitals the anta caps of the crowning architrave or lintel of the Altar-Base III entablature would rest. That there had been indeed six sculptures in relief on each of the north and south pilasters of Altar-Base III was suggested also by the close parallel of Qasr el-Bint Far'un at Petra.[112]

We had first seen the crowning lintel of the entablature of Altar-Base III at the bottom of the pile of important architectural pieces that someone had assembled on top of the surface debris of Khirbet Tannur (Pl. 86b). It was similar in general form to that of Altar-Base II. Its chief decoration, beneath a narrow panel with the egg and dart design, which appears thus for the first time at Khirbet Tannur, consists of a long, horizontal, sunken panel of alternating types of formalized leaves and vines on either side of a central rosette. They are very closely related to the decorations on the engaged quarter columns and jambs connected with the pilaster blocks bearing the goddess reliefs.

The vine and leaf panel of this lintel must have been closed at either end of the jambs of the south and north anta caps, on which, in turn, there may have been repeated the thunderbolt motif of the anta caps of the Altar-Base II lintel. They were not recovered. This thunderbolt motif may well have looked something like the one on a decorated stone of uncertain location also found among scattered surface stones at Khirbet Tannur (Pl. 105a). Its central, horizontal thunderbolt, with each end arrow placed between two small rosettes, is bordered by an upper panel of egg-and-dart design and a lower one of alternating types of leaves—at once both related to and dissimilar from those on the lintel of Altar-Base III. It is, of course, also possible that the south and north anta caps of the lintel of Altar-Base III may have continued and finished the design of the lintel and contained its concluding border lines.

d. The Altar Proper

Elevated (probably on a plinth) over the top of the base or pedestal of Period III (about 3.40 m. above the pavement of Sub-II), stood the altar proper. It seems to have repeated in smaller scale the main features of the east façade of its base and of other façades of the same period at the Temple of Tannur. Common to them all were corner pilasters with engaged quarter columns, vertical sunken panels on the pilasters, molded bases and floriate Corinthian capitals. The engaged quarter columns and Corinthian capitals occurred only in Period III. These main features of Altar III, with the exception of the engaged quarter columns, were reflected in the small, votive, Alexandros Amrou altar (Pls. 187, 188) found among the Khirbet Tannur ruins, as we shall see later on. This beautiful little incense altar may have stood on one of the two old Altar-Bases, sunk upside down into the Sub-II pavement of the raised inner temple-court, in front of the north and south pilasters of the east façade of Altar-Base III (Plans A; C bottom; B; Pl. 111a).

Enough pieces of the altar of Period III (which we shall henceforth call Altar III, to distinguish it from the base or pedestal which supported it) were discovered to give a fair approximation of its original appearance. Among them was part of a pilaster base (Plan C: 23b), three Corinthian pilaster capitals, and drums of pilasters with engaged fluted quarter columns, and vertical sunken panels on the faces of the pilasters. A very small sculpture of the head of a goddess projected in high relief from the center of the abacus of one of the three floriate Corinthian capitals [113] (Pl. 133). Reliefs of similar small goddess heads had been broken off the other two capitals (Pl. 134). The double end horns of these capitals, with their exaggerated abacus projections, were reminiscent of the purer Nabataean-type capital of the preceding Period II (Pl. 173a, b, c).

One of these pilaster capitals of Altar III had been hewn separately, that is, without any part of the pilaster shaft attached to it (Pl. 134a). Each of the two others (Pls. 133a, b, 134b), one with and one without the small projecting goddess relief, had been hewn, together with the top division of the pilaster and engaged quarter column, out of one block of stone. On each pilaster, commencing beneath the capital, was a vertical sunken panel with plain borders, which, together with its continuation, was decorated with eight rosettes of two alternating types, each contained within a continuous scroll of acanthus leaves (Pls. 133a, 134b). The better preserved of the two (Pl. 134b) had two and a half rosette divisions. The continuation, consisting of a middle section of the pilaster, with the lower part of its engaged fluted quarter column broken off, had five and a half more rosette divisions, making thus a total of eight. The molded, horizontal, closing line of this sunken panel may have appeared at the very top of the lowest missing section of this pilaster, whose face, above the base, was presumably plain up to this point.

These capitals, with their pilasters and engaged quarter columns, could have belonged to the same east façade of the altar only if the engaged quarter columns could be conceived as returning on the outer north and south sides, which, however, seems contrary to all convention. In any event, the presence of three capitals, with obviously a fourth missing, indicates that the altar of Period III was ornamented certainly on its east and west sides in a manner imitative of the decorative schemes of the east façade of its supporting pedestal and to a certain degree of that of Period II. Common both to Altar III and the east façade of its pedestal, as we have seen, was the use of engaged quarter columns, Corinthian capitals, and high reliefs of heads of goddesses.

Common to the pilasters of Altar III and of the east façade of the Altar-Base of the preceding period was the appearance on both of eight divisions of acanthus enclosed rosettes. It will be recalled that there were related rosette divisions on the crowning lintel of Altar-Base II. It seems possible, therefore, that the pilasters of Altar II, no traces of which were found, may also have been decorated with vertical, sunken panels of rosettes similar to those on the pilasters of Altar III. Altar III would then have combined decorative elements of Periods III and II. It may have been about 1.50 meters high, enabling the officiating priest, who mounted the pedestal of Altar III by the steps on its south side, to reach it easily.

3. OPEN TO THE SKY

a. *Pylon Character*

The careful examination of all the fallen building stones and those still in position, showed clearly that the east façades of the inner and outer temple-courts were higher than any of their other walls. The façade of the sunken east forecourt in the two main periods of its history was closely related to the Period II and Period III façades of the raised inner temple enclosure. It was only after unravelling the three distinctive construction periods of the inner court and altar-pedestal and becoming acquainted with the characteristic, architectural styles of each period, that it became possible or much easier than it would have been otherwise to determine the building periods of the east façades of both the elevated inner and sunken outer courts. It became clear that these façades were built first in Period II and then rebuilt in Period III as pylons, with the pylon of the inner temple-court undergoing much more radical changes than that of the outer one. The raised inner temple-court with its central altar was contained within a walled enclosure, whose south, north and west walls were appreciably lower than its elaborate east façade.

b. *Significance of Sloping Pavements*

There is not a shred of evidence that the inner raised temple enclosure was ever roofed over. All indications point to the contrary, including particularly the existence of the carefully planned and executed slope from west to east of the pavements in and outside the temple enclosure designed to carry off rainwater.

The north side of the pavement of the raised inner temple enclosure sloped 12 centimeters between its west and east ends and 17 centimeters on its south side. This would have made no sense unless it provided for the easy drainage of rainwater which was not kept out by a roof over the enclosure. The very strong rubble foundations beneath the pavement made it impossible for the sloping of the pavement to have been caused by sinking. By the same token, a pronounced difference existed in the levels between the west and east ends of the pavement of the east forecourt below the inner temple-court, amounting to 26 centimeters on the north side and 38 centimeters on the south side. The rainwater drained into two shallow gutters, one on each side of the entrance way, just inside the outer east wall of this forecourt, and was led outside through two outlets which pierced it. Both sections of the gutter drained from their north and south starting points, respectively, towards the outlets on either side of the entrance way.

A comparison of the different levels of each of the four corners of the forecourt pavement seems to indicate that the original intention in Period II was to drain the forecourt pavement from the northwest to the southeast corner. For all we know, there may possibly have been an outlet through the outer east wall at this corner in that period, before the outer east wall was largely rebuilt in the subsequent period. In any event, in Period III, if not already sometime in Period II, commencing near the north and south walls, two halves of a downward sloping gutter were cut into the flagstones just inside the outer east wall as far as either side of the entrance way which they did not cross. The rainwater that was led to them was, as already mentioned, carried outside via outlets pierced through the outer east wall (Plan A; Pl. 93a, b).

c. Sloping Pavements

Indeed, the slopes of all the pavements and paved floors of the Temple of Tannur seem to have been planned very carefully. Thus the pavement immediately outside and below the north side of the raised inner temple enclosure sloped 19 centimeters from west to east and the one below the south side sloped 21 centimeters from west to east. The east continuations of these pavements took the form of narrow platforms on the north and south sides of the forecourt and two steps high above it. The slope of the north platform amounted to 15 centimeters from west to east. The northwest corner of the forecourt proper was 37 centimeters below the platform at its north end, and the southwest corner of the forecourt was 34 centimeters below the platform at its south end. The platforms and the forecourt they paralleled followed thus the general scheme of drainage of the raised, paved, inner court and the pavements outside it, below its north, south and west sides.

The pavement of the inner temple-court suffered little damage from the collapse of the east façade or of the side walls. The east façade or pylon seems to have tumbled outward on to the forecourt both in Periods II and

III. We have already noted that this pavement was first laid in the Sub-II period, with a purposed slope of some 17 centimeters between its west and east ends to carry off the rainwater. This fact supports the evidence that the inner temple-court was never roofed over and that its east façade was built as a pylon in Periods II and III.

Some changes did occur, to be sure, in the paving of the inner temple-court during Period III, when its enclosure walls were rebuilt. The most obvious changes were the two slabs from old altar-bases placed upside down in the pavement and protruding above it, directly in front of the east pilasters of Altar-Base III (Pls. 101a, b; 102a; 111a; Plans A, C, bottom), as we have already mentioned above. We have suggested, furthermore, that they may have served as bases for small votive altars, several of which were recovered in complete or fragmentary form.

In addition to these obvious changes, it is probable that several rows of paving slabs on the north and south sides of the inner temple-court and several rows between the Altar-Base and the east and west walls were relaid in Period III. When the enclosure walls of the inner temple-court were re-built in Period III, the outer rows of paving slabs of the original Sub-II floor were cut into, and those adjacent to the inner faces of the walls had to be relaid or renewed altogether. Generally speaking, the paving slabs of Period III are larger than those of Period II.

d. Periods of Construction

In order to determine the nature of the artificial platform over which the Sub-II pavement of the inner temple-court was laid, we lifted four of the flagstones between the west wall of Altar-Base III and the west wall of the court enclosure—to the south of the underground offering box on that side. The paving blocks had been laid with plaster between them, over a rubble fill. About 20 centimeters below the Sub-II pavement was a rude, flint block floor or level. Immediately above and below it was a layer of ashes, several centimeters thick, composed mostly of burned kernels of wheat. Among the ashes were fragments of fine, delicate, painted and plain Nabataean pottery of the most excellent and sophisticated types of this extraordinary ware. The rough, flint block foundation floor—if it may be called that—and the ash deposits with fragments of Nabataean pottery could not possibly be later than Period I, whatever time lag there may have been between the two layers of ashes. We dug then through the stone block rubble, in which we found nothing, until we came to virgin soil resting on native rock. The same results were obtained in two similar soundings below the Sub-II pavement in the northeast and southwest corners of the inner temple-court (Plans A; D, Section E-W; E, Section S-N; Pls. 101a, 108).

The conclusion forced upon us by these soundings was that sometime before the end of Period I and preceding the laying of the Sub-II flagstone

Pl. 57

a, b.   Aretas IV coin, enlarged (p. 11)
c, d.   Aretas IV coin, natural size (p. 11)
e, f.   Enlarged coin of Antiochus III, Abda (p. 12)
g, h.   Antiochus III coin, actual size (p. 12)
i.   Bronze spatula
j, k.   Bronze ring, Byzantine

129

Pl. 58   Enlargement of bronze coin of Aretas IV and Shaqilat I, Petra, obverse (p. 165)

Pl. 59   Aretas IV coin, reverse (p. 165)

Pl. 60 Enlargement, Nabataean
bronze coin of Malichus II and
Shaqilat II, Qasr Rabbah, obverse
(p. 165)

Pl. 61 Qasr Rabbah coin, reverse
(p. 165)

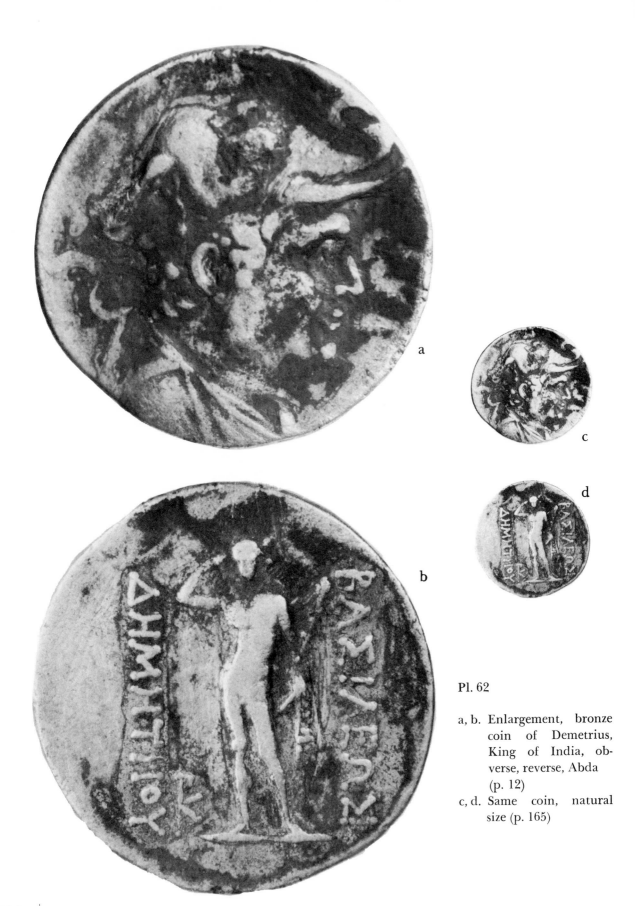

a

c

b

d

Pl. 62

a, b. Enlargement, bronze coin of Demetrius, King of India, obverse, reverse, Abda (p. 12)

c, d. Same coin, natural size (p. 165)

a   b

g   h

c   d

i   j

e   f

k   l

Pl. 63   Nabataean coins *(actual size)* (p. 165)

a, b.   Aretas IV-Shaqilat I, Petra
c, d.   Aretas IV-Shaqilat I, Petra
e, f.   Aretas IV-Shaqilat I, Kerak
g, h.   Aretas IV-Shaqilat I, Qasr Rabbah
i, j.   Malichus II and Shaqilat II, et-Telah
k, l.   Malichus II and Shaqilat II, Petra

a   b

c

a

b

c

d

Pl. 65

a, b. Sinope silver coin, enlargement (p. 61)
c, d. Natural size (p. 61)

Pl. 64 (*opposite*)

a. Tyrian didrachmon, Wadi Daliyeh, obverse (p. 61)
b. Tyrian didrachmon, Wadi Daliyeh, reverse (p. 339)
c. Taras on a dolphin, reverse (n. 64)

pavement, the Nabataeans had become masters of the art of pottery making and had produced beautiful and distinctive wares which bore the unique imprint of their genius. It is necessary thus to distinguish the following periods of the inner temple-court at Khirbet Tannur, which must apply naturally to the entire site: (a) Period I, during at least the latter part of which fine Nabataean pottery was produced whose excellence was not surpassed in the subsequent periods; (b) Sub-II, when the fine flagstone pavement was laid over the raised inner temple-court enclosure; (c) Period II, marked, among other things, by the inner Altar-Base with steps on its west side, which as we have seen, was built around the preceding one; and (d) Period III, to which the inner Altar-Base, enlarged for the third time, with steps on the south side, belonged.

That Period II must have come into existence shortly before 7 B.C. is indicated also by the date of a Nabataean dedicatory inscription we found at Khirbet Tannur (Pl. 194c). Deciphered by the late Père R. Savignac and revised by Abbé Starcky, it reads as follows:

"(The Monument) built by Netir'el the son of Zayd'el, *r's'yn l'aban,* (Master of the Spring of La'aban), for the life of Haretat, king of the Nabataeans who loves his people, and for the life of Huldu, his wife, in the year II." That is the equivalent of 8/7 B.C., which is the second year of the reign of Aretas IV, who ruled from 9 B.C. to A.D. 40,[114] and had two successive queens, the first named Huldu and the second called Shaqilat.

The fine Altar-Base of Period II was, as we have seen, built over the Sub-II pavement, whose flagstones touched the edge of the beveled plinth of the Altar-Base of Period I. Working backwards then, if Altar-Base II, built around the core of Altar-Base I, was constructed shortly before 7 B.C. then the Sub-II pavement that went under the walls of Altar-Base II (with whose building blocks its flagstones are closely related), could hardly have been constructed much later than 15 or 10 B.C.

Period I, to which the Nabataean pottery under the Sub-II pavement obviously belonged, would then have had to come to an end approximately between 25 and 10 B.C., and have commenced possibly a century earlier. Some time then around the end of the second century B.C. or perhaps around the beginning of the first century B.C. the first rude, rubble platform was constructed, on top of which the box-like Altar-Base of Period I was built. At that time, apparently, the general plan of the entirety of Khirbet Tannur came into being, and was maintained during the subsequent two main periods of history that followed it.

Period III at Khirbet Tannur can be dated by its architecture and sculptures to about the first quarter of the second century A.D. Its construction started probably, although not necessarily, before A.D. 106/107, when the Romans conquered the Nabataean kingdom and incorporated it into their Provincia Arabia. It could, of course, have been started some years later, too, before the full consequences of the Roman victory made themselves felt through diversion of trade routes and the consequent weakening and then disintegration of the Nabataean economic structure.

e. Earliest Pottery Evidence

Corroborative but not conclusive evidence of the dating of the initial appearance in Period I of fine Nabataean pottery, which, to be sure, continued to be used, in addition to somewhat coarsened forms, during the rest of the history of Khirbet Tannur and of the Nabataean kingdom, was also obtained from the excavation of the unpaved sections of the narrow platforms below the raised, inner temple enclosure on its south, north and west sides. We have already referred to the difference in level between the Sub-II pavement of the raised inner temple enclosure and that of the pavement outside of and below it. The outer pavements on the north and south sides of the enclosure are 34 centimeters lower at the west end and 30 centimeters at the east end than the inner temple-court pavement. The gap between the paved sections of these outer and lower platforms and the walls beyond them delimiting the entire temple area are too regular to have been accidental. This is particularly true on the north and south sides, with the unpaved section being more irregular on the west side. One wonders whether these empty spaces (Plan A; Pl. 98a, b) could have been occupied by benches, transforming the platforms outside the raised temple enclosure, which perhaps were originally colonnaded and roofed over, into the equivalent of sacred dining areas, related to the triclinia characterizing the rows of attached, outer side rooms.

Digging into the unpaved area on the north side of this outer pavement we came across a rude stamped lime floor, on top of which was a layer of burned earth and ashes. This extended under the flagstones of the outer pavement, as we were able to ascertain when we lifted some of its paving blocks to see whether it did so or not. Above and below this stamped floor we found numerous fragments of the finest types of Nabataean pottery, including some of the painted Nabataean plate (Pls. 73a, 74a). The latter, however, need not belong to Period I. These findings would have had no significance for dating the extremely fine Nabataean pottery, were it not for the complete similarity of some of them to those found under the Sub-II pavement of the inner temple-court to which we have referred, and were it not also for the fact that some of them came from the seemingly undisturbed bottom of the ditch. The possibility, nevertheless, exists that many sherds from this unpaved stretch and from the other unpaved areas are intrusive from Periods II and III (Pl. 75a, b).

f. Squatters' Houses

On the north and south sides of the pavements outside and below the inner temple enclosure were parts of several free standing columns, probably not in place at the time we uncovered them (Pl. 98a, b). There were other column parts scattered about in the vicinity. They consisted of two main types, the one with drums varying from 51 to 50 centimeters and the other with drums varying from 45.5 to 39 centimeters. A whole group of column drums of these main dimensions had been dragged together after the final destruction of the Temple of Tannur to form the curving front wall of a squatter's house, built against the intact portions of the walls at the southwest corner of the inner temple enclosure. This squatter's house had been constructed some time during the Byzantine period before the seventh century A.D., to judge from fragments of Byzantine pottery and pottery lamps found in the debris there. It possessed a crude fireplace (Pl. 110a; Plan A), built against the west end of its pillar-drum wall and separated by a single stone from the inner face of the remains of the west wall of the inner temple enclosure.

Some large column drums were placed, probably also in the Byzantine period, under the sagging steps on the south side of Altar-Base III (Pl. 102a), on top of which perhaps a squatter's hut had been built. In addition, we assembled from various sections of the ruins of Khirbet Tannur a number of column drums, several severely damaged capitals and a base from the debris on the north side of the outer pavement (Pl. 113c). Some of these columns may have belonged to a narrow colonnade with roof sloping inward, which may have covered the two narrow platforms on the north and south sides of the forecourt. These forecourt platforms can, for all practical purposes, be considered extensions of the outer south and north pavements located below the raised inner temple-court, being almost exactly on the same level.

g. Inviolate Area

The inside area of the raised inner temple-court remained the same in Periods II and III, measuring 10.38 m. from west to east and 9.72 m. from south to north. The enclosure walls of dressed stones with rubble filling between the inner and outer faces were 72 cm. thick on the south, west and north sides and 85 cm. on the front side. These dimensions apply to the Period III walls, which completely replaced those of Period II, reusing many of the earlier stones. A type of building block common in Period III construction was the one edged with beveled bands, sometimes used to subdivide the pecked faces of larger stones [114a] (Pl. 102b). There seems to have been a covering of stucco over the inner and outer faces of the Period III walls, hiding many imperfections and some shoddy work. The tooling on the faces of these blocks probably served to hold the stucco in place. It is also evident that parts of the Period III enclosure walls were repaired or built over again at least once during that time.

The paving blocks of the Sub-II pavement of the inner temple-court abutted against the inner faces of the outer Period III enclosure walls (Pls.

101a, b, 108, 109b). It will be recalled that the Sub-II pavement went under the walls of Altar-Base III and II up to the plinth of Altar-Base I. Parts of some of its paving blocks had been cut through when the Period III enclosure wall was built. The line of the inner face of that wall may already previously have been more or less determined by that of a Period I rubble wall, which would have been continued then when the Period II wall was built and followed in turn as much as possible in Period III. A trace of the Period I rubble wall can be seen under the south enclosure wall of Period III. The Sub-II pavement would then originally have been built up to the face of the Period I rubble wall, even as it had been up to the plinth of Altar-Base I. Parts of this Sub-II pavement were repaired with new paving blocks in Period III.

Each of the three side and rear walls of the inner temple enclosure had four pilasters, two in the middle and a returning one at each corner, with three indented panels between them. The outer edges of the torus of each pilaster were flush with those of its supporting plinth or ledge; and the faces of the panels agreed with the inner edges of this plinth which was returned on each of the three side walls (Pls. 113c, 114a). No capitals at all were found for the northwest and southwest corner pilasters of the enclosure walls. Each wall probably had a crowning architrave on the top of it, that simply returned around the projection of each pilaster. The pavement laid against the outer rear and side walls of the raised inner enclosure was some 20-30 cm. below the inner Sub-II pavement abutting their inner faces. This outer pavement was probably also first laid in the Sub-II period.

Near the east end of the south wall of the inner temple enclosure is a small side entrance (Pl. 109a, b). It is related in type to the smaller of the two side entrances in the north half of the outer east façade of the forecourt, both of which were used in Period II and blocked up in Period III (Pls. 95a, 96, 97). The possibility, indeed likelihood, exists that at least in part of Period III it too may have been blocked up and plastered over. It may have served as a special entrance for the temple priests, who at appropriate times would open the large double doors of the main gateway on the east façade to permit worshippers to ascend the steps from the east forecourt and gain entrance into the raised inner temple-court and access to the central altar on its high base.

The faces of the upper stones of this side entrance showed the beveled edges and diagonal lines of tooling common in Period III that served to hold a plaster covering. Cut through half of the length of the bottom of the plinth stone on the outer west side of the entrance frame was a rectangular opening that may have served as a door socket. There may have been a similar socket at its top, when the wall was intact. The door swung outward and fitted, when closed, in the space left for it in the plinth. The torus of the molded base of each pilaster projected to the outer edge of this plinth, with the indented panels of the S, N and W walls between the pilasters being flush with its inner edge (Pls. 109a, 114a, Plan A).

h. East Façade

There were sufficient remains of the rear and side walls of the inner temple enclosure to make it possible to date them to Period III. Their equivalent in Period II had disappeared completely, with perhaps some of its stones having been incorporated into the later walls. Enough remained also of the fine east façade or pylon of Period II to furnish a good idea of what it looked like originally. There was even a greater quantity of architectural remains of the much more ornate façade or pylon of Period III. We shall commence, therefore, with the latter, and return then to a consideration of the Period II, which it replaced.

When the debris was cleared away, we saw that the east façade had been destroyed, probably by a violent earthquake, down to the bases of three of its columns. Fortunately, a considerable number of its most important pieces were found on the pavement of the forecourt immediately below it, where the façade's superstructure had fallen. Still in position were the bases of two corner pilasters with attached quarter columns of the type characteristic of Period III, and on the left side of the entrance was the base of a column engaged half of its diameter. The missing half base from the right side was on the pavement below. In the pile of collapsed masonry there we found parts of capitals, of the main architrave, crowning cornice, features of decorated niches between the capitals and most of a very large, semicircular Atargatis panel that originally surmounted the entire entablature (Pls. 31-34; Plan B: 33, 35, 32).

The entire façade rested on a ledge or plinth, 70 cm. deep, which remained over from Period II and was the front of the built-up platform of the raised inner temple-court (Pls. 98a, 99a, b; Plan B, bottom). The bases of the pilasters and half engaged columns were of the Attic type and larger undoubtedly than their predecessors in Period II. The column drums above them seem to have been plain. Professor Fisher suggested, by reason of a few broken fragments found in the debris, that there might have been a foliate band just above the base, as seen for example on the Triumphal Arch and South Gate at Jerash.[115] That seems questionable, however, to judge from the striking parallel to this entire façade of the face of the Tomb of Sextus Florentinus at Petra (Pl. 200b).[116]

The two corner pilasters were 80 cm. wide and the drums of the attached half columns were 80 cm. in diameter and both projected 45 cm. from the main wall. The bases and capitals of the corner pilasters with attached quarter columns had carefully worked returns to correspond to the quarter columns. The capitals were in two horizontal blocks (Plan B:49, 44), the lower with double rows of acanthus leaves (Plan B:49; Pl. 176a) and the upper with wide spreading volutes whose projecting ends had been broken off [116a] (Plan B:44; cf. Pl. 175a, b, c). Paralleling it was a cornice (Plan B:6; Pls. 172a or 172b) which may have returned and crowned the very top of the side and rear walls, whose height apparently did not equal that of the east façade.

1) ATARGATIS PANEL

At this point, above the cornice over the capitals and the top of the walls between them on the east façade, there rose an extraordinary entablature, a restoration of which Professor Fisher has essayed in his plan. We found parts of an architrave (Plan B:17), of a frieze of large busts in relief, including a corner piece with sculptures on two adjacent sides (Plan B:34; Pl. 53a, b), and of another cornice (Plan B:15 of the type of Pl. 172b), which Professor Fisher has put together in that mounting order, with a beak molding (Plan B:12) adjacent to the cornice (Plan B:15). The entire Period III east façade, as Professor Fisher has reconstructed it, mounting from the surface of the platform on which it rested to the top of the crowning cornice, attained a height of 7.5 m. We shall return later on to a discussion of the frieze with the large busts in relief.

These three sections, however, from above the top of the capitals to the top of the cornice, formed only one part of the amazing entablature of the east façade of the inner temple enclosure. Together with many other pieces of masonry from the east façade that had fallen on the pavement of the lower, east forecourt in front of it, we found most but not all of the parts of a large, semicircular, carefully sculptured panel. It must have been located above the crowning cornice that capped the frieze of busts of deities, and occupied a space equivalent to the width of the central panel of the east façade, in which the gateway into the inner temple-court was located.

The central and largest section of this grandiose, semicircular panel, featured a larger-than-life size bust in high relief of Atargatis, whose face and bosom were partly covered with leaves. On each side of her head, the top of which rose above the radius of the panel and extending to four other connecting sections (Pl. 31), was an intricate pattern of interlaced vines and acanthus leaves encircling separate rosettes, figs and pomegranates. The goddess was thus in the center of an elegant, spreading floral scroll. At least one piece of the semicircular panel, namely the one between the two end pieces of the bottom blocks, is missing. It formed the continuation of the central Atargatis panel, and must further have carried out the decoration of leaves which not only, in effect, veiled her face, but adorned her neck, and seemed to form a bodice covering her body while leaving her breasts bare. Her hair, parted in the middle, was trained into carefully separated tresses, framing her face and falling over the front of her shoulders. The tresses of the attendant lion of another Atargatis and of other lions, too, were modeled in the same fashion of carefully trained locks coming to a point, cascading over one another in orderly profusion (Pls. 160, 165). The hair of Saturn, for example, was similarly portrayed (Pl. 153a).

At the back and bottom of the central panel, from the front of which the Atargatis bust in relief rises, there is a very large dowel (Pl. 33a, b) that must have fitted into a hole made to receive it in the center of the now missing block below it. It may be that the six pieces of the semicircular panel, including the missing one into which the Atargatis section proper was rabbeted, rested directly on the cornice below, even as the closely related semicircular panel is represented as doing in the strikingly parallel façade of the Tomb of Sextus Florentinus at Petra.

2) EAGLE FINIAL

In the heap of masonry where we found most of the pieces of the semicircular Atargatis panel was a finial with the relief of an eagle with outspread wings. The bottom side was horizontally grooved and it could have fitted exactly on top of the center of the wide rim of the main Atargatis section, from which and above which the head of the goddess protruded (Pl. 34a). We also found there two complete sections of a curved cornice of the same radius as the top of the semicircular panel. Each of them had a projecting triangular horn, set at an outturned angle. They probably represented rays of the sun (Pl. 34b), or possibly, although less likely, symbolized the horns of bulls associated with Zeus-Hadad. Both the rays and the eagle could stand for the god, himself.

There is a relationship to the bust of a solar god from Hatra[117] with a circular radiate halo behind his head and a circular medallion on each shoulder bearing a standing eagle with outstretched wings, in left profile. A closer parallel is the relief of the youthful, beardless Helios from Khirbet Tannur (Pl. 136), with a torch over each shoulder, representing probably the evening and morning stars, respectively, and wearing a radiate crown,[118] and also the Helios relief from Qasr Rabbah (Pl. 137a).

The closest parallel occurs on the Cerberos relief from Hatra showing in part an enthroned Atargatis flanked by two lions, with two dolphins in heraldic juxtaposition underneath her feet and a frontally positioned eagle with spread wings surmounting her head. It is also significant that in her right hand she holds a leaf, relating her also in this fashion to the Khirbet Tannur Atargatis with her veil of leaves (Pl. 10a, b).[118a]

The eagle finial crowns the impressive semicircular Atargatis panel that rises thus strikingly above the top cornice of the east façade of the inner temple-court pylon and, as has already been mentioned, spans the area set back between the two central engaged half columns which flank the main entrance way into the raised inner temple area. We believe it possible that the semicircular Atargatis panel with its superimposed eagle finial and curved cornice of projecting horns was only part of an elaborate attic addition, which would raise the east façade of the inner temple enclosure of Khirbet Tannur much higher than is presently shown on the plan of the architectural reconstruction.

Decisive for us in this matter is the appearance of the entire façade of the Tomb of Sextus Florentinus at Petra (Pl. 200b), to which reference has already been made above. There is a striking similarity between it and the east façade of the inner court of the Temple of Tannur. They are much alike in the position of the semicircular panel, located in each instance above the crowning cornice of the main story, with its corner pilasters, Corinthian capitals and central entrance. The figure of what may be an Atargatis or Tyché bust in relief, wearing perhaps a crown, occupies the center of the Petra panel, with an urn (?) on a ledge directly above the top center of the curved cornice. The Petra panel, however, is located in the lower part of an elaborate second story or attic addition which is marked by corner pilasters with Corinthianized Nabataean capitals [119] and is capped by a fine pediment.

Much the same type of attic addition may have been incorporated in the upper part of the east façade of the inner court of the Temple of Tannur. Some of the loose sculptures found in the ruins there may originally have belonged alongside the curved cornice of the Atargatis panel, as is the case in the Petra parallel. Other fragments of architectural stones, for which no definite place could be found in the restoration, might have been parts of this second story. To its corner pilasters then would belong, we think, the Corinthian capitals decorated with exactly the same kind of foliage and fruit as the Atargatis panel (Pl. 175a, b). The double pronged horns (cf. Pl. 175c) had been broken off when the capitals fell to the ground. There is a relationship in general form to those of the inner temple-court altar of Period III (Pls. 133, 134), to which an isolated architrave section with apparently similar decoration may have belonged (Pl. 174d).

3) ARCHITRAVES WITH BUSTS IN RELIEF

We shall reserve discussion of the entrance way in the center of the east façade between the two inner, engaged half columns, until we deal with its appearance in the preceding Period II. On each side of it, however, between each engaged half column and the corner pilaster with attached quarter column was a shallow niche, of 91 centimeters overall width, with plain pilasters resting on a base. Above each niche was an architrave, topped by a dentilated pediment (Plan B:26; Pl. 178a), which had two side brackets and another on the finial above its apex to support small sculptures of goddesses or eagles or something similar. The architrave over each niche is decorated with two rosettes, spaced between three triglyphs (of two divisions each instead of the three of the usual Doric style). These in turn are set between two small, probably female busts in relief contained within plain bordered panels (Plan B:19; Pl. 12a, b; cf. Pl. 166b).

The neckline of the bodice on each of the two busts of the one comparatively intact architrave has the same triangular ornamentation (Pl. 12a) as that of the dolphin-goddess of Altar-Base III (Pl. 1). The decoration over the shoulders and arms of the two busts on the architrave cannot be distinguished from the overlapping rows of feathers on the body and part of the underside of the outstretched wings of the eagle on the finial above the semicircular Atargatis panel in the attic above these niches. Both the triangular neckline ornamentation and the one that looks like a series of overlapping feathers appear on the bodice of one of the much-damaged dolphin (?) goddesses (Pls. 27a, b, 28a). The busts of the second architrave also have the triangular ornamentation over the neckline of their bodices, but different lines of draperies over their shoulders and forearms (Pl. 12b).

There are also several other slight differences between the two sets of busts of these two architraves. In the case of those of the second architrave, the hair is parted in the middle and set in wavy tresses like that of the dolphin and grain goddesses (Pl. 12b), but is not covered with a sky veil (Pls, 1, 2a, b, 25, 26). This is true, at least, of the bust on the right side of the second architrave (although something seems to have been broken off from the top of the frame or panel against which her head rests). The bust on the left side of this architrave has been badly disfigured, but the likelihood is that it looked like the one on the right side. In the instance of the first architrave, however, the hair is covered by a pointed Athena or Mercury-type helmet,[120] set against three rectangular projections, the top one of which is broken off on the left side of the photograph. The helmets permit the fronts of the evenly spaced rows of curls to be seen. Careful examination reveals also slight differences of the inner edges of the panels, in which the two pairs of busts are set.

4) GATEWAY

A flight of three steps led up from the west end of the forecourt (Pls. 91, 99a, 100a) to the gateway in the east façade opening into the raised, inner temple-court. These steps were built into the plinth of the front of the pylon's low, raised platform. The width of the entrance was 1.75 meters in Periods II and III, and the height, as restored by Professor Fisher from the coursing of the masonry, was almost 4.5 meters. This was increased in Period III by a pediment (Plan B:36), which was closely related to the two smaller ones over each of the niches in the face of the Period III pylon (Plan B:36). It is likely that over this gateway in Period II was a decorated architrave or lintel much similar to the one over the Period II base of the altar in the inner temple-court (Plan C:25b; Pl. 104a).

There were two sills at the entrance, with L-shaped cuttings at their ends, into which iron sockets were fitted for the doorposts of the doors that swung inward (Plans A; B, bottom). The outer and higher (Pls. 99b, 100a) one undoubtedly belonged to Period II, with a hole in the center of the sill for a supporting vertical, iron bar. A horizontal beam undoubtedly locked the two doors of each gateway in place when they were closed. The inner sill for the doors of the Period III gateway was lower than the outer one, and the L-shaped cuttings at either end were correspondingly larger. They extended under the walls at either end and were grooved and tongued (Pl. 100b) to hold the large iron sockets placed in them to give support to the massive doors used in this period. Two holes at the edge of the center of the sill indicate where vertical iron bars were placed to strengthen and help lock the Period III doors in place when they were closed (Pls. 99b, 100a).

A rectangular, burned patch on the Sub-II pavement floor immediately beyond or west of the double doors indicated where they had fallen and burned in the conflagration ensuing from the earthquake that brought the history of Khirbet Tannur to an end in Period III. The heavy, supporting, stone buttresses placed on each side of the gateway in this period, against the inner face of the east façade, were unable to prevent its collapse when the earthquake occurred (Plans A; B, bottom).

5) EARLIER FORM OF FAÇADE

We have seen that the side and rear walls of the inner temple enclosure of Period III completely replaced those of Period II. Some of the building blocks of Period II were recut and reused and, occasionally, sandstone blocks were introduced. Fortunately, there remained some clear cut building-stones that could only have belonged to the Period II east façade of the inner temple enclosure. They would not have sufficed, however, to make a reasonable reconstruction possible, as in Period III, were it not for the east façade of the forecourt, which retained in Period III much the same appearance it had in Period II, and indicated thus, for instance, what the capitals of the east façade of the inner temple enclosure of Period II must have looked like. Further discussion must therefore await the description of the east façade of the forecourt.

i. *Outer, West Altar*

Sunk into the outer part of the existing section of the pavement beyond and below the west side of the raised inner temple-court enclosure is a square plinth of two equal parts supporting the base of a comparatively small altar, formed of several separate pieces. It is located on the axis of the altar-base of the inner court and faces westward. It would have been seen by those entering the gate that is presumed to have existed in the outer west wall of the entire temple area, of which, to be sure, no absolutely certain

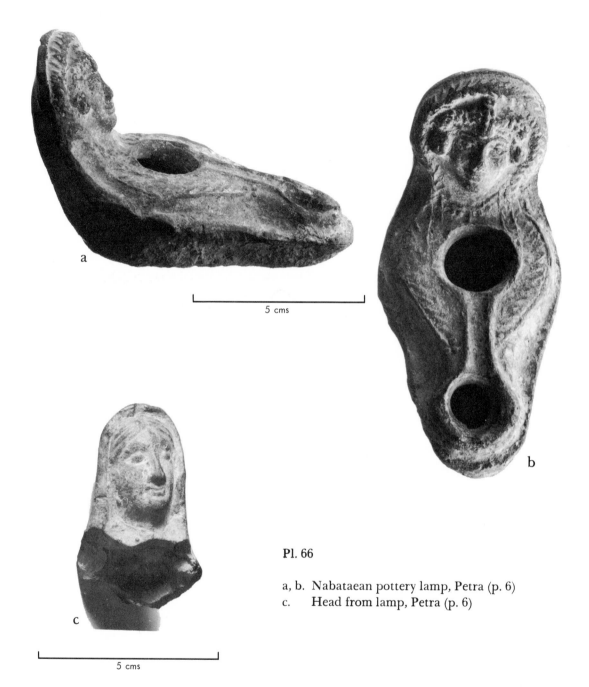

a

b

c

5 cms

5 cms

Pl. 66

a, b. Nabataean pottery lamp, Petra (p. 6)
c.   Head from lamp, Petra (p. 6)

Pl. 67 (*opposite*)

a. Enlargement, head from Nabataean lamp (p. 6)
b. Natural size (p. 6)
c. Right profile (p. 6)

149

Pl. 68   Crown of Nabataean pottery lamp, enlargement, Petra (p. 6)

c   d

Pl. 69

a, b.   Front view and right profile of head of Moabite pottery figurine,
        el-Medeiyineh (p. 222)
c.   Head of Moabite pottery figurine (p. 222)
d.   Head of Moabite pottery figurine (p. 222)

Pl. 70   Ammonite stone figurine (p. 222)

Pl. 71   Stone figurine, Amman (p. 222)

a, b

c, d

5 cms

154

traces remain (Plans A:6; D, Section E-W; Pl. 114a, b, c). There are, however, definite indications as to where its line must have been. It may be taken for granted that the outer west pavement continued originally to the face of this projected wall.

The plinth of this outer west altar was sunk into the soil, and the flagstones around it seem to have been relaid in Period III. It will be noticed that one paving slab was cut to fit around its southeast corner and that the two slabs against the rest of its south side were laid sidewise instead of lengthwise in accordance with the normal procedure (Plan A:6; Pl. 114b). Indeed, it seems obvious that this altar, probably first constructed in Period II, was radically repaired in Period III. It was traditional at the Temple of Tannur to preserve from period to period objects of enduring sanctity.

Looking at the south side of the base of the altar, one sees that it is composed of two main parts, with a molded plug in between. On the north side the two parts come together. Just when it became necessary to insert a plug on the south side is impossible to figure out exactly. Our guess is that this plug and the east half of the altar-base nearest the outer west side of the raised inner temple enclosure stem from Period III. It can be seen that their lines of molding simulate but do not completely repeat the lines of molding of the west half, probably to be ascribed to the preceding Period II. Was the reverence for their past so great among the Nabataeans that they followed the practice, common in our own times, of inserting only partly shaped building stones when reconstructing ancient structures, in order to establish clearly their difference from the authentic, original parts they replace? The possibility exists that the major east part of the base and the plug into it were originally one piece, but that they got broken into two somehow or other, possibly even before they were put into place. Their outer surfaces are completely identical.

The central shaft of the altar was completely missing. Belonging apparently to the top of it was part of a cap, whose lines of molding on the sides resemble those on the front of the base (Pl. 114c). On the face of this broken cap is a little more than half of three rods fanning out from a bound center, above which is the design of a "shield," or "axe" such as may also have been repeated below it, too. This design appeared at Khirbet Tannur also under the horns of one of the Nabataean pilaster capitals, which adorned the attached columns of the east façade of the inner temple and outer forecourt enclosures (Pl. 173a, b). The representation of bound rods undoubtedly signifies a multipronged thunderbolt, a commonly repeated motif in the ornamentation of Khirbet Tannur and other Nabataean temples. The most striking example at Khirbet Tannur is the thunderbolt over the left arm of Zeus-Hadad, its chief male god. (Pl. 41). It is noteworthy in this connection that the enlarged "shield" or "axe" which decorates a building block at the Nabataean site at Khirbet Brak near Petra [121] contains the

Pl. 72 (opposite)

a, b. Limestone head with unusually long neck, Amman (p. 222)
c, d. Torsos designed to receive separate heads, Amman (p. 222)

duplicate of half of the double pronged, twelve leafed thunderbolt design (Pl. 174c) that is repeated a number of times at Khirbet Tannur (Pl. 105a, b). The thunderbolt symbol repeatedly employed at Khirbet Tannur occurs also at the nearby Nabataean site of Khirbet edh-Dherih (Pl. 178d).

4. PLACE OF ASSEMBLY: EAST FORECOURT

a. Dimensions

The outer east forecourt, inside the line of its north and south platforms which are two steps high above it (Pl. 91; Plan A), is almost square. Oriented west-east, it measures 15.68 by 15.47 meters. Including the width of the platforms, the total distance between the north and south walls bounding the platforms is 20.05 meters. We shall refer later to the side triclinia or sacred rooms attached to these walls, with entrances into them from the platforms. These platforms represent the continuations of the pavements below the north and south sides of the raised inner temple enclosure. We have suggested previously that the platforms were probably colonnaded and roofed over, as possibly may have been the pavements below the north, south and west sides of the walled and elevated inner shrine area.

The east and west portions of the forecourt pavement were revealed when we cleared the debris covering it, but the middle portion of it had apparently been carried away and used for building purposes elsewhere. The rows of paving slabs of the two opposite sections of the forecourt pavement do not correspond with each other, as do the rows of the pavements of the inner temple area. The explanation may be that when the ornate pylon of the east façade of the raised inner temple enclosure collapsed at the end of Period II, it damaged the pavement of the west end of the forecourt below it severely enough to require the relaying of that section in the reconstruction which took place during Period III. When that was done, the rows of paving slabs were not kept in alignment with those at the east end of the forecourt. We have already mentioned the care taken when the forecourt was first paved in Period II to have it slope so that the rainwater drained from west to east, or more particularly from northwest to southeast. That same slope was retained in Period III. There was, for instance, a drop of 38 centimeters between the west and east ends of the south side of the forecourt. The possibility exists that the pavement of the forecourt may have been laid at the same time as the raised inner shrine, namely in Period Sub-II.

It was clear, too, after the debris had been removed from the side platforms, that such paving as remained on them at the end of Period III was of an irregular and at times even crude nature. The outer slabs of paving blocks on the platforms were laid lengthwise to the steps leading up to them. The west end of the south platform was particularly badly paved with reused flagstones and parts of old pedestal bases (Plan A). Part of this patchwork paving extended into the unpaved space at the edge of the extant pavement below the south side of the raised inner temple enclosure. We have remarked about a similar unpaved space at the edge of the north pavement below the raised, inner temple enclosure and of a related, but more irregular, unpaved space left at the edge of the pavement below the west end of the raised, inner temple enclosure. We have wondered whether benches for sacred dining purposes could have occupied these unpaved spaces, particularly on the north and south sides, both in Periods II and III, and which disappeared somehow at the end of the latter period. In that case, the pavements around and below the raised, inner temple enclosure and the platforms on the sides of the forecourt would in effect belong to a great, public triclinium, with the smaller triclinia or sacred dining chambers attached to the outer north and south side walls being reserved for special groups.

b. Forecourt Altar

Near the northeast corner of the forecourt are the remains, now only one course high, of the outline of a 2 m. square altar, seeming originally to have belonged to Period II. Destroyed or badly damaged at the end of that period, it was repaired and enlarged in Period III, measuring then 2.45 m. square. The foundation stones of this enlargement can be seen on the west, north and south sides of the altar base. The enlargement required the lifting of the original flagstones of the pavement bordering the Period II altar and replacing them in changed form to fit against the one of Period III. Those on the north side of the enlarged altar base were laid sideways instead of lengthwise as usual (Plan A; Pl. 91). The retention of the Period II Altar-Base inside of the enlarged one of Period III in the forecourt corresponds to the building process, according to which the altar-pedestal in the raised inner temple-court was erected in the form of three boxes of three successive periods placed one over the other. In his excavations of the "Conway High Place" at Petra, Albright found that there, too, successive builders were careful to cover up or enlarge and not to destroy previous installations. Others, as a result of later excavations, have held that this may not be a "high place" after all, but rather a circular corner bastion of Roman military construction.[122]

c. East Façade

It appears that the east façade of the forecourt did not suffer the same complete destruction in Period II that befell the inner temple enclosure façade then as the result of an earthquake. Aside from the blocking of two secondary entrances in the forecourt façade in Period III, north of its central entrance, its main features seem to have been retained. On either side of the main entrance (Plan A; Pl. 95b) were two engaged columns, projecting only about a third of their diameters from the face of the wall. They rested on bases of Attic type, which continued in use in Period III. Equidistant from them were two pilasters, projecting the same distance from the face of the wall. It seems that the position of the north one of them was determined in Period II by the fact that it was on the south side of the secondary entrance opening into the forecourt (Pls. 93b; 95a, b; 96). We shall see that the other secondary entrance beyond it in the outer east façade opened on to the platform on the north side of the forecourt (Pls. 95b; 96b; 97a, b). The bases, both of the pilasters and columns, had been reused in Period III, as well as their distinctive Nabataean capitals.

These capitals, well known from Petra and elsewhere, were composed of two blocks, the lower one containing the moldings and the upper one having the characteristic horned projections, suggesting an exaggerated Corinthian abacus. Two of the capitals were found outside the east façade of the forecourt and on the south slope of the hilltop, one for an intermediate, attached pilaster (Pl. 173a, b) and the other for a square pilaster (Pl. 173c). The latter served as the model for the capitals of the corner pilasters also of the Period II façade of the inner temple-court enclosure. The measurements of these pilasters, corresponding with those of the capitals, were less than those of their successors of the inner court, Period III façade, to which also engaged quarter columns were added. The detached Nabataean capital (with the center horn broken off) served as the model for the capitals of the correspondingly still narrower, engaged middle columns of the inner court, Period II façade that projected about a third of their diameters. Their missing bases were restored on paper by Professor Clarence S. Fisher, in accordance with the *in situ* ones of the Period III forecourt façade, which had first been placed there in Period II and were reused in Period III.

A simple cornice was found (Plan B:13) which could have crowned the top of the side walls of the inner temple enclosure of Period II. Their height paralleled that of the Nabataean capitals of its east façade, which, however, was possessed of an additional entablature and attic story. The entablature consisted of an architrave with a simple crowning molding (Plan B:10). Above it must have been a frieze of some kind with a simple molding (Plan B:7) of its own and over which, in turn, rested a large, overhanging, Doric-type cornice with a sloping soffit and a deep channel for carrying off rainwater (Plan B:18). Then came, apparently, as Professor Fisher has reconstructed it, an attic story crowned by a large, cavetto cornice block of Egyptian style (Plan B:14). In effect, thus, the east façade of the inner temple enclosure of Period II formed a high pylon which towered above its side walls. They supported no roof, however, leaving the inner temple-court and its central shrine open to the skies.

The reconstruction of this façade, as worked out and drawn by Professor Fisher on the basis of Carl Pape's measurements of every architectural stone uncovered in our excavations, brought the height of this east façade or pylon of the inner temple-court enclosure of Period II to almost eight and a half meters. We have already seen that the one that replaced it in Period III was still higher.

d. Main and Side Entrances

When we cleared the outer east wall of the forecourt, we found, as has been mentioned, that in addition to the main entrance in the center there were two side entrances in its north half. These latter two had been used in Period II, but had been blocked up and probably plastered over, together with the other plain parts of the outer wall in Period III. Most of the outer wall had probably been plastered over also in Period II. Just why these two side entrances in the outer east wall were blocked up in Period III is impossible to explain. The same thing had occurred at that time in the case of the side entrance in the south wall of the raised, inner temple enclosure.

The one side entrance in approximately the center of the north half of the outer east wall opened directly into the forecourt and towards the altar in its northeast corner. Three paving slabs laid lengthwise and two other cut stones laid sidewise over part of them—all of them hailing from Period II—had been used among other stones to block this doorway in Period III (Plan A; Pls. 93b, 95b, 96a). The second side entrance was located at the north end of the outer east wall and opened on to the north platform. When the stones blocking it were removed, the steps leading up to it and the door-sill and door-jambs were clearly visible (Plan A; Pls. 95b, 96b, 97a, b).

Had we judged only from the appearance of the remains of the inner face of the outer east wall as seen from the forecourt (Pl. 91), we never would have learned of the existence of two side entrances in the north half of that wall. They became apparent only when we cleared the outer face of the wall (Pls. 93b, 95a, b). There was never any question, however, about the location of the main entrance or gateway in the center of the outer east wall of the forecourt. On each side of it, on the outer façade of Period II, as we have already pointed out, was an engaged column and a pilaster with a Nabataean capital which were retained also in Period III.

Broad steps led up to the gateway proper. One of them is still more or less in place directly below the doorsill. In front of it is a broken block, which could not originally have been in that position (Pls. 94b, 95a). The doorsill itself consisted of two long slabs, the inner one, found in badly preserved condition, seems to have had shallow door sockets. This gateway apparently remained more or less the same both in Periods II and III.

5. ANTECEDENTS

If the three successive altar-bases in the center of the raised inner court may be said to have consisted of a series of three open end boxes, the first and oldest being enclosed by the second and that in turn by the third, the entire architectural plan of Khirbet Tannur can also be thought of as being composed of a series of boxes open at the top and contained within one another.

In the center of the raised inner court is the box-like altar-base or pedestal that, as we have mentioned, was enlarged twice, each time preserving the previous original. This raised inner court or platform was completely enclosed by walls, with a pylon forming the east side. A corridor surrounded the west, north and south sides of this walled inner court, with steps leading down from the east pylon to a large, sunken forecourt below it. The north and south corridors outside the walled inner court continue along the north and south sides of the sunken forecourt. This entire scheme was bounded on the north and south and possibly on the west sides by series of triclinia, with the front east side of the sunken forecourt and of the entire enclosure consisting of another pylon.

We have referred several times to the close relationship of Khirbet Tannur not only to the Zibb Atuf high-place of Petra but also to the tiny, Nabataean temple in the Wadi Ramm, where a simplified form of the Khirbet Tannur scheme prevailed. Consisting of a square cella in the center of a walled area, its plan, like that of Khirbet Tannur and the ones of each of the temples of Sur and Sahr and of the two Ba'al-shamin and Dushara temples of Si'a in Nabataean Syria, seems to have been characteristic of Nabataean temple architecture till about the middle of the second century A.D.[123] The antecedent of this type of temple plan, like so much else of the Nabataean civilization, seems to have been Parthian and, earlier still, Achaemenean or Persian.[124]

V. DINING WITH DIVINITY

1. Triclinia: Religious Banquet Chambers
    a. *A Main Feature of the Temple Architecture*
    b. *Parallels*
    c. *The Role of Women*
    d. *On the North Side*
        1) Rooms 8, 9, and 10   2) Room 11
    e. *Burned Level and Nabataean Pottery*
    f. *South Triclinia Chambers*
        1) Rooms 14 and 15   2) Rooms 12 and 13
    g. *Uniformity of Furniture*

V. *Dining with Divinity*

1. TRICLINIA: RELIGIOUS BANQUET CHAMBERS

a. A Main Feature of Temple Architecture

There is a series of rooms on the north and south sides of the outermost walls enclosing the inner temple area and the forecourt together with its platforms. They served primarily as sacred banquet chambers, where priests and pilgrims joined in feasts of religious significance. Not all of the fruits and grains and flesh of fowl and beasts set before the deities of the temple were consumed by fire on its central and side altars. Much or most of the offerings were eaten by the temple functionaries and the worshippers in these rooms, set aside especially for this purpose. Known as triclinia because of the high, narrow bench or platform going around three sides of each room, these sacred dining halls played an important role in the temple ritual, aside from the possibility of affording lodging to the permanent attendants of the temple. There is no proof for this last surmise. Remnants of pillars with courses composed of three triangular stones found in one of these rooms indicate that they may once have been roofed over, unlike the raised, inner temple platform with its central altar open to the skies.

The triclinia, or more exactly the chambers with triclinia, were originally well paved, with a short flight of steps in each of them leading up to the banquet benches on three sides. Seated or reclining, and afterwards resting on the benches, the faithful dined literally on the food of the gods, breaking the bread and wine and meat of communion with those whom they fondly conceived to be the sources of their welfare.

On occasions marking the advent of spring or fall, when the blessings of fertility were besought or acknowledged and at other propitious times, the Temple of Tannur on its hilltop of age old sanctity was a lodestar of attraction to multitudes who climbed to its precincts bearing gifts to the gods.

The cult meal marked the culmination and conclusion of their pilgrimage, occupying as it did a position of central importance in Nabataean religious observance, as also in that of the related and surrounding Hellenistic-Semitic world.

b. Parallels

There seems to be no question that the practice of the cult meal was observed at triclinia and biclinia at every Nabataean temple throughout the entire Nabataean kingdom. The Nabataean temple in the Wadi Ramm in southernmost Transjordan, resembling in miniature the Temple of Tannur, and dating in its present form probably to early in the second century A.D., also had rooms around its sides. They must have served as triclinia chambers,[125] although no traces of banquet benches remained when the site was excavated.[126] In front of the main altar in the raised inner court, approached by a flight of steps, must have been placed the sandstone sculpture of a seated goddess found there, with an unrecognizably damaged figure at the bottom of her tunic (Pl. 52c). One thinks in this connection of the well known relief on the Tyché of Antioch, with her right foot resting on the neck of the personification of the Orontes River (Pl. 52a).[127] Whether the Wadi Ramm figure was known at Tyché, Atargatis, Allat or by some local name,[128] it is clear that some part of the offerings brought to her on the altar in front of which she was enthroned must have been consumed by the celebrants in the course of ritual feasts on the adjacent triclinia.[129]

The triclinia of the Temple of Tannur are of course directly related to those found in large numbers at Petra (Pls. 92a, 202b, 205b, 206a, b).[130] The only difference between the triclinia of the two places is that the banquet benches at Petra were hewn out of easily workable sandstone, while those at the Temple of Tannur were constructed of well dressed and coursed limestone blocks of the same excellence as the flagstones of the pavements of the triclinia chambers. The triclinia and biclinia of Petra, however, need not all have been connected with ritual meals of religious significance. Some may have formed the equivalent of dining tables of private dwellings.[131] Most of them, however, were integral parts of tombs or were constructed in their proximity for commemorative feasts to the dead.[132]

The connection of Nabataean wakes with triclinia in burial tombs at Petra is illustrated by the Nabataean inscription on the front of the Turkomaniyeh Tomb there.[133] It refers to the *"space with couches for funeral repasts"* as *"the consecrated and inviolable possession of Dushara."* [134] An excellent triclinium with rebated edges and with an arcosolium burial place cut into its rear wall is visible in the Qattar ed-Deir in Petra.[135]

The cult or sacrificial meals in connection with worship of the gods were celebrated on the triclinia platforms or benches, and apparently no temple or altar was considered complete without provision for triclinia. A striking example of that is furnished by the Great High Place of Zibb Atuf at Petra. The benches of the outer east court formed a large triclinium.[136] Indeed, the platforms, raised two steps high above the north and south sides of the great forecourt of the Temple of Tannur, may be considered as forming a biclinium, in addition to the triclinia chambers attached to their outer walls.

The importance of the ritual meal in the religious practices of the Nabataeans, held especially on calendrical occasions,[137] with which feasts commemorative of the dead, as well as the departure and resurrection of some of the gods on the two autumn and spring equinoctial days must be associated, is evidenced by the prevalence of triclinia in contemporary temples of related architecture and worship both inside and outside the Nabataean kingdom. They were all embraced within the circle of a common Hellenistic-Semitic culture.

Triclinia occurred in Syria in such places as Antioch, Dura-Europos, Palmyra, Khirbet Semrin and probably Byblos, among other places.[138] The temple of Abgal at Khirbet Semrin furnishes evidence of a third century A.D. date for its triclinia.[139] They are known to have existed in Alexandria in the third century B.C.[140] Egypt, Greece, Rome and the ancient Near East in general knew the triclinia well.[141] There is little doubt but that they were to be found also in temples in Arabia of the first centuries B.C. and A.D., and certainly at Nabataean sites such as Meda'in Saleh. Participation in sacred meals in a sanctuary was well known to the Israelites of old.[142]

c. The Role of Women

Little is known about the actual character of the sacred meals eaten in triclinia at Nabataean and related sanctuaries. The participation of two female singers at Nabataean communal banquets of thirteen persons each is reported by Strabo,[143] not, however, on the basis of his own experience. The statement may or many not be true and, in any event, is in itself no indication of licentious behavior on such occasions.

The advanced position of women in the Nabataean body politic is evidenced, at least among the royalty, by the prominent role that the Nabataean queens played in public life, alongside of their kings. The heads of the reigning king and queen were frequently emblazoned on Nabataean coins (Pls. 58-63).[144] It may thus not have been unusual for women to have taken a more active role than normal in the Semitic world even in the most sacred religious ceremonies and in the cult meals, although there is no proof for it.[145] In general, however, the role of women in the contemporary, Hellenistic-Semitic, ancient Near East was an important one. Herodias in Judaea was certainly no less influential than her counterpart, Huldu or Shaqilat, in Nabataea. It is known from Nabataean inscriptions that married women could hold and bequeath property, and that the genealogy was sometimes traced through the female line.[146] Pagan temples, whether inside or outside the Nabataean kingdom, were dedicated both to Dushara and Allat or to localized versions of Zeus-Hadad and Atargatis, such as were worshipped at the temples of Tannur or of Dura.[147] Indeed, in general, Atargatis seems to have outranked her consort by far.

It may be taken for granted that both men and women visited the Nabataean temples, and there can be little doubt but that they pilgrimaged together to the especially sacred Temple of Tannur. The role of women in pagan religious ceremonies in the ancient Near East is well attested. "For it came to pass," we read, "when Solomon was old, that his wives turned away his heart after other gods . . . after Ashtoreth . . . and after Milcolm . . . And so he did for all his foreign wives, who burned incense and sacrificed unto their gods" (I Kings 11:4-8). The excitement of pagan worship and participation in feasts of sacrificial offerings apparently often led male and female worshippers to join together in feverish consummation of fertility rites.

Rich food in plenty and strong wine without stint on these occasions helped bring the deities and their devotees into a perfervid relationship. The Bible may be taken literally when it inveighs against those who played the harlot upon every high hill and under every green tree (Jeremiah 2:20) and who ate of the sacrifices of the gods (Exodus 34:15; Ezek. 16:16, 17). It is in the light of this background that there may possibly be some basis to the perhaps overly righteous comment of Bar Hebraeus on Nabataean women. Employing as his text Psalm 12:8, "The wicked walk on every side when vileness is exalted among the sons of men," he castigates their promiscuousness on the occasion of the cult meals after they had danced around a representation of Baltis or Aphrodite on a mountain top shrine.[148]

d. On the North Side

1) ROOMS 8, 9, AND 10

From the remains of the triclinia chambers on the north side of the temple area, it is possible to reconstruct their appearance in considerable measure in Periods II and III. The best preserved chambers are rooms 8, 9 and 10, the latter being obviously the latest addition, with the entrance on its south side facing the open area in front of the outer east façade or pylon of the forecourt. Rooms 8 and 9 also had entrances on the south, each wide enough for a single door, opening on to the north platform of the forecourt. The bases of the door jambs of the entrance of room 8 would seem to belong at the earliest to Period III and not to have been made especially for the purpose, being wider than the entrance sill and overlapping the ends of it (Pls. 115, 116). They were perhaps dragged there, when squatters oc-

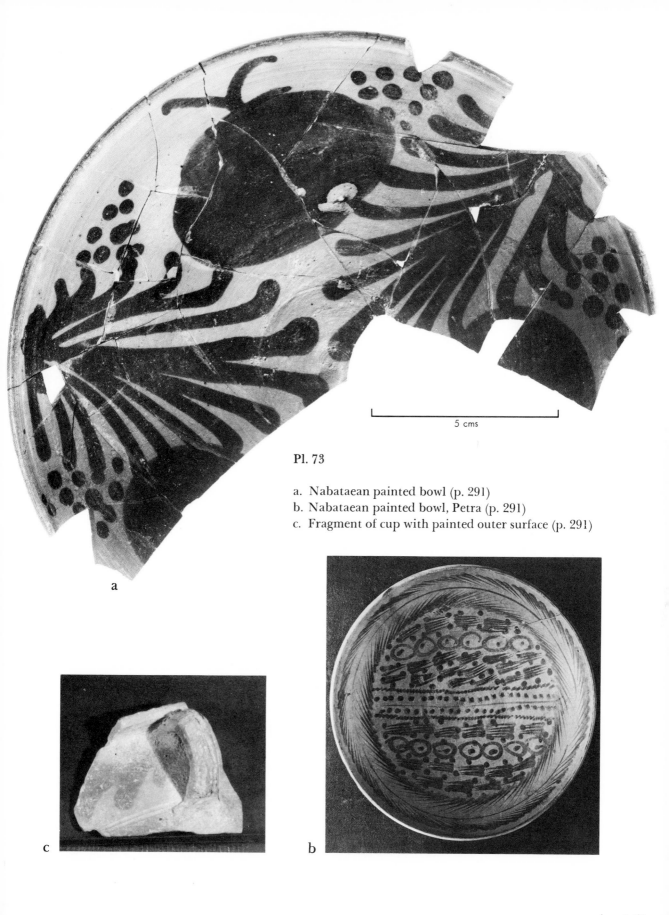

Pl. 73

a. Nabataean painted bowl (p. 291)
b. Nabataean painted bowl, Petra (p. 291)
c. Fragment of cup with painted outer surface (p. 291)

5 cms

a

c

b

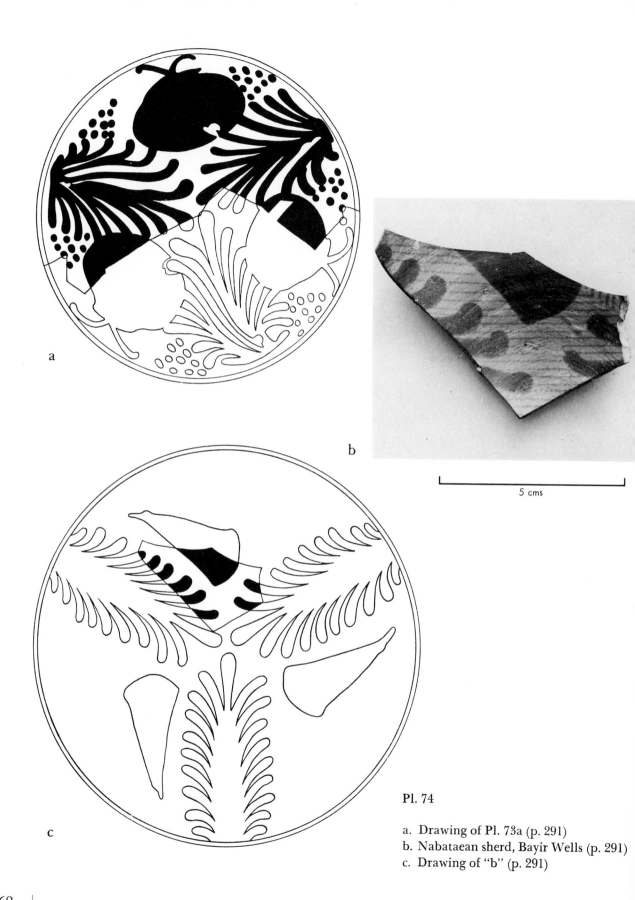

a

b

c

5 cms

Pl. 74

a. Drawing of Pl. 73a (p. 291)
b. Nabataean sherd, Bayir Wells (p. 291)
c. Drawing of "b" (p. 291)

168

a

b

Pl. 75   a, b. Fragments of Nabataean painted bowls (p. 291)

5 cms

3 cms

Pl. 76   Nabataean painted bowls, Petra (p. 291)

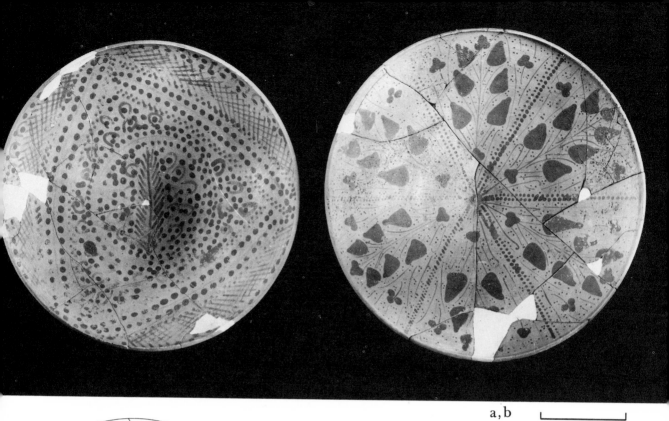

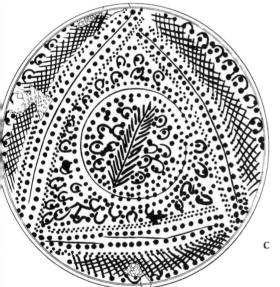

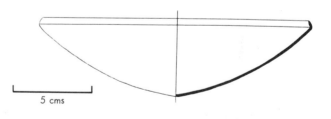

a, b

5 cms

Pl. 77

a, b. Nabataean painted bowls, Amman (p. 291)
c.   Drawing of Pl. 77a (p. 291)
d.   Plain Nabataean bowl, Petra (p. 291)

c

5 cms

5 cms

d

a

b

c

5 cms

Pl. 78

a. Large fragment of painted Nabataean bowl, Petra (p. 291)
b. Three small plain Nabataean bowls, Petra (p. 291)
c. Small plain Nabataean juglet, Petra (p. 291)

Pl. 79   Painted, plain and rouletted Nabataean sherds, Petra (p. 291)

5 cms

5 cms

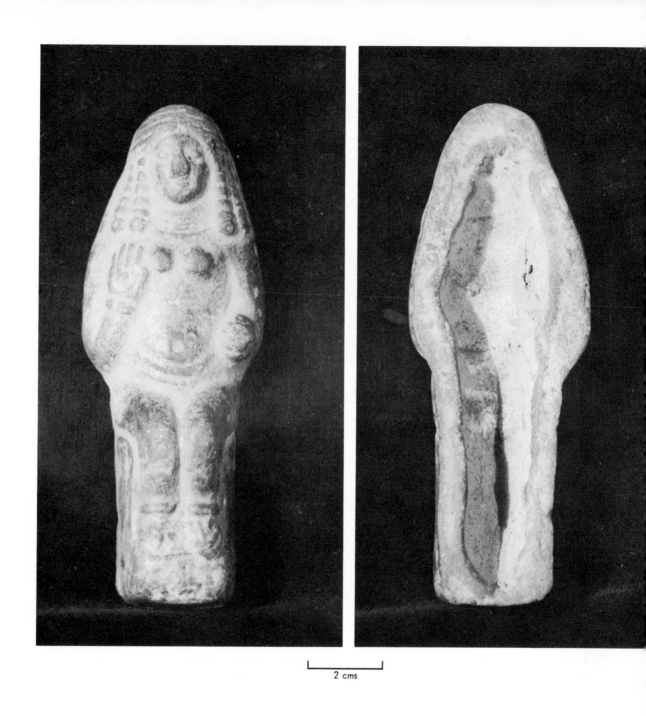

2 cms

Pl. 81   Petra figurine (p. 508)

Pl. 80 (*opposite*)   Painted Nabataean sherds, Petra (p. 291)

a   ⊢——⊣ 5 cms

b

c

5 cms

Pl. 82

a. Byzantine pottery lamps (p. 183)
b. Broken Byzantine lamp (p. 183)
c. Part of animal figure (p. 183)

cupied and possibly rebuilt part of the room in the Byzantine period and built a fireplace in its southeast corner (Pl. 116a).

Room 8 was the best preserved of the triclinia chambers. Its pavement was the finest in the entire temple. It had undoubtedly been laid first in Period II, and, with the exception of the replacement possibly of one flagstone immediately inside the entrance, had remained intact during the last two periods of the history of the Temple of Tannur. Its flagstones were well cut and well fitted and the alignment of their rows was completely straight. The floor had been levelled and the pavement laid so that there was a slope for drainage from the entrance at the south to and through an outlet in the north facing wall of the room and the outer north wall beyond it and the filling of debris between them (Plan A; F, Section S-N¹; Pl. 116b). Were it not for the remains of four pillars in the adjacent triclinium chamber of room 9, which meant that there had to be a roof over it and therefore probably over the other triclinium chambers also, this distinctive slope of the pavement in room 8 might have been used as proof to indicate that it was not roofed over originally. This still remains a possibility.

Around the west, north and south sides of rooms 8, 9 and 10 were stone benches with rebated edges. The priests and pilgrims sat and reclined on these triclinia benches while participating in the cult meals, and may have slept there afterwards. The benches are about 90 centimeters high and two meters wide, and consist of an inner and outer wall with a dirt filling in between. The inner wall is composed of rubble, covered on the side facing the interior of the room with two rows of finely coursed and dressed limestone blocks. Extending over the entire width of this inner wall is a crowning ledge, about 11-12 centimeters deep, projecting 8 centimeters beyond the face of the wall (Plan F, Section S-N¹; G:a-d; Pls. 115b; 116a; 118b; 120a). Dishes with food and drink may have been placed on these ledges by attendants within the room.

Whether or not the rest of the top of each bench extending to the inner face of the outer rubble wall was covered with dressed slabs of stone similar to that of the crowning ledge is problematic. Both in rooms 8 and 9, parts of a continuously beveled headrest, 26 centimeters high, were found (Plan G:d), set back some 40 centimeters from the outer edge of the crowning ledge. This afforded space not only for the serving up of dishes and drinks from the room proper, as we have already mentioned, but also for passing along the top of the benches without disturbing the occupants seated or reclining beyond the headrests. When they lay down, their feet would be pointed to the rear wall of the triclinium bench.

At the northwest and northeast inner corners of rooms 8 and 9, a lower course block projected or a corner block was added, apparently as a sort of a pedestal on which something could be placed (Plan G:b; Pl. 116a). A small relief of a deity or a statuette or perhaps a small incense altar could be placed on such corner blocks or socles.[149] In room 10, such a block is visible only in the northeast corner and is absent in the northwest corner (Pl. 119b).

These inner corner blocks were not used as steps to reach the top of the triclinia benches, because in rooms 8 and 10 there were special flights of steps for this purpose at the south end of the west wall adjoining the entrance door (Pls. 115b, 119a, b). These steps, for which room was made in each of the west facing walls of these rooms, led up to the back of the triclinia benches. They are missing in room 9, where some other provision must have been made, with steps probably having been built against the south end of the west facing wall rather than in it. There is space for them there along the inner face of the south wall adjoining the entrance (Pl. 117a, b).

The fine paving of the type in room 8 is completely missing in room 9, having possibly been removed later on as were the paving slabs in the center of the forecourt. Present, however, in room 9 are the remains of four square pillars, which must have supported a flat, wooden beam roof. They are peculiarly formed of three triangular stones, fitted and plastered together to form a square (Pl. 118a, b). They were plastered over on the outside also, so that the form of their composition was not visible originally. The surfaces of the facing walls in all of these triclinia chambers seem also to have been covered with plaster.

In room 8, where the original pavement of Period II is still intact, there is no remnant whatsoever of pillars like those in room 9, nor can any traces be discerned on its paving blocks as to where they might have stood. The possibility remains therefore that room 8 was not roofed over originally, which would make its pronounced drainage slope and outlet at the base of the north wall more understandable. If it were roofed over at all, that may well have taken place only during Period III. We regard that as likely despite the absence of traces of where the supporting pillars stood.

Had the square pillars of room 9 been built in Period II, it seems to us that they would have been constructed on top of a flagstone pavement such as exists in room 8. The fact that they rest on the hard packed dirt floor means either that they were constructed after the original stone pavement had disappeared or that they were sunk down through it and that the stone slabs of the pavement disappeared after the end of Period III, as did those of the center of the forecourt. We have seen how some of the paving blocks of the forecourt were rearranged in Period III to accommodate the enlarged foundations of the altar in its northeast corner. We believe, therefore, that room 9 was first roofed over in Period III.

There is neither pavement nor remains of any original pillars in the triclinium chamber of room 10, which was added as an afterthought on to the east side of room 9. The pillar drum and damaged capital in it are intrusive and do not belong there. Its triclinium arrangement is patterned after that of the other rooms, and indeed is more intact. The inner west and north facing walls are better constructed than the other two walls, which incorporate building stones from earlier periods. Stuck upside down into the outer south wall, east of the entrance, is a building block with the classical Nabataean lines of tooling at a 45 degree angle (Pl. 120b). The west end of this south wall was built against the south end of the outer east wall of room 9, probably either at or shortly after the time that the north gate in the outer east wall of the forecourt opening on to the north platform was blocked up (Pl. 119a).

It is obvious that the east and south sides of room 10 were reconstructed in Period III, but the inner north and west facing walls seem to belong to the previous period. The plinth on which they rest protrudes slightly, and it would seem that originally a stone slab pavement, of which no traces are left, was laid against them in Period II (Pl. 120a).

The outer facing of the north wall of room 10 had also been reconstructed in Period III, being built against the east end of the outer north wall of room 9, with reused stones of Period II being employed in part for the purpose and being used also in the debris fill between the inner west end of the outer north wall of room 10 and outer east wall of room 9 (Plan A; Pl. 121a).

It was across this kind of fill, found in every triclinium chamber between the inner walls with their facing of dressed blocks and the inner faces of the outer walls, on the north, west and east sides of the rooms, that the major part of the triclinium benches extended. We have commented before about the difficulty of determining now whether or not the tops of these fills were covered with paving blocks. It is possible that rugs or blankets or straw mats were stretched across these spaces, on which the celebrants wined and dined and lolled and slept after partaking of the sacred meals (Plan G; Pl. 115a).

While it is clear that the triclinia chambers 8 and 9 and perhaps 10 belonged first to Period II and then to Period III, there is reason to believe that cruder predecessors may have existed already in Period I. Indeed, it seems that the entire outline of the Temple of Tannur was established then. The slanting line of the cross wall between rooms 8 and 9 can be explained in no way except that the builders of Periods II and III were following the direction of a wall that existed there already in Period I. That they could build a wall straight and true is demonstrated by the character of their work, for instance, in the triclinium benches and in the pavement of room 8 (Pl. 116a, b).

The south wall of room 10 was also not built in a straight line, apparently on purpose. The angle may have been occasioned by an earlier wall of Period I underneath it, part of which protrudes below the west half of its outer south side. We discovered also that the east end of the south wall cut through an earlier cross wall, whose width extended slightly beyond the outer face of the outer east wall of room 10. This section of an early rubble wall, whose south, southeastward extension we were able to follow only for a short distance, must have belonged to Period I (Plan A; Pl. 120b). It will be recalled that a trace of the Period I rubble wall is visible under the south wall of the inner temple enclosure of Period III.

2) ROOM 11

On the west side of Room 8 is a large, long, completely destroyed room whose outermost walls of rude flint and limestone blocks can barely be traced. The west end of the south wall is of poorer construction than the rest of that wall. The point where the finer construction ceases may mark the place where the outer west wall, of which no traces whatsoever remain, may have been built against it. There was an entrance in the south wall, and its sill, door jambs, and a step leading down into the room are still in place (Plan A; Pl. 121b). This part of the wall, together with the entrance, may originally have belonged to Period II. Room 11 is wider and longer in its present form than the other triclinia chambers on the north and south sides of the Temple of Tannur. The greater width was gained by extending the north end of the outer west wall of room 8 and lining up the north wall of room 11 with it.

A short distance west of the outer west wall of room 8, we came across the remains of another cross wall, and designated the intervening space at the east end of room 11 as room 7. One wonders, in the complete absence of remains of triclinia benches, pavement, pillars or stone dishes in the limited area of the so-called room 7, whether it could not have been occupied originally by one of the triclinium benches. The excavation of the debris in room 7 and room 11, to which the former should probably be assigned, revealed some mixed Nabataean and Byzantine sherds and the existence of a squatter's fireplace in the southwest corner of the room. In its present outline, room 11 belongs in all probability to Period III. At that time, it was not only widened but lengthened beyond the originally walled-in temple area of Periods I and II, and may originally have been subdivided into several rooms. At the bottom of the mixed debris inside this room were traces of a slight burning. To judge from the level in which it occurred, it is the same as the one ascertained in the open space immediately outside its south wall, which continues under the flagstones of the partly stripped, outer pavement of the platform, located below the north side of the raised, inner temple enclosure.

e. *Burned Level and Nabataean Pottery*

This fact reminds us that when we dug down into the fill between the inner and outer walls of room 8 (Pl. 115a), we came across at first a mixture of Nabataean and Byzantine sherds, in addition to some broken parts of various Nabataean sculptures. At the bottom of the fill, however, we encountered a slight burned level intermixed with fine Nabataean sherds, which continued under the paved floor of room 8. We did not, however, lift any of the flagstones, as we probably should have, because the same phenomenon occurred on three sides of the room, and it seemed clearly evident that the burned level with fine Nabataean sherds in it undoubtedly continued underneath the entire pavement, which we were most reluctant to harm.

The presence of this burned level at the bottom of the fills and underneath the paved floor of room 8 may be compared to the same phenomenon underneath the Sub-II pavements inside and immediately outside the raised inner temple enclosure. It will be recalled also that some of the most nearly complete specimens of fine painted Nabataean pottery plates were recovered from near the bottom of the ditch at the north side of the pavement below the north side of the raised inner temple enclosure. It would seem to us, although the proof is less certain than in the case of the fine Nabataean sherds found underneath the Sub-II pavement of the raised inner temple-court, that the fine Nabataean sherds in the slight, burned level at the bottom of the fills in room 8, which continues under the pavement of that room, must also be assigned to sometime preceding Period II. The original triclinium chamber of room 8 must first have been constructed early in Period II, and the bare possibility exists that it was built at the same time as the Sub-II pavement of the raised inner temple-court was laid up to the edges of the beveled plinth of Altar-Base I.

It needs to be pointed out that there was a thin layer of ashes, partly of wood, mixed with other debris, directly on top of the flagstones of the pavement of room 8, which may have come in part from the fire that destroyed the wooden roof over it. The burnings on the dirt floors of the other triclinia prove nothing with regard to the possibility of wooden roofs over them, because these burnings may have been there in part before the stone pavements laid over them were removed probably after the destruction of the Temple of Tannur at the end of Period III, or they may be even later. As we have already pointed out, the square pillars in room 9 were proof sufficient that they supported a roof over it in Period III and give basis to the presumption that there were wooden roofs over the rest of the triclinia of the Temple of Tannur at least in this period.

f. South Triclinia Chambers

1) ROOMS 14 AND 15

The height of the walls, levels of the sub-floors and condition of the rooms on the south side of the inner temple area and of the south platform of the forecourt reflect the sharp descent southward and eastward of the slope of the top of Jebel Tannur. The probability is that all the rooms on the south side also served as triclinia chambers, as seems to have been the case with all the rooms on the north side. Remnants of the well-dressed and well-coursed inner facing of triclinia benches are visible on the west side of room 14 and on the south sides of rooms 14 and 15 (Pls. 124a, b, 125, 126). There are no cross walls left in rooms 14 and 15, and the possibility exists that this long narrow, rectangular area may have been subdivided into three instead of two rooms.

The inner facing of the wall of the triclinium bench on the south side of rooms 14 and 15 is two courses high at its west end and one course high in its eastward continuation. It is supported by a steadily deepening foundation wall, made necessary by the sharply descending slope eastward of the south side of the hilltop. Both this triclinium bench wall and its supporting foundation and the outermost south rubble wall behind it have disappeared from the easternmost end of room 15, where the slope of the hill becomes precipitate both on the east and south sides (Plan A; Pl. 126). The central part of the outermost south wall has also collapsed and bulges out.

The height of the existing north wall of rooms 14 and 15 increases steadily as it goes from west to east, accommodating itself to the increasingly downward slope eastward of the hilltop. This wall joins that of the outer east pylon façade of the forecourt (Pl. 94a). One can see that the forecourt itself had to rest on correspondingly high foundations. It was bounded on the south by the north foundation wall of room 15, in order to achieve the almost imperceptible drainage slope that the measurements of the surface levels of the pavements of the forecourt and of its platforms revealed (Pl. 91). The west extension of the south platform, forming the continuation of the outer south pavement below the raised inner temple enclosure, also required an expertly constructed rubble foundation beneath it to ensure its carefully planned drainage slope.

That the extent of the reconstruction which took place at the Temple of Tannur after the end of Period II was very considerable can be judged from the nature of the outer south wall of the south platform of the forecourt, which forms the north wall of rooms 14 and 15. At the point where the foundation courses of this wall begin to increase in number because of the sharpening angle of descent of the slope of the hill, marking perhaps where room 14 ends and room 15 begins, building blocks first placed there in Period III begin to be visible. They have the lines of drafting and beveling (Pl. 125) that were particularly clear on the faces of the stones forming the steps and the south side of Altar-Base III in the inner temple enclosure (Pl. 102b). The marks of repair and patchwork at this line of division are quite clear. Different sized stones were used, making for uneven courses. One of them was cut at its lower right corner to fit over the top of larger building blocks next to and below it.

The earlier kind of drafting with lines of tooling at a 45 degree angle that seems to be especially characteristic of Period II, can be seen near the east end of this wall. The lines of tooling in both periods served to hold in place the plaster which covered the inner and outer faces of the walls.

At the very eastern end of room 15 are several stones of a rude wall of greater width than the outer walls of this room or than the outer wall of the forecourt. It is impossible to determine whether or not they belong to an earlier period than the Period II-III remains of the triclinia chambers. Their greater size may have been occasioned by the necessity of providing the firmest possible footing for the wall erected above them at this south-easternmost corner of the temple, where the hillside begins to fall away so abruptly. It is also possible that they hail from a crude, Byzantine squatter occupation, of which there was considerable evidence in room 15. This latter possibility was heightened by finding a small, round column drum among the row of stones along the conjectured line of the inner face of the tri-clinium bench at the east end of room 15 (Plan A). Between these two rows, squatters in the Byzantine period had built a fireplace against the north wall. In the debris that filled this corner of the room was found a Zeus-Hadad head showing Parthian influences (Pl. 127).

A small crude broken animal figurine of uncertain period, perhaps Byzan-tine, was found in the debris of this room (Pl. 82c), together with a small Byzantine lamp with a Byzantine cross on it (Pl. 82b), Nabataean to Byzan-tine sherds and also a worn coin of Antiochus IV, the Seleucid king also known as Antiochus Epiphanes. As we have already seen, his attempt to introduce the worship of the Olympian Zeus into the Temple at Jerusalem sparked the explosion of the Maccabean rebellion in 168 B.C. that led to the ephemeral independence of a restored Judaean kingdom.

The floor level of rooms 14 and 15 may be assumed to have been flush with the bottom of the first course of the well hewn and well coursed stones of the inner facing of the triclinia benches on the west and south sides of room 14. There was little information of value concerning levels and periods that could be gained from the debris filling these rooms, with their admixture of a Seleucid coin, a Nabataean sculpture and mixed Naba-taean and Byzantine potsherds (Pl. 82a). The various lines of burning visible could have stemmed from squatter occupation in the Byzantine period.

The inner face of the north wall of rooms 14 and 15 was built, as we have already seen, of rough hewn blocks laid more or less in straight rows, that increased in number in accordance with the sharply descending slope of the hilltop eastward. Its height at the west end was 110.5 cm., near the middle was 171 cm., and at its east end was 226 cm. The manner in which

this north wall of rooms 14 and 15 had to be built up can be seen par-
ticularaly well at its junction with the outer east wall of the forecourt at its
southeast corner. Looking at it from the outer east side, one can see the
southeasternmost extension of the pavement of the built-up forecourt and
then the very substantial three to four courses high foundation of the outer
east façade wall (Pls. 94a, 95b). We recall that in Period II steps ascended
to three entrances through the outer east wall into the forecourt, namely,
the main central gateway, a smaller side one to the north of it that led to
the altar in the northeast part of the forecourt, and the second side-entrance
which opened on to the north platform. We recall also that in Period III,
both of the side entrances were blocked up, with only the main central one
being retained (Pls. 91, 93b).

2) ROOMS 12 AND 13

It would seem likely that all the rooms on the south side of the temple
were originally filled with debris purposely to bring their floors to a uniform level, with entrances on their north side. One entrance has been indicated on Plan A, leading directly to the triclinium bench at the west end
of room 14. We feel that such an entrance should rather have been placed
approximately opposite the small one in the south side of the raised inner
temple enclosure. Actually, no remains of entrances into rooms 14 and 15
from the south platform of the forecourt are visible, although they must
have existed at one time. Only in the instance of room 13 was there clear
evidence of one on its north side (Plan A; Pl. 122b).

The pronounced slope downward of rooms 12 and 13 is to the southeast,
with the hillside falling steeply away below them. Room 12 is the westernmost of the chambers on the south side of the temple. It was impossible to
determine whether or not there had ever been an additional one beyond it,
although the west end of its north wall seems at one time to have continued
farther. The projected entrance of room 12 opens on to the present edge of
the outer west pavement below the raised inner temple enclosure, leading
to the small altar at the outer edge of this pavement (Pls. 114a-c, 122b). Because of the sharp downward slope, the walls converging at the southeast
corner of room 12 are necessarily higher than the other sections of the walls
(Pl. 122a). It may be presumed, however, that the floor itself was fixed on a
level plane. The outer west wall was built against the north wall, which,
as we have already pointed out, seems originally to have continued farther
westward (Plan A; Pl. 122a). No remains are left of triclinia benches that
may have existed in this room. The west, east and south foundation walls of
this room are of rude rubble construction and inferior to the north wall.

The floor of room 13 slopes downward in much the same fashion and
direction as that of room 12 (Pls. 122a, 123). The south wall is also of rude
rubble construction, with systematic use being made of small stones between

Pl. 83   Jebel Tannur, looking northwest (p. 74)

Pl. 84   Ruins on top of Jebel Tannur (p. 74)

Pl. 85   Ruins of Khirbet Tannur on top of Jebel Tannur (p. 74)

a

b

Pl. 86

a. Air view of Khirbet
   Tannur excavations (p. 74)
b. Surface remains (p. 104)

Pl. 87   Basalt (?) outcrop on the north slope of the Wadi Hesa (p. 86)

larger building blocks. There is a narrow shelf formed by a setback along most of its length. This shelf may well mark the bottom of the built-up floor level in this room. It is paralleled by a similar narrow shelf along most of the length of the inner face of the west wall. There was no evidence of triclinia benches in this room either, but it may be assumed that they were present at one time.

g. Uniformity of Furniture

As has already been remarked, there is a close relationship between triclinia extending from the Orient to the Occident. The sacred meal [150] was held in these specially designed banquet chambers in sanctuaries reaching from Dura to Delos to Rome and from Petra and Khirbet Tannur to Palmyra, among other places.[151] Little wonder then that among the names of a religious brotherhood listed in inscriptions from Palmyra there should be mentioned those of the head-cook and cup-bearer,[152] and that sacred repasts should be featured on numerous burial monuments and tesserae from there [153] and elsewhere.[154] The triclinia of Khirbet Tannur, for example, dating in their final form to no later than the end of the first quarter of the second century A.D., and some of those of the Temple of Abgal at Khirbet Semrin about 50 kilometers to the NNW of Palmyra,[155] belonging to the third quarter of the third century A.D.,[156] could for all practical purposes have been constructed by the very same builders—so much are they alike.

A most striking parallel in almost every respect can be drawn, for instance, between the triclinium of room 8 of Khirbet Tannur and the one of room "X" of the Temple of Abgal at Khirbet Semrin. This latter temple, incidentally, seems to have been a regional one,[157] as was also the temple of Khirbet Tannur, if indeed that site did not possess national significance. Both of these triclinia had the following features in common: a high sill at the doorway, a short flight of steps close to the entrance inside the room leading up to the bench on the left side, the three side platforms or benches with outer and inner walls and debris in between, probably paved on top and covered with rugs and cushions upon which the celebrants reclined, stone head-rests or raised curbstones near the inner edges of the benches, stone ledges to hold dishes and cups, protruding beyond the faces of the inner triclinia walls on three sides of the room, corner socles on which votive objects, statuettes or small incense altars may have been placed, and finally, a great stone vat or crater used in all probability for wine.[158]

The one at Khirbet Semrin stood near the rear center of room "X." The large, oval shaped stone vat or crater at Khirbet Tannur had been inserted into the face of the bench on the west side of room 8, near the steps in the southwest corner, and is now partly broken (Plan D: Section S-N¹). Resting on the stone-block pavement, it reached to the top of the second course of the facing wall, and had a bung hole at the bottom of its south side. One wonders whether or not there was a particular reason for the outlet there, because otherwise it should have been on the north side, facing the direction of the drainage slope to the north. Part of a stone lid with a large semicircular opening in it was found nearby on the pavement. The other half of the heavy stone lid, which seems purposely to have been divided into two parts, was missing. On top of the triclinium bench, adjacent to the steps, was a large stone bowl that probably had some connection with the vat (Pls. 115b; 116a). We are inclined to believe that this vat was inserted into the facing wall in Period III, although it may originally have been in use in the preceding period too.

A large stone jar found at Petra has been called a "Roman vase," [159] but we feel certain that originally it was located in one of the triclinia chambers there. It has a striking resemblance, even so far as its side handles are concerned, to the stone crater in room "X" of Khirbet Semrin.[160] Nearly a century and a half intervened between the times of employment of the stone wine vats of Khirbet Tannur and Petra on the one hand and that of Khirbet Semrin on the other, but the religious purpose to which they were put was the same. On the rim of a stone wine crater in triclinium "I" of the Temple of Abgal at Khirbet Semrin was a very clearly incised Syriac inscription dedicating it to the god Abgal in the equivalent of the month and year of A.D., July 257.[161] Hence the name of the Temple of Abgal was suggested by its excavator, Daniel Schlumberger. Fragments of more or less similarly inscribed stone wine craters from other triclinia in this Temple of Abgal were recovered.[162] Among them was one large fragment bearing a mask in relief,[163] reminiscent of one found on a small Nabataean altar at Abda (Pl. 8a).

VI. BY THEIR GODS SHALL YE KNOW THEM

VI. *By Their Gods Shall Ye Know Them*

1. VARIETY OF RELIGIOUS EXPERIENCE

a. Roman Tolerance

The absolute uniformitarianism of the Pax Romana could not brook even the circumscribed freedom of Nabataean political independence, isolated almost like a tiny island in the sea of its authority, and therefore erased its corporate existence once and for all near the beginning of the second century A.D. This did not mean, however, as we have seen, that the Nabataeans and their culture disappeared forthwith from off the face of the earth. Totalitarian genocide is an aberration of modern culture and not of ancient civilization. The Romans, in accordance with their general policy towards subject peoples, continued to give full leeway to Nabataean worship, as long as it interfered in no wise with their political and economic control. For well over a century after their political eclipse, the Nabataeans continued thus to prostrate themselves before the pantheon of their gods in temples which they repaired or raised anew.

While their kingdom gave way before Roman conquest, marking the beginning of a very gradual but ultimately disastrous decline in their economy, their religious practices and deities disappeared only when the Nabataeans were completely absorbed by the mighty forces of early Christianity. In the efflorescence of Roman Byzantium and Byzantine Christianity, the descendants of the Nabataeans figured prominently, peopling the cities erected on foundations their fathers had laid, cultivating the soil their ancestors had tilled, repeating or replacing to an even greater degree the terraces and cisterns and dams their forebears had constructed, engaging essentially in the same trade activities that had once enriched Petra and Abda and other Nabataean cities located on age old caravan routes, and

193

forming the chief membership of congregations of the Byzantine churches often built over and sometimes incorporating remains of Nabataean temples.

We have seen that numerous political, economic and cultural factors conditioned the development and collapse of the Nabataean kingdom, although obviously all of them can never be known. Many of the variables must lie in the realm of the irrational and intangible, defying understanding and explanation. The innate abilities of the Nabataeans themselves must strongly be reckoned with to explain their rapid rise to power and position, enabling them to become in a short span of time builders, engineers, traders, artists of distinction, soil and water conservationists and agriculturists without superior. The experiences and accomplishments of their predecessors from Edom to Sinai were of great advantage to them. Others like them, however, of related origins and opportunities, never emerged from their desert backgrounds, remaining as unknown and impersonal as its grains of sand.

b. *Comparison with the Israelites*

In many ways, the story of the Nabataeans is similar to that of the Israelites before them. Both appeared during periods of political disaster or disorganization, when major and minor powers were too bruised or beaten or exhausted to exercise authority and maintain order in their territories or keep out infiltration from infertile lands. It was then that the Bedu, lurking over the rims of the Sown, could alight like locusts on the gardens of ploughmen and eat their fill of grains and fruits they themselves had never cultivated. Indestructible as fleeting shadows and endlessly persevering in the fullness of their hunger, they could always capitalize instantly on the weaknesses and catastrophes of their political and cultural peers. At such junctures, they would make haste to overrun areas emptied of military restraint and stake them out as their very own with utter impunity. Soon, however, if they settled down, the comparative richness of the new environment and the compulsions of possessions would transform them as if by the touch of a magician's wand. Imperceptibly their flimsy tents would give way to fixed abodes of brick or stone. Palaces of royalty, sanctuaries of worship, centers of trade and industry would arise and the hum of civilized activity resound throughout the land—until the wheel of fortune turned again and they were overwhelmed or displaced by newcomers, who themselves sooner or later reached the end of the same cycle.

c. *By Their Gods Shall Ye Know Them*

Israelites and subsequently Nabataeans progressed swiftly in this pattern of change from nomadic conditions, with at first little need of many possessions and much contempt for manual labor, to an agriculturally based state of complex nature and inescapable cultural contacts. There was, however, a vast difference between the two peoples, even as there had been between the Israelites and their Canaanite contemporaries. In Israel, a small handful of intellectual and spiritual giants had undeviatingly succeeded in implanting at long last into the minds and hearts of their people more or less their own prescient understanding of the existence, order and mandates of the one God of all mankind and of the entire universe. The people of Abraham and Moses and the Prophets and the Rabbis proved to be unique in this respect. The Nabataeans, even as the Edomites, Moabites and others, took the diametrically opposite tack, gladly accepting with significant adaptations the gods of their new surroundings and circumstances and steadily enlarging horizons.

The fruitful union of their native genius with the dynamic Hellenistic and Oriental cultures they came in contact with yielded marvelous results. On the one hand, they absorbed much from a creative Hellenism that had disregarded territorial boundaries and had spread irresistibly from Greece to Arabia and Afghanistan and to the borders of India and beyond. On the other hand, their most direct and animating contacts were with an unconquerable and incandescent Orientalism (powerfully expressed by a Parthian renascense and efflorescence). It rebounded after the ebb of Alexander's advances to stem with fluctuating but in the main impressive success the renewed Western push to the East, invigorated by Roman expansionism. They exchanged the featureless stones of their desert devotion for the sculptured approximations of Greek deities with profound Semitic characteristics. Of the Nabataeans it might be said: "By their gods shall ye know them."

2. ZEUS·HADAD·JUPITER

a. Greek at First Glance

The first god we encountered in the excavation of the Temple of Tannur was its chief male deity. Completely covered under fallen building blocks, damaged sculptures, fragments of pottery and accumulated soil, his statue had survived comparatively intact for almost two millennia after the destruction of the sanctuary dedicated to him and his consort. Carved in almost three quarters relief on a large friable sandstone block (a meter long and 45 centimeters wide), the foreshortened figure of the deity was represented as being seated on a throne, flanked by two bulls. The disproportionately small body about 35 centimeters long is dominated by a magnificent life size head about 29 centimeters long. Handsome, virile, regal, serene, the head is a striking, stylized portrait in stone of an idealized king transformed into a god (Pl. 41). The impact of the statue was heightened when it was completely freed of the debris which had entombed it (Pl. 42). I could imagine a worshiper standing spellbound before this king of the gods, whose powerful head commanded attention and respect. At first glance, it appeared to be that of a Greek Zeus.

b. Oriental on Second Look

Further examination quickly revealed that influences of the Orient as well as of the Occident had molded the visage and determined the proportions, position and accoutrements of the body. All in all, this god was obviously more of a product of the East than of the West, however Hellenistic his coiffure and attire were on the whole. The hair strongly waved and curled, the beard set in three curving rows of tight spiral curls,[164] and the ends of the flowing moustache terminating in snail curls could have, if viewed alone, marked the well-barbered deity of Occidental antiquity, even as the low polos or kalathos on top of the head and the high-girdled chiton and the himation draped over his shoulder could have marked the well-dressed one.

Other features, however, immediately obtrude themselves as being out of place in this picture. The low forehead, heavy eyebrows, shallow eye-sockets with traces of red paint remaining in them, flattened nose, immobile expression and rigid carriage contribute to the appearance of a powerful but remote ruler of absolute and impersonal authority, whose prototype is to be sought "on the other side of the Jordan, towards the rising of the sun." He was a Hellenized, Oriental deity. The totality of his dress and form and the sum of attributes stamped him as being essentially an Oriental, however superficially at first sight he may have appeared to be an Hellene. We have called him Zeus-Hadad-Jupiter because of the merger of oriental and occidental elements in his makeup.[165]

The attention paid to the Greek style of the hair dress of the paramount deity of the Temple of Tannur and of the lesser gods associated with him there is striking and is indicative of the spread of cultural forces of the Mediterranean world to the variegated peoples of the land masses of Asia. Almost all of the deities of the Temple of Tannur had their tresses fixed in more or less the same style. It looked as if they had all patronized the same beauty parlor. The hair of some of them fell over their shoulders in carefully curled, overlapping locks, each of which curved gracefully to a point (Pls. 31, 153a), while in others the long locks reached the shoulders in carefully twisted, ringletted form (Pl. 153b).

In the case of the male deities, the beards and moustaches were arranged and trimmed in generally uniform manner, with some variations among them—all closely related to those of the main god, namely Zeus-Hadad-Jupiter. In one particularly Oriental looking face, the comparatively closely trimmed beard of separate, carefully waved, double strands and the heavy, ornately trained moustache with twirled ends terminating in snail curls enclose an open mouth and clean shaven chin. The hair on top of the head is parted in the middle and combed in ordered, undulating waves on either side (Pl. 127), as occurs among other male and female deities of the Temple of Tannur (Pls. 1, 2, 44a, 46, 135a, 179). The deeply furrowed forehead, blank pupils slightly depressed in the center of the protruding irises, coupled with the open, drooping mouth give this essentially Oriental head the staring appearance of a person in a deep trance.

In a sculpture much like it (Pl. 128), and perhaps the work of a different craftsman, the eyes are represented in much the same manner, the eyesockets being recessed through careful chiselling, and the depressed centers of the protruding irises representing the pupils. It is more or less in this manner that the eyes are fashioned in all the rest of the Khirbet Tannur sculptures, with faint traces of red paint remaining in the eyesockets of some of them. In this latter sculpture, the lips are closed and one can glimpse or at least imagine an almost imperceptible smile. In further contrast to the previous portrait, the moustache is more simply represented and a fuller beard completely covers the chin. A crown of stylized leaves encircles the head, instead of the hood or fillet of the one it resembles.

A fine example of the beard combed in separate, ringletted strands is displayed in the sculpture of the head of yet another god (Pl. 129; cf. 153a). Both the upper and lower lips are clean shaven. Below the strongly flaring nostrils of the virile, somewhat flattened nose commences a comparatively thin, elegant moustache, culminating in two incomplete or broken spirals touching the tops of two strands of the beard. With mouth slightly open between well formed but not too full lips, the sculpture seems in this particular instance to be more of a portrait of a real person than most of the others, despite the various stylized features it shares with them. It looks like the face of a worldly wise patrician courtier, possessed of strength, patience, humor and cunning.

Definitely, although not exclusively, Eastern is the appearance of a head (Pl. 130), smaller than the ones thus far mentioned, which has suffered to some extent from vandalism. The spiral curls of the hair are of the same type as those of the chief Zeus-Hadad-Jupiter figure (Pl. 41) and testify to Occidental influence. The full and carefully trained moustache and the elaborate arrangement of the beard bespeak Oriental attention to intricate detail. Viewed *en-face,* it can be seen that the part of the beard extending from ear to ear and covering the lower part of the face is arranged in two parallel rows of curls, looking like a series of open six's and some nine's. The underside of the face, reaching down to the top of the neck is covered with columns of curls, depicted in profile.

1) INTERMINGLING OF STYLES

The points of difference between Nabataean and Parthian sculptures are noticeable, but the similarities are too close to be accidental. The close relationship evidences itself among other things in the stylized ornateness of the elaborately trained beards and full moustaches of both. In sculptures from the Parthian trade center of Hatra, approximately a long day's journey by camel to the west-northwest of Assur on the northern Tigris River, there is great emphasis upon carefully serrated moustaches and intricately fixed beards. The striking beard, set in alternating rows of quarter spirals, looking something like exaggerated regular and inverted commas, and the heavy, drooping, but meticulously trained and trimmed moustache of a magnificent bust of a royal personage from Hatra [166] bring to mind the even more elaborate beard and moustache of one of the Nabataean sculptures from Khirbet Tannur (Pl. 130). To be sure, the distinctively projecting Parthian spade-beard is different in type from the Nabataean one common at Khirbet Tannur that hugs the face, but both are closely connected to each other in general style.

To the clearly Oriental or Parthian type of beard and moustache belong those of several, almost identical busts from Khirbet Tannur (Pls. 127, 128), closely related in some particulars and in general impact to the one just mentioned above (Pl. 130). The drooping moustache and long beard of separately braided locks of the Parthian god sculptured in relief on the face of an altar at Hatra, with a double axe in his right hand and two serpents in his left,[167] need to be examined in this connection. Furthermore, the separate locks of hair of this fearsome-looking god, which fall along the sides of his head down to his shoulders, are closely related in style to those of the Goddess of Vegetation (Pl. 31), the damaged sculpture of Saturn with the harpé from Khirbet Tannur (Pl. 153a), and the elaborate manes of the lions at both Hatra and Khirbet Tannur (Pl. 165a-d). These carefully tressed locks [168] of hair are, however, by no means exclusive to Parthian or Nabataean sculpture and can be found throughout most of the Hellenistic world. They seem on the whole, however, to be better executed at Khirbet Tannur than at Hatra. Excellent Hellenistic-Scythian examples exist of a type with which the Nabataeans must have been familiar (Pl. 161c).

While the moustache and beard with its carefully separated, ringletted strands of the magnificent, small sculpture of a head of a deity from Khirbet Tannur (Pl. 129) are reminiscent of those of other sculptures from there mentioned above (Pls. 127, 128), there is a considerable degree of difference in excellence of artistry between the former and the latter. We have already taken notice of this head. More than almost any other single sculpture from Khirbet Tannur, it escapes or perhaps better transcends the bonds of stylization imposed upon its companions there. In feeling and form and general felicity, it moves much nearer the idealized sculptures of the Hellenistic West, but remains nevertheless essentially Oriental in spirit and in its obvious remoteness from the workaday world.

Comparable to it in form and forcefulness seems to be the upper right hand mask sculptured on the wall of the great "Iwan" at Hatra.[169] Closely related is the beard arrangement of both, consisting of carefully separated, ringletted strands, with the Hatra beard fuller and more spread out than the Nabataean one from Khirbet Tannur. The drooping moustache of the former also seems to be fuller than that of the latter. Common to both are the stylized full cheeks, deep set eyes, low foreheads and patrician appearance. The damaged nose of the Hatra figure may have been of the same flattened type as the Nabataean one, to judge from other examples of this Parthian site.[170]

In all of these hair and beard fashions, there is an intermingling of Greek and Semitic stylistic elements. The latter come to the fore in the accentuated spiral curls, formalized beards and florid moustaches, not to speak of the staring eyes, generally stiff and stylized features and rigidly frontal posture, aside from the carefully wrought disproportion of the size of the head in relationship to the rest of the body, as in the relief of the main Zeus-Hadad-Jupiter figure. In the final analysis, this particular treatment of the hair and beard arrangements with sharply separated parallel wavy lines, spiral curls and ringletted locks may be traced back to the Achaemenid Persians and to the Assyrians.[171] The Persian influence especially, as transmitted through Parthia, exercised a very strong impact upon the Nabataeans.

The separate cultural influences in these sculptures vie with each other at times for predominance. Sometimes it is like recognizing one particular parent in the features of a child, only suddenly to behold in them the lineaments of the other also. All in all, however, the sum of the characteristics of these portraits in stone seems to spell the predominance of the East over the West in their total effect.

Even though occasionally a flicker of individuality can be discerned or read into the faces of these gods, they all partake of an impersonal, or, perhaps better, de-personalized uniformity, which is essentially Oriental. They give the impression almost of having been cast in a mold rather than of having been hewn by hand. With some exceptions, the presence or absence of beards and moustaches are the only distinguishing differences between the faces of the mature male and female deities of Khirbet Tannur. Common to them all were low foreheads, heavy eyebrows, deep set eyes, rounded cheeks, flattened noses, flaring nostrils, full lips.

For all practical purposes, the same model of a face served for the portrayal of the features of every deity of the Nabataean pantheon of Khirbet Tannur. This also applied apparently at least to all the other Nabataean temples in the southern part of the Nabataean kingdom—to judge from the sculpture of a mask in relief on a small Nabataean altar found at Abda (Pl. 8a) in the central Negev [172] and from the outlines of the faces, ravaged by vandals, of the Nabataean gods at Petra.

Pl. 88   Roman road ascending Wadi Mojib (p. 55)

Pl. 89   Roman road and fortress on Edomite plateau (p. 75)

Pl. 90   Roman road to Lisan, Dead Sea (p. 55)

The artful magnification of the Khirbet Tannur head of Zeus-Hadad-Jupiter in relationship to the rest of the body accentuates the oriental character of the deity. He is not merely a superhuman figure, stronger, handsomer, more vigorous, infinitely longer lived than perishable mortals. His features and those of Atargatis are not just idealized replicas of kings and queens, of heroic warriors and noble women, of founders of dynasties and masters and mistresses of domains. Both of them are not only more than that, but they are essentially apart from and basically above the human species. Zeus-Hadad-Jupiter of Khirbet Tannur, for instance, possesses a distinctiveness of his own, which is not dependent upon the multiplicity of individual differences setting one person apart from another. In the sameness of his face, which he shared with a panel of his divine companions and in the unnatural disproportions of his body, the bond of connection with flesh and blood reality is weakened. The idea of endless divinity is emphasized over the ennobled likeness of transient mortality. In this general respect of difference from human beings in degree and dimension, the gods of the Nabataeans are Oriental in essence, however imitatively Occidental in appearance they may at first glance and in many respects appear to be. It is not surprising thus that the Zeus-Hadad-Jupiter head has striking resemblance to a bearded male deity at Dura-Europos.[173]

The Eastern character of Zeus-Hadad-Jupiter emerges, however, not only through factors of impersonal sameness and sophisticated disproportion making for minimizing if not negating bondage to mortal elements, but also through distinctive and tangible features which are the equivalent, in their totality, of a stamp of "Made in the Orient." Three of them stand out, namely the thunderbolt over his left arm, the two bulls flanking or forming the side pieces of the throne on which he is depicted as being seated, and finally, particularly, the torque ending in lions' heads around the top of his chiton. There was a fourth feature, too, held in the raised right hand of the statue, which was found broken off at the elbow. The missing object held aloft may have been a double axe [174] or a bundle of wheat,[175] or it may have been a sceptre (Pls. 112b, 185), such as was found at the base of the Zeus-Hadad-Jupiter stele. Neither the last feature nor the first two are in themselves peculiarly Oriental.

2) THUNDERBOLTS

Giving clear evidence of the authority and power of the bearded deity enthroned between his accompanying bulls is the symbol of the thunderbolt. Affixed to the outer edge of the end of the himation draped over his left shoulder is the stylized representation of a multi-branched thunderbolt culminating originally in an arrow head at either end, with the top one, which extended beyond his shoulder, now broken off. The bottom arrowhead reaches down to the side of his most awkwardly sculptured hand which protrudes below the corner of the himation and points to the right ear of the comparatively intact bull guarding the left side of the throne (Pl. 42). We have seen that the theme of the thunderbolt was emphasized in the architecture of Khirbet Tannur (Pls. 187a, 105a, b, 174c), of Khirbet Dherih (Pl. 178d) and Khirbet Brak (Pl. 178c).[176] It occurred also on the small altar at the edge of the pavement on the west side of Khirbet Tannur (Pl. 114c).

The god of the heavens, Ba'al-shamin-Hadad, whose thunderbolt and lightning accompanied the rain of fertility that transformed the desert into gardens sustaining life for man and beast, could have found no more suitable location for a sanctuary devoted to him and his consort, Atargatis, than the sacred mountain site of Jebel Tannur.[177] And it was natural that in the temple erected partly in his honor on its summit, the theme of the thunderbolt should be emphasized repeatedly in the main periods of its existence. The Ba'al-shamin, the god of the heavens, was, among other characteristics, the lord of rain, whose might was manifested in thunder and lightning. And the thunderbolt of his authority is visible in representations of him throughout the Semitic world, where he was conceived of as exercising his authority almost always from the lofty seat of the peak of the sacred mountain.

Armed with his magic and potent rod of power, the thunder and lightning rain-god of the heavens appeared in many places and under various names in the ancient Near East. Dura-Europos, at the eastern end of Syria, knew him well. Another great center of his worship was located at the western end of Syria in the age-old city of Baalbek, whose very name, meaning the Valley of Baal, reflects the impact of his presence. He was the master or Baal of the Valley, the Beq'ah, one of Asia's best watered and most fertile stretches, locked between the Lebanon and Anti-Lebanon mountains. In the Hellenistic period, he was identified there in part with the Greek sun-god Helios. Indeed the entire site was renamed Heliopolis, only to revert to its former appellation after the Greek cultural sun had set. Known as Jupiter Heliopolitanus, he was worshiped there in the magnificent Temple of Jupiter. Six of its mighty columns, each about 21 m. high and 2.5 m. in diameter, still tower over the watered greenness of the rich valley.[178]

The Jupiter Heliopolitanus of Baalbek was an older contemporary and kin of the mountain god of Jebel Tannur, whom we have arbitrarily named Zeus-Hadad-Jupiter,[179] but for brevity's sake will henceforth term Zeus-Hadad. The name of Zeus-Hadad is merited, we believe, because of the commingling in his figure of Hellenistic and Semitic forms and features. Among the chief of them, as we have seen, is the thunderbolt, possessed by the two main gods of both places.[180] The insignia of the thunderbolt was particularly suitable to Hadad, whose very name connotes thunder, with its concomitant of lightning and rain.[181]

Actually the name of this paramount male god of the ancient Near East varied from country to country and frequently from place to place. The appellations of Baal Gad, Baal Hermon, Baal Pe'or represent some of them.[182] Sometimes the original Semitic name and the subsequent Greek name of the same deity have survived and other times one or the other. Thus Baal Zafon became known as Zeus Kasios (Casius), a name mentioned indeed in the Nabataean inscription found in the great Zeus temple on Jebel el-Aqra (Mount Casius) in Phoenicia.[183]

The Nabataean Zeus-Hadad of Jebel Tannur was most properly worshipped on that sacred mountain, which commanded the springs and wadi of La'aban. Its name was reflected in his local title. He was at once the mountain god of Jebel Tannur, armed with the thunderbolt, and the fertility god who made the rain to fall and the springs to flow and the women and flocks and fields to be fertile. His composite nature, as that of his like everywhere, is reflected in the attributes of the God of Mt. Sinai, at whose appearance the heavens shook and the clouds dropped water.[184]

The merging of Zeus with Hadad among the Nabataeans and their contemporaries in Parthia, Syria, Palestine and elsewhere was more than a merely superficial one resulting in the Hellenistic hair dress and garments of the chief male gods of Khirbet Tannur and of Dura-Europos, for instance. It was a thoroughly natural one, because the symbol of the thunderbolt has of old also been associated with Zeus. In his sculptured forms, Zeus is frequently represented as being armed with the thunderbolt.[185] It was not only natural, therefore, but almost inevitable during the period of the flood of Hellenistic influences which inundated much of the Orient, for this form of Zeus to be equated with the familiar figure of Hadad. He would have appeared almost naked without the multi-leaved rod which was the conventional representation of lightning not only among the Semites but also among the Greeks.[186]

3) BULLS

The high significance of the bull in the cult of Zeus as a fertilizing power[187] also assisted in the easy transition of the Zeus of the Greeks and the Hadad of the Nabataeans, Parthians and Syrians into the superficially Greek but essentially Semitic form of Zeus-Hadad.

The thunderbolt symbol of the might of Zeus-Hadad of Khirbet Tannur was emphasized by the frontal sculptures of the two bulls, one at each side of his throne. Only the forequarters of their bodies are depicted. The head and most of the right foot of the one on the right side were missing, as indeed was the outer right side of the entire length of the stele, involving the loss of the upper right arm. The right side of the base is also missing, including part of the lower left limb of the bull. It may be assumed that the proportions of the stele on the left side were duplicated on the right side.

The bull[188] on the left side of the enthroned deity is a strong-faced animal, with a character of its own. Here again, as in the case of the figure of the deity, the head is disproportionately large compared to the rest of the body. In conformity with the principle of frontality that characterizes the Nabataean sculptures of Khirbet Tannur, the forefront alone of the animal is represented, consisting of the head, the chest and the forelegs in approximately three quarter relief. The rather fine lines indicating the hair on top of the bull's head have been somewhat obscured by the weathering of the sandstone, causing pitmarks and holes elsewhere in the figure. The tip of the left ear has been broken off. A band of stone leads from the top of the right ear to the left hand of the deity, which protrudes beneath the lower edge of the corner of the himation over his left shoulder. The palm of the hand and the inner side of the fingers grasping the connecting band are turned outward, with the middle finger alone not being visible.

Much of significance was conveyed to the worshippers of Zeus-Hadad by the presence at his side of the two bulls. The reverberating thunder and crashing violence of the elements of nature were associated with them in their natural form.[189] Particularly was it felt that the brute strength and tremendous virility of these animals were at the command of the deity, in whom these qualities were magnified. Human beings were dependent upon their being exercised in their behalf, so that they and their beasts might be strong and fruitful and multiply.

The presence of bulls in the pantheon of the gods appeared therefore natural and proper to the supplicants for the blessing of protection and fertility. A Nabataean altar has been found, ornamented understandably with a bull's head.[190] We recall that the upper corners of one of the underground chambers at Abda were decorated with crude reliefs of bulls, whose horns rest on the ceiling. Their features had been accentuated by paint. The Nabataean occupancy of Abda [191] has been fully attested, but whether or not these reliefs are Nabataean in origin is not absolutely certain. The golden calf which the Israelites fashioned and worshipped when Moses delayed returning from the summit of the sacred mountain he had ascended to seek converse with God, incorporated for them the divine protection and the promise of green valleys they sought in the despair and fright that gripped them in the burning desert of their homelessness (Exodus 32:4).

4) LIONS' TORQUES

One distinctive feature of the dress of several of the Nabataean gods of the Temple of Tannur is the use of the torque. It is worn by Zeus-Hadad, among others. Immediately the question arises concerning the source whence the Nabataeans obtained it. While there are certain symbols such as the thunderbolt and the bull which occurred simultaneously both in the Orient and the Occident, the one employed at Khirbet Tannur stems solely from the East. It is the ornamental, twisted, metal neckpiece known as a torque. The Nabataeans seem to have borrowed it from the Parthians [192] who inherited the domain and geopolitical compulsions of the Persians before them, and who maintained and transmitted many of their artistic and religious traditions.

Circling the shoulders of the figure of Zeus-Hadad near the very top of his chiton is a twisted torque,[193] whose terminals consist of lions' heads touching either side of a circular object that may have planetary significance (Pl. 41).[194] In real life, this circular object or brooch may have consisted of a precious stone.[195] The fold of the himation thrown over the god's left shoulder conceals part of the torque on that side. Obviously a symbol of high authority and power, the torque is undoubtedly modeled after originals of gold or baser metals worn by royalty or nobility.[196]

The lions' heads at the terminals of the torque emphasize the fullness of the might of Zeus-Hadad, which is underscored in the first instance, however, by the thunderbolt over his left arm and the bulls at the sides of his throne. The figure of his consort, Atargatis, who probably also wore a torque, was, as we shall point out below, accompanied by lions at the sides of her throne. Little more than parts of one of them and very little of her entire stele remain (Pls. 160, 161a, b). It is interesting to know that the Parthian warrior god, Aphlad, found in a Dura-Europos shrine datable to A.D. 54, is also represented as wearing a torque (and in addition is pictured as standing on two winged lions).[197]

The lions' torque was worn not only by Zeus-Hadad at Khirbet Tannur but also by several of the goddesses of the Nabataean pantheon there. It can be seen encircling the shoulders of a finely sculptured relief of a small Atargatis of classical Nabataean appearance, who also was apparently depicted as being seated on a throne guarded by lions (Pl. 44a, b). Another lions' torque ornamented the figure of a Tyché. She wears a long veil or hood over her hair, and over her right shoulder is a cosmic standard or semeion (Pl. 45a). The headdress is symbolic of the covering of the skies.

The lions' torque at Khirbet Tannur, therefore, is to be interpreted as an ornament of divine power, rather than a symbol associated with any particular god. In general, however, lions form the accompaniment of Atargatis in the Nabataean-Syrian-Parthian world of the Hellenistic period and bulls the companions of Zeus-Hadad. The famous stele of Zeus-Hadad and Atargatis from Dura-Europos on the Tigris shows just these very animals as the respective body-guards of the enthroned couple.[198] Incidentally, it furnishes part of the indirect evidence that an Atargatis figure, seated between lions, must have accompanied the stele of Zeus-Hadad with his bulls at Khirbet Tannur.

It was particularly from Parthia, I believe, that the Nabataeans borrowed the torque symbol of royal and divine authority, with which they probably adorned themselves and certainly embellished their gods.[199] The forces of commerce and culture that supported the rise and prosperity of the desert emporium of Parthian Hatra, near the northern Tigris, made possible also the rise and amazing, if brief, prosperity of Dura-Europos to the southwest of it on the Euphrates. These economic and cultural influences flowed west-southwestward to Damascus and beyond, enriching also Palmyra in-between. The further connections southward between the rich oasis of Damascus and distant Petra, the capital of the Nabataean territory that straddled the approaches to Arabia and Egypt and the Red Sea, were strong and direct and continuous for centuries.

The appearance of the torque in sacred and royal precincts of the Nabataean kingdom was natural and perhaps inevitable under the circumstances. I cannot imagine the brilliant and rich Nabataean king, Aretas IV (9 B.C.-A.D. 40), appearing in public without a Parthian-type torque being draped over the top of his Hellenistic chiton to demonstrate the loftiness of his position and the divine source of his authority.

The Parthian sculpture of Hercules at Hatra depicts him as being clothed with nothing but a quizzical look and a torque around his neck. Otherwise he is as bare as a newborn babe, except that the remnant of what was probably intended to represent a lion skin is draped over his broken left arm, while his right hand rests on a knobbed club.[200] There is, incidentally, a striking similarity between his beard and moustache and those of some of the Khirbet Tannur deities (Pls. 41, 130). His eyes, however, as those of some other gods at Hatra, were inlaid with shell and stone,[201] in contrast to the simpler fashion of representation through sculptural planes and depressions and lines, which was the rule at Khirbet Tannur. The decorative torque is worn also by other Parthian deities [202] and members of royalty [203] at Hatra, but over their regular attire.

The Parthians themselves came by the torque naturally. This decoration seems to have been fairly common among the Scythians of southern Russia during the Hellenistic period. The Scythians who had early settled in Persian Iran, which the Parthians eventually took over, and who had risen to high rank in the Persian and Parthian establishments, may well have introduced the use of torques there. The Achaemenians and Parthians continued the decorative tradition introduced by the Scythians. Furthermore, the Parthians probably had lively trade connections with their Scythian relatives and naturally were cognizant of the torques they employed. Indeed, the only other torques with terminals shaped like lions' heads that I have been able to find, comparable to those at Khirbet Tannur, are Scythian ones along the shores of the Bosphorus.[204]

The use of torques was widespread. Not only do they reach as far south as the Temple of Tannur, but they can be traced from Pergamon in Asia Minor to as far east as Gandhara in northwestern India,[205] and as far west as Ireland and Gaul.[206] It is conceivable also that their westward penetration

may in minor part at least be attributed to Nabataean and Syrian or Phoenician tradesmen who ventured far afield in the pursuit of trade. They
worshipped Hadad and Atargatis at the temple devoted to the Syrian gods
in Delos, which has been dated to the second half of the second century
B.C.,[207] and in Nabataean sanctuaries which we have reason to believe
existed at Rhodes and still farther west at Puteoli near Naples,[208] among
other places. It seems reasonable to believe that the Nabataeans would have
decorated the deities they set up abroad with the same torques of authority
and distinction as adorned the gods they worshipped in their sanctuary of
Khirbet Tannur. To the Scythians must be attributed the major role in
introducing the use of the torque in westernmost Europe.[209]

From Hatra in Parthia to Petra in southern Transjordan to Puteoli in
Italy, and in all probability farther westward, too, the Nabataeans conveyed
their merchandise and their gods. Both goods and deities found ready
acceptance in the market places and sanctuaries of distant lands that must
have appeared to many as being at the very edge of the boundaries of light.
The traffic of interchange followed thus a two-way lane, enriching and in-
fluencing in various degrees both the East and the West, and coursing also
in less clearly understood but increasingly better comprehended fashion
between the distant North and South. It dealt not only with ivory, incense,
slaves, wine, wheat, marble, gold, copper, iron, precious stones and other
articles of exchange, but also with the coins of ideas, the keys of language, the habiliments of fashion, the weapons of battle and the figures of
divinity.

In addition to the use of the originally Scythian torque on many of the
sculptures of Hatra and some of those of Khirbet Tannur, they have in
common a fullness of cheeks, stiffness of carriage and military manner of
facing front. There is an affinity between them in hair, beard and moustache
arrangements. These are characteristics which in general separate Nabataean, Syrian and Parthian statues or reliefs from those of the Hellenistic
West of the same era.

VII. SCULPTURES ANONYMOUS

VII. *Sculptures Anonymous*

1. DIADEMS

The similarity to one another of Nabataean sculptures from Khirbet Tannur and Petra and various other Nabataean sites in the southern part of the Nabataean kingdom is not limited to the deities we have thus far dealt with. It is evidenced also in other sculptures from the same or different Nabataean sanctuaries and settlements.[210] Their identity is not always clear, but the relationship is quite apparent. This can be demonstrated by examples from Petra, Kerak and Ma'in in southern Transjordan and Abda in the Negev. Some of them are sculptures of gods and others are memorial reliefs of deceased humans.

There is, for instance, at Petra a sandstone bust in high relief (Pl. 153c), that can closely be likened to others at these various places. Its face has been carefully destroyed, but the figure is otherwise comparatively intact. It is clothed with tunic and himation. Reaching down from the right side of the head are two ribbons belonging to a diadem or fillet [211] originally on top of it. Similar ribbons can be seen on the right side of the head of the flute-playing figure on the Qanawat stele from the Jebel Druze, which features an eagle holding in its claws a serpent, whose length spans the entire face of the relief.[212]

Visible also on several reliefs from Palmyra and its vicinity are ribboned ends of such diadems or fillets,[213] crowning the heads of the deities identified, respectively, as Bel (Ba'al-shamin), and the moon god, Aglibol (Malakbel) on his right side and the sun god, Jarhibol, on his left.[214] One of these reliefs, which are practically identical with each other, has been dated correctly, we think, to the first half of the first century A.D.[215] Another diadem with braided ribbons, knotted at the ends, one on either side of the head, as in the Palmyra examples just mentioned, can be seen on the head of the bottommost of the three masks on a wall of the Parthian palace at Hatra.[216]

211

A striking example of the diadem with a ribbon on each side is seen in the relief of the deity, Aphlad, from Dura-Europos.[217]

Almost exactly similar to the diadem ribbons on the right side of the defaced Petra relief are those on the right side of the broken-off head of the limestone bust of a male figure in high relief at Kerak (Pl. 155a, b). It is built into one of the walls of the castle of the Crusader town there,[218] which superseded the earlier Nabataean city, erected in its turn over the still earlier, walled, Moabite fortress of Qir of Moab (Qir-hareshet). I have found fragments of Nabataean pottery in the lime between the building blocks of the Crusader castle, and feel certain that this sculpture is Nabataean, too.[219]

In general configuration and style of workmanship and clothing, it is very much like that of the Khirbet Tannur Helios with a torch above each shoulder (Pl. 136). It is even more closely related to a Saturn sculpture from there (Pl. 153a), which we shall discuss below. As in the case of the latter two examples, one can make out, particularly on the left side of the head, the curled locks of hair falling down to the shoulders. Extending diagonally from the right shoulder, over the front of the bust at Kerak, is a sash, which is a feature often encountered on Parthian sculptures,[220] as also are embroidered bands on representations of Nabataean and Parthian garments (Pls. 157b, 159).[221] Like almost every other symbol in Nabataean and related art, this sash probably has astral significance. It is to be related to the one bearing the signs of the zodiac worn diagonally over the torso of the Vatican copy of the so-called "Apollo with the Goose" (Pl. 158).[222]

The use of the diadem or fillet with ribbons, which were sometimes plaited and in addition knotted at the ends, originally probably to prevent unravelling and to facilitate firmer tying, emphasizes again thus the Parthian influence on Nabataean art. The Nabataean reliefs at Petra, Kerak and Abda (Pls. 8a; 155a-c)[223] showing part of this type of headdress bear a direct relationship also in this respect to sculptures from Palmyra, Hatra and other Parthian sites.[224]

a. Horses

The Kerak bas-relief, however, possesses also another feature which may be attributed to direct Parthian influence and indirectly again to the underlying Scythian background. Over the left shoulder of the Kerak figure can be seen the neck and head of a horse in profile. The upper part of the neck and all of the head have suffered damage, but not sufficiently to obscure the identity of the animal. Even part of the bridle is still visible (Pl. 155a, b). The horse was obviously intended to accompany the deceased on the journey through after-life.

This funerary bust of a Nabataean cavalryman from Kerak finds its parallel in a Parthian [225] funerary plaque from Palmyra (Pl. 156a, b). On it, above the left shoulder of a bust, rise the head and neck of a horse, while a palm branch [226] extends above the right shoulder. Surmounting the relief of the deceased person's head is an eagle [227] in completely frontal position,[228] with partly opened wings. The horse's head and bridle and neck on this relief from Palmyra are much like those occurring on numerous other Parthian [229] and Scythian [230] and Nabataean [231] parallels, among the latter of which an example from Nabataean Si'a in the Hauran is striking.[232]

Another Parthian funerary bust in relief of a horseman, also from Palmyra, dated between A.D. 150-180, is particularly similar to the Nabataean one from Kerak. The date is comparable, too. We assign the Nabataean sculptures of Khirbet Tannur and Petra and other Nabataean sites we have mentioned to approximately the second quarter of the second century A.D. Above the left shoulder of this Palmyra figure there appear again the neck and head of a horse.[233] The horse's head has been severely damaged and the greater part of it is completely broken off, but there can be no question with regard to its identity. The eye, mouth and head rein are visible on the side of its head, shown in profile. The short, thick neck of this horse is characteristic of the distinctive type of horse the Parthians bred and the use of which spread far and wide (Pl. 156A).[234] Above the left shoulder of still another funerary bust from Palmyra can be seen a camel's neck and head.[235]

Closely resembling the funerary bust in relief from Kerak of a Nabataean cavalryman (Pl. 155a) are several sculptures of male figures in relief from Ma'in, not many miles away. They are built into various walls of the modern village and must have belonged to an important Nabataean temple there.[236] On one of them is an elaborately ornamented sash, extending diagonally across the chest from the right shoulder (Pl. 157b),[237] recalling the much worn and probably originally closely similar one across the chest of the Kerak figure. It may be likened, too, to the diagonal sash on a plaster statue of Artemis of Graeco-Parthian style from Dura-Europos.[238] We have wondered whether the four visible rectangular divisions or frames on this Ma'in sash may not have contained signs of the zodiac. All of the 12 signs of the zodiac are contained, for example, in frames or "houses" on a diagonal sash decorating the torso of a nude Apollo in the Vatican Museum, that has been mentioned.[239] It would seem possible that this particular Ma'in bust also belonged to a similar figure. On the molding above the right shoulder of the Ma'in figure are visible the lower part of the left foot and the claws of an eagle, reminiscent of the claws on part of the body of an eagle on the damaged column above the right shoulder of Hadad in the famous Atargatis-Hadad stele from Dura-Europos.[239a]

The garb of another Nabataean sculpture from Ma'in (Pl. 159) is marked by bands of embroidery, which seem to indicate Parthian influence.[240] That is further evidenced by the bracelets on the upper arms.[241] The body is clothed with a short-sleeved cloak, whose loosely fitting neckline is edged

Pl. 91   Khirbet Tannur (p. 184)

a

Pl. 92

a. Zibb Atuf, Petra (p. 63)
b. Altar shrine of Zibb Atuf (p. 63)

b

Pl. 93

a. Entrance and gutters of forecourt
   (p. 127)
b. East side of paved forecourt (p. 127)

a

b

a

Pl. 94

a. Foundations of southeast corner of east forecourt (p. 184)
b. Main entrance (p. 159)

b

Pl. 95

a. Foundations of pylon of east forecourt (p. 141)
b. Main entrance and two side entrances to east forecourt (p. 184)

a

b

a

Pl. 96

a. First side entrance, east forecourt (p. 158)
b. Second side entrance at north end of east forecourt (p. 158)

b

Pl. 97

a

a. North side entrance, east forecourt (p. 158)
b. Inside north side entrance, east forecourt (p. 158)

b

with three rows of pearls.[242] These were often employed in Parthian dress for ornamental purposes.[243] The cloak is partly covered by a himation draped over his left shoulder, with an elaborately decorated band on its outer edge. The loosely fitting ornamented neckline of the cloak or chiton is very much like one on a basalt bust of a woman, which may have come from the Nabataean Hauran or Jebel Druze.[244] On the molding at the right side of the damaged head of this sculpture are the remains of what possibly may have been eagle's claws, although much less clear than on the molding above the other Ma'in bust in relief just mentioned.

Earlier influences encountered in Transjordan by the Nabataeans are evidenced in the clothing of two small stone torsos from Amman (Pl. 72c, d) with openings at the top into which separate heads with necks purposely made unusually long were inserted (Pl. 72a, b). Moabite pottery figurines of approximately the same period between the ninth and sixth centuries B.C. were similarly put together (Pl. 69a-d) and reveal the same type of dress, as do several small intact foreshortened stone figurines from Amman (Pls. 70a-d, 71a-d). The similarity of garb between the earlier groups from Amman and Moab and the later Nabataean ones from Ma'in in former Moabite territory, separated in time by half a millenium and more, seems to be too striking to be accidental.[245]

Interestingly enough, the stylized locks of hair reaching down over the shoulders of the Ma'in relief with the diagonal sash (Pl. 157b), each of which is composed of three separate strands coming together at the end to form a rather sharp point, are much the same as those visible on the left shoulder of a badly broken, flattish relief from Khirbet Tannur (Pl. 157a).

Careful examination of the Ma'in bust with the diagonal sash reveals the lower part of the leg of an eagle and its claws on the molding above the right shoulder of the figure, whose head has been completely broken off. We are reminded of course of the eagle above the head of the Atargatis of Khirbet Tannur in her role as Vegetation Goddess, and of the eagle standing on the head of the bust on the above mentioned funerary plaque from Palmyra, with the horse's head and neck over the left shoulder and the palm frond over the right shoulder, and also of the eagle above the head of the deity sculptured in relief on an altar found at Soueïda.[246] One can cite also the sculpture of the eagle surmounting the head of a deified king at Hatra, and the one on the head of the Atargatis figure on the Cerberos relief from there (Pl. 10a, b).[247]

More particularly, however, we are reminded of the stele from Dura on which is a relief of Hadad and Atargatis, with the latter taking up most of the space and the former occupying a decidedly secondary position. Of interest to us at this point, however, is the fact that on the damaged column behind his right shoulder are traces of the claws and part of the body of an eagle.[248] This would seem to us to heighten the possibility that the first mentioned Ma'in bust with comparable remains in the same position represents a deity rather than a human being.

That horses should be depicted at Si'a in the northern part of the Nabataean kingdom and at Petra and Kerak in the southern part is not surprising thus in view of the numerous Parthian parallels, which must be added to other evidence of Parthian influence on Nabataean art. Cavalrymen obviously formed an important part of the Nabataean military forces [249] and it is most likely that they joined forces with Parthian horsemen on more than one military campaign.[250] The spearhead that can be made out above the right shoulder of the Nabataean relief at Kerak, in addition to the neck and head of a horse above his left shoulder, indicates that an armed cavalryman was being represented, of the type characteristic of the Scythian-Parthian mounted warrior elite. This Kerak relief calls to mind the sandstone one from Petra [251] (Pl. 155c) showing in profile the much-damaged head of an oriental-looking warrior equipped with two spears [252] and a bow. One or both types of these weapons may have been standard equipment for Parthian and Nabataean cavalrymen.[253]

To judge from the remaining intact lock of hair streaming outward at the back of his head, the Petraean warrior may well have been presented originally as mounted on a horse and charging into battle. The identity of this figure is uncertain; [254] one wonders whether it is Nabatean in origin, because it departs from the generally prevailing principle of frontality which characterizes late first and particularly second century A.D. Parthian and Nabataean sculptures of gods and people.[255] To be sure, at the Nabataean site of Soueïda in the Hauran, there is a relief of a helmeted warrior in combat posture, armed with a short sword and a rectangular shield, whose face is shown in three quarters profile.[256] And we are reminded of the fact that the type of human head of the anguiped from Nabataean Soueïda and of other sites is shown in three quarters profile.[257]

2. CAPITALS WITH FIGUREHEADS

The general uniformity of features of the deities at Khirbet Tannur, both of smaller and larger size, is reflected in the tiny figurehead replacing the central horn of the abacus of a pilaster capital of an engaged column belonging to the elevated, innermost altar there. The top of the capital has been marked out with incised lines into squares divided into triangles and connected with arcs. An incised line runs from its top back side to the edge of the protruding head (Pl. 133a, b).

The head itself is intact, with the same bulging forehead, flattened nose, filled out cheeks and thick lips as the larger Atargatis or Tyché sculptures. The hair is parted in the middle and combed in separate rows of curls extending from the front to the back of the head, as on a number of related sculptures from Khirbet Tannur (Pl. 131a, b). The protruding irises of the deeply countersunk, almond shaped eyes are left blank, as is commonly the case with this type, with the exception of the right iris of a closely related head perfunctorily holed to indicate the pupil (Pl. 132a, b). Unlike the heads of the Hellenistic-type Nikés (Pls. 183a, 184b) and of the smaller, disproportionately bodied Nikés and Niké-Tychés, the eyebrows of the head on this capital and of other heads akin to it are not accentuated respectively by a grooved line near the top of the canted plane leading down sharply to the top of the raised eyelid below it.

The tiny heads at the top, front center of the other pilaster capitals of the pedestaled altar of the raised inner shrine of Period III, have all been broken off (Pl. 134a, b). This type of ornamentation seems to have occurred fairly frequently on late Corinthianized Nabataean capitals. A diminutive male bust with oversized head and hands decorates a capital from the Decapolis city of Qanawat in the Hauran[258] and similar ones or heads alone can be seen on ornate Nabataean pilaster capitals from Si'a,[259] Soueïda,[260] and Salkhad[261] in the Hauran. Another perhaps masculine head is visible at the top front center of the abacus of a Corinthianized Nabataean capital from Ma'in (Pl. 132c) southwest of Madeba in Transjordan[262] where, also, several other fine although mutilated Nabataean sculptures have been found (Pls. 157b, 159).[263] Heads of related type appear at the top front center of Corinthianized pilaster capitals on a third century A.D. relief from Igel near Trier, Germany, with a counterclockwise zodiac encircling a portrayal of the apotheosis of Heracles.

Inside the zodiac, Minerva is shown emerging from the clouds to meet Heracles in his chariot in order to help him ascend to heaven. Inasmuch as it was thought that the souls of the departed might become wind spirits, there is reason for the inclusion of the busts of the wind gods in the spandrels above and below the zodiac. This entire relief on a funerary monument concerns itself thus with the triumphant progress of the soul of the departed heavenward, after having, like Heracles, completed the cycle of mortal existence and endeavor. The Hellenistic-Semitic concern with life after death is once again underscored by this insertion into the zodiacal cycle of Heracles who became identified by the Greeks with the Tyrian Melqarth, and who is sometimes identified with Dushara.[264]

3. IDENTICAL TWINS

Among the sculptures found at Khirbet Tannur were two mask-like heads in such high relief as almost to be in the round. Their measurements and impressiveness made them appear almost life size. In one instance the front of the head alone remained (Pl. 132a, b). In the other the head was almost completely intact, including the rear attachment joining it to the remaining fragment of the stele, from which the relief arose (Pl. 131a, b).

The faces of these two sculptures duplicating each other are distinguishable practically only in dimension from the tiny head protruding from the pilaster capital and from the busts on the two architraves on the east façade of the pylon of the raised inner temple court. The hair dress on all of them is much the same, except that in the case of the larger of the two heads (Pl. 131a, b) it can be seen, especially when viewed in profile, how the waved and curled sidelocks are swept back over the nape of the neck. In miniature, and with less detail, the fashion of combing the hair back in this manner was incorporated in the instance of the tiny bust in relief on the above-mentioned altar capital. Almost all the other features, even to the down-turned pouting lips, are common to most of the company of the Khirbet Tannur sculptures. The irises of the more intact head have been left blank, while slight indentations were made in those of the companion piece to represent pupils (Pl. 132a, b).

In these heads there is a marked absence of the curved grooved line which represents the eyebrow in several other sculptures [265] (Pls. 129, 135, 145, 150). It is located just below the bottom of the forehead, near the top of the canted plane that is slanted down steeply to the ridged upper eyelids. The lack of this grooved line accentuates the staring aspect of the eyes whose raised lower lids curve more sharply than the upper ones (cf. Pls. 130, 184d). The presence of this grooved eyebrow line, however, does not alone guarantee a more naturalistic expression (Pls. 127-129). The artificial stiff appearance of the faces is heightened by the very ornate coiffure. The hair on these heads looks as if it had been put up in curlers, being carefully divided with military precision into separate rows of individual curled locks. This, however, is meant to convey the impression of wavy locks. The hair arrangement does not cover the large, rounded ears. The wavy locks are combed back along the sides of the head and neck, as can be seen in the case of one intact head. Furthermore, they are divided into two thick ropes of differently aligned curls in an attempt to show them in profile. The downward turned, pouting mouths of these two heads accentuate the mask-like character of the faces.

The feature which distinguishes these two heads from all the others at Khirbet Tannur is the presence of large rounded ears on both of them. They are fashioned in three successively descending planes. In the center of each ear a round hole was bored, perhaps to represent the ear-drum and also probably to serve as an inset for a jewel of some kind. Analogies for these ears may be found, reaching back to early Assyrian history,[266] but we believe they may be found nearer at hand. Ammonite, Moabite and Edomite gods (Pls. 69, 70), contemporary with the period of the Kingdom of Judah between the tenth and sixth centuries B.C. furnished, we think, the immediate examples followed by the Nabataeans. Indeed, the entire tradition of disproportionately large heads and foreshortened bodies that characterized Nabataean sculptures, exemplified particularly by the stele of their main Zeus-Hadad deity enthroned between two bulls, may have been transmitted in considerable measure by Nabataeanized Moabites and Edomites.[267]

Whether or not these two Nabataean heads (Pls. 131, 132a, b) are masculine, as we are inclined to believe, or feminine, is difficult to decide. The coiffure is identical in part with that of the feminine busts of the two architraves (Pl. 12) and of the tiny, protruding head of the pilaster capital of the central altar (Pl. 133a), but that is not decisive. Nor are the facial characteristics that could belong equally well to a Helios or to a Medusa (Pl. 39). The blank irises of the larger of the two heads (Pl. 131) are repeated in the instance of a bearded, Parthian-type head (Pl. 130), but it is not possible to arrive at a judgment on that basis. Nor is it possible to adjudge these heads as being masculine because of the visibility of the large ears, such as feminine coiffures frequently but by no means invariably concealed.[268] We are constrained therefore for the present to leave this question open, although several authorities have held these heads to be masculine.[269] It is noteworthy that these are the only two sculptures among all of those at Khirbet Tannur that are depicted with ears.

I am not at all certain that the Nabataean mask on one side of the small altar from Abda[270] need be that of a goddess. This uncertainty is caused by the presence of the ribboned diadem on the head of the mask (Pl. 8a). It is a type of headdress that with very few exceptions, seems to have been predominantly employed both for Nabataean and Parthian warriors and kings and gods. The highly stylized griffin in the frieze above the mask of the small Abda altar, which simulates the façade of a temple, bears a strong resemblance to the tiny bronze lion or leopard found there by Negev and Avi-Yonah.[271] It is very closely related to the reliefs of Petra griffins on either side of figures of Eros or Dionysus (Pl. 167a, b),[272] to the two lions on the sides of the entrance to the Lion Triclinium at Petra (Pl. 166b) and to the monumental relief of a lion, with tail raised and curled in griffin style, carved into the face of a sandstone cliff at Petra (Pl. 166a) and also to the large limestone lion or feline discovered by Paul Lapp at Araq el-Emir in Jordan (Pl. 168).[273] The griffin, derived from much earlier backgrounds,[274] and like so many other symbols in Nabataean and related cultures, must be related to the concept of life after death. It served to convey the dead to the bourne of the beyond.[275]

The general uniformity of sculptural representation prevailing at Khirbet Tannur in the third and last period of its history extended also to other parts of the Nabataean kingdom and particularly to southern Transjordan in the areas of ancient Edom and Moab and to the Negev of southern

Palestine. The close interrelationship with the contemporary Nabataean sculptures of Syria is demonstrable, but there are many examples of variations attributable mainly to the far more difficult basalt material generally used there. Other factors included the colonial-type overlordship of the Hauran by Nabataeans rather than their intensive settlement of it, and its greater nearness to Parthian territory and influences. Many of the sculptors in Nabataean Syria need thus not have been Nabataeans at all and have been much more familiar with and affected by Parthian rather than Nabataean artistic patterns.

4. GODS AS DECORATIONS

The use of deities for decorative purposes at Khirbet Tannur is exemplified by a bust in high relief (Pl. 135a, b),[276] projecting from a limestone block inserted at one time into a wall. The hair is parted in the middle and wavily combed to the sides, where it is divided originally into two long, curled locks of shoulder length,[277] only one of which now remains. The rest of the hair is swept backward in curled locks to the rear sides of the head, where they merge with the stone from which the bust rises. There is thus a striking similarity to the mask in high relief just discussed, whose wavy locks of hair are combed back over the nape of the neck in much the same fashion, permitting, however, the rounded ears to be seen (Pls. 131b, 132b).[278] A comparison of the left profiles of both sculptures shows that they also have much in common so far as facial features are concerned.

Although the countenance of this particular figure has also much in common with that of Helios, for instance, from the same site (Pl. 136) and with the possibly masculine mask in relief on one side of the small altar from Abda (Pl. 8a), it could be a female face and, indeed, bears close similarities to several of the goddesses of Khirbet Tannur. A separate sculptural fragment (Pl. 184c) consisting of the broken top of a head shows the beginnings of the same hair fashion as on the head of this gargoyle.

5. POTTERY FIGURES

The sculptural materials most frequently employed in the southern part of the Nabataean kingdom were limestone and sandstone, the latter especially although not exclusively at Petra and Meda'in Saleh (Hejra). Several of the most important sculptures at Khirbet Tannur were of sandstone. Molds were also employed for metal (Pl. 191d) and pottery representations of animals and gods and for lamps with or without figureheads, as can be seen particularly from objects found at Abda [279] and Petra.[280] At the latter place,

I once purchased from local Bedouins several Nabataean pottery lamps, each decorated with a facial mask corresponding in its salient features to those of stone from there and elsewhere in the southern part of the Nabataean kingdom.

In each instance, a mask of a person or more probably of a deity adorned the nearly vertical handle of the pottery lamp. In two cases only the handle with the mask remained, while the rest of the lamp had disappeared. One of them shows a head, whose features resemble those of numerous Nabataean stone sculptures (Pls. 67, 68).[281] The low, bulging forehead, flattened nose, deeply sunk eye-sockets, protruding irises with indentations in them for the pupils, rounded cheeks, slightly opened mouth, full lips and pronounced chin are typically Nabataean.

Certain slight differences may be attributed to unevennesses in the mold and above all to smallness in size. A coronet is set on top of the head over an elaborate fillet or snood, looking like a modern Arabic *kafiyeh,* whose ends billow out parallel with the bottom of the chin. Beneath the fillet, a long, curled lock of hair can be seen on each side of the face. Over the headdress is a multiroped head-band, *'uqal,* which is held together at the top center of the forehead by a circular brooch.

There is striking similarity in style between this fillet and the one on the head of a pottery figurine of a Moabite king or deity (Pl. 69a, b) found on the surface of the ancient, Moabite site of el-Medeiyineh, overlooking the Wadi Themed during the course of our archaeological explorations of Transjordan.[282] It, too, billows out at the bottom on both sides of the head and is fastened at the top center of the forehead by a bow knot. It seems likely that in our lamp handle we have a mask portraying a Nabataean king or god.

We have suggested that the Nabataeanized Moabites and Edomites used or adopted this type of figurine and this style of head gear. The descendants of Moabite and Edomite royalty may have achieved high or even highest station among the Nabataeans, with whom they merged. It is worth noting in this connection that Herod the Great, who became the king of Judaea, was ethnically part Judaized Idumaean and part Nabataean.[283]

Behind the coronet that surmounts the fillet on the head of the mask on the Nabataean lamp handle rises what might be described as a lyre. It is shaped like a double harp and has three strings. We have encountered seven-stringed lyres at Khirbet Tannur in connection with reliefs of Mercury (Pl. 146a) and of Tyché[284] (Pl. 53a). It is quite in keeping with the ancient concept of the muscial harmony prevailing among the zodiacal systems and between the planets associated with the deities after whom the days of the week have been named,[285] that several of them should be adorned with lyres.[286] It is difficult to determine whether this mask represents a royal personage or is meant to portray Dushara-Dionysos.

At the bottom of the so-called lyre are two volutes. They touch the ends of the outer strings and reach to the top of the sides of the coronet which projects beyond them. The motif of volutes [287] is repeated on several lamps from Petra,[288] and appears on the broken stand of what may originally have been an incense altar or thymiaterion from Khirbet Tannur (Pl. 191a). Stereotyped faces of lesser clarity than the striking one with the lyre appear fairly frequently on Nabataean and imported Hellenistic lamps found at Petra.[289]

Particularly interesting in connection with the volutes or spirals on this lyre headdress is the discovery in an approximately eighth-century B.C. tomb at Amman of a pottery figurine, representing, it has been said, apparently an hermaphrodite deity. Its headdress consists of four up-turning spirals set at right angles to each other. There may have been another tier of spirals above them. One wonders whether this form of crown and others like it, which may well have existed at the same time in Moab and Edom, could have helped bring about the use of spirals in the lyre headdress on the lamp head from Petra.[290]

The lyre headgear as such, if it is that, might possibly be considered pseudo-Egyptian in style. It is reminiscent of crowns on such Egyptian gods as Amon, Seth-Khnum, Osiris and Horus.[291] A closer connection may perhaps be glimpsed in the headgear of a bronze Isis-Tyché figurine from Luristan, holding a cornucopia in her left hand. On her head and resting on two feathers or horns joined together in the form of a crescent moon, is a double-harp shaped ornament, with a lotus flower in its center.[292] On her forehead are leaves, recalling those on the forehead and face of Atargatis of Khirbet Tannur in her appearance as Vegetation Goddess. A very closely related Isis-Tyché figurine in the Berlin Egyptian Museum shows almost exactly the same head ornament, with the goddess holding two cornucopias in her left hand and grasping a rudder in her right.[293] This is duplicated by a small winged bronze figure of Isis Panthea in the Staatliche Museen, Berlin.[294]

The entire headdress of this Petra pottery lamp relief is reminiscent also of the general shape and volutes of a white marble acroterion with the relief of a Gorgon head in the center at Cyrene, Libya. It is thought originally to have adorned the pediment of one of the earliest Doric temples known.[294a] That the pottery head with the lyre on top of it from Petra might possibly be feminine has occurred to us, but we regard it as doubtful. The fillet on it is almost always found on masculine figures, and closely parallels others on the heads of earlier Moabite [295] and Ammonite [296] figurines (Pls. 69a, b, 70a-d). We believe that this type may have become familiar to the Nabataeans and exercised an influence on their art particularly through the medium of Nabataeanized Moabites and Edomites, as we have previously suggested. The mask on the pottery lamp may mirror the appearance of a Nabataean king or nobleman, if it is not meant to portray Dushara-Dionysos or Hermes-Mercury.

A feminine face of Nabataean stereotype appears on another handle, this time of an intact pottery lamp from Petra (Pl. 66a, b). Her side tresses culminate in poufs or buns touching the middle of her cheeks.[297] There is a remarkable similarity between her coiffure and that of Mesopotamian goddesses of several millennia earlier. Between and above her eyes and heavy eyebrows, which are the duplicates of those of an ancient, Mesopotamian predecessor of hers from Tello (Lagash),[298] and covering the middle of her low forehead, is a double jeweled frontlet that extends to the top of her head. It brings to mind the Egyptian uraeus, a sign of nobility,[299] and it is of a type that may have been attached to a jeweled tiara. She also wears a necklace with several pendant beads or jewels on either side of a central lavalier.

Encircling the head of this goddess on the handle of the lamp is what appears to be a hood of herringbone design. This particular type of design is employed to represent braided locks of hair and eyebrows and is used for other decorative purposes in ancient Sumerian and Babylonian art.[300] Each of the ends of this braided headdress merges at the bottom of each side of the goddess's neck into a widened band of diagonally striated lines.[301] These bands, in turn, continue separately along the rest of the top sides of the lamp, curving past its mouth and reuniting around the circular lip of its nozzle. The blackened nozzle shows that the lamp was once lit. The mask on the handle of this lamp may mirror the image of a Nabataean goddess or queen.

On still another pottery handle, which originally was attached to a Nabataean pottery lamp from Petra, is impressed a well-molded, feminine face (Pl. 66c). She is represented as wearing a shawl or hood over her head, which may possibly have been considered a part of her entire, outer garb. Only the front part of her hair is visible under it, being parted in the middle and combed low over her forehead to the sides. She may have worn long earrings and possibly a necklace. Her features differ from those of the other pottery lampheads from Petra only insofar as her lips are up-turned and closed instead of being slightly parted and down-turned in more or less pouting fashion. Her aquiline and fairly prominent nose is of a type generally encountered in Nabataean representations, although it appears in more flattened form in Nabataean stone sculptures. This type of nose manifests itself strikingly in the tiny reliefs of some of the signs of the zodiac at Khirbet Tannur.

a. Influence of Edom and Moab

There is little question, as we have previously suggested, that the Nabataeans early became familiar with effigies in stone and pottery of the gods that had been worshiped in the kingdoms of Edom and Moab and incorporated them into their own religious system. The downfall of these states as political entities in the sixth century b.c. certainly did not bring about the complete disappearance either of their inhabitants or their gods. Both remained to a considerable degree, to be absorbed in large part by the newcomers. Imagine how many figures of Moabite and Edomite gods the Nabataeans must have encountered, if approximately two millennia later we were still able to find some of them on the surfaces of ancient sites in southern Transjordan.

A pronounced feature of the heads of pottery figurines we discovered in Moab was their large ears. The head of a pottery figurine of a Semitic deity or king we picked up on the ground at el-Medeiyineh in ancient Moab (Pl. 69a, b) reveals not only the large ears, but a type of head cover and hair dress perpetuated centuries later in purely Nabataean representations, as we have previously noted.[301a]

We shall discuss shortly a head broken off a Nabataean pottery lamp from Petra which has a striking relationship in these last two and other respects to its Moabite precursor.

While the size of the entire pottery figurine to which the Moabite head from el-Medeiyineh belonged could have been guessed at from related figurines found at Edomite Buseirah, a subsequent discovery at Amman revealed what it must have looked like when intact. Four stone sculptures were brought to light there, dated to no earlier than the ninth century b.c., and one is particularly pertinent to our present discussion (Pl. 70a-d).

b. Ammonite Predecessors

It consists of a small, limestone statuette with oversize head, originally inlaid eyes, foreshortened and tunic- and shawl-clothed body, crude hands and legs, holding a long stemmed lotus flower in his left hand and standing on an inscribed base.[302] The Moabite el-Medeiyineh figurine must have been fashioned in much the same proportions, or, perhaps better said, disproportions. These were transposed, we are convinced, to Nabataean sculptures and are reflected, for example, in the relative measurements of the relief of the main Zeus-Hadad figure of Khirbet Tannur, as we have already suggested. Carefully trained locks of hair falling down to the shoulders, fillet around the head, large ears, side locks, shape of lips, general type of beard and of physiognomy characterize the heads both of the Ammonite and Moabite figurines. There is a direct relationship between them and Nabataean sculptures both in specific features, such as large ears of the two Nabataean heads discussed above, and in the persistence of disproportionate forms of representation, despite the powerful influence of Hellenistic naturalism.

Among the four stone sculptures found at Amman, dating between the

a

b

Pl. 98

a. Paved platform on south side of east forecourt (p. 139)
b. Paved platform on north side of east forecourt (p. 139)

a

b

Pl. 99

a. Steps to raised inner temple court (p. 146)
b. Door sills of Periods II and III of gateway at top of steps
into raised inner court (p. 147)

233

a

Pl. 100

a. Steps from paved forecourt to raised inner temple court, showing also door sills of Periods II and III. (p. 146)
b. Grooved socket and tongue for door post of Period II gate (p. 147)

b

a

Pl. 101

a. East and north sides of Altar-Pedestal (p. 128)
b. East and south sides (p. 128)

b

a

b

Pl. 102

a. Period III staircase on south side of Altar-Pedestal (p. 121)
b. Tooling on building blocks (p. 182)

Pl. 103   East façade of Altar-Pedestal
of Period II (p. 103)

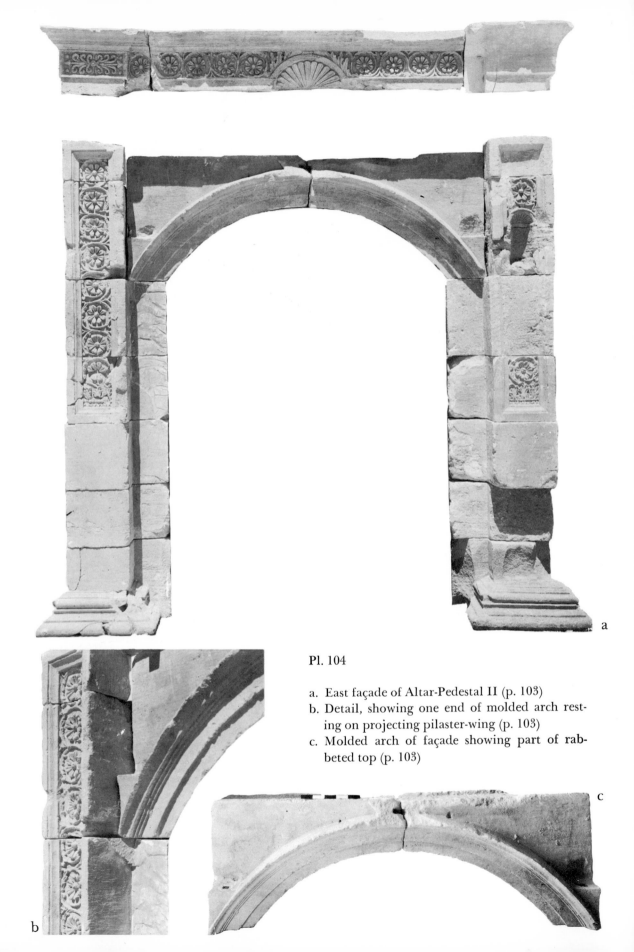

Pl. 104

a. East façade of Altar-Pedestal II (p. 103)
b. Detail, showing one end of molded arch resting on projecting pilaster-wing (p. 103)
c. Molded arch of façade showing part of rabbeted top (p. 103)

a

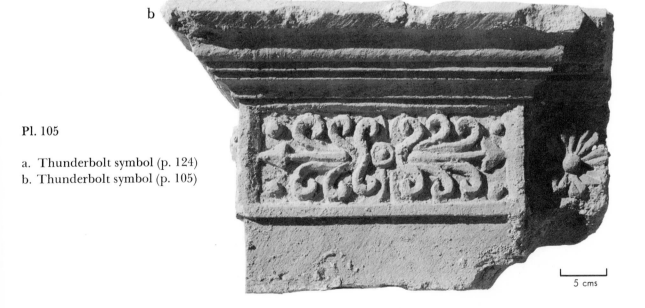

b

Pl. 105

a. Thunderbolt symbol (p. 124)
b. Thunderbolt symbol (p. 105)

a

b

Pl. 106

a. Concealed "offering box" near northeast corner of Altar-Pedestal (p. 98)

b. "Offering box" with paving stone lid removed (p. 98)

a

b

Pl. 107

a. "Offering box" near northeast corner of
   Altar-Pedestal (p. 98)
b. "Offering box" near southeast corner of
   Altar-Pedestal (p. 99)

ninth and the sixth centuries B.C., to which the above mentioned one belonged, were several others paralleled in much later, Nabataean examples of the second century A.D. It was not necessarily these particular pieces that influenced Nabataean art. Others like them may be assumed to have existed in Moab and Edom. Several of the sculptures were nearly life size and were fashioned in separate sections, so that the head could be inserted into the top of the torso.[303] As previously noted, we have found heads of pottery figurines of this type in Moab, meant to be inserted in this fashion into separately made bodies (Pl. 69a-d).

A nearly life size stone head of this type was found previously in Amman, with an exceedingly long neck (Pl. 72a-d), which was obviously intended to be inserted into a space cut out between the shoulders of a separately fashioned body.[304] Bearded, moustached, possessing very large ears and wearing a pseudo-Egyptian Osiris crown, this detached head is very similar to that of a complete, gray stone statuette, one of the above mentioned four sculptures (Pl. 71a-d), found in an excavation outside the city walls at the north end of the Amman citadel.[305] Assuming that this large, detached stone head is an authentic piece, it is important to note the striking resemblance between it and a detached, sandstone head found in the great Nabataean emporium of Meda'in Saleh in northwestern Arabia.[306]

6. MASKS FOR IMMORTALITY

The concern with after-life led the Nabataeans and the Palmyreneans among others, as we have seen,[307] to add horses and camels to the commemorative reliefs of their dead, with the hope that the familiar and tried means of transportation might facilitate the journey through the vale of the beyond. The emphasis placed by the Nabataeans and the Parthians upon dolphin deities and the dolphin symbol in their inland sanctuaries is also to be connected, as we shall see, with their desire to secure survival and safety for themselves along the unknown routes they would have to traverse after quitting their mortal coil.[308] The Nabataean use of the tragic mask furnishes yet another example of their preoccupation with immortality and their intense desire to become identified with divinity. The sacred meal partaken of on zodiacal and memorial occasions in the triclinia banquet chambers of all their temples served this purpose especially. The use of the tragic mask suggesting the face of death was another means to the same end of achieving immortal status. The mask served as a portrait of the deathless god, of Dushara, Dusares, Dionysos, and its wearer became united with him through its use for life everlasting, escaping thus the limitations of the mortal span.[309] Sarcophagi decorations in Lebanon apparently frequently included dolphins (Pl. 24a).[310] A Nabataean mask appears on the tiny commemorative altar found at Abda, even as a related one is carved on the triclinium crater at Khirbet Semrin in Syria [311] and others on the temple wall at Parthian Hatra.

A Nabataean basalt tragic mask of astounding artistry and intensity is known from the Hauran [312] (Pl. 7) and another occurs on a sandstone lintel from the south suburb of Petra, called es-Sabra [313] (Pls. 5, 6). At the side of the relief of this Petraean tragic mask, there appears a number of dolphins in foliate bowers. It seems certain that the tragic mask and the dolphins together magnified the significance conveyed by each alone, among other meanings, to the Nabataeans and their world "that the dead are really living and that being and not living are themselves so closely united as to be one." [314] This theme is repeated in a painted panel from Herculaneum, showing a feminine tragic mask accompanied by a fish and a dolphin.[315] Incidentally, the position of the body and tail of the dolphin there duplicates almost exactly that of the bronze body and tail of a dolphin found at the Nabataean temple in the Wadi Ramm at the entrance to Arabia [316] (Pl. 8b).

Noteworthy in this connection, too, is the presence of two dolphins at one end of a Jewish sarcophagus (Pl. 24b) in one of the Jewish catacombs of Beth She'arim at Sheikh Ibreiq near Haifa.[317] Above their heads are two serpents whose bodies, bound together in a Hercules knot, entwine the bottom of a wreath centering around a shell, and the tips of whose tails touch those of the dolphins. The dolphin motif is repeated also on a mosaic pavement at Beth She'arim,[318] reflecting the earlier and widespread popularity of this sea creature. In far removed Rome, a sarcophagus has been found with a relief on it of dolphins bearing a garland on their tails, showing thus an interesting parallel to the Beth She'arim example.[319] It was especially from the West that the East borrowed the dolphin theme. This symbol underscored in part the profound Nabataean and Parthian concern with life after death.

7. INHABITED SCROLLS

Sculptures in relief are the general rule and in the round are rare exceptions in Nabataean art.[320] Frequently encountered are Nabataean decorations in low relief of birds and beasts and of figures like Eros [321] (Pls. 167c, 203) or Pan, among others,[322] contained within wreaths or bowers or spirals of stylized acanthus or other leaves and vines in what have become known as "inhabited scrolls" or "peopled scrolls." [323] None of these was discovered at Khirbet Tannur, to be sure, but we imagine that some of them must have existed there before the temple was destroyed. Several attractive examples of such "inhabited scrolls" are known to us from various Nabataean sites, and especially from the ruins of Qasr Rabbah, located in the rich plains of Moab to the north of Khirbet Tannur.[324]

One of them there (Pl. 169b) featured the relief of the head and upper part of the body and forelegs of a lion. The head has been somewhat damaged, without really detracting from the vivid representation of a powerful animal at rest, with its forelegs stretched out in front of it. Considerable skill was exercised to compress the front half of its body within the confines of a nearly circular bower and yet not detract from its striking qualities of strength and naturalism.[325] A related relief from the Nabataean temple of Si'a in the Jebel Druze in Syria, showing a lion in similar posture but with head turned backward, is equally vigorous in style, although inferior in execution.[326]

Of comparably high quality at Qasr Rabbah is a relief contained within a highly stylized leaf and vine bower showing the front half of a gazelle [327] (Pl. 169a), with its forelegs stretched out in front of it and its head turned backward. The craftsman who carved this sculpture may have been the same one who fashioned the above mentioned lion relief. He was an artist of considerable ability. The naturalistic appearance of both animals is in harmony with the sculpture in the round made out of sandstone of a gazelle at Khirbet Tannur (Pl. 170a). The position of the head in profile, turned to the rear in this Qasr Rabbah example, serves as an excellent device to portray it on a much larger scale than would otherwise be possible within the limited space available in the "inhabited scroll." This scheme was commonly employed in Hellenistic art, from which the Nabataeans borrowed it.[328]

Nabataean sculptures in the Hauran and the Jebel Druze, be they in the round or in relief, or be they of gods, fauna or flora are generally cruder [329] than those of the southern part of the Nabataean kingdom in such places as Qasr Rabbah, Khirbet Tannur and Petra. There is first of all, as we have previously mentioned, an important difference in materials that generally affected the form of the sculptures to a considerable degree. In the Hauran and the Jebel Druze, they were almost always made out of basalt, a stone very much harder to work than the limestone or sandstone of the heartland of Nabataea in southern Transjordan.

There are, to be sure, exceptions to the general rule that the Nabataean basalt sculptures from Nabataean Syria are cruder than those made out of softer stone in Nabataean Transjordan. Such an exception can be seen in the half-length relief of an ibex in a reclining position, with its forelegs stretched out in front of it, emerging from a circle of petals in the center of a nearly circular scroll of vines and stylized acanthus leaves (Pl. 170b) on a basalt block from Nabataean Atil, near Qanawat in the Jebel Druze.[330] The front part of the head has been broken off, as has most of the left leg and part of the right one, but the relief exhibits the same kind of artistic excellence that characterizes the related ones at Qasr Rabbah.

Much similar to it is one from Nabataean Si'a in the Jebel Druze, showing an animal emerging from a circle of petals. Its head, which seems to be turned to the rear, has been so badly damaged as to be unrecognizable. Its left foreleg has been broken off too. It would appear to have represented originally an ibex or a gazelle, but certainly not a lion.[331]

The practice of filling acanthus leaf scrolls with half-length, reclining animals was continued in Coptic art,[332] sometimes with striking analogies to earlier Nabataean examples.[333] The inhabited scrolls of Coptic art cannot, however, be attributed solely to Nabataean influence inasmuch as they were widely employed both in the East and the West in the second century A.D.[334] The fact remains, however, as we have already pointed out, that the enduring impact of Nabataean art, even after the downfall and absorption of the Nabataean kingdom and the disappearance of the Nabataeans as a separate people, was definitely one of those that had a powerful effect upon the development of Coptic art.[335] We believe also that strong Nabataean influence is evident in the inhabited leaf and vine and fruit bowers, among other aspects, of Omayyad art.[336]

A Nabataean style capital with an exaggerated abacus and projecting horns or bosses was employed by the eighth-century A.D. Omayyads in the mosque they erected at Qasr Hallabat in the desert east of Amman in Transjordan.[337] The presence of Nabataeans there at one time is demonstrated by a Nabataean funerary fragment discovered on the site. The probably third-century A.D. heraldic type of relief of two eagles with patterned wings at Qasr Hallabat [338] also testifies to Nabataean antecedents there.

Just as we were able in the case of the Nabataean torques from Khirbet Tannur to detect Parthian and Scythian influences,[339] so do we find them reflected in many instances of the Nabataean portrayal of animals in the round and in relief and especially of those in reclining position, with the legs folded beneath the body or with the forelegs stretched out in front of the body. There are numerous Scythian representations of the ibex, both with head pointed forward or turned to the rear, that remind one very much of the sculpture in the round from Khirbet Tannur and of the sculpture in relief of a gazelle from Qasr Rabbah (Pl. 169a).[340] This is also true with regard to the relief of a lion at Qasr Rabbah.[341] The chief source, however, exercising a formative influence upon the Nabataean inhabited and peopled scrolls must be regarded as Hellenistic, to which the Scythian-Parthian one was subject, too.[342]

It must be recognized that these Hellenistic influences were not only preserved but also partly transformed by their contact with the native ideological and artistic forces of the ancient Near East and North Africa.[343] "It is evident," wrote Toynbee and Perkins concerning the history of the peopled acanthus-scroll, "that in many respects the Eastern Mediterranean retained under the Empire a certain priority of invention and stylistic practice." [344]

VIII. CLEARLY DIFFERENT

VIII. *Clearly Different*

1. DISTORTION BY DESIGN

a. *Nabataean Models*

Thunderbolts and bulls are generally connected with Zeus-Hadad. Lions usually served as animals-in-waiting to his consort, Atargatis. Together with the other members of the Nabataean pantheon, they are all depicted as if on drill parade, so rigid in posture [345] and unbending in facing front [346] are they. One basic model seems to have served the Nabataeans for both their gods and goddesses. Despite the usual distinguishing features of their sexes, the facial lineaments of all of them remain so much alike,[347] that they appear almost to have been cast in a mold rather than hewn by hand.

Little importance was attached to fashioning the gods in relationship to normal human dimensions.[348] Purposed distortion was readily resorted to. As already noted, the head of Zeus-Hadad was approximately one third as large as all the rest of his body. It is difficult to believe that the Nabataeans who knew how to paint or carve flowers, leaves and fruits with such excellence (Pls. 30, 73a, 169, 203, 204), and were so skillful in creating most delicate and sophisticated types of pottery, could not, had they so desired, have fashioned their deities in accordance with the classical standards of the Hellenistic cultural world, with which they were thoroughly familiar. Certainly they could have approximated these standards more closely than they obviously cared to.

The purely Hellenistic gods were known to the Nabataeans both from near and far. They encountered them from Damascus to Scythopolis and Jerash, from Jericho to Ascalon and Gaza, and from Alexandria to Athens and Rome. They chose, however, to fashion their gods primarily in accordance with their own traditional loyalties and religious convictions and the dictates of their origins and environment, however much they responded to cultural factors and examples of non-Semitic sources. They preferred their familiar gods, altered as they may have been by Hellenistic influences, above all others. Traveling much abroad, they even established sanctuaries for them in Rhodes [349] and Puteoli [350] near Naples, and it would not be surprising if a Nabataean one were discovered some day at Delos, where a Syrian temple to Hadad and Atargatis is known to have existed.[351] We have seen that there was a Nabataean reference to Zeus-Casius found in the temple devoted to him on Mt. Casius in Phoenicia, indicating the presence of Nabataean worshippers there. They brought offerings to their native Dushara in the Delphinium of Apollo at Miletus. They worshipped native gods in their sanctuaries at various places in Egypt, where they functioned mainly as traders and mercenaries.[352]

Among the Nabataeans and others of their general culture, the artistic interpretation of the function and authority of the deities took precedence over the idealized but fairly accurate portrayal of the image of man. From Arabia to Asia Minor and from Parthia to Palestine and Egypt, the Oriental emphasis upon the concept and attributes of divinity was generally expressed in forms that took precedence over the need to glorify the appearance of the gods in accordance with Occidental standards. The distortions usually manifest in the Nabataean, Syrian and Parthian sculptures of their gods and goddesses stemmed not so much from lack of ability to portray them more naturalistically as it did from conscious desire to separate the representations of the deities from glorified verisimilitude to mortal man.

The Nabataean gods shared a community of likeness with their Syrian and Parthian counterparts. They would have been almost as much at home in Palmyra, Dura-Europos and Hatra in greater Syria and Parthia as they were at Khirbet Tannur, Petra, or Abda in the Nabataean kingdom proper. Generally speaking, but by no means always, the native Syrian and Parthian sculptures were cruder and less elegant than the Nabataean ones, but the relationship between them is clear. The Zeus-Hadad and Atargatis of Dura-Europos, for instance, have the same equipment and companions as those of Khirbet Tannur. They, too, respectively, are enthroned between bulls and lions, and the thunder-god in both places is armed with the thunderbolt.[353] By and large, however, most of the contemporary Syrian and Parthian deities are not as smooth of countenance and finished in form as the Nabataean ones of Khirbet Tannur, Petra, or Abda. A few of the sculptures of Hatra and Palmyra are, to be sure, of an excellence equalling or even surpassing the sculptures of the Temple of Tannur.[354]

Indeed, the Nabataean gods themselves differ in this respect from area to area. Those found at Si'a and Soueïda in the Nabataean province of Jebel Druze in southern Syria are not in the same class as those worshiped in the mountain-top Temple of Tannur. The more difficult basalt stone out of which they were hewn may explain the comparative crudity, as we have previously suggested. They are comparable more to the generality of their Syrian and Parthian counterparts than to their southern equals in the heartland of the Nabataean kingdom. The Nabataeans apparently governed the Jebel Druze almost as if it were a foreign colony inasmuch as it was not a country settled thickly by themselves. It is only in this wise that I can explain the seemingly total lack in the Syrian part of their kingdom of the delicate and unmistakably distinctive painted, rouletted and plain Nabataean potsherds that litter the surface of almost every Nabataean site in southern Transjordan, the Wadi Arabah, the Negev and Sinai.

Too many unknown factors exist to accord definitely the stamp of sculptural superiority to the gods of the southern Nabataeans over those closely related to them in contemporary Syria and Parthia. On the whole, however, it may be said, at least at the present time, that in excellence of execution and artistry the Nabataean gods of Khirbet Tannur stand midway between the purely Hellenistic ones of classical proportions of some discovered at places like Ascalon and Jerash (Pls. 43a, 49b) and those of more definitely Oriental type at Dura-Europos and Hatra of the same period. This does not apply to the portraits in stone of some of the kings of Hatra,[355] surpassing in one instance at least in every respect anything ever found at any Nabataean site.

b. Parthian Counterparts

There are profound differences also between the Parthian sculptures of Hatra and the Nabataean ones of the Temple of Tannur, manifesting themselves both in styles of execution and details of dress. Among the Parthian sculptures of Hatra there is a range of quality extending from superb to pedestrian to poor. This does not find its parallel at Khirbet Tannur, where the level of craftsmanship is much more uniform and median. At Khirbet Tannur, for example, there does not exist the wide range of difference that at Hatra separates the copper Medusa mask[356] and the fine stone portrait of a king[357] and the splendid masks on the wall of the great "Iwan" from the graceless figures of deities and personages also found there.[358] Comparable also to the best of the Hatra sculptures is a magnificent bronze bust of a Parthian chieftain from southern Iran, now located in the Teheran Museum. The splendid torque around his neck obviously corresponded to his high rank.[359]

The Medusa head, the "Iwan" mask and the sculpture of the king at Hatra demonstrate a high order of skill and interpretation, corresponding to the strong Hellenistic influences that permeated the ancient Near East. Together, however, with cruder figures from Hatra,[360] to which must be added the Dura-Europos relief of Hadad and Atargatis[361] and still others from there and Palmyra,[362] they nevertheless reflected the ineradicable tradition of the Orient. In accordance with it the face of the king or of the god became more of a stylized mask than an idealized likeness of a human being.

Another noticeable difference between the sculptures of Khirbet Tannur and Hatra is that at the former place they reveal styles of clothing clearly Hellenistic in origin, although rigidly and formalistically patterned. They lack almost completely the fluidity of line that accentuates grace of body and limbs. At the latter site both coarsened Hellenistic and indubitably Parthian styles can be seen, either separately or commingled. The natively Parthian garments at Hatra consist of trousers, tunics, cloaks and even crowns of distinctive and native character.[363] The overriding impression of the garb of the goddesses at Hatra is Parthian, even when the conscious or unconscious intention may have been to make it Hellenistic in effect. Had the flesh and blood models of the Parthian goddesses joined the fashion parades of their sisters under the skin in Ascalon or Athens they would most assuredly have felt terribly out of place. Much less so their Nabataean cousins from Petra or Khirbet Tannur or Abda, very many of whom, at least so far as manner of dress is concerned, could have vied with the Herodians in their eager acceptance of Hellenistic styles. Only in one instance at Khirbet Tannur was there a sculpture with garment modeled in Parthian fashion (Pl. 43b).

c. Unique Characteristics

The sharp opposites of form and attire and the patent differences of degree of skill in workmanship manifesting themselves at Parthian Hatra, do not appear at Khirbet Tannur. The Nabataeans borrowed both from Hellenistic and Parthian or Oriental sources, but changed what they took into something different from both. It is for this reason that we place the art of Khirbet Tannur in a midway position between them. In the overall image of its pantheon of deities, in the distinctive capitals that adorned the columns of its buildings, in the easily recognizable forms of its generally exquisite pottery, in the adaptability and amazing industriousness and enterprise of its people, the Nabataean civilization represents an exhilarating and unique phenomenon in the pageant of history it graced for all too few centuries.

The symbols of the thunderbolt and of the bull in association with the deity can of course, as we have seen, belong to the Hellenistic West as well as to the Nabataean and Parthian East,[364] being differentiable more in the manner of their portrayal than in the fact of their mutual employment. It is, however, in the emphases and frequency of their use, in the adaptation of Hellenistic styles in hair fashions and garments, in the magnification of certain physical features at the expense of the proper proportion of others, in the frozen, uniform, staring faces and in the rigid frontality of posture, that they combine in their totality to fashion the unmistakable, predominantly Oriental character of the Nabataean, Syrian and Parthian gods—however relatively much or little these reveal the impact upon them of Hellenistic influences. One feature, as we have seen, namely, that of torques, is exclusively Oriental in origin.

There was nothing hazy or indefinite about the appearance and nature of the Nabataean deities of the Temple of Tannur. Once recognized as such, they stand revealed as being as outstanding in their way as Nabataean pottery is in its. While they all shared attributes indicating their membership in a community of gods spread far and wide in the Orient and the Occident, they also possessed characteristics which set them apart in a distinctive pantheon of their own. Each of the Nabataean gods of Tannur represents a fusion into a new entity of widely divergent forces as different from each other as the places of their origin are far apart—ranging from the lands bordering the Mediterranean on the one hand to those of the Fertile Crescent on the other.

The Nabataean sculpture and pottery and civilization in general represented something more than the eclectic product of cultural forces coming together from opposite directions. In their totality, they add up not merely to a sum of parts but to something uniquely different that is Nabataean. And, in due course of time, when the distinctive identity of the Nabataeans became completely lost in the magnificent developments of the Byzantine renaissance of the eastern Roman empire, they nevertheless unquestionably contributed to its enrichment with their fine artistic traditions.[365] In this fashion, we believe the Nabataeans added materially to the shaping of Byzantine and Coptic art and subsequently of Omayyad art.

Each area of the ancient Near East sooner or later acquired its own character, compounded of survivals of the past, overlapping cultural patterns of changing times and circumstances and of new developments. The physical, artistic and ideological forces of Hellenism that pushed powerfully eastward, particularly but not exclusively from the Aegean end of the Mediterranean, were constantly countered or altered by others no less dynamic and ultimately more durable, that were at home in the areas of their penetration. From Arabia to Iran and from beyond their confines, too, there was an interchange of goods and an irrepressible interplay of ideas and techniques and tendencies. There was no possibility of blocking off all avenues of travel and trade between them either because of vagaries of weather, violence of wars or impediments of seas or deserts. The compulsions of geography and the pull or push of international politics and cultural forces bound these lands together for good or ill, making for confederation or conquest.

We begin to understand how and when and why and by whom the centrally located Nabataeans were influenced and to appreciate their native genius. They developed into a people with an art, a pantheon of deities, a character and a niche in history of their very own. Arabians, Judaeans and Syrians were their next-door neighbors, Parthians and Hellenes their constant associates, Aramaic and Greek the languages that bound them and their more distant contacts together, the struggle between the Seleucids and Ptolemies, the Romans and Parthians their saving grace. The impact of

Pl. 108

"Offering box" near west end of raised inner temple court (p. 99)

a

b

Pl. 110

a. Byzantine squatters' room (p. 140)
b. Pavement on north and west sides of Altar-Pedestal (p. 120)

a

b

a

b

Pl. 111

a. Period I-III walls of Altar-Pedestal and Sub II pavement,
   south side (p. 87)

b. Period I-III walls of Altar-Pedestal and Sub II pavement,
   east side at north end (p. 87)

Pl. 113 (*opposite*)

a. Steps bonded into west wall of Altar-Podium II (p. 103)
b. North and west sides of raised inner temple court (p. 103)
c. North side of Altar-Pedestal, showing walls of Periods III, II and I (p. 103)

a

b

Pl. 112

a. Sub-II pavement laid against base of north side of Altar-Pedestal of Period I (p. 87)
b. East façade of composite Altar-Pedestal of Periods I-III (p. 87)

a

c

b

a

b

Pl. 114

a. Altar base at outer edge of west pavement (p. 142)
b. Plugged south side of west altar base (p. 155)
c. Thunderbolt symbol on west altar base (p. 155)

c

Hellenism and the influence of the Orient and especially of Parthia were the most important, particularly in the latter stages of their extraordinary career. Ultimately the power of Rome was the direct cause of their defeat, decline and disappearance.

2. IN THE EYE OF THE STORM

a. Perpetual Expansionism

To understand more fully the areas of interdependence between the Nabataeans and the Parthians and also to mark the boundaries of divergence between them clearly, it is well to examine in somewhat more detail than we have previously the times and circumstances of their appearance as historical forces of mature strengths and accomplishments. They lived in closest communication with each other, although physically separated by hundreds of miles. They worshiped many of the same gods, spoke essentially the same languages, derived much of their economic life blood through interconnecting trade routes and were exposed to the same Hellenistic influences, although not in equal degree. The difference of their ethnic origins, of which they were probably not aware, never interfered with the cords of connection which laced them together. However, the circumstances of their geographical locations, historical backgrounds, numerical size and relative political strengths were acutely unlike and made them dissimilar in the midst of their considerable sameness.

Ever present in their lives was the enduring fact of international conflict that affected their economic vitality, cultural complexion and physical survival. Both were caught—or gladly engaged as the case may be—in a pull of opposites that knew little or no surcease in their times, nor in those that preceded or followed them. The very avenues of trade by land and sea to and from markets of all kinds also gave access to armies seeking to dominate and exploit areas of interest and security, which were always expanding by the very nature of the process. The compulsions of geographical location, the imperatives of commercial and cultural objectives, the force of politics and the drive of religion seem often separately or in various groupings to keep countries or continents engaged in endless conflict, be it thrust upon them or sought. This has long been true especially of the more or less rich lands of the Fertile Crescent that bends like a bow between Mesopotamia and Egypt.

Follow the history of the Assyrians and Babylonians on the one hand and of the Egyptians on the other. See how they marched and countermarched endlessly against each other and succeeded only in preparing the way for their ultimate eclipse by others. The Persians then continued, after their conquest of the Babylonians, this repetitive pattern of self-defeating expansionism. With the base of their power reaching from the Euphrates River to the Indus, they, too, felt compelled to extend their mastery south-westward to the banks of the Nile. Thin success was gleaned by them late in the sixth century B.C. Attainment and fear, like appetite growing with the feeding, impelled them thereafter to expand the circle of their security. They sought further to consolidate victory with conquest farther afield and undertook the assault of the mainland of Europe. Its history might have developed far differently had their armies not been decimated at Marathon in 491 B.C. and their fleet not been defeated at Salamis in 480 B.C.

Just a year short of a century and a half later, fortune was violently reversed. Having consolidated his position by relentless victories from Asia Minor to Egypt, Alexander of Macedon and his war-tempered troops marched irresistibly eastward into Persia, toppling over its fat cities like tenpins, before moving on several years later to India. The spoil taken from Persepolis alone was immense, requiring, according to Plutarch, 10,000 pairs of mules and 5000 camels to carry it away. Whatever the truth of that account may be, it must have represented a great treasure indeed.[366]

And then, in 323 B.C., in the thirty-third year of his frenetic life, Alexander died, consumed like a quickly burned-out meteor. The empire that had been fused by the flame of his spirit disintegrated, with the captains of his hosts grabbing its major segments as their personal booty. They established their own dynasties—among them the Ptolemies in Egypt and the Seleucids in Syria. Soon they were at each other's throats in the endless battle for the evanescent control of the entire Fertile Crescent. The prize was always the same. Only the contestants were different. At the next turn of the wheel of time and fortune, the center of the struggle for domination of the rich lands and trade routes from India to Egypt and from Arabia to Asia Minor shifted somewhat and raged between the Seleucids and, wonderful to relate, Persia, risen anew but ruled now by the Iranian Parthians. A little over two and a half centuries later, the scope and intensity of the senselessly tragic combat was enlarged when the Romans replaced the Seleucids in Syria after Pompey had annexed it in 64 B.C. The Roman protagonists of the Greek tradition attempted in vain to succeed against the Parthians where the Seleucids had failed.

Once again it was a wrestling match unto death between the West and the East, that wasted their substance and vitality in the futile fight for the quicksilver of unstable supremacy over distant lands of perpetually retreating horizons. It continued for some seven centuries more, with the reinvigorated forces of Byzantium replacing the legions of Rome late in the third century A.D. Opposing them, early in the same century, were the resurgent neo-Persians, who were to become known as the Sassanians. They substituted for the closely related Parthians in the age-old conflict. The fury over Eden died down for a while when the flame of Islam vaulted barriers of land and sea to penetrate eastward into Asia and westward to the outer rim of Europe. It became in due course restricted to narrower confines, that still remain continental in scope. The restless seeking for absolute power is, however, a continuous one to this very day. The scenes have shifted and the contestants have changed, but the repetitive account has remained the same macabre epic of folly and futility.

b. *Opportunity out of Conflict*

We are, however, less concerned with the reasons for this protracted struggle than with demonstrating the fact of its existence and its bearing upon the rise and fall of the Nabataeans. In eras of weakness caused by the exhaustion of the embattled protagonists, vacuums of power were created into which newcomers, driven by hunger and hope, moved with amazing dispatch. They had otherwise not dared enter the areas of contention. It was in such a period that the Israelites found providential occasion to make their way to the Promised Land. Under similar circumstances, the Nabataeans pitched their tents in cultivable fields they had otherwise never been permitted to trespass. Through intense labor and with swiftly acquired skills, through brilliant imitation and creative genius, they enlarged their squatters' holdings to the magnitude of a glittering kingdom. It was destined, however, after a few centuries of astonishing growth to collapse like a sand-pile palace.

During the confusions and uncertainties attending the colorful procession of changing masters of the ancient Near East, among whom the Babylonians, Persians, Greeks, Romans and Parthians were foremost, in the range of our immediate concern with the shrill notes of change piped by the dissonances of war, the Nabataeans infiltrated and made themselves the masters of Sinai, the Negev, the Arabah, the lands of former Edom and Moab in southern Transjordan abutting the desert of Arabia, and the Jebel Druze highlands with their approaches to the Damascus oasis. Consolidating their swift advance, this urgent and enterprising people managed to entrench themselves particularly strongly in their southern base centering around their capital city of Petra, before the next turn of fortune endangered their shallow security. That occurred after the break-up of the empire of Alexander the Great, with, among other regional alignments, the establishment of Ptolemaic Egypt and Seleucid Syria at opposite ends of the Fertile Crescent. Out of the debilitating struggle that ensued between them, with the Seleucids ultimately gaining complete control for a while of Palestine, there emerged two factors of disproportionate importance in the story of the ancient Near East.

1) THE RISE OF PARTHIA AND NABATAEA

The major factor was the resurgence of Iranian strength in distant Parthia south of the Caspian Sea, resulting in its being catapulted into the eminence of a world power. It arose on the foundations of the earlier Achaemenian Persia, which, we remember, had been conquered by Alexander. The other was the emergence of the flickering political independence of the Nabataeans. They would never, however, have been able to maintain it for long, had they stood alone. The preoccupation of the Seleucids in Syria with the Ptolemies in Egypt over Palestine weakened their ability to prevent the rise of Parthia and preclude its inevitable surge westward. Indeed, not only the coming into being but especially the expansionism of Parthia engaged the strength of the Seleucids to an exhausting degree. It definitely saved the Nabataean kingdom from being taken over by them as completely and early as Palestine was at the very beginning of the second century B.C. The Nabataeans might also have succumbed to the Hellenism that the Seleucids so strongly espoused, had there not been the counterforce of Parthian Orientalism to confront and confound it. They did not possess the heritage of age old religious consciousness and historical and cultural continuity that enabled the core of the Judaeans successfully to resist not only immense political power and intense physical pressure, but also complete cultural assimilation.

The Parthians, throughout the nearly half millennium of their rule from the middle of the third century B.C. to about the end of the first quarter of the third century A.D., remained essentially Oriental in faith, imagery and traditional outlook. Taking advantage of the protracted contest between the Seleucids of Syria and the Ptolemies of Egypt, the Iranian Parthians seized control of Persia under the leadership of Arsaces (c. 250-248 B.C.), who founded the Arsacid Dynasty. It endured for nearly five centuries, from about 250 B.C. to about A.D. 229.[367] Despite the powerful inroads of Hellenism, they remained firmly attached to the character of their origins and the backgrounds of their history. It was inevitable that they would exercise a tremendous impact upon the Nabataeans, with whom they had long and intimate contact. The Nabataeans, nevertheless, remained selective in their borrowings from Parthian cultural possessions.

It may be said that the Nabataeans stood midway between the cultural worlds of the Seleucids and then of the Romans on the one hand and of the Parthians on the other, being profoundly subjected to the influence of both. Practically from the very beginning, they were at once much exposed to the Orientalism of the Parthians and to the Hellenism of the Ptolemies and particularly of the Seleucids—all of whom vied for the spirit and possessions of this gifted people. The result was neither a felicitous mixture of the best of both worlds nor a hodgepodge of the worst, but, as we have seen, something new and different. It was distinctively Nabataean, revealing, however, on the whole more of the imprint of the East than the stamp of the West. Not so in the instance of the Parthians who were also strongly exposed to the culture of the Greeks, but who remained fiercely and successfully resistant to it, as did their Sassanian successors after them.

The fact that the ruins of the sometime capital of Parthia are known only by its Greek name of Hecatompylos [368] (the "hundred-gated") is misleading if it conveys the impression that the Greek influence was the dominant one there during the period of Parthia's existence, even taking into cognizance that this city may have been founded by Seleucus I, one of the great captains of the hosts of Alexander the Great.[369] The latter was himself the most militant evangelist of Greek culture of his times, regarding it correctly as a unifying factor in the variegated complexity of his enormous empire. The Greek speaking inhabitants he left behind him in Parthia and the Greek towns established there by Seleucid monarchs were never enough, however, as numerous as they were, to change the character of the overwhelming majority of the population. It was sufficiently mature and strong enough both to resist their Hellenistic influence and ultimately to absorb the Greek settlers into their own bloodstream and culture.[370]

The rise of the Nabataeans to a unique niche in history was thus largely but not completely fortuitous. The happenstance of their location at the edge of the desert, the existence of trade routes of intercontinental importance traversing it and the slackening and disappearance of the military capability and inhibiting strength of major political powers in their area, gave them an opportunity which they could neither have expected nor planned, but which they exploited to the full with feverish skill. The success they achieved was rocket-like but ephemeral. The miracle of the Nabataeans is not that they lasted as long as they did, but that they lasted for any length of time at all. The foundations of the structure of their state were very shallow, even as were those of many of their buildings, and simply could not withstand any major disturbances.

The Tyché goddess of good fortune, whom they worshipped among others, served them well. Almost any one event of many could have spelled final disaster for them, so subject were they to factors completely beyond their control. If the attack on their capital city of Petra in 312 B.C. by Antigonus Cyclops, who was one of the immediate successors of Alexander the Great, had been successful, there would have been little of their subsequent story to tell. The extension either of the Seleucid absorption of Palestine in 198 B.C. to the other side of the Jordan or later on of the Roman annexation of Syria by Pompey in 64 B.C., followed immediately by his reduction of Judaea to a state of dependency, could have occasioned the immediate downfall and eclipse of the Nabataean kingdom.

The saga of the Parthians is entirely different. Their rise to power was the inevitable consequence of their deep rootedness and sturdy development in their homeland to the south and east of the Caspian Sea. They were the natural successors of the Achaemenian Persians before them. Already in the latter third of the third century B.C., they had begun to consolidate much of the territory of Iran that Alexander the Great had conquered. Not only were they able to withstand the attacks of the Seleucids, who felt probably correctly that they must defeat them in good time or perish themselves, but were soon able to mount counter-attacks with considerable success.

The spearhead of the strength of their terrifying army was its cavalry of archers.[371] These were apparently, for the most part, descendants of Scythian nomads who had become transformed into a ruling class of landed gentry that sustained the throne. Together with other heavily armed horsemen and foot soldiers, they formed an effective striking force, that beat its way eastward as far as the borderlands of India, and by the second half of the second century B.C., in their westward advance, had taken possession of the entirety of the fertile plains of Mesopotamia, which are so blessedly veined by the Tigris and Euphrates Rivers.[372]

There seems little doubt that the Parthians, advancing westward like a flow of lava, would have conquered the Syrian base of Seleucid power, had not the legions of imperial Rome, advancing in the opposite direction, stayed their forward thrust. Rome pressed eastward with the same compulsiveness that made Parthia strike westward towards the enemy's bases, and soon they were locked in the age-old battle for continental supremacy. It has been seen that it was just this kind of fierce embroilment of world powers with each other that gave the flourishing little Nabataean kingdom a longer lease on life than might otherwise have been expected.

The intense Hellenism of the Seleucids found new champions in the Roman conquerors of Syria, who took it over from them in 64 B.C. They lifted on high the banner of Greek culture that Alexander the Great had carried to the edge of India. It became in effect a symbol of their endeavor to push back or at least to contain the Parthians, who kept penetrating westward as if indeed they were the indestructible companions of the rising sun.[373] The Roman campaigns against them failed. When in 54/53 B.C., Crassus, the Roman legate of Syria, joined battle with them at Haran (Carrhae) of Biblical fame,[374] at the northwestern corner of their empire on an upper branch of the Euphrates (that once had served as the last capital of the Assyrians before falling to the Scythians),[375] he suffered ignominious defeat. The brilliant Marc Anthony fared no better in his Parthian campaign of 39 B.C.

The power and boldness of the Parthians is evinced by their direct intervention in 40 B.C. in the tortuous Judaean politics. The audacity and self-confidence of their undertaking is revealed, among other things, by the fact that their sometime capital city of Hecatompylos is nearly a thousand miles in a straight line distant from Jerusalem. They helped to capture Jerusalem from Herod's brother, Phasael, who thereupon committed suicide, and to install Antigonus, the second son of Aristobulus II, as its ruler. His reign there, as the last of the Hasmonean rulers, came to an end three years later. That occurred when Herod, who was to become known in history as "the Great," and who had earlier been confirmed in the rank of king of Judaea by the Roman senate, drove him out and, assuming the crown, began a career that became Solomonic in scope and accomplishment. Antigonus, for his pains, was beheaded by the Romans at Antioch.[376]

The attempt to suppress the Parthians became a fixed but woefully unsuccessful part of Roman foreign policy. Finally, in A.D. 165, the Romans conquered northern Mesopotamia and transformed the Parthian fortress of Dura-Europos into a Roman stronghold.[377] It availed them but little to win this victory. They were not able to achieve their goal of crushing the Parthians, who remained strong enough to permit them no further gains.[378] For nearly three centuries, less about a dozen years, the bitter confrontation between the two powers continued, commencing with Pompey's annexation of Seleucid Syria in 64 B.C., but, nevertheless, with the Parthians keeping the upper hand. It was all that the Romans could do to maintain their position of power along the western hills and plains of Asia and keep open the land routes to Arabia and Egypt and the sea lanes to Rome. They failed not only to destroy but even to blunt the Scythian-edged striking power of the Parthians.

We have seen that the Nabataeans occupied fortunately an offside position in the struggle between the Parthians and the Romans. This did not mean that the Nabataeans stood by supinely to watch the outcome of the conflict. They fought the Seleucids, resisted the Romans and battled with their Judaean neighbors at the drop of a hat. They intervened repeatedly in the mazes of Judaean politics, no less than the Romans and Parthians, as we have seen, to try to determine which particular Hasmonean or Herodian should sit on the throne in Jerusalem. The fortunes of all of them were mutually interdependent, with the political fate of the Nabataeans and Judaeans, however, being determined more by Parthia and Rome than by their own actions. The achievements of the Nabataeans cannot, nevertheless, be disassociated from their own native genius.

3. JUDAEAN SEPARATENESS

In the acceptance or absorption of Hellenistic or Oriental cultural influences, the Nabataeans made their own knowing or unconscious choices, aped in many respects by multitudes of Judaeans. One group among the latter, however, was immune to the blandishments of popular conformity and not only indifferent but immovably antagonistic to the adoption either of practices or fashions, beliefs or injunctions not in harmony with their spiritual heritage. That group consisted in the main of the simple folk of Judaea. They were the followers and disciples of Rabbis like Hillel and John the Baptist. Among their company were the Essenes. They dwelt, as did Jesus, in the world of the imperatives of the Bible and the straightforward ethics and profound moral simplicity of the Mishnah and the Midrash.

As the physical and spiritual descendents of the Rechabites, they turned to the teachings of the Prophets, such as Isaiah and Jeremiah for their religious direction and moral instruction and ways of life. Some of them sought seclusion for contemplation and prayer in monastic settlements like that of Qumran overlooking the Dead Sea. Many others similar to them in spirit and belief were engaged in the humble pursuits of the workaday world. They studied Sacred Writ and prayed to the God of their fathers in tiny synagogues scattered about the countryside. Their inner fortitude surpassed the power of armed might. Their faith in the God of Israel and all mankind knew no compromise, and they adhered to it undeviatingly. Brutal force failed to change them. Nor did they succumb to the far more subtle appeal of their general environment and of daily contact with the eclectic paganism of Greeks, Romans, Parthians and Nabataeans. The contrast between such normative Judaeans and the Nabataeans is astonishing.

Out of the welter of influences that assailed them both from all points of the compass came diametrically opposite results. The Nabataeans fashioned a brief future with brave old-new gods that reflected both the impact of their environment and the surge of their own creativity. The hard core of the Judaeans, however, resisted both the allure and even more so the imposition of pagan customs and allegiances and clung with intensified firmness to the sustaining essentials of the faith of their fathers. It gave them a future whose end is not yet in sight.

IX. FIRST AMONG EQUALS

IX. *First Among Equals*

1. PARAMOUNT QUEEN

a. Lions in Waiting

The regal figure of Zeus-Hadad, attired with flowing vestments, decorated with a lions' torque, armed with a thunderbolt and enthroned between two bulls at his mountain top Temple of Tannur, shared his eminence and authority with his queen. Certainly no less impressive and powerful, she was seated next to him between her two attendant lions. In addition to the stele bearing his figure in high relief, there was room also for her monument in the panel of the east façade of the raised, inner court altar. Whenever the gates in the pylon on the east side of the platform of the inner temple court were pushed ajar at the break of dawn, the penetrating rays of the rising sun would swiftly chisel away the darkness from the faces of these two reigning deities. Their prominent features were carved to catch and reflect the changing light of the growing day.

I speak of Atargatis, queenly and serene, at the side of Zeus-Hadad at the Temple of Tannur, without being able to produce her. I know she was there and I believe I can describe her looks faithfully and with the homage of admiration. It is, nevertheless, impossible to present her visibly in the sturdiness and grace of her physical form. Broken into bits as a result of the collapse of the temple about her during a shattering earthquake, almost every trace of her body has disappeared, the sandstone of its substance smashed for the most part into formless debris.

The proof of the existence of Atargatis at the side of Zeus-Hadad can be substantiated in several ways. Important, but not in itself sufficient is the fact that there is enough room next to the Zeus-Hadad stele for another of approximately the same size, bearing the form of the goddess in three quarter relief. Of additional weight is the fact that Hadad and Atargatis are often represented in physical juxtaposition.[379] The Parthian relief of both of them on a single stele at Dura-Europos shows them enthroned next to

269

each other, together with the bulls and lions and sundry insignia of their offices. It furnishes a fair approximation of what must have been their family portrait in stone at the Temple of Tannur.[380] The likenesses of the divine couple with their familiar beasts were also impressed on coins current throughout the ancient Near East in the Hellenistic period. Several of them, for example, have been found at Hierapolis-Bambyke in southwestern Asia Minor.[381]

The most convincing proof, however, of the presence of a properly attired Atargatis, accompanied by the lions of her authority, ensconced next to Zeus-Hadad at the Temple of Tannur, was the discovery among the ruins near the inner altar there of several sandstone fragments, which could have belonged to nothing else except the stele on which she was carved.

The largest fragment consisted of what was obviously part of the lower left base of the Atargatis stele. On its upper right side is visible the corner fold of a himation. Below it, there protruded in high relief the dramatic sculpture of the front part of the body of a small lion (Pls. 160, 161a, b). In size it was comparable to the relatively intact small bull at the left side of the Zeus-Hadad stele, although it was superior to it in excellence of execution. Even with the lower part of its jaw broken away and parts of its forelegs missing, it reflected in miniature the aura of majesty and beauty of its mistress.[382] Its duplicate on the right side of the stele was never found.

The carefully combed locks of hair of this lion are almost exactly like those of the great bust of Atargatis as the Goddess of Vegetation, that surmounted the east pylon of the raised inner temple court (Pls. 31, 32). The low, sloping forehead, deeply grooved eyes with protruding irises and perforated pupils, the rounded cheeks, flattened nose with flaring nostrils, are closely related to the outstanding features of the generality of sculptures of the Temple of Tannur. The artfully carved grooves and curves and concaves were calculated to increase the contrast of light and shadow and enhance the impression of power. The full likeness of this guardian lion with its open mouth and menacing fangs, one of which is still visible, can be gathered from sculptures of lions' heads at the Temple of Tannur, or for that matter at Qasr edh-Dherih, Qasr Rabbah or Petra, among other Nabataean sites (Pls. 162-166).[382a]

The careful examination of the debris revealed several additional pieces from the bottom of the missing Atargatis stele. On one of them were the remnants of the paw and toes of the left foot and the ends of two of the toes of the right foot of the lion. On the other, resting on a low pedestal, was the front part of the sandaled right foot of a person, with four toes still intact, and the place where the left foot clearly had stood. There can be little question that this latter fragment belongs to the figure of Atargatis. It parallels the bottom part of the Zeus-Hadad stele, which shows feet of similar type in the same relative position.

Pl. 115

a

a. Room 8, looking south, showing Byzantine fireplace at southeast corner of
   paved floor (p. 180)
b. Arrangements of Room 8, showing broken lid, crater, bowl, and steps (p. 191)

b

a

Pl. 116

a. Crater lid, crater and bowl, and later fireplace in Room 8, looking south (p. 177)
b. Looking through entrance of Room 8 across paved floor to north wall with outlet for water at its base (p. 177)

b

a

Pl. 117

a. Composite square pillars in unpaved Room 9 (p. 178)
b. Looking northeast into Room 9 (p. 178)

b

a

Pl. 118

a. Looking west in Room 9 at composite pillar and west wall of triclinium (p. 178)
b. Southwest composite pillar and west triclinium wall, Room 9 (p. 178)

b

Pl. 119

a. Steps to west triclinium bench, Room 10, and to left of it the north side entrance to outer east forecourt (p. 178)

b. Room 10, showing steps at southwest corner (p. 178)

a

Pl. 120

a. Room 10, entrance on south side (p. 179)
b. Diagonal Nabataean tooling on reused building stone in outer south wall of Room 10, which cuts through Period I (?) crosswall (p. 179)

b

a

Pl. 121

a. Reused building stone in outer north wall of Room 10 (p. 179)
b. Inner north side of entrance, destroyed Room 11 (p. 180)

b

Pl. 123 Looking southeast at foundations of Room 13 (p. 184)

Pl. 122 (*opposite*)

a. Rooms 12 and 13, looking southeast (p. 184)
b. Room 12, looking north and Room 13 to right, with entrance at northeast corner (p. 184)

a

Pl. 124

a. West end of Room 14, south wall (p. 182)
b. West end of Room 14, north wall (p. 182)

b

Pl. 125   Area of Rooms 14 and 15, showing also west end of Room 14 (p. 182)

Pl. 126   Looking east at area of Rooms 14 and 15, with view of Wadi Hesa (p. 182)

And, finally, it is striking that all three pieces attributed to the stele of Atargatis were of friable sandstone, as was the entire Zeus-Hadad stele. With these exceptions and that of one small, crouching animal figure, possibly that of a gazelle (?) (Pl. 170a), also made of sandstone, every other sculpture found at the Temple of Tannur was made out of crystalline limestone quarried probably in the vicinity of Jebel Tannur. The sandstone had to be fetched from farther afield, and perhaps from as far as Petra itself. It may be that some special sanctity was attached to this material, particularly if it came from the central shrine of metropolitan Petra. Be that as it may, the presupposition that an Atargatis stele must have existed to match the Zeus-Hadad one is borne out by reason of the space left next to the Zeus-Hadad stele on the east side of the inner altar, by the discovery nearby of the lion and fragments of feet, and by the sameness of the sandstone out of which the reliefs of both deities and their companion animals were carved and by analogies elsewhere. It is difficult not to read some special significance into the fact that of all the sculptures of deities at the Temple of Tannur, only the two companionate steles of Zeus-Hadad and Atargatis and one of a reclining gazelle (?) were carved out of sandstone.

Confident now of the existence of this sandstone stele of Atargatis, seated between two lions and next to the related stele of Zeus-Hadad, we can reconstruct her facial appearance from the analogies of other goddesses who dwelt with her at the Temple of Tannur. All of them were carved in essentially the same manner. Some of them represented her in different guises, and one of them seems indeed to have mirrored her exact likeness, but in smaller dimensions (Pl. 44a, b).

In addition to the famous Dura-Europos stele, further confirmation of the fact that the sandstone fragments of lions at Khirbet Tannur represented the animals-in-waiting of a missing sandstone sculpture in high relief of an enthroned Atargatis on a stele next to that of Zeus-Hadad with his bulls, is furnished by the lower part of a basalt plaque found at Raha in the Jebel Druze, bearing a related relief.[383] It shows a seated goddess, with a lion on either side of her throne. The one on her left side is comparatively intact, but only the left foot and claws of the lion on her right side remain. There is abundant evidence in Syria that the worship of Atargatis took precedence over that of her consort Hadad.[384]

Zeus-Hadad (Ba'al-shamin) was essentially the sky-father and Atargatis the sky-mother. Manifesting herself in numerous forms, she appears to have been the paramount deity of Khirbet Tannur, assuming the superior rank there that she generally held elsewhere. At Palmyra, Dura and Hierapolis, for instance, Hadad was definitely of secondary importance compared to Atargatis, being an associate of necessity and not an equal, much less a superior in position.[385]

One of the Atargatis sculptures in particular from Khirbet Tannur duplicates almost exactly, we believe, her appearance next to Zeus-Hadad, except that it is smaller and is carved out of limestone instead of sandstone. Only the upper half of the stele in question was found (Pl. 44a, b) and depicts the goddess in a seated position. The lower half, extending from just below her knees is missing, together with the two lions which probably stood at the bottom of it, one on each side of her. Her right arm is broken off below the elbow and the one forearm that had been doweled into a hole in the elbow is missing. The goddess is dressed in a high-necked, loosely draped chiton, very similar to that worn by the sandstone Zeus-Hadad (Pls. 41, 42). The high sash or girdle of the latter is now absent from her costume, but it or something like it must have been affixed to her dress, as can be seen from the holes along a horizontal line across it into which dowel pins fitted (Pl. 44a).

Around her neck and over the top of her chiton was a lions' heads torque with a rosette brooch or medallion [386] between the terminals, as we have already mentioned. Both of the lions' heads were somewhat damaged. It was exactly the same kind of torque as the one on the sandstone Zeus-Hadad figure, and it seems most likely, therefore, that the sandstone Atargatis on the adjacent stele must also have worn a lions' torque around her neck. Otherwise, at the Temple of Tannur, the torque is clearly worn by only one other deity, namely, a goddess wearing a high-necked chiton, with a separate "sky" veil covering her head and a long, narrow, tuning fork type of symbol, its two prongs bound together near the top, over her right shoulder (Pl. 45a). She may be a Tyché, having many similarities, including the bound, double pronged symbol, to the Zodiac-Tyché (Pl. 46). The symbol probably represents a planetary standard, called a semeion. The torque insignia of distinction is found unmistakably only on these three figures at the Temple of Tannur, namely, the last one mentioned, the first on Zeus-Hadad and the other on the figure of what seems beyond all question to have been a smaller replica of Zeus-Hadad's companion, Atargatis.

Her features are youthful, rounded, reflective, strong, attractive and stylized. Her hair, parted in the middle, is combed in graceful waves terminating in separate locks on the side of her head, which is topped by a high floriate crown or polos (Pl. 44a). The almond shaped eyes on either side of the straight, short, slightly flattened and damaged "Grecian" nose are skillfully executed, giving the face a pensive, withdrawn look. The arching eyebrows are indicated by grooved lines and a downward sloping change of plane between them and the eye sockets that show traces of red paint in them. The eyes are deeply countersunk. The eyelids are clearly etched by skillfully canted grooves of varying planes on their top and bottom sides, raising them above the eyesockets. The irises are represented by raised, concentric circles and the pupils by the circular depressions inside them. The full lips, curved in an emphatic bow, as in other instances from this site, are slightly parted (the upper one broken partly on the left side), with deep grooves along their sides accentuating them as well as the rounded cheeks above a firm, well formed chin. A long patrician neck completes the appearance of the bust.

This small limestone Atargatis represented, as must have her large sandstone likeness, a goddess of calm beauty, quiet strength and infinite bounty. She reflects knowledge of the savor of ecstasy, the joyousness of fertility, the calm of fulfillment. The very tilt of her head, however, seems to indicate that she was not complete in herself. It is bent slightly to the right towards the god with whom she shared the responsibilities and reward of creativity. Next to her must have been placed a similarly proportioned Zeus-Hadad of limestone, just as next to the sandstone Zeus-Hadad there must have been enthroned the Atargatis figure to whom the sandstone fragments belonged. Theirs preëminently was the rule over nature and human affairs. To them were offered the supplications and sacrifices of dependent mortals.

1) SCULPTURES IN THE ROUND

Of all the representations of beasts and birds in stone at Khirbet Tannur, only one was sculptured in the round, the others being rendered in low or high relief. It represented a comparatively small sculpture of a cloven-hoofed, reclining animal, with its feet folded beneath it (Pl. 170a). Unfortunately, the head had been broken off and we found no traces whatsoever of it. That was a pity because this particular sculpture [386] seems to have been one of the best executed of any at Khirbet Tannur in its artistic life likeness. There is a charm and delicacy and excellence of form about this particular work making it stand out among the highly stylized sculptures which are common at Khirbet Tannur and other Nabataean sites. There is a flow of line and a subtlety of features that almost invest this animal of stone with the grace of living reality. There is no question that the head, had it been preserved, would have possessed and perhaps surpassed the fine quality of the backward turned ibex head in the inhabited scroll of an unusually good relief at Qasr Rabbah (Pl. 169a). Indeed, the decapitated sculpture in the round may originally have represented an ibex or a gazelle.[387]

One striking thing about it, as has already been noted, is that it is made of sandstone instead of the limestone out of which almost all the other sculptures at Khirbet Tannur were fashioned. The only other objects made out of sandstone there were the stele of Zeus-Hadad enthroned between two bulls and the remnants of the stele of his consort, Atargatis. Of the latter there remained, as we have seen, only her left foot (Pl. 161b), part of the body and head, one paw and traces of several toes of the lion that also originally guarded the left side of her throne. There must originally have been another lion on the right side.

One wonders whether any special significance attaches to the fact that this small sculpture of an animal couchant was hewn out of sandstone. There would seem to be a possibility of its being specially important because sandstone is not native to the Khirbet Tannur area and a block of it would have had to have been brought in perhaps from the Petra region. It will be recalled that the most important steles at Khirbet Tannur, namely the above mentioned ones of Zeus-Hadad and Atargatis with their attendants and with their lions' torques, were made out of sandstone. We have suggested that this was done in order to emphasize their holiness and connect them with the supremely important and especially sacred Nabataean sanctuary at the capital of Petra.

b. Lion Gargoyles

Lions were frequently sculptured by the Nabataeans and others as stand-ins for the paramount goddess of their pantheon. A number of limestone gargoyles of heads of lions in high relief were found at Khirbet Tannur. One of them (Pl. 165), with the top of its head broken off, formed, together with its mane, the front of a large, stone water basin. The open mouth of the lion, pierced all the way through, served as a spout through which water could be poured or drained from the basin, which too had suffered damage, particularly on its left side. The upper teeth of the lion are carved in complete relief, with the protruding tongue making it unnecessary to show the lower ones. Between the upper and lower sides of the wide open mouth a curtain of stone remains, on which the upper and lower side rows of teeth have been carved in relief. The distance between them affords the illusion of a wide-open mouth even when viewed in profile.

Another lion's head in high relief, with part of the neck at the back of it still remaining, is almost a duplicate of the one just mentioned, except that the lower front fangs are shown, as well as the upper ones. The side rows of teeth are depicted again at the bottom and top of a curtain of stone remaining between the upper and lower sides of the mouth (Pl. 165c, d). The differences between the two reliefs, aside from the different positioning of the side teeth, are minimal. Both reliefs were fashioned in exactly the same style as the head of the sandstone lion, originally one of a pair, that guarded the two sides of the throne of Atargatis at Khirbet Tannur (Pl. 160).[388] Her stele, as we have seen, stood in all probability beside that of Zeus-Hadad enthroned between his two guardian bulls.

Similar lion gargoyles of limestone were found at Qasr Rabbah and undoubtedly came from either the Nabataean temple or other Nabataean public buildings there.[389] At the base of an arch inside one of the modern buildings at Qasr Rabbah is a well fashioned lion's head in high relief, extending from a decorated block, which may have belonged originally to a cornice of the Nabataean temple there (Pl. 164a). At the base of the other side of the arch is another large, limestone block, bearing on a raised medallion the relief of a bust of Helios-Apollo, with the sun's rays extending from the sides and top of his head (Pl. 137a).

Placed upside down in the wall of another building at Qasr Rabbah is a large, decorated building block with a massive lion-gargoyle in high relief rising from it (Pl. 164b),[390] whose mouth once served as a water spout. In still other walls in this village are several other reliefs of lions' heads, in more damaged condition than the last two mentioned (Pl. 163b, c). It will be remembered that these are in addition to the two beautifully rendered half-length bodies in relief of a lion and a gazelle located there. Furthermore, in the tumble-down litter of the ruins of yet another Nabataean temple, namely that of Khirbet edh-Dherih, is a similar lion's head rising in high relief from the center of a badly damaged, Corinthianized pilaster capital (Pl. 163a).

Almost all of these reliefs of heads of lions are much the same wherever they occur in Nabataean sites in southern Transjordan. This applies also to the frontally positioned, exceedingly worn head of a huge relief of a lion carved otherwise in profile on the face of a sandstone cliff at Petra (Pl. 166a) [391] and to the extant head of one of the two reliefs of lions on either side of the entrance to the Lion Triclinium there (Pl. 166b).[392] In the latter, the entire front of the lion's body, including head, chest and forelegs, is presented in full view, while the rest of the body is shown in profile. These lion reliefs can be duplicated in Nabataean Syria, allowing for differences in most instances resulting primarily from being sculptured in basalt instead of in limestone.[393]

Their likeness appears also on torques carved on some of the sculptures of deities at Khirbet Tannur. There are numerous parallels extending far beyond the territory and in many cases preceding the era of the Nabataean kingdom. They can be traced, for instance, in the Hellenistic period, from Baalbek in Coele Syria [394] to Timna in South Arabia [395] and occur in many other places both in the Orient and the Occident.[396] The lion as a solar symbol became a hallmark of Hellenistic influence. The South Arabians alone seem to have persisted in assigning to it a secondary rank in order to emphasize their continuing belief in the primacy of their lunar male god of the heavens.[397]

c. Badges of Distinction

We have seen that the Nabataean torques with lion terminals on sculptures of Zeus-Hadad, Atargatis and Tyché at Khirbet Tannur represent an important element in the cultural forces merged in the unique amalgam of the Nabataean civilization. Demonstrably influenced both by the Orient and the Occident, this civilization was, nevertheless, on the whole, markedly more than the sum of its parts, as we have previously maintained. Some of the motifs and symbols employed in the art and architecture of Khirbet Tannur occurred simultaneously in each of the worlds from which the Nabataean kingdom drew much of its strength and character, while others may be pinpointed as belonging to only one of these major sources. To the latter category belong the lions' torques from Khirbet Tannur. Together with other features of Nabataean art, which we shall discuss later on, they are directly Parthian and indirectly Scythian in origin.

The Nabataeans occasionally ascribed the same attributes and insignia with fine impartiality not only to different deities of the same pantheon but also to gods and goddesses alike. This applies at Khirbet Tannur to the use of the lions' torque, worn not only by Zeus-Hadad but also, as we have seen, by Atargatis and Tyché. Types of the radiate crown worn by Helios there appear also on particular forms of these female deities (Pls. 32, 136).[398] And by the same token, although Atargatis is strikingly portrayed as the wheat goddess at Khirbet Tannur (Pl. 25), it is possible that her consort, Zeus-Hadad, who wears the thunderbolt symbol of his power over his left arm, may possibly also have held aloft in his right hand a sheaf of wheat.[399] In the related bas-relief of Zeus-Hadad and Atargatis at Dura-Europos, he does indeed hold a bundle of wheat in his right hand.[400] A wheat god is pictured on one of the tesserae of Palmyra,[401] and a sheaf of wheat is one of the attributes of Hadad on a Syrian intaglio,[402] as it is of the related deity, Gad, the protectress of Alexandria.[403] Actually, however, we believe that the sandstone Zeus-Hadad held loft in his right hand a limestone scepter, the fragments of which we found in the immediate proximity of his stele and were able to put together again (Pls. 112b, 186a). The bottom is whiter than the rest of it, showing that it was inserted into a hand or into some sort of socket and thus escaped being slightly darkened by exposure to the elements. The possibility of course also exists that the scepter was held in one of the hands of the relief of the enthroned Atargatis,[404] although that seems less likely to us.

2. FERTILITY GODDESS

a. Chief in Rank

Atargatis had many costumes as befitted a queen of the gods. In his description of the cult-statue of Atargatis to whom the great temple at Hierapolis-Bambyke in northern Syria was primarily dedicated, Lucian calls her Hera, but knows that she has another name. He reports further that she wore a mural crown and that "she borrowed particular traits from a variety of goddesses—Athena, Aphrodite, Selene, Rhea, Artemis, Nemesis, and the Moirei." [405] Indeed, it may be more correct to speak of her as the reigning monarch of the Temple of Tannur and of Zeus-Hadad as her royal consort.

The largest and perhaps the most striking sculpture of the Temple of Tannur was that of the veiled or masked Goddess of Vegetation (Pls. 31-33), crowning the east façade of the inner temple-court pylon. It was the dominating representation of Atargatis, to whom the Temple of Tannur was probably primarily devoted in the first place. This was the case in many other temples in Syria and Asia Minor, as illustrated by the splendid temple dedicated to her at Hierapolis-Bambyke and by the one she presided over at Dura-Europos,[406] where the previously mentioned stele of Atargatis and Hadad was found.

Her bust in high relief, which was larger than life size, rose from a massive, limestone block. It formed the central section of a semicircular panel of considerable size, consisting of at least six main parts, of which five were recovered. This impressive group, together with several other pieces obviously attached to it, may have been the central feature of the entablature crowning the ornate pylon on the east side of the raised inner temple-court. Nearly all the pieces belonging to this Atargatis panel were found near the bottom of the steps leading up to the pylon gateway giving access to the innermost sanctuary. They had remained where they had fallen as the result undoubtedly of a catastrophic earthquake. One piece was not recovered.

Perched on top of the central Atargatis block, but somewhat behind and below the crown of her head, is another carefully sculptured relief of an eagle with extended wings. On either side of it was one of two and perhaps originally more parts of the complete panel. They consisted of curved pointed stone equivalents of horns or sunrays extending above and beyond their retreating, beveled bases. I have pointed out above that the bottom side of the eagle finial was horizontally rabbeted, enabling it to be fitted closely on top of the main Atargatis section. Furthermore, these two complete sections of a curved cornice, each of them with a projecting, triangular, outturned horn, had exactly the same radius as the top of the semicircular panel and must have been placed on top of it. There is no doubt in our mind that all of these pieces were conceived and executed as belonging together.

The very size and centrally featured position of Atargatis on this semicircular panel emphasized the preëminent position this goddess occupied in the Temple of Tannur. She was its paramount deity, even as in other temples in the ancient Near East [407] and elsewhere.[408] We can understand thus why Lucian reports with regard to the Dea Syria of Hierapolis that sacrifices brought there to Zeus (Hadad) were offered in silence, but those brought to Hera (Atargatis) were accompanied by exultant declamations and manifestations of ecstatic joy.[409] His inferior or secondary position in comparison to her is emphasized by Lucian in his description of her role as "fish goddess." He reports that when Hera went down to look at the sacred fish in the lake nearby the temple of Hierapolis, Zeus was not even permitted to view them before she did and that indeed he was held off from preceding her by various artifices on her part.[410]

We found no sculpture of Zeus-Hadad of comparable size in the Temple of Tannur, nor do we believe that one existed to share with Atargatis the star billing, strikingly given her by the practically exclusive position of her relief placed high in the crowning entablature of the east façade of the innermost sanctuary. That Zeus-Hadad was her royal consort is clearly shown by the two relief panels of both of them, standing doubtlessly side by side in front of the base of the main altar in the center of the raised, inner temple court. It seems certain, however, that Atargatis was the first in rank and foremost in representation and probably most featured in worship of the deities of the Temple of Tannur. Indeed, in connection with the great entablature relief of Atargatis, it is noteworthy that the figure of Zeus-Hadad is reduced to the secondary status of a superimposed ornamental appendage in the form of an eagle accompanied by a series of stone horns as the symbols of sunrays. It may be said of the Atargatis both of Dura and Tannur that she was most emphatically the more important figure. In the famous relief of Hadad and Atargatis from Dura, the thunder god appears as the anaemic, undersized, henpecked and melancholy mate of the much bulkier, full-chinned, firm-featured, superior-appearing Atargatis. She looks as if she were accustomed to leading him by the nose. She not only dominated his person but his animal servitors. Even her attendant lions are much larger than his sickly-looking bulls, one of which has indeed been completely squeezed out of position at his left side and pokes his head out like a frightened puppy from behind the pillar framing the left side of the panel.[411]

Atargatis appears on the elaborate, multisectioned, semicircular panel at the Temple of Tannur as the Goddess of Vegetation, the mother of nature, the matrix of leaves and vines and fruit and flowers. Leaves sprout from her face, neck and chest in the center of an elaborate, attractive, spreading floral scroll. The floral scroll background from which her high relief emerges consists of an intricate bower of interwoven vines encircling formalized acanthus leaves or completely or partly open rosettes of various sizes, possessing eight or less double petals. Pomegranates or occasionally figs appear in the composition. This elaborate bower of vines and foliage and fruit forms a luxuriant setting for Atargatis as the source of fertility.

The pomegranate especially has of old been considered a symbol of fecundity,[412] reflected in the abundance of its seeds and possibly in the redness of its color.[413] At Petra, there was discovered a relief of Eros waving a pomegranate branch (Pl. 171b).[414] In the Greek world, Athena-Niké is represented as holding a pomegranate in her right hand[415] and Persephone as pressing one between her breasts.[416] Hera of Argos was distinguished by a scepter in one hand and a pomegranate in the other.[417] The association of pomegranates with Atargatis (Hera) of our panel is seen thus to be a natural one. Particularly interesting to us, furthermore, in view of the connections of the Nabataeans with Parthian Iran, are several, small, bronze water goddesses from Luristan, each having a circle of pomegranates around her navel.[418] The pomegranate, both in the East and the West was viewed as the regenerative fruit of the tree of life.[419] Was it perhaps the original of the famous apple of the Garden of Eden?

The fig symbol on this panel, if indeed it is a fig, does not seem to have quite the same religious and ritualistic significance as is associated with the pomegranate in the literature and sculpture of antiquity. It serves however, to underscore the phenomenon of birth and ripening in general. The grape motif was similarly but even more frequently employed in Nabataean art. All of these features, together with and perhaps especially with the highly sophisticated and stylized designs of the palm branch and leaf frequently employed, symbolized perpetual rebirth and fecundity in this life and the next. They became the hallmark of most of the Nabataean painted pottery. It was generally almost eggshell thin, masterfully wheel thrown, thoroughly baked and on the whole absolutely unique (Pls. 73-80).

The most beautiful and naturalistic example in Nabataean art of the theme of vines and leaves and flowers, to which are added birds and various mythological figures, is to be found in a superb mural painting (Pls. 203, 204) at the site of Siq el-Bared, a suburb of Petra. The artistic and scientific excellence of representation of flora and fauna and the warmly life-like depiction even of mythological figures such as Pan, Eros and Ganymede in the el-Bared mural surpasses normal Nabataean craftsmanship. The wall paintings there may possibly have been executed near the beginning of the first century A.D. or later by an Alexandrian craftsman who was steeped in and master of the finest Hellenistic artistic traditions, and skills.[419a] An exuberant Nabataean lintel with reliefs featuring gods and foliage and olive branches laden with fruit, which is closely related to the Siq el-Bared mural, has been found in Syria in the Jebel Druze and could possibly have been a part of the Nabataean temple at Si'a.[420] The "inhabited scrolls" of Baalbek and Palmyra and of Nabataean Atil, Qanawat, Si'a and Soueïda in the Syrian Jebel Druze and of Qasr Rabbah in Transjordan belong in this category (Pls. 169a, b, 170b).[421] Others occur, for instance, at Sardis in Asia Minor [422] and at Beth-shan in Palestine.[423]

Especially striking are the large, serrated leaves covering the face, neck and body of the Atargatis relief, leaving only her breasts bare. One of the leaves, broader than it is long, hangs like a great jewel over the front of her forehead. It extends from below the sides of the front of her centrally parted hair nearly down to the top of the bridge of her nose. The sides and bottom of the leaf form six separate triangles, reminding one of the sun rays forming the crown of Helios (Pl. 136). They recall also the two sections of the curved cornice with projecting, triangular horns, that may have belonged on either side of the eagle finial surmounting the top of the Atargatis head. Two additional leaves, with four and originally possibly five triangular edges at their bottoms, completely cover her cheeks and reached to her nostrils. Her nose has been chiseled away by vandals. Another large leaf covers the lower part and bottom of her large and firmly rounded chin. Two others encircle all but the central, front part of her long, patrician neck, looking like two halves of a high, open throated collar. Her entire open-bosomed bodice consists of or is almost completely covered with leaves. The remaining locks of her hair fall over the top of each shoulder.

The head and face of this Vegetation Goddess are in every major respect similar to those of other forms of Atargatis as Dolphin, Grain, Guardian, Victory or Queen Goddess, who wears the lions' torque of her royal status. The short, separate, flame-like locks of her hair, composed of two to five strands each, are of a type common both to the deities and lions of Khirbet Tannur (Pls. 31, 39, 150, 160). The deep, countersunk eyes, with their raised, circular irises and depressed pupils conform to those of all the rest of the deities of the Temple of Tannur, as do the rounded cheeks and full, slightly parted lips curved in the shape of a bow above the firm chin. Traces of red paint still remain in the sunken cornea of the eyes.

Carved more massively than the other Khirbet Tannur sculptures, this relief of Atargatis was obviously meant to be placed on high and viewed from below as part of the tympanum or entablature over the entrance to the raised, inner court of the sanctuary. When looked at on the ground, the chin of the goddess seems unduly large, although actually it is no larger in proportion than those of her sculptures in other guises. The length of her neck also helps maintain the proper perspective with regard to the features of her countenance. She was clearly the leading deity in the pantheon of gods of the Temple of Tannur. Her figure commanded the forecourt and the entrance into the raised, inner temple area with its central altar. No other sculpture of comparable dimensions was found, nor any other deity discovered there who appeared in so many closely related roles, each of which required distinctive accessories.

b. Duplicate Models

The stellar position she occupied at the Temple of Tannur seems to have been repeated at the important suburb of Petra, called Khirbet Brak. To judge from the sculptures and other architectural pieces scattered among its ruins, another Nabataean temple, closely related to that of the Temple of Tannur in style and period must have existed there. Among them was a large, limestone relief, 52 centimeters wide and 56 high, of the head of a goddess, who in size and appearance could almost have been a twin sister of

Pl. 127 (*opposite*)   Parthian-type head (p. 183)

5 cms

Pl. 128   Parthian-type head (p. 197)

Pl. 129 (*opposite*)   Parthian-type relief (p. 197)

2 cms

a

Pl. 130 (*opposite*)   Parthian-type bust in relief
(p. 198)

5 cms

Pl. 131   a, b. Mask *en-face* and left profile
(p. 226)

b

5 cms

5 cms

a,b

c

a

Pl. 133

a. Mask in front top center of capital (p. 125)
b. Mason's markings on top of above capital (p. 125)

5 cms

b

Pl. 132 (*opposite*)

a, b. Mask *en-face* and
left profile (p. 224)
c. Nabataean capital
with mask, Ma'in
(p. 60)

5 cms

Pl. 134

a. Pilaster capital with front top central mask broken off (p. 125)

b. Horned pilaster capital minus front top central mask (p. 125)

a

b

5 cms

5 cms

Pl. 135

Mask on front of basin
(p. 227)

5 cms

Pl. 136   Helios relief with torches (p. 144)

|__ __|
5 cms

Pl. 137

a. Helios relief, Qasr Rabbah
   (p. 58)
b. Badly damaged Helios relief (p. 417)

a

b

Pl. 138   Ba'al-shamin, Luna and Helios relief, Nabataean Jebel Druze (p. 472)

Pl. 139   Damaged relief, Khirbet el-Mesheirfeh (p. 59)

a, b

c

Pl. 141

a, b. Eagle and serpent sculpture, Zaharet el-
        Bedd (p. 480)

c.   Eagle and serpent graffito, Dura-Europos
        (p. 481)

Pl. 140 (*opposite*)   Eagle and serpent sculpture
                         (p. 479)

Pl. 142   Eagle and serpent, Ausan, South Arabia (p. 489)

Pl. 143 Eagle shrine, Petra (p. 474)

a, b, c

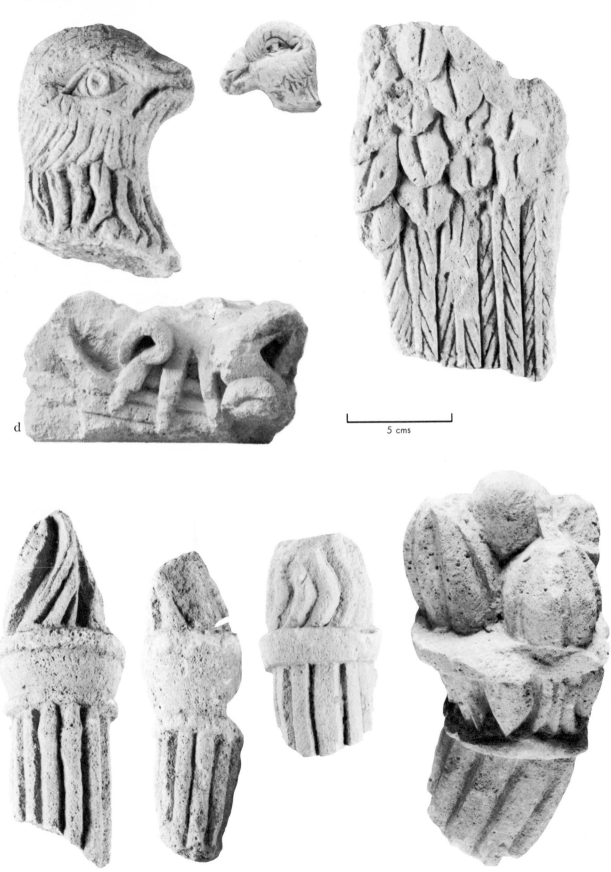

d

5 cms

e, f, g, h

the great Vegetation Atargatis of the Temple of Tannur with face and body nearly completely veiled with leaves.[424] She had suffered even more from wanton vandalism than the Vegetation Goddess had, but the resemblance is striking and unmistakable. The right top of her head has been broken off and damage inflicted on her eyes, nose, mouth and chin.

Her hair was arranged differently from that of her twin. Although likewise parted in the middle, it is combed in undulating, wavy fashion to either side of her head, with three tight locks curving in toward the middle of the left side of her face and one remaining long, twisted braid falling down over her now missing right shoulder. This type of hair arrangement occurs frequently at the Temple of Tannur among other goddesses and gods as well (Pls. 53b, 55). There is a particularly striking similarity to the hairdress of a female bust in relief decorating a water trough (Pl. 135a) and to the top of the head of an otherwise completely destroyed deity from there (Pl. 184c).

Another difference between the two sculptures of Atargatis lies in the plain background of the stone panel from which the Khirbet Brak relief emerges. Different, too, are the ringlets,[425] one on each cheek near the ear, which are missing on the Tannur sculpture. They occur there, however, on the cheeks of the Grain and Dolphin Goddess versions (Pls. 1, 2a, b, 3a, 25, 26b, c), which harken back to Hellenistic originals.[426]

Otherwise, the proportions and features of the Khirbet Brak goddess are similar to those of the one from the Temple of Tannur. She, too, was obviously meant to be located high up and looked at from below. Seen on the ground, the heavy chin of the Atargatis of Khirbet Brak seems too large for the rest of her face, as does that of her sister at the Temple of Tannur. We may assume that the former, too, gazed from her elevated vantage place in the tympanum or entablature above the entrance of the sanctuary over which she presided. She, too, had a veil of leaves over her face, failing to conceal her features. It covers her forehead, upper cheeks and lower part of her chin in almost exactly the same way as on the Atargatis of Tannur. So strikingly alike in most important respects are these two reliefs of Atargatis from the temples of Tannur and Brak that it almost seems possible to attribute them to the handiwork of the same sculptor. They certainly belong to the same artistic school, the same period and the same religious preconceptions. A similar Leaf or Vegetation Goddess has been found at Petra.[426a]

We thought at first that the phenomenon of these leaf masks might be based upon a long lingering Semitic tradition, according to which the deity had to be listened to, but could not be looked at. Moses was thus adjured not to gaze at the face of God: "for a man shall not see me and live. And the Lord said, Behold there is a place by me, and thou shalt stand upon the rock. And it shall come to pass, while my glory passeth by, that I will put

Pl. 144   Sculptural Fragments (*opposite*)

a, b. Eagles' heads (p. 445)   c. Fragments of eagle's wing (p. 445)

d.   Eagle's claws (p. 480)   e-g. Tops of torches (p. 464)   h. Cornucopia thee in a cleft of the rock and will cover thee with my hand until I have passed by. And I will take my hand away and thou shalt see my back, but my face shall not be seen" (Exodus 33:20-23). Even more specifically does the Bible relate that after this experience the face of Moses shone so that "he put a veil on his face" to mask the effulgence that had become his through close contact with the Lord and that mortal men dared not behold with impunity (Exodus 33:22-23, 34:30, 33-35).[427] We are reminded, too, of Elijah's standing with covered countenance at the entrance of the sacred cave on Mt. Horeb, hearkening to the word of the Lord (I Kings 19:8, 9, 13).

I am convinced, as has previously been stated, that the Nabataeans of the second century A.D., had they so desired, could have given their deities much the same noble proportions and idealized beauty that the Hellenistic gods possessed. These were familiar to them from many places such as Jerash (Pl. 43a), Philadelphia-Amman (Pl. 51), Ascalon (Pl. 49b) or Antioch (Pl. 52a) and from numerous points on the Mediterranean littoral they visited so frequently. They chose, however, to follow their own bent and not slavishly imitate any single artistic tradition but selectively to adopt or adapt what appealed to them.

Nabataean sculpture revealed a commingling of cultural influences of polar disparity, among which the Hellenistic ones exercised a very powerful impact. This is evidenced, also, in the employment by the Nabataeans of masks of leaves and also of dolphins and probably of crab's claws in connection with their gods. The most direct source of these features was Mediterranean and Hellenistic. Sea gods, both male and female, sported one or more of them, and their worship ranged from England to Iran and from Africa to Asia. The Nabataeans, Syrians, Parthians and others transferred them to dry land and transmuted their significance in accordance with their own past and predilections and convictions. At Hatra, for instance, there is a stone, male mask with acanthus leaves springing from his hair, cheeks and beard (Pl. 35a).[427a] It can be paralleled by another from Aurelian's Temple of the sun in Rome (Pl. 35b) [428] and by comparable sculptures from the shores of the Mediterranean and elsewhere.[429] In like manner, the Nabataeans and their Semitic contemporaries near and far also adopted the playful dolphins as guarantors of well-being and safety in travel in this world and in the hereafter and introduced representations of them in extensive areas of their domicile and dominion. They can be traced on dry land at sites as distant from one another as Petra in southern Transjordan, Hatra in Parthia and Sardis in Asia Minor.[430]

The characteristics and areas of authority of all these deities with attributes of leaves, dolphins and crab's claws, not to mention others, such as cornucopias and lyres, seem to disregard differences of sex. Indeed, the competencies of male and female gods often overlapped or were indistinguishable. There remained, nevertheless, pronounced divergencies between the Hellenistic deities of the Mediterranean littoral and the Hellenistic-Semitic ones of the Nabataeans, as much alike in many ways as they superficially appeared to be. The veil of leaves on the Atargatis of Khirbet Tannur may be most directly, to be sure, ascribed to Hellenistic influences. Its complete explanation cannot be found, however, in its similarity to seaweed clinging to marine deities and its origins must be sought much farther back in time and much farther afield in significance. The Vegetation Goddess and the Dolphin Goddess are obviously closely related to the goddess from Leptis Magna in Tripoli, for example, marked by crab's claws, dolphins and a veil of leaves.[430a] The Nabataean peasant or desert dweller, however, who never glimpsed the sea, could not but have seen in the veil of leaves an augury of the lush crops or abundant grazing he hoped the gods would provide for him.

The Hellenistic-Semitic gods of the zenith of Nabataean development in the second century A.D. were far removed from the rough-hewn, rectangular blocks of the Dhu Shara (Dushara, Dusares) deity of their earlier history. His ultimate identification with bibulous Dionysos marked the complete transition from desert simplicity and severity to comparative opulence and sophisticated adaptation to cultures of widened horizons.[431]

X. AFFINITY WITH DOLPHINS

X. *Affinity with Dolphins*

1. AS DOLPHIN AND GRAIN GODDESS

In any kind of a fashion show for goddesses of the ancient Near East, the Atargatis of Khirbet Tannur would easily have won the prize as the best dressed one of them all. She had a different and striking costume for apparently every conceivable occasion, with changes for every day of the week and more. We know of nine different garbs that were used by her at Khirbet Tannur and there may have been others to judge from the number of fragments of busts of goddesses found there damaged beyond recognition.

In one appearance, as we have seen, she had a transparent veil of leaves on her face and body, that rose from a background of fruit and foliage contained in an elaborate floral scroll (Pl. 31). In another, she wore a mural crown and was encircled by a ring of the signs of the zodiac (Pls. 46-48). In a third manifestation, she chose as additional ornament a lion's torque (Pl. 44a); in a fourth she carried a horn of plenty (Pl. 55) and in yet another, in addition to a lions' torque, a planetary standard over her right shoulder (Pl. 45a), which in another appearance with the mural crown and the signs of the zodiac is shown over her left shoulder. In two additional, much damaged versions, she carries a now indefinable object, perhaps a rudder, in her left hand (Pl. 45b) in one instance, and in the other what appears to be a lyre (?) over her left shoulder, while on her head can be seen the remains of a mural crown (Pl. 53a, b).

In two of her most beguiling costumes, she could be either one of a pair of twins, separately recognizable mainly by the different tiaras in their hair. The accessories set the tone and made for a clear distinction between the two sisters. In one costume she appeared as the Grain Goddess (Pl. 25) and in the other as the Dolphin Goddess (Pl. 1), with the latter being the most unusual of them all. On the small top of a steep-sided hill, in a canyon-split land edged on several sides by immense deserts and bordered on another by a wild, deep, practically waterless rift difficult of access, in an isolated sanctuary many weary miles removed from any sea and its creatures, this Atargatis of Tannur wore a headdress of dolphins!

When the sculpture of Atargatis as Grain Goddess came to light in our excavations at Khirbet Tannur, it occasioned delight but no particular surprise. In that capacity and under various names, among some of which are Atargatis, Hera, Fortuna, Tyché and Demeter, she was extremely popular and rapturously idolized in the Hellenistic-Semitic world. To portray her with stalks of grain came natural to the Nabataeans, Parthians and many others.[432] The phenomenon of making seed sprout, grain grow, fruit ripen and the womb yield its young in plenty was largely attributed to her, whose importance surpassed that of her consort, Zeus-Hadad, or however he was variously known. He, too, as the protector of crops, was often shown to be holding stalks of wheat in his hand,[433] even when, as at Dura-Europos, he was definitely pushed into the background by the forward-thrusting Atargatis.

The appearance, on the other hand, at Khirbet Tannur of Atargatis as the Dolphin Goddess, who, both by pride of looks and position, was obviously the twin sister of the Grain Goddess, was at the time completely unexpected. This was not the familiar mainstay and benefactress of abundant nature. Meeting her, as we did, practically in the middle of the desert, flaunting dolphins on top of her head, seemed at first almost as strange as it would have been to have encountered a camel swimming far out at sea. It took considerable scientific detective work to ascertain that the ornament of dolphins was as highly esteemed by the Nabataeans as were the symbols of fruit or foliage or grain and that worship of the Dolphin Goddess was held to be as important for travel by land as for voyage by sea. Indeed, especial reverence was accorded dolphins for the help they were supposed to be able to give on the journey that every one sooner or later had to undertake into the blue beyond of life after death.

The Dolphin Goddess and the Grain Goddess and a number of their replicas were located, as we have previously mentioned, on the front sides of opposite, attached corner-pilasters of the east façade of the base of the altar in the center of the elevated, inner court of the Temple of Tannur. The bust of the Grain Goddess is tilted slightly to the left and that of the Dolphin Goddess slightly to the right, indicating their respective positions and the fact that they were inclined towards each other. To this minor degree, they depart thus from the orientalizing pattern of immobile frontality [434] that applies in general to all the gods of the Temple of Tannur. Only the heads of some of the animals are occasionally presented in profile. The Dolphin Goddess and the Grain Goddess were very much like each other in many ways, but to carry the analogy of their relationship farther, they were totally dissimilar twins with different associations and with widely divergent although strangely interrelated purposes. But let us describe their physical make-up first before turning to a consideration of their place in the Hellenistic-Semitic world and their religious significance in the essentially inland kingdom of a basically Semitic people.

There was very little difference in the coiffure of the two goddesses. In each case the hair was parted in the middle, wavy, combed to the side and fell in two curled locks, one on each side of the face, down to the shoulders. The bottom end of each of these twisted side-locks of hair consisted of two carefully waved strands, set in a formal pattern. The sister goddesses did not, however, wear exactly the same clothes. The Grain Goddess had on a high-necked blouse or chiton, fastened apparently at the top center, with the lines of the garment conforming to the contours of the breasts. The plain band at the top gave way in the dress of the Dolphin Goddess to a dentilated neckline, while the rest of it seemed to be formed of triangularly shaped segments superimposed on top of each other in scale-like fashion.

Each of the high reliefs of the goddesses emerges from a nearly circular, multisectional shell, with stylized half acanthus leaves at each corner, all of which is set in a slightly sunken panel between broad borders on three sides, with whose surfaces the top of the shell and leaves are flush.

The role of the acanthus leaf in Nabataean and related Hellenistic-Semitic sculpture is an exceedingly important one, as is that of the vine, laurel and other leaves. The acanthus leaf is particularly emphasized on the Grain and Dolphin Goddess panels of Khirbet Tannur, on the faces and bodies of the Vegetation Goddesses there and at Khirbet Brak, and on numerous other Nabataean sculptures. It was rendered apparently to convey the idea of irrepressible fertility and of continuous regeneration and renewal in this life and in the hereafter. This applies also to other repeatedly depicted leaves.

The stylized acanthus leaf of Nabataean sculpture at Khirbet Tannur appears in the form of an acanthus cup or base in numerous Graeco-Roman and in related Hellenistic-Semitic sculptures. It substitutes for the Egyptian lotus blossom associated with the concept of birth and renewal of life on earth and in the world beyond.[435] Dependent directly apparently upon the Egyptian influence in this respect is the bust of a Parthian king dated to the first part of the Christian era.[436] A striking example of an acanthus cup replacing a lotus cup or blossom is furnished by a Hellenistic bronze of Semitic background. It shows a Scylla, accompanied by four griffins, with her right arm upraised and her left one holding up a rudder, rising from a multipetalled acanthus cup or base [437] (Pl. 171a).

Emerging from a base or cup of double acanthus leaves on an ornately carved lintel at Nabataean Qanawat in the Jebel Druze is the head and nude torso of a winged deity, who is probably to be identified with Dushara-Dusares-Dionysos.[438] With both arms outstretched, the figure grasps vines laden with clusters of grapes. On either side of it is an intricate pattern of "inhabited" scrolls of grapevines and clusters of grapes enclosing winged vintaging Erotes. There is a very close connection between this lintel and the murals of el-Bared near Petra, which portray even more elaborate leaf and vine scrolls enclosing birds of various kinds and figures such as a flute-playing Pan or a goose-clasping Ganymede.

This winged, acanthus-based deity from Qanawat represented, it seems certain, the ever vigorous, newly reborn god of fertility and vegetation, whose endless reproductivity is symbolized by the self-renewing and self-perpetuating tendrils, leaves and fruit of the grapevine. Its entire artistic theme conveys the intimations and explicit promise of immortality. This is frequently expressed elsewhere by the use of acanthus and other leaves, by the symbols of dolphins and griffins, for instance, on sarcophagi (Pl. 24a, b) or as attributes or ornaments of the deities, and by the relationship of the entire pantheon of the gods to the seven planets and to the constellations of the zodiac. The abundance of the good life on earth and the assurance of its continuation in the hereafter were the endless concern of the Nabataean cosmogony.

On each of the cheeks of the Grain and Dolphin Goddesses are small carefully waved locks or ringlets of hair.[439] They are present also on the cheeks of the Atargatis of Khirbet Brak in the suburbs of Petra, who, with her veil of leaves and in most other respects, parallels the monumental relief of Atargatis as the Vegetation Goddess of the Temple of Tannur. It is fascinating to follow, as we shall later on, the connection between the Dolphin Goddess and the Vegetation Goddess of this sanctuary with Hellenistic deities, particularly of the contemporary, Mediterranean world.

In the main, the features sharply separating the Dolphin Goddess from the Grain Goddess are to be found in the two dolphins that face each other on the top of the veil or shawl, covering the head of the former, and the stalks of wheat that grace the top and the left side of the head of the latter. One complete wheat stalk arises above the left shoulder and left side of the head-veil of the Grain Goddess and four abbreviated double ones sprout from the upper sides and top of her head, with the two shortest, central ones being almost completely broken off and the outer left one partly damaged. These replace the two dolphins with their serrated tails resting on the upper sides and top of the head-veil of the Dolphin Goddess, and with their beaks meeting above the line of the central part of her meticulously waved hair.

The physical differences between the two goddesses are practically nonexistent. The cast of countenance of the one goddess is essentially a duplicate of that of the other. It happens that the irises protruding above the sunken corneas of the eyes of the Dolphin Goddess are less indented than those of the Grain Goddess. In all other respects, aside from their headgears, there is little or nothing to set them apart from each other. This similarity of form and feature holds true also for the rest of the pantheon of goddesses of Khirbet Tannur and for that matter for its male deities, too. Forehead, eyes, nose, cheeks, lips, chin are the same with all of them. The badges of their identities are to be seen in particulars of head dress, clothes, equipment, ornaments and attendants and not in individual peculiarities of facial features. A beard, of course, tells its own story, but the absence of one can be very misleading so far as the determination of the sex of the deity is concerned. So basically similar to one another are most of the gods, that nearly all of them could have been fashioned by the same sculptor or at least been the product of the same studio.

Even the dolphins take after the goddess they adorned insofar as their bulbous eyes are concerned. These are large in relationship to the size of their heads and have about the same shape and measurements as those of the host goddess herself. To be sure, the circular irises of her eyes protrude more sharply and are less indented than the conical ones of the dolphins, but it is clear that a certain, mutual resemblance reflects the intimacy of the bond between the sea-creatures and their mistress.

The large mouths and distinctively shaped heads and beaks of the two dolphins leave little doubt with regard to their identity (Pls. 1, 2a, b). We shall see later how much alike they are to other representations of dolphins and particularly to the two dolphins in almost exactly the same position on top of the head of the Goddess of Aphrodisias. The tail of the dolphin on the right side of the veil covering the goddess's head has three dentilated edges, while the one on the left side has five. They resemble the triangular decorations on the neckline of her dress, which appear otherwise, as has been mentioned, on some defaced busts of the same type (Pls. 27a, b, 28a) and also on two small reliefs of goddesses on the east façade of the pylon of the raised inner temple court (Pl. 12a, b).

2. DOLPHINS ON DRY LAND

a. Khirbet Brak

It would indeed have been strange if the Nabataeans had utilized the symbol of dolphins in their religious art only at Khirbet Tannur. It is no less a rule in archaeology than in philosophy that there is no such thing as a *Ding an sich,* totally separated from anything else in existence and complete in itself. Even those works of art bearing the uniqueness of the stamp of genius are the result in part of an endless series of prior influences. Where then did the Dolphin Goddess of Khirbet Tannur come from? With what juncture of events and impacts is she to be connected? She was no Athena sprung full-blown from Zeus's head. An innumerable series of overlapping circles of political and cultural and religious conditions and circumstances were intertwined in her coming into being and occupying a place of central symbolic prominence in the family of deities to which the Nabataeans and countless others paid glad homage.

Like a magnet pulling isolated particles into the field of its attraction, the discovery of the Dolphin Goddess of Khirbet Tannur drew into the orbit of her significance a series of hitherto more or less isolated items and invested them with new meaning. Separate pieces began to fit into a meaningful pattern, solving the puzzle of their proper place and resulting in a vastly improved understanding of Nabataean civilization. It was natural, under the circumstances, to remember an earlier find I had made in southern Transjordan of a Nabataean dolphin sculpture and relate it to our discoveries at Khirbet Tannur. I had chanced across it while exploring the Nabataean hill suburb of Khirbet Brak on the outskirts of Petra. Rumor reached me in Arab tents of the existence of fabulous statues there, and I had visited it to attempt to determine whether or not they were real or imaginary. I found none at the time, although years later it was demonstrated that the report was based on fact. The story had persisted, and following its lure, the English scholar, Peter J. Parr, went to Khirbet Brak to be shown a stone, which, when rolled over, turned out to be the leaf-veiled and ringletted Atargatis of Brak, whom we have mentioned above.[440] Her nearly identical twin had in the meantime been rescued from the limbo of the past in excavations at Nabataean Petra,[441] that had risen to prominence on the site of Biblical Sela, one of the chief cities of the kingdom of Edom.[442] The translation of both names, whether in the Greek form of Petra or the Hebrew form of Sela, is "the Rock"—which correctly expresses a good deal about the nature of the site.

My own excursion to Khirbet Brak, however, had not been in vain. Scattered among its ruins were numerous building stones of excellent cut and elegant decoration (Pls. 174c, 178c). We surmised then that they belonged to a small, fine temple, which was Nabataean in date, as were practically all the beautiful fragments of pottery littering the surface of the ground. It seems likely now that the Atargatis of Khirbet Brak, with her veil of leaves and the ringlets on her cheeks, was its chief goddess. Among these architectural stones, we saw a Nabataean pilaster capital, whose central horn was broken off, but each of whose end horns supported a carving of a highly ornate dolphin's head (Pl. 4a, b). The left one was fairly intact, together with its stylized fin (?), while the other was almost completely broken off. The comparatively intact head of the one dolphin is skillfully decorated with differently oriented sets of wavy grooves to accentuate its various contours (Pl. 4b). In general appearance, and specifically in the treatment of the eye, it belongs to the same genre of dolphins as those of Khirbet Tannur.

b. *Petra*

The list of Nabataean sites where terrestrial dolphin figures occur begins to grow impressive. It is natural that there should have been discovered also in Petra proper a Nabataean capital with dolphins on its end horns, similar

Pl. 145 Hermes-Mercury (p. 465)

a

b

5 cms

Pl. 147   Hermes-Mercury with side-locks
          (p. 469)

Pl. 146 (*opposite*)   5 cms

a. Hermes-Mercury with lyre (p. 228)
b. Crude relief of Hermes-Mercury (?) (p. 467)

Pl. 148   Hermes-Mercury, Nabataean Syria (p. 469)

Pl. 149

a. Winged Hermes-Mercury, Petra (p. 469)
b. Same, three-quarter right profile (p. 469)

b

Pl. 151   Hermes-Mercury, Petra (p. 467)

5 cms

Pl. 150 (*opposite*)   Hermes-Mercury (p. 292)

a

5 cms

c

b

Pl. 152   Caduceus symbols

a. Petra (p. 466)
b. Petra (p. 466)
c. Ramat el Halil, Hebron (p. 466)

5 cms

a   └──────┘
      5 cms

b   └──────┘
      5 cms

c   └──────┘
      5 cms

Pl. 153

a. Cronos-Saturn (p. 198)
b. Hermes-Mercury (p. 417)
c. Damaged sandstone bust, Petra, with ends of fillet over right shoulder (p. 211)

Pl. 154   a, b. Jupiter (p. 470)

a

b

5 cms

330

to the one found at the Petraean suburb of Khirbet Brak.[443] That these creatures should have been reproduced likewise in pottery form in view of the Nabataean skill in ceramics is not at all surprising. One discovery has already been made at Petra of dolphins in low relief on a plaque featuring a tragic mask (Pls. 5, 6).[444] It is most probable that a dolphin goddess will be brought to light there some day, similar to the one of Khirbet Tannur and related to the dolphin goddess of Aphrodisias in Asia Minor and of Leptis Magna in Tripoli and to the other Mediterranean dolphin gods of Aquileia, Puteoli and Lixus.[445]

This likelihood is heightened when one recalls the discovery among the ruins of the thermal baths at Petra of a broken section of a rectangular stone frieze in relief, depicting what has been described as a Nereid mounted on a Sea Centaur.[446] Numerous parallels can be cited, including those on the superb round silver dish from the fourth-century A.D. Mildenhall treasure in England.[447] Around the dolphin- and leaf-decorated head of Oceanos in its center are two concentric bands of various figures, with the inner and narrower one showing Nereids on Sea Centaurs and also some other marine beasts.[448]

The Petraean feminine figure on a sea animal could, however, also be identified with an Atargatis or Aphrodite mounted on a fish-tailed Capricornus.[449] There is an example of this on one of the panels in relief on the tunic of the very large, marble cult statue of the paramount Carian Aphrodite at Aphrodisias on the Maeander River near the western coast of southern Asia Minor.[450] Her posture, with her right hand resting on the back of her mount and her raised left hand holding the loose end of the "sky" veil billowing over her head, is almost exactly the same as that of the Petra parallel. In front of the latter there can be made out the tail of another sea-animal or of a Triton. This adds to the likelihood that the Petra frieze more or less duplicates the panel on the Aphrodisias statue of Aphrodite, showing a Triton in front and a dolphin behind the Aphrodite mounted on her charger. In addition to the Triton on one side of the Petra Nereid or Aphrodite, there may have been a dolphin on the other side, too. Rising in low relief from a panel on the skirt of a smaller statue of the Carian Aphrodite from Aphrodisias is another Nereid or Atargatis-Aphrodite frontally seated on a fish-tailed Capricornus, with her head turned to the left. Her left arm outstretched and bent, she grasps the end of her "sky" scarf or veil that billows over her head (Pl. 23b).

There can properly be mentioned here, too, the figure, interpreted to be that of Thetis, the mother of Achilles, astride a sea creature, embossed in the center of a bronze vessel of Roman origin (Pl. 22). It was found, together with other vessels, objects and documents of the second century A.D. in the Cave of the Letters in the Nahal Hever above Ain Gedi overlooking the center of the west side of the Dead Sea.[451]

Closely connected with the reliefs of the above-mentioned Nereids and with the late fourth-century A.D. Mildenhall example, is a most unusual one of Ino and Melicertes (Pl. 21a), whom she is nursing, on a sea-centaur or ichthyocentaur, embossed on a silver plate, located in the Benaki Museum, Athens, Greece. It has been dated to the late sixth or early seventh century A.D., as have the winged Erotes holding tridents and standing on or astride dolphins, embossed on other silver plates in the same museum (Pls. 20a, b, 21a).[452]

Originating probably in the Nile Delta region of Egypt, these Byzantine representations, with their frontally positioned and disproportionately rendered bodies, and with the head of Ino shown in profile, reveal the persistence of the orientalizing tradition, that characterized late Hellenistic-Semitic art.[453] The general posture of Ino and the position of her raised left hand grasping the edge of her hood or "sky" veil are similar to those of the Nereids or Aphrodites in the earlier Aphrodisias and Petra reliefs.

Dolphins formed beloved and not infrequent decorative and religious motifs at inland Nabataean temples, as we have seen. They were certainly no less highly regarded at Aphrodisias in Asia and at numerous Mediterranean sites. There was indeed a very close relationship between the dolphin-crowned Atargatis or Aphrodite of Aphrodisias and the Dolphin Goddess of the Temple of Tannur. In addition to the dolphin visible on the tunic of the colossal Aphrodite statue of Aphrodisias, the very arm rests at the ends of the top tier of seats of its small semicircular auditorium were shaped in the form of dolphins, sometimes mounted by an Eros.[454] For much of the first millennium B.C. and well into the first millennium A.D., representations of deities with dolphin symbols or of dolphins by themselves are found from Iran to England in sculptures of stone or bronze or pottery or on coins,[455] lamps, mosaics and murals. Much religious importance was attached to them for safety and succor on the journey through life first by sea and then by land and perhaps even greater significance for assistance on the much more perilous, uncharted routes through the world of after-life.[456]

c. Abda

There is a charming dolphin relief above an arched opening on one of the two existing sides of a tiny Nabataean altar from Abda (Eboda, Ardat) in the center of the Negev.[457] A fascinating city of Nabataean origin, which probably incorporates the name of one of the great Nabataean kings, written Obodas in its Greek form, this fantastic desert emporium flourished under changing rule and with changing architecture for about a thousand years, from approximately the second century B.C. till the eighth century A.D. Literally hundreds of additional Nabataean and later towns and settlements, some larger and most of them smaller, substituted during this millennium of pagan to Jewish and Christian enlightenment and rule, the productive order of civilized trade and agriculture for the intermittent anarchy of the Negev wasteland. Many of these places are located on or near still older Judaean or even earlier Abrahamic sites. In almost every Nabataean city and village there must have been a temple, with dolphin figures in many of them, even as subsequently there must have been Byzantine Christian churches and basilicas in nearly all of them, and to a lesser degree Byzantine synagogues in some of them. These sites testify even in their ruins to the creative ability of human beings when properly directed in periods of peace. Above the relief of the dolphin's head on this lovely little altar at Abda is a fragmentary Nabataean inscription ending with the consonants of the word "s l m," meaning "Peace." [458]

In this expressive altar at Abda, with its upper border of heraldic figures and centrally placed relief of a Parthian-type mask of Khirbet Tannur likeness on one side and the animated relief of a dolphin's head, topped by a Nabataean inscription on the adjacent side, and with one of two remaining, simulated, attached corner-pilasters and composite capitals facing two ways between them, there is manifested something of the high quality of the Nabataean civilization. The Nabataeans, as is becoming increasingly clear, took the dolphin figure to their hearts and placed it in the forefront of their religious adoration. The dolphin sculptures, appearing, apparently frequently also in hinterland areas, far removed from the sight or even smell of the sea, add range and depth to the scope and character of Nabataean achievement.

Abda, to be sure, is on the great Nabataean trade-route leading from the Nabataean capital of Petra in southern Jordan to Gaza and Ascalon on the Mediterranean shore of Palestine, but it is located in the midst of the marginal lands of the Negev,[458a] where scarce water must be garnered with the patience of penury. The dolphin theme was repeated on a piece of sigillata from Abda.[458b] The dolphin became definitely one of the major religious symbols of the Nabataeans and played an important role in their concept of destiny.

d. Wadi Ramm

Imagine stopping at a small Nabataean temple by the side of a remote wadi passageway in the Arabian desert and finding there the figure of a bronze dolphin! Such a sanctuary existed once in the Wadi Ramm, far south of the fertile hill-country of Khirbet Tannur and Petra with its hundreds of other Nabataean sites and sacred places. Sculptures of a lion, a bull, an eagle or a serpent might have been expected there, together with the effigies of the deities they attended or adorned, but surely, at least to the uninitiated, not a bronze dolphin, which had been skillfully conjured into shape out of molten metal poured into a carefully prepared form! But there it was, to be seen and worshiped in the company of the deity of its attachment.

When the little temple was excavated nearly two millennia after its construction, the tail of a bronze dolphin was recovered there (Pl. 8b) [459] that may have served as the handle of a ritual implement. The main find was the lower part of the sandstone cult statue of an enthroned Atargatis or Tyché (Pl. 52c). The excavators thought they discerned a serpent entwined around the bottom of her garment. [460] I fail to make it out, although the possibility of its existence must be taken into account. [461] One wonders whether it could have represented a personalized figure such as that signifying the river Orontes in front of the enthroned, mural-crowned Tyché of Antioch (Pl. 52a).

The location of the Wadi Ramm temple made sense. Nearby was the small but perennial spring of Ain Shellaleh. The track leading to it from Edom, and ultimately to the oases deep in the Arabian desert, passed along a whole series of seepages of sweet water emerging between the granite base and the sandstone body of the range of the Jebel Ramm.

Was it because of the nearness and wonder of drinkable water in the midst of the desert that the widely traveled Nabataean caravaneers, trafficking between the Persian Gulf and the Red and Mediterranean Seas, introduced the images of dolphins into the fabric of their worship? That hardly seems sufficient reason. Or was it because of a very direct connection that had been established between dolphins and travel as such whether by sea or land, whether in this life or beyond it?

Why a dolphin altar at Abda in the desert of the Negev, which depended upon waters painfully garnered through unbelievably extensive and intricate devices from the desert's brief season rains? Why sculptures of dolphins in the deep clefts of the earth's crust that marked the location of Petra, as hidden as could be from the sound and smell and roll and fury of the sea? Why the reliefs of dolphins on the head of Atargatis at the mountaintop temple of Khirbet Tannur, that used cistern water for immediate purposes? The permanent stream at the bottom of the deep canyon of the Wadi Hesa (River Zered) below it to the north was a good hour's walking distance away and more down and back again in each direction.

It would seem then that it was neither the nearness nor the remoteness of living waters either in the comparatively fertile highlands or in the unrelievedly sere deserts of the Nabataean kingdom that determined the presence of dolphin sculptures in Nabataean temples. Such sculptures or related mosaics depicting dolphins exist at inland sites as different from one another as Khirbet Tannur, Petra, Khirbet Brak, Wadi Ramm and Abda in the southern parts of Eastern and Western Palestine, at Syrian Antioch on the Orontes, at the great Parthian trade emporium of Hatra on the

Euphrates River and at the Hellenistic site of Aphrodisias in Asia Minor. It will be necessary to examine these and consider others, especially in the Mediterranean area, some of which have already been mentioned, before venturing an answer.

3. ELSEWHERE IN THE ORIENT

a. Hatra in Parthia

In view of the extremely intimate connections between the Parthian and the Nabataean kingdoms and cultures, it comes as no surprise that dolphins have been found at Hatra. The wonder is not that they occur there but that many more examples have not been found. The ones we have reference to are inconspicuously located at the bottom of a representation of Atargatis on a second-century A.D. Cerberos relief from that site (Pl. 10a, b).[462] Enthroned between two lions,[463] with an eagle on top of her head, as is repeated another time there [464] and as is gloriously exemplified by the eagle on top of the panel of the Vegetation Goddess at Khirbet Tannur, and as occurs elsewhere in the Nabataean kingdom,[465] this Parthian Atargatis has a small pair of horns,[466] one on each side of her head, holds a leaf in her right hand, and rests her feet on a base that is decorated with two small dolphins in low relief facing each other. They are paralleled by two dolphins facing each other at the bottom of a relief at Atargatis in a niche in an African funerary stele.[467]

We construe the leaf in the right hand of the Hatra goddess to be a symbol of fertility. This leaf and another one in the left hand of a statuette also from Hatra [468] bring to mind naturally the leaves on the face of Atargatis in her various appearances as Vegetation Goddess at Khirbet Tannur, Petra and its suburb of Khirbet Brak. The phenomenon of leaves on the face of a deity occurs in yet another instance at Hatra. Built into the façade of its great central temple is the high relief of a male, moustached Medusa with leaves sprouting from his cheeks and from underneath his chin and with serpents entwined in his hair and facing each other on top of his head [469] (Pl. 35a). It is attributed to the third quarter of the first century A.D.

With his moustache and serpents, he somewhat resembles the second-third century A.D. male Medusa at Bath, England (Pl. 36a),[470] which however is distinguished further by wings and trident-like or flame-like locks of hair on top of his head. The bearded and winged male Medusa from Dorchester (Pl. 36b) needs also to be considered in this connection.[470a] There are resemblances also to the bearded and moustached, male Medusa from Chester, England, with eight writhing serpents framing its face [471] and to the moustached Oceanos of Mildenhall, with leaves covering his beard (Pl. 15b). We shall return later to a consideration of the four dolphins that peer through the side locks of the hair of this English Oceanos.[472] Much like these various male Medusas in general appearance is also the winged, moustached and bearded head in low relief of the wind god, Boreas, who, together with the winged wind god, Zephyrus, can be seen in the lower corners of a second-third century A.D. Mithraic stele from London.[473]

We shall see that the leaves and dolphins connected with Nabataean and Parthian deities find their parallels in Asia Minor and Mediterranean lands. There certainly was an intermingling of motifs, even as there was an inter-twining of relationships evidenced by them between the Orient and the Occident. The leaves on the faces and in the hands of the Nabataean and Parthian deities could easily in the Oriental mind have been symbolic of lushness of vegetation on land, as is underscored by the presence of pome-granates sculptured on the panel of the leaf-veiled Atargatis of Khirbet Tannur. By the same token they could have appeared as emblems of sea deities to much of the population of the western, Hellenistic world and have been considered as seaweed of the type associated with Poseidon or Triton or Oceanos. The full significance of the presence of sculptures of dolphins at Nabataean sites remains to be explained in the light of their frequent occurrence in Asia Minor and along the shores of the Mediter-ranean and elsewhere.

b. *Aphrodisias in Asia Minor*

The dolphins on the head of the Dolphin Goddess of Khirbet Tannur are, as we shall see in detail later on, clearly the same in kind and general appearance as those appearing with the Mediterranean deities of Aquileia, Puteoli, Ostia, Pompeii, Leptis Magna and Lixus and elsewhere and as featured frequently on mosaic representations. The latter include, for in-stance, the mosaic floor of Yakto near Antioch in Syria,[474] which shows a dolphin on either side of the goddess, Thalassa, who also holds a dolphin in her left hand and a rudder in her right. The rudder is also one of the attributes of Isis-Tyché-Aphrodite.[475]

If any additional evidence is required as to whether dolphins or fishes crown the head of the Dolphin Goddess of Khirbet Tannur, it is furnished by the marble bust of Atargatis from Aphrodisias in Caria in south-western Asia Minor.[476] Emerging from the front locks of the wavy hair on top of her head are two dolphins (Pl. 11), facing each other in heraldic juxtaposi-tion.[477] They duplicate almost exactly the position of the two dolphins at Khirbet Tannur. The right hand of the Goddess of Aphrodisias presses an-other dolphin or some other sea-creature against the bottom of her breasts and she cups its head with its interlocking upper and lower fangs in her right hand reaching over to her left side. A fragment of a sculpture has been found in Syria (?) showing an Eros astride a dolphin, which has a similarly shaped head and teeth.[478] Over the left shoulder of the Goddess of Aphrodisias is the much-damaged head of another large dolphin or sea animal.[479]

The relationship of the two Atargatis sculptures from Khirbet Tannur and Aphrodisias with their tiaras of dolphins is too striking to be fortuitous. It would seem obvious that somehow or other a common tradition embraced them both. We have previously taken note of the fact that the dolphin theme is repeatedly employed at Aphrodisias. The very arm rests at the ends of the tiers of seats of the semicircular auditorium there are fashioned in the form of dolphins, and at times with an Eros astride one of them.[480] Furthermore, sculptured on one of the decorative panels of the tunic of the colossal marble statue of Aphrodite are a dolphin and a Nereid sitting side-ways on a fish-tailed Capricornus or sea centaur and a Triton in front of it.[481] A smaller statue of Aphrodite discovered there previously also shows, as has been mentioned, a Nereid astride a fish-tailed Capricornus in one of the panels of her dress (Pl. 23b).[482] Curving above the head of each of these Nereids is a banderole or veil, the ends of which are held in their hands. Symbolic of the canopy of the heavens, it is met with constantly in represen-tations of Nereids and of various deities, some of whose backgrounds hail back to Assyrian antiquity.[483]

A scarf or banderole of the heavens envelops the top part of the upright figure of a Tyché or Atargatis on a Baalbek coin between two Nikés on pillars some distance removed from each other, holding its ends.[484] A closely related graffito from Dura-Europos shows another Atargatis in much the same posture under the arch of the heavens, supported by two pillars, one on each side of her.[485] On each of her shoulders is a dove,[486] and there is an eagle with spread wings on her head. One is reminded of the monumental Atargatis relief of Khirbet Tannur with the eagle finial on her head and the two remaining stone horns, representing perhaps rays of the sun. They may have been part of a series forming the equivalent of a heavenly canopy over the top of the curved sides of this Atargatis panel (Pls. 32, 34b). It is interesting to note that the Dura graffito, just mentioned, shows inside the curved arch a series of narrow triangles, with their points at the top. They also may have been symbolic of the rays of the sun. The representation of Venus, synonymous with Astarte and Atargatis, wearing the shawl of the skies over her head, is contained among the seven planetary figures sur-rounded by the zodiac in the Temple of Bel at Palmyra.[487] A curved line over the head of one of the figures in a bas-relief dedicated to Ba'al-shamin at Palmyra has the same significance.[488] The heavenly scarf occurs also in connection with mermaids.[489]

The use of this symbol was very extensive, being evidenced in places as far apart as Ostia, Italy,[490] where it appeared over the head of a Venus in a Mithraeum, and Safa in Arabia,[491] in a graffito over the head of an Allat, surrounded by Safaitic inscriptions. In two particular reliefs of Mithras, the scarf or banderole is replaced by a cloak. Billowing out in an arc behind him, it clearly depicts the heavens, augmented by a crescent moon and seven simple rosettes standing for the seven planets, namely, the Sun, Moon, Mercury, Venus, Mars, Jupiter and Saturn.[492] A Roman coin from Dura displays the seven planets in the form of simple rosettes above a crescent moon.[493] This theme is repeated on the handle of a Roman lamp, impressed with the likeness of the god, Caelus, holding the banderole of the heavens above his head, on top of which is a large crescent moon with the seven planetary rosettes.[494] These rosettes can be seen also, for instance, under the equivalent of the heavenly canopy over the head of a deified Faustina.[495]

The scarf or shawl over the head of any Nabataean goddess would seem to bear the same connotation. One of the clearest examples of this is furnished by the scarf or shawl over the mural crown of the Zodiac-Tyché of Khirbet Tannur [496] (Pls. 46, 48). There is a striking parallel to it on a small plaque from Syria. [497] The Zodiac-Tyché of Khirbet Tannur and the entire assembly of gods there may indeed be interpreted in the light of the prevailing astral cosmogony. This applies also to rosettes and other symbols connected with sacred objects and sanctuaries.[498]

All of them formed an interwoven complex, in which the heaven above, the earth and seas below together with their creatures, and especially human beings were brought into relationship with the deities. Through the planets and constellations, they governed the mysteries of life and death, of fertility and well-being, or rebirth and renewal in this world and in the life beyond.[499] Nothing was beyond the pale of their power. In ivy, laurel, acanthus, oak and vine leaves, in grapes and figs and pomegranates, in all the friendly and fearful phenomena of nature, in objects of fact and figures of fancy, the Nabataeans and their like saw the handiwork or agents or portents of the deities, upon whose favor their fortunes depended in the visible now and the curtained hereafter.

c. *Olbia on the Black Sea*

Dolphin representations on tokens placed in the hands of the dead [500] and on coins ranging in date from the sixth to the first centuries B.C. have been found at the coastal town of Olbia at the northwest corner of the Black Sea, where the River Dnieper and the River Bugh empty their waters. Some, belonging primarily to the sixth century B.C., come from the nearby island of Berezan, abandoned at the beginning of the fifth century B.C. Excellent fifth/fourth-century B.C. examples, as previously mentioned, stem also, for instance, from Sinope on the north coast of Asia Minor.[501] The examples on coins usually show on the reverse side a sea-eagle with extended wings standing on the back of a dolphin (Pl. 65), while on the obverse side there can be seen representations of Medusa [502] or of Demeter with stalks of wheat.[503] A first-century A.D. coin from the Bosporus region has a dolphin on the reverse side and a Poseidon(?)-like figure with a trident on the obverse side.[504] Early fourth-century B.C. Tyrian coins of the type bearing a dolphin representation have been found together with palaeo-Hebrew documents from Samaria in the Nahal Daliyeh cave near Jericho (Pl. 64a, b), as we have already noted.[505]

The dolphin symbol was well known in southwestern Asia. The finds at Kerch, which overlooks the northwest end of the channel between the Sea of Asov and the Black Sea, included wooden dolphins and sea centaurs or hippocamps,[506] and among the discoveries at the related site of Anapa were wooden Nereids riding on such sea creatures.[507] They are reminiscent of the type of Nereid mounted on a fish-tailed Capricornus carved on the tunic of each of several statues of the Aphrodite-Atargatis of Aphrodisias (Pl. 23b), and of other Nereids astride sea centaurs at Baalbek,[508] and of still another at Petra.[509] In the extremely rich, Greek barrow, called the Great Blitznitsa, located near the Bosphorus, was a wealth of elaborate jewelry. It included, among other objects, a gold temple ornament, showing a calathos-crowned and veiled Demeter riding a hippocamp sideways, with a dolphin on either side of it.[510]

It is evident, therefore, that the frame of reference in which the Nabataean and Parthian dolphins and other sea creatures are contained must be widened to include Hellenistic places as distant from Khirbet Tannur and Petra and Hatra as Aphrodisias and Olbia and Kerch. The latter two places especially and others of the same type, a few of which we have mentioned, must have been frequented also by Scythians as well as by Greek colonists and traders.[511] It is possible, therefore, that the significance of the dolphin may have been transmitted in part to the Nabataeans through Scythian-Parthian sources, even as was unquestionably the emblem of the torque, before its importance was impressed upon them by their constant journeying through the Aegaean and Mediterranean in the heyday of their foreign undertakings and affluence. There is little doubt, however, that the most immediate background of the use of the dolphin by the Nabataeans is Greek. The purpose of placing dolphin tokens in the hands of the dead seems to have been to assure a safe voyage for those who had to traverse the uncharted regions of after-life.[512]

4. MEDITERRANEAN CONNECTIONS

a. Aquileia

The presence of sculptures of dolphins and of the Dolphin Goddess among the Nabataeans predicates their thorough acquaintance with the role played by the dolphin in the religious life of their Hellenistic-Roman con-

a

Pl. 155

a. Damaged memorial relief from Kerak with horse's head and neck over left shoulder (p. 59)
b. Drawing of above (p. 59)
c. Relief of warrior, Petra (p. 212)

b

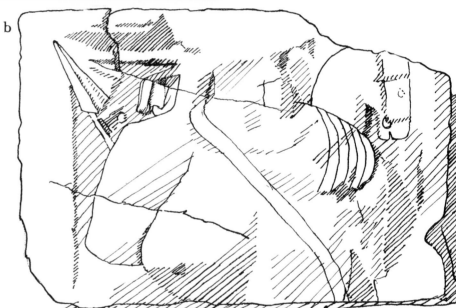

c

Pl. 156

a. Memorial relief surmounted by eagle,
   and with horse's head and neck over
   left shoulder, Palmyra (p. 212)
b. Drawing of above (p. 212)

Pl. 156A Memorial relief with horse's head and neck in relief over left shoulder,
Palmyra (p. 213)

5 cms

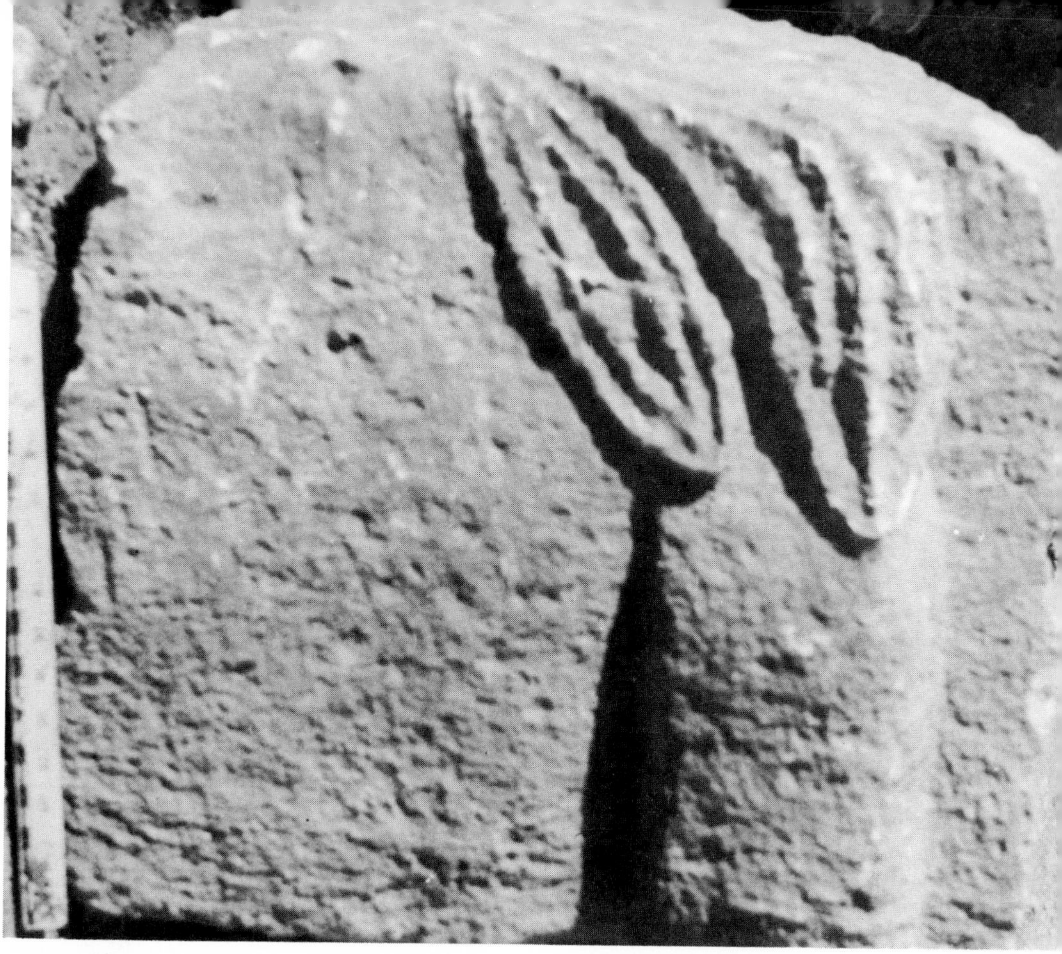

a

Pl. 157

a. Left half of crude bust (p. 222)
b. Damaged relief with sash, Ma'in (p. 222)

b

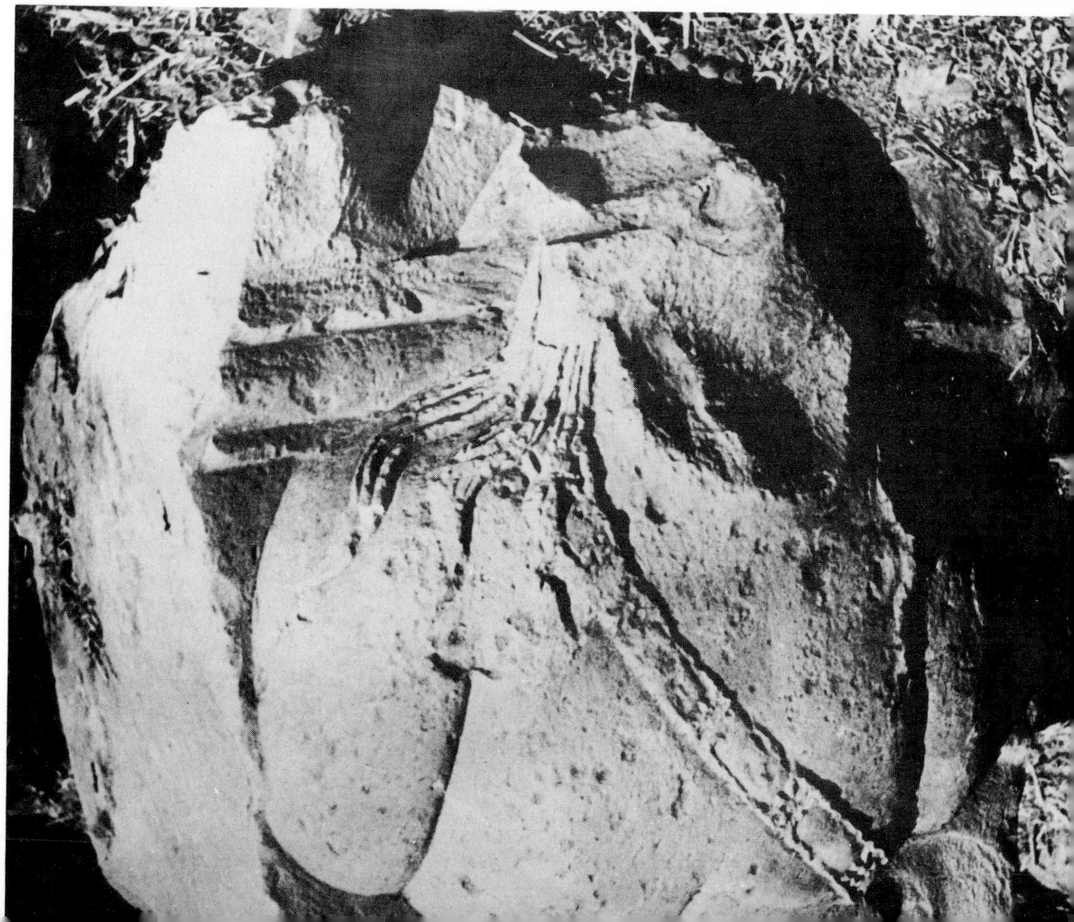

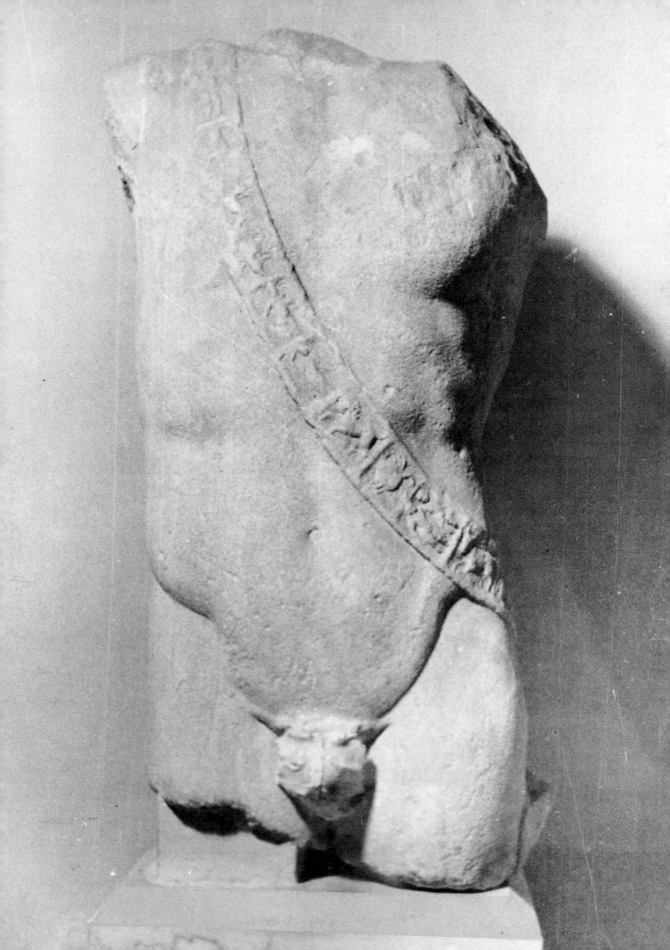

Pl. 159   Bust in relief, Ma'in (p. 213)

Pl. 158 (*opposite*)   Apollo with sash of twelve signs of the zodiac (p. 212) temporaries. One looks seaward, naturally, for the source of the dolphins that decorated Nabataean sanctuaries and finds them disporting themselves in the waters of the Mediterranean and deified in the lands that border it. Other attributes of divinity, common among the gods of the western world, were also adopted by the Nabataeans for the deities of their own fashioning. The veil of leaves, in addition to the dolphin, was among the most striking of them.

Where the Mediterranean deities were richly endowed with many characteristics, the Nabataean ones were far more sparing in their display. That marks, fundamentally, the difference between the Desert and the Sown. The abundant water resources and lush growth of the latter can be prodigally spent. Not so in the desert, where the scarce water is carefully apportioned and death hangs on its dearth and the simplest fare is shared in scarcity. We shall encounter various gods along the shores of the Mediterranean possessed of many characteristics, some of which at Khirbet Tannur are separately allocated to individual members of the Nabataean pantheon.

A fascinating example of the contrast and connection between Mediterranean and Nabataean deities is furnished by the small, bronze bust of the God of Aquileia (Pl. 13). A little less than twenty centimeters high and labeled as a "Triton," it is now located in the British Museum.[513] It was found at Aquileia, some six miles inland from the north shore of the Adriatic Sea, being connected originally with it by a canal. Established by the Romans early in the second century B.C., it is located some twenty-two miles west-northwest of Trieste. It became a commercial and military center of first rank and is purported to have had a population of nearly half a million during the reign of Hadrian. Its importance may be judged by the fact that it shared with Rome alone the right to mint coins.[514] There must have been heavy sea traffic between it and Egyptian Alexandria and Palestinian Ascalon, whence, as we shall see, Nabataean ships departed to engage in the lucrative Mediterranean trade.[515]

Leaves, crab's claws and dolphins are attached to the bust of this so-called Triton. Generally designated as seaweed, a series of overlapping leaves almost completely cover but do not conceal his face, merge with others that overlay his eyebrows and culminate in a five-pointed leaf that almost reaches to the top of his forehead. The strong, finely molded, beardless chin is covered with leaves and two additional ones cling to the top of the sides of his neck and the bottom of his cheeks. Others cover almost the entire front of his chest. The separate, flame-like locks of his hair resemble those of the Atargatis of Tannur and descend in wavy tresses to the top of his shoulders. The youthful countenance of classical beauty, undimmed by the addition of the transparent mask of leaves, could be identified with Dionysos, who delighted in the forms of nature, or could be equated with a youthful Zeus-Hadad, who was thought to command its creative forces.

The Triton aspect is emphasized by two crab's claws rising from the top of his head and facing each other and by two dolphins extending outward from the sides of his temples. The bodies of the dolphins rest on and reach out beyond the stylized shells of circular leaves or flowers covering or replacing his ears. The dolphin head on the right side, with one eye clearly visible, is better cast than the one on the left. It is seen that this god combines in himself various features which, with the apparent exception only of crab's claws, are apportioned to individual goddesses at Khirbet Tannur. The crab, however, is present also at Khirbet Tannur as one of the signs of the unusual zodiac there, encircling the bust of Atargatis as Tyché, the guardian goddess of the site. The veil of leaves can be seen at Khirbet Tannur, Petra [516] and Khirbet Brak [517] on Atargatis as the Vegetation Goddess. The dolphins crowning another bust in high relief of Atargatis, as the Dolphin Goddess, at the mountain sanctuary of Tannur indicate yet a different manifestation of her form and function.

All three of these goddesses at Khirbet Tannur as Zodiac Tyché, Vegetation Goddess and Dolphin Goddess were essentially the same Atargatis, wearing, so to speak, different costumes. She was a lady of a large wardrobe and an extensive repertoire. In many ways, these Nabataean goddesses, worshipped far inland from the eastern Mediterranean coast and perfectly at home also under various names in Asia-Minor, Syria and Parthia, and the God of Aquileia with his multiple attributes, who was worshipped on the north shore of the Adriatic, were, despite the difference in their sexes, one and the same deity.

b. Puteoli

There was yet another god, Greek in countenance but undoubtedly considered also Oriental by the Nabataeans in the sum of his attributes, whose face and body were covered with leaves (Pl. 14). Made of yellowish, crystalline marble and 91 centimeters high, it was found at Puteoli (Pozzuoli) on the north shore of the Gulf of Puteoli, several miles to the west of Naples, and is now in the Vatican Museum in Rome.[518] Of interest to us in this connection is the fact that Puteoli was one of the main European points of call for large vessels coming from Egypt. It marked the final stop of the ship that took Paul of Tarsus from Caesarea in Palestine to Italy, where he visited Rome (Acts 28:13). It was also frequented by enterprising Nabataean and other merchants from the east [519]—a subject to which we shall return later. One of the principal sources of such widely spread, reddish glazed, and highly burnished earthenware, known technically as *terra sigillata*, which the Nabataeans may have imported, is perhaps identifiable with the famous Italian pottery of Puteoli.[520] Some of it, to be sure, was of Nabataean manufacture.[521] The Nabataeans left records of their stay behind them [522] and seem to have instituted the worship of their own gods there.

The appearance of the veiled god of Puteoli probably also contributed to the style of leaf veil worn by the Vegetation Goddess of Tannur. But then, we are far ahead of the proper sequence of our story and must retrace our steps to its beginning.

The God of Puteoli was par excellence a fertility god and not merely a sea god or Oceanos.[523] In attractiveness of appearance, he may be compared to the colossal bust of Zeus-Serapis in the Vatican, presumed to have been modeled after the reputed statue of Serapis of Alexandria, sculptured by Bryaxis.[524] There is also considerable although not complete likeness to the noble and expressive head of Serapis, found in the temple of Mithras in Roman London, where the worship of this Egyptian corn-god had been introduced.[525] The God of Puteoli represented, however, like the one of Aquileia, a different and more complex entity.

Moustache, beard, hair parted in the middle and reaching down to the top of his shoulders, and two carefully trained ringlets on his forehead were composed of graceful, wavy, pointed locks, whose harmonious lines were repeated over the back top of his head and even on the sides and bottom front of his bust. His hair was garlanded with a wreath of vines and leaves and grapes. Two rounded horns protrude from the top of his head and two dolphins in heraldic juxtaposition seemed to swim out from the bottom of his beard. The horns, however, clearly represent a later repair and may originally have been crab's claws.[526] Added to all of this was a covering of leaves over the upper part of his body and a veil of leaves over his face. Its irregular triangular edges covered and reached beyond his eyebrows and pointed to the upper center of his forehead, and, at the bottom, overlapped the upper part of his beard, below his full, parted lips.

c. Lixus

Closely related to the bronze sculpture of the God of Aquileia, with the crab's claws, dolphins and veil of leaves, is a bronze medallion mask in relief (Pl. 15a),[527] from the originally Phoenician site of Lixus (Larache)[528] on the Atlantic coast of Morocco. Less classically Hellenistic and more Eastern or Oriental in appearance than the God of Aquileia on the north shore of the Adriatic Sea, the bronze from Lixus would seem, nevertheless, to belong approximately to the same, late Hellenistic or early imperial, Roman period.[529] Among the carefully trained locks of hair and of beard, projecting like separate, short tongues of flame from the broad, more or less circular face to give it an unprepossessing, rather fierce appearance, there disport themselves a whole series of sea denizens.

At the top of this god's forehead, two crab's claws confront and almost touch each other, in much the same position as the tiara of two dolphins in heraldic juxtaposition which surmount the bust of the Atargatis of Khirbet Tannur and of the Atargatis of Aphrodisias. The closest parallel, of course, are the two crab's claws emerging from the top of the head of the bronze Hadad of Aquileia and curving towards each other. In this respect alone, not to mention others now, the two deities from Lixus on the Atlantic, and Aquileia on the Adriatic, obviously belong to the same cultural tradition.

Another similarity, among others, between the gods of Aquileia and Lixus, making them almost exact twins in form and absolutely so in function, is the appearance of dolphins also in the hair of the latter. On the right side of his face, parallel with his right eye, a dolphin emerges from his locks, in a downward swimming position, with the top of its head and beak visible. On the left side of his face, coming out of the waves of his locks of hair, there appears the head of another dolphin, shown in profile, with its beak pointing over the side of the god's face towards his left eye. The location of these two dolphins parallels closely that of the dolphins emerging from the sides of the head of the God of Aquileia, except that the latter face outward. The god of Lixus, however, has a larger contingent of dolphins than his counterpart at Aquileia. A third and a fourth dolphin can be seen in his beard at the edges of his drooping moustache, with the one on the right swimming, as it were, towards it, and the one on the left swimming away from it. In between them, at the very bottom of his beard, is still another dolphin, with its head pointed to the left.[530]

It is almost as if the sculptor had intentionally portrayed the sequence of movements of a single dolphin, which, commencing at the upper right, continues downward, to reappear alongside the moustache, then to round the point of the god's chin, come up for a breather at the left side of the moustache, and surface finally at the upper left side of the god's face in order to survey it partly. The dolphins visible in the beard proper call to mind the two protruding from near the bottom sides of the beard of the god of Puteoli. The dolphin alone or in association with male and female deities occurred frequently in sculptural or mosaic or painted form on the mainlands and islands of the entire Mediterranean.

The sculptures of these gods from Puteoli, Aquileia and Lixus were related to each other, however, not only by the dolphins attending all three of them and by the crab's claws common to the latter two, but also by the practically transparent veil of leaves on the face of each of them and on their bodies. In this particular, too, they must be included within the cultural configuration embracing the deities of Khirbet Tannur, and numbering, among others, one form of Atargatis with dolphins and another with a veil of leaves. In each instance, the veil of leaves on these gods is slightly different in detail, but essentially the same in general appearance and specific purpose. Three overlapping sets of leaves rise above each other on the face of the god of Lixus, mounting from his cheeks and the upper part of his nose to the top of his forehead.

The "seaweed" explanation given to this veil of leaves on these Oceanos figures of the Mediterranean area, certainly cannot apply completely to the Atargatis of Khirbet Tannur. The covering of leaves on all of these deities is at once a veil of divinity and a symbol of vegetation made possible by divine grace. To relegate those wearing it at Lixus, Puteoli, Aquileia, and, as we shall see, at Leptis Magna, to the role merely of "sea gods" is to do them an injustice. It would, furthermore, increase the difficulty of making sense of their obvious relationship to some of the most important members of the Nabataean pantheon, worshiped at home in inland centers from Arabia to Syria and Sinai and abroad from Egypt and Asia Minor to Italy.

These deities, and others, too, from Mediterranean and Atlantic seaports, where also, it must be remembered, Oriental influences long proliferated, were syncretistic in the variety of their attributes and cosmic in the scope of their authority. This was true also of the Atargatis of Parthian Hatra, with two dolphins facing each other on the base panel of her throne, and with a guardian lion on each side (Pl. 10a, b),[531] and of the leaf-veiled male Medusa from there [532] (Pl. 35b). It applies definitely to the totality of the manifestations of Atargatis at Khirbet Tannur, in association with those of her male consort there, Zeus-Hadad.

d. Mildenhall

Closely related to the gods of Aquileia, Puteoli and Lixus is the central Oceanos mask of the superb, silver, fourth century A.D., round dish or plate, nearly two feet in diameter, from the Mildenhall treasure in England (Pl. 15b). Four dolphins emerge from between the serpentine locks of hair of the Mildenhall Oceanos, two of them parallel with his mouth and above his completely leaf-covered beard and two of them projecting outward from his temples. With these gods it shares dolphin and leaf and other characteristics and also has much in common with the male Medusas of Parthian Hatra and Roman Bath in England and of Pompeii in between.[533] We shall refer to it again in further consideration of the theme of dolphins, Nereids, Medusas and Atargatis-Aphrodite at Khirbet Tannur, Petra, Baalbek, Aphrodisias and related sites.[534] A similar Oceanos, or perhaps a male Medusa, occurs at the bottom of a bronze handle from London. The heads of two sea serpents, whose bodies twist in a coil over the position of his ears, appear above his temples, facing each other, each beneath a wing at either side of his head (Pl. 37a).

We saw in the case of the God of Aquileia that two dolphins likewise protrude outward from his temples and that in the instance of the God of Puteoli two dolphins poke their heads through the locks of his beard, while in the example of the God of Lixus six dolphins make their appearance among the tresses of his hair and beard. Another illustration of the latter profusion can be seen in connection with another Oceanos head on an altar of Diana Lucifera from Rome.[535] Two crab's claws confront each other at the top of his head, as they do on the tops of the heads of the gods of Aquileia and Lixus, and leaves can also be seen on his forehead and cheeks, as well as a whole series of dolphins playing hide and seek among the locks of his beard.

e. Leptis Magna, Tripoli

A very close likeness of the Dolphin Goddess of Aphrodisias, and related thus to the Dolphin Goddess of Khirbet Tannur, was found at Leptis Magna in the form of a relief on a bronze (?) medallion.[536] At the top of her head were originally two crab's claws in heraldic juxtaposition. Only the left one remains, the other having been broken off. On her cheeks, and apparently on her forehead, is a covering of leaves, appearing also in a scroll pattern encircling her head. This veil of leaves is very similar to that of the Vegetation Goddess of Khirbet Tannur but is absent from the visage of the Atargatis of Aphrodisias.

Emerging from her hair and almost touching her left cheek is the head of a dolphin. Below it, turned towards the chin of the goddess, is the large head of a sea creature, with mouth partly open, showing the large, serrated, intermeshing teeth of the upper and lower jaws. The head of this sea monster, duplicated perhaps also on the right side of the medallion, is almost exactly like the one held by the Goddess of Aphrodisias in her right hand below her left breast. The same type of head appears in a fragment from Syria, showing originally an Eros riding on a dolphin.[537] This is a recurrent theme, beautifully represented on a Hellenistic basalt sculpture from Egypt (Pl. 17b) [537a] and on a related one from the Hermitage Museum (Pl. 18).[537b] Another example of an Eros on a dolphin occurs on the right side of a beautiful statue of a nude Aphrodite at Leptis Magna.[538] One can cite also in this connection a fine, Hellenistic pottery figurine from Tunis showing a lovely Aphrodite, nude from the waist up, and with a long "sky" veil over her head billowing out behind her, tranquilly seated on a dolphin (Pl. 23a).[539] A second-century B.C. limestone Punic stele from Carthage, dedicated to Baal-hammon and Tanit, shows a figure with a caduceus (?) above a dolphin (Pl. 17a).[539a]

The importance of the dolphin was heightened, furthermore, by the astral significance anciently ascribed to it,[540] as well as to the fish and crab symbols. It is well to bear this in mind when considering the reasons for the high regard that the Nabataeans entertained for the dolphin attribute, apparently wherever they erected sanctuaries in honor of Atargatis.

The Goddess of Leptis Magna, with her dolphin, leaf and crab claw decorations, and the one of Aphrodisias are obviously sisters in divinity, sharing the attributes of dolphins and sea creatures, but each being outfitted with something not worn by the other. The goddess from North

Africa, however, was also, as we have seen, distinguished by crab's claws and a veil of leaves, while the clear-faced one from Aphrodisias in south-western Asia Minor had, draped over her left shoulder, a large, now damaged sea creature, which may possibly have been a very large dolphin, in addition to the two small dolphins facing each other on the top of her head after the fashion of the Dolphin Goddess of Khirbet Tannur.

In their company must be included the goddess, Thalassa, the Greek personification of the sea, who appears in the center of a mosaic floor at Antioch on the Orontes in Syria with two crab's claws among the flame-like locks of her hair at the top of her head, a rudder in her right hand and a dolphin in her left.[541] Another mosaic representation of her there shows her with wings on her head,[542] a serpent-like creature coiled around her neck, and, below her, a winged Cupid on the back of a dolphin angling for fishes. A relief on a cornice from Salikiyeh in Syria shows a row of shells, with open-beaked dolphins facing the right and left sides of each of them.[543] Another use of dolphins as significant symbols is visible on a lead sarcophagus of the Hellenistic period from Tyre (Pl. 24a), and many more examples could be cited.[544] The previously mentioned dolphin symbols on the Jewish stone sarcophagus from Beit She'arim (Pl. 24b) will be described in more detail below.[544a]

Dolphins and/or leaves are repeated among the attributes of the gods of Aquileia, Puteoli, Lixus, Mildenhall and Hatra,[545] and the goddesses of Antioch, Aphrodisias, Leptis Magna, Ostia-Pompeii, with the addition of crab's claws among those of Aquileia, Lixus, Leptis Magna and Antioch.

With one possible exception, namely that of crab's claws, the connection of all these attributes with the pantheon of deities of Khirbet Tannur becomes clearer with each comparison, or perhaps the order should be in the reverse. The major difference seems to be that individual attributes or symbols such as dolphins and a veil of leaves are assigned at Khirbet Tannur to separate goddesses, each of whom in effect represents a different facet of Atargatis. It seems likely under the circumstances that there might well also have been present at Khirbet Tannur a goddess with crab's claws sprouting from the top of her head.

Under the aegis of the deities of Khirbet Tannur, the differences between dominion over sea and land, between control of water routes and overland or desert roads and trails were erased. Atargatis, together with her consort Hadad, was conceived by the Nabataeans as reigning supreme over both, transcending in her multiple appearances differences of scene and even of sex. Even male Medusas, such as those of Hatra in Parthia and Bath in England,[546] must have been familiar to them, and the possession by gods in Mediterranean ports of characteristics of various forms of their own Atargatis would not have caused them much surprise. In particular, the attributes of leaves or vegetation and of dolphins, together with others which the Nabataean deities possessed or assumed, enabled their worshippers to turn to them with prayers and sacrifices of importunity that life might be made possible, the pursuit of livelihood secure and rewarding, and travel and sojourn certain and safe, also in life after death.

Wherever they turned or might have visited, the Nabataeans were confronted with or would have seen the dolphin symbol and from the beginning would have been impressed with its significance. On mosaic floors at Sardis [546a] or Delos (Pl. 16b),[546b] on votive models of temples at Italian Teanum Sidicinum, Teano (Loreto), or on a bronze *trapezophoros* at Pompeii [546c] (Pl. 19), at Sabratha on the south side of the Mediterranean, to the west of Leptis Magna and Tripoli,[540d] among many other places and examples, some of which have been mentioned and others of which we shall further refer to, the dolphin symbol could be seen. It became an attribute of their chief goddess, standing for succor in peril, safety in danger, security and promise of blessing in the unknown and hereafter.

5. MEDUSAS

a. Hellenistic-Roman

The advantage of being able to fashion a deity in painted, mosaic or sculptural form enabled the ancients on occasion, as we have seen, to attach a wholesale quantity of attributes to a single figure. Nowhere is this better illustrated than in a relief of the head of a goddess at the base of a bronze handle from Rome's port city of Ostia at the mouth of the Tiber. The top side-prongs of the handle are embossed mainly with acanthus leaves and each of their ends is marked by a relief of a double-horned goat's head. The main arm of the handle is embossed with a delicately wrought vine and leaf scroll.[547]

This goddess of Ostia, as we shall name her, has almost everything (Pl. 16a). On top of her head, above her temples, are two sea creatures or dolphins facing each other in the same manner as those on the dolphin goddesses of Khirbet Tannur and Aphrodisias. Two other sea creatures or dolphins touch each side of the bottom of her chin, and farther down still are two more of them, nuzzling a seashell. Knotted together, immediately underneath her chin are the bodies of two sea serpents, whose heads emerge through her hair near the middle of the sides of her cheeks. These would identify her as a Medusa, who frequently appears with this kind of a necktie.[548] Furthermore, above the two sea creatures or dolphins surmounting her head, and between three upswept locks of hair are two wings, which also are frequently associated with Medusa representations,[549] such as occur at Khirbet Tannur (Pls. 38a, 39) and Petra (Pls. 37b, 38b, 40). Wings are also often attached to representations of Hermes-Hercules.[550] Leaves decorate the cheeks and chin of the Goddess of Ostia, as in the instance of the Vegetation Goddess of Khirbet Tannur, and cover her ears.

Clearly belonging to her type is the relief of another Medusa-like head at the bottom of a bronze jar-handle from Pompeii.[551] In front of the two wings on top of her head, between which three undulating flame-like or trident-like locks of hair rise, two dolphins face each other. Intertwined below her chin and around her face are two serpents, the uppermost parts of whose bodies, together with their heads, curve around at the top sides of her head as if they were ears. The two dolphins in heraldic juxta-position at the top of her head relate her closely to the dolphin goddesses of Aphrodisias and Khirbet Tannur. Like them, she also lacks leaf decoration on her face.

At the base of another Roman period bronze jug handle, this time from Cairnholly, Kircudbrightshire, Scotland, is a much similar Medusa head. She has trident-like locks of hair crowning her head, fins or crab's claws on her cheeks and a collar of leaves.[552] Like the heads on the shields from the Severan Forum at Leptis Magna, identified as portraying Atargatis Derketo,[553] she has fins for eyebrows, leaves on her cheeks, and six sea creatures emerging from her hair, namely, two sea-hounds at the bottom, two sea lions at the top and a pair of dolphins in the middle.[554]

We have previously referred to a closely related mosaic head of a Medusa from the Dodecanese, having sea serpents and wings on her head.[555] Crowning her head, as in the case of the Goddess of Ostia, are three upstanding, pointed locks of hair, looking like the tines of a trident such as is usually carried by the sea god, Poseidon.[556] Medusa heads seem to be ubiquitous both in the Occidental and Oriental cultural spheres [557] and were adopted also by the Nabataeans.

b. Nabataean

In view of the wide range of Medusa heads with wings and/or serpents, extending from Scythia and Parthia and Syria to the Roman West,[558] it is not surprising to find examples of various kinds among the Nabataeans. Closely related to several from Parthian Hatra [559] and one from a Roman necropolis near Nawa in the Hauran,[560] and also strikingly similar to the Medusa from the Dodecanese, and in some respects like the bronze relief of the goddess of Ostia, are several Nabataean Medusas from the Hauran. They have wings on their heads, with trident-like locks of hair between and above them, and knotted serpents under their chins, whose heads peer through the upper locks of their hair.[561]

Medusa heads have been found at Petra, one of them on each side of a capital of an apparently square column (Pl. 40). A pair of wings is visible on top of each head, with two knotted serpents under each chin. The lines of the serpents' bodies that enclose the lower part of the face in each instance and then disappear underneath the outflaring, separate locks of hair, framing most of each head, re-emerge together with the outward-facing heads of the serpents above the temples [562] of each Medusa. The damaged faces of these Medusas conform to the fixed Nabataean style of representation. [563]

Two more Medusa heads appear at Petra at either end of the architrave of the entablature above the Corinthianized pilaster capitals of the Lion Triclinium there [564] (Pl. 38b). The similarity of their faces and hair dress to the appearance of one of the Medusas of Khirbet Tannur with ribbon bows in her hair (Pl. 38a) is striking. It cannot be determined with certainty whether or not either one of the Medusa heads on the Lion Triclinium had wings on top of it, although it seems possible to discern remnants of them on the top of the head on the left side of the architrave of the entablature.

It is also impossible to determine beyond all question of doubt whether the heads of serpents can still be seen emerging from the tresses near the tops of the heads of these two Medusas at Petra in their present physical state. There is, however, no doubt that the lower parts of the bodies of two serpents can be seen emerging from below the ends of the curled side-tresses of each of the two Medusas and being joined below their chin. More of the lines of their bodies can be seen below the lower part of the face of the Medusa on the left side of the base of the entablature of the Lion Triclinium and more of the knot binding the two serpents together can be seen under the chin of the Medusa on the right side.

Very similar in appearance to the Medusa heads of Petra is another one from Khirbet Tannur. It shows two serpents confronting each other on top of her head, with the remnants of two wings still visible above them (Pl. 39). The serpents' heads are fashioned in the same wise as the larger one in high relief on the eagle-serpent sculpture (Pl. 140). To judge from the intact right side of this Medusa head, the bodies of the serpents, partly concealed by her outflaring, pointed side-locks, encircle her face and are knotted together under her chin. The position of the lower parts of their bodies parallels that of the serpents knotted together below the chins of the Medusas on the Lion Triclinium at Petra.

This Medusa relief at Khirbet Tannur is located in the center of the breastplate of what may originally have been a sculpture in relief of Mars [565] or of Jupiter Dolichenus. [566] A related Medusa relief occupies a similar position on the upper part of the peplos of Athena-Allat-Atargatis at Parthian Hatra. [567] Almost exactly duplicating the Khirbet Tannur relief is a winged, serpent-enclosed Medusa on the serpent-scaled back of the suit of armor of Ashur-Bel or Ba'al-shamin, garbed as a Roman emperor, from Hatra. [568]

The Medusa appendages of wings and serpents of the goddess of Ostia by no means complete the list of her interrelationships with the Nabataean gods at Khirbet Tannur and elsewhere and also with other deities. Among the latter are the gods of Lixus, Leptis Magna, Aquileia, and Puteoli. At the latter place, as we have seen, the Nabataeans probably had a temple of their own. One of the most important features the Goddess of Ostia shared with them was a veil of leaves [569] on her forehead, cheeks, chin and hair. It will be recalled that a veil of leaves was the most striking characteristic of the great bust of Atargatis at Khirbet Tannur in her role as Vegetation Goddess, and of her counterparts of equally massive size at Petra and at one of its suburbs, now known as Khirbet Brak.

It is seen thus that all of the attributes of the goddess of Ostia, including the one of dolphins, and excepting perhaps only that of crab's claws, were distributed among various deities at Khirbet Tannur. They illustrate the impact of the Mediterranean cultural world upon vast stretches of the Orient, extending from Arabia to India and the farthest reaches of Iran. To find dolphins at Khirbet Tannur, on top of an isolated hill in the broken high-lands of Nabataean Transjordan, most of whose inhabitants probably never saw the sea, and to encounter contemporary dolphins at stations in the desert or semidesert as far removed from one another as Abda in the Negev, Petra and Khirbet Brak in southern Edom, Wadi Ramm at the entrance to Arabia and Hatra in interior Mesopotamia is to be impressed forcibly with the powerful influence of pervasive Hellenism. Widespread commerce and intercontinental conflict were equally effective in the intermingling of the goods and the religions of the Orient and the Occident.

XI. ATARGATIS-APHRODITE

1. In Dolphin Form
2. Widening Horizons
   a. *On Land*
   b. *By Sea*
3. Economics and Diplomacy
   a. *Syllaeus*
      1) Miletus   2) Rhodes and Puteoli
4. Goddess of Fair Weather
5. Half Woman-Half Fish
   a. *Fecundity and Faith*
   b. *Appearance at Ascalon*
   c. *Mermen*
   d. *Sacred Pools*

XI. *Atargatis-Aphrodite*

1. IN DOLPHIN FORM

Be the explanation of the spread of the dolphin-cult among the Nabataeans whatever it may, the fact remains that the dolphin cult or the worship of deities with the dolphin attribute in one form or another does not seem to appear among the Nabataeans before the second century A.D. It manifested itself, however, much earlier in Greek, Hellenistic and Roman sources. Aristotle in his *History of Animals* in 330 B.C. accurately describes dolphins, classifying them as mammals, with the female of the species producing her single offspring after many months of gestation and nursing it in human fashion for a considerable period thereafter.[570] The Roman scholar, Pliny the Elder, who died in the eruption of Vesuvius in A.D. 79, wrote in a similar vein, although not as clearly or as comparatively scientifically. He relates in his *Natural History* how a dolphin would daily carry a boy on his back across the Bay of Baiae to Puteoli, which is near Naples (Pl. 9).[571] One wonders whether the Nabataean traders who frequented Puteoli and probably worshipped Atargatis in a temple of their own there were, as seems likely, acquainted with this fable or for that matter with the gods of Puteoli and Aquileia, and their various attributes, including also the one of dolphins.

The Nabataeans were conditioned by cultural experience and economic undertakings that led them far beyond the confines of their land-locked territory to accept and cherish the inclusion of dolphins as companions or attributes of their deities. Atargatis, who seems to have been foremost in their favor, being venerated more than the other members of the pantheon she belonged to, was above all the creator and sustainer of life. And life was impossible without the generative power of water, with which the dolphin was so inseparably associated, although the dolphin itself could hardly be considered a fertility symbol. Furthermore, the Atargatis, whom they gradually substituted for or perhaps merged with their native Allat, as they abandoned the rigorous simplicities of nomadic and seminomadic existence

359

for the complexities of a sophisticated, agricultural civilization, seems to have appeared in mermaid form at several famous shrines, including Ascalon.[572]

And as the Nabataeans, from about the beginning of the modern era some two thousand years ago, began more and more and farther and farther to venture abroad in pursuit of trade, they encountered a goddess often accompanied by or seated on a dolphin, who proved to be both extremely attractive and acceptable. She was none other than Aphrodite, who represented one of the main forms in which the Atargatis familiar to them had penetrated from western Asia to the Mediterranean area.[573] At Leptis Magna, in Roman North Africa, as noted above, there was a beautiful statue of her, with a dolphin on her right side carrying an Eros.[574] A pottery figurine from Tunis, as we have seen, shows her gracefully and relaxedly riding side-saddle on a complacent dolphin carrier (Pl. 23a).[575] And numerous other examples could be cited, such as the Metropolitan Aphrodite with the dolphin (Pl. 9A).[575a]

Lucian, himself, in his *De Dea Syria,* informs us that Aphrodite under various names was, in effect, synonymous with Atargatis.[576] And she, too, as Atargatis in one of her manifestations, was closely connected with the sea. Indeed, she was supposed to have sprung from its foam. Among her titles, in this connection, was that of Anadyomene (rising from the sea), Euploia (guarantor of prosperous voyages) and Galenaia (goddess of fair weather) who was represented as possessing the dolphin attribute.[577] The dolphin, however, was not associated with the matrix of life, fulfilling the reproductive role of the mother goddess, but was considered rather the harbinger of fair weather, the guarantor of successful enterprise, the guardian of safe journey across expanses of water and land and through the unexplored stretches of after-life. In dolphin form, Atargatis-Aphrodite with her dolphin symbol or attribute or quality was worshipped by all who went down to sea, including, of course, the Nabataeans. On a Punic stele of the second century B.C. from Carthage, dedicated to Baal-hammon and Tanit, as previously mentioned, is a dolphin above which is a deity holding up a caduceus (Pl. 17a).[578]

2. WIDENING HORIZONS

a. On Land

The Nabataeans, it is seen, ventured far overseas and over distant lands in their mercantile undertakings, and were much influenced in their course by the phenomenon of dolphins and of the extremely important even though subsidiary dolphin attribute of some gods and goddesses. The fabled country of Sheba in Arabia Felix, with its access to India and Africa, and the Parthian successor state of ancient Persia far to the northeast were within the range of their activities. Extremely well known to them were Palestine and Syria and the territories of the Cities of the Decapolis, including among others such centers as Gadara and Gerasa and Philadelphia (Rabbath-Ammon, Amman) in between. The southern border of the Decapolis touched upon their kingdom's base in the areas of the former kingdoms of Moab and Midian, which they early made intensively their own. From there they spread across the Negev westward to the outer edges of Sinai or at least to the River of Egypt (the Wadi el-Arish), that cleaves it in two from north to south (Joshua 15:4, 47, Numbers 34:4, 5). They also established themselves in southern Syria. Furthermore, Egypt and Italy, Greece and Asia Minor became the constant targets of their unflagging and successful business endeavors.[579]

Numerous cities on or near the banks of the Jordan and Nile and Tiber and Maeander Rivers were frequented by them, as were those on the Tigris and Euphrates, too. By military right or diplomatic agreement, they were at home in such widely scattered trading centers as Damascus in Syria, Hatra on the Euphrates in Parthia, Gerrha on the west shore of the Persian Gulf, Leuce Come on the east shore of the Gulf of Aqabah that bounds the peninsula of Arabia, Berenike on the west shore and Ascalon on the Mediterranean coast of southwestern Palestine. Other Mediterranean seaports such as Alexandria in Egypt, Miletus in Asia Minor and Puteoli in Italy were visited by them regularly. One of their chief seaports, Aila,[580] with its plenitude of spring water and refreshing greenery of extensive date-palm groves, was located in the lee of the hills of southernmost Edom at the northeast corner of the Gulf of Aqabah. It was but a few miles east of the remains of Solomon's seaport, and those of others later on, whence his ships sailed through the Red Sea to fabulous Ophir and back.[581] The lodestar of all these cities, so far as the center of the East-West trade was concerned, was their fantastically beautiful capital of Petra, hewn out of multicolored sandstone cliffs, and located at the ancient Edomite site of Sela in southern Transjordan. Most of their caravans converged or commenced there.

The Nabataeans made much profit by transporting and trading goods from and to all these places and others, too, in addition to the wealth they gained from taxes levied on the transit trade along the highways of their control. To provide food for the cities and hamlets that sprang up along and spread beyond the routes of their travel, they engaged in large areas in dry agriculture, assisted by intensive water-gathering techniques, on a scale hitherto unknown. With unerring knowledge of the arteries of commerce that crisscross the vast emptiness of Arabia, only sparingly relieved by occasional oases, they brought the spices and other precious goods of the East to their capital city of Petra for redistribution in many directions, including the countries bordering the shores of the Mediterranean.

Pl. 160

Sandstone lion (p. 144)

⊢————⊣
3 cms

a, b

c

Pl. 161

a, b. Lion
and a foot of
Atargatis,
see Pl. 160
(pp. 207, 508)
c. Kerch
marble lion
(p. 198)

a

b

Pl. 162

a. Lion's hindquarters (p. 270)
b. Lion's paw (p. 270)

5 cms

a

⊢———⊣
5 cms

b

Pl. 163

a.   Khirbet edh-Dherih lion (p. 287)
b, c. Qasr Rabbah lions' heads (p. 57)

c

365

a

b

366

a, b

5 cms

5 cms

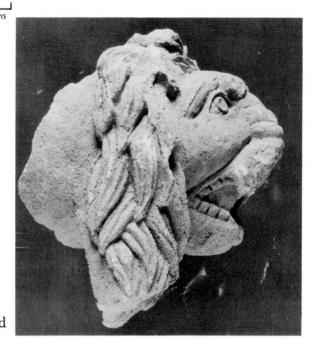

5 cms

d

Pl. 165   a-d. Lion reliefs (p. 144)

Pl. 164 (*opposite*)

a. Lion relief, Qasr Rabbah (p. 286)
b. Lion relief, Qasr Rabbah (p. 57)

a

b

Pl. 166

a. Lion Monument, Petra
   (p. 226)
b. Lion's Tomb, Petra
   (p. 226)

a

b

Pl. 167

a, b. Winged Eros between two winged griffins, Petra (p. 226)
c. "Inhabited scroll" with winged Eros, Qasr Rabbah (p. 57)

c

Pl. 168   Feline, Araq el-Emir (p. 7)

Pl. 169

a. "Inhabited scroll" with gazelle relief, Qasr Rabbah (p. 244)
b. "Inhabited scroll" with lion (?) relief, Qasr Rabbah (p. 244)

a

b

5 cms

371

5 cms

a

b

Pl. 170

a   Damaged gazelle (?) (p. 285)

b. "Inhabited scroll" with ibex, Nabataean Jebel Druze (p. 244)

372

a

b

b. By Sea

Their contacts by land alone made their acquaintance with the Dolphin Goddess certain. Whether they first met her in Ascalon or were introduced to her from Hatra, Aphrodisias, Sardis, or Alexandria cannot be ascertained. Their contacts by sea made their acceptance of her inevitable. They sought her benison for the lanes of trade that crossed the Great Sea and also furrowed desert wastes with faint lines of passage. She was the supreme patroness of travelers to distant horizons that rimmed difficult and sometimes dangerous expanses of land and restless and often turbulent stretches of sea.

Sprung originally from the desert, the Nabataeans took to the sea as though to the forecastle born. From Gaza and Ascalon and perhaps Caesarea in Palestine or from Alexandria in Egypt they embarked in foreign ships across the frequently stormy Mediterranean with their baggage of goods for barter and gold and some of their familiar gods for comfort and guidance. Disaster at sea during voyages that could not wait for favorable seasons or during storms which overtook them even after the best of auguries at the outset, were all too common occurrences. Paul learned this to his sorrow, when he was sent in chains by boat from Caesarea Maritima in Palestine to defend his case before the emperor in Rome. Raging seas resulted in shipwreck. As a result, there was a three months involuntary stay at Melita (modern Malta), before Paul and his shipmates were picked up by a vessel from Alexandria wintering there and brought to the Italian seaport of Puteoli, a few miles west of Naples. From there he was sent overland for his audience with the emperor in Rome.[582]

Intrepid Nabataean tradesmen, as well as ambassadors or opponents of the royal court in Petra and others, too, were constantly setting forth on Mediterranean voyages to places as remote as any that Paul visited by force or choice during his various voyages to Europe and Asia Minor. His path and theirs may have crossed frequently in these foreign cities so distant from home. One cannot help being constantly amazed at the enterprise and achievements of the Nabataeans. It seems most proper for the swift and graceful dolphin to have become the protective symbol of their bold undertakings on land, their venturesome movements across seas to centers of exchange and enrichment, and the inevitable pilgrimages of all mortals through the unknown of the hereafter.

3. ECONOMICS AND DIPLOMACY

a. Syllaeus

Economic interests and diplomatic missions led both the Nabataeans and their Judaean neighbors to voyage frequently to Italy across the Mediterranean both in temperate and turbulent seasons. The two peoples had much in common, including especially the fickle overlordship of Roman emperors. The Nabataeans and Judaeans did business together, befriended or fought each other intermittently, and sometimes intermarried with each other, at least once with disastrous results, as we have seen. For all the contiguity of their territories and the intermittent closeness of their political relationship, they remained worlds apart in fundamental religious orientation.

Underscoring the cleavage between them was the refusal of the Nabataean princeling, Syllaeus, apparently the most powerful individual in the immediate entourage of his king, Obodas III, to meet the condition of conversion to Judaism to gain the hand of Salome, the sister of Herod the Great. She was apparently no less brilliant and beautiful and determined than any of her kin, including her luscious, vindictive half niece, Herodias, whose memory is perpetuated in infamy. The whole family, with the exception perhaps of the half uncle-husband whom Herodias abandoned in Rome to wed another half uncle in utter disregard of Jewish law, was as able as it was endlessly ambitious and ruthlessly brutal and violent. Some of them were merely more so than others.

It was one thing for a Nabataean princess to marry a Judaean, but it was entirely different and apparently impossible for a Nabataean of royal lineage to conclude such a union by renouncing the gods of his people and remain a member of the kingly household and a possible claimant of the Nabataean throne. The very love that Syllaeus professed for Salome and that she seems to have entertained for him, made him suspect in the eyes of the paranoid Judaean king, Herod the Great, three of whose own sons, aside from other members of his family, were executed at his command because of his sickly fears.

One of the weapons of puppet kings of countries under the shadow of Roman authority, and of members of their ruling cliques who were permitted to batten upon the gains of their limited and unstable power, was to accuse each other, sometimes correctly, but more often than not with no basis other than envy or malice, of the most sinister plots and heinous crimes against the peace of the realm and directly or indirectly against the prerogatives and even the person of the Roman emperor himself. And Herod the Great, who murdered the nearest and dearest to him with feverish abandon, and then, when they were safely dead, reared monuments to their memories in heart-rending contrition, was also a past master of character assassination. He began to employ his talents against Syllaeus and soon was joined in this respect by the new, Nabataean king, Aretas IV, called Philopatris or *Rahemammu*—Lover of His People, who ascended the throne in Petra in 9 B.C. He was a brother of Obodas III, who died that year, poisoned perhaps at the instance of Syllaeus, who may have sought to supplant him, and for alibi's sake, made it his business to be out of the country at the time. It may have been in memory of Obodas that there was established at an important crossroads point in the Negev the Nabataean hilltop town of Eboda (Abda, Avdat), with a great temple and an encampment for Nabataean troops. Over its ruins, and partly out of them, rose subsequently a magnificent, church adorned, Christian Byzantine emporium.

The weapon of denunciation to the Roman authorities was a double-edged one and could often be turned against its wielder. The final but some-times perilous recourse of malcontents, as well as of other petitioners, was to seek the ear of the emperor, himself. Often the difference between life and death, between increase in power or effacement in exile, depended upon which petitioner reached him first and elicited his approval. It was a gamble for high stakes, frought with much danger, because royal favor was notori-ously changeable. Herod Antipas, for instance, was to experience how un-accountably and disastrously it could veer.

Yielding to the importunities of his inordinately ambitious wife, Herodias, as we have already noted, this ablest of the surviving sons of Herod the Great, each of whom inherited a third of their father's kingdom, took the long and difficult trip to Rome to beseech the emperor, Caligula, to change his title of tetrarch to that of king, in order to match the one bestowed upon his nephew, who was also his wife's brother, Herod Agrippa I. The latter, however, apprised of his uncle's intent and not minded to be equaled or perchance outranked by his uncle, raced ahead of him to Caligula and accused him falsely but convincingly of treason. When Herod Antipas arrived at the Roman court, he found himself not only out of favor but also out of office. He was stripped of all authority and banished to Lyons in Gaul, together with Herodias, there to be lost to history, while his tetrarchy of Galilee and Peraea was added to the lands of his detractor.

The Nabataean, Syllaeus, pursuing a similar course of action, suffered an even worse fate at an earlier date. He repaired to Rome on two separate occasions. The first time was shortly before the death of the Nabataean king, Obodas III, whom he would have liked to have succeeded. He apparently was bent upon bolstering his position in advance for the purpose. The second time was several years after Aretas IV had ascended the Nabataean throne in 9 B.C., without prior approval by the Roman emperor, following the death of Obodas III.[583]

Thinking to exploit the royal displeasure, which Aretas's negligence had incurred, Syllaeus sought to retrieve his former position of power at home and perhaps even by some legerdemain or falsehoods to secure the Naba-taean crown for himself. He found himself confronted, however, at the Roman court by the envoys of Aretas IV, together with Antipater, the most beloved son of Herod the Great, whom the mad father nevertheless added later on to the list of his children whom he caused to be murdered. The representations of Syllaeus failed. The charges against him of crimes against the state, of poisoning Obodas III and even of killing a brother of Herod the Great, sealed his fate. The result was his execution by order of Augustus and the belated confirmation, although for different reasons, of course, of Aretas IV as king of the Nabataeans. The second long and difficult voyage by sea of the Nabataean nobleman, which had been undertaken in peril, was concluded in tragedy.[584]

The offerings we know that Syllaeus brought to an especial sanctuary at Miletus, when his ship anchored at this Asia Minor seaport on the first leg of its way to Italy from Palestine or Egypt, proved to have brought him no blessing for his mission in Rome. But why should his ship have halted at Miletus and not have sailed in a straight and much shorter line directly to Italy, which Syllaeus was so desperately anxious to reach with all possible dispatch? In seeking the answer to this question, we have learned much about the seemingly strange but nevertheless wholly sensible and only possible way of sailing in the eastern Mediterranean in classical times, and the relationship of prayers for safety in travel and success of undertakings to deified dolphins or to the gods that bore them as symbols of their power.

1) MILETUS

The numerous journeys by Nabataeans across the Mediterranean hastened their glad acceptance of the dolphin as an attribute or symbol of the pantheon of gods to which their loyalty and love were devoted. With one exception, however, there is no record of their actual contact with any of the dolphin deities, male or female, located at such places as Aquileia, Puteoli, Ostia, Leptis Magna, Lixus and wherever else they may have existed. The one fortunate exception consists of a bilingual inscription in Nabataean and Greek [585] on a stone block dedicated to the Nabataean god, Dusares, found in the Delphinium of Apollo at Miletus.[586] It had been placed there by Syllaeus as a thanksgiving offering for his safe arrival at this prominent seaport, located near the mouth of the Maeander River on the Aegean coast of southwestern Asia Minor. Because of courtesy, custom or perhaps the necessity of establishing an alibi, he also included in his prayer a salute to his king, Obodas III.[587]

The question needs to be asked as to why Syllaeus chose the Delphinium of Apollo at Miletus as the depository of his gift. The first answer of course is that his ship had anchored at Miletus. The second is that the sanctuary there was one of the sacred places, including Athens and Cnossus among others,[588] where Apollo was accompanied by or appeared in the guise and under the name of Delphinios, the dolphin god. The spring festival of Delphinio was celebrated in Attica in honor of this god.[589] Legend has it that Apollo had once turned himself into a dolphin, that is, "Delphin." [590] Plunging dolphins, painted on an early fifth-century B.C. red, figured hydria, together with a figure of Apollo, uplifted on a winged tripod above the sea, mark him as an Apollon Delphinios.[591]

The uninitiated may wonder, as I did, why Syllaeus took a boat via the very indirect route to Miletus in Asia Minor, when he obviously wanted to get to Rome as directly and quickly as possible. The way to do that would seem to have been to sail straight to Puteoli, the Italian seaport near Naples, and then make the brief overland trip north to the capital on the Tiber. Miletus was, of course, an important commercial center, undoubtedly well known to Nabataean and other traders from abroad. Paul's ship anchored there, while he was homeward bound from one of his far-ranging missionary journeys.[592] For Syllaeus, however, to interrupt his journey at Miletus, or even to go there at all, unless it were compellingly necessary, could at this particular juncture of his life have meant only a chafing and perhaps fatal delay in securing the audience with the emperor in Rome, upon the outcome of which his career and possibly his life depended.[593] The answer is that he had no choice, and particularly so since starting out in winter.[594]

Apparently no ship could keep to a fairly straight course, it mattered not under whose command or for what purpose, when it sailed from Caesarea or Gaza or Ascalon in Palestine or from Alexandria in Egypt to Europe in inclement weather. Apparently, too, even under clear skies and with favorable winds and in good weather, the merchantmen heading from these harbors to Puteoli or other distant ports, reached their goals by following the equivalent of the rule, that "the longest way around is the shortest way home." The direction of the prevailing winds and the inability to make progress forward by tacking against them for lack of proper swinging sails, not known then, left no other choice. Those employed then and for a long time thereafter were unchangeably positioned and could not be shifted on a boom from side to side to make progress diagonally forward by catching the breezes from quarter directions.[595]

It becomes clear then that it was common practice for every ship setting forth from Ascalon or Alexandria on the way to Puteoli to sail first towards Asia Minor and put in at a seaport such as Miletus on its Aegean coast or anchor in harbors at such nearby islands as Cos or Rhodes or Delos. After halting at one or more of these places for unloading of cargo, taking on new freight and supplies and making whatever repairs might have become necessary, it would then head westward, hugging Greek shorelines for part of the way, till finally it reached its destination in Italy.

Even in good weather, each voyage was an adventure, and particularly in stormy season was it attended by danger, terror and occasionally catastrophe. Little wonder, then, that Syllaeus deposited a thanksgiving offering to Dusares in the Delphinium of Apollo at Miletus after completing the first and perhaps the most difficult leg of his wintry odyssey. There was no faster or more direct route negotiable in that era for travellers from Palestine and Egypt who wished to reach Rome. Little wonder, too, that Nabataean tradesmen were wont to follow his example and at journey's break or end give tangible expressions of gratitude to their gods for having brought them in safety to their intermediate or final goals.

And would not Syllaeus naturally have sought out the dolphin-deity of Miletus because of its affinity to the dolphin-goddess, whose vogue was so great throughout the Nabataean kingdom? Every Nabataean traveler seems to have been devoted to her, to judge from the frequency of her appearance at such inland and unquestionably Nabataean sanctuaries as Abda in the Negev, the temple by Ain Shellaleh in the Wadi Ramm on the way to Arabia, Khirbet Brak and es-Sabra in the suburbs of Petra, and especially Khirbet Tannur, where she appears in a classic posture, with a tiara of heraldic dolphins on her head. Noteworthy, too, is the fact that Aphrodisias, where a dolphin-crowned Atargatis was found, is but a comparatively few miles inland to the east, northeast of Miletus.

The difference in sexes of the dolphin-gods of Miletus and Khirbet Tannur, for example, so far removed from one another in space if not in time, is not important in this connection. We have seen that each of the Hellenistic male gods of Puteoli and Aquileia and Lixus on opposite sides of the Mediterranean possessed the characteristics of practically all the goddesses of the Nabataean temple of Tannur, being paralleled in this respect by the Parthian Atargatis of Hatra. The emphasis was upon their attributes and functions rather than upon the sexual features which were supposed to have separated them. The goddess of Leptis Magna possessed all their attributes, too.

2) RHODES AND PUTEOLI

Nabataean travelers visited all kinds of seaports and commercial centers on the Mediterranean, Aegean and Adriatic shores and other emporia located probably farther inland, and Nabataean inscriptions have been found at some of them testifying to their presence. I am confident that more records of this kind, including the delicate, unmistakable Nabataean pottery, will turn up in time at places of this type, where they have as yet not been discovered or perhaps recognized. The Graeco-Nabataean inscription at Miletus has already been referred to. Another has been located at the town of Rhodes, on the island of that name not far from Miletus, and several at the Italian seaport of Puteoli,[596] near Naples. Puteoli seems in Hellenistic-Roman times to have been the home port for ships with grain and frankincense and spices and other goods from the southern and eastern sides of the Mediterranean. In one of the Nabataean inscriptions from Puteoli, mention is made of an offering of two camels to the Nabataean god, Dusares.[597] They were probably gold miniatures, rather than the actual animals themselves. It might have been difficult to find camels in Puteoli for the purpose, and the presiding priest would probably have been happier with the smaller gift in precious metal rather than the larger one in the flesh.[598]

It is not at all impossible that there may have been a small Nabataean temple at Puteoli, where Nabataean tradesmen and other countrymen of theirs on different missions, far from home, could have worshiped their native gods in familiar surroundings. Indeed, fair-sized colonies of Nabataeans and other Orientals may have been resident in Puteoli and Rome, as also in Delos, where there was a Syrian temple devoted to Atargatis, and in Rhodes and Miletus and elsewhere. And even if opportunities for religious ceremonies could not always be afforded them on foreign soil in sanctuaries of their own, there were plenty of others of sufficient similarity where Nabataeans abroad must always have been welcomed and would have felt themselves completely at home. We have seen the relationship, for example, between the Vegetation and Dolphin Goddesses of Khirbet Tannur and the God of Puteoli with his veil of leaves and his dolphins.

4. GODDESS OF FAIR WEATHER

Through her dolphin attribute, Galenaia-Aphrodite-Atargatis was the goddess of fair weather, upon whose favor depended the safety of travelers by sea, and, through an easy transition, also by land and in the realm of the hereafter. The surmounting of the difficulties and dangers of long journeys and the deliverance of precious cargoes or the attainment of sorely cherished goals evoked the need to propitiate the deity at the beginning of the trip and utter words of praise and bring sacrifices of gratitude at its successful conclusion. Her favor was probably equally or even more importunately sought, as we may remark again, for safe conveyance to and in the bourne of the beyond.[599] As travelers and traders with international interests, as purveyors of precious goods between Arabia and southern Europe, between Persian Gerrha and Roman Puteoli, it was natural for the impressionable Nabataeans to adopt and adapt as their own many aspects of the gods and much of the garb and other cultural belongings of the peoples they encountered.

The impact of the Nabataeans upon the countries of their commercial association or penetration is much more difficult, if not impossible to assess, but it must, nevertheless, have been considerable. The spread of the worship of Atargatis westward, be it under her own name and form or those of various forms of Aphrodite,[600] may be attributed in part at least to the extension of Nabataean enterprise throughout much of the Mediterranean world and the establishment of their own sanctuaries and the worship of their own gods in many of its most important seaports and trading centers.

They were not the only people of the Orient that incorporated the dolphin within their religious framework, as we have already seen from the connection of dolphins with a relief of Atargatis in Parthian Hatra. Indeed, the adoption of the dolphin in the East seems to have been a general one. One can cite the relief of a dolphin and two fishes on the funerary stele of an Asiatic soldier buried by the side of the Danube, who had belonged to Vespasian's XV Appolinaire Legion.[601] Two dolphins decorate the right end of a sarcophagus in one of the Jewish catacombs of Beit She'arim near Haifa, belonging to the second century A.D. They form the outer part of an ornamentation in low relief, which includes also a half shell in the center of a wreath, the bottom of which is contained in a "Hercules" knot [602] of two serpents, whose tails touch the tails of the dolphins [603] (Pl. 24b).

The dolphin symbol was known and venerated in much of Hellenistic Europe, Africa and Asia long before the Nabataeans established their kingdom, and it continued in use long after the Nabataean identity had been erased and forgotten.[604] The dolphin in the divine capacity attributed to it spelled out the equivalent of *bon voyage* for journeys by sea, on land, and in the realm of the beyond which could be entered only after the bonds of mortality had been broken.

5. HALF WOMAN-HALF FISH

a. Fecundity and Faith

Atargatis was a many-faceted goddess, who appeared in multiple forms. Veiled with leaves and decorated with pomegranates and other fruits, she also presided over the mystery of birth of man and beast and all living things. Her favor was a prerequisite for the blessing of birth and sustenance. Arrayed with stalks of grain, her good will had to be sought, that fat crops might grow and ripen in due season. Wearing a crown resembling the turreted wall of a fortified city, she could, if she would, safeguard it from ill, and the seeking of her favorable disposition was, therefore, the earnest concern of its every inhabitant.

Her power extended over every season of the year, over every month of its passage, with the moon and the stars amenable to her will. The signs of the zodiac were beholden to her control, including the two fishes she had had placed in it as the symbol par excellence of her prodigality.[605] She was above all the goddess of fertility, and functioned in this respect also as the Fish Goddess, in an all-embracing, fecundizing fashion, that had originally little or nothing to do with her dolphin role. She was both Fish Goddess and Dolphin Goddess. As the one, she was the female incarnate, whose bountiful womb made her the progenitress supreme. As the other, she was a gracious sprite, who calmed the seas and cleared the skies and conducted the traveler to safe havens during the limited span of mortality and through the endless reaches of afterlife.[606] We wonder, however, whether the distinction between the two was clearly retained in the popular mind and whether or not by the time of the Nabataeans, the line of demarcation between them had not become too blurred in the general public consciousness to be recognized.[607] In any event, it is not clear to us how sharply, if at all, the Nabataeans differentiated between Atargatis as the Dolphin Goddess and Atargatis as the Fish Goddess.

b. *Appearance at Ascalon*

It is easily understandable why the goddess reflected in dolphin shape or bedecked with the dolphin symbol was most attractive to and widely worshipped by the much traveled Nabataeans. One might say that essentially she was the object of their obeisance even before their intrepid mercantile enterprises made them as familiar with the sea lanes as with caravan trails. Long before they knew Galenaia as the dolphin form of Aphrodite or knew Aphrodite as the Atargatis-Derceto of such places as Carian Aphrodisias in southwestern Asia Minor[608] or of Leptis Magna in North Africa, or had come into contact with such dolphin ornamented forms of Zeus-Hadad as those of Puteoli, Aquileia and Lixus, the Nabataeans were thoroughly acquainted with what may possibly be her eastern, sea-connected prototype at Ascalon on the southwestern Palestinian coast and others like her or closely related to her in Syria.

The Atargatis of Ascalon is described by Diodorus Siculus[609] as being half woman and half fish. We wonder without too much conviction whether it might not have been more correct to describe her as half woman and half dolphin. The same reservation applies to Lucian's mention of a Phoenician Atargatis-Derceto as being "one half woman, but the part which extends from the thighs to the feet ends in a fish's tail." [610] The relationship of Atargatis of the famous shrine of Hierapolis in Syria to water ceremonies is stressed by Lucian when he reports how her statue was brought down during the vernal season to a lake and immersed in it. He alludes also to the fact that the greatest of the sacred assemblies in which these rites were practiced took place on the sea coast. They may have marked the opening of the shipping season in April.[611]

It seems certain that the Nabataeans must have been familiar with the marble statue of Artemis of Ephesus found at Caesarea, on the lower part of whose body in low relief are depicted feminine figures grasping what appear to be their bifurcated tails in their hands.[612]

The clearest of the reliefs of this type is the one in the front center of her chest. It shows on close examination a winged figure rising out of a stylized acanthus cup. There is a strong resemblance to a bust of Athena of

Eleusis.[613] Both hands of the winged figure rest on the ends of the two outward extended and curved petals. In some of the panels of the dress of this statue of Artemis of Ephesus are much similar but non-winged figures grasping what definitely seem to be the ends of bifurcated tails.

Related figures are visible on a statuette of this goddess from Ephesus, located north of the Maeander River on the west coast of Asia Minor,[614] and there are other widespread Greek and Hellenistic examples.[614a] Bernard Goldman has called attention to a small bronze mermaid from Luristan in ancient Persia similarly grasping in each hand one of the ends of her bifurcated tail, revealing the influence of Assyrian art of the first half of the first millennium B.C.[615] The worship of Atargatis as Artemis was popular and widespread, extending in classical antiquity from the east as far west as Spain. Troops, tradesmen and slaves were the purveyors of her piquant cult.[616]

Whether the Nabataeans regarded the Atargatis of Ascalon as Fish Goddess, which is probable, or as a different form of the Dolphin Goddess, which seems less likely, it is clear that they were familiar with the fish symbol, to judge from their use of the Pisces or Fishes in their Khirbet Tannur zodiac. It is difficult, if not impossible, to distinguish the difference in form between them and the dolphins on the head of the Dolphin Goddess. It is only because the Pisces division of zodiacs in general is almost always occupied by two fishes or occasionally one, that those of the Khirbet Tannur zodiac must be adjudged as belonging to that category.

c. Mermen

There were not only mermaids like the Goddess of Ascalon, but mermen, too, of related type.[617] The tradition of the fish-man of Luristan [618] and perhaps of the still earlier one of the personage of Lagash [619] (Tello), north of Ur in Sumer, holding two serpents and with two fishes suspended from his torque, may indirectly have become part of the cultural background of the Nabataeans, via their exceedingly close connections with the Parthians, and through them with the Scythians. It is interesting in this connection to note that Scythian bridle trappings are occasionally shaped like fishes.[620]

There is little question that the Nabataeans must have been acquainted with the Hellenistic Triton of Massa'id, south of Gaza, whose bearded face, inlaid eyes, agonized expression, beautifully carved body and two contorted, scaly fish tails, with their ends twisted up to his back side, could not fail to have left an indelible impression upon all who viewed him.[621] It would appear that his figure was part of a magnificent frieze of gigantomachy, portraying a combat for supremacy among various groups of gods, very similar to the one decorating the walls enclosing a fountain at Aphrodisias.[622] This Gaza sculpture may possibly be connected with the legend of Perseus slaying the sea-monster and rescuing Andromeda as thought to

a

b

Pl. 172

a. Cornice with mason's mark (p. 480)
b. Related type of cornice (p. 143)

5 cms

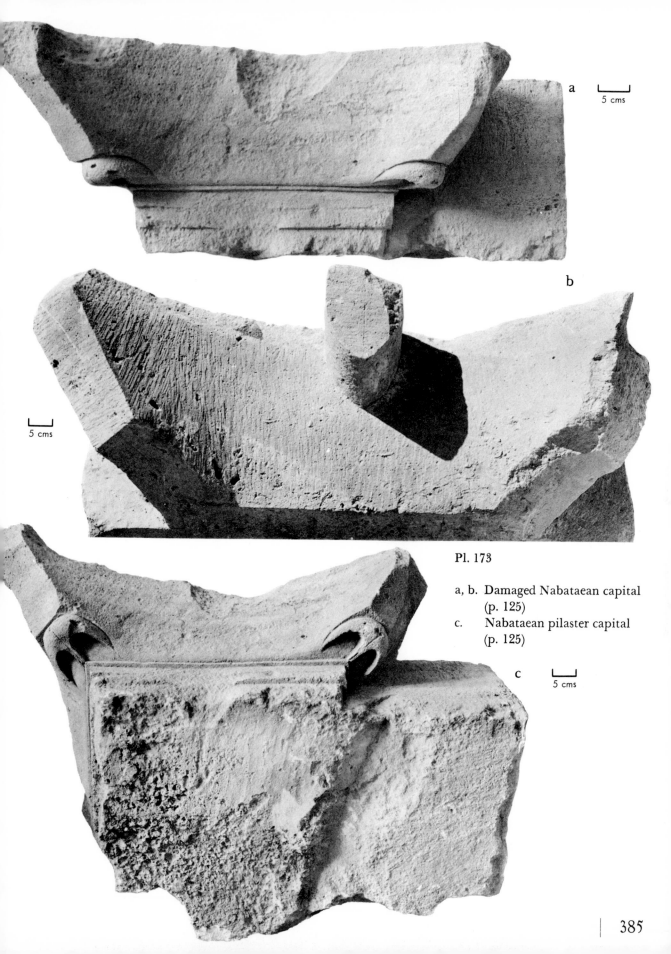

a

b

Pl. 173

a, b. Damaged Nabataean capital
(p. 125)
c. Nabataean pilaster capital
(p. 125)

c

5 cms

5 cms

5 cms

385

a

5 cms

b

Pl. 174

a. Nabataean pilaster capital (p. 105)
b. Bottom side showing mason's lines (p. 105)
c. Thunderbolt shield (?), Khirbet Brak (p. 156)
d. Decorated horn of a pilaster capital (p. 145)

c

d   5 cms

a

5 cms

Pl. 175

a, b. Nabataean pi-
laster capitals
(p. 143)

c. Cornice frag-
ment, with acan-
thus leaves and
rosettes (p. 143)

b

c   5 cms

387

a

b

c

Pl. 176

a. Section of pilaster capital (p. 142)
b. Architectural stone turned into watering trough, Qasr Rabbah (p. 57)
c. Nabataean capital, Khirbet edh-Dherih (p. 48)

a

b

Pl. 177

a, b. Architrave sections, Qasr Rabbah (p. 57)
c.   Cornice section, Qasr Rabbah (p. 58)

c

Pl. 178

a. Pediment on east pylon (p. 145)   c. Stylized thunderbolt, Khirbet Brak (p. 204)

b. Period III architrave (p. 48)   d. Stylized thunderbolt, Khirbet edh-Dherih (p. 156) have been represented on a coin from nearby Joppa (Jaffa).[623] It was from a ship sailing from Joppa that Jonah was cast overboard to quiet the raging sea and was swallowed by a sea-monster, a "great fish" (Jonah 1:3, 17, 2:10). One is reminded of the related scene of a gigantomachy on the monumental frieze of the altar at Pergamon in Asia Minor, dated to about 180 B.C.[624]

d. Sacred Pools

The association of water with fish and fish with fecundity is obviously a natural one. It comes as no surprise, therefore, to find traditions placing the birthplace of Aphrodite-Atargatis in the waters of the Euphrates River. In one account, her origin was ascribed to an egg fallen from heaven into it and saved by fishes, which brought it to shore, where it was hatched out by a dove. Later on, in response to the importuning of the grateful goddess, Jupiter is said to have placed the fishes in the zodiacal circle.[625] According to another story, the goddess fell into the pond at Hierapolis-Bambyke and was saved by fishes, which later on were transported to heaven as a result.[626] Diodorus relates the legend that the Dea Syria, out of shame over an affair with an attractive young Syrian, threw herself into the sacred pool at Ascalon, where she was transformed into a fish.[627]

The above accounts do not exhaust the stories of the relationship of the Mother Goddess to the symbol of fish. It is one which is deeply rooted in the mythology both of the Orient and the Occident.[628] As a sign of exuberant fecundity, the fish was particularly sacred in the Atargatis cult.[629] It would seem that no sanctuary of hers was complete without having attached to it a sacred pond, in which untouchable fish swam about.[630] It will be recalled that Lucian refers to the annual baptismal ceremony, during which the statue of Atargatis was immersed in the sacred lake belonging to her temple.[631] And at Ascalon, where, as we have seen, she was worshiped in mermaid form, there was, according to Diodorus, "a large and deep lake full of fish," which must have been connected with her sanctuary.[632] We believe that there may have been a sacred pond in the center of the outer courtyard at Khirbet Tannur, and that such a pool of greater or lesser size may well have been connected with every Nabataean temple devoted to Atargatis, no matter where located.[633]

While there may have been in every Nabataean and related temple a sacred pool devoted to Atargatis, in some of which perhaps sacred fish were kept, it would have been difficult for the land-locked Nabataeans to stock their sacred pools with fish. It was, however, generally believed that Atargatis took ritual baths in the sea or lake by the side of which her temples were located or in the pools that were specially constructed for the purpose within their sacred precincts. There was no conflict between her functioning in this particular fashion, in which water and fish and fecundity formed a trinity of features united in her person, and various other phases of her complicated make-up. In the relief of Atargatis at Parthian Hatra, for example, almost all of her attributes are attached to a single body,[634] unlike the situation at Khirbet Tannur, where they are divided among a whole company of goddesses, as has previously been remarked.

It is possible that Atargatis could be worshipped at one and the same sanctuary both as Dolphin Goddess and as Fish Goddess and in other forms, too. The Dolphin Goddess and the Fish Goddess, with their respective virtues and competencies, may in the public consciousness have merged into each other. When Atargatis was depicted as the former, it is barely possible that she was considered also as fulfilling the functions of the latter, or vice versa. She had become a cosmic goddess, it mattered not in what form she appeared.[635]

XII. IN THE CENTER OF THE FIRMAMENT

1. A Divine Fashion Plate
   a. *Crown, Torque, Standard*
   b. *Guardian Goddess*
      1) *Hellenistic Imprint*   2) *Cornucopia*
   c. *The Focus of Attention*
   d. *Arrangement Without Parallel*
2. The Signs of the Zodiac
   a. *Aries*
   b. *Sagittarius*
   c. *Capricornus*
   d. *Taurus, Leo, Gemini, Cancer, Libra, Scorpio*
   e. *Virgo*
   f. *Aquarius*
   g. *Pisces*
3. Niké Caryatid
   a. *Bracelets*
   b. *Cultural Imprints*
      1) *Forms and Feathers*   2) *Patterning of Drapery*
4. Other Nikés
   a. *Hellenistically Inclined*
   b. *Common Types*
   c. *Discoid Bases of Niké Reliefs*

XII. *In the Center of the Firmament*

1. A DIVINE FASHION PLATE

a. Crown, Torque, Standard

The features of the sandstone Atargatis (Pl. 44) from the Temple of Tannur can be seen also in those of the guardian goddess who appears in the form of Tyché there, wearing a turreted crown and surrounded by a circle of the figures of the zodiac (Pls. 46, 48). This crown is covered by a scarf or shawl, the sides of which reach down over the front of the bust of the goddess. It denotes, we believe, the canopy of the heavens, as it does in the reliefs of the Grain and Dolphin Goddesses and all comparable instances (Pls. 1, 25). The Tyché of Palmyra, wearing a turreted crown [636] (Pl. 52b) and also the Tyché of Dura-Europos [637] have many features in common with the one of the Temple of Tannur. Almost any one of these goddesses could have served as the model for the reconstruction of the head of the sandstone Atargatis of the Temple of Tannur, whose stele must have stood next to that of Zeus-Hadad.

The lions' heads forming the terminals of the torque on one of the Tychés of Khirbet Tannur (Pl. 45a) have lost much of their original comparative sharpness of features. They are easily recognizable, however, because of the two other torques of this kind on the Zeus-Hadad and Atargatis figures (Pls. 41, 44). The Tyché with the lions' torque has been severely damaged. The top of her head is broken off and the features of her face rendered indistinguishable. Over her hair is a shawl or a veil, whose ends fall gracefully in double folds over the front of her shoulders and the sides of her peplos. The torque encircles the top of her highnecked dress, with a circular medallion or precious stone separating its terminals of lions' heads.[638]

This goddess may well have worn a mural crown, now broken off. The probability of its existence is heightened by the presence of one on the intact relief of the Tyché, encircled by a zodiac panel (Pls. 46, 48), also found at Khirbet Tannur. Indeed, the two Tyché reliefs may be said to be almost exact duplicates of each other. Their entire configuration is the same. It would seem not too venturesome to say that both were fashioned by the same sculptor. Alike are the patrician neck, the rounded cheeks, the long locks of hair, the same type of shawl or veil. The lines of the folds of the peplos of the Zodiac-Tyché and of her shawl or veil are, however, slightly different from those of the Tyché with the lions' torque. Otherwise the two sculptures seem to represent one and the same goddess. The chief difference between them is the absence of the lions' torque from the Zodiac-Tyché relief, and, of course, the absence of the zodiac circle in the other one.

Both of those reliefs have one feature in common that seems further to substantiate their single identity. It looks like a double pronged tuning fork or a long wishbone, joined together at the bottom and open at the top, with the two sides of the "v" tied together by a double band near the upper third of their length. One side of the symbol consists of a wand which is topped by a crescent moon, while the other side could represent one of many things such as a scepter,[639] a torch,[640] a stalk of wheat [641] (Pl. 25), a spindle,[642] or possibly a musical instrument. With the exception of the latter, Tyché sculptures are frequently adorned with one or another of them and sometimes with several of them.[643] The possibility of its being a spindle or distaff is heightened by Lucian's description of Hera (Atargatis) of Hierapolis-Bambyke as holding a mirror (?) in one hand and a spindle in the other. The spindle of fate naturally belonged to her, particularly in her identification with Nemesis and the Fates which he mentions.[644]

There is a similarity between this symbol and a musical instrument borne by a Coptic, female figure in relief of the fifth century A.D.[645] In view of the close connection between Nabataean and Coptic art,[646] one wonders whether the Coptic figure and musical instrument may have any connection with earlier Nabataean models. We know that musical instruments, especially the lyre, are associated not only with some representations of Hermes but also occasionally with Tyché-Niké figures.[647] Indeed, the remnants of what may originally have been a seven stringed lyre can be seen on the left shoulder of the much-battered, mural-crowned Tyché on one side of a corner cornice stone (Pl. 53a).

This double-pronged symbol extends immediately above the right shoulder of the Tyché with the lions' torque, and has the crescent-moon wand on the outside. It appears also in the same order on the Zodiac-Tyché relief, but this time immediately above her left shoulder. In the field above the latter's right shoulder and to the right of her head is a crescent moon (Pl. 46).[648] The faint outlines of a similar crescent moon can be made out in the field above the left shoulder of the Tyché with the lions' torque (Pl. 45a), indicating its presence there before it got broken off. In this particular relief the crescent-topped wand is bent to fit it into the stone frame from which the Tyché bust springs. Its counterpart in the Zodiac-Tyché relief is straight because there is plenty of room for it in the frame above her left shoulder.

The moon-goddess role of Tyché was a familiar one for her in the sanctuaries of the ancient Near East. Together with a star she is represented by a crescent moon, for example, on tesserae from Palmyra, and on coins from there by a crescent moon and by a lion.[649] Elsewhere a crescent moon tops her head.[650] At Parthian Hatra there is a lunar goddess in relief on a circular medallion, with the bottom of her bust enclosed within the shallow arc of the crescent.[651] The reverse position of the crescent moon behind the bust of the moon-goddess can be seen on an altar from Tyre and on a coin from Jerash.[652]

The fact that the outer side of each of the symbols above the left and right shoulders, respectively, of the Zodiac-Tyché and the Lions'-Torque Tyché of Khirbet Tannur consists of a wand topped by a crescent moon, and that there is a crescent moon in the field above the other shoulder in each case may be taken as indicating in part the moon-goddess identification of Tyché with Selene. Her name is mentioned by Lucian as being one of those synonymous with Atargatis-Artemis, the Syrian goddess of the famous Hierapolis-Bambyke temple, to which we have just referred.[653] It is noteworthy that Selene was worshiped on the days of the full and new moon.[654]

The kind of wand topped by a crescent moon associated with Tyché-Selene-Atargatis is visible also on the famous Dura relief of Zeus-Hadad and Atargatis. She is portrayed there wearing a rayed mural crown, and seated on a throne between two lions with the crescent-moon wand topping the standard between her head and Hadad.[655] She practically crowds him and his bulls out of the picture. This crescent-bannered wand is strikingly portrayed on a separate limestone relief from the Temple of Atargatis at Dura, which shows a pillar, topped by a crescent moon, with a small lunar disc in the field above it.[656]

All in all the symbol is perhaps best to be identified with the equivalent of the planetary emblem, known as a *semeion*,[657] which is associated with Zeus-Hadad or Atargatis-Tyché-Venus or with both of them. Composed of two wands bound together, the one topped by a crescent room and the other being possibly a torch and representative of the sun or of a star, such a symbol could comport well with the essentially astral nature of the Zodiac-Tyché. This is reflected in everything about her, her scarf, crown and indeed her entire figure. The scarf signifies, as we have pointed out, the canopy of the heavens. The crown stands for guardianship and protection in this life and for victory over death.[658] As the paramount Atargatis-Tyché-Venus, she was associated with one of the main groupings of the planetary system. The double band holding the two wands together at their base may be similar to the ribbon or fillet tied in a bow around the wand of a *semeion* from Carthage.[659] A crescent-topped wand projects above each shoulder of the "Tyché of Taimei" at Palmyra.[660]

Not only the crescent moon and the turreted crown distinguish the sculptures of Tyché, but, as we have pointed out, the lion symbol is also included among some of them. The lion symbol in particular relates her to the paramount goddess, Atargatis. She was above all the guardian of her peoples, and in particular personified the matrix of life itself. Especially clear at Khirbet Tannur is the inseparable connection between its chief deity, Atargatis, together with her lions' torque and attendant lions, and several of the individual Tyché reliefs with their mural crowns and lunar attributes. The fact that one of the Tychés wears a lions' torque, too, as we have seen, merely emphasizes their consanguinity. Indeed, it may be noted in this frame of reference that the Tyché of Palmyra, who in the paintings in the temple of Palmyrene gods at Dura is depicted side by side with the Tyché of Dura, has a lion at her left side [661]—a fact which again identifies her with Atargatis.[662] The names and forms of Tyché are varied, as we have seen, representing different or specially emphasized facets of essentially the same goddess. At one place, thus, she appears as "Artemis, the Tyché of Gerasa," [663] and at another place, in the temple of Artemis at Dura-Europos, in the form of a statuette of Fortuna.[664]

b. Guardian Goddess

Outstanding among the Tychés of Khirbet Tannur is the central jewel-like one surrounded by a zodiacal circle, the bottom of which is broken off. The story of the recovery of the missing portion will be told later on. The only damage suffered by the central Tyché herself reveals itself in the absence of most of her nose. Her face proper could otherwise be that of any of the numerous Nabataean goddesses of Khirbet Tannur. This similarity of features extends beyond the confines of this temple, as an examination for instance of the Vegetation Goddesses of Petra and Khirbet Brak, to which we have previously referred, and of the mask of a deity on the tiny Nabataean altar found at the comparatively distant Abda in the Negev,[665] demonstrates. It seems certain, on the whole, that a single school of sculptors created all the Nabataean deities in southern Transjordan and the Negev within a fairly brief span of time early in the second century A.D. There is little variation in the features of any of them.

The facial lineaments of the Zodiac-Tyché of Khirbet Tannur are among the clearest of all the Nabataean goddesses there, although the Vegetation Goddess (Pl. 31), the small Lions' Torque Goddess (Pl. 44), and the Grain and Dolphin Goddesses (Pls. 1, 25), are very close to her in excellence of features. Her wavy hair is parted in the middle and combed down over the sides of her forehead, with spiral locks descending over her shoulders and the front of the upper part of her *peplos,* and culminating in carefully curled strands, arranged in all related instances also with ritual exactitude. This hair fashion exposes a diamond-shaped expanse of low forehead of a type common to all the deities of the Temple of Tannur.

Concentric grooves accentuate the top of her eyebrows, with sharply canted planes leading down to the eyelids. These are strongly emphasized by deep incisions above and below them to make them stand out above deep eye-sockets, from which circular irises with pupils represented by drilled depressions protrude prominently, resulting in an expectantly in-quisitive look. The cheeks are full and the firm chin rounded. Deep grooves around the sides of the mouth set off the voluptuous, parted lips and the flaring nostrils of what we know to have been a somewhat flattened nose above them. There may well have been red paint between her lips and on them and in her eyeballs, accentuating her attractiveness and appeal. The same holds true, incidentally, for the main Zeus-Hadad figure. Probably all of the sculptures of Khirbet Tannur were similarly "made up" for their public appearances. The face of the Zodiac-Tyché seems in general to be that of a deity who has savored much of life and confidently awaits further gratification. This appearance is characteristic of all the gods and goddesses of Khirbet Tannur.

The popularity of the Tyché figure at Khirbet Tannur is indicated by the presence there of several other considerably damaged sculptures, aside from those we have already mentioned, which may well belong to the category of the Guardian Goddess. Among the surface ruins was found a much battered sculpture in relief of a goddess (Pl. 45b), which would seem to belong to the Tyché type. The lower part of the back of her head rests against the face of the uppermost segment of a wide raised curved band, the top of which rises well above her shoulders. She wore a high girdled peplos with the end of the superimposed chlamys folded over her upper left arm. Her right arm was broken off. She may possibly have held a rudder in her left hand. A much better executed and more plastic form of the same dress combination can be seen on a damaged Niké relief, probably originally winged, and most of whose body and the right half of whose head we found in separate pieces in our excavations and were able to join together again (Pl. 184a, b).[666]

It is clear that the bas-relief of this Tyché or Atargatis figure belonged to a larger composition of several limestone building blocks, on one of which her right arm must have been portrayed. Even in its present badly mangled state, the sculpture has a regal poise. It is manifested in the finely shaped head turned slightly to the right, the long patrician neck, the erect posture, the manner of holding some kind of a sacred emblem in her left hand, several fingers of which are now missing. Only an enigmatic outline remains of the object she holds against her left side. In the tilt of her head, in the remnants of the diadem crowning it, in the two long twisted locks of hair reaching down to her shoulders, this goddess bears a distinct resemblance to the busts of several notable Tychés (Pls. 45a, 46), and of an elegant small Atargatis or Tyché (Pl. 44) from Khirbet Tannur.

I have not yet been able to determine the nature of the object held between the fingers of the left hand of the goddess, resting against the left side of her bosom and reaching to the top of her left shoulder. It could be any one of many things, including a widely spreading palm branch (Pl. 188a, b), a lyre (Pl. 53a) comparable to the one on the shoulder of a bas-relief of Mercury (Pl. 146a), a double-pronged quiver (?) or distaff (?) or semeion (Pls. 45a, 46), or possibly even a wide horn of plenty (Pls. 54, 55, 185)—all of which accompany one deity or another at Khirbet Tannur. It might well also have represented a rudder, not otherwise found there, but frequently associated with Tyché as the goddess of fortune and fate.[667]

The mural crown on the Zodiac-Tyché and on the other Tychés of Khirbet Tannur delineates her role as its guardian goddess. Almost every Hellenistic-Roman town and temple in Syria, Parthia and Palestine, among other areas, was graced by her presence. With her regal headdress of the replica of turreted fortification walls, she is known from such diverse places, to mention some of them, as Petra,[668] Amman,[669] Madeba,[670] and Gerasa[671] in Transjordan; Philoteria (Beth-yerah)[672] in Palestine; Antioch,[673] Hierapolis-Bambyke,[674] Soueïda[675] in Syria; Palmyra,[676] Dura-Europos,[677] and Hatra[678] in Parthia; and from many others, too.[679] Especially closely related are the Tychés of Palmyra and Dura-Europos, with the one from Palmyra being particularly like the Zodiac-Tyché of Tannur insofar as hair style, parted lips and general expression are concerned. Nevertheless there are differences between them. The Tyché of Palmyra is more stylized and expressionless and that of Dura is cruder. All of them bear the stamp both of the East and the West, but more of the former than the latter.

1) HELLENISTIC IMPRINT

It is important to remember that in the Orient there were many places where Hellenistic culture was implanted and took root and long retained much of its native hue. It was strongly furthered even in Parthia by Macedonian Greeks settled there by Alexander the Great in the wake of his conquest of Iran. The process of the settlement in Iran and elsewhere of Greek army veterans and immigrants, which he instituted, was methodically continued by his Seleucidian successors. A certain amount of intermarriage among the city-dwellers naturally contributed to the Hellenizing of the Iranians and by the same token to the Iranization of the Greeks. The intermingling of the Hellenistic and Iranian cultures, stemming from coloniza-

Pl. 179   Winged Niké relief with chignon (p. 445)

Pl. 180   Winged Niké on globe
(p. 431)

a

5 cms

Pl. 181   a, b. Defaced Niké reliefs
(pp. 447, 450)

b

a

b

5 cms

c

d

Pl. 182   a-d. Niké-Tyché reliefs (pp. 410, 445)

a,b

5 cms

c

Pl. 183   Niké heads in relief

a. Right profile (cf. Pl. 184b) (p. 448)
b. Right top broken off (p. 449)
c. With chignon (p. 445)
d. Chignon broken off (p. 445)
e. Same head with part of body (p. 445)

5 cms

d

e

a

b

5 cms

2 cm

c

5 cms

d

Pl. 184   Sculptural fragments

a. Winged (?) Niké without head (p. 399)
b. Winged (?) Niké with head (cf. Pl. 183a) (p. 399)
c. Fragment of top of head (p. 227)
d. Fragment of face of relief (p. 225)

Pl. 185   Winged Niké-Tyché, Petra (p. 410)

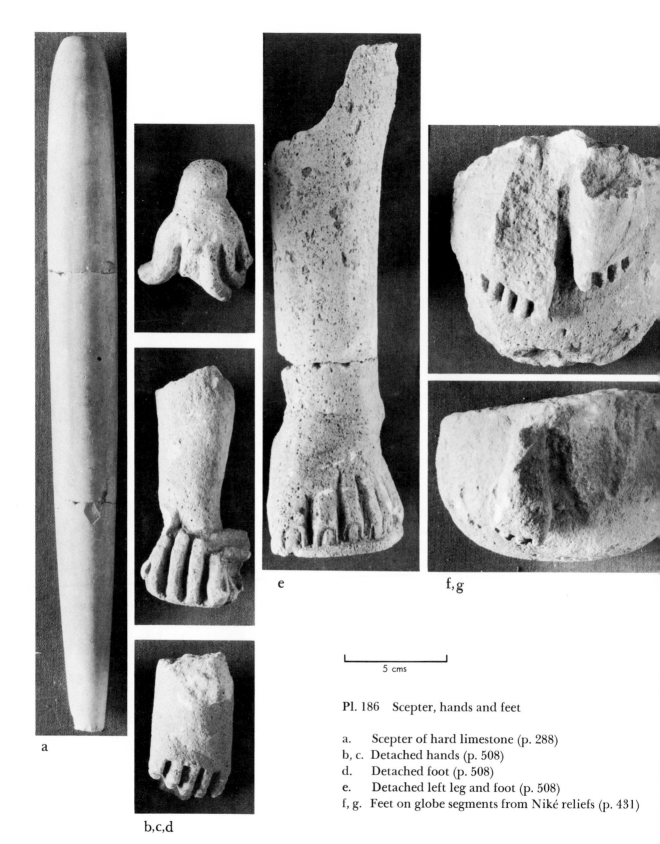

a

b,c,d

e

f,g

5 cms

Pl. 186   Scepter, hands and feet

a.   Scepter of hard limestone (p. 288)
b, c. Detached hands (p. 508)
d.   Detached foot (p. 508)
e.   Detached left leg and foot (p. 508)
f, g. Feet on globe segments from Niké reliefs (p. 431)

tion, couches and commerce, was not and could not have been interdicted by the Parthians, when they in turn pushed out the Seleucids, withstood the Romans and raised up a new kingdom over much of the territory of former Persia. The Greek strain, especially of the urban population, remained naturally and probably unconsciously philo-Hellenic even when the Sassanians succeeded the Parthians.[680] It is noteworthy that the early Parthians called themselves "Philhellenes" on their coins.[681]

Revealing pronounced Western as well as some Eastern characteristics is the Tyché crouched at the feet of the marble statue of Ba'al-shamin from Parthian Hatra,[682] who has a torque around his neck, a bust of a Helios on his breast and a head of a winged Medusa on his back. In this category from there are a splendid copper Medusa mask [683] and stone reliefs [684] of various other gods. Joined with them at Hatra were numerous other deities,[685] including another relief of the sun god.[686] These latter, however, bear the strong imprint of their eastern nativity, tempered in the case of some of them to a lesser degree by the mark of Occidental impact.

Purely Hellenistic is the marble Tyché of Antioch (Pl. 52a),[687] fashioned by Eutychides, a pupil of Lysippus. It dates from the founding of Antioch by Seleucus I Nicator about 300 B.C. This type of sculpture must be considered a predecessor of the Tyché of Hatra, dated in the first century A.D.[688] There was also, for instance, the beautiful Tyché of the Decapolis city of Philadelphia (Amman) (Pl. 51a, b), with her mural crown and classical expressive features, modeled seemingly after those of an attractive woman.[689] The Tyché of another magnificent Decapolis city of Gerasa is comparable. [690] Many of the Parthians and particularly the Nabataean merchants and caravaneers without number undoubtedly were intimately acquainted with the nobly proportioned Hellenistic sculptures of the gods of Ascalon (Pl. 49b) [691] at the end of one of their most important trade routes, leading westward from Petra to the Mediterranean coast.[692]

The contact of the Nabataeans with the forces of Hellenism was vigorous and constant and superficially could appear to have been compelling. The lands bordering the eastern Mediterranean were very familiar to the Nabataeans during the Hellenistic period and especially during the first centuries B.C. and A.D. Alexandria in Egypt, Miletus on the Asia Minor coast, Rhodes and Delos in the eastern Mediterranean and Puteoli in Italy, among other places, served them as regular ports of call.[693] Greek was their second language. As merchants extraordinary, their affairs and interests were cosmopolitan in scope and they could easily have become completely imitative in culture. That, under the pressure of all these circumstances, heightened by the fragility of their political fortunes, they were able to retain and furthermore sharpen their distinctive identity, is little short of a miracle.

The journey between the metropolis of Antioch in Syria and the great

Nabataean capital city of Petra in southern Jordan was regularly undertaken by merchants and other travelers of many nations, including of course the enterprising Nabataeans. Nevertheless, while the distance between the dramatically Hellenistic cities of Gerasa (Jerash) and Philadelphia (Amman) on the one hand and the sacrosanct Nabataean temple of Khirbet Tannur on the other was shorter still, they were, despite all their bonds of connections, worlds apart from each other, especially in sculpture and pottery. The Tychés and other deities of Antioch, Philadelphia, Gerasa, Ascalon and similar cities were recognizably different from those of the Temple of Tannur.

Subjected largely but not completely to the same powerful Oriental and Occidental influences as their immediate neighbors, the Nabataeans, nevertheless, went their own way with regard to the deities they sculptured, the temples they erected and the very script they employed in their separate version of the Aramaic language. They were Semites who were Hellenized to a considerable degree, but their native character was so strong that almost everything they touched was transmuted into something unquestionably Nabataean. Dramatic evidence of this fact is furnished by their exquisite, highly sophisticated and absolutely unique pottery.

2) CORNUCOPIA

The Tyché figure, so prominent among the sculptures of Khirbet Tannur and elsewhere in the Nabataean kingdom, as for example at Petra (Pl. 185), functioned not only as the Guardian Goddess but also as the Goddess of Fortune and Fate. As the Goddess of Fortune, she was often depicted holding a cornucopia, filled to overflowing with fruit. The horn of plenty had long been one of the badges of distinction of Tyché[694] and occurred at Khirbet Tannur frequently in connection with a whole series of smaller, winged Tyché-Nikés (Pl. 182b, d). However, not every figure holding a cornucopia can be identified as a Tyché. Numerous examples can be cited to demonstrate that the male of the species in the form of Zeus or Jupiter or Dionysos-Dusares carried it too, as one who was also a "giver of wealth."[695]

The horn of plenty occurs in striking fashion on two large reliefs at Khirbet Tannur, each of which forms one of the sides of two end cornice stones, with two other reliefs occupying the adjacent sides. We have already referred to a mural crowned Tyché relief with a lyre on one side of one of these end cornice stones (Pl. 53a). On the adjacent side is another, even more defaced sculpture in equally high relief of a deity, holding against its left side what appears to be a horn of plenty, the top of which is broken off (Pl. 53b). The entire head of the sculpture is missing. Still visible are the lower parts of four long curled locks of hair descending over the shoulders, with the very ends of the two inner ones on either side of the neck being comparatively intact. Over a closely fitting tunic is a himation, fastened at the right shoulder and then draped apparently over the left one.

An almost exact duplicate of this figure is repeated on one side of a second end cornice stone, which also bears two reliefs, one on each adjacent side. The main difference is that the horn of plenty, this time intact, is carried against the right shoulder (Pl. 55). Otherwise the two cornucopia-bearing reliefs on these end cornice stones can hardly be distinguished from one another, except to a minor degree. The heads and faces of both reliefs have been so radically destroyed as to make identification from this point of view difficult, if not impossible.

Fortunately, examples of cornucopia-carrying sculptures from Nabataean Syria enable us to arrive at a likely identification of these two particular reliefs, each occupying one of the two sides of the two end cornice stones. At Nabataean Si'a [696] in the Jebel Druze, there is an intact bearded Dusares relief with a cornucopia against his left side and shoulder, paralleling the position of the cornucopia on the left shoulder of one of the defaced cornice reliefs at Khirbet Tannur (Pl. 53b). There are striking similarities between the two reliefs, including the shape of the stem of the cornucopia and the lines of the folds of the chiton, over which in each instance there is a himation, whose end is draped over the left shoulder. The Khirbet Tannur cornice relief could easily have had a bearded face similar to the one of the Nabataean Dusares from Si'a and have represented the same deity.

Another intact relief from Si'a, now located in the museum at Soueïda, also in the Nabataean Jebel Druze, obviously depicts a Tyché or an Allat and has a cornucopia against her right side and shoulder.[697] The broken lintels, from which the Dusares and Tyché-Allat reliefs with their cornucopias extended, were obviously originally of one piece. The heads of the two deities, located at either end of this lintel, were slightly turned towards each other. We believe that the two Khirbet Tannur reliefs with their cornucopias are the counterparts of the two from Nabataean Si'a and Soueïda. The one bearing the cornucopia against the right shoulder is to be identified with Tyché and the other with the cornucopia against the left shoulder must represent Dionysos-Dusares.

Each end-cornice stone has a male and female figure on its two sides. The one bears on one side a relief of a mural-crowned Tyché with a lyre on her left shoulder (Pl. 53a) and on the adjacent side originally a male figure of Dionysos-Dusares with a cornucopia against his left shoulder (Pl. 53b). The other cornice stone has a Tyché on one side with a cornucopia against her right shoulder (Pl. 55) and on the other side what seems to be a relief of a Zeus-Hadad-Jupiter with a stylized thunderbolt over his left shoulder (Pl. 56). There come to mind the two defaced Tychés (?) at either end of the lintel of the entablature of the ed-Deir monument at Petra, with a cornucopia against and over the right shoulder of one and the left shoulder of the other.[697a] (Pl. 54)

c. The Focus of Attention

The bas-relief of the Zodiac-Tyché, with her mural crown and probably astral symbol over her left shoulder, rises from a nearly circular sunken panel, which is surrounded by a raised zodiacal band. The twelve signs of the zodiac, divided into counterclockwise and clockwise halves, rise from slightly depressed frames, separated from one another by raised grooved bars. One or two raised dots on the sides of some of the small reliefs of the zodiacal signs accentuate their presence and probably were to be found originally in each separate frame. It seems most likely that these dots, which in every instance may have been present in pairs, signify, respectively, the evening star and the morning star.[698]

This zodiacal circle or oval, signifying the celestial sphere, rested on the upraised hands of a winged Niké, who performed an Atlas-like function. We shall return to a fuller discussion of her later on. Suffice it to say at this juncture that the back of her head, which is slightly tilted to the left, rests against the bottom of the zodiac, between the original frames containing Virgo and Pisces. All of the sculpture, with the Tyché gazing through her zodiacal show window, was carved originally out of a single block of limestone and set into the face of a wall of the temple. The Virgo figure is badly damaged and the Pisces division completely missing in the upper part of the relief found by us.

The entire stele with its central Tyché, zodiacal circle and supporting Niké, testifies to the nature of the Nabataean civilization, born of the marriage of many antipodal elements. The faces and forms of planetary and astral deities employed in this zodiacal composition are much alike in their stiffness, sameness and comparatively crude execution, but they reflect nevertheless a feeling of maturity and independent sturdiness. Subject to their will were the seasons of the year and its divisions into months. We shall see that there were seven special planetary deities to whom the Nabataeans were above all attached. In addition to their Semitic names these deities may possibly have been known to the Nabataeans by the equivalents of the familiar Sol, Luna, Mars, Mercury, Jupiter, Venus and Saturn,[698] so clearly reflected in the names of the days of the week.

The role of the Zodiac-Tyché, whose functions were inseparable, as we have seen, from those of Atargatis, was that of *prima inter pares* among the select company of the seven planets, to which were subject the phenomena of the universe, the fate of the quick and the dead in their sojourn on earth and their peregrinations beyond its boundaries.[699] Sometimes, to be sure, for various purposes and in different places, Tyché yielded the center of the stage to one of her divine companions, about whom then the zodiacal figures would revolve.[700] Zeus himself often displaces Tyché in the center of the zodiacal circle (Pl. 49a).[701] In another instance a horned goat-footed flute-playing Pan occupies the middle of the circular zodiacal stage.[702] There is a whole series of second-century A.D. coins from Asia Minor, featuring Zeus in this pivotal position, around which the signs of the zodiac revolve.[703] In one instance, in the Temple of Bel at Palmyra, the seven planets in the form of busts in relief occupy the circle around which the figures of the zodiac revolve.[704]

d. Arrangement Without Parallel

The story of the zodiac and of astrological determinations based upon it encompasses the length of many centuries and the breadth of many lands. Originating in Babylonia, it spread with growing refinement and increasing popularity to Egypt and Greece and Rome and their dependencies. By the beginning of the Christian era, the use of the zodiacal calendar was practically ubiquitous in the cultural worlds of the Orient and the Occident and remained so during the Byzantine period.[705] There was hardly a church or a synagogue of that period that did not possess a mosaic floor ornamented with the signs of the zodiac and of the seasons. The far reaching influence of Mithraism, whose beliefs and rituals were based upon observations of the stars, further intensified the importance of the zodiac in the minds and lives of millions of many faiths during the early centuries A.D.[706] Illustrative of this is a second- or third-century A.D. counterclockwise zodiacal circle from the London Mithraeum, enclosing a central panel in which Mithras is featured as the Bull Slayer (Pl. 50) [706a]

It is therefore natural that the zodiac should have occupied a central position in the religious life of the Nabataeans. They were well acquainted with its significance, if only from their intimate contact with the great centers of Syria and Parthia, where it seems to have been featured in every sanctuary.[707] The unusual character of the zodiac at Khirbet Tannur, therefore, makes it all the more intriguing and significant because thus far I have not been able to find any exact parallel to it.

The normal sequence of the zodiacal signs is to commence with number one and in progressive and undisturbed order conclude with number twelve. That can be done from either end of a sometimes divisible straight or curved line,[708] or by starting at any given point on a circle or oval and then, proceeding either from the right, that is, clockwise, or from the left, that is, counterclockwise, and making a complete and uninterrupted revolution back to the point of departure.[709]

In the zodiac of Khirbet Tannur, however, neither of these normal possibilities is completely followed, but rather both of them in part. Starting from the top left center of the zodiac, immediately above the right side of the top of the head of the turret-crowned Tyché, the sequence of the signs of the zodiac is counterclockwise and goes as follows: (1) Aries, (2) Taurus, (3) Gemini, (4) Cancer, (5) Leo and (6) the top of the head and left shoulder of a figure, undoubtedly that of Virgo, with a damaged spica (spike) of grain above that shoulder.

In the normal sequence of the signs of the zodiac, the seventh one, namely, the Scales, known as Libra, should then have occurred, followed in turn by the eighth one, the Scorpion or Scorpio, and so on till the twelfth. Continuing counterclockwise, however, from Virgo, the next one met with is the broken but unmistakable figure of Aquarius, which is the eleventh in the customary lineup of the zodiacal signs. The previous missing twelfth one, Pisces, was later on recovered, together with the missing sections of the Virgo and Aquarius divisions, in the bottom segment of the zodiac retained in the hands of the supporting Niké.

It quickly became apparent that something was radically different in this particular zodiac as compared to all others. Indeed, it was literally a revolutionary zodiac, with the ordinary sequence turned upside down. A glance revealed that its seventh sign, Libra, which, in the continuation of the counterclockwise order, should have been at the bottom of the zodiac, was instead at the very top, adjacent to the first one, Aries.

Libra, thus, commenced a new, this time clockwise, progression of its own, around the left side of the zodiacal circle. In a word, we were confronted with a zodiac of two diametrically opposite and completely separate halves. The counterclockwise half included numbers 1 to 6 and the clockwise one included numbers 7 to 12. This was something definitely new under the zodiacal heavens. It was also obvious that the twelfth sign, which was broken off altogether, and which should have followed that of Aquarius near the bottom of the clockwise half, could be none other than the one of the fishes, namely, Pisces. The next sign immediately adjacent to Pisces in this dual arrangement of two opposite halves should have been number 6, namely, that of Virgo, but obviously something had intervened to separate the two.

The presence of the extraordinary zodiac at Khirbet Tannur would not seem to be the result of happenstance, but must be connected somehow with the uncommon importance of the sanctuary itself. It must have been felt that the main members of the Nabataean pantheon, identified with the seven, major planets, delighted to visit the Temple of Tannur on signal occasions, when the twelve zodiacal constellations had assumed their most benign positions. It was at such times, we think, that all those who could escape the confinement and pressures of their daily concerns would forsake temporarily the familiar altars of their own home-town temples to make pilgrimages to this isolated highplace of regional distinction and ancient holiness. They would bring with them offerings of devotion and desire in order to break the bread and drink the wine and thus share the food of communion with their deities, whom they thought to be more sharply attuned then than normally to the needs and fears and dreams of their supplicants.

The general significance of the two contrary halves of the Khirbet Tannur zodiac seems to denote the existence and invite the celebration of two New Years, one in the spring and another in the fall.[710] These high holy days may have been invested there with profounder meaning than elsewhere, because it was a place particularly favored by the gods themselves. In all events, this zodiac served as a powerful reminder of the need for periodic religious reorientation. It may have underscored the advisability of seasonal withdrawal from everyday pursuits for purposes of wholly undistracted and uninhibited communion with the company of the gods, who seemed to be more approachable and more amenable at certain times and places than otherwise.

2. THE SIGNS OF THE ZODIAC

a. Aries

The importance and attractiveness of the central Tyché panel of the Khirbet Tannur zodiac tend to overshadow and even obscure the individuality and charm of the separate divisions in their counterclockwise and clockwise order. Three of the symbols of this zodiac, namely, Aries (1), Sagittarius (9) and Capricornus (10) differ considerably from the forms in which they are usually portrayed, respectively, as a ram, a four or two-legged centaur with drawn bow and arrow, and a goat with fish's tail.[711] Instead, they are rendered with bas-reliefs in human likeness.

Aries was depicted as an Athena-Minerva figure.[712] An enlargement of a photograph of her relief in the zodiacal band reveals that the sculptor took considerable pains with her, as, indeed, he did with every single symbol of the twelve constellations. Her head is placed between two raised circular dots of the kind that are or probably orginally were present in every one of the other divisions of the zodiacal circle. It has been suggested that they stand for the evening and morning stars, or even of the sun and the moon, with comparable significance being invested in the single dots.[713]

Some damage has been done to part of the raised double-grooved border framing her panel. Each of the other symbols was similarly enclosed, with the exception of the two bottom ones of Pisces and Virgo. We shall see that they were bordered only on three sides by this raised grooved line and on the other by the head of the Niké resting against the bottom face of the upper part of the stele containing the zodiacal circle.

There can still be made out, above the left shoulder of Athena-Minerva, the line of the slightly raised lance or sword, with which she was armed, reaching up behind the side of her head to the top of the panel. Above the wavy hair of her head there may once have been a diadem. Her long full face, with rounded cheeks and pointed chin has suffered slight damage, but its character is clear and its impression firm and sharp. Her patrician head and neck place her very much in the noble tradition of the queenly bust of the Tyché below her in the circular central panel. She is clothed with a chiton, overlaid with a himation.

The spring festival was known of old to the Nabataeans in their Bedouin days. It inaugurated the season when the lambs were born and the grazing was good and the earth was green with the seasonal rains. Its importance was not lessened but rather heightened for them later on in their more sophisticated development, when, in addition to rearing flocks, they learned to till the soil more successfully than any of their predecessors. Symbolic of this familiar New Year in the spring was the ram of Aries, whose form appeared in the first frame of the usual zodiac. The Nabataeans substituted in its stead in their zodiac the bust of Athena-Minerva, with her lance.[714] She was generally recognized as the goddess of rainclouds and lightning and the patroness of spring,[715] who occasionally was depicted together with or seated on a ram.[716]

The motivating reason, in all probability, was that they had come to see in Athena-Minerva their own Allat, the consort of their beloved god, Dushara, or Dusares. His native habitat was the Jebel Shara in the southern hills of the land of Edom, which became the center of their kingdom and the seat of their capital city, Petra, known in Biblical times as Sela, the Rock.[717] After they had seized and settled the comparatively rich farm lands of the Edomites and Moabites and learned with amazing skill to exploit them, as well as the marginal lands they occupied elsewhere, it became natural for the Nabataeans to adopt also the harvest festival and autumnal New Year of the agricultural economy of their predecessors, whom they partly displaced and partly absorbed.

It was during this process that they identified not only Allat with Athena-Minerva and occasionally with Tyché-Atargatis, but at the same time merged their Semitic Dushara (Dusares) with the Greek Dionysos.[718] The change was marked by their transition from a people with profound religious prepossessions against the use of wine, coupled with an antipathy to dwelling in stone houses, to a nation that made viticulture one of its foremost preoccupations. The grapevine and its leaves and fruit became a primary motif of their artistic endeavors (Pl. 30a, b). The zenith of their transformation occurred when the drink of their preference became wine instead of water. The ecstasy it often induced when freely imbibed, especially at religious ceremonies, afforded them an otherwise unobtainable intimacy and even identification with their gods and the assurance of their limitless survival and well-being beyond the bounds of mortality.[719]

b. Sagittarius

The familiar centaur of Sagittarius (9), with a drawn bow and arrow, gives way in our zodiac panel to the bust of a young man with round face, somewhat damaged lips and rather jovial expression. His hair, which is parted in the middle and twisted into separate, curled locks ending in a point, like those of Saturn, for instance (Pl. 153a), reaches down along the sides of his face. Over a tight-fitting tunic he wears a chlamys. It is fastened at the right shoulder by a faintly indicated brooch, with the opposite end draped over the left shoulder in a manner reminiscent of several Helios and Mercury busts of Khirbet Tannur (Pls. 136, 137b, 139). Jutting above the top of his left arm, and surpassing in height the entire length of the bust proper, is a spear or a greatly enlarged arrow with sharp point and pronounced barbs. The arrowhead rests in part on the inner beveled side of the raised, originally grooved, outer section of the panel border. The skill and originality of the craftsman is clearly evident in this sculpture, too. In general appearance, this bust with the spear or long arrow above its left side, resembles that of Minerva with her spear held against her right side.[720]

c. Capricornus

In the instance of Capricornus (10), the customary fish-goat has been displaced by a carefully coiffured bust in relief, appearing at first glance to be feminine. It has withstood the passage of the years quite well, with the exception of the loss of the thick upper lip. On the left side of the head is one of the tiny raised solid circles, similar to the two that appear in the firmament on either side of the head of the Athena-Minerva-Allat-Aries bust. The face may be a dulled replica in miniature of that of the central Tyché; and the garb, much of which has been worn away, could possibly duplicate her chiton and overlapping himation. The hair is combed into pronounced locks, two of which reach down to the middle of the cheeks. Two others rise like horns above the head, with perhaps a central one missing.[721] If this small bust is indeed a feminine one, it may picture one of the Nereids of the Capricornus constellation.[722]

It is, however, not at all certain that this is a female bust. The beardless countenances and bulging breasts of some of the gods of Khirbet Tannur can hardly be distinguished from those of its goddesses. It is often only through such elements as a caduceus over one of the shoulders of a god (Pls. 152a, b, c, 153b), side locks on the cheeks (Pls. 147, 148, 149a, b), the arrangement of hair on the head and neck (Pl. 131a, b), or the use of a chlamys, worn at Khirbet Tannur chiefly by males, that a distinction can be made or reasonably attempted.

I am inclined to think that this particular bust was meant to be a Pan figure, with the two top outturned locks of hair intended perhaps to convey

Pl. 187a   Alexandros Amrou Altar, with Zeus-Hadad on front panel (p. 125)

Pl. 187b Incense basin on top, Zeus-Hadad front panel and winged
Niké relief on right side panel of Alexandros Amrou Altar (p. 125)

a

Pl. 188

a, b. Winged Niké reliefs on left and right side panels of Alexandros Amrou
    Altar (p. 125)

a

b

Pl. 189

a, b. Round altar with damaged winged
       Niké reliefs (p. 447)

a

b

5 cms

5 cms

c

5 cms

Pl. 190

a, b, c. Damaged Niké reliefs (p. 509)

422

Pl. 191   Altar fragments and mold

a. Part of a thymiaterion (?) (p. 229)
b. Part of a thymiaterion (?) (cf. p. 229)
c. Fragment of a rounded altar (p. 509)
d. Stone mold (p. 227)

a

5 cms

b

5 cms

5 cms

c

d

5 cms

5 cms

Pl. 192　Incense altars

a. Gabled (p. 511)
b. Horned (p. 510)
c. Small altar with deep basin (p. 510)

b

c

5 cms

5 cms

a, b

5 cms

d

e

Pl. 193   Incense altars

a. Four-legged base of small altar (p. 511)

b. Small incense altar (p. 511)

c. Tiny incense altar with crisscross decorations
    (p 511)

d. Incense altars, Petra (p. 511)

e. Tiny incense altars, Tell el-Kheleifeh
    (Ezion-geber:Elath) (p. 511)

5 cm

425

the impression of horns, with which he is so frequently adorned.[723] Such a figure would indeed most appropriately serve as a stand-in for the fish-goat of Capricornus. Legend has it that Pan once changed himself into a goat, whereupon the gods named him Aigipan and transplanted him to the stars.[724] The possibility of the correctness of this suggestion is heightened by the existence of a number of counterclockwise zodiacs, which enclose a central panel featuring the figure of a horned Pan with goat's legs.[725]

d. *Taurus, Leo, Gemini, Cancer, Libra, Scorpio*

The remaining symbols of the Khirbet Tannur zodiac conform generally to the pattern of others elsewhere, but they are enlivened by touches of original artistry. Thus, Taurus, the Bull (2) and Leo, the Lion (5) are carefully positioned in artistic counterpoint, the one facing the inside of the zodiac circle and the other turned to the outer rim. The bellies of both animals are grooved to show the folds in the skin. Several of their limbs can be made out only with difficulty, but their recumbent positions are excellently portrayed, with the head of the bull facing front and that of the lion shown in profile. The tail of the former touches the lower end of the raised, outer border of the panel in which it is enclosed, while the tail of the latter rests against the edge of the raised, bottom border and over the end of the crossbar separating its panel from that of Virgo, the Virgin (6), immediately below. In the field above the body of Leo, the Lion, whose erect ears touch the top of its cage or frame, is a single, raised dot of a star or a sun.

Such a star shines also in the center of the sky above the two bodies of the Gemini, the Twins (3). Only the twin on the left side is intact, with his features being something like those of Sagittarius (9). Over his curled locks, that seem originally to have reached down to his shoulders, is a helmet or hood. The head of the twin on the outer side has been completely broken off. The bodies of both seem to have been left bare, which is not uncommon in their representation. It is a moot question as to whether or not they represent Castor and Pollux, two of the brightest stars of the constellation of the Gemini, or two legendary heroes such as Heracles (Hercules) and Apollo, or possibly still others.

Another apparently bare bodied male figure is the one with the scale over his right shoulder, belonging to Libra, the Balance or Scale (7), representing a southern zodiacal constellation between Virgo and Scorpio. Actually, there are traces of a chlamys on his upper right arm and shoulders. It is comparable to that on the bust of Sagittarius (9), armed with an arrow or spear, whose hair-dress is similar. The nose of Libra seems particularly large because of the breaking away of most of the thick lips under it. Most of the raised border line between Libra and Scorpio, as well as the border enclosing the top of both of their panels has been destroyed.

Even Cancer, the Crab (4), is rendered with a flair in this zodiac. Two of the legs on its right side are broken off altogether, but the head is intact, and its two protruding eyes, separated by a prominent, pointed nose, stare at a partly destroyed world. Scorpio, the Scorpion (8), on the other side of the circle, has fared even worse so far as its head is concerned, having a hole in it, but better so far as its limbs are concerned. Two of them on its right side have been damaged, but otherwise Scorpio seems to be clambering right out of its sunken cell.

e. Virgo

We have already remarked that in the main section of the zodiac stele recovered in the excavations, the remaining part of Virgo, the Virgin (6), consists of the top of her head and the top of her left shoulder, above which the stalk of an ear of wheat extends, in consonance with her familiar appearance.[726]

Of much interest are the two projections that can clearly be seen at the top of her head. The possibility that they may be ribboned topknots such as occur on one of the Khirbet Tannur Medusas must be considered and will be adverted to again. It seems doubtful that they could have been meant to represent the kind of ribbons belonging to fillets or diadems, sometimes encountered on Nabataean and Parthian sculptures, and worn usually, although not exclusively, by male figures.[727] Nor does it seem likely that Virgo would be decked out with the plumed helmet worn on occasion by Minerva.[728]

Virgo was thought of primarily as the creative mother-goddess,[729] with one or more stalks of wheat as her chief attribute, being in effect often equated with Atargatis-Astarte.[730] She is identified as such on the famous stele featuring Mithras slaying the bull, found at Heddernheim, Germany.[731] It has been suggested that the Babylonian version of her name and of that of the star, Spica, can be translated as "furrow." Be that as it may, there seems to be no question that the name "Spica," which means "ear of grain," is of Babylonian origin.[732] Virgo, thus, in history and by attribute, is a fertility goddess.

One wonders whether the two projections on top of her head could possibly stand for a sea-connected fertility symbol, namely, that of crab's claws. We have seen that such claws protrude from the heads of the fertility gods of Aquileia, Leptis Magna and Lixus and may well originally have been present on the head of the god of Puteoli, only to be replaced by its present horns of obviously secondary origin.

A goddess, often pictured with crab's claws on her head, is Thalassa. We have previously referred to a striking representation of her on a first-century A.D. mosaic floor of a triclinium at Yakto near Antioch on the Orontes in Syria. She holds a rudder in her right hand, a dolphin in her left and has crab's claws sprouting from the top of her head.[733] A headdress of crab's claws is her familiar ornamentation on numerous Asia Minor and other coins of the second and third centuries A.D.[734] A personified representation of Hellenistic-Roman Alexandria as a goddess reveals the same embellishment.[735]

The importance of the symbol of crab's claws is highlighted, for instance, by their presence on the chest of a statuette of an Ephesian Artemis, whose popularity in the East spread in classical antiquity to the outer edges of the known West.[736] In related fashion, there can be seen on a sixth-century A.D. Byzantine church mosiac at Qasr el-Lebia (ancient Olbia), near Cyrene in Libya, a picture of a merman, with crab's claws protruding from his abdomen. He is portrayed also as shouldering a rudder and spearing a fish with a trident, and manifestly reflects a flashback to a pagan Poseidon.[737]

There is undoubtedly also a clear relationship between the symbol of the crab's claws and the astral sign of the crab (Cancer) in the zodiacal circle. This relationship pervaded Nabataean, Parthian, Hellenistic and Roman art and its earlier predecessors. I am convinced that the absence of a sculpture of a deity with crab's claws at Khirbet Tannur does not mean that such a sculpture never existed there. In all probability, it was destroyed in the earthquake that brought the history of this Nabataean temple to an end, and it seems likely that excavations at other Nabataean sites will sooner or later come across such a sculpture.

It is intriguing to consider identifying Virgo with Thalassa and equate her with the Tyché-Atargatis, who is featured in the panel enclosed by the zodiac of which Virgo is an integral part. Through her stalk of wheat Virgo also reflects the nature of the Wheat or Grain Goddess of Khirbet Tannur (Pl. 25). Had Virgo's face not been obliterated in this zodiac, it would undoubtedly have been essentially the same as that of the zodiac's central Tyché-Atargatis and of the other goddesses of this temple.

It needs to be repeated in this connection that all the various goddesses of Khirbet Tannur seem to be different representations of one and the same goddess, namely, Atargatis, or whatever her native designation there may have been. Particular qualities of her composite nature were represented by a series of separate sculptures. Basically, however, they all indicate facets of a single deity, whether they appear in public with headgears of turreted walls, dolphins or crabs in heraldic juxtaposition, ears of grain or with veils of leaves.

In spite of all these considerations, however, it must be emphasized that the two projections on the top of the head of Virgo in the Khirbet Tannur zodiac may not be crab's claws at all. We suggest that they represent rather a type of coiffure of voluted topknots such as appear on a sculpture of a Syrian Venus.[738] They could also be ribboned topknots such as seem to appear on the head of the comparatively intact relief of the Niké on the right side of the Alexandros Amrou altar (Pls. 187b, 188a), and such as incontestably appear on top of the head of one of the two Medusas of Khirbet Tannur (Pl. 38a).[739]

f. Aquarius

It is evident from the total picture of the Khirbet Tannur zodiac, made possible by putting together its two broken parts, which will be discussed in more detail below, that Aquarius is shown with his upraised left hand, holding his bucket of water upside down above the left side of his head. The top part of the panel showing his head and the overturned bucket with the lines of water pouring out of it are contained in the remaining part of the Aquarius frame at the left end of the main zodiac section encircling the Tyché. His face is partly worn away, but can rather clearly be made out, with his curled locks descending along the sides of his head. His features conform to those of the others in the zodiac and in general at Khirbet Tannur, and may be likened in particular, for example, to those of a young Mercury (?) head from Khirbet Tannur (Pl. 147).

The bottom part of his bust, which was contained in the lower section of the zodiac recovered later on, together with the supporting Niké, is much more worn than the upper part, but is still sufficiently intact to be discernible, although the top fragment of it is missing. It shows the frontally positioned body and the left arm bent outward and upward from the elbow to raise on high and hold on to the overturned water bucket.

g. Pisces

Careful examination shows that the twelfth sign of Pisces, the two fishes, is the best preserved of our restored zodiacal circle. Their bodies stand out clearly in the sunken panel, which is bordered on one side by the head of Niké and on the other three sides by a raised, narrow border, part of which is still faintly grooved. Lying on their sides in parallel position, with their backs near the edges of the enclosing frame, the tails of the fishes point toward the raised crossbar that separates their panel from that of the sign of Aquarius (11) above it. The workmanship on the tiny figures of this constellation is excellent. The fins on the back of the lower one, and those barely suggested on the top of the upper one, and the raised sliver of stone connecting the undersides of both of them can easily be made out. Their deep set eyes reflect the shape and manner of execution of the orbs of the Tyché goddess in the central circular panel.

Indeed, insofar as the shapes of their bodies, the forms of their eyes and especially the line of the mouth of the upper one of them are concerned, there is little to distinguish these two fishes from the two dolphins located on the top of the head of the Dolphin Goddess in a heraldic design (Pl. 1). The certainty, however, that she was crowned with dolphins and not fishes is underscored by her relationship to the Dolphin Goddess of Aphrodisias.

This is further borne out by the closely connected gods of Aquileia, Puteoli, Ostia, Leptis Magna and Lixus. Apollo, too, as we have seen, was worshiped in dolphin form at the Delphinium of Miletus, particularly at the beginning of spring, when sea traffic was resumed after the cessation of the winter storms.[740]

The similarity between the dolphins and fishes at Khirbet Tannur raised the question, however, as to whether the sculptor had fishes or dolphins in mind for the twelfth panel of the zodiac of Khirbet Tannur, even though the name of the constellation of Pisces calls obviously for the former rather than the latter. The answer may well be that it must often have been difficult there and elsewhere in the Hellenistic-Semitic cultural world to separate Atargatis as the Dolphin Goddess from Atargatis as the Fish Goddess. The salient features and functions of both must frequently have merged in the public mind, however different from one another they were in reality.

As the Dea Syria, the Fish Goddess was widely known and happily worshiped from the shores of the Mediterranean to the banks of the Euphrates. At places as far apart as Ascalon on the southwestern coast of Palestine and Heliopolis-Baalbek and Hierapolis-Bambyke in Syria,[741] to mention only a few, temples were erected to house her effigies, and pools of water were prepared for her sacred fish. There is reason to believe, as we have previously remarked, that a small sacred pond existed at Khirbet Tannur.[742] Her names were many, among them being Atargatis, Derketo, Aphrodite and Venus, but they all referred to the same fertility goddess, whose popularity was immense and whose supremacy in the pantheon of Hellentistic-Semitic gods was undisputed.[743] As the Dolphin Goddess her appearances were no less widespread, extending from desert stations to sea-washed lands and islands.

At Khirbet Tannur the dolphins on one hand and the fishes of the zodiac on the other were obviously different in origin and aim, but indistinguishable in appearance and perhaps interchangeable in public adoration and and affectionate regard. At Abda, for instance, as we have seen,[744] in the middle of the semidesert of the Negev in southern Israel, a dolphin appears on one side of a small Nabataean altar, and a mask of a deity on the adjacent side. There too a piece of sigillata ware was found, with a raised decoration of a tiny, but excellently defined dolphin. I have also picked up on the surface there another fragment of Arretine ware, on which in low relief was the bottom half of a fish with a pronounced double-fluked tail.

3. NIKÉ CARYATID

The missing bottom part of the circular zodiac of Khirbet Tannur turned up, wonderful to relate, in Amman. It had been among the sculptures removed from Khirbet Tannur before we began to excavate the site. One of the finest of them, made available through the good offices of Abdullah Rihani Bey of the Arab Legion, was the bust in high relief of Atargatis as the Dolphin Goddess. Not till much later did the rest of them come to the attention of Sir G. Lankester Harding, formerly Director of the Government Department of Antiquities of the Hashemite Kingdom of Jordan, who had photographs made and most graciously sent copies to me. He had participated actively in our excavations on several visits as the then Chief Curator of Antiquities in Transjordan.

All of the photographs he sent me were important but one of them was especially intriguing. It showed a somewhat damaged sculpture in high relief of a strongly winged Niké wearing a high-girdled peplos with diaphanous skirt. Her arms, stretched out horizontally from the shoulders and then bent upwards from the elbows, held up behind and above her head what was obviously the broken section of the bottom of a circular zodiac. The braceleted left arm of the Niké was completely intact except for some damage to the palm of the inward turned hand. Her right arm, to be sure, was almost entirely broken off, with just enough remaining, however, to show that its position paralleled that of its mate. Her feet are missing, and probably rested originally on a globe or discoid base (Pls. 47, 180, 186f, g).

After the first swift glance, my attention was riveted on the fragment of the bottom, outward-curved segment of the zodiac being carried on high by this poised female version of Atlas. Unlike him, she seemed as pleased as she could be with her burden. It was immediately clear that the section of the zodiac being held aloft by the Niké had originally been a part of the damaged circular zodiac we had previously excavated and the bottom of which was missing. There was no question that the two pieces would fit together to make a complete and significant whole.

I had photographs of both blown up to the same size and placed in proper juxtaposition to create an almost complete reunion (Pl. 48). They belonged together like members of a long separated family. The scar of the break which separated them still remains in the photographic restoration. The two sections have not, however, been brought together physically. The larger section of the zodiac, enclosing the Tyché panel is in the Cincinnati Art Museum and the bottom piece which the Niké is lifting up in her raised hands is in private possession in Amman, Jordan.

It has previously been pointed out that the top of the head and left shoulder of Virgo (6), together with most of the stalk of wheat above her left side, were all that remained of the sixth division of the counterclockwise half of the nearly complete zodiac. Furthermore, we had noted that immediately above the broken bottom of the clockwise half, there appeared the entire head and part of the neck and upper shoulders of Aquarius (11), with his bucket of water depicted upside down above his left side, and the water pouring from it. And lastly, we had posited the existence of the sign of Pisces, the Fishes (12), below that of Aquarius, and of something occupying the space between Pisces at the end of the clockwise order and Virgo at the end of the counterclockwise one. The discovery of the Pisces sign merely corroborates thus an obvious conclusion. The presence of the back of the head of the Niké between the Pisces and Virgo signs was, however, completely unexpected and all the more welcome. In the reassembled zodiac it is seen that Virgo holds her stalk of wheat in her left hand and that the upside down bucket of Aquarius is held aloft by his raised left arm, paralleling the position of the left arm of the supporting Niké.

The uniting of the nearly complete zodiac with its missing Niké-borne bottom segment, resulted in the imperfect completion of the Virgo and Aquarius panels. Their long missing parts had suffered physically and the figures had lost most of the details of their attire. Enough remained, however, to make it clear that their busts had been frontally presented, as in the case of the other likenesses of human figures in this zodiac. In contrast to this arrangement are, for instance, the full length, diagonally placed figures in the arched, clockwise zodiac above the niche of the Heddernheim relief of Mithras slaying the bull.[745]

The Niké Caryatid has lost her feet and the globe or discoid base they must have rested on. Furthermore, almost every vestige of her right arm and the outer part of her right wing above it have disappeared. Gone, too, are the very top of her head and the tip of her nose. In addition, her chin and the palm and fingers of her left hand have suffered some damage. Her patterned hair, like that of her mistress above her, is parted in the middle and, combed on either side of her typically low forehead, reaches down in carefully twisted locks along the sides of her head.

Her head is disproportionately large. It is about one and a half times as big as the mural crowned one of her queen. This is quite in the tradition of the head measurements of Zeus-Hadad, which, although life size, is set on a disproportionately small three-quarter length body.[746] The head of the Niké is turned slightly to her left side, in a manner rather unusual at Khirbet Tannur, but which is repeated in the opposite direction in the instance of a much-damaged Tyché, with a rudder (?) in her left hand (Pl. 45b). Her features are coarser in a subtle way than those of her mistress, who gazes so fixedly from her circular zodiacal window. Basically, however, both of them share almost exactly the same cast of countenance, which is a characteristic common to all the other deities of the site.

Her high girdled, apparently windblown peplos, fastened at each shoulder by a brooch in the form of a multipetalled rosette, was of a strictly conventional type, worn by almost every well-turned-out goddess, regardless of class distinction. In its Nabataeanized or Orientalized form, her garment was neither especially chic nor becoming. Despite its diaphanous skirt, through which the legs can be glimpsed, it added little or nothing to her allure. Nor was it supposed to! It was a garb that neither beautified nor accentuated her desirability. It served rather merely to clothe her nakedness and indeed negate its importance by means of its patterned uniformity and stiffened folds.[747] It helped proclaim with Semitic insistence that exalted authority rather than the glorified image of the deity was of paramount importance for the mortal worshipper, who sought communion and identification with the gods.

There is little fundamental difference, as we have seen, in the faces and forms of many of the deities of Khirbet Tannur, and sometimes it is difficult to distinguish their sexes. They all exude an earthy quality of resolute strength, that would seem to correspond to the character of the people who made them. The Niké of the zodiac stele mirrored no lithe and fashionable city dweller, accustomed to the comparative ease of urban living, nor yet a lean and restless daughter of the desert, always ready to strike her tent and pitch it again elsewhere far off. She was a peasant, rooted in the soil, whose hands had been roughened and body thickened by arduous toil and endless tasks. Her gaze was direct. She was sturdy, unafraid and impassive. Her outlook on life was uncomplicated, her faith in the gods of fertility unwavering. These Nabataean women and Nabataean divinities understood and appreciated each other and were profoundly secure in their essential sameness.

There is a startlingly close parallel to this sculpture of a Tyché in the center of a zodiac, supported by the uplifted arms and hands of the Niké Caryatid of Khirbet Tannur. It consists of a Roman relief of an enthroned Jupiter of the Zeus Marnos type[748] in the center of a zodiac, which rests on the upraised arms and hands and on the back of the shoulders of an Atlas (Pl. 49a). The back of the head of the Atlas occupies the same relative position between the two halves of the Roman zodiac as does that of the Niké Caryatid at the bottom of the Khirbet Tannur zodiac. While marked differences between the two sculptures are apparent in excellence of execution, in the order of rotation of the signs of the zodiac (that of the Roman one being completely counterclockwise), in the presence of an eagle perched on top of the latter and its absence in the former, and naturally in the substitution of Jupiter and Atlas for Tyché and her supporting Niké, the general plan of the two sculptures is so much alike, that one must assume a very close relationship between them in time and contact and ideology.

Both of them belong to the same period. We have dated the Khirbet Tannur ensemble to the first quarter of the second century A.D. and the Roman equivalent has been assigned to the second century A.D. The close contact between the Nabataeans and Romans, between Petra and Puteoli has already been pointed out. Everything we have learned about the Nabataeans points to their complete involvement with the deities personifying the seven planets and the twelve signs of the zodiac. Through these heavenly bodies, the gods governed the universe and everything therein, including the lives and fortunes of all human beings in this life and in the continuation of personal existence beyond the conclusion of mortal being.

Nothing could more dramatically epitomize the involvement of the Nabataeans with their entire cultural world, embracing in one way or another most of the Orient and the Occident, than these two sculptures featuring zodiacs from Khirbet Tannur and Rome. Related to both of them is a fine Hellenistic relief from Ascalon of classical style showing an Atlas supporting a sphere on which stands an elegant winged Tyché (Pl. 49b). The dominating concern with the heavenly bodies and their everlasting effect upon human destiny, preceded the period of the Nabataeans by many centuries and continued to affect the religious life of myriads long thereafter. The zodiac was a central feature of almost every Byzantine church and synagogue. Our own involvement with the starry belt called the Zodiac by the Greeks [749] is reflected every time we thank "our lucky stars."

a. Bracelets

The winged Niké with head tilted to the left, upholding, like a peasant Caryatid, the zodiacal sphere with its central Tyché panel, wears a striking ornament on her upper left arm, consisting of a chain bracelet (Pl. 48). It is, aside from the burden she supports, her most singular possession and the only one of its kind at Khirbet Tannur. Like the lions' torque on three sculptures there, namely, the major stele of Zeus-Hadad, the smaller one of Atargatis and the high relief of yet another Tyché with a planetary standard on her right shoulder, it must have served as a symbol of especial distinction both for deities and human beings.

Similar or related bracelets or armlets grace other Nabataean sculptures from the northern part of the Nabataean kingdom in the Jebel Druze, and I am confident that additional ones will be discovered there and in the southern part, too, in time. Thus, on the upper right arm of a seated male figure from Qanawat are two armlets,[750] while a straight chain of three interconnected links of the Khirbet Tannur type is suspended from the right shoulder of the upper of two superimposed male busts found at Nabataean Si'a in the Jebel Druze.[751] The bust is clothed with a chlamys fastened at the right shoulder, with the loose end folded over the left shoulder, such as we have seen on Helios and Hermes busts at Khirbet Tannur and elsewhere. There is also a bracelet on each wrist of a feminine, funerary bust from Kafer.[752] Striking, too, are the bracelets and anklets on the various figures, including especially Pan, Eros and Mercury (?) in the Nabataean murals at el-Bared, a suburb of Petra (Pl. 203).

In view of the close relationship between the Nabataeans and the Parthians and the direct connections, for instance, between Nabataean torques on the one hand and Parthian and Scythian ones on the other, it is not surprising to find Parthian and Scythian parallels to the Nabataean brace-lets. In this instance, too, we believe that the Nabataeans borrowed this ornament from the Parthians, who in turn obtained it from the Scythians. We have seen that the Scythians had early become an important part of the original Persian population and remained to form an essential element of the Parthian. On the relief of an Atargatis from Parthian Hatra, there can be seen a chain extending from her shoulders to the center of her belt.[753] A solid silver bracelet or armlet is visible above the right elbow of a small copper statuette of Hermes from Hatra.[754] It parallels in general position the chain armlet above the left elbow of the Zodiac-Niké from Khirbet Tannur. Bracelets were sculptured also on the wrists of other male and female figures from Hatra,[755] with one of them simulating a bracelet of twisted metal.[756]

In the excavations of Parthian Dura-Europos, too, there were found fairly numerous paintings and sculptured reliefs of deities and people with brace-lets on their arms or wrists. Some appeared on the left wrist only, as in the instances of a bronze statuette of a warrior [757] and of a partly broken, plaster Niké of Graeco-Parthian type,[758] and others on the right wrist,[759] and still others on both wrists. The latter can be seen in a painting of one of the goddesses [760] of Palmyra and on reliefs of its mural-crowned Tyché and attendant Niké, found in the Temple of Gaddi at Dura-Europos. As the chief goddess, this Tyché, with the personification of Dura's powerful spring at her feet, seems to have combined the characteristics both of Tyché and Atargatis.[761] Elsewhere, bracelets occur also on the wrists of a Helios figure, depicted as one of the seven planets, including, in addition, Luna, Mars, Mercury, Jupiter, Venus and Saturn, whose figures are embossed on a gold vase found years ago in Switzerland, which undoubtedly belongs to the late Hellenistic period and may well stem from a Graeco-Parthian background.[762] The order of the planets is listed also on a gold bracelet from Syria.[763]

The most striking parallel, however, to the bracelet or armlet of the Khirbet Tannur Niké, who holds above her the zodiacal sphere and its central Tyché, is an actual silver bracelet of interconnected links found at Dura-Europos. The links were formed by twisting a silver wire back upon itself in chain pattern, with the open ends soldered to close the circle and with its joint being concealed by a cone-shaped silver button.[764] In its pristine state, it would have made an excellent ornament for a Parthian lady, either in flesh or sculptured form.

Numerous examples of Scythian originals of these bracelets can be cited,[765] which does not mean of course that they were not common in the Hellenistic world, too. There is, for instance, the bracelet on the arm of the Aphrodite of Knidos, sculptured originally by Praxiteles in the fourth century B.C.[766] Bracelets, thus, were familiar to the Nabataeans not only because of their contacts and community of interest with the Parthians, but also because

a,b

5 cm

c

Pl. 194   Mati'a'el altar

a, b. Incense altar bearing name of donor, Mati'a'el, in Nabataean script (p. 509)

c. Copy of inscription by Père M. R. Savignac (p. 138)

d. Nabataean Netir'el inscription, ending "in the year 2" (p. 7)

O m. 12

5 cms

a

b

Pl. 195

a. Damaged Nabataean inscription, mentioning Netir'el (p. 513)
b. Copy of inscription by Père M. R. Savignac (p. 513)

Pl. 196   Horned stele with Nabataean Qosmilk inscription (p. 91)

Pl. 197   Back of horned stele (p. 91)

5 cms

439

Pl. 198   Broken horned stele (p. 91)

a, b. Front and back of stele with grooves (p. 91)
c, d. Back and front of stele base (p. 91)

c

5 cms

b

d

b

c

Pl. 199

a. Stele with Greek inscription (A) **R A Y** (p. 516)
b. Mason's mark "k" (p. 480)
c. Anthropomorphic idols, Petra (p. 516)

of their intimate association with the entire Mediterranean cultural world. In the main, however, we would say that they adopted the usage of bracelets from the Parthians. Whether or not these ornaments possessed a religious significance escapes us.

The ultimately decisive cultural influence upon the Nabataeans seems to have been derived from the Eastern background of the Parthians, which in turn was shot through frequently with the golden threads of Scythian connection. Torques and bracelets, griffins and plaques of stylized human beings or of recumbent animals, pictured alone or locked in combat, diadems and pendants and amulets, beads, buckles, rosettes, palmettes and other kinds of jewelry without end were commonplace among the Scythians, including some which were definitely "Irano-Greek" or "Graeco-Oriental" in style and workmanship.[767]

Through the Parthians, many of the Scythian motifs and designs were handed down thus to the Nabataeans, as we have seen in the instance of the Nabataean lions' torques. No claim is being made, however, that the Scythians should be regarded as the sole originators of the bracelet ornament. An early bronze Phoenician figurine, for instance, from Minet el-Beida on the Phoenician coast of the eastern Mediterranean, belonging to the second half of the second millennium B.C., is shown wearing a bracelet around the middle of his raised right arm.[768]

b. Cultural Imprints

The Nabataeans, it is seen thus, permitted themselves a certain leeway in the patterning they employed, although it was of minor consequence. Such limited differences as existed, stemmed from the swing between the Oriental tendency to rigid formalism, accentuated by Parthian nationalism or orientalism, on the one hand, and the Hellenistic tendency to emphasize beauty of form, on the other hand. The convention of stylization was of course not solely Nabataean or Parthian, even if derived clearly from an earlier eastern background, but was practiced also in Egypt and Greece. The Niké of Breccia, for instance, exemplified the attractive, Hellenistic type of fixed fashion of reproduction.[769] One of the main factors which set the Oriental and Occidental culture worlds apart was therefore not the existence of fairly rigid patterns of portrayal in the one or the other, but rather the manner of expressing them. The Semitic predisposition was to underscore the centrality of the idea that animated the object, and the Greek inclination was to emphasize the harmony of proportion and the attractiveness of appearance.

Khirbet Tannur and Parthian Hatra[770] differed only in degree from one another in stiff and mechanical depiction of wings, for example, or, for that matter, of gods and men and beasts. Both, however, were far removed from the graceful and relatively more naturalistic reproduction of a Hellenistic, winged Niké from Ascalon (Pl. 49b), or of a winged Eros on a stele featuring a confrontation of Helen and Paris,[771] or, in yet another example, especially of the eagle of Zeus flying skyward with Ganymede.[772]

It becomes clear in the comparison of these separate, cultural traditions that despite all Western overlay or influence, the artistic creations of the Nabataeans, and even more so of the Parthians, remained Eastern to the core. The Parthians revived and reinterpreted the older formalism of their ancient origins;[773] and the lure of their religious beliefs and practices penetrated military camps and fortified cities as far as the westernmost reaches of Europe.[774] The Nabataeans also prepared effigies of their gods in accordance with Eastern tradition, but incorporated Western influences far more than their powerful, northern neighbors.[775] In addition, they considerably modified what they embraced in accordance with their own predilections. As a result, they brought into being types that, by and large, became unmistakably and distinctively their own.

The forms they created were, indeed, different both from those of the lands of the rising and setting sun, with which they had such constant and intimate contacts. Furthermore, the unique character of their artistic endeavor and achievement proved to be so virile, that it persisted long after their political collapse. This was demonstrated by the fact that despite the progressive effacement of their identities as Nabataeans in the brilliant renascence of Byzantine Rome, more or less crude copies of their sculptures appeared at that time in even such far flung places in their former kingdom as border caravanserais in eastern Transjordan and desert emporia in the Negev of southern Palestine. Their influence on Byzantine art in general, and Coptic[776] and Omayyad[777] art in particular, persisted for hundreds of years after they had ceased to exist as a separate kingdom and culture, as has been correctly surmised.[778]

1) FORMS AND FEATHERS

The general uniformity in appearance of the gods of Khirbet Tannur and other Nabataean temples extended understandably also to the wings which some of them had, as evidenced by those of the Zodiac Niké and numerous others related to her there. It seemed also not to matter whether the wings belonged to gods fashioned in the images of human beings or to eagles as frequent embodiments of the gods, or to Erotes or griffins that danced attendance on them. The pattern was much the same for all of them, allowing for slight variations, and was repeated with occasional minor changes at other Nabataean sites, both near and remote. It prevailed, too, in places such as Palmyra, Dura-Europos and Hatra, with which the Nabataeans had the closest possible commercial and cultural connections.

It must not be imagined, however, that the exchange between these places was so great as to make for nearly complete similarity in their art forms.

There were not only notable likenesses but also deep and striking differences between them, even as there was considerable polarity within their own camps. It is probably correct to say that the Nabataeans were closer spiritually to the Parthians than they were to the Romans, but above all they pursued their own bent. They catered to and were served by both the East and the West, but yielded themselves completely to neither. It was their particular genius, coupled with a rare, once in a millennium concatenation of geopolitical forces, that made their brief success and cultural uniqueness greater than the sum of their borrowings.

The Nabataeans copied, for example, the Hellenistic peplos, which many of the Nabataean woman must have worn, but reproduced its folds generally in stiffly unnatural lines, because it served their purpose to do so. They may not have possessed the same high sculptural skills as contemporary Greek and Roman craftsmen, but there was also ideological method in their persistent repetitiveness of frozen forms. When they fashioned wings of gods and birds in stone or bronze or clay, they deliberately chose, I believe, not fully to imitate models of comparatively high artistic excellence such as they must have seen at places like Gerasa, one of the nearby cities of the Decapolis, which we know they frequently visited (Pl. 43a).[779] They copied Hellenistic-Roman representations of wings, but stiffened their shapes and reduced the harmony of dissimilar and more naturalistic gradations of feathers to an orderly and monotonous array of equally sized segments, overlapping each other like tiles on a roof.

This is apparent in the upper feathers of the strong, extremely large, partly spread wings of the Zodiac-Niké (Pl. 48). The lower feathers were originally outlined like diagonal spikes on long pointed quills, placed over each other like pieces of cordwood. With unfailing regularity and fewest changes, the Nabataeans kept on repeating this stiff style of representation. It can be seen also in the feathers on the wings and breast of the eagle with the serpent (Pl. 140), and even better on the nearly undamaged, finial eagle over the head of the Vegetation Goddess (Pls. 32, 34a). In the latter two examples the neck and leg feathers are rendered like smaller versions of the wavy horn-like tresses on some of the gods and lions of Khirbet Tannur, such as are visible, for instance, on the Vegetation Goddess herself. Lions with carefully trained locks of hair occur in more elegant form at places like Baalbek and were commonly employed throughout the Hellenistic-Semitic world.

The pattern of the wings on the Zodiac-Niké and on the eagles, that we have discussed, was used over and over again. Whether the figure is represented as a Niké, the goddess of victory, with her laurel wreath and palm branch, or as a Tyché, the goddess of fortune, bearing aloft her horn of plenty, or even as a Niké-Tyché, in a combination of both, the design and decoration of their wings are nearly always the same. Examine the Niké reliefs on a round altar from Khirbet Tannur (Pl. 189a, b), or those on the side panels of the altar dedicated to Alexandros Amrou (Pl. 188a, b), and see how their wings conform to the convention! Nor is there much difference in a whole series of winged Nikés at Khirbet Tannur, each on a separate rectangular limestone block, that may have belonged to a frieze on one or several of the temple walls (Pls. 179-182, 183c, d, e). The stereotype is manifest also on several fragments of wings (Pl. 144c), that must once have been part of excellent and sizable sculptures. Indeed, more reliefs of eagles with this type of wings must have existed there, to judge from two detached heads (Pl. 144a, b) found in our excavations.

This rigidity of representation was by no means limited to Khirbet Tannur, but can be seen at other Nabataean sites, quite distant from it and far removed from one another. In the southern part of Nabataea it can be seen in the wings of the eagle dominating the Eagle Shrine at Petra (Pl. 143).[780] It appears in those of the comparatively large and mechanically windblown Niké-Tyché from there, who holds a spreading palm branch in one hand and an overflowing cornucopia in the other (Pl. 185).[781] There is an example of it to the north at Qasr Rabbah, south of the Wadi Mojib (the River Arnon of the Bible), in the wings of an Eros, rising from an acanthus frame on a decorated limestone block, now inserted in a wall of a rude modern house there (Pl. 167c).

This fashion of representation also occurs frequently at various sites in the northern part of the Nabataean kingdom in the Jebel Druze and Hauran districts of Syria. The relief of a winged figure from Qanawat bears evidence of it,[782] as does that of an eagle with a serpent in its claws from there.[783] It occurs on the wings and body of a sideways-faced eagle from Atil,[784] and it must have been present, too, in the opened wings of a sideways faced eagle surmounting the head of an apparently masculine bust from Soueïda.[785] It calls to mind, furthermore, the sideways-faced but otherwise frontally positioned finial eagle over the Vegetation Goddess, Atargatis, of Khirbet Tannur (Pls. 32, 34a), and also the frontally faced one standing on the head of a deified king from Parthian Hatra.[786] There is an analogy also in a relief from Palmyra of a frontally faced eagle with spread wings standing on the head of a deceased warrior or hunter, with a palm branch over his right shoulder and a horse's head over the left one [787] (Pl. 156a, b). The pattern is repeated on the wings of still other eagles facing sideways [788] or frontally [789] at Nabataean Siʻa in the Jebel Druze. Still other examples could be cited.

It is possible that there were at Khirbet Tannur itself some noticeable, although essentially minor differences of workmanship and elegance in the details of the generally adopted wing pattern. No examples of such variations have survived there, however, such as exist at Petra or Siʻa, for example, near the southern and northern limits of the Nabataean kingdom. They show up at the former place in two striking sandstone reliefs, each depicting a winged Eros holding a serpent, which is being touched by a raised paw of a winged griffin on each side of him (Pl. 167a, b).[790] A small bronze leopard with left paw uplifted in related fashion has been found at Abda, and a large stone lion or leopard, very similar in appearance and posture to the Petra griffins, has been found by Paul Lapp at Araq el-Emir [790a] (Pl. 168).

Similar refinements of forms of feathers mark a wing fragment of a broken Niké (?) torso from Petra of strongly Hellenistic spirit,[791] closely related in type to the outstretched wing and flowing drapery of a broken Niké (?) relief at Nabataean Si'a.[792] Another example from Si'a [793] is furnished by a splendid relief of an eagle with partly spread wings standing on a laurel wreath, facing left and with its head resting against the middle of adjoining acanthus leaves (Pl. 138).[794] Still other examples can be cited from there and from Qanawat [795] and Soueïda,[796] all located in the Nabataean Jebel Druze, and from Mejdel,[797] in the jagged hill country of the Ledja.

2) PATTERNING OF DRAPERY

Persistent formalism and rigidity of pattern are exemplified in the peplos worn by the Zodiac-Niké of Khirbet Tannur. Had this garment been stamped out by machine during the Nabataean period instead of being shaped by hand, it could hardly have been more uniform in appearance. The Niké's legs are visible through the diaphanous cloth of the lower part of the peplos, with the right knee slightly bent. The pleats of the lower section of the peplos covering the legs succeed, in a mechanical manner, in giving the illusion of motion, although their stiff curves look like congealed ripples in a suddenly frozen pond.

The top overfold repeats this pattern of pleats, but in a wholly irrelevant fashion. The two central ones are curved, as if to outline a protruding belly with central navel,[798] while the outer ones bend much less. The abdominal features, incidentally, appear quite plainly in several of the Niké reliefs (Pls. 179, 188a, 189a, 190b). In general, however, the pleats of the upper and lower parts of the drapery of the peplos-clad figures of Khirbet Tannur are treated in a rigidly patterned fashion, regardless of different positions and movement of various parts of the body. This is especially evidenced in the matching of the bottoms of the ridged pleats of both the lower and upper parts of the peplos, regardless of the relationship to the continuation of the lines of the pleats in between.[799]

The damage done to the bottom of the lower part of the peplos of the Zodiac-Niké figure prevents this phenomenon from being seen clearly. It is, however, a feature quite evident on some of the less-damaged Nikés from Khirbet Tannur and other Nabataean sites,[800] as are the other characteristics referred to (Pls. 180, 184b).

This parallelism of the bottoms of the pleats on the upper and lower parts of the peplos occurring in more artistic fashion in Hellenistic sculptures (Pl. 49b) is pronounced on each of the Niké reliefs of the Alexandros Amrou altar (Pl. 188a, b) and on one of the Niké reliefs of the round altar (Pl. 189a). We mention, passingly, because of its application here, but reserve for fuller discussion later on, the matching oppositeness of the stance of the feet of the Nikés on these altar panels. It is noteworthy that the feet of each still existing pair are set at right angles to one another.

As in the case of the portrayal of wings at Nabataean sites, there must also have been a certain leeway with regard to portrayal of clothing at Khirbet Tannur, although only the most stereotyped patterning is visible on the extant sculptures. In general it may be said that only a very limited amount of artistic freedom prevailed among the Nabataeans and the Parthians and those who long thereafter perpetuated their artistic traditions. It did exist, however, and extended from the usual mechanical repetitiveness and purposeful disregard of natural proportions to the occasional employment of more graceful and Hellenistic stylization. Nevertheless, even when the Nabataeans attempted to imitate the Greek style, they never completely succeeded in transcending their own, basically Oriental approach.

This is illustrated by the high relief of a much-damaged Niké from Khirbet Tannur, whose head, wings, right arm, right leg, left forearm and left foot were missing when we first dug it up. We came across its partially broken head later on. The rest of the figure, however, was intact. It was clothed with a high girdled peplos, in almost exactly the same manner as the rest of the Nikés of Khirbet Tannur. The garment was, however, more elegantly styled than usual. The overfold, looking like a masculine type of short chlamys or paludamentum [801] (Pl. 184a, b), must originally have been fastened at the right shoulder by a fibula. It was then draped over the left shoulder and around the left elbow, behind and below which its end dangled.

There was a gracefulness of form and excellence of execution about this figure that bring it close to the approach to Hellenistic style evidenced in the winged Tyché of Petra (Pl. 185).[802] Its arms, to judge from the remnant of the left one, seem to have had the natural fullness and femininity of those of the Petra sculpture and of several smaller Nikés of Khirbet Tannur (Pl. 181a). They lack the angular stiffness [803] of the arms of the Zodiac Niké relief and of those of the Nikés on the Alexandros Amrou (Pl. 188a, b) and round (Pl. 189a, b) altars. That is to be attributed, we feel, not so much to inexperience as to preconceived purpose.

Despite its approximation of Hellenistic style, this comparatively elegant relief did not escape the general pattern of fixed and formal stylization. The pleats of the lower part of the drapery, however, depart from the usual pattern, in order to conform to the lines of the bent, right knee, visible underneath the cloth of the garment. As a result, with the exception of two pleats that enfold it on either side, and of several above it which logically have been deflected to the extreme right, all the rest of the pleats billow out to the left side. Despite the precision and orderliness of their arrangement, they still manage to convey a sense of forward motion.

The pleats of the overfold of the peplos, however, bear no relationship in comparative naturalness to those of the bottom of the garment. Furthermore, except for a distinct refinement of workmanship, they cannot be distinguished in position and direction from the pleats of the upper part of the drapery of the Zodiac-Niké or of similar figures at Khirbet Tannur. The resulting impression, therefore, is, that while the lower part of the body of this particular figure seems to be moving ahead, the upper part is in effect standing stock still. Nevertheless, the formally patterned bottom of the ridged pleats of both the upper and lower parts of the peplos are in line with one another.

It is necessary to bear in mind that the patterning of drapery prevailed as much in the Occident as in the Orient, and that indeed it was borrowed from the West. Nabataean and Parthian gods were frequently dressed with coarsened copies of Hellenistic-type garments.[804] Sometimes, as we have just seen, a reproduction adheres more closely to the Hellenistic than to the Semitic fashion, but both fashions were subject to stylistic formalization.

An examination of the Hellenistic relief of the Tyché of Ascalon (Pl. 49b) reveals that the bottoms of the pleats of the overfold of her peplos match those of the lower parts, in much the same wise as in the Khirbet Tannur draperies. There is clearly more harmony of line and motion and proportion in the shape and hang of her garment than in the Nabataean equivalents, but the fact remains that it is cut in accordance with a definite, unnaturalistic pattern. To be sure, it is a more plastic one than that employed at Khirbet Tannur. Numerous examples could be cited to show that even in Greek sculptures of greater realism of representation, the matching of the bottoms of pleats of the upper and lower parts of the same drapery was in vogue before it appeared in Oriental renditions.[805] The clear purpose was to effect a relationship between all the folds of the entire garment so that it might appear as a single plastic unit.[806]

4. OTHER NIKÉS

a. Hellenistically Inclined

A considerably damaged head of the most Hellenistic of the winged Niké reliefs recovered at Khirbet Tannur (Pls. 183a, 184b) was found some distance from its body. The right half of the head was moderately well preserved, but the other half was never recovered, having probably been smashed to bits. Its chin, mouth and all the nose except a bit of the nostrils are gone, but a sufficient amount of the rest of the face and head and neck remains to give a clear picture of the appearance of the whole. The long well-modeled aristocratic neck supports what was once one of the most charming heads among the sculptures of Khirbet Tannur.

The rounded right cheek, the almond-shaped right eye, the right half of the forehead and the front top of the head are comparatively intact. The hair is arranged upward in individual flame-like locks, bunched out at the sides to cover the ears. The top of the head has been damaged, but it looks as if the hair had been caught in a knot at the back. The deeply sunk socket of the right eye, with protruding iris and hollowed out pupil is characteristic of the type generally employed at Khirbet Tannur, but is executed with greater care than is usual there. The pupil was not drilled as deeply as were the pupils of the zodiac-encircled Tyché (Pl. 46), and, as a result, does not have the rigidly staring appearance that characterizes most of the Khirbet Tannur eyes.

Seen from the right profile, the head appears much more complete than it is, and gives the impression of belonging to a young person. It has not been fashioned with the stiff fullness of cheeks and lips and chin that seems to come with the representation of more mature figures among the busts of Khirbet Tannur.

The youthfulness of appearance and comparative delicacy of features were fortunately caught again in a more complete manner in another and almost exact duplicate head (Pl. 183b). The body to which it originally belonged would most probably have been similar to the one mentioned above with the half broken head turned slightly to the left. Still a third relief of a winged Niké-Tyché of this general type and size lay near the surface of the rubble at Khirbet Tannur, with its individual features of head and dress so hammered away, however, as to be almost unrecognizable (Pl. 182d).

The upper right part of the more intact duplicate head is missing, as well as the outer side of the right eye, almost all of the nose and some of the chin, but the full cast and charm of its face can still be made out. The lips are open and not abnormally full. Again, the eyes have been especially well rendered, with enough of a grooved line drawn for the arched eyebrow over the intact left eye to give it a comparatively natural appearance. The presence or absence of such grooved eyebrow lines (Pls. 130-132a, b) can make a considerable difference in appearance. The delicacy of the eyebrow line, the care with which the pupils are cut into the irises protruding from the countersunk eyesockets and the naturalness with which the slightly parted lips are modeled result in a portrait somewhat different from the usual stereotyped sculpture at Khirbet Tannur. Even one of the clearly Parthian-type gods from there, with its highly stylized beard of separate spiral locks and downward flowing moustache with curled ends is given the look of a real person (Pl. 129). That is achieved by the skillful rendering of the eyes, with the main curve in the upper eyelid, and by the slightly parted, not too full lips which do not give the impression of having been stamped out in a cookie mold. In general, the employment by Nabataean sculptors of canted planes, sharp grooves and deep cavities to render eyebrows and eyes was carefully designed to take full advantage of the resultant dramatic opposites of lights and shadows that emphasized salient features in almost startling fashion.

b. Common Types

Hardly any of the small amount of individuality incorporated into this more Hellenistic type of Niké sculpture at Khirbet Tannur is left in the rest of the fairly numerous, comparatively small Niké and Niké-Tyché reliefs found there. Several of their bodies and heads were recovered separately in the excavations, and it was fun to join together what accident or malice had sundered. In one instance it was possible to reunite three separate parts, namely, a truncated body, a broken off head and an orphaned pair of feet resting on a global disc, and to recreate thus a nearly complete whole (Pl. 180).

This reassembled winged Niké had once held aloft in her right hand a bannered wreath, the outline of which can still be made out, and a palm branch in her left hand, reaching above her left shoulder. Her nose and the top of her coiffure had been broken off, but otherwise her head is intact. Her face duplicates in miniature the features of larger figures of goddesses from this temple, differing slightly only insofar as her protruding irises have been left blank—not an uncommon phenomenon there. In other instances of small Niké reliefs the wreath was held up in the left hand and the palm branch jutted above the right shoulder (Pl. 181b).

The coiffure of our reconstituted Niké was quite elaborate. Her wavy combed hair, twisted into short locks over her ears and the nape of her neck, was parted in the middle above her forehead and then caught at the top of her head in a fancy chignon. That this was so, even though it cannot presently be seen, is demonstrated by the hair-dress of an intact relief of the head of a sister Niké. She, too, at one time, carried a bannered wreath in her right hand, but perhaps a horn of plenty instead of a palm branch in her left (Pls. 179, 182b, 183e). The head and upper part of the torso in relief of yet a third Niké of this type (Pl. 183d, e) was found, but none of the rest of it was recovered. She, too, undoubtedly wore a chignon. The faces of all of these Nikés are practically identically the same.

Some of these small reliefs of winged goddesses possess not only the characteristics of Nikés with the wreath and/or palm of victory, but also the cornucopia of plenty and good fortune of the Tychés. In one instance, the much battered Niké-Tyché holds aloft a cornucopia in her left hand (Pl. 182d). In a clearer example, the goddess carries a horn of plenty in her right hand (Pl. 182b) and may have held a palm branch aloft in her left.

In another relief, the goddess holds a garlanded wreath in her left hand and what may have been a horn of plenty in the right (Pl. 182a). A larger relief from Petra shows a Niké-Tyché with a palm branch in her right hand and a cornucopia in her left (Pl. 185), as we have previously seen.

c. Discoid Bases of Niké Reliefs

The spherical segments that serve as bases under the feet of numerous Nikés at Khirbet Tannur (Pls. 180, 186f, g) and elsewhere, and in connection with Tychés [807] and eagles,[808] too, at various places, apparently symbolize celestial globes or spheres. They are frequently associated also with Zeus-Hadad or Jupiter in his capacity as the Ba'al-shamin, the master of the heavens.[809] Commonly employed in the first centuries B.C. and A.D. and also in the Byzantine period, both in the Orient and the Occident,[810] they incorporate Mesopotamian and Egyptian concepts of the world. Basically, however, the celestial globe is the creation of Greek cosmography. Its general adoption by the Nabataeans, Palmyreneans and others of the ancient Near East may be attributed to the pervasive power of widespread Hellenism,[811] which renascent and particularly Parthian Orientalism could not eradicate.

It may be going too far, however, to assume that all of these spherical segments signify celestial globes or solar discs, upon which the eagles of Helios or Zeus-Hadad, or the Niké and Tyché figures associated with them could with propriety repose.[812] Some of these discoid bases may symbolize sacred mountain tops, where Zeus-Hadad and other deities loved to dwell. A possible indication of this seems to be furnished by a remarkable Syrian bronze sculpture showing a solar eagle perched on a discoid base, on the front of which, incised in large Greek letters, is the name HELIOS.[813]

XIII. THE ASTRAL BASIS OF NABATAEAN BELIEF

XIII. *The Astral Basis of Nabataean Belief*

1. THE SEVEN PLANETS

The zodiac, with its counterclockwise and clockwise halves, indicating among other things probably the observance of two New Years, one in the spring and one in the fall, and the presence of its central Tyché panel, dramatize the great importance attached by the Nabataeans to the heavenly firmament. They beheld in its orbs the reflections of their gods, whose powers governed the mysteries of nature and the conditions of mankind during life on earth and its continuation in the hereafter. The select company of their supreme deities was identified above all with the seven planets, known to them and their near and distant connections by various Semitic, Greek and Latin names. In the Hellenistic-Roman cultural environment, in which the Nabataeans, Syrians, Parthians and others of the Orient were deeply immersed, the designations or equivalents of the names employed for these planets were, as we have already mentioned and as is commonly known, Sol, Luna, Mars, Mercury, Jupiter, Venus and Saturn.

Venus was the Nabataean Atargatis-Aphrodite-Allat, or by whatever other names she may have been called; Jupiter, the Zeus-Hadad; Luna, the Tyché of multiple forms. There remain to be considered the other luminaries of this divine directorium, who ruled without particular gradations of rank, but among whom nevertheless the authority of Atargatis was unquestionably the primary one. These deities governed the seasons of the year, the zodiacal sequence of its changes, the moods of nature, the vagaries of fortune, the exigencies of life, the unexplorable unknown of the world beyond death, whose concealing curtain could not be penetrated by mortal gaze. The lives of the Nabataeans and their like were suffused with the awareness of personified divinity and of the infinite power of the pantheon of deities and of their surrogates. One of them, who, in addition to Atargatis, Zeus-Hadad

453

and Tyché, figured prominently in their thoughts and acts of propitiation and whose likeness they delighted to set up in sculptural form in their temples and dwelling places was the sun god, Sol or Helios-Apollo, or whatever they called him in different places and under different circumstances.

a. Helios

The importance of the role of the sun god in the Nabataean pantheon of Khirbet Tannur was emphasized by the discovery there of a limestone bust in high relief of Helios. Rising from a practically square panel, it may have been part of a frieze that included sculptures of gods, set in the upper face of the side walls of the raised, inner temple enclosure. The head proper had been broken off completely. We were fortunate enough, however, to find two main parts of it, which, when put back into place, restored much of its original likeness (Pl. 136).

In most respects, the face of this deity is essentially the same as that of the sandstone sculpture of Zeus-Hadad (Pl. 41), minus the latter's beard. Common to both sculptures are the slightly furrowed forehead, pronounced ridges on either side of the top of the flattened nose, flaring nostrils, rounded cheeks, recessed eye sockets, irises indicated by raised, concentric circles and pupils by circular depressions, eyebrows and eyelids portrayed by canted grooves of varying planes, and full and slightly parted lips and strong chin.

While obviously individually sculptured, most of these gods, as we have previously remarked, could almost have been hewn by the same hand in accordance with a single pattern. Fine degrees of distinction, however, manifest themselves in the countenances of the gods and goddesses of this Nabataean sanctuary. A comparison of this Helios bust, for instance, with that of the Atargatis with the lion's torque (Pl. 44), reveals that her forehead is smoother and her chin less squared than his. The appearance of the female of the species is not unexpectedly less rugged than that of the male, despite the fact that the rank and worship of Atargatis seem to have taken precedence over those of her consort.[814]

Above the low forehead of Helios rise the carefully trained, upswept, curving and flame-like [815] locks of his hair, which also originally reached down to the top of his cheeks and covered his ears. Crowning his head, and extending between its extreme left and right sides, was a rayed tiara, now partly broken. Twelve shafts or spokes are still visible and there must have been at least two more in the missing section on the top left side of his head (Pl. 136). We are reminded of the separate stone horns on either side of the eagle finial surmounting the relief of Atargatis as the Vegetation Goddess, which are, as we have previously suggested, to be interpreted as belonging to the symbols of the solar deity.[816] The crown or tiara or halo of the sun's rays is the familiar and fitting badge of identification of Helios, Mithras,

Jarhibol and Serapis in the Nabataean, Parthian, Egyptian and related worlds.[817]

Worn over the close-fitting, low-necked tunic on this Helios sculpture is a shoulder cape or chlamys, fastened in front by a rosette brooch at the right shoulder and then draped backward over the left shoulder. This type of mantle is visible, for example, on a relief of Asklepios to be seen on an altar fragment from the Hauran,[818] on a relief from Palmyra, featuring a triad of gods,[819] and on the famous one of Antiochus I, Epiphanes of Commagene and Mithras.[820] One effect of the body-hugging tunic of the Helios relief is to emphasize the comparatively prominent breasts of the god and make it appear at first glance as if it were a female rather than a male figure. This is not borne out, however, by closer examination, and there is no question that this is a sculpture of Helios-Apollo.[821]

Practically indistinguishable in general characteristics from the high relief of Helios-Apollo of Khirbet Tannur (Pl. 136) is one (Pl. 137a) that can be seen at the base of an arch in a house of the modern village of Qasr Rabbah,[822] a goodly number of miles to the north of it, located between Kerak and the Wadi Mojib. Part of the original Nabataean temple still stands at Qasr Rabbah, and many of the houses of the present day village incorporate plain or decorated building blocks, which come either from the temple or from other structures of the former Nabataean settlement there. Despite the damage to the face of this Qasr Rabbah sculpture, it is unmistakably to be identified with the sun god. A halo of nine rays surrounds his head, which rests against a raised disc, in a fashion visible on reliefs from Palmyra and Hatra.[823] The shoulder cape or chlamys over the tunic and the now damaged, rosette type brooch fastening it at the shoulder are essentially the same as those on the Helios-Apollo reliefs of Khirbet Tannur.

Still other closely related Helios busts in relief have been found at various Nabataean sites throughout the Nabataean kingdom, and many more must have existed or will yet be discovered. Brünnow and Domaszewski reproduce a poor photograph of a defaced Helios figure with radiate crown at Mahaiy in southern Transjordan. It was lying upside down among the ruins of a Nabataean temple and settlement built by the Nabataeans on the remains of an earlier Moabite site.[824] It is just several miles ESE of the very large Nabataean and later town of Dhat Ras, itself only a few miles north of Khirbet Tannur, on the opposite side of the Wadi Hesa, the River Zered of the Bible. As we have seen, the main Nabataean temple of Dhat Ras was devoted to the worship of Atargatis.[825]

There is, furthermore, no question in our mind that excavations would reveal an entire pantheon of Nabataean gods, including one or more reliefs of Helios, particularly at the extensive Nabataean site of Khirbet edh-Dherih, a few miles to the south of Khirbet Tannur, where numerous Nabataean sculptures and elaborately decorated building blocks still litter

a

Pl. 200

a. Umm el-Biyara, Petra (p. 43)
b. Tomb of Sextus Florentinus, Petra (p. 142)

b

Pl. 201

a. Nabataean tomb at Siq el-Bared,
   near Petra (cf. p. 164)
b. Nabataean tomb at Siq el-Bared,
   near Petra (cf. p. 164)

a

b

a

b

Pl. 202   Pl. 203 (*opposite*)

a. Façade of "Painted House," Siq el-Bared (p. 5)   a. Mural in "Painted House," Siq el-Bared (p. 6)

b. Vaulted alcove in "Painted House" (p. 5)   b. Reconstruction, highlighting details (p. 6)

Pl. 204

a. Extension of mural from "Painted House" (p. 6)
b. Reconstruction, highlighting details (p. 6)

a

b

Pl. 205

a. "Painted House" at Siq el-Bared showing tooling (p. 5)
b. Triclinium and Arcosolium in Qattar ed-Deir, Petra (p. 5)

462

Pl. 206

a. Triclinium, Round House, Petra (p. 164)
b. Dorotheos House, Petra (p. 164)

a

b

the surface. Like Khirbet Tannur it seems to have been an almost purely Nabataean site. Additional work at the great Nabataean emporium of Abda in the Negev is bound to bring to light sculptures other than those on the small altar found there,[826] with its reliefs of the mask of a deity and of a dolphin that could just as well have come from Khirbet Tannur.

Garbed in exactly the same fashion as the Khirbet Tannur busts of Helios is a Nabataean sculpture built into the top of a gateway at modern Mesheir-feh in central Moab, on the east side of the Jordan (Pl. 139).[827] This former Nabataean settlement is but a few miles ESE of Dhiban, the Biblical Dibon. It was there that the Mesha stele, commemorating the independence briefly regained by the earlier Moabites from Ahab of Israel, was discovered. The Nabataean city that succeeded the prominent Moabite one came to an end itself in due course and has served as a quarry of ready-cut stones for structures of later periods.[828]

b. Morning and Evening Stars

One of the completely defaced figures from Khirbet Tannur seems to have borne on its shoulders somewhat the same kind of flaming torches[829] as on the outstanding, relatively well preserved and similarly garbed, Helios sculpture from there (Pl. 136). They are longer and far less distinct. The one on the left shoulder has been gouged out completely and need not necessarily be a torch, although the likelihood is that it parallels the one over the right shoulder. That one, too, has been much damaged, but it is possible to make out the lines of the flame at the top of it, curving to the right. It would seem to have been more like the long torch held in the right hand of a Niké relief on one of the panels of a round altar at Khirbet Tannur (Pl. 189a).

The possibility of the existence originally of several additional Helios figures at Khirbet Tannur with torches above their shoulders is heightened by the discovery there of three detached torches (Pl. 144e-g), each different from the other and from the two on the comparatively intact Helios relief. They could also, however, have belonged to Niké figures bearing torches, such as can be seen on one of the bas-reliefs on the damaged, round altar at Khirbet Tannur (Pl. 189b). There are also examples elsewhere of representations of the moon-goddess, accoutered with a crescent moon and a torch.[830] Be that as it may, it is clear that each pair of torches depicted above the shoulders of the Helios sculptures at Khirbet Tannur must convey a distinctive meaning.

They symbolize the morning and evening stars, respectively, as we have already mentioned, and as is generally, and we believe correctly, held. These shining stars attended the rising and setting of the sun, one of the seven planets worshiped in personified form by the Nabataeans and by multitudes of others of the Hellenistic-Semitic world. The flickering light of these stars was reflected by the torches attached to the shoulders of the sun god, Helios. Mithras, too, as the Parthian sun-god, is portrayed with two torches,[831] or is accompanied by two figures bearing respectively an upraised and lowered torch, representative of the evening and morning stars. This can be seen, for example, in a classical representation of Mithras as the Bull-Slayer, enclosed by a zodiacal circle, on a second- or third-century A.D. stele from the London Mithraeum. At the lower corners of this stele are depicted the frontal busts of two wind gods, possibly Boreas and Zephyrus (Pl. 50).[832]

c. Hermes-Mercury

Wearing the same kind of garb as on the Helios busts is one of several Khirbet Tannur reliefs that can be identified with Hermes-Mercury. It rises from a sunken panel framed by a beveled molding (Pl. 146a). Aside from the fact that the entire front of the head and neck has been broken off, the bust is otherwise intact, with the chlamys over the body tunic being fastened by a brooch or fibula at the right shoulder and its end draped over the left shoulder.

Above the left shoulder appears a partly damaged lyre of seven strings,[833] being the main reason for our identifying this bas-relief with Hermes-Mercury. It is well known that he was frequently represented with this instrument, and tradition has it that he was its inventor.[834] While this sculpture evinces strong Hellenistic influence both in the garb and the lyre, it is noteworthy, in view of the pronounced Parthian impact on the Nabataeans, that Mercury was connected by the Parthians with Mithras.[835] Considered to be, among other things, the protector of roads, market places and merchants, it was natural for the commerce-minded Nabataeans to worship Hermes-Mercury, in addition to all the other reasons bound up with his inclusion among the seven planetary figures of their cosmogony.

Another Khirbet Tannur bust in relief, this one completely intact, whose attire is almost identical with that of the Helios sculptures and the above mentioned Hermes-Mercury (Pl. 146a), represents a youthful, contemplative Hermes or Mercury figure (Pl. 145).[836] It rises from a sunken panel, with parts of the body reaching over the beveled inner moulding enclosing it and also over the still higher, straight surfaced outer moulding on the top and the right sides of the stone block. The beardless, pensive face is almost feminine in its youthfulness, with none of the furrows of maturity wrinkling the brow. The hair is fixed in double rows of spiral curls, whose open sides face each other at the part of the hair in the middle and whose closed ends in the back descend gracefully to a point just above the exposed ears. The folds of the shoulder cape or chlamys are not worked as carefully as those of the Helios busts, and it is fastened in front of the right shoulder by a simple, circular brooch instead of the more ornate rosette type.

In yet another instance, a similar circular brooch or medallion is used to fasten the chlamys, this time on top of the right shoulder of a bust in relief of what well may be a Nabataean Mercury figure (Pl. 152c), found at Haram Ramat el-Khalil, two miles north of Hebron.[837] Hebron was one of the great trading centers of antiquity and must have been frequented by Nabataeans en route either to or from Gaza. Over the left shoulder of the much worn relief, rising from a roughly worked, rectangular, limestone block, there projects a wand with a wing [838] near the upper end of its left side and the remaining hint of one on its right side and with a broken crescent (?) surmounting its top. The crescent may, however, be only a remnant of something else. It reaches over the lower part of the comparatively large raised circle above it, whose left side is still fairly intact. Inside this circle is a small horizontal slit, into which something seems at one time to have been dowelled. It may well be that the wand with its present crescent-shaped top and wing (?) may be the healing, caduceus symbol of Hermes or Mercury.[839] Indeed, we think we can discern the outline of the upper part of the caduceus, indicating originally the confrontation of two serpents. It can be seen in this form, for example, at Petra [840] (Pl. 152a, b).

There is a much damaged figure from Petra of Hermes-Mercury in high relief, with a caduceus above the right shoulder, clothed in similar fashion, namely with a tunic, over which is a chlamys fastened at the right shoulder by a circular brooch and then draped over the left shoulder.[841] Almost all of the head and part of the neck have been broken away, but the rest of the bust in high relief is still intact (Pl. 152b). The chlamys and circular brooch are reminiscent of those on the Hermes-Mercury figures from Khirbet Tannur (Pls. 136, 145, 146a). The heads of the serpents of the caduceus of the Petra Hermes are clearly defined, and even more so on a fragment of what must have been another Hermes sculpture from there (Pl. 152a) [842] of the same kind.

Dalman reports the existence of yet another, much-damaged Hermes-Mercury relief from Petra, carved on a marble medallion, once built into the wall of a mosque at Elji at the entrance to Petra. His drawing [843] shows a bust in relief, clad with tunic and chlamys, and bearing a double-winged caduceus over its right shoulder, paralleling the above-mentioned caduceus fragment from Petra, which, too, must have extended over the right shoulder of a Hermes-Mercury relief.

Very similar to the probably Nabataean Ramat el-Khalil relief is a Syrian one of Mercury, carved on the front side of a small altar found in the Heliopolis-Baalbek region. On three of the sides of this altar were reliefs of deities commonly worshiped in the ancient, Hellenistic-Semitic world.

On the right side is a representation of the sun, with a seven rayed nimbus encircling his head and a whip jutting above his left shoulder.[844] The figure of the moon, with the crescent behind her back and with its horns appearing above her shoulders, is on the left side of the altar. On the front side, in between them, is a relief of Mercury with a clear cut caduceus above his left shoulder. As in the case of the Ramat el-Khalil sculpture, there appears to be a crown or headpiece of some sort on his head; and in this instance, too, the chlamys is fastened with a circular brooch on top of his right shoulder.

The worship of this triad of deities, namely, Helios, Luna and Mercury, was, among that of others, popular at Heliopolis-Baalbek and many other places in Syria in Hellenistic-Roman times,[845] just as it was among the Nabataeans of Khirbet Tannur and elsewhere. The Khirbet Tannur examples included a limestone bust in relief (Pl. 153b), whose face has been obliterated by vandals, but whose figure is otherwise intact. It is clothed with a tunic, over which is a himation, the end of which is draped over his left shoulder. Above that shoulder extends a wand, entwined by a serpentine vine or perhaps more correctly a serpent.[846] Near the top of the left side of the wand is a slight, raised projection, which may originally have been a wing.

Very similar to this wand with serpentine decoration is one which appears on each of two sculptures in relief at Petra. One of them is of a god of superficially Hellenistic appearance, whose beard of tightly rolled snail curls betrays Orientalizing influence (Pl. 151).[847] The head of this bearded but youthful deity is crowned with a laurel wreath, and his body is clad with a tunic and himation, the end corner of which is draped over his left shoulder. Above that shoulder is a wand, with what we take to be a stylized serpent coiled around it from bottom to top. It is, thus, almost exactly similar to the one over the left shoulder of the Hermes figure from Khirbet Tannur (Pl. 153b), clothed in the same manner. This wand may be a variant form of the caduceus wands from Petra (Pl. 152a, b)[848] and of what may well be a caduceus wand over the left shoulder of the relief from Ramat el-Khalil (Pl. 152c), which, as previously mentioned, we consider to be Nabataean. A similar serpentine or "twisted" wand appears by the left side of a much-damaged relief on the front face of an altar at Petra.[849]

Yet another bust in relief from Khirbet Tannur (Pl. 146b) is clothed with tunic and chlamys in basically the same fashion as the Mercury (?) (Pls. 145, 146a) and Helios (Pl. 136) sculptures there, although in a much more crudely patterned fashion. Headless, as a result of accident or vandalism, this particular bust, with one exception, to be dealt with later on, is cruder than any others found on this hilltop sanctuary. Although the missing head must have projected almost in the round from the larger than usual, rectangular, limestone block to which the relief was attached, the rest of the bust was carved in comparatively low relief.

On the whole, it is flatter and less plastic than the generally prevailing style of sculptures at Khirbet Tannur. Its shoulders and arms are stiffer and less rounded and less properly proportioned than is customary even in the restrained and formalized fashion in vogue there. The shoulder cape or chlamys over the tunic, while fastened at the right shoulder with a circular brooch as on the Ramat el-Khalil (Pl. 152c) and youthful Hermes-Mercury (?) figures (Pl. 145), is even less carefully rendered than the one on the latter—which, in turn, does not measure up to the comparative excellency of the rosette and chlamys on the Helios bust (Pl. 136).

The folds of the chlamys on this flat and rather crude and graceless sculpture are by contrast merely suggested by arbitrary grooves. The varying width of the front part of this garment is indicated by two separated, raised and curved bands of different sizes at its outer edges. Furthermore, the sides of the back of the garment extending beyond the body are executed with more than usual rigidity and look like tacked-on side strips. Their lines differ completely from the comparatively natural flow of the descending, side folds of the back of the chlamys visible on the Helios sculpture.

Extending above the left shoulder of this crude bas-relief is the remnant of a broken object, that originally was obviously longer than it is now. It could be part of one of many things such as a scepter, whip,[850] caduceus or horn of plenty.[851] This flat relief seems in general most closely related to the Hermes-Mercury busts of Khirbet Tannur (Pl. 153b) and Ramat el-Khalil (Pl. 152c). It is possible, therefore, that the broken rod above the left shoulder was part of a caduceus. There seems, however, also to have been part of a staff over the right shoulder too, recalling the two torches over the shoulders of Helios (Pl. 136). In style of execution, this relief and another fragmentary one, discussed immediately below, are more closely related in their flat and completely stiff proportions to many of the Nabataean sculptures of southern Syria [852] than to most of those from Khirbet Tannur.

There is only one other badly damaged sculpture in low relief (Pl. 157b) at Khirbet Tannur, that is closely related to the above-mentioned one (Pl. 146b). It formed approximately the left half of an apparently male bust. Its head, which may have been carved in high relief and almost in the round, has been completely broken off. Two locks of hair fall over the left shoulder and the top of the left arm. These locks have none of the stylized grace and plastic contours of those of Zeus-Hadad (Pl. 41) or of the Vegetation Goddess (Pl. 31), or, as we shall see, of the Saturn relief (Pl. 153a). They are, however, much similar to those on a Nabataean sculpture from Ma'in (Pl. 157b).

The sculptures of Khirbet Tannur are by and large, we believe, no different from others occurring particularly in those parts of the Nabataean kingdom embracing the former territories of Moab and Edom and most of the area of the Negev of southern Israel. We doubt very much whether they can be set apart from the Nabataean sculptures of Petra, although it has been thought that there are "many features which distinguish the orientalizing art of Petra from that of Tannur." [853]

We have remarked above about the close relationship, for instance, between the Hermes figures of the two places, and especially those clothed with the tunic and the chlamys, fastened at the right shoulder by a circular brooch or clasp. There is, furthermore, such a wealth of other similarities between the sculptures of the comparatively isolated sanctuary of Khirbet Tannur and the great central emporium and capital of Petra that we do not feel it necessary to labor the point. To be sure, there are unique individual pieces, or at least thus far unique at each of these centers.

Some leeway was exercised in the manner in which also the Hermes-Mercury figures were sculptured at Khirbet Tannur. A comparison of the two attractive Niké heads (Pl. 183a, b) with that of a youthful Hermes-Mercury one (Pl. 147), shows that it belonged to the same sculptural tradition. Despite the damage wrought to his eyes, nose, mouth and to a lesser degree to his chin, his head, in many respects, is hardly distinguishable from theirs. A minor difference is that his hair is arranged in snail curls and theirs in upswept, flame-like locks. These heads belong to the more comparatively Hellenistic style existing to a minor degree at Khirbet Tannur, while the majority of the sculptures there belong to the more Oriental or Parthian style. Both types there share characteristics stamping them as being distinctively Nabataean. In general it may be said that the sculptures of Khirbet Tannur point more to Syria and Parthia than they do to the more purely Hellenistic west.

There is one distinctive feature, however, aside from such trademarks as the caduceus separating the Hermes-Mercury head from those of the Nikés, that makes it possible to identify it. On its cheeks are side locks looking like sideburns, without which it might have been difficult to establish that this was a male and not a female head. Each consists of two rather long narrow halves of locks, twisted or plaited in mutually opposite directions. Known among modern Bedouins as "love locks," they often occur on Hermes-Mercury sculptures and are visible on the face of a magnificent winged Hermes-Mercury head from Petra [854] (Pl. 149a, b). They also appear on the sides of the face of a bust from Nabataean Si'a (Pl. 148), which, too, is probably to be designated as a Hermes-Mercury figure. A Hermes-Mercury mask from Hatra, with two small wings on top of its head,[855] is very similar to the Petra one.

A small, pottery plaque of a Nabataean cavalryman from Petra [856] shows sideburns on his face. They appear also on two poorly rendered profiles of heads in low relief at Nabataean Bostra [857] and can be seen also on a sculpture of a male head from Dura-Europos.[858] The tradition of the representation of sideburns long precedes, however, their employment in the Parthian-Nabataean period. They are present, for example, on a pottery portrait from Brak, Syria,[859] among other places,[860] which has been dated to the middle of the second millennium B.C. and appear on the cheeks of Moabite (Pl. 69a, b) [861] and Ammonite figurines [862] (Pl. 70).

d. Saturn (Cronos)

Included among the male deities in the Nabataean cosmogony, paralleling the Parthian one, in addition to Zeus-Hadad-Jupiter, Helios-Apollo and Mercury-Hermes, is the figure of Saturn-Cronos (Pl. 153a), as we have already in passing mentioned. He figures prominently in the Parthian Mithraeum at Dura-Europos,[863] armed with a harpé. It looks like a pronged scimitar or harpoon with a heavy curved side-hook near the end which was intended apparently to engage the blade once it had penetrated the body.[864]

In the Nabataean sculpture of Saturn-Cronos at Khirbet Tannur, the harpé is prominently displayed above the right shoulder of Saturn. The bearded face of the god has been much damaged. Part of the right eye is still visible. The bust rising in high relief from a plain panel is otherwise intact. The beard consists of separate twisted locks. Carefully trained long curved separate locks of hair, coming to a sharp point at their ends, reach down over each shoulder. They are completely like those of the Vegetation Goddess (Pl. 31).

Very similar in appearance to the Saturn-Cronos bust with the harpé over his right shoulder is another bas-relief from Khirbet Tannur, to which we have previously referred (Pl. 154a, b). The face and front top of the head have been much damaged. The eyes are discernible and part of the nose and the mouth can be made out. The beard and hair are fairly intact, particularly on the sides. On each side of his head, twisted locks of hair fall down to just above his shoulders. The beard is composed of rows of tightly twisted snail curls, being very similar to the beard of the enthroned, main Zeus-Hadad figure (Pl. 41).

The body is clothed with a tight fitting doublet, and the end of a superimposed himation is thrown over the left shoulder. Above that shoulder are the much-damaged remains of what may possibly have been a thunderbolt symbol, identifying the bust then in that case as representative of Zeus-Hadad-Jupiter-Ba'al-shamin. Belonging to this latter group is another bust in high relief, with a stylized thunderbolt over his left shoulder, located on one of the two adjacent sides of an end cornice stone at Khirbet Tannur (Pl. 56). On the other side was a defaced bas-relief of what we believe to be a Tyché with a cornucopia against the right shoulder (Pl. 55). The counterpart of this end cornice stone also bore two high reliefs, one of a mural-crowned Tyché and the other a Dushara-Dionysos-Zeus-Hadad with a cornu-copia against his left shoulder (Pl. 53a, b). Reference has previously been made to these cornice stones with their sculptures. We recall that the popular Zeus-Serapis, whose worship was especially widespread in Egypt,[865] was represented not only with a calathos on his head in the form of a standard grain container but also with the symbol of the thunderbolt,[866] as is visible on several Khirbet Tannur sculptures (Pls. 41, 187a). There was a Serapion, a temple devoted to him, very close to Puteoli, where the Nabataeans probably also had a sanctuary of their own, and where, it will be remembered, Paul landed upon his arrival in Italy (Acts 28:13).

e. Mars

The only one of the seven planetary deities of Mesopotamian background and intensive Greek acceptance and adoration that cannot be identified with any single sculpture at Khirbet Tannur is Mars. We have dealt with the other six, but find it impossible to fix with certainty upon the seventh. There is no doubt, to judge from the example of Parthian Hatra alone,[867] that also this particular member of the sacred seven, whose complete authority was recognized with fervor from India to England, must also have been present and worshiped at Khirbet Tannur.

We have wondered whether perhaps the limestone fragment of a breast-plate, bearing in its center a winged, serpent-encircled Medusa head (Pl. 39), might have belonged to a sculpture in relief of Mars. Our conclusion, however, was that there was just as much or even more reason to assign it to a relief of Jupiter Dolichenus or of Zeus-Hadad-Ba'al-shamin or of an Athena-Allat-Atargatis.[868] We are nevertheless confident that a representation of Mars must have existed at Khirbet Tannur and that a recognizable one will yet be found in a future excavation at some Nabataean site such as Petra or Khirbet edh-Dherih in Jordan or one of the great Nabataean emporia in the Negev of Israel such as Abda.

2. SURROGATES AND SYMBOLS

a. Eagles

The role of the eagle was a most important one in Nabataean religious symbolism, as indeed it was throughout the entire Hellenistic-Semitic world. We first encountered it in connection with the eagle finial rabbeted into the back of the top of the head of the veiled Vegetation Goddess, with a stone horn on either side of it (Pls. 32, 34).

We have seen that the bottom of the eagle finial was horizontally dowelled to fit into the top of the panel bearing the high relief of the Vegetation Goddess. The triangular horns were projections of two sections of a carved cornice of the same radius as the top of the semicircular Atargatis panel. It seems likely that originally there were additional sections of this curved cornice, each with a projecting triangular horn, but no others were recovered in our excavations of the site. There is little question that the relief of the eagle with opened wings, together with the projecting horns, represents the solar Zeus, accompanied by rays of the sun. These were found in close proximity to the various pieces of the semicircular Atargatis panel, to which they belonged by dimension, design and spirit. We discovered nothing else at Khirbet Tannur to which they could be attached.

That the eagle in the Hellenistic-Semitic world was representative of Zeus and Ba'al-shamin is well attested.[869] Because of these Western and Eastern characteristics, we have called him Zeus-Hadad at Khirbet Tannur,[870] where, however, he probably bore a local Semitic name. The identification of the eagle with this god is often evidenced by sculptures of eagles with thunderbolts in their claws.[871] The thunderbolt symbol occurs strikingly at Khirbet Tannur, and can be seen twice there over the left arm of reliefs of Zeus-Hadad. In eagle form, this deity was frequently sculptured together with the sun and moon gods, Helios and Selene (Pl. 138),[872] and often as the solar deity [873] himself, as we saw in connection with the Vegetation Goddess of Khirbet Tannur. The two stone horns by the sides of the eagle finial above her head may reflect, as we have also suggested, the radiate crown that appears so frequently in representations of Zeus-Hadad (Ba'al-shamin), Helios, Mithras and Serapis.[874]

It should be remembered that just as Atargatis assumed many forms, such as Grain Goddess, Vegetation Goddess, Guardian Goddess and Dolphin Goddess, so did Zeus-Hadad take on different guises, expressive in his case, too, of numerous, separate functions. He was considered to be not only the ruler of the heavens but the master of the entire world. As such, he controlled the elements, manifesting himself in thunder and lightning and governing the planets and the stars in their courses.[875] In Syria, one particular form of the syncretistic Zeus-Hadad of Baalbek, for instance, bore, among other features, a solar disc, an eagle and two bull's horns.[876] The latter distinguished also the Syrian Ba'al of Hama.[877]

In view of the multiplicity of Hellenistic, Parthian and Egyptian factors that shaped the concepts and images of the gods of the ancient Near Eastern world, including the Nabataean pantheon, it is not surprising to find Parthian mention of the consort of Atargatis as "Zeus the sun, Mithras, Serapis," underscoring the solar attribute common to all of them.[878] The Parthian influence in that respect is emphasized by the discovery in front of the ruins of the Nabataean temple of Dushara at Si'a in the Hauran in southern Syria [879] of a basalt relief showing the slaying of the bull by Mithras. On this relief are also a radiate bust of the sun god, accompanied by an eagle, and a representation of the moon goddess with a crescent moon on her head.

Beneath the former is a figure in relief holding a torch, indicating perhaps the evening star, and beneath the latter, hidden partly behind the neck of the bull is yet another partly damaged figure, possibly also originally having held a torch, which then would have been the equivalent of the morning star [880] (Pl. 50).

The Nabataean Zeus-Hadad or Ba'al-shamin, as we have already pointed out, was repeatedly pictured in eagle form, together with representations of the lesser gods of the sun and the moon. Several other steles with reliefs of this type have been found at or are supposed to have come from the Nabataean site of Si'a just referred to. On one of them are the reliefs of three figures, including the lunar goddess on one side, the sun god on the other and the eagle of Ba'al-shamin with spread wings in between.[881] The bust of the moon goddess is set in a crescent moon.[882] Her face, with her curled locks reaching down to her shoulders, has been damaged, and her eyes are barely visible. In the center of a raised, circular concave shield on the opposite side is the relief of a much worn Helios mask, with twelve rays or petals extending from it. The eagle, dominating the scene, is shown with head turned in left profile and claws gripping the leading edge of the architrave of the tiny shrine pictured on this stele.

Still other sculptures on basalt blocks thought to have come from Nabataean Si'a (Pl. 138), but built now into a chieftain's house at the village of Ire in the Hauran, repeat the above pattern, although their arrangement is obviously not the original one.[883] Below a long lintel with stylized vine, leaf and fruit designs, is a beautifully executed relief of an eagle with spread wings, head turned to the left in right profile against a background of two large stylized acanthus leaves, shown in a sunken panel. The eagle stands on a protruding wreath, in a fashion reminiscent of the serpent-eagle sculpture from Khirbet Tannur, which we shall discuss later on (Pl. 140). Below it, although obviously not immediately connected with it, are two long blocks, bearing in high relief the busts of the moon and sun gods. At the side of each of them, on the same block, is a sunken panel containing a bust in relief, beneath a floral piece, which is entwined by a serpent (?) twisted in a Hercules knot. On the one block, the partly broken crescent of the moon rises behind the top of the back of the lunar goddess, on the front of whose right shoulder the end of a long torch rests. The pronounced curls or ringlets on the cheeks of the lunar goddess call to mind similar, if smaller ones on the cheeks of some of the goddesses of Khirbet Tannur (Pls. 1, 2a, b, 25, 26b, c, 51a).

On the adjacent block of stone is the equally high relief of the radiate sun god, with a similar torch commencing over the outer front of his left shoulder and with a sinuous serpent (?) on either side of the front of his chiton. In the sunken panel next to his left shoulder is a male bust of almost beatific appearance, with curled hair, beard and moustache. This is counterbalanced on the right side of the lunar goddess block by a similarly located relief of a bust, whose head and cheeks are covered by a helmet, leaving only the lower part of the forehead, the lips, nose, mouth and chin exposed. We surmise that these sunken panel reliefs, coupled with the torches, represent the evening and morning stars, the former in connection with the lunar goddess and the latter with the solar deity.[884]

The eagle on the finial above the head of Atargatis as the Vegetation Goddess at Khirbet Tannur is strikingly paralleled on a previously mentioned funerary plaque from Palmyra [885] (Pl. 156a, b). Forming its triangular top is an eagle, in completely frontal position, with lowered spread wings. It stands on the head of a male bust, its claws resting in his upward combed hair. A palm [886] branch extends diagonally upward from the outer edge of the right shoulder, and the neck and head of a horse in right profile can be seen above the left shoulder, now broken off, as is indeed the entire lower part of the plaque. The horse is much similar to one found at Nabataean Si'a [887] and to pottery figurines of horses from the Nabataean capital of Petra.[888]

A Nabataean sculpture from Kerak (Pl. 155a), in Biblical times the site of the Moabite capital of Moab,[889] shows, as we have already indicated, much the same decoration of the head and neck of a horse visible on this funerary plaque from Palmyra, emphasizing thus the common Parthian influence that binds them together.[890] In the Kerak relief, the considerably damaged head and neck of the horse appear above the left shoulder of the figure, and are turned in right profile to the left side of the framed sunken panel from which the sculpture protrudes. Most of the horse's neck is intact, but the rest of the relief of the animal has to be looked at attentively to be seen. The outline of all of the horse's neck and head, including some of its head harness, can then clearly be made out. The horses on these reliefs and camels [891] on others undoubtedly signify that they were meant to convey their riders through the world of after-life.

As a familiar symbol of divinity, the eagle, as we have seen, was well known in the ancient Near East,[892] and nowhere more so than among the Nabataeans, be it at Si'a in the Syrian Hauran, Khirbet Tannur or Petra in southern Transjordan, or Meda'in Saleh in northern Arabia.[893] The bold relief of an eagle, with opened wings, dominating the Eagle Shrine (Pl. 143), cut into the face of a sandstone cliff at Petra,[894] is indicative of its importance.

Two detached limestone heads of different sizes belonging originally to high reliefs of eagles were found in the debris of Khirbet Tannur (Pl. 144a, b). The body of the smaller one seems completely to have been destroyed in the cataclysm that brought the history of the temple to an end. A left wing fragment was recovered that may, however, belong to the body of the larger of the two (Pl. 144c). It is even possible that it belonged to the type

5 cms

10 cms

Pl. 207

a. Nabataean (?) rock drawing of spearman on camel, near Abda (p. 7)
b. Nabataean (?) rock drawing of ostrich hunt, Negev (Site 297 A) (p. 7)

475

Pl. 209 (*opposite*)

a. Nabataean rock drawing of horse and rider, with much later drawings around it, Negev (Site 297) (p. 7)
b. Nabataean memorial inscription, Negev (Site 415) (p. 7)

Pl. 208

a, b. Rock drawing of hunting scene, Negev (Site 262) (p. 7)

Pl. 210 Nabataean-Byzantine cave-cistern, Negev (Site 30), still water-tight. Byzantine Greek inscription BOETHON and Byzantine crosses superimposed on originally Nabataean pillar (p. 5)

of serpent-eagle sculpture from Khirbet Tannur (Pl. 140), dramatizing the solar characteristic of Zeus-Hadad in the role of Helios, the sun god, in the Nabataean pantheon.[895]

b. Serpents

Particularly striking was the discovery during the excavations of Khirbet Tannur of a sculpture in high relief of an eagle, representing the solar Zeus-Hadad, with opened wings, entwined by a serpent (Pl. 140). Both of them stand or rest, respectively, on a laurel wreath, in the center of which is a plaster basin. The laurel wreath is a symbol of victory and immortality.[896] Most of the pieces of this sculpture that had been broken and scattered about in a radius of several square meters near the east façade of the pylon of the raised, unroofed, inner temple-court, were recovered in our excavations and put together again, but some could not be found. Missing are the eagle's beak, most of the breast, part of the lower right foot, and a segment of the serpent's body near the eagle's lower left foot. The front, outer left top side of the eagle's left wing was damaged and repaired with plaster while the temple was still standing. It is furthermore clear that the bottom of the wreath rested on a ledge of some kind, while the back of the sculpture was embedded in a wall. Some of the original plaster or stucco holding it in place and concealing the very clear chisel or toothed adze marks visible especially on the back side of the eagle's left wing, can be seen at the rear and side of the top of the left wing and of the wreath on which it rests. The entire sculpture was originally hewn out of a single limestone block.

Clinging by its tail to the front of the wreath, the speckled serpent coils, in effect, around the right leg of the eagle, emerges under its left leg and rises upward diagonally to rest its head against the top of the center of the eagle's right wing. Some of the serpent's body has been sculptured in the round, cut free in part from the top of the wreath and from the eagle's right wing. Its head is turned upward in right profile, toward the eagle's head above it, shown in left profile. The sculptor seems to have attempted to invest the serpent with an attitude and gaze of starry-eyed, partly open-mouthed adoration.

The eyes of the eagle and of the serpent, as a matter of fact, were carved in a manner familiar to us from the sculptures of the gods, dolphins, animals and fishes of Khirbet Tannur. Behind the left side of the eye of the eagle is an exaggeratedly large auricle or ear opening, comparable to the one next to the eye of the smaller of the separate two eagle heads recovered in the excavations (Pl. 144a, b). No such auricle appears on the head of the eagle relief on the finial above the panel of the Vegetation Goddess (Pl. 34a).

The plumage on the bodies of both of these eagles is much the same. The long lower inside wing feathers are on vertical spaced ridges, narrowing from the top to the bottom, with those of the finial-eagle showing more detail than in the case of the serpent-entwined eagle. The smaller formalized feathers of these eagles are otherwise duplicated by the type of stylized ornamentation, looking like overlapping leaves divided in the middle, that can be seen on the shoulders and arms of two small busts in relief on an architrave above a niche in the east face of the inner temple-court pylon of Period III of Khirbet Tannur (Pl. 12a, b). This type of ornamentation appears also on the shoulders of several of the mutilated busts of what may be a Dolphin Goddess at Khirbet Tannur (Pls. 27a, b, 28a).

The legs of the serpent-entwined eagle end in three tremendous claws, which are half covered by tufts of feathers. The upper halves of the legs are covered with wavy curled feathers, that have the appearance of locks of hair on many of the Khirbet Tannur deities and animals. The legs of the eagle in relief on the finial above the Vegetation Goddess panel are similarly decorated, although the three claws on each of them have been much damaged (Pl. 34a). Short irregular incisions, producing a stippled effect, mark the seemingly bald heads of both eagles, being, however, larger and deeper on the crown of the head of the serpent-entwined eagle. A limestone fragment was found of what must have been a large eagle sculpture, to judge from the claws of one foot of an eagle visible on it (Pl. 144d).

Strikingly similar to the Khirbet Tannur sculpture of a serpent-entwined eagle standing on a wreath is another one (Pl. 141a, b), also of limestone, found at Zaharet el-Bedd in North Gilead, on the east side of the Jordan. Enfolding the right leg with two complete loops of its tail, the serpent bends around the back of the left leg and rears up sinuously across the breast of the eagle to rest its head against the right side of the top of the eagle's neck. Only the top and the back end of the broadened head of the serpent are visible. The indentations serving in lieu of spots on the body and head of the Khirbet Tannur serpent are fashioned more deeply in this case. The head of the eagle is shown in left profile, and once again the serpent seems to be reaching forward in utter adoration of the eagle as the solar deity.

The Zaharet el-Bedd eagle differs somewhat from the Khirbet Tannur one through the ornate coxcomb on its head. Otherwise, it is very much like it in posture, opened wings and general manner of depiction of the plumage on the inner surface of its wings and on its body, although there are some clear-cut differences in the shape and arrangement of the feathers. The three claws on each leg are also fashioned in much more detail and are shown grasping a ledge rather than a wreath. On the back of the left wing are two Greek letters, the equivalent of "p" and "x," probably representing the sculptor's identifying marks. There is a Greek "k" sculptor's mark, too, on one of the building stones at Khirbet Tannur (Pl. 199b) and a Greek "p" on another (Pl. 172a). The Zaharet el-Bedd sculpture is probably to be dated, like its Khirbet Tannur parallel, to the first part of the second century A.D.[897] It too was probably embedded originally in a wall, with its base resting on a stand or ledge.

There is no reason to believe that the Zaharet el-Bedd eagle-and-serpent sculpture comes from a Nabataean temple, but there is every reason to believe, as we have suggested, that both the Zaharet el-Bedd and the Khirbet Tannur examples belong to the same period, being intimately connected in general form and specific features and religious purpose. Nabataeans may well have worshiped in whatever pagan sanctuary existed at Zaharet el-Bedd during their frequent visits there. Travel and trade and regional politics made it natural for numerous Nabataeans to frequent the territory and cities of the Decapolis and their dependencies, most of which lay between the Syrian and Transjordan parts of their kingdom. The fact that the Nabataeans apparently had a sanctuary of their own at Gerasa (Jerash),[898] southeast of Zaharet el-Bedd, is indicative of the heavy Nabataean traffic in the Decapolis area. The sanctuaries and gods of the Nabataeans were closely related to those in vogue throughout most of the ancient Near East. As a result, peoples of many lands could find common ground and worship together in places far removed from their native hearths. Particularly during the first two centuries B.C. and A.D. they enjoyed a far ranging community of culture. Despite pronounced and recognizable differences, they had much in common, insofar as literary language, religion, architecture, art, political and economic interests and interdependence are concerned. It comes as no surprise, therefore, to find at Dura-Europos a drawing of an eagle and serpent closely related to those of Khirbet Tannur and Zaharet el-Bedd (Pl. 141c).[898a]

The Judaeans alone were set apart or set themselves apart from their contemporaries near and far by reason of the Judaism they espoused and practiced in varying degrees. It rejected, by virtue of the ultimately decisive influence of a minority of purists, all physical representations of the divine and was fiercely opposed to all pagan gods. To be sure, in the purest distillation of its philosophy the contemporary Judaism was practiced only by a fraction of the total population of Judaea. It was this small group, however, that perpetuated the deep rooted strength and the clear vision of their ancient faith and provided the leadership that guaranteed its future.[899]

The Nabataeans for their part, with their many close contacts with the Judaeans, must have been familiar with the nature of their worship of an invisible God, even as the latter must have been cognizant of the Nabataean and other closely related deities.[900] The very similarities and mutuality of interests of the two peoples resulted in their joining together frequently for cooperation, but did not prevent them, under varying circumstances, from often being ranged against one another in bitter conflict. In the final analysis, it may well have been the dissimilarity of religious orientation that spelled the crucial difference between survival for the Judaeans and their descendants and cultural effacement for the Nabataeans and others like them.

Both the eagle and the serpent in their roles as surrogates of gods were foreign and vile to the puritanism of the spiritually invincible minority of the Judaeans whose time-and-tempest-tested Judaism was essentially that of the Prophets and the Rechabites and Essenes. This remained true during the Hellenistic-Nabataean-Roman periods with which we are particularly concerned in this book, even though it was not uncommon for many Judaeans to pay obeisance then, to a greater or lesser degree, to these and other pagan deities and to include them and others in their protective amulets and familiar prayers.[901]

For the Nabataeans, however, and multitudes of others of related cultures, near and far, the eagle and the serpent were enduringly divine symbols and supremely sacred objects of profound worship. To them the posture of the serpent in relationship to the eagle signified adoration and supplication. The serpent represented, among other things, the movement of the sun across the skies.[902] It attested also to the universal and eternal qualities of the sun god it served and symbolized.[903] The aspect of immortality was concretized in the periodic renewal of its skin, in its amazing ability to shed the old one in favor of the new. The very armor of Ba'al-shamin was conceived of as being composed of a series of overlapping serpent scales, testifying thus to his undying divinity and to his power to perpetuate life.[904]

The sanctity of the serpent is emphasized by a striking example in the great Nabataean center of Meda'in Saleh in northern Arabia, where, too, the solar eagle is repeatedly employed.[905] Both occur, for example, on a crenellated tomb façade of a type common there, where, as at Petra to the north of it, related structures of elaborate fronts and comparatively shallow depths were cut into the sides of sandstone hills. The eagle on this particular shrine or tomb appears above the tympanum of the façade, while in the center of the tympanum is a bust with now indistinguishable features, flanked on each side by a serpent.[906]

A splendid relief from Aden, which will be alluded to again (Pl. 142), shows two serpents enfolding a frontally positioned eagle with head turned in right profile.[906a]

The serpent in general was considered of old to be an agent of healing [907] and fertility,[908] and was connected, as we have seen, with the promise of immortality, of life after death, of endless renewal. It was held in high repute in Egypt, Syria, Mesopotamia and Asia Minor, whence it was transported to Greece to become identified or associated with Zeus Milichios or Zeus-Sabazios.[909] Egyptian [910] and especially Parthian [911] influences, added to earlier ones, made the serpent an object of intense veneration among the Nabataeans, to judge particularly from the eagle-and-serpent sculpture of Khirbet Tannur.

The excavators of the small Nabataean temple at Ramm in southernmost Transjordan discovered the statuette of a seated goddess there (Pl. 52c) and reported that they could make out the presence of a serpent coiled around the bottom of her tunic.[912] We consider this goddess to be the same type of enthroned Atargatis as the one that must have been placed next to the Zeus-Hadad stele at Khirbet Tannur. It is difficult to see the serpent in any of the published photographs.[913] If it was indeed depicted, it would seem to have been related in background and meaning to the type of python coiled around the legs of the goddess on a sixteenth-century B.C. stele found by Albright at Tell Beit Mirsim.[914]

More directly connected with the Khirbet Tannur eagle-and-serpent sculpture and indicative of the strong Parthian influence in one direction on Nabataean culture, are the numerous Parthian representations of serpents,[915] including one beneficently coiled around the Mithraic sun god, Zarvan, who became known among the Greeks as Cronos or Aion.[916] There are still others, such as the one underneath the horse of the mounted Mithras,[917] another of fertility significance under the bull being slain by Mithras,[918] and a third above the left side of the head of the sun god, with the crescent of the moon on his shoulders, from Palmyra.[919]

The possibility of the existence of a bas-relief of a serpent coiled around the bottom of the tunic of a goddess, such as the excavators of the temple in the Wadi Ramm thought they saw on the statuette they found there, is, to be sure, heightened by the apparent existence of a unique monument at Petra. Concerning it, Kennedy writes: "The snake monument itself is unique among Petraean carvings. The coils of the serpent wind around a central block on the top of a plain four-square block." [920] With the exception of a passing reference to this snake monument in Brünnow and Domaszewski,[921] I find no other reference to it, nor any clear photographs. If Kennedy's description is correct, it would seem to be that of a serpent around a Dushara block, and an earlier predecessor of the one entwined around the solar eagle of Khirbet Tannur. The sculptures of Zeus-Hadad and of Helios there and throughout the entire Nabataean kingdom and the sculptures of the eagle that variously represented one or the other of them, replaced in the final, major period of Nabataean history the pristine representation of the chief Nabataean god in the form of a roughly hewn, rectanglar block. I know of no Nabataean example, however, where Zeus-Hadad-Ba'al-shamin alone is unmistakably represented by a serpent.[922]

The serpent theme occurs clearly at Petra, as we have already seen, also on two sculptured building blocks, on each of which is shown in relief a winged Eros (?), standing between two griffins (Pl. 167a, b), and holding in each hand a serpent rearing itself upward from the ground.[923] The raised front left foot of each griffin touches the serpent in front of the Eros (?) figure.

These serpents remind one of the two held in the left hand of a god from Parthian Hatra, who wields a peculiarly shaped double axe in his right hand. Represented on one of the sides of a funerary altar, this god has been interpreted as a chthonic god, and identified with the Iranian Ahriman or Nergal.[924] The axe is similar to the one held in the right hand of another god from Hatra, the cutting edge of which is on the outside, with the other side forming the upcurved head of a serpent. The god himself, standing in a welter of serpents, and between a complex standard on his right side and an enthroned Atargatis on his left, seated above two dolphins and holding on to a leashed dog below her, has been identified with the Parthian god, representing a composite Nergal-Ahriman-Hades.[925] (Pl. 10a, b)

To judge, therefore, from these Parthian examples from Hatra, it is possible, although we do not consider it likely, that the serpents by the sides and in the hands, respectively, of the winged Eros (?) figures at Petra are not to be considered in the same light as the one in the serpent-and-eagle sculpture of Khirbet Tannur. It is nevertheless difficult not to ascribe to them a fecundizing and solar significance.[926]

Whether or not it is correct that the serpents connected with these Eros (?) figures find their most direct spiritual relationship with those of the chthonic gods from Hatra, it is possible that these particular Parthian gods can be described as being more Eastern and insularly Parthian [927] than any of the Khirbet Tannur sculptures and than some from Hatra itself.[928] If then within Hatra and the Parthian kingdom Hellenistic-Semitic cultural influences on the one hand and more exclusively Parthian on the other manifested themselves differently at the same time, it is not surprising that the same state of affairs should be found to have prevailed within the heart of the Nabataean kingdom, too, although to a more attenuated degree. In both countries, there seem to have been differences between the solar and subterranean connections or functions of serpent representations, with the former, certainly among the Nabataeans, being more widespread and general than the latter.

To the category of netherworld [929] and occasionally inimical or combative character, belongs a rather crudely fashioned relief of two serpents at Petra, shown attacking a small, four-footed animal, with one of them reaching for its head and another seizing one of its rear legs and pulling it backwards.[930] They may have belonged to a crude Mithraic symbol, showing serpents licking the life blood. Another instance is recorded from Petra of a serpent represented as having slithered up above the back of a horse and striking the person leading it.[931] The inference seems reasonable, therefore, that these particular examples from Petra, if they have been correctly reported, give evidence of direct chthonic influence from Parthia.

We have seen, thus, that there is evidence in the Nabataean capital of Petra itself of serpent symbols with two, main, dissimilar connotations, resulting respectively from the distinctive and harmonious merger of Hellenistic-Semitic influences on the one hand and the direct impact of more natively Parthian ones on the other hand. It should, therefore, not be surprising to encounter the same phenomenon in other parts of the Nabataean kingdom, or even to find the balance weighted notably against the one and in favor of the predominant Hellenistic-Semitic cultural element.

1) REGIONAL FACTORS

Many factors need to be considered in this connection. Among the most important of them was the degree to which a thoroughgoing Hellenistic-Semitic culture prevailed in any particular region or was resisted or altered or confounded by a renascent East, which out of the exuberance of its growing strength and mounting self-pride introduced ideas and forms and fashions conforming inherently to the compulsions of its nativity. This manifestation of confident awareness of its indigenous strength, rooted in the rich soil of its origins and antecedents, characterized the swift growth of newly arisen Parthia. Having inherited and in some ways magnified the power and enlarged the territory of former Persia, after the collapse of the empire of Alexander the Great, it soon proved able to halt the forward thrust eastward of expansionist Rome and contain it and at times even endanger its Asiatic foothold.

Hellenism was employed by the western state as an imperial weapon, and the Parthians at first instinctively and then by design blunted it and beat it back more or less successfully with the Orientalism of their cultural inheritance and conscious purpose. In the sculptures and paintings of their gods and royalty and remembered dead, they frequently incorporated fashions of garb and hairdress, casts of countenance, types of jewelry, weapons and style of portraiture that were unmistakably Parthian. To be sure, in many instances and at numerous sites, they did not or could not eradicate completely the reflection of strong Hellenistic-Semitic influences, as opposed to what I should like to call more purely Parthian ones. Among the latter, for example, is the use of the torque as insignia and ornament and the very significant introduction and insistent emphasis upon the spiritual principle of stylized frontality in their artistic compositions.[932] Parthian, too, was the widely penetrating effect of their concept of the conflict between the forces of good and evil.

That the generally happy marriage of Hellenistic and Semitic cultural elements exemplified in the harmony of art and architecture of Khirbet Tannur was not characteristic of all the parts of the Nabataean kingdom, becomes apparent, as we have already pointed out, when one compares the sculptures of that shrine with those of Nabataean temples in southern Syria. This might have been expected, perhaps, as a result of the considerable differences in population, pottery and political control existing between the northernmost part of the Nabataean kingdom in the Hauran and Jebel Druze on the one hand and its main, southern division on the other hand, that extended through the former territories of Moab and Edom into northern Arabia and across the Negev in southern Palestine and Sinai to the edges of Egypt.

The wide disparity between the two is eloquently revealed by the seemingly complete absence in the north of the characteristic and generally exquisite Nabataean pottery found in great quantities on hundreds of sites in the south. To pass from the uniformity of Hellenistic-Roman wares in Syria and most of Eastern and Western Palestine to the absolutely unique, flashing and sophisticated artistry of Nabataean earthenware found from Edom and Moab to the Wadi Arabah, the Negev and Sinai, is like passing from a dull reach of sameness to a gladdening oasis of glowing flowers.

I have never come across any of the hundreds of Nabataean sites we were able to discover and place on the map in the southern part of the Nabataean kingdom, without finding many or a multitude of Nabataean potsherds, that fairly shouted out the story of their once unbroken shape and significance and the skills and sophistication of the Nabataean potters and people. Nabataeans lived or lodged in all these southern hamlets, villages and towns in the course of their frequent and wide ranging trade journeys and their flourishing agricultural and economic development. They built kilns and houses and temples. They erected dams and terraces and dug cisterns without number. These served many purposes, to keep the cultivable earth in place, to catch and conserve the rare rainwater and to sustain their crops and nourish their flocks and themselves. Stone piles (Pl. 213) mistakenly known today as *teleilat el-anab,* "hillocks on which grapevines were trained," were swept together on uncultivable slopes to provide swifter and more complete runoff of infrequent rainwater to arable lands in terraced dry stream beds or *wadis* (Pls. 212, 214). The Nabataeans tilled the reluctant soil with almost incredible intensity and transformed the face of the earth from grim wilderness to gardens yielding grain, grapes, olives, pomegranates and figs for human beings, and fodder and grazing for herds and flocks.

The reason that none of the typical Nabataean pottery has as yet been encountered in Nabataean Syria, and a rare discovery would make no difference in this regard, is, as I have already suggested, because the Nabataeans never formed the bulk of its population. Their role during the approximately two centuries of their control of the Hauran and Jebel Druze from 85 B.C. on was that of colonial rulers and administrators. This state of affairs was altogether different from the one which prevailed in the agricultural heartland of their kingdom, much farther south, whose capital was Petra. There, together with many of the former Moabites and Edomites who became fully Nabataeanized in time, they themselves became the farmers and shepherds, the traders and caravaneers, the artisans and artists, the governing class as well as the more or less happily governed.

Despite the long enduring Nabataean overlordship, the people of the land in the Hauran and the Jebel Druze remained basically unchanged and stubbornly provincial. They were more exposed and perhaps more receptive to Parthian than to Hellenistic influence, which, however, they could by no means completely escape. They apparently gladly worshiped in the Nabataean temples, such as those of Si'a and Soueïda,[933] erected by their masters, but inevitably introduced into them the character and coloration of their own prepossessions. In the gods fashioned almost exclusively by local craftsmen for these sanctuaries, there were incorporated qualities which made them distinguishable from the deities of Khirbet Tannur, however closely related to each other in many respects they nevertheless remained.

The examination of several sculptures from the Jebel Druze which may well be Nabataean, and contemporary with those of Khirbet Tannur far to the south, illustrates both the striking relationship as well as the radical difference, at times, in the two areas of treatment. This applies, for example, to the important theme of the relationship of the eagle and the serpent to one another. At Khirbet Tannur, as at Zaharet el-Bedd, it was a complementary and sympathetic one, with the serpent represented as a beneficent agent. This harmony of connection is further demonstrated at Qanawat, in the northern extension of the Nabataean kingdom in the Jebel Druze in Syria.[934]

A basalt stele was found there, which shows the damaged relief of an eagle in the center, with body intact but head broken off, portrayed in a frontal position, with wings opened against its sides, and holding firmly in its claws a serpent, whose head, touching the outer edge of the eagle's right wing, has suffered damage but can still clearly be made out. Twisting downward below and beyond the eagle's left wing, the serpent coils around in a double or pretzel-like loop on the lower left side of the stele. Its tail extends diagonally upward to just below and beyond the left foot of a nude, male figure above it.

The upper half of the head of this apparently divine figure is missing. In the disproportionately large fingers of his left hand, he holds a spear diagonally, the tip of which points to the serpent at a point below the outermost, bottom edge of the eagle's left wing. Above the top of the spear can be seen five petals or rays and the edges of two more. It seems certain that originally there were twelve of them, forming a radiant circle around a mask of Helios.[935]

At the upper right side of this stele is a relief of another nude figure, apparently male, serving as a counterpart to the nude, male spearman on the other side. Wearing a beribboned fillet, it is represented as holding a flute. The figure has been identified by some as a "Selene." [936] I am reminded, however, of the flute-playing Pan in the Nabataean mural at el-Bared (Pl.

203) near Petra in southern Transjordan. Protruding from behind the right side of this figure is what has been called a tail,[937] a most doubtful designation. Could it possibly be part of the serpent? On a raised panel at the lower right side of this stele is a deeply engraved Greek inscription of theophoric Nabataean names.[938]

It seems possible to identify the holder of the spear with the morning star,[939] and the other figure with the evening star. We think, too, that the symbol for the moon, paralleling that of the broken, radiant circle suggesting the presence of the sun god, may also originally have been present on this stele. We cannot agree with some to the effect that the serpent on this stele seems to be synonymous with the forces of darkness or evil, which the auxiliary of the sun god exorcizes or expels with the shafts of dawning light.

A striking example of the solar eagle with its symbolic bodyguard of the morning and evening stars occurs on yet another basalt stele recovered from the Nabataean temple site of Soueïda in the Jebel Druze, with the likelihood although not the certainty that it actually came from the Nabataean temple there. It shows an eagle in flight, with completely outstretched wings, flanked by two winged youths. The one on the right side of the eagle holds a torch upright, while the one on the left grasps a torch turned downward. These two torches have been interpreted, correctly we think, as symbols of the morning and evening stars on either side of the sun.[940]

Whether our explanation of the nude figures on the Qanawat stele from the Jebel Druze be correct or not, the chief importance of this stele for us lies in the parallel of mutually warm relationship between the eagle and the serpent, such as prevailed at Khirbet Tannur. If our interpretation is mistaken, however, and the serpent is to be conceived of as being inimical to the eagle, then the antecedent background of the Qanawat stele could be reflected in Job 9:13 in the enmity to the monster Rahab. The relationship between the eagle and the serpent at Qanawat would then be one of sharp antagonism, of the conflict of good against evil, of light against darkness, of the creatively divine against the destructively demonic. We do not, however, believe this latter version to be the correct explanation of the Qanawat stele and hold to the above mentioned one.

The beneficent relationship between the eagle and the serpent shown in the Nabataean sculptures of Khirbet Tannur and Qanawat is emphasized again in a small bas-relief of the sanctuary of Aglibol and Malakbel at Palmyra. Over the fruit laden altar between the two figures there hovers an eagle with a palm branch in its claws and a serpent in its beak. The serpent's head and tail touch the crowns of the heads of the two gods.[941]

The same, mutually warm relationship is shown in an Arabian stone relief in a collection in Aden.[942] Rising in low relief from a sunken panel is a frontally positioned eagle with half-opened wings and with its head in right profile, whose body is completely encircled by two serpents, one on each side. Their tails touch the outer claws of each foot of the eagle and their heads touch the back and front sides of the top of the eagle's head. The wings of the eagle cover to a greater or lesser degree part of the bodies of the serpents (Pl. 142).

There is a fascinating, near-duplicate of the Khirbet Tannur and Zaharet el-Bedd eagle-serpent reliefs at Yugoslavian Pula, at the southern end of the Istrian peninsula, about midway by sea between Rijeka and Trieste, near the northeast end of the Adriatic Sea. At the top of the ceiling of the magnificent Triumphal Arch of Lucius Sergius the Younger, dated to no later than the end of the reign of Augustus (72 B.C.-A.D. 14), is a low relief of a frontally positioned eagle with opened wings, clasping a serpent in its claws. The serpent twists gracefully in an inverted "S" fashion across the front of the eagle's body to gaze in worshipful admiration at the eagle, whose head, in left profile, is inclined downward towards it.[943]

This eagle-serpent relief, executed with more classical excellence than its Khirbet Tannur and Zaharet el-Bedd parallels, is placed inside a square, tilted on end, whose sides are formed by two parallel, raised lines. Particularly amazing in view of the title and subject matter of this book is the fact that above or below each side of the square is portrayed a lively dolphin. We recall that not very far from Pula, near the center of the north shore of the Adriatic Sea, there was discovered the bronze bust of the God of Aquileia, with his dolphins and crab's claws and transparent veil of leaves over his face (Pl. 13). There comes to mind in this connection also the Dolphin Goddess and the leaf masked Fertility or Vegetation Goddess of Khirbet Tannur, whose backgrounds, together with others of the pantheon there, were in considerable part strongly Hellenistic.

The presence on the soffit of the Triumphal Arch at Pula of the reliefs of elaborate rosettes set between acanthus and other leaves in squares or rhomboids, paralleled by fantastic sea-creatures, some of the upper parts of whose bodies consist of the busts of winged, nude females, brings to mind the presence at Petra of Nereids riding on centaurs.[944]

Griffins and lions and other animals of fact or fantasy fill triangular spaces of other tilted squares, which are ornamented with a series of small rosettes in separate, square frames.[945] Still other reliefs on the Pula Triumphal Arch portray armor and weapons of various kinds, among which a type of shield or possibly battle-axe is featured that occurs at Nabataean Khirbet Brak (Pl. 174c), a suburb of Petra.

All of these features on the Arch of Pula, either in direct or related form, occur in Nabataean representations, too, with the probability that the laurel, acanthus, oak and ivy leaves, floral and vine designs and the ubiquitous rosette and various fruits employed both in the West and the East conveyed, at least to the initiated, particular significance, namely, in addition to ornamentation and distinction, that of renewal, resurrection and immortality.[946]

A fourth-century A.D. lead sarcophagus from Mohalib, north of Tyre, in

Lebanon, has decorations of myrtle and vine leaves; an eight-rayed sun at one end, together with rosettes at the end of each ray, centering in a ninth one in the middle; a Satyr's head between Corinthian columns of a simulated temple-front at the other end; and a winged Medusa head entwined by serpents on the front side, with a pair of dolphins facing each other above it and a similar pair below it (Pl. 24a).[947] Dolphins occur also on other sarcophagi from Tyre.[948]

The Medusa head, especially, symbolizing victory over death, the various leaves indicating perpetual renewal, the serpent achieving immortality by shedding its old covering and finding new youth, and the dolphins auguring well-being and safety of travel in this life and the next, underscore the hope for immortality, which so strongly animated the Hellenistic-Semitic cultural world.

c. Anguipeds

Although the relationship between eagle and serpent in the reliefs and stele thus far discussed has been a mutually favorable one, there is expressed on one of the basalt steles from the Nabataean site of Soueïda [949] a strong antipathy to a monstrous creature, part serpent and part human in form, known to us as an anguiped. The likelihood, although not the certainty, is that it is indeed a Nabataean sculpture, reflecting, however, a dominantly Parthian background. We judge it to be approximately contemporary with the second-century A.D. period of the eagle-serpent sculpture of Khirbet Tannur. The center of the scene on this stele is occupied by two combatants engaged in mortal battle.

The one on the stele's right side is represented as a mounted bowman shooting arrows, one after another at the body of his enemy. Above him is visible a rosette with five double petals, seeming to enhance his divinity. The object of his attack is a monstrous male anguiped, part human and part multiple serpent. His head is turned in profile towards his attacker but otherwise the anguiped is depicted in frontal position. The upper part of his body is that of a human, while the lower part is composed of two serpents twisted upward in striking position. The head of the left one has been broken off, but the head of the other, shown in left profile and pointed to the right side of the stele, is still intact, with its left eye deeply carved and its tongue realistically protruding in flashing anger.

One of the arrows has pierced the monster's body,[950] whose face has been mutilated by vandals, but whose carefully combed hair and side locks are intact. The wounded anguiped clutches two circular stones in his raised hands,[951] and is about to hurl them at the charging horseman, from whose bent bow a second arrow has just been released to follow the one that has already found its target. The carefully tressed tail of the horse touches the outer edge of the right side of the stele, with its two hind legs resting on a raised panel and its two front ones reared high in a galloping position.

Between the two antagonists on the Soueïda stele is a male bust in relief, in whose hands is a circular medallion, bearing in turn the relief of a twelve-petaled rosette. The latter consists really of two rosettes, one on top of the other, of six petals each, arranged in alternating order. We believe with Seyrig,[952] that this bust with its double rosettes represents the sun god, Helios, and that the attacking horseman, blazing away with his bow and arrows at the aroused and counterattacking anguiped, is to be identified with the morning star. Dunand, however, followed by Dussaud, would equate the mounted warrior with the sun god, accompanied by the morning star in the form of the bust with its rosette-decorated medallion.

We wonder about this viewpoint, being mindful of the damaged rosette on the Qanawat stele and the complete one on the Si'a stele,[953] which, in the form of radiate circles or radiate crowns, are to be connected with heads of Helios. By the same token, we think that the rosette connected with the Soueïda bust heightens the possibility of the identification of the latter with Helios. His figure replaces on this Soueïda stele the solar eagle on the Qanawat one. Be that as it may, the fact remains that both of these steles repeat essentially the same theme, namely the fight of light against darkness, of good against evil.

Almost exactly the same scene of a gladiatorial contest between the equivalent of an angel and a demon, as depicted by a combat between a mounted archer and a malevolent anguiped on the Soueïda stele, is repeated on a marble relief in the temple of Bel in Palmyra.[954] There are differences between the two, but they are minor.

On the Palmyra one, the archer stands, it is assumed, in a chariot, instead of being mounted on a charging horse as on the Soueïda stele. Otherwise, the action is much the same. The charioteer-archer is pictured as being about to shoot an arrow from his drawn bow, another arrow already in flight is about to pierce the anguiped's neck and one has already penetrated the creature's breast.

The head and right arm of this anguiped have been broken off, with the lower part of the left one also having been much damaged. The lower part of its body is not composed of two serpents coiled to attack, as on the Soueïda stele, but five of them. They emerge from underneath three acanthus leaves, marking the division between the monster and human parts of the creature. One of these serpents has grasped and is strangling a small figure of a deity or of a human being, which is being further attacked or is being devoured by a small dog.[955] It reminds one of the scenes of Mithras slaying the bull, with a dog rearing up in front in order to consume the blood or life force.

It is interesting to compare the Soueïda and Palmyra portrayals of an attack by solar powers against the inimical anguiped with an European bas-relief of Mithraic background, representing much the same confrontation. It shows the sun god, Ahura-Mazda, fighting with demons of anguiped form. One of them, as in the case of the Soueïda relief, holds round missiles in his hands as weapons.[956]

Telling evidence of the very direct impact of Parthian Mithraism upon the Nabataeans was furnished by the discovery in their Dushara temple at Si'a in the Hauran, of a familiar type of relief in basalt, showing the solar deity, Mithras, slaying the bull in the presence of sundry attendant deities, with his dog leaping at its throat, and underneath the dying beast a serpent drinking its blood, and a scorpion biting its testicles,[957] all of them absorbing or consuming the life force.

As the popularity of Mithraism grew, propagated by eastern merchants and Roman soldiers and slaves of eastern experience or origin, the more or less exact replicas of this stele spread from the Orient to the farthest reaches of the Occident,[958] including even England.[959] The possibility of the existence of a Nabataean temple at Aquileia on the north shore of the Adriatic, whence came a bust of Zeus-Hadad with a veil of leaves on his face and body like the one worn by Atargatis at Khirbet Tannur, is fortified, although hardly proven, by the fact that an excellent bas-relief closely similar to the one of Si'a was found there.[960]

The anguiped in each of the Soueïda and Palmyra steles, to return to a consideration of them and their parallels, is in effect the Leviathan, whose head God crushed,[961] according to Psalm 74:14. It is kin to the type of seven-headed dragon of evil against which the forces of good contended, as we read in Revelation 12:3-17. Noteworthy in connection with the attack of the sun god on the anguiped are the statements in verses 1 and 14 in Revelation 12 that the "woman arrayed with the sun and the moon under her feet, and upon her head a crown of twelve stars" was given "the two wings of the great eagle" to escape this monster. And particularly pertinent is the passage in Isaiah 51:9, which reads: ". . . O arm of Jehovah, . . . is it not Thou that didst cut Rahab in pieces, that didst pierce the monster?"

The story of this conflict between the deity or his agent and the dragon, reflected in the Bible and also occurring in ancient Canaanite, Syrian and Akkadian mythology,[962] finds its analogy in Greek mythology too, in the legend of the slaying of the many headed monster by Heracles, with the assistance of Iolaus.[963] There are also the Syrian accounts and representations of the combat of Zeus with Typhon, of Perseus with the sea monster of Jaffa,[964] and, of course, later on of St. George with the dragon.[965] Whether or not the basis for this tradition is to be traced back to the ancient Near East,[966] the fact remains that both from Semitic and Hellenistic sources, conflicting influences converged upon the Nabataeans dealing on the one hand with the interrelationship of the eagle and the serpent and the benevolent forces they represented, and on the other with the combat of the gods against the evil powers of the anguipeds.

The emphasis of Parthian Mithraism on the dualism of good and evil and light and darkness reflects, as we have seen, a profound interest in these problems, which was expressed in Biblical and related Semitic sources. It formed one of the main preoccupations of Judaism of the Hellenistic-Roman period and of earliest Christianity. Additional information on this dualism and of the confrontation between God and Satan, has come from the Dead Sea Scrolls.[967] The Nabataeans, too, for all we know, may have been conversant and concerned with this philosophy. Tangible expression of it seems to be reflected in some of their Jebel Druze sculptures and perhaps in several of their Petra reliefs. It is not evident, however, in their sculptural portrayal of the ardent relationship between the solar eagle and the solar serpent at Khirbet Tannur, mirroring the similar connection between the Mithraic Cronos and the serpent.[968]

The forces of life and death were represented as being at war with each other in the anguiped representations. One is reminded of various portrayals of a gigantomachy, with gods engaged in internecine conflict, such as can be seen on friezes at Aphrodisias and Pergamon.[969] The theme is repeated in the struggle of Laocoön and his two sons against the serpents sent by Apollo to destroy them.[970] The reverse situation is portrayed in pictures of the slaying of the serpent by Apollo.[971]

The serpent and serpentine creatures, it seems, were cast in mutually contradictory roles in Nabataean and related sculptures, frequently as the subject of adoration and occasionally as the object of attack. It seems strange, therefore, at least at first glance, to find that many people considered as helpful or saving graces the very serpent-legged creatures at first treated as hostile demons. Nevertheless, partly perhaps as a result of Egyptian influence, large numbers of people of the Hellenistic-Roman-Semitic world, including Jews, made fond use of protective amulets featuring the originally inimical anguipeds.[972]

A reasonable explanation of the widespread usage of such charms to ward off evil or requite a hurt or win a lady's favor or recapture a languishing or lost love, lies in the very "apotropaic value of monstrous forms, among which the Gorgon's head is the obvious example," as has been suggested.[973]

Responsive then in function to varied cultural influences, emanating sometimes from a single source or again from opposite points of the compass, the serpent, either by itself or in concert with other mythological beings, appears in the final analysis to have embodied the ambivalent forces that seem first to create and then to destroy every society. Fiery serpents were sent to punish the wayward of Israel and a copper serpent was fashioned to heal its conscience stricken (Numbers 21:6, 9). And was not the Nehushtan, the copper serpent, long worshiped in the sanctuary at Jerusalem (II Kings 18:4)?

XIV. MEANINGFUL NAMES

XIV. *Meaningful Names*

1. ON ALTARS

a. Alexandros Amrou Altar

The most dramatic and obvious example of the intermingling of Hellen-istic and Oriental elements in Nabataean art and architecture is furnished by a small, free-standing, incense altar decorated on three of four sides with striking reliefs and bearing on the top of the front panel a clear Greek in-scription.[974] The residue of the incense burned on top of the altar testifies to the frequent use made of it (Pl. 187b). Analysis has determined that it is of an oleoresinous variety, and consists of the resin of frankincense which resolidified after having been melted by fire without being entirely con-sumed. The Nabataeans obviously made much use themselves of the incense they purveyed to their immense profit from Arabia to Syria and Palestine and beyond.

Rising from three rectangular panels set between attached pilasters, capped with uniquely Nabataean, Corinthianized horned capitals, and rest-ing on Attic bases are reliefs of a central Zeus-Hadad (Pl. 187a) and two Niké figures, one on either side of him (Pl. 188a, b). Horizontal lines across the face of each pilaster above the base simulate the existence of two lower courses of building blocks, with a long, narrow, rectangular inset decorating the upper face of the pilaster. The pattern is very much like that of the pilasters of the east façade of the altar-pedestal of Period II, without the ornate floral and rosette design in the insets above their bottom courses.

Two corner acroterions, each apparently composed originally of four curved and voluted branches, decorate the sides of the upper face of the altar above the sunken panel containing the inscription. The other two worked sides of the altar have the same triangular panels and bordering acroterions, but lack any inscription.

It is noteworthy that the same type of acroterion decoration occurs on a fragment of a raking cornice from the Nabataean temple of Si'a in the Hauran.[975] It appears also at the corners of a gable from Coptic Ahnas,[976] whose art, we believe to have been strongly influenced by Nabataean influences, although probably not in this particular facet.[977]

On the upper face of the front side of this altar, occupying a narrowing triangular space between the corner horns,[978] was originally a four-line inscription in Greek letters, the first line of which is now missing. It had been hammered away, leaving only traces of grooves of several letters, but there can, however, be little doubt about their identification. The entire inscription reads, *(alexa) ndros amro u,* namely, Alexandros Amrou. The latter part of the name is typically Nabataean or Semitic, while the former, of course, is typically Greek. It is not surprising to encounter the name of Amrou or Amru also at Nabataean Abda [979] and in the Nabataean Jebel Druze,[980] among other places,[981] and generally as part of Nabataean theophoric names.[982] It is closely related to the name of one of the most famous of Israelite kings, Omri, whose repute was so widespread that the name of his country was preserved in Assyrian annals as Omriland.[983]

1) Zeus Marnos Panel

The reliefs on the front panel and on the two side panels of this altar, which was donated by or dedicated to Alexandros Amrou, are as indicative of the mutual cross fertilization of Hellenistic and Semitic cultural forces as the name itself, with its Greek and Semitic components. The central figure combined features of the Greek god, Zeus, and of the Semitic god, Hadad. His torso is bare, and the rest of the body is covered with a himation, folded around the waist and then draped under his right arm, around his back, and over his left shoulder and arm, with its end hanging below his left hand. Over the lower part of his himation-covered left arm is the symbol of the thunderbolt.[984] It parallels the thunderbolt in similar position on the main Zeus-Hadad stele, which, together with the Atargatis relief that once stood beside it, graced the front of the altar pedestal of the raised inner shrine of the last period of Khirbet Tannur (Pls. 41, 101).

In several respects, also, there are similarities between the two Zeus-Hadad figures. The elaborately curled hair of the incense-panel Zeus-Hadad duplicates that of the larger figure. The head of the former is not covered, however, as is that of the latter, with a crown or calathos of some kind. The position of the outstretched, upward-bent right arm is also the same in both. In the case of the larger relief of the enthroned Zeus-Hadad, the raised right forearm is broken off and it is conjectural as to whether or not there was held in its hand a double axe or, as we think, a sceptre. The Zeus-Hadad of the incense altar holds a long staff in his upraised right hand,[985] both, fortunately, being intact.

The differences between the two reliefs, however, are far greater than the resemblances. The face, perhaps originally bearded, of the Zeus-Hadad on the Alexandros Amrou altar has been much damaged, but enough remains to fix the outlines of the head, particularly on the left side, part of which is still intact. He is portrayed in a standing position, and without the calculated disproportions of body of the larger, bearded Zeus-Hadad enthroned between two bulls. The curved top of a simulated niche appears behind him.

His right hand, in which he grasps the long staff, is the most naturalistically portrayed one on any of the sculptures at Khirbet Tannur. All of the fingers of the hand can be seen, with the forefinger extended outward full length. Protruding beneath the thunderbolt symbol and from underneath the lower part of the end of the himation, there is visible part of the back of the left hand, although it is hardly more than outlined. Part of the left leg is outlined through the comparatively naturalistic folds of the bottom of the himation.

The feet, enclosed in open-toed, double-thonged sandals, are partly damaged, with most of the toes of the left foot broken off and those of the right foot being more intact. Unable to solve completely the problem of presenting the feet and toes frontally on the same plane, which would have involved the necessity of foreshortening the feet or placing one foot slightly in advance of the other, the sculptor elevated them so that the figure seems to be standing on an inclined plane.

In effect, he has depicted the deity as if he were standing on the balls of his feet or dancing on his toes. Clark Hopkins has shown that this type of representation was introduced by the Parthians, whose purpose was to remove the necessity of foreshortening the feet when the entire figure was being frontally shown.[986] It would seem that the Nabataeans took over this practice from the Parthians.

In the case of the feet of the Nikés on the opposite panels of the altar, the sculptor depicted one foot of each figure in a completely flat sideways position, while the other foot, frontally presented, is shown raised in the same manner as on the central front panel, with the result that the heel of one foot of each pair is higher than that of the other foot shown in profile.

In general, however, the appearance of the Zeus-Hadad of the front central panel of the incense altar is more Hellenistic than Semitic, and much more pronouncedly so than the larger Zeus-Hadad in high relief on the stele belonging to the façade of the inner altar pedestal. We have already commented on a Roman relief of the Zeus-Marnos type in the center of a zodiac, resting on the back and hands of an Atlas.[987] It not only affords an amazing parallel to the zodiac-encircled Tyché upheld by a winged Niké at Khirbet Tannur, but reveals that the Nabataeans, in addition to adopting the general format, must have known the form of representation of Zeus or Jupiter, with bare torso, himation draped over the left shoulder and with staff clasped in one of the hands.

There is a striking resemblance also to the free standing statue of Zeus, now headless, found in the temple of Hera at Pergamon,[988] built under Attalus (159-138 B.C.). The originally raised right arm, bare torso, thick overfold at the waist of the himation which is then draped behind the body and over the left shoulder and arm, the sandled feet and shape of the body seem almost to have been copied by the Khirbet Tannur sculptor. The folds of the himation of the Nabataean figure were far more stiffly depicted than those of the Pergamon figure and the position of the feet far less naturally portrayed, but in general appearance the two sculptures of Zeus are much alike. The Khirbet Tannur relief may be categorized as a provincial imitation of the earlier Pergamon sculpture and of the contemporary Roman one of Jupiter. The Hellenistic model shows clearly the Nabataean overprint.

Similarly attired is a representation of Jupiter Dolichenus embossed on a silver plate from Heddernheim,[989] where an extremely fine Mithras relief with a zodiac was found.[990] The god holds a long staff in his left hand and a thunderbolt in his right hand, and an eagle stands beside his right foot. It would seem likely too that the Zeus-Hadad of the Alexandros Amrou altar was similar to the paramount god of Gaza, known as Zeus Marnos. Very many Nabataean caravaneers and tradesmen and travelers must have been familiar with him and with his temple, known as the Marneion.[991]

a) Gaza Model

Familiar to the Nabataeans and others before and after them from close acquaintance with the Marneion temple in ancient Gaza, and other pagan temples there, not destroyed till 401 A.D.,[992] was a large, marble statue of the god, seated on a throne, holding probably a thunderbolt in his right hand and a staff in his raised left hand. He was represented as a comparatively young man, of classical visage, with hair and beard arranged in curled locks and sporting a full moustache with curled ends. The brawny torso was bare, with the lower part of the body swathed in a himation. It encircled his waist and was draped then under his right arm and behind his back to fall over his left shoulder and along the left side of his body.

The upper half of the original Zeus-Marnos statue[993] was discovered at Tell el-Ajjul, near Gaza. There is little question, however, that in its original state it looked like various intact sculptures of Zeus, holding a thunderbolt in one hand and a long staff in the other.[994] Dated to about the second century B.C.,[995] it seems reasonable to believe that this Tell el-Ajjul sculpture in particular and others like it exercised considerable influence upon the art of the Nabataeans. They must have seen it and perhaps worshiped it frequently. It could have had a direct effect upon some of their

a

b

Pl. 211

a. Nabataean-Byzantine reservoir, Umm
   el-Jemal (p. 5)
b. Judaean-Nabataean-Byzantine cistern
   and channel leading rainwater to it,
   Negev (Site 149 C) (p. 5)

a

b

c

Pl. 212

a. Nabataean terraces, Negev (Site 270) (p. 5)
b. Nabataean wall-enclosed and terraced section of a wadi in the Negev (p. 5)
c. Nabataean terraces, side view, Negev (Site 415 A) (p. 5)
d. Nabataean terraces, front view, Negev (Site 415 A) (p. 5)

a

b

c

Pl. 213

a, b.   *"Teleilat el-anab,"* Qetsiot, Negev (p. 5)

c.   *"Teleilat el-anab,"* Mishrefeh, near Isbeita, Negev (p. 5)

Pl. 214 Grain growing in anciently terraced Wadi Raviv, Negev. Abrahamic and Judaean sites on hilltops in background (p. 5)

a

Pl. 215

a. Dushara throne, Sela, Transjordan (p. 61)

b. Partly rock-hewn Nabataean house with cistern, Sela (p. 5)

b

representations of Zeus-Hadad and in particular upon the one occupying the central front panel of the Alexandros Amrou altar.

In the heads and dress and proportions of the bodies of the two Zeus-Hadads of Khirbet Tannur, namely, the larger one of the main altar-base and the smaller one of the Alexandros Amrou altar, can be seen the measure of diversity of cultural influences affecting Nabataean art. The pronounced accent on the sculpture of the enthroned Zeus-Hadad is Oriental, while, conversely, the pronounced accent on the other is Hellenistic. Both, however, while evincing strong effects of the cultural impacts of the Orient and the Occident, remain in their total make-up definitely Nabataean.

2) Niké Panels

In the panels on the left and right sides of the central front relief of Zeus-Hadad of the Alexandros Amrou altar are two Nikés, holding palm branches and laurel wreaths (Pl. 188a, b). Both of these goddesses of victory are winged, peplos-clothed and stiffly positioned. The Niké on the right of the Zeus-Hadad panel is almost completely intact, having suffered only the loss of her nose and slight damage to her eyes and forehead. Her upswept hair culminates in two top-knots, in chignon fashion, which her sister Niké in the panel on the opposite side must also have had before most of her face and the top of her head were chiseled away.

There is an artistic diversification of arm position in the reliefs of the two Nikés. The one on the right side of the Zeus-Hadad relief grasps the end of the long palm branch in her lowered left hand and holds it diagonally across her body over her right shoulder. Her right arm is crooked in front of her, and her right hand, resting on her left arm, holds up a laurel wreath above her left shoulder. One wonders if the Virgo of the Khirbet Tannur zodiac could have had such top-knots on her head.

The other Niké, whose bent left arm extends beyond her body, holds the bottom end of a palm branch in her left hand. It rests on her left shoulder, with its leaves extending beyond it. Her right arm is stretched out full length, and in her clumsily portrayed hand she holds a double ribboned laurel wreath. The stiff angularity of the arms may be due as much to Oriental tradition as to lack of skill in execution.[996]

It is difficult to make out whether the lady is, so to speak, all thumbs or not. It would appear as if the sculptor or artisan had gotten his hands mixed up and added to her right arm the back of a left hand instead of the proper one. Either that or the fingers are so poorly carved that it is difficult to make out which is supposed to be the thumb and which the little finger. If there really were a mixup, it would seem to have been repeated in the portrayal of the outward turned palm and fingers of the left hand of the larger, enthroned Zeus-Hadad. If the mixup were purposed, it may be attributed to ancient Oriental tradition, as illustrated, for example, as we believe to be the case, in the case of one or two Assyrian warriors on a relief of the period of Tiglath-Pileser III (746-727 B.C.).[997]

The two Nikés are distinguished, furthermore, by a matching oppositeness of the stance of their feet, in both instances, placed at right angles to one another. The Niké with the palm branch over her right shoulder is pictured with her left foot in profile and the right frontally depicted, and, with the heel raised considerably above the line of the toes, as if the foot were resting on a steep incline (Pl. 188a). Both feet of the Zeus-Hadad-Marnos in the central panel follow this fashion, as we have seen. The other Niké, with the palm branch over her left shoulder (Pl. 188b), is shown with her right foot in profile, flat on the ground, and with the left foot frontally positioned and inclined in much the same manner as the right foot of her opposite number.

The presentation of one foot of each Niké in profile can be related in effect to Hittite examples in which both feet are placed sideways, one before the other and flat on the ground, although the bodies are presented frontally. With the other foot of each Niké frontally inclined as if she were standing on her toes, there is a carrying out of the Parthian influence. The Nabataeans never learned or perhaps never chose to copy successfully the Greek fashion of portrayal of feet.

In a Greek statue, such as that of Zeus from the Temple of Hera at Pergamon, to whom, as we have seen, the Zeus of the Alexandros Amrou altar may be compared so far as bare torso and drapery are concerned, the problem of the relationship of two differently positioned feet is solved. The right foot, flat on the ground, is frontally positioned, while the left is raised and set back a bit as if a step forward were about to be undertaken.[998] In fifth-century B.C. Greek vase painting, as Hopkins has pointed out,[999] when a frontally depicted figure was shown moving to the right or left, one foot was portrayed in profile, while the other was raised slightly for the step, exposing thus the broad, comparatively flat surface of the foot.

In our Nabataean examples, however, as has been noted, while one foot in each case is shown in profile, the other is frontally presented, with the heel elevated considerably to avoid foreshortening. There was no attempt to show any kind of movement, and the limitations of space brought into being a device, which in effect meant merging ancient Oriental precedent with coexistent Parthian fashion. This furnishes another example of the essentially Eastern character of Nabataean art.[1000]

The depiction of hands seems always to have been difficult for the Khirbet Tannur sculptors. The damaged right hand of one of the Niké reliefs (Pl. 188b) is only a little less awkwardly fashioned than the almost impossibly twisted left hand of the main Zeus-Hadad figure, which, as already pointed out, is shown grasping the projection leading to the right ear of the bullock on the left side of his throne (Pl. 42). No more successfully fashioned are several broken-off hands found in our excavations. One of them shows the back of a left hand with only the outsize, somewhat grotesque thumb still completely intact, and the other, to which is still attached part of a forearm and a right hand, shows the hand with the palm turned inward, clasping the corner of a garment (Pl. 186b, c). That this style of fashioning and positioning of hands and feet is purposed, is evidenced by a rather crude Nabataean plaque of a nude, enthroned Atargatis, with anklets and one visible bracelet, holding up her right hand with palm turned outward in a gesture of blessing. This fashion is encountered in Hatra, Dura and Palmyra (Pl. 81a, b).[1000a]

Equally crudely fashioned are the feet of various sculptures, be they those of Zeus-Hadad or of various Nikés. The feet of many of the latter are still attached to a segment of a global or discoid base, protruding from the limestone steles on which they and the Nikés they belonged to were sculptured in high relief (Pls. 180, 186f, g). Comparable also to the poorly wrought feet of the main Zeus-Hadad figure is a single right foot of sandstone with four toes remaining (Pl. 161b), which is all that is left of a relief of Atargatis, once enthroned beside him. The detached left foot in high relief of an otherwise completely destroyed sculpture looks as if it had one toe too many (Pl. 186e).

The uniformly crude portrayal of hands and feet is characteristic of the workmanship of Nabataean sculptors, who never escaped or perhaps never tried to escape the dilemma of straddling two cultural worlds with differing orientations. Their art reflected the perplexity of incomplete compromises. It developed a flavor and on the whole a form of its own, but never transcended the provincial.[1001]

a) Related Types

The two Niké reliefs on the side panels of the Alexandros Amrou altar are closely but not completely paralleled by two others on a fragment of a round altar (Pl. 189a, b), which, too, may originally have borne an inscription. The back side of the altar was hollowed out for attachment to a projecting support of some kind, which probably extended from a wall. Both reliefs on this rounded altar were much damaged. The face of the Niké in the panel on the right side has been battered away, and the bottom part of the column, which must have shown the lower part of her peplos and of her legs with the feet, is missing altogether. The head of the other, better preserved relief is missing, too.

The panels featuring these two Nikés are framed between three semicircular, attached columns, each capped by a crude Corinthianized capital. Each of these columns, to judge from what is left of them, seems to have been represented as standing on a base of three beveled divisions of equal proportions. Above each base was a smooth portion of the column culminating in a protruding, rounded molding, beyond which the main portion of the column extended. This upper part of the column was decorated with four long narrow panels with rounded ends, each contained within raised borders.

The most interesting thing about the more intact of the two reliefs on this rounded altar is that again the feet are depicted at right angles to one another, in exactly the same fashion as those of the Niké in the panel on the right side of the Alexandros Amrou altar. The left foot is shown in profile, while the right foot is frontally positioned, but elevated as if the Niké were walking or dancing on her toes, so far as that one foot is concerned. The front of this right foot has been somewhat damaged but it is clear that it was elevated as if placed on an inclined plane.

The legs of both of the Nikés on this round altar and those of a Niké that belonged to another round altar of the same type (Pl. 190a), as also other Niké reliefs (Pl. 190b, c), are revealed very noticeably through the bottom drapery of the peplos. They are fashioned in much more detail than usual, with an obvious attempt having been made to show their muscular formation. The wings of one of the two Nikés on the round altar are partly opened, with the right wing being completely intact, in comparison with the left one, the top of which is partly damaged. The wings of her companion Niké are closed, being visible in part only at her sides.

The latter bears a torch in her downward stretched right hand and holds in her left hand a palm branch projecting behind her left arm and left shoulder. The right arm of the other Niké is angularly bent across her waist, but the hand and whatever it may have held are gone. Her left arm rests on the opened left wing, but it is not clear what is being held in her left hand.

There was also a fragment of a small round limestone altar (?) that still had broken sections of engaged rectangular columns; the upper part of each contained a sunken rectangular panel framed within raised borders (Pl. 191c). On one of the columns there remained a much worn Corinthianized capital, such as the other columns must also have had. These engaged columns and capitals seem to have been much similar to, although not exactly the same as, the columns and capitals of the Alexandros Amrou altar. It is to be observed, although it is not readily explicable, that the one broken column with a capital on this fragmentary round altar terminates at a lower level than the other two columns.

b. Dedicated by Mati'a'el

Resembling in general shape the Alexandros Amrou altar is another small rectangular, three-paneled one of limestone, whose untreated back side must have been placed against or inserted into a wall (Pl. 194a, b). Engaged rounded columns separate the three panels, the central or front one of which bears a damaged Nabataean inscription. The top basin is much broken and shows no traces of incense having been burned in it. Plain double triangular horns decorate the top of each side. Each pair of them encloses a narrowing triangular space such as was employed for the Greek inscription on the top of the front side of the Alexandros Amrou altar. Below the attached columns and the inset panels and above and extending beyond the plain base of the altar is a moulding of three narrow horizontal divisions, separated from one another by deep grooves running around the three open sides of the altar. Another moulding of four such divisions or horizontal layers appears above the tops of the attached columns and below the double triangular horns on the sides of the top of each panel.

In the front inset panel is a Nabataean inscription reading: "[The altar] which Mati'a'el [the son of 'U]t'el gave as a thanksgiving offering." The suggested restorations and translation of the text stem from the late Père R. Savignac, O.P., who graciously consented at the time to publish the Nabataean inscriptions from Khirbet Tannur. All of them have previously appeared in print [1002] except this one (Pl. 194c).

It is doubtful, to judge from the clean condition of its basin, whether this Mati'a'el altar was ever actually employed at Khirbet Tannur. The great earthquake which we believe utterly destroyed the temple sometime during the second quarter of the second century A.D., may have resulted in the burial of this altar under a mass of debris shortly after it had been put into place. The suddenness of the catastrophe is testified to, for example, by the presence of several unfinished sculptures, roughed out in various degrees (Pl. 3a, b), but never finished.

c. Without Designation

1) Another limestone altar (Pl. 192b) of the same general type as the Mati'a'el one, but smaller, was recovered in the excavations. It, too, has three panels, with, however, no engaged columns separating them, and with the back side plain and unworked. A circular depression in the top served for offerings. The altar bears no inscription and is completely plain except for a moulding around the base and another just below the triangular horns at the top of each side. As in the previous two examples, a triangular space is left between them, employed sometimes, as we have seen, for a dedicatory inscription. Part of the upper portion of this small altar has been broken away, including two of the horns.[1003]

2) There was found a small, rather crude, soft limestone altar, of a type that must have been donated and utilized by less affluent pilgrims to Khirbet Tannur. It is completely plain, with an offering basin hollowed out on the top, blackened by the fire of small burnt offerings (Pl. 192c).

3) Several tiny limestone altars were also recovered. One of them (Pl.

193c) is partly broken, and retains only two of its originally four, very low, square legs. There are traces of reddening, caused by burning, in the basin of the altar. Diagonal crossed lines form an "x" on the sides of each outer face of the altar.

4) In addition, we came across another very small, limestone altar (Pl. 193b) of a type not unexpectedly discovered also at Petra [1004] (Pl. 193d), indicating that probably numerous ones of this type were used by the worshipers who came to Khirbet Tannur for special occasions and participated in sacred meals. Originally it was square and had four legs and a comparatively deep basin on top. Only half of the tiny altar and two of its legs remain. It seems to have been reddened to a considerable depth below the surface by the immense heat of the great conflagration which apparently raged when Khirbet Tannur was destroyed apparently by a very severe earthquake. Some blackening visible in the basin may have stemmed from incense offerings burned in it. Just below the top of the altar, there is an incised line running around the sides. These small altars call to mind the tiny stone and pottery incense altars we excavated at Tell el-Kheleifeh (Ezion-geber:Elath) on the north shore of the Gulf of Aqabah, the eastern arm of the Red Sea (Pl. 193e).

5) The molded base of what may have been a fairly small incense altar of limestone was found (Pl. 193a) with three of its originally four square stone legs remaining. On this base stood apparently four attached pillars, which in turn supported the main block containing the incense basin at the top of it. One can imagine that it looked something like one of several small incense altars or burners from the Timna cemetery in Arabia, uncovered by the expedition of the American Foundation for the Study of Man.[1005] Even more closely related (by means of its engaged columns, remaining worn Corinthianized capital and recessed panels) to the incense altar from Timna in South Arabia is the previously mentioned fragment of what may be part of an engaged column of a rounded, comparatively large, limestone incense altar from Khirbet Tannur (Pl. 191c).

6) Among the most interesting of the discoveries of altars of various kinds at Khirbet Tannur was a small, broken limestone incense burner (?) hewn out of a single block of stone. It looked like a model of a rectangular temple or perhaps sarcophagus with a gabled roof or lid (Pl. 192a). The eaves of the two long sides of the gabled top are raised and thickly rounded or rolled. There were apparently walls on only three sides. The blank, topmost part of them extends slightly beyond the face of the rest of the walls, perforated with irregular rows of slightly diagonal holes. Only one of the two, long, perforated side-walls is comparatively intact, although it too has suffered damage. Almost all of the perforated part of the rear wall is gone, but remnants of a row of perforations remain just below the edge of the slightly

overhanging ledge of the blank section of the wall above it, showing that it once existed. On that blank section are traces of the typical, diagonal, Nabataean tooling.

The perforations in the rear wall and the two side walls seem to prove that this model was once employed or was meant to be used as an incense burner. Its shape is an ancient one, recalling the Chalcolithic, fourth-millennium B.C. pottery burial urns in Palestine, some of which had gabled roofs.[1006] Remains of actual houses of the seventh century B.C., some of them rectangular and others apsidal, with gabled roofs, have been found at Old-Smyrna in Anatolia.[1007] The heavy lid of the fourth-century B.C. Alexander sarcophagus from the Royal Cemetery at Sidon, imitating the architecture of an Ionic temple,[1008] brings the tradition of the gabled roof or lid closer to the period of influences underlying this Nabataean incense burner (?) and perpetuated through and beyond the Nabataean period.[1009]

7) We have previously mentioned the square altar plinth composed of separate parts, sunk into the pavement beyond the west side of the raised inner temple-court. Only part of the altar proper resting on this plinth remained, with remnants of a thunderbolt design on it (Pl. 114c).

The existence of a large altar near the northeast corner of the great fore-court of Khirbet Tannur has also been referred to, and the central podium altar on the raised inner platform has been dealt with at length. Altars large and small, highly ornate and plain, stationary and movable, obviously existed in large numbers at Khirbet Tannur, as could have been expected from a site which was obviously a sanctuary of extraordinary sacredness. There must have been numerous other altars, including some dedicatory inscriptions, that were completely destroyed in the ultimate earthquake catastrophe.

2. DEDICATORY PLAQUES

a. *The Spring of La'aban*

The most important of the Nabataean inscriptions from Khirbet Tannur was a four-line one in a sunken panel on a limestone block (Pl. 194c). It contains information relevant to the history and location of the site. On it are the name of the donor, Netir'el the son of Zayd'el; [1010] his title as master or official in charge of the spring of La'aban, namely, the *r's* of *'yn l'aban;* [1011] the names of the king and queen whose well-being it besought, namely, Haretat and Huldu; and the date in the second year of the king's reign. There is no question that the king referred to is Aretas IV, 9 B.C. to A.D. 40. The second year of his reign is the equivalent of 8/7 B.C. The inscription belongs thus to near the beginning of the second period of construction of Khirbet Tannur, which, as has been previously stated, could not have been much earlier than 15 or 10 B.C.[1012] The entire inscription in translation reads:

1. "(   ) which was built (by) Netir'el son of
2. Zayd'el, Master of the spring of La'aban for the life of Haretat,
3. king of the Nabataeans, who loves his people and for the life of Huldu
4. his wife in the year 2."

There is one word in particular in the inscription, namely, *l'aban*, that serves eloquently to demonstrate the living continuity of the past in the present. As Père Savignac recognized at once,[1013] it is still retained to this day in the name of the Wadi La'aban (Wadi el Aban), that passes below the west side of the almost completely isolated Jebel Tannur. Descending from the edge of the northern top of the highlands of Edom, this south-north tributary canyon, with its usually dry stream bed, carves its way downward to join the greater main east-west canyon of the Wadi Hesa, the Biblical River Zered, whose perennial stream flows past the north base of Jebel Tannur to empty finally into the Dead Sea.

There is, furthermore, still in existence the name of a spring, called Ain La'aban. It is situated close to the ruins of the Nabataean temple and village of Khirbet edh-Dherih, on the east bank of the Wadi La'aban, about six kilometers to the north of Khirbet Tannur. The spring of Ain La'aban mentioned in this inscription, however, may possibly refer to the powerful springs of Aineh, on the opposite north slope of the Wadi Hesa, several kilometers northeast of Khirbet Tannur. There is little doubt, however, that still another Nabataean sanctuary existed at Aineh, as part of a rather large Nabataean settlement. Its shabby ruins are now commingled with others; both of earlier and later times.

b. Built by Netîr'el

Another Nabataean inscription, this one in a very poor state of preservation, was found at the surface of a soft limestone block at Khirbet Tannur. It was incised on the face of a sunken panel or cartouche of rectangular shape, with a tongue or flap extending from the middle of either narrow end of the panel (Pl. 195a, b). Of the original four lines of the inscription, only the first can be read with some degree of clarity, the second much less so, the third practically not at all with the exception of parts of several letters and the fourth having been weathered away completely. The name of the donor of the tablet is clear enough, being Netir'el. We recall that a Netir'el figured as the donor of the *r's'yn l'aban* inscription, designated there as "Netir'el the son of Zayd'el." Whether or not this "Championed by God," which is what Netir'el means, was the same person in both inscriptions is debatable. The possiblity, however, makes plausible the restoration of his patronymic. A date may have been mentioned in the worn-away fourth line.

As translated by Père Savignac with suggested restorations and revisions by Abbé Starcky,[1014] the Nabataean inscription reads as follows:

1. "(which) (was) built (by) Netir'el the son of
2. (Zayd'e)l for the life of Haré(tat)
3. (King of the Nabataeans, who loves) his people.
4. ── "

c. *Which Qosmilk Made*

The clearest of the Nabataean inscriptions from Khirbet Tannur was on a broken limestone stele of small size (Pls. 196, 197) and of strikingly unusual form. Its roughly hewn base had apparently been inserted into a foundation of some kind and would not have been visible. The Nabataean letters had been cut deeply into the otherwise carefully smoothed face of the stone. It had also been cemented into position, to judge from the remnants on its back side of some plaster cement, into which tiny bits of pottery had been mixed for binding purposes.

The shape of the stele is most interesting. There were originally two horns extending from the base of its smooth portion, with the one on its left side having been completely broken off. Above the point where the topside of the horn begins to project from the body of the stele, there commences a semicircular indentation, rising five centimeters high, before it ends in a sharp break. A similar curve is visible in part on the much more damaged left side of the stele. There is no question that both of these indentations led to two additional horns or projections indicating perhaps arms and parts of shoulders, with one such horn on either side. The shaped inner parts of shoulders are still visible, particularly on the left side. Rising above them is a narrowed neck or shaft with rounded back and top, eleven centimeters high and eight and a half centimeters wide and deep.

The general impression of the entire stele is one of a very crude, anthropomorphic figure. It may be representative of the beginning of a development from the plain Dushara blocks of Nabataean beginnings to the sophisticated Hellenistic-Semitic sculptures in relief of deities prevalent at Khirbet Tannur and Petra, among other Nabataean sites, during the second century A.D. One is reminded of what appears to be a small "face idol" of stone found at Petra.[1015]

Père Savignac has suggested two slightly varying translations for the inscription on this stele: [1016]

"(the stele) which Qosmilk made for Qos, the god of Huru (the sculptor)";
or
"(the stele) which Qosmilk made for Qosallah.[1017] Huru (the sculptor)."

The name, Huru, occurs in two inscriptions from Meda'in Saleh, in

Arabia, dated, respectively, to the years 37 and 40 of Aretas IV (9 B.C.-A.D. 40) as Père Savignac points out.[1018] The Khirbet Tannur inscription with that name could, but need not necessarily belong to the same period, and it is most unlikely that one and the same person is referred to in both places.

Whether or not "Qosallah" in the second version of the Khirbet Tannur inscription is to be considered as the full name of the deity or is to be translated in accordance with the first suggestion as "Qos, the god of . . . ," the fact remains that "Qos" or "Qaus" is the name of a familiar Edomite, Nabataean and Arabian deity and occurs also in numerous related composite names. We came across the name Qos or Qaus in the course of our excavations of Tell el-Kheleifeh (Ezion-geber:Elath), the site originally built by Solomon on the north shore of the eastern arm of the Red Sea. On the handle of each one of a whole storeroom full of pottery jars was stamped the inscription: "Belonging to Qos'anal, the servant of the king."

Numerous examples of such composite theophorous names either beginning or ending with Qos occur in Biblical, Assyrian, South Arabian, Nabataean and Greek texts. Because of their own background and that of the Moabites and of the Edomites whom they supplanted and largely absorbed, it was completely natural for the Nabataeans to refer to one of their main gods as Qos or Qosallah and to some of their own people with names such as Qosmilk, as in this particular inscription, or Qosnatan in another one.[1019]

A Greek inscription from the island of Delos apparently mentions a Nabataean god and gives his name as Pakeida Kos.[1020] This would seem to be the very same Nabataean deity, Pakeida (Pakida), mentioned together with the goddess Hera in two Greek inscriptions from Gerasa (Jerash), in connection with a Nabataean shrine there.[1021] The reference to a Nabataean deity of this name at Delos is all the more interesting because it underscores the probability of the existence of a Nabataean shrine, visited regularly by Nabataean sea travelers when their ships by intention or because of storms made port there. Such a sanctuary would have been related to various way-station Nabataean shrines such as those at Rhodes and Puteoli, frequented by Nabataean sailors, merchants, officials and refugees enroute to or from Italy.

3. ANTHROPOMORPHIC STELES

a. Double-sided

A much-damaged, horned stele from Khirbet Tannur had incised lines on the smoothed surface of an inset panel on each of two sides (Pl. 198a, b). It had two horns, one at each corner of one end and there may have been two more at the opposite end. It is difficult to decide which end is up. On each of the two main sides, above the rough-hewn base, which apparently was not visible when in proper position, was a smoothed surface extending to the tops of the horns. Beneath them was the remaining part of a sunken inset panel. On the smoothed surface of each of the two sunken panels were what appear to be deeply incised rectangles connected to a deeply incised horizontal line.

One wonders whether they could belong to the type of incised squares representing eyes and the narrow vertical rectangle representing a nose that appear on the crude anthropomorphic idols found at Petra (Pl. 199c).[1022] Whether these incised lines belonged to letters of words or are to be connected with a representation on each side of a crude stone idol of an intermediate Dushara type, like the above-mentioned one with the deity's name of Qos or Qosallah on it, is difficult to determine. We are inclined to believe that such anthropomorphic idols persisted in use even when Hellenistic-that they belong to the latter [1023] rather than the former. It is quite possible Semitic sculptures of Nabataean gods such as those of the pantheon of Khirbet Tannur were generally worshiped by the Nabataeans.

Yet another end piece of a horned stele with two smoothed faces was found, without enough of it being left to show whether it had any inscription or incised lines of any kind on it (Pl. 198c, d). In general appearance, it resembles the Qosmilk, Qos(allah) Huru horned stele, which, however, was smoothed only on one side. The beginning of the projection of one horn can clearly be seen on the left side of the more intact panel of one face of the stele (Pl. 198d). The shape of the base as shown at the bottom of both the reverse and obverse sides, indicates what the base of the horned stele with the Nabataean Qos(allah) dedication may have looked like.

b. In Greek, too

One small limestone fragment of what may have been a similar type of horned stele bore on the smoothed surface of a sunken panel four rather crude deeply incised Greek letters (Pl. 199a), the first one much damaged, which read *(a) r a y*. There is no question that they were preceded by other Greek letters. Indeed, there are some indications of parts of incised lines of one of them at the top of the break beyond the right side of the initial letter that seems to have been an *alpha*. It seems doubtful that any letters followed them on the left side of the top of the inset panel ending with an *upsilon* (?). There were, however, undoubtedly other lines of letters underneath the first line. The backside of this broken stele was rough, indicating that originally it had been set into a wall.

XV. AFTERGLOW

XV. *Afterglow*

1. OUTPOSTS OF CHRISTENDOM

a. *Byzantine Negev*

When the Romans swept away the political independence of the Nabataeans, a gradually developing decline ensued, which for long was hardly
perceptible. It culminated ultimately in the almost complete absorption
of the Nabataeans by the burgeoning economic and religious forces of
Byzantium. Nabataeans and their sites and sanctuaries, pottery and sculptures, in time lost the uniqueness of their identity but not the splendor
of creative spirit which had brought them into being and helped to raise
them to considerable heights of relative prestige and power. Byzantine art
and initiative perpetuated it. The new and expanding Christian culture
could not do otherwise than be enriched by it in the areas where the Nabataeans had placed the stamp of their personality and productivity.

By the fifth century A.D., the Byzantines had reared structures of their
own upon almost every center and settlement established by Nabataean
endeavor, and were inevitably profoundly influenced by their predecessors.
The achievements and example of the Nabataeans for Byzantine undertakings and advancement were immense and incalculable. Nabataean influence can be traced in part by virtue of the fact that the Byzantines repaired and reused or built over or incorporated almost everything that the
Nabataeans had left behind. Much was transmitted in altered fashion by the
Nabataeans themselves through what gradually must have become their
mass conversion to Byzantine Christianity. Wherever I have wandered in the
former domain of the Nabataean kingdom, I have found abundant evidence
of the commingling of Nabataean and Byzantine remains or proof that the
latter replaced or built over or made use of the former.

A lasting recollection of the presence of Nabataeans in the Negev of southern Palestine is preserved in fifth-sixth century A.D. sculptures at predominantly Christian Byzantine towns such as Abda and Isbeita (Pl. 216a),

among others, than had been erected over Nabataean ruins. At Abda, for example, they include, on one side of a capital, a relief of a man, whose head was inordinately large in comparison with his body [1024] (Pl. 219b), a round-bodied eagle with spread wings and stylized feathers,[1025] a peacock or ostrich(?),[1026] and two lions confronting each other.[1027] Among other reliefs of this type may be mentioned one of fishes found at Isbeita (Pl. 219a).[1028] Another showed a damaged fish on the intact side of a partly broken circle enclosing a Byzantine cross at the bottom of each side of which were replicas of the *Alpha* and *Omega* (Pl. 217b) referred to in chapters 1:8, 21:16, 22:13 of The Revelation of John. All of them mirror in crude and provincial but forceful manner the works of the Nabataeans several centuries earlier. A Byzantine lintel from Nabataean-Byzantine Elusa (Khalasa) (Pl. 218a) shows clear relationship to Nabataean forerunners. The leaf and vine, grape, pomegranate and rosette decorations have numerous parallels in Nabataean art at Khirbet Tannur and elsewhere.[1028a] The feminine bust in a circular frame with braided locks under an ornamented shawl, low forehead, full cheeks and flattened nose crudely mirrors composite examples of Nabataean Tychés.

Some of the Byzantine sculptures of human figures were better formed than others, as illustrated by the reliefs of St. Theodore and St. Longinus on capitals of a Byzantine church at Aila (Pl. 216 b, c), built next to the now hardly noticeable remains of an extremely large Nabataean site on the northeast shore of the Gulf of Aqabah. The Nabataean influence manifests itself in the patterning of the feathers of the phoenixes appearing with the saints and in the position of the feet of the latter at right angles to each other, approximating closely, for example, the stance of one of the Niké reliefs on the Alexandros Amrou altar (Pl. 216 b, c).

These Byzantine sculptures are only relatively less sophisticated than the originals of their Nabataean background. Nabataean sculpture as a whole may be termed provincial and crude, particularly when compared to the purely Hellenistic parallels of the West. It is, however, a crudity that conveys a feeling of strength and a forcefulness of conviction derived from a vigorous, Oriental heritage of ancient vintage. There is an earthy and native quality to the superficially Hellenistic appearance of much of Nabataean sculpture, that reappeared in even cruder form several centuries later in its Byzantine Christian counterpart.

It was completely natural for the influence of the Nabataeans to be so strongly preserved in the art forms of the Byzantine Negev, which they had so intensively settled and farmed with such astounding success. We have seen that even after the Romans erased their independence, the Nabataeans did not disappear into the bowels of the earth. They and their children's children remained to till its soil under the aegis of Roman Byzantium and engage also, in the places they kept on inhabiting, in all manner of other activities. Among them were included for a considerable period the continued construction and repair of their own temples. Many of the finest Nabataean temples were constructed after A.D. 106, when Trajan made the Nabataean kingdom a part of the Provincia Arabia.

The last and finest period of construction of Khirbet Tannur, which we have designated as Period III, and to which we believe all the sculptures of deities belong, is to be dated probably to the first quarter of the second century A.D. It could possibly have come into being after A.D. 106 and been destroyed about a quarter of a century later, perhaps in the earthquake that is known to have occurred in Palestine in A.D. 130.[1029] There was no immediate radical change. Everything remained much the same, or even more so after the Roman conquest, except that the final authority was in the hands not of a Nabataean king enthroned in Petra but of a Roman legate in residence there. Some remarkable Nabataean documents, dating to the post A.D. 106 period were found by Yigael Yadin in a large cave in the canyon of Nahal Hever, near Ein Gedi, on the west side of the Dead Sea, together with others in Hebrew, Aramaic and Greek. They deal with events in the years before and during the Bar Kochba rebellion against the Romans, which began in A.D. 132 and lasted for three years and included dispatches from the leader, who signed his name as "Shim'on Bar Kozibah," rather than "Shim'on Bar Kochba." [1030]

These Nabataean documents help to inform us that the affairs of the Nabataeans did not undergo a sudden drastic deterioration as a result of the reduction of their kingdom to provincial status. Long before that a progressive decline had commenced, culminating in the Roman conquest of Nabataea in A.D. 106. The greatest flowering of the Nabataean economy occurred some time before the reign of Aretas IV (9 B.C.-A.D. 40). The change for the worse took place particularly under his successors, the last two Nabataean kings, Malichus II (A.D. 40-71) and Rabbel II (A.D. 71-106). The most direct cause was the increasingly successful Roman undertaking to bypass overland caravan routes that led through Nabataean territory by shipping Arabian goods to Roman emporia in Egypt via the Red Sea and then alongside or down the Nile. Nabataean commerce in southern Nabataea and cities and settlements more or less dependent upon it suffered as a result, although gradually and for years almost imperceptibly.

This state of affairs continued and worsened naturally after the takeover of Nabataea by Trajan. It followed too that certain areas such as the Negev were considered of less importance to the Romans than to the Nabataeans and were therefore less well protected by armed forces than previously. An inevitable consequence ensued that had manifested itself under similar circumstances in earlier periods of history whenever the central political and military authority was weakened or destroyed. Like buzzards appearing out of the blue to feast on a new carcass, nomads flock into lands richer

Pl. 216

a. Byzantine church, Isbeita (p. 579)
b, c. Byzantine capitals showing Saints Theodore and Longinus, Aila (p. 520)

c

b

a

b

Pl. 217

a. *Alpha* and *Omega* from Byzantine church, Isbeita (p. 71)
b. Byzantine cross and rosettes, Isbeita (p. 71)

a

b

Pl. 218

a. Byzantine lintel, Khalasa (Elusa) (p. 520)
b. Wine-press, Byzantine Isbeita (cf. p. 520)

Pl. 219 (*opposite*)

a. Raised medallion with three fishes in low relief, Isbeita (p. 520)
b. Byzantine capital with relief of a man, Abda (p. 520)

a

b

5 cms

a

b

Pl. 220

a. Dolphin on Byzantine marble chancel, Susita (cf. p. 361)

b. Eagle on Byzantine capital, Abda (p. 520)

than their own when no longer restricted by superior power. At this particular juncture, Thamudic and Safaitic Arabs moved in wherever they could. The destruction of Nabataean Abda in the Negev, probably at the end of the first quarter of the second century A.D., may be attributed to them. Rock-drawings and inscriptions by the hundreds marked their advent and tenuous stay. It was not till the Romans found it fit to reintroduce military controls in areas once safeguarded by Nabataean troops, that the nomadic invaders were contained and driven back to the desert whence they had come.[1031]

In spite of all of this, however, Nabataean achievement persisted long after their always fragile political independence had been destroyed. Gradually, however, as the second century came to an end and the third century A.D. ran its course, the Nabataeans began to lose their cohesive identity. Under the new conditions of more direct administration of the eastern Roman empire, introduced by Constantine I (A.D. 288-337), when he removed his capital from Rome to Byzantium (soon to become known as Constantinople), a great economic renascence commenced throughout his realm. The former Nabataeans labored mightily wherever they were rooted to their own advantage and that of their rulers, whose new religion of Christianity they ultimately adopted and helped to propagate.

Little wonder then that direct descendants of the Nabataeans should have retained in their traditions and memories and incorporated into the sculptures of the churches they erected and attended some distinctly recognizable characteristics and features of deities their forefathers worshiped in Nabataean sanctuaries of their own at the very same sites. It is possible to trace in a very direct and unbroken line the history of art at Abda in the Negev from the approximate time when a Nabataean temple was first erected there in honor of Obodas, one of several kings of that name,[1031] to the time, some three or four centuries later, when a great Byzantine church was erected on its ruins. In the misshapen form of a relief of a man on the face of one of its capitals (Pl. 219b), to which we have referred, there is roughly outlined in miniature the configuration of a Zeus-Hadad of an earlier day. And much the same sequence of events can be documented throughout all the territories of the former Nabataean kingdom, extending from southern Syria to northern Arabia.

b. In Egypt

1) COMMERCE AND CONFLICT

In Egypt, too, where many Nabataeans found their livelihoods and homes, the impact of their art exercised a profound effect upon the character of fifth-century A.D. Coptic art.[1032] Their contacts with Egypt had been of long duration and considerable extent. Indeed, their relationship with Egypt manifested itself in their very first appearance in recorded history. It had to do with the peripheral and at the time completely innocent and indeed aggrieved part they played in the internecine struggle between the generals of Alexander the Great for mastery over some or all of the parts of his kingdom, which had disintegrated after his death.

One of Alexander's satraps, known as Antigonus Cyclops, who, after the death of the Macedonian genius, rose temporarily to the top of the heap in Syria and Babylonia in the murderous scramble for power, sought to remove Ptolemy, a former companion in arms, from his command over Egypt. The plan comprised military and economic means. Both elements were employed in a rear-guard action involving the Nabataeans. It was known, for instance, that they exercised a most profitable monopoly in securing and transporting the Dead Sea bitumen, so highly prized in Egypt particularly for embalming purposes.[1033] If they could have been conquered, the lucrative and strategically invaluable trade-route they dominated, leading from Arabia via Aila or Petra and Gaza to Sinai and to Egypt would have been taken over, with the bitumen and carrying-trade profits accruing to Antigonus' enrichment.

I, myself, have come across large and small chunks of asphalt near the southwest corner of the Dead Sea, spewed forth from fissures opening up somewhere in its depths. Kammerer[1034] is correct in denying its export in modern times. It is quite possible that in Nabataean times much more asphalt came to the surface than is presently the case. In the times of Josephus the Dead Sea was known as the Asphalt Lake.[1035]

Had Antigonus succeeded in his design, the Macedonian ruler of Egypt, Ptolemy I, would have suffered both in his prestige and his pocket, and his countrymen would have been deprived of a commodity more precious to them than much gold. In addition, no assistance could come, escape be possible or a counterattack be mounted across this ancient highway, which at Petra turned not only southward to Arabia, but northward to Bostra and Damascus and elsewhere, in addition to leading westward to Egypt. Antigonus stood to gain much at little cost, but he reckoned without his hosts. The attacks, launched at his command against Petra, were decisively repulsed, as previously noted.

This entire series of events was duly noted by Diodorus, who even mentioned the year of their occurrence. It was 312 B.C. The net result was that the Nabataeans were catapulted into the record of history, although they probably never knew it. Antigonus failed utterly in his overall plan, which collapsed completely when he died. He was followed, as we have seen earlier, in Syria by yet another of Alexander's generals, Seleucus by name, who founded the dynasty that engaged the Ptolemies in the renewal of the age-old struggle between Asia and Egypt for domination of the Fertile

Crescent. It was never lastingly secured by either, even as complete and permanent control of it has ever remained elusive.

If it were possible to list all of the activities of Nabataean traders and residents in Egypt it would undoubtedly be necessary to compile a formidable catalogue. Bitumen was only one of the commodities traded. Elephants' teeth formed another, if we may accept a chance remark of the Roman satirist, Juvenal, who lived long in Egypt and died there.[1036] The commercial and diplomatic missions which had the Nabataeans crisscrossing the Mediterranean must have resulted in a fairly constant stream of Nabataean visitors to Alexandria. These consisted in the main probably of merchants and government officials, together with some priests who ministered in Nabataean sanctuaries established in foreign places. We shall see, too, that Nabataean merchants and mercenaries were much at home in Egypt and frequented numerous places and important caravan trails between the Nile River and the eastern part of the Red Sea that separates Arabia from Africa.

2. TRADE-ROUTES

Some of the Egyptian ports on the west side as well as on the east side of the Red Sea were frequented by Nabataeans, and their merchants must have trafficked over its waters, too. Not only were the spices of Arabia and the exotic imports from Persia and India transported overland by Nabataean caravans to Aila and Petra for further dispersal,[1037] but some of the precious cargos were in all likelihood shipped across the Red Sea directly from a port such as Leuce Come on the Nabataean Arabian coast to Egyptian shores on the opposite side. There is no question that much valuable freight came directly by sea to Egyptian ports on the Red Sea. The Romans were to succeed in furthering this sea commerce at the expense of Nabataean traffic on land. Their unsuccessful campaign in 25 B.C. to conquer Arabia and seize control of its lucrative incense and spice trade was directed to this purpose.[1038]

Two famous trade-routes through the Arabian peninsula converged at the great Nabataean emporium of Meda'in Saleh (Hejrah), near its northwestern side. One led from the eastern Arabian port of Gerrha [1039] on the Persian Gulf opposite the islands of Bahrein and crossed the width of the Arabian peninsula, via the oases of Hail and Teima to this great inland commercial center, that was lastingly marked by Nabataean monuments. Another traversed the length of the Arabian peninsula, passing not far from its western Red Sea side to reach the same point. There at Meda'in Saleh in the heart of the Arabian territory of the Nabataean kingdom, the caravans would make a long halt before proceeding with Nabataean personnel, fresh beasts of burden and renewed supplies to other market places and distribution points.[1040]

The route from Meda'in Saleh northward led through the desert to the oasis of Tebuk and then either to the Nabataean seaport of Aila [1041] on the northeast shore of the Gulf of Aqabah, and splitting off thence in various directions, or directly via Tebuk to the magnificent Nabataean capital of Petra, ensconced among colorful sandstone clefts in the southern highlands of Nabataeanized Edom. From Petra one track turned westward across the Negev to Gaza and/or Rhinocolura (el-Arish) in Sinai on the shore of the Mediterranean, and thence along the coast of Sinai to Egypt.[1042] Another continued northward to the cities of the Decapolis and beyond. Yet another heavily traveled track turned almost due westward from Meda'in Saleh to reach the Nabataean port of Leuce Come [1043] on the east side of the Red Sea. This port was also a transshipment point for Red Sea cargos, unloaded and sent by land to Meda'in Saleh (Hejrah) for further distribution. Across the comparatively narrow finger of the sea, some 125 miles to the southwest, was the Egyptian harbor of Berenike,[1044] or across the sea to the northwest was the harbor of Myos Hormos.[1045] Berenike had been established by Ptolemy II Philadelphus in the third century B.C. to facilitate the exchange of goods between Egypt and India and beyond.[1046] Later on, as we have seen, Rome manifested a deep interest in the very same sea-route.[1047]

From Berenike, there was a caravan road that debouched northeastward through unsafe territory to Coptos on the Nile. The exotic goods carried there by beasts of burden were then transported by boat to Alexandria. It took 24 days to negotiate the entire distance from the Red Sea port to the Mediterranean metropolis. Half that time was required for the much shorter part of the trip between the Red Sea and the Nile. Military posts and soldiers along the way guaranteed safety of travel, according to Pliny.[1048]

It is quite possible that Nabataeans participated to a considerable degree in the movement and disposal of goods along this route. As long as they had anything to say, they would hardly have permitted the diversion via Leuce Come of any appreciable part of the Arabian trade which did not yield them profit. A Nabataean official resident in Leuce Come collected there a twenty-five per cent tax on all imports.[1049] This sea-front town must therefore have served the export as well as the import trade, and Nabataean merchants and merchantmen could well have set out from there for Berenike, Myos Hermos or Leucos Limen, across the sea from Leuce Come. The fluctuating increase or decrease or control of sea piracy may have conditioned their choice of sea or land routes. It cannot presently be proven, but it seems likely that the Nabataeans either had ships of their own or hired them, making themselves thus a force to be reckoned with at least in the northern section of the Red Sea. In any event, at least according to one account,[1050] it was possible for them to destroy by fire the fleet that Cleopatra had previously assembled there.

3. MERCHANTS AND MERCENARIES

Be that as it may, the drastic curtailment of the power of Cleopatra and her subsequent suicide, following that of Mark Antony, attendant upon his defeat the year before in the naval battle off Actium in Greece, must have been welcomed by the Nabataeans. Like other small nations, they were all too often compelled to gamble on the success of one of the periodic contenders for supreme power in Rome and bolster his cause with contingents of troops. Mark Antony, who showered Cleopatra with gifts of Judaean and Nabataean lands for the price of her embraces,[1051] seems to have requisitioned their help in his ill-fated contest with Caesar, without their earning her gratitude. Only once did the Nabataeans pick a winner. That occurred in 47 B.C., when the Nabataean king, Malichus I, sent some of his cavalry to support Julius Caesar in his campaign against Alexandria, Egypt.[1052] Caesar's victory over Pompey and Egypt and his pleasure in Cleopatra lasted only two brief years, before assassins struck him down.[1053]

Actually, however, the identity of the changing masters in Rome mattered little to the Nabataeans, whose kingdom continued to exist in the final analysis only by imperial sufferance. The governing authorities, whoever they might be, could not but look with jaundiced eyes at what was practically a Nabataean monoply of the rich Arabian trade and seek, as had others before them, to curtail or destroy it if some or much of its profits did not accrue to them. The day would come when they would succeed in their purpose, shaped by compulsions of empire.[1054]

Forced to join battle all too frequently with Romans against Romans, the Nabataeans managed nevertheless to promote their commercial interests in Egypt and elsewhere by endless diligence and with enviable gain. It was also their practice to hire themselves out as mercenaries.[1055] Several Nabataean funerary inscriptions memorialize some of their number who served as guards along the Berenike-Coptos trade-route from the Red Sea to the Nile.[1056] It was used, as we have seen, by caravans laden with goods, which perhaps in part, at least, had been expedited by their own countrymen from Arabian Leuce Come on the east side of the Red Sea.[1057]

It is known, furthermore, that among the permanent officials or hired agents of the Ptolemaic government in Egypt both before, during and after the time of Cleopatra, there were numerous border guards and customs inspectors, known as "Arabarchs." [1058] There is reason to believe that many, if not most of them were Nabataeans, who are frequently equated with Arabs by Josephus. He refers to Petra, for instance, as "the royal seat of the king of Arabia" and to the Nabataeans as "Arabians." [1059] One of their qualifications, shared with the Parthians [1060] and the latter's Scythian intermixture, was their skill as cavalrymen, either on horse [1061] or camels. [1062] Their riding ability fitted them particularly for border and highway patrol and they must have been welcome adjuncts to the armies deployed in the East by successive contenders for supreme power in Rome.

It was indeed prudent and wise of the Ptolemies to permit and undoubtedly to encourage some of the Nabataeans to settle in a permanent colony in the Wadi Tumilat, which gives direct access from Sinai to the land of Goshen in northern Egypt. [1063] Their aptitudes and connections made them extraordinarily valuable to the Egyptian governmental and economic apparatus.

The children of Israel may indeed have commenced their Exodus through the Wadi Tumilat. From earliest historical times on, it was the most convenient avenue of entry and departure between Egypt and Sinai. There was a constant stream of Nabataean caravans passing through this important pass, either coming from or returning to Petra, among other places. It was natural, therefore, for some Nabataeans to establish residence in the Wadi Tumilat and enter into the service of the rulers and priests of Egypt. Who better than the Nabataean caravaneers knew what was transpiring in the Sinai desert, [1064] or could more sensitively feel the pulse of events in the making, or with greater experience facilitate the import and export of goods between Egypt and Asia and Arabia and India?

This Nabataean settlement became buried in time in Tell esh-Shuqafiyeh in the Wadi Tumilat. It is less than two miles from Tell el-Kebir, [1065] with Bubastis in the Delta to the east of it. To the south of Bubastis, there were located on the banks of the Nile such places as Heliopolis and Memphis and Heracleopolis and Oxyrhynchus, which figure in our story. We shall return in particular to the mention of the latter two. [1066]

A small, damaged Nabataean stone inscription of eight lines was found at Tell esh-Shuqafiyeh. It contains a name or title that has been rendered in effect as "Arabarch-in-chief." The inscribed stone would seem to be dedicated to a Nabataean deity, with a localized name. The ruins of a Nabataean temple dedicated to him may be buried in the mound of Tell esh-Shuqafiyeh. [1067]

All in all, what is clear from this inscription, and from others found in Egypt, and from other evidence such as that referred to above, is that many Nabataeans frequented Egypt. Large numbers of them traveled there in various capacities. Some of them who had been engaged as mercenaries settled on the land, and others established themselves permanently in centers such as the one now covered in all probability by Tell esh-Shuqafiyeh. It is reasonable to believe that in the course of time proof of the existence of still other Nabataean settlements in Egypt will be forthcoming.

With the Nabataeans traveled their gods, in whose honor, as we have seen, they sometimes erected sanctuaries in foreign places. Such a temple probably existed not only in the Wadi Tumilat, but perhaps also at Alexandria and elsewhere in Egypt. The Nabataeans did not disappear from Egypt when the Romans took over their kingdom in A.D. 106, any more than they immediately disappeared from the Negev or Transjordan or other parts of their former realm as a result of that event. Those who remained were simply absorbed into the continuing life there.[1068] They lived on in their accustomed places, accepting and contributing to the culture and religion of their environment, even as did others of Nabataean ancestry in early Byzantine Christian sites in the Negev of Palestine.

We are convinced that one of the consequences of the presence of Nabataeans in Egypt as caravaneers, merchants, officials, religious functionaries, mercenaries and settlers was the impact their sculpture continued to exercise, even after their disappearance as members of a separate entity, upon the Coptic art of the fifth century A.D. In the art forms of Coptic Ahnas in Egypt [1069] are definitely mirrored those prevailing several centuries earlier in Nabataea and closely related countries such as Parthia. It needs to be emphasized in this connection, however, that the Nabataeans formed only one of fairly numerous Oriental groups trading and living in Egypt at the same time as they did. Syrians, Parthians, Palmyrenians, Armenians and Scythians were among the foreign colonies resident there.[1070] The direct and indirect impact of highly advanced South Arabian civilization, which long preceded that of the Nabataeans and from which they undoubtedly derived much of their own background and skills, must also be considered in this connection. Throughout history there has been much cultural and commercial intercourse between Egypt and Arabia.[1071a]

It must be remembered, too, that there was a lively commercial and cultural interchange between Coptic Egypt and the Byzantine Negev and southern Transjordan, which had been such a flourishing part of the Nabataean kingdom and where the descendants of the Nabataeans continued to dwell and transmit, although in much altered fashion, their cultural heritage. In similar fashion, Nabataean and related styles can be traced in the eighth-century A.D. Omayyad art of Khirbet Mafjar in the Jordan Valley,[1071] in the mosque of Qasr Hallabat in the eastern desert of Transjordan and at Qasr el-Heir el-Gharbi in Syria.[1072]

The climate for the acceptance of Oriental influences in general and perhaps of Nabataean in particular in such an early Christian community as Coptic Ahnas in Egypt may have been created in part by a conscious turning away from the purer Hellenistic forms, dominant in Alexandria, in favor of those from the Orient, where Christianity was native and whence so many of its first adherents came.[1073] It was among the Semitic colonies scattered around the Mediterranean and throughout Egypt that the new faith found many of its first and most zealous converts. Among the earliest crosses in Christendom are the Byzantine ones found at some of the approximately three hundred early Christian Byzantine sites I discovered in the Negev. The cross on one of the building blocks at Byzantine Isbeita in the Negev (Pl. 217b) and the one with the eloquent *Alpha* and *Omega* on another from there, that has a fish symbol on the intact side of the circle enclosing these letters (Pl. 217a), give tangible evidence of the impact of burgeoning Christianity in the Negev in the fifth and sixth centuries A.D.

4. REFLECTED IN COPTIC ART

Evidence of some continuing memory of the presence of Nabataeans, and particularly of their sculpture and that of related peoples in Egypt as late as the fifth century A.D., is revealed in the clearly related Coptic reliefs of that period. These are even closer in likeness to the original sculptures of Khirbet Tannur than the generally cruder and perhaps somewhat later ones from Byzantine churches in the Negev. The latter hailed back, both in character and location, as we have seen, to Nabataean derivatives. The connection between Coptic sculptures of Christian Ahnas in Egypt and the distinctively Nabataean ones of the Hellenistic-Semitic Near East of several centuries earlier is too definite and too close to be accidental.[1074]

Part of the explanation may lie in the background of the Orientalized and Egyptianized Hellenism [1075] of Ahnas itself, located near the Nile, some 75 miles to the south of the position of Cairo. Its name in classical times was Heracleopolis.[1076] The Ahnas sculptures do not, despite their church associations, reflect a profoundly Christian consciousness. They may possibly denote the fact that the acceptance of the new religion was superficial in many respects. A fifth-century A.D. exponent of it, Apa Shenoute, by name, inveighed against his contemporaries,[1077] much as the prophets of Israel in an earlier age had lambasted their people for their continuous backsliding. The Ahnas-Heracleopolis sculptures were more Greek than Egyptian, more Oriental than Greek, and more pagan than Christian. This is also true of the reliefs of winged Erotes on dolphins and of Ino and Melicertes on a sea centaur embossed on the late sixth-century A.D. plates in the Athens Benaki Museum (Pls. 20, 21).[1078] It is not yet possible to show in detail every link of the chain of connection which we believe existed between the sculptures of the Nabataean kingdom and some of the earlier examples of the Coptic art of the Nile Valley, or more particularly between those of Hellenistic-Semitic Khirbet Tannur and Byzantine Christian Heracleopolis-Ahnas, but the fact of its existence is incontrovertible. Among other factors, as we have pointed out, the physical presence and cultural influence of Nabataean travelers and residents in Egypt are incontrovertible, as are the strong connections that existed between the Byzantine Negev and Coptic Egypt in the period following the disappearance of Nabataean identity. A very direct antecedent lies in the Orientalized sculptures of Oxyrhynchus,[1079] located close to the Nile, about 85 miles to the south of Heracleopolis-Ahnas. Dated to about 300 A.D.,[1080] they represent a coarsened form of earlier Hellenistic-Semitic art. This can be seen, for example, by comparing some of the Oxyrhynchus reliefs of inhabited" scrolls,[1081] as well as those of Ahnas, containing recumbent animals, with the earlier and far more excellent ones of the Nabataean temple of Qasr Rabbah (Pl. 169a, b).

To gaze at a series of reliefs from Coptic Heracleopolis-Ahnas is to see a reflection of the distinctive but provincial art of the Nabataeans. The deep set eyes with protruding irises, the low forehead, flattened nose, rounded cheeks, very full lips and exceedingly long chin characteristic of the Atargatis of Khirbet Tannur in her various guises as Vegetation, Grain, and Dolphin Goddess have been reproduced in a Coptic bust now in the Cairo Museum.[1082] The arrangement of the hair of the Grain Goddess and the Dolphin Goddess in regular waves on either side of a central part and collected above the ears in two, thick, twisted locks, which then fall down to the shoulders, is repeated in much the same form in the relief of a female head from Ahnas.[1083] The snail curls of the beard of the main Zeus-Hadad of the Temple of Tannur (Pl. 41) and of related Parthian gods [1084] are reflected in yet another bust from Ahnas.[1085]

c. At the Beginning of Islam

1) OMAYYAD ART

Although many of the features of the Coptic art of Egyptian Ahnas can be ascribed to Hellenistic-Semitic influences in general, it seems probable that there is a clear-cut connection with Nabataean art in particular, especially as exemplified by that of the Temple of Tannur.

There is, furthermore, strong evidence of Nabataean influence in the stucco sculptures in relief and in the round at the eighth-century A.D. Omayyad site of Khirbet Mafjar in the Jordan Valley, as has been previously suggested. [1086] It also manifests itself in the similarly dated Omayyad site of Qasr el-Heir el-Gharbi in southern Syria.[1087] We have also noted that the Omayyads built some of their caravanserais and hunting lodges on sites of former Nabataean occupation, such as that of Qasr Hallabat at the edge of the desert in Jordan.[1088] It seems possible that they may well have absorbed into their own bloodstream some of the distant descendants of the Nabataeans, who, under varying governments and religions, maintained and transmitted some of the skills and forms of their continuing artistic tradition.

As in the case of the Temple of Tannur, there is a certain leeway of variation in the conventional patterning of the Khirbet el-Mafjar sculptures. It ranged from the more purely Hellenistic to the more pronouncedly Oriental. One fragment of a small female figurine belongs to the former category, to judge from her comparatively graceful drapery of Graeco-Roman style,[1089] through which her shapely limbs can be glimpsed. It is closely related to the model worn centuries earlier by the Zodiac-Niké of Khirbet Tannur and by others there. The apparel and shape of almost all the other female and male sculptures of Khirbet Mafjar are pronouncedly Parthian-Nabataean in character, with the strong accent being on the Eastern rather than the Western in their make-up.[1090]

5. IN RETROSPECT

However much or little of Nabataean influence can be traced in Coptic and Omayyad art, the fact remains that the advent of Islam brought in its wake the beginnings of what developed into an absolute break with the Nabataean past. Most of the southern part of the Nabataean kingdom, revitalized by the rule of Christian Byzantium, reverted to the form of wilderness out of which it had originally been fashioned. The very existence of hundreds of former Nabataean settlements in the ancient Moab and Edom parts of Transjordan, the Wadi Arabah, the Negev and Sinai became forgotten for more than a millennium and a half. It was widely believed that the Nabataeans had been little more than a seminomadic people, engaged mainly in the incense and spice caravan trade, with their capital at Petra, and several cities or settlements along their main travel routes. They were rescued from oblivion mainly by employing on a country-wide scale the modern twentieth-century A.D. tool of identification of surface finds of pottery fragments. As a result these territories and the hamlets, villages and towns that once dotted them were placed within the framework of history.

Unmistakably recognizable Nabataean potsherds of vessels requiring high skills and sophistication to produce were found among the ruins of Nabataean sites that in the course of time were usually razed to the ground or subsequently built over. Occasional inscriptions, many rock drawings, and more frequent remains of water and soil conservation works also served to open the way to the Nabataean past. All of them helped make possible the clear delineation from surface finds alone of much of the nature and extent of the Nabataean kingdom and civilization. Subsequent excavations in depth at places like Khirbet Tannur, Dhiban, Petra, the Wadi Ramm and Abda substantiated and implemented the conclusions arrived at from such surface finds.

During the entire period of Nabataean history and thereafter, and as we have reason to believe during all of the last ten millennia, the factor of major permanent climatic change has played no role whatsoever in the rise and fall of civilizations anywhere in the ancient Near East. Aside from unknown variables of catastrophic epidemics or natural cataclysms, they must be attributed to human behavior and especially to the consequences of wars. The spirit of alert enterprise was the chief asset of the Nabataeans, and their appearance in a strategic area at an opportune interval in history their good fortune.

As long as they could they exploited to the full the extraordinarily favorable juncture of their time and location during the seesaw battle of world powers for mastery of the heartlands of Asia and Africa. Crops grew under their amazingly skilled hands even in previously unploughed wildernesses. Developing water and soil conservation to a high art, they constructed innumerable cisterns to store the rare rainwater and countless terraces to anchor the earth. Commerce flourished because of their imaginative and hard driving initiative. There was an enriching interchange of goods and cultural influences especially between their capital of Petra and international emporia. Wealth and power and position came to them more quickly than they could possibly have dreamed of in their desert days.

The quickly risen kingdom of Nabataea collapsed when Trajan in A.D. 106 shoved it like a shot-down and retrieved bird into the nondescript game-bag of the Roman Provincia Arabia. Nevertheless, for considerably over a century thereafter, the momentum of their achievements and the productivity of their undertakings enabled the Nabataeans to escape the anonymity of complete ethnic and cultural absorption. But the end of their existence as a separate people with an art and architecture and a place in the sun of their own was, from that moment on, inexorably determined, although not immediately consummated.

Their system of society lacked the indestructible ideas of Greek philosophy, Roman law and Hebrew religion that bore within themselves the elements of cultural or physical perpetuity or both. The Nabataeans never succeeded in building a system of values and a structure of faith whose enduring rightness could withstand the attrition of time and the indifference or antagonism of mortals.

Their concern with the worship of the divine in physical form was directed almost entirely to supplication for food and fortune in this world and in the hereafter. It carried with it even in the midst of a brilliant period of efflorescence the irresistible causes of disintegration and disappearance.

In their deities and dolphins and all manner of closely connected symbols, the Nabataeans found sufficient promise for their wellbeing in all the ways of life on earth, and safe passage and endless continuity in the hereafter. Their gaze was literally heavenward toward the planets and constellations they identified with their gods, whose forms they worshiped and whose blessings they sought in sanctuaries such as that of the Temple of Tannur.

CHRONOLOGY

Nabataea *

Palestine

332 B.C. Alexander the Great occupies Palestine.

312 B.C. Nabataeans of Petra repel two attacks of Seleucid Syrians.

321 B.C. Ptolemy I Soter (323-285 B.C.), one of successor generals of Alexander the Great, took control over Palestine. He established the dynasty of Ptolemies or Lagidae, that ruled Egypt till it became a Roman province in A.D. 30.

350 B.C.

c. 150 years. No mention of Nabataea or Nabataeans as such.

300 B.C.

(PARTHIA)

250 B.C.

(c. 250 B.C.-A.D. 229.) Arsaces (c. 250-248 B.C.) established Parthian kingdom, which flourished in Iranian lands freed from Seleucid control, and lasted till A.D. 229; fought and contained Roman expansionism eastward and at times threatened its foothold in western Asia. Strong connections with Nabataeans.

Parthian king, Orodes II, (c. 57-37/6 B.C.), put Hasmonaean Antigonus (40-37 B.C.) on throne in Jerusalem, in opposition to Roman supported Herod (the Great).

198 B.C. Palestine became subject to Seleucid Syria under Antiochus III, the Great (223-187 B.C.). The Seleucid dynasty was established by Seleucus I Nicator (312-281 B.C.), another of the successor generals of Alexander the Great. It ruled Syria till Pompey made it a Roman province in 64 B.C.

200 B.C.

c. 169 B.C. Aretas I, "tyrant of the Arabs" (II Macc. 5:8), also called "king of the Nabatu."

* Based on Starcky, *BA*, XVIII:4, Dec. 1955, pp. 81-106

Nabataea

Palestine

168 B.C. Revolt sparked when Seleucid ruler, Antiochus IV Epiphanes (175-164 B.C.), established Greek polis in City of David in Jerusalem.

167 B.C. Temple polluted by Syrians. Maccabaean rebellion broke out, led by Hasmonaean priest, Mattathias and his five sons, the greatest of whom was Judas Maccabaeus (166/5-160 B.C.).

162 B.C. Temple returned to Jews.

c. 157 B.C. Hasmonaean Jonathan (160-143 B.C.) makes peace with Seleucids, but was executed by Antiochus VI Epiphanes (145-142/1 B.C.) in 143 B.C.

150 B.C.   gap of c. half a century.

142 B.C. Demetrius II Nicator (145-139/8 B.C.) gives autonomy to Judaea.

140 B.C. Hasmonaean Simon (142/1-135/4 B.C.) appointed Ethnarch of Judaea.

134 B.C. Autonomy of Jerusalem confirmed by Antiochus VII Sidetes (139/8-129 B.C.), the last strong ruler of the Seleucids. He had conquered Jerusalem. Ultimately, he died fighting the Parthians.

134-104 B.C. John Hyrcanus I, son of Simon and grandson of Mattathias.

104-103 B.C. Aristobulus, son of John Hyrcanus I.

100 B.C.   c. 100 B.C.

(120-96 B.C.) Aretas II ("Erotimus, king of the Arabs" (?)), to whom people of Gaza, besieged by the Hasmonaean king, Alexander Jannaeus (103-76 B.C.), appealed in vain for help.

c. 90 B.C. Obodas I, "king of the Arabs," son of Aretas II, defeated Alexander Jannaeus and gained control of Hauran and Jebel Druze.

c. 87 B.C. Rabbel I, another son of Aretas II, fought successfully against Seleucid Antiochus XII Dionysus (87-84 B.C.) and against Alexander Jannaeus.

87-62 B.C. Aretas III ("Philhellene") occupied Damascus in 85 B.C. De-

103-76 B.C. Alexander Jannaeus, brother of Aristobulus. His reign marked high point of development of Hasmonaean kingdom of Judaea.

Nabataea

feated Alexander Jannaeus in battle in maritime plain east of Lydda in Palestine, but came to terms with him and withdrew to his own territory.

70 B.C. Nabataean occupation of Damascus intermittent; in 70 B.C. troops of Aretas III evacuated the city in face of invasion of Coele-Syria by Armenian king, Tigranes.

62-30 B.C. Malichus I (62-30 B.C.) ascended throne a year after Pompey made Judaea a Roman dependency and two years after he made Syria a Roman province. When Octavian (Caesar Augustus) made Egypt a Roman province in 30 B.C., ultimate Roman absorption of Nabataea in A.D. 106 was foreshadowed.

Malichus I sent cavalry to help Caesar in Egypt in 48 B.C. at request of his friend Idumaean Antipater. Pompey had previously made Antipater the procurator of Judaea, at same time as he had made Hyrcanus II its hereditary high-priest. Both appointments were reconfirmed by Caesar.

30-9 B.C. Obodas III (30-9 B.C.) was

Palestine

76-67 B.C. Salome Alexander, widowed queen of Alexander Jannaeus.

67-63 B.C. Aristobulus II, younger son of Alexander Jannaeus.

64 B.C. Pompey (106-48 B.C.) annexes Syria.

63 B.C. Pompey made Judaea a Roman dependency, and Aristobulus II was sent by him as prisoner to Rome.

63-40 B.C. Hyrcanus II, older brother of Aristobulus II, was installed by Pompey as high-priest of Judaea.

50 B.C.

47 B.C. For the support given to Julius Caesar (c. 102-44 B.C.) against Pompey, who was defeated in 48 B.C. and murdered when he fled to Greece in 48 B.C., Caesar confirmed Hyrcanus II as hereditary high-priest and ethnarch of Judaea and the latter's friend, the Judaized Idumaean, Antipater, as its procurator.

Soon thereafter he appointed two of Antipater's sons, Phasael and Herod (to become known as the Great) as governors of Jerusalem and Galilee, respectively. Their mother, Kypros, was a Nabataean.

(44 B.C. Caesar assassinated)

40-37 B.C. As a result of direct Parthian intervention by Orodes II (c. 57-37/6 B.C.), Antigonus (40-37 B.C.), the son of Aristobulus II, was enthroned in Jerusalem. He was to be the last of the Hasmonaean rulers. Herod's brother, Phasael, committed suicide and Herod fled to Rome, where the Senate gave him the title of King of Judaea. It was left to him, however, to get rid of the Parthians and of Antigonus.

37-4 B.C. Herod (the Great) (37-4 B.C.) captured Jerusalem in 37 B.C. and soon established his rule over all of

Nabataea

probably poisoned by his chief minister Syllaeus, who was beheaded in Rome in 5 B.C.

Name of Nabataean Abda (Eboda) in the Negev may reflect burial and deification there of Obodas. Nabataean coins with king and queen jugate first appeared during his reign.

A.D. 1

9 B.C.-A.D. 40 Aretas IV, ("Philopatris"), (9 B.C.-A.D. 40), was called "the king, king of the Nabatu, who loves his people." His two successive queens, Huldu and Shaqilat I, appeared with him jugate on some of his coins.

During his reign, temporary control apparently was regained over Damascus, where his ethnarch attempted to imprison Paul.

A.D. 40-71 Malichus II (A.D. 40-71) apparently lost control of Damascus, but retained territory to east and southeast of it, in addition to southern part of Nabataean kingdom. His coins picture him with his queen, his "sister," Shaqilat II. His reign marks waning of power of Nabataean kingdom.

Palestine

Palestine. The Hasmonaean Antigonus fled and was beheaded by the Romans at Antioch.

(30 B.C. Suicide of Anthony and Cleopatra and annexation of Egypt by Rome)

(27 B.C.-A.D. 14 Octavian sole ruler of Rome under name of Caesar Augustus)

4 B.C.-A.D. 39 Herod the Great's kingdom divided among his three surviving sons:
  a) Herod Antipas (4 B.C.-A.D. 39) was made tetrarch of Galilee and east Jordanian Peraea;
  b) Herod Philip (4 B.C.-A.D. 34), tetrarch of Batanaea, Trachonitis, Auranitis, and Ituraea;
  c) Archelaus (4 B.C.-A.D. 6), ethnarch of Samaria, Judaea, Idumaea.
A.D. 6-41 Judaea under Roman procurators.
A.D. 27-37 Pontius Pilate, procurator of Judaea.
A.D. 41-44 Herod Agrippa I, son of Aristobulus, who had been executed in 7 B.C. by his own father, Herod the Great, was made ruler by Rome over all his grandfather's realm. In A.D. 37 he had inherited the tetrarchy of one uncle, Herod Philip. In A.D. 39, he was given the tetrarchy of another uncle, Herod Antipas, who was banished to Gaul. In A.D. 41, he received the ethnarcate of his third uncle, Archelaus, who much earlier had been banished to Gaul.
A.D. 44-66 Judaea under Roman procurators, among whom was Porcius Festus (A.D. 60-62). He was married to Drusilla, the sister of Berenice and Herod Agrippa II (A.D. 50-100).
A.D. 66-73 Jewish War (A.D. 66-73), caused by harshness of Roman procurators, climaxed by Titus' destruction of Jerusalem and Temple in A.D. 70 and fall of Masada in A.D. 73.

Nabataea

Palestine

A.D. 50-53 Herod Agrippa II, son of Herod Agrippa I, ruled as king of Chalcis.

A.D. 53-100 Herod Agrippa II then became king of former tetrarchies of Herod Philip and Lysanias. After his death, his kingdom was incorporated into Roman province of Syria.

(ROME)

(A.D. 37-41   Gaius (Caligula)

A.D. 41-54   Claudius

A.D. 54-68   Nero

A.D. 68-69   Galba, Otho, Vitellius

A.D. 69-79   Vespasian

A.D. 79-81   Titus

A.D. 81-96   Domitian

A.D. 96-98   Nerva

A.D. 98-117   Trajan

A.D. 117-138 Hadrian)

A.D. 71-106 Rabbel II ("who gives life and salvation to his people"), (A.D. 71-106). Extant coins show him with his queen-mother, Shaqilat II, and then with Gamilat, one of his two successive queens, his "sisters," Gamilat and Hagiru.

Like his father, Malichus II, he spent much time at Bostra in Nabataean Syria, attesting to further decline of Nabataean power.

A.D. 50

A.D. 100

A.D. 106 Roman legate of Syria, A. Cornelius Palma, on behalf of Trajan (A.D. 98-117), annexed Nabataea and incorporated it into Provincia Arabia, with its capital in Bostra, Syria.

Petra gradually yielded its position as a great desert emporium to Palmyra and by end of third century A.D. was no longer of major importance.

A.D. 132-135 Bar Kochba rebellion against Rome, incited when Hadrian (A.D. 117-138) began to construct pagan city of Aelia Capitolina on site of Jerusalem.

A.D. 150

A.D. 300

A.D. 323-337 When Constantine I (the Great) (A.D. 323-337) emerged as sole ruler of Roman empire, and in A.D.

Nabataea

330 moved its capital to Byzantium (Constantinople), and made Christianity the official state-religion, an economic and religious efflorescence manifested itself in former Nabataea, including the Negev, and the rest of Palestine, among other places.

ABBREVIATIONS

AAA	*Annals of Archaeology and Anthropology.* Institute of Archaeology, University of Liverpool.
AAS	*Les Annales archéologiques de Syrie.*
AASOR	*Annual of the American Schools of Oriental Research.*
ABSA	*Annual of the British School of Archaeology at Athens.*
Ac. Or.	*Acta Orientalia.*
ADAJ	*Annual of the Department of Antiquities of Jordan.*
AE	*Ancient Egypt.*
Aegyptus	*Aegyptus, Rivista italiana de egittologia e di papyrologia.*
AfO	*Archiv für Orientforschung.*
AI	*Ars Islamica.*
AJ	*The Antiquaries Journal.*
AJA	*American Journal of Archaeology.*
AK	*Antike Kunst.*
ANEP	*The Ancient Near East in Pictures Relating to the Old Testament.*
ANET	*Ancient Near Eastern Texts Relating to the Old Testament.*
An. Or.	*Analecta Orientalia.*
AO	*Der alte Orient.*
A. Or.	*Archiv Orientalni, Journal of the Czechoslovak Oriental Institute.*
APS	*Proceedings of the American Philosophical Society.*
Archaeology	*Archaeology,* Archaeological Institute of America.
Arch. Anz.	(see JDAI).
Atiqot	*Atiqot, Journal of the Israel Department of Antiquities.*
BA	*The Biblical Archaeologist.*
BAAAC	*Bulletin de l'association des amis de l'art copte.*
BASOR	*Bulletin of the American Schools of Oriental Research.*
Berytus	*Berytus, Archaeological Studies.*
BIES	*Bulletin of the Israel Exploration Society.*
BMB	*Bulletin du Musée de Beyrouth.*
BMC	*British Museum Catalogue.*
BMMA	*Bulletin of the Metropolitan Museum of Art.*
BSOAS	*Bulletin of the School of Oriental and African Studies.*
CIS	*Corpus Inscriptionum Semiticarum.*
CRAI	*Comptes rendus de l'Academie des Inscriptions et Belles-Lettres.*

EPH-Tel	*Encylopédie photographique de l'art I. Le Musée du Louvre.*
GA	*Gazette archéologique.*
HGR	*Histoire générale des religions.*
HUCA	*Hebrew Union College Annual.*
IB	*The Interpreter's Bible.* New York: Abingdon Press, 1954.
IDB	*The Interpreter's Dictionary of the Bible.* New York: Abingdon Press, 1962.
IEJ	*Israel Exploration Journal.*
ILN	*The Illustrated London News.*
Iraq	*Iraq.* British School of Archaeology.
JA	*Journal asiatique.*
JAOS	*Journal of the American Oriental Society.*
JBL	*Journal of Biblical Literature.*
JDAI	*Jahrbuch des deutschen archäologischen Instituts.*
JNES	*Journal of Near Eastern Studies.*
JHS	*Journal of Hellenic Studies.*
JOAI	*Jahreshefte des österreichischen archäologischen Instituts.*
JPOS	*Journal of the Palestine Oriental Society.*
JRAS	*Journal of the Royal Asiatic Society.*
JRS	*Journal of Roman Studies.*
LXX	*Septuagint.*
MS	*Mélanges syriens offerts à monsieur René Dussaud.* Two volumes. Paris: Paul Geuthner, 1939.
MUSJ	*Mélanges de l'Université St. Joseph,* Beyrouth.
PA	Brünnow and Domaszewski, *Die Provincia Arabia.*
PAAJR	*Proceedings of the American Academy for Jewish Research.*
PAES	*Syria: Publications of the Princeton University Archaeological Expedition to Syria in 1904-1930 and 1949.* Leyden: E. J. Brill.
PBSR	*Papers of the British School at Rome.*
PEFQS	*Palestine Exploration Fund Quarterly Statement.*
PEQ	*Palestine Exploration Quarterly.*
QDAP	*Quarterly of the Department of Antiquities in Palestine.*
RA	*Revue archéologique.*
RAO	*Recueil d'archéologie orientale.*
RB	*Revue biblique.*
RHR	*Revue de l'histoire des religions.*
RN	*Revue numismatique.*

Syria	*Syria. Revue d'art oriental el d'archéologie.*
TAPA	*Transactions of the American Philological Association.*
VT	*Vetus Testamentum.*
ZDMG	*Zeitschrift der deutschen morgenländischen Gesellschaft.*

310 / PLATE 144
Sculptural fragments
a. b. Eagles' heads c. Fragment of eagle's wing d. Eagle's claws e-g. Tops of torches h. Cornucopia

321 / PLATE 145
Hermes-Mercury
322 / PLATE 146
a. Hermes-Mercury with lyre
b. Crude relief of Hermes-Mercury(?)
323 / PLATE 147
Hermes-Mercury with side-locks
324 / PLATE 148
Hermes-Mercury, Nabataean Syria. *Daniel Schlumberger*
325 / PLATE 149
a. Winged Hermes-Mercury, Petra. *Peter J. Parr*
b. Same, three-quarter right profile. *Peter J. Parr*
326 / PLATE 150
Hermes-Mercury. *G. L. Harding*
327 / PLATE 151
Hermes-Mercury, Petra. *Peter J. Parr*
328 / PLATE 152
Caduceus symbols
a. Petra b. Petra c. Ramat el-Halil, Hebron. *Peter J. Parr*
329 / PLATE 153
a. Cronos-Saturn
b. Hermes-Mercury
c. Damaged sandstone bust, Petra, with ends of fillet over right shoulder
330 / PLATE 154
a. b. Jupiter

340 / PLATE 155
a. Damaged memorial relief from Kerak with horse's head and neck over left shoulder
b. Drawing of above
c. Relief of warrior, Petra. *Peter J. Parr*
341 / PLATE 156
a. Memorial relief surmounted by eagle, and with horse's head and neck over left shoulder, Palmyra. *Daniel Schlumberger*
b. Drawing of above

342 / PLATE 156A
Memorial relief with horse's head and neck in relief over left shoulder, Palmyra. *Louvre*
343 / PLATE 157
a. Left half of crude bust
b. Damaged relief with sash, Ma'in. *Père R. deVaux*
344 / PLATE 158
Apollo with sash of twelve signs of the zodiac. *Vatican*
345 / PLATE 159
Bust in relief, Ma'in. *Père R. deVaux*

362 / PLATE 160
Sandstone lion
363 / PLATE 161
a. b. Lion and a foot of Atargatis, see Pl. 160
c. Kerch marble lion. *State Hermitage Museum*
364 / PLATE 162
a. Lion's hindquarters
b. Lion's paw
365 / PLATE 163
a. Khirbet edh-Dherih lion
b. c. Qasr Rabbah lions' heads
366 / PLATE 164
a. Lion relief, Qasr Rabbah
b. Lion relief, Qasr Rabbah
367 / PLATE 165
a-d. Lion reliefs
368 / PLATE 166
a. Lion Monument, Petra. *Department of Antiquities, Palestine*
b. Lion's Tomb, Petra. *Department of Antiquities, Palestine*
369 / PLATE 167
a. b. Winged Eros between two winged griffins, Petra. *Peter J. Parr*
c. "Inhabited scroll" with winged Eros, Qasr Rabbah
370 / PLATE 168
Feline, Araq el-Emir. *Paul W. Lapp*
371 / PLATE 169
a. "Inhabited scroll" with gazelle relief, Qasr Rabbah
b. "Inhabited scroll" with lion(?) relief, Qasr Rabbah
372 / PLATE 170
a. Damaged gazelle(?)
b. "Inhabited scroll" with ibex, Na-

436 / PLATE 194
Mati'a'el altar
a. b. Incense altar bearing name of donor, Mati'a'el, in Nabataean script
c. Copy of inscription by Père M. R. Savignac d. Nabataean Netir'el inscription, ending "in the year 2"

437 / PLATE 195
a. Damaged Nabataean inscription, mentioning Netir'el
b. Copy of inscription by Père M. R. Savignac

438 / PLATE 196
Horned stele with Nabataean Qosmilk inscription

439 / PLATE 197
Back of horned stele

440 / PLATE 198
Broken horned stele
a. b. Front and back of stele with grooves c. d. Back and front of stele base

441 / PLATE 199
a. Stele with Greek inscription (A) R A Y
b. Mason's mark "k"
c. Anthropomorphic idols, Petra. *Peter J. Parr*

456 / PLATE 200
a. Umm el-Biyara, Petra. *Agnes and George Horsfield*
b. Tomb of Sextus Florentinus, Petra. *Department of Antiquities, Palestine*

457 / PLATE 201
a. Nabataean tomb at Siq el-Bared, near Petra. *Department of Antiquities, Palestine*
b. Nabataean tomb at Siq el-Bared, near Petra. *Department of Antiquities, Palestine*

458 / PLATE 202
a. Façade of "Painted House" Siq el-Bared. *Department of Antiquities, Palestine*
b. Vaulted alcove in "Painted House." *Department of Antiquities, Palestine*

459 / PLATE 203
a. Mural in "Painted House," Siq el-Bared

b. Drawing of mural

460, 461 / PLATE 204
a. Extension of mural from "Painted House." *Department of Antiquities, Palestine*
b. Line drawing of mural

462 / PLATE 205
a. "Painted House" at Siq el-Bared showing tooling. *Department of Antiquities, Palestine*
b. Triclinium and Arcosolium in Qattar ed-Deir, Petra. *Department of Antiquities, Palestine*

463 / PLATE 206
a. Triclinium, Round House, Petra. *Department of Antiquities, Palestine*
b. Dorotheos House, Petra. *Department of Antiquities, Palestine*

475 / PLATE 207
a. Nabataean(?) rock drawing of spearman on camel, near Abda. *HUC Expedition*
b. Nabataean(?) rock drawing of ostrich hunt, Negev (Site 297 A). *HUC Expedition*

476 / PLATE 208
a. b. Rock drawings of hunting scene, Negev (Site 262). *HUC Expedition*

477 / PLATE 209
a. Nabataean rock drawing of horse and rider, with much later drawings around it, Negev (Site 297). *HUC Expedition*
b. Nabataean memorial inscription, Negev (Site 415). *HUC Expedition*

478 / PLATE 210
Nabataean - Byzantine cave-cistern, Negev (Site 30), still water-tight. Byzantine Greek inscription BOETHON and Byzantine crosses superimposed on originally Nabataean pillar. *HUC Expedition*

499 / PLATE 211
a. Nabataean - Byzantine reservoir, Umm el-Jemal. *Department of Antiquities, Palestine*
b. Judaean-Nabataean-Byzantine cistern and channel leading rainwater to it, Negev (Site 149 C). *HUC Expedition*

BIBLIOGRAPHY

Abdul-Hak, *Catalogué Damas.*
  Abdul-Hak, Sélim and André. *Catalogué Illustré du Département des Antiquités Greco-Romaines au Musée de Damas.* Damas: Directeur Général des Antiquités de Syrie, 1951.

Abel, *Géographie.*
  Abel, F. M. *Géographie de la Palestine.* Paris: J. Gabalda et Cie.
  Tome I: Géographie physique et historique, 1933.
  Tome II: Géographie politique. Les villes, 1938.

Aelian.
  Aelian. *On the Characteristics of Animals.*

Ainalov, *Art.*
  Ainalov, D. V. *The Hellenistic Origins of Byzantine Art.* Trans. Elizabeth and Serge Sobolevitch. Ed. Cyril Mango. New Brunswick: Rutgers University Press, 1961.

Ainé and Barré, *HP.*
  Ainé, H. Roux and Barré, L. *Herculanum et Pompéi.* Paris: Librairie de firme Didot frères, fils, et Cie., 1862.

Akurgal, *Anatolien.*
  Akurgal, Ekrem. *Die Kunst Anatoliens von Homer bis Alexander.* Berlin: Walter de Gruyter and Co., 1961.

Albright, *AP.*
  Albright, William Foxwell. *The Archaeology of Palestine.* Revised. London and Baltimore: Penguin Books, 1954.

————, *ARI.*
  ————. *Archaeology and the Religion of Israel.* Baltimore: The Johns Hopkins Press, 1953.

Alexander, "Aphrodite."
  Alexander, Christine. "A Statue of Aphrodite," *The Metropolitan Museum of Art Bulletin*, May 1953, pp. 241-251.

Alpers, *Dolphins.*
  Alpers, Anthony. *Dolphins: The Myth and the Mammal.* Cambridge: The Riverside Press, 1961.

Altheim, Stiehl, *Araber.*
  Altheim, Franz and Stiehl, Ruth. *Die Araber in der Alten Welt.* Vol. I. Berlin: Walter de Gruyter and Co., 1964.

Andrae, *Hatra.*
  Andrae, Walter. *Hatra.* Leipzig: J. C. Hinrichs, 1912.

Appian.
  Appian. *Roman History.*

Aristotle.
  Aristotle. *Historia Animalium.*

Arndt, *Register.*
  Arndt, Paul. *Register zu Denkmäler griechischer und römischer Skulptur.* München: F. Bruckmann, 1897.

Avi-Yonah, *IWB.*
  Avi-Yonah, Michael (*et al.*). *Illustrated World of the Bible.* New York: McGraw-Hill Book Co., Inc.
    I. The Law, 1959.
    II. Former Prophets, 1960.
    III. Later Prophets, 1960.
    IV. The Writings, 1961.
    V. New Testament, 1961.

————, *Or. Art.*
  ————. *Oriental Art in Roman Palestine* (Studie Semitici 5). Rome: 1961.

————, *QDAP.*
  ————. "Oriental Elements in the Art of Palestine in the Roman and Byzantine Periods." *QDAP*, Parts I-III, Vols. X, XIII, XIV, 1944-1950.

Bachmann, Watzinger, Wiegand, *Petra.*
  Bachmann, W.; Watzinger, C.; Wie-

gand, Th. *Petra*. Berlin and Leipzig: Walter de Gruyter and Co., 1921.

Bacon, *DFH*.
Bacon, Edward. *Digging for History*. New York: John Day Co., 1960.

Barnett, *ADAJ*.
Barnett, R. D. "Four Sculptures from Amman," *ADAJ* (Amman), I, 1951, pp. 34-36 and Plates X-XIII.

Bechi, *Real Museo Borb*.
Bechi, Guglielmo. *Real Museo Borbonico*, V. Napoli: Dalla Stamperia Reale, 1829.

Bellinger, *Troy, Coins*.
Bellinger, Alfred R. *Troy, the Coins*. Princeton, N. J.: Princeton University Press for University of Cincinnati, 1961.

Berghe vanden, *Iran*.
Berghe vanden, L. *Archéologie de l'Iran ancien*. Leiden: E. J. Brill, 1959.

Bieber, *Sculpture*.
Bieber, Margarete. *The Sculpture of the Hellenistic Age*. Revised edition. New York: Columbia University Press, 1961.

Bonnard, *Dieux de Grèce*.
Bonnard, André. *Les Dieux de la Grèce*. Mermod, Lausanne, 1946.

Bonner, *Amulets*.
Bonner, Campbell, *Studies in Magical Amulets, Chiefly Graeco-Egyptian*. Ann Arbor: The University of Michigan Press, 1950.

Borovka, *SA*.
Borovka, Gregory. *Scythian Art*. Trans. V. G. Childe. New York: Frederick A. Stokes Co., 1928.

Bossert, *Altsyrien*.
Bossert, Helmuth Th. *Altsyrien*. Tübingen: Ernst Wasmuth, 1951.

Bowen, Albright, *ADSA*.
Bowen, Richard; Albright, Frank P. (et al.). *Archaeological Discoveries in South Arabia*. Baltimore: The Johns Hopkins Press, 1958.

Breccia, *Musée*.
Breccia, Evaristo. *Le Musée Gréco-Romain*. Bergamo: Instituto Italiano d'Arti Grafiche, 1925-31 (pub. 1932) and 1931-32 (pub. 1933).

Brunn, *Götterideale*.
Brunn, Heinrich. *Griechische Götterideale*. München: Verlagsanstalt für Kunst und Wissenschaft, 1893.

Brunn, Bruckmann, *Denkmäler*.
Brunn, H.; Bruckmann, F. *Denkmäler Griechischer und Römischer Skulptur* (Continued by P. Arndt and G. Lippold). Munich, 1888-1947.

Butler, *PAES*.
Butler, Howard C. *PAES* II, A, 6, 1919.

Cantineau, *Nabatéen*.
Cantineau, J. *Le Nabatéen*. Paris: Ernest Leroux. Vol. I. Notions générales—Écriture grammaire, 1930. Vol. II. Choix de Textes—Lexique, 1932.

Casson, "Voyage."
Casson, Lionel. "The Isis and Her Voyage," *TAPA*, LXXXI, 1950, pp. 43-56.

Chatelain, *Maroc*.
Chatelain, Louis. *Le Maroc des Romains*. Paris: E. de Boccard, 1944.

Cicero.
Cicero, *De Divinatione*.

Clark, *Myth*.
Clark, R. T. Rundle. *Myth and Symbol in Ancient Egypt*. London: Thames and Hudson, 1959.

Clermont-Ganneau, *RHR*.
Clermont-Ganneau, Ch. "Les Nabatéens en Égypte," *RHR*, LXXX, 1919, pp. 1-29.

Cleveland, "Conway High Place."
Cleveland, Ray L. "The Excavation of the Conway High Place," *AASOR*, XXXIV-XXXV, 1960, pp. 57-78.

Contenau, *CP*.
Contenau, Georges. *La civilisation phénicienne*. Paris: Payot, 1926.

_____, *Déesse*.
_____. *La Déesse nue Babylonienne*. Paris: Paul Geuthner, 1914.

_____, *ELBA*.
_____. *Everyday Life in Babylon and Assyria*. London: Edw. Arnold, 1954.

_____, *MAO*.
_____. *Manuel d'Archéologie ori-*

entale. Vols. I-IV, 1927-1947. Paris: Auguste Picard.

Cook, *Zeus.*
Cook, Arthur Bernard. *Zeus.* Vols. I-III, 1914-1940. Cambridge: University Press.

Cook, *RAPLA.*
Cook, Stanley A. *The Religion of Ancient Palestine in the Light of Archaeology.* London: Oxford University Press, 1930.

Cooke, *N-S Inscr.*
Cooke, G. A. *A Text-Book of North-Semitic Inscriptions.* Oxford: The Clarendon Press, 1903.

Cross, *Library.*
Cross, Frank Moore. *The Ancient Library of Qumran and Modern Biblical Studies.* Garden City: Doubleday and Company, Inc., 1958.

Cumont, *After Life.*
Cumont, Franz. *After Life in Roman Paganism.* New Haven: Yale University Press, 1922.

————, *Doura.*
————. *Fouilles de Doura-Europos* (1922-1923). Texte et Atlas. Paris: Paul Geuthner, 1926.

————, *Études.*
————. *Études syriennes.* Paris: Auguste Picard, 1917.

————, *MM.*
————. *The Mysteries of Mithra.* Trans. Thomas J. McCormack. Second edition. Chicago: Open Court, 1910.

————, *OR.*
————. *The Oriental Religions in Roman Paganism.* With an Introductory Essay by Grant Showerman. Chicago: Open Court, 1911.

————, *RO.*
————. *Les Religions orientales dans le Paganisme romain.* 14th edition. Paris: Paul Geuthner, 1929.

————,
————. *La Stèle du Danseur d'Antibes et son Décor Végétal.* Paris: Paul Geuthner, 1942.

————, *TM.*
————. *Textes et monuments figurés relatifs aux Mystères de Mithra,* Tomes I and II, 1899 and 1896, Bruxelles: H. Lamertin.

Dalman, *NPF.*
Dalman, Gustaf. *Neue Petra Forschungen und der heilige Felsen von Jerusalem.* Leipzig: J. C. Hinrichs, 1912.

————, *Petra.*
————. *Petra und seine Felsenheiligtümer.* Leipzig: J. C. Hinrichs, 1908.

Daremberg-Saglio: *Dict.*
Dictionnaire des Antiquités Grècques et Romaines d'après les Textes et les Monuments. Eds. C. Daremberg and C. Saglio. Paris: 1873-.

Debevoise, *Parthia.*
Debevoise, Neilson C. *A Political History of Parthia.* Chicago: The University of Chicago Press, 1938.

de Vaux, see Vaux.

Dio Cassius.
Dio Cassius. *Roman History.*

Diodorus.
Diodorus of Sicily. *The Library of History.*

Dölger, *Der Heilige Fisch.*
Dölger, Franz Joseph. *Der Heilige Fisch in den antiken Religionen und im Christentum.* Vols. I-V, 1910-1943. Münster in Westfallen: Aschendorffschen Verlagsbuchhandlung.

Doughty, *Travels.*
Doughty, Charles M. *Travels in Arabia Deserta.* Two volumes. New York: Random House, 1938.

Drioton, *BAAAC.*
Drioton, Étienne. "Art syrien et art copte," *BAAAC,* III, 1937, pp. 29-40 plus 8 plates.

Drower, *Book of Zodiac.*
Drower, E. S. *The Book of the Zodiac.* London: Royal Asiatic Society, 1949.

Dunand, *Soueïda.*
Dunand, Maurice. *Le Musée de Soueïda.* Paris: Paul Geuthner, 1934.

Dussaud, *Arabes en Syrie.*
Dussaud, René. *La pénétration des arabes en Syrie avant l'Islam.* Paris: Paul Geuthner, 1955.

———, *Art phénicien.*

———, *L'Art phénicien du IIe Millénaire.* Paris: Paul Geuthner, 1949.

———, *Notes Myth. Syr.*

———. *Notes de mythologie syrienne.* Paris: Ernest Leroux, 1903.

———, *Topographie.*

———. *Topographie historique de la Syrie antique et médiévale.* Paris: Paul Geuthner, 1927.

Dussaud, Macler, *Mission.*

Dussaud, René and Macler, Frédéric. *Mission dans les régions désertiques de la Syrie moyenne.* Paris: Ernest Leroux, 1903.

Eisen, *Seals.*

Eisen, Gustavus A. *Ancient Oriental Cylinder and Other Seals.* Chicago: The University of Chicago Press, 1940.

Eisenberg, *ECS.*

Eisenberg, Jerome M. *A Catalog of Late Egyptian and Coptic Sculptures.* New York: Royal Athena Galleries, 1960.

Eisler, *Weltenmantel.*

Eisler, Robert. *Weltenmantel und Himmelszelt.* 2 Bände. München: C. H. Beck, 1910.

Eissfeldt, *Baal Zaphon.*

Eissfeldt, Otto. *Baal Zaphon, Zeus Kasios und der Durchzug der Israeliten durchs Meer.* Halle (Saale): Max Niemeyer, 1932.

Elderkin, *Antioch.*

Antioch on the Orontes, I. Ed. Elderkin, George W. Princeton: Princeton University, 1934.

Eliot, *Life Int.*

Eliot, Alexander. "The Creative Adventure: The Wine in the Marble," *Life International,* June 8, 1962, pp. 71-74.

Euting, *Inschriften.*

Euting, Julius. *Sinaitische Inschriften.* Berlin: Georg Reimer, 1891.

Evenari, Shanan, Tadmor, *Runoff-Farming in the Negev.*

Evenari, Michael; Shanan, Leslie; Tadmor, Naphtali, H. *Runoff-Farming in the Negev Desert of Israel.* Rehovot, 1963.

Finegan, *LfAP.*

Finegan, Jack. *Light from the Ancient Past.* Princeton: Princeton University Press, 1946.

Frankfort, *Art and Arch.*

Frankfort, Henri. *The Art and Architecture of the Ancient Orient.* Baltimore: Penguin Books, 1955.

Ghirshman, *Bichâpour.*

Ghirshman, Roman. *Les mosaiques sassanides.* (Musée du Louvre—Département des antiquités orientales. Série archéologique . Tome VII. *Fouilles de Châpour.* Publiées sous la direction de Georges A. Salles et R. Ghirshman. *Bichâpour.* Vol. II.) Paris: Paul Geuthner, 1956.

———, *Iran.*

———. *Iran.* Trans. Stuart Gilbert and James Emmons. London: Thames and Hudson, 1962.

Glueck, *AASOR.*

Glueck, Nelson. *Explorations in Eastern Palestine,* (AASOR).

I	Vol. XIV	1934
II	XV	1935
III	XVIII-XIX	1939
IV	XXV-XXVIII	1951

———, *OSJ.*

———. *The Other Side of the Jordan.* New Haven: American Schools of Oriental Research, 1940.

———, *RITD.*

———. *Rivers in the Desert.* New York: Farrar, Straus and Cudahy, 1959.

———, *RJ.*

———. *The River Jordan.* Philadelphia: The Westminster Press, 1946.

Goldman, *AK.*

Goldman, Bernard. "A Luristan Water-Goddess," *AK,* III, nr. 2-3, 1960, pp. 53-57.

Goodenough, *Symbols.*

Goodenough, E. R. *Jewish Symbols*

in the Graeco-Roman Period. Vols. I-VIII, 1953-. New York: Pantheon Books.

Grant, *World of Rome.*
Grant, Michael. *The World of Rome.* London: Weidenfeld and Nicolson, 1960.

Gressmann, *AOB.*
Altorientalische Texte zum Alten Testament. Ed. Gressmann, Hugo. Zweite Auflage. Berlin und Leipzig: Walter de Gruyter and Co., 1927.

_____, *AOT.*
Altorientalische Texte zum Alten Testament. Ed. Gressmann, Hugo. Zweite Auflage. Berlin und Leipzig: Walter de Gruyter and Co., 1926.

_____, *OR.*
Gressman, Hugo. *Die orientalischen Religionen im hellenistisch-römischen Zeitalter.* Berlin und Leipzig: Walter de Gruyter and Co., 1930.

Halliday, "Artemis."
Halliday, W. R. "A Statuette of Artemis Ephesia in the Possession of Dr. Robert Mond," *AAA,* XIX, 1932, pp. 23-27.

Hamilton, *QDAP.*
Hamilton, R. W. "The Sculpture of Living Forms at Khirbet al Mafjar," *QDAP,* XIV, 1950, pp. 101-119 and Pls. XXXV-XLV.

Hammond, *BA.*
Hammond, Philip C. "The Nabataean Bitumen Industry at the Dead Sea," *BA,* XXII, 1959, pp. 40-48.

Harding, *Antiquities.*
Harding, G. Lankester. *The Antiquities of Jordan.* London: Lutterworth Press, 1959.

Hausmann, *Weihreliefs.*
Hausmann, Ulrich. *Griechische Weihreliefs.* Berlin: Walter de Gruyter and Co., 1960.

Heichelheim, *Wirtschaftsgeschichte.*
Heichelheim, Fritz M. *Wirtschaftsgeschichte des Altertums.* Vols. I and II. Leiden: Sijthoff's Uitgeversmaatschappij N.V., 1938.

Herodotus.
Herodotus. *History.*

Hill, *BMC: Palestine.*
Hill, George Francis. *Catalogue of the Greek Coins of Palestine.* London: British Museum, 1914.

_____, *BMC: Phoenicia.*
_____. *Catalogue of the Greek Coins of Phoenicia.* London: British Museum, 1910.

_____, *Greek Coins.*
_____. *Catalogue of the Greek Coins of Arabia, Mesopotamia and Persia.* London: British Museum, 1922.

Hill, *London.*
Hill, William Thomson. *Buried London: Mithras to the Middle Ages.* London: Phoenix House, 1955.

Hinks, *Catalogue.*
Hinks, R. P. *Catalogue of the Greek, Etruscan and Roman Paintings and Mosaics in the British Museum.* London: British Museum, 1933.

Hogarth, *Hittite Seals.*
Hogarth, D. G. *Hittite Seals.* Oxford: The Clarendon Press, 1920.

Hollis, *Temple.*
Hollis, F. J. *The Archaeology of Herod's Temple.* London: J. M. Dent and Sons Ltd., 1934.

Hopkins, *Berytus.*
Hopkins, Clark. "Aspects of Parthian Art in the Light of Discoveries from Dura-Europos," *Berytus,* III, 1936, pp. 1-31.

_____, *Berytus.*
_____. "The Parthian Temple," *Berytus,* VII, 1942, pp. 1-18.

_____, "Frontality."
_____. "A Note on Frontality in Near Eastern Art," *Ars Islamica,* III, 1936, pp. 187-196.

Horsfield, *QDAP.*
Horsfield, G. and A. "Sela-Petra, The Rock, of Edom and Nabatene," *QDAP,* VII, 1938, pp. 1-42; VIII, 1938, pp. 87-115; IX, 1942, pp. 105-204.

Ingholt "Hatra."
Ingholt, Harald. "Parthian Sculp-

tures from Hatra, Orient and Hellas in Art and Religion," *Memoirs of the Connecticut Academy of Arts and Sciences,* XII, 1954, pp. 5-55.
———, "Palmyra."
———. "Inscriptions and Sculptures from Palmyra," *Berytus,* III, 1936, pp. 83-125.
Ingholt, Seyrig, Starcky, *RTP.*
Ingholt, Harald; Seyrig, Henri; Starcky, Jean. *Recueil des tessères de Palmyre.* Paris: Paul Geuthner, 1955.
Ipser, *VA.*
Ipser, Karl. *Vatican Art.* Trans. Doireann MacDermott. New York: Philosophical Library, 1953.

Jaussen, Savignac, *MA.*
Jaussen, Antonin and Savignac, Raphael. *Mission archéologique en Arabie* (Mars-Mai 1907). Vols. I, 1909, and II, 1914. Paris: Ernest Leroux.
Josephus, *Antiq.*
Josephus, *Antiquities of the Jews.*
———, *War.*
———. *Wars of the Jews.*
Jucker, *Blätterkelch.*
Jucker, Hans. *Das Bildnis im Blätterkelch.* Lausanne and Freiburg i. Br.: Urs Graf-Verlag Olten, 1961.

Kammerer, *Pétra.*
Kammerer, A. *Pétra et la Nabatène.* Paris: Paul Geuthner, 1929.
Kantorowicz, *Gods in Uniform.*
Kantorwicz, Ernst H. "Gods in Uniform," *APS,* CV, 1961, pp. 368-393.
Kawerau, Rehm, *Milet.*
Kawerau, Georg and Rehm, Albert. *Milet.* Ed. Theodor Wiegand. Heft III. Berlin: Georg Reimer, 1914.
Kennedy, *Petra.*
Kennedy, Alexander B. W. *Petra.* London: Country Life, 1925.
Kitzinger, *Coptic Sculpture.*
Kitzinger, Ernst. "Notes on Early Coptic Sculpture." Oxford: John Johnson, 1938. (Taken from *Archaeologia,* LXXXVII, 1938, pp. 181-215.)
Kraeling, *Gerasa.*

Gerasa, City of the Decapolis. Ed. Kraeling, Carl H. New Haven: The American Schools of Oriental Research, 1938.
Kraeling, Adams, *City.*
City Invincible. Eds. Kraeling, Carl H. and Adams, Robert M. Chicago: The University of Chicago Press, 1960.
Kraeling, *Atlas.*
Kraeling, Emil G. *Rand McNally Historical Atlas of the Holy Land.* Chicago: Rand McNally and Company, 1959.
Kramer, *MAW.*
Mythologies of the Ancient World. Ed. Kramer, Samuel Noah. Chicago: Quadrangle Books, 1961.

Lapp, *BASOR.*
Lapp, Paul W. "The Second and Third Campaigns at 'Araq el-Emîr," *BASOR,* 171, 1963, pp. 8-39.
Lawrence, *Pillars.*
Lawrence, T. E. *The Seven Pillars of Wisdom.* New York: Doubleday, Doran and Company, Inc., 1935.
Lidzbarski, *AT.*
Lidzbarski, Mark. *Kanaanäische Inschriften* ("Altsemitische Texte" I). Giessen: Alfred Töpelmann, 1907.
Lieberman, *HJP.*
Lieberman, Saul. *Hellenism in Jewish Palestine.* New York: Jewish Theological Seminary, 1950.
Lilly, *Man and Dolphin.*
Lilly, John C. *Man and Dolphin,* New York: Worlds of Science pub., Pyramid Publications, 1962.
Lilly, "Dolphins."
Lilly, John C. "Modern Whales, Dolphins, and Porpoises, as Challenges to Our Intelligence," in *The Dolphin in History.* Los Angeles: University of California, 1963.
Lippold, *Skulpturen vat.*
Lippold, Georg. *Die Skulpturen des vaticanischen Museums.* Band III, 1. Text. Berlin und Leipzig: Walter de Gruyter and Co., 1936.
Littmann, *BSOAS.*
Littmann, Enno. "Nabataean In-

scriptions from Egypt." (With an Introduction and Classical Notes by David Meredith). *BSOAS*, Part 1, XV, 1953, pp. 1-28; Part 2, XVI, 1954, pp. 211-246.

————, *Sem. Inser.*

————. Part Four of the Publications of an American Archaeological Expedition to Syria, 1899-1900. *Semitic Inscriptions.* New York: Century Co., 1904.

————, *PAES.*

————. *PAES*, IV, A: Nabataean Inscriptions. Leyden: E. J. Brill, 1914.

Löwy, *Triumphbogens.*
Löwy, Emanuel. *Die Anfänge des Triumphbogens.* Wien: Anton Schroll and Co., 1928.

Lullies, *Greek Sculpture.*
Lullies, Reinhard. *Greek Sculpture.* New York: Harry N. Abrams, Inc., 1960.

McCown, *AASOR.*
McCown, C. C. "The Goddesses of Gerasa," *AASOR*, XIII, 1931-1932, pp. 129-166.

Ma'ayeh, *ADAJ.*
Ma'ayeh, Farah S. "Recent Archaeological Discoveries in Jordan," *ADAJ* (Amman), IV and V, 1960, pp. 114-116 and plate III.

Macrobius.
Macrobius. *Saturnalia.*

Mader, *Mambre.*
Mader, Evaristus. *Mambre.* Freiburg im Breisgau: Erich Wewel Verlag, 1957.

Mallowan, *Iraq.*
Mallowan, M. E. L. "Excavations at Brak and Chagar Bazar," *Iraq*, IX, 1947, pp. 1-259.

Matthews, Cook, *CS.*
Matthews, Kenneth D. and Cook, Alfred W. *Cities in the Sand.* Philadelphia: University of Pennsylvania, 1957.

May, *Atlas.*
Oxford Bible Atlas. Ed. May, Herbert G. London: Oxford University Press, 1962.

Mazar, Dothan, Dunayewski, *'Ein-Gedi.*
Mazar, B., Dothan, T., Dunayewski, E. *'Ein-Gedi.* (Hebrew). Jerusalem: The Israel Exploration Society, 1963.

Mendel, *Catalogue.*
Mendel, Gustave. *Catalogue des sculptures grècques, romaines et byzantines.* Vol. II. Constantinople: Musée impérial, 1914.

du Mesnil, *TMP.*
du Mesnil du Buisson, Comte. *Les tessères et les monnaies de Palmyre.* Paris: E. de Boccard, 1962.

Milik, Seyrig, *RN.*
Milik, J. T. and Seyrig, Henri. "Trésor monétaire de Murabba'at," *RN*, VI, 1958, pp. 11-26.

Miller, *Greek Horizons.*
Miller, Helen Hill. *Greek Horizons.* New York: Royal Greek Embassy Press and Information Service, 1961.

Minns, *S. Gr.*
Minns, Ellis H. *Scythians and Greeks.* Cambridge: University Press, 1913.

Montagu, Lilly, *Dolphin in History.*
Montagu, Ashley and Lilly, John C. *The Dolphin in History.* Los Angeles: University of California, 1963.

Moortgat, *Kunst.*
Moortgat, A. *Die bildende Kunst des alten Orients und die Bergvölker.* Berlin: Hans Schoetz and Co., 1932.

Morey, *Mosaics.*
Morey, C. R. *The Mosaics of Antioch.* New York: Longmans, Green and Co., 1938.

Morgenstern, *JBL.*
Morgenstern, Julian. "The 'Son of Man' of Daniel 7:13f.: A New Interpretation," *JBL*, LXXX, 1961, pp. 65-77.

Murray, *Petra.*
Murray, M. A. *Petra.* London and Glasgow: Blackie and Son, Ltd., 1939

Musil, *AP.*
Musil, Alois. *Arabia Petraea.* Vol. I: Moab. Vol. II: Edom. Wien: Alfred Hölder, 1907.

Naville, *Ahnas.*
Naville, Edouard. *Ahnas el-Medineh*

(*Heracleopolis magna*). London: Egyptian Exploration Fund, 1894.

Negev, *'Avdat.*
Negev, Abraham. *'Avdat.* (Hebrew.) Jerusalem: Department of Education, Israel Defense Forces, 1962.

————, *Hist. of 'Avdat.*
————. "Chapters in the History of 'Avdat," in *Elath: The Eighteenth Archaeological Convention,* October 1962, pp. 118-148 (Hebrew), 1963.

Neumann, *Great Mother.*
Neumann, Erich. *The Great Mother.* Trans. Ralph Manheim. New York: Pantheon Books, Inc., 1955.

Newell, *Num. Notes and Monographs.*
Newell, Edward T. *Late Seleucid Mints in Ake-Ptolemais and Damascus* ("Numismatic Notes and Monographs," No. 84.) New York: The American Numismatic Society, 1939.

O'Callaghan, "Statue."
O'Callaghan, R. T. "A Statue Recently Found in 'Ammân," *Orientalia* (Rome), XXI, 1952, pp. 184-193.

von der Osten, *Seals.*
von der Osten, Hans Henning. *Ancient Oriental Seals in the Collection of Mr. Edward T. Newell* ("The University of Chicago Oriental Institute Publications," Vol. XXII.) 1934.

Parr, *ADAJ.*
Parr, Peter J. "A Cave at Arqub el Dhahr," *ADAJ* (Amman), III, 1956, pp. 61-63; "Excavations at Khirbet Iskander," IV and V, 1960, pp. 128-133; "Nabataean Sculpture from Khirbet Brak," pp. 134-136.

————, *PEQ.*
————. "Recent Discoveries at Petra," *PEQ* (London), LXXXIX, 1957, pp. 5-16.

Parrot, *Sumer.*
Parrot, André. *Sumer.* ("L'univers des formes.") Paris: Gallimard, 1960.

————, *Tello.*
————. *Tello,* vingt compagnes de fouilles (1877-1933). Paris: Albin Michel, 1948.

Pauly-Wissowa.
Paulys Real-Encyclopädie der classischen Altertumswissenschaft. Ed. G. Wissowa, Stuttgart, 1894-.

Pelekanides.
Pelekanides, Stylianos. *The Silver Plates in the Benaki Museum.* Anatyposis ek tes Archeologikes Efermeridos. Athens, 1948.

Periplus.
The Periplus of the Erythraean Sea. Trans. from the Greek and annotated by Wilfred H. Schoff. New York: Longmans, Green, and Co., 1912.

Perkins, *City.*
Perkins, Ann L. In discussion, "The Greek and Roman Orient." *City Invincible.* Eds. Carl H. Kraeling and Robert M. Adams. Chicago: The University of Chicago Press, 1960. pp. 165-223. (Perkins section: pp. 207-210.)

Petrie, *Oxyrhynkhos.*
Petrie, Flinders. *Tombs of the Courtiers and Oxyrhynkhos.* London: British School of Archaeology in Egypt and Bernard Quaritch, 1925.

Phillips, *QS.*
Phillips, Wendell. *Qataban and Sheba.* New York: Harcourt, Brace and Co., 1955.

Picard, *CL,* II.
Picard, Charles. "Sur l'Atargatis-Derkétô des Thermes d'Aphrodisias en Carie," *Hommages à Joseph Bidez et à Franz Cumont.* (*Collection Latomus,* II.) Brussels: (n.d.), pp. 255-264.

————, *RA.*
————. "Les sculptures nabatéennes de Khirbet-et-Tannour et l'Hadad de Pouzzoles," *RA* X, (Paris), 6th series, July-Dec., 1937, pp. 244-249; "Une Atargatis méconnue à Leptis Magna," XXXVII, 1951, pp. 231-233.

Piggott, *Dawn.*
The Dawn of Civilization. Ed. Piggott, Stuart. New York: McGraw-Hill, 1961.

Pliny, *Nat. Hist.*
Pliny. *Natural History.*
Plutarch.
Plutarch. *Lives.*
Polybius.
Polybius. X, II, 31.
Potratz, *Kunst.*
Potratz, Johannes A. H. *Die Kunst des Alten Orients.* Stuttgart: Alfred Kröner, 1961.
Powell, *Celts.*
Powell, T. G. E. *The Celts.* New York: Frederick A. Praeger, 1958.
Pritchard, *ANEP.*
See Abbreviations *ANEP, ANET.*

Reinach, *CMIA.*
Reinach, Salomon. *Catalogue du musée impérial d'antiquités.* Constantinople: La direction du musée, 1882.
———, *Répertoire.*
———. *Répertoire de la statuaire grècque et romaine.* Vols. I and II, 1897; III, 1904; IV, 1913; V, 1924. Paris: Ernest Leroux.
Rice, *Scythians.*
Rice, Tamara Talbot. *The Scythians.* London: Thames and Hudson, 1957.
Richter, *Sculpture.*
Richter, Gisela M. A. *The Sculpture and Sculptors of the Greeks.* New Haven: Yale University Press, 1950.
Ridder de, *Bronzes.*
Ridder de, A. *Les Bronzes Antiques du Louvre.* Vol. I—Figurines, Vol. II—Instruments. Paris: Ernest Leroux, 1915.
Robinson, *Sarcophagus.*
Robinson, George Livingston. *The Sarcophagus of an Ancient Civilization* (Petra, Edom and the Edomites). New York: The Macmillan Co., 1930.
Ronzevalle, *MUSJ.*
Ronzevalle, P. S. "Notes et études d'archéologie orientale (troisième série, 11): Jupiter héliopolitain, nova et vetera," *MUSJ* (Beyrouth), XXI, 1938, pp. 1-162; "La couronne ("nemara"?) d'Atargatis à Délos," XXII:5, 1939, pp. 107-121.

Roscher, *Lexikon.*
Ausführliches Lexikon der griechischen und römischen Mythologie. Ed. Roscher, W. H. Leipzig: Teubner, 1884-1937.
Rossini, *Dedalo.*
Rossini, Carlo Conti. "Dalle Rovine di Ausàn," *Dedalo,* Rassegna d'arte di retta da Ugo Ojetti, Milan-Rome, Anno VII, volume Terzo 1926-1927, pp. 727-754.
Rostovtzeff, *CC.*
Rostovtzeff, Mikhail I. *Caravan Cities.* Trans. D. and T. Talbot Rice. Oxford: The Clarendon Press, 1932.
———, *DPPA.*
———. "Dura and the Problem of Parthian Art," *Yale Classical Studies,* V, pp. 157-304. New Haven: Yale University Press, 1935.
———, *Dura.*
Dura. The Excavations at Dura-Europos. Conducted by Yale University and the French Academy of Inscriptions and Letters. Eds. Rostovtzeff, M. I.; Baur, P. V. C.; Bellinger, A. R.; Brown, F. E.; Hopkins, C.; Welles, C. B. Vol. I, 1929; II, 1931; III, 1932; IV, 1933; V, 1934; VI, 1936; VII and VIII, 1939; IX, 1944, with Parts 2 and 3 in 1946 and 1952. New Haven: Yale University Press.
———, *Dura Art.*
Rostovtzeff, Mikhail I. *Dura-Europos and Its Art.* Oxford: Clarendon Press, 1938.
———, *Iranians and Greeks.*
———. *Iranians and Greeks in South Russia.* Oxford: Clarendon Press, 1922.
Roussel, *Délos.*
Roussel, Pierre. *Délos, colonie athénienne.* Paris: Fontemoing and Cie., 1916.

Sarre, Herzfeld, *Felsreliefs.*
Sarre, Friedrich und Herzfeld, Ernst. *Iranische Felsreliefs.* Berlin: Ernst Wasmuth A.-G., 1910.

Savignac, *RB.*
 Savignac, R. "Le Haut-Lieu de Pétra," *RB,* XII, 1903, pp. 280-291; XIV, 1915, p. 242.
 _____. "Notes de voyage.—Le sanctuaire d'Allat à Iram," *RB,* XLI, 1932, pp. 581-597.
 _____, "Le dieu nabatéen de La'aban et son temple," *RB,* XLVI, 1937, pp. 401-416.
Savignac, Horsfield, *RB.*
 Savignac, R. and Horsfield, G. "Le temple de Ramm," *RB,* XLIV, 1935, pp. 245-278.
Savignac, Starcky, *RB.*
 Savignac, R. and Starcky, J. "Une inscription nabatéenne provenant du Djôf," *RB,* LXIV, 1957, pp. 196-215. Note additionnelle, pp. 215-217: "Y a-t-il un dieu Rêš 'ain La'aban?"
de Saulcy, *Numismatique.*
 de Saulcy, F. *Numismatique de la terre sainte.* Paris: J. Rothschild, 1874.
Schalit, *Land of Israel.*
 Schalit, A. "On the Conquests of Alexander Jannai in Moab," *The Land of Israel* (Hebrew), 5711.
Schlumberger, *Palmyrène.*
 Schlumberger, Daniel. *La Palmyrène du nordouest.* Paris: Paul Geuthner, 1951.
 _____, *Syria.*
 _____. "Les formes anciennes du chapteau corinthien en Syrie, en Palestine et en Arabie," *Syria,* XIV, 1933, pp. 283-317.
 _____. "Les fouilles de qasr el-Heir el Gharbi (1936-1938), rapport préliminaire," *Syria,* XX, 1939, pp. 324-373.
 _____. "Descendants non-Méditerranéens de l'art grec," *Syria,* XXXVII, 1960, pp. 253-318.
Schreiber, *Toreutik.*
 Schreiber, Theodor. *Die alexandrinische Toreutik.* I. Teil. Leipzig: S. Hirzel, 1894.
Segall, *South Arabia.*
 Segall, Berta. "The Lion-Riders from Timna'" in Bowen, *ADSA.*

Seyffert, *Dictionary.*
 Seyffert, Oskar. *A Dictionary of Classical Antiquities.* New York: Meridian Books, 1956.
Seyrig, *Antiquités syriennes.*
 Seyrig, Henri, *Antiquités syriennes,* I-VI, 1934-1959 in *Syria,* XII-XXXVII, 1931-1960.
Smith, *HGHL.*
 Smith, George Adam. *The Historical Geography of the Holy Land.* New York: A. C. Armstrong and Son, 1895.
Smith, *Kinship.*
 Smith, W. Robertson. *Kinship and Marriage in Early Arabia.* London: Adam and Charles Black, 1903.
Sourdel, *Hauran.*
 Sourdel, Dominique. *Les cultes du Hauran à l'époque romaine.* (Institut français d'archéologie de Beyrouth). Paris: 1952.
Starcky, *BA.*
 Starcky, Jean. "The Nabataeans: A Historical Sketch," *BA,* XVIII, New Haven, 1955, pp. 84-106.
 _____, *RB.*
 _____. "Un contrat nabatéen sur papyrus," *RB,* LXI, 1954, pp. 161-181.
 _____, *Syria.*
 _____. "Autour d'une dédicace palmyrénienne à Sadrafa et à Du'anat," *Syria,* XXVI, 1949, pp. 43-85.
Stebbins, *Dolphin.*
 Stebbins, Eunice Burr. *The Dolphin in the Literature and Art of Greece and Rome.* Baltimore, Md.: Johns Hopkins Press, 1929.
Stève, *LWB.*
 Stève, M. J. *The Living World of the Bible.* Trans. Daphne Woodward. Cleveland and New York: The World Publishing Co., 1961.
Stocks, *Berytus.*
 Stocks, H. "Studien zu Lukians 'De syria dea'," *Berytus,* IV (Copenhagen), 1937, pp. 1-40.
Strabo.
 Strabo. *Geography.*
Strong, *Apotheosis.*
 Strong, Mrs. Arthur. *Apotheosis and*

After Life. London: Constable and Company, Ltd., 1915.

Strong, Garstang, *Syrian Goddess.*
Strong, Herbert A. and Garstang, John. *The Syrian Goddess.* Translation of Lucian's "De Dea Syria" with a Life of Lucian. London: Constable and Co., Ltd., 1913.

Sukenik, *Beth Alpha.*
Sukenik, Eleazar L. *The Ancient Synagogue of Beth Alpha.* Jerusalem: University Press, 1932.

Tcherikover, *Hellenistic Civilization.*
Tcherikover, Victor. *Hellenistic Civilization and the Jews.* Trans. from Hebrew by S. Applebaum. Philadelphia: The Jewish Publication Society, 1959; Jerusalem: The Magnes Press, the Hebrew University, 5719.

Toynbee, *Art.*
Toynbee, J. M. C. *Art in Roman Britain.* London: Phaidon Press, 1962.

Toynbee, Perkins, *PBSR.*
Toynbee. J. M. C., and Perkins, J. B. Ward. "Peopled Scrolls: A Hellenistic Motif in Imperial Art," *PBSR,* XVIII, 1950, pp. 1-43, Pls. I-XXVI.

Tushingham, *BASOR.*
Tushingham, A. Douglas. "Excavations at Dibon in Moab, 1952-53," *BASOR,* CXXXIII, Feb. 1954.

van Beek, *JAOS.*
van Beek, Gus W. "Frankincense and Myrrh in Ancient South Arabia," *JAOS,* LXXVIII, 1958, pp. 141-152.

Van Buren, *Symbols.*
Van Buren, E. Douglas. *Symbols of the Gods in Mesopotamian Art, An. Or.* 23, 1945.

Vanden Berghe, see Berghe

de Vaux, *RB.*
de Vaux, Père R. "Une mosaïque byzantine à Ma'in (Transjordanie)," *RB,* XLVII, 1938, pp. 227-258.

Vermeule, *Berytus.*
Vermeule, Cornelius C., III. "Hellenistic and Roman Cuirassed Statues, the Evidence of Paintings and Reliefs in the Chronological Development of Cuirass Types," *Berytus,* XIII, 1959-1960, pp. 1-82, plus 26 plates.

della Vida, *Clara Rhodos.*
della Vida, G. Levi. "Une bilingue greco-nabatea à Coo," *Clara Rhodos,* Studi e materiali pubblicati a cura dell' instituti storico-archeologico di Rodi (Bergamo), IX, 1939, pp. 137-148.

de Villard Monneret, *Ahnas.*
de Villard Monneret, Ugo. *La scultura ad Ahnas.* Milano, 1923.

Vincent, *RB.*
Vincent, L. H. "Le dieu Saint Paqeidas à Gérasa," *RB,* XLIX, 1940, pp. 98-129.

Virolleaud, *Syria.*
Virolleaud, Charles. "Les Travaux archéologiques en Syrie en 1922-1923," *Syria,* V, 1924, pp. 113-122.

Vlasto, *Tarentine Coins.*
Vlasto, M. P. *Descriptive Catalogue of the Collection of Tarentine Coins.* Compiled by Oscar E. Ravel. London: Spink and Son, Ltd., 1947.

de Waele, *Magic Staff.*
de Waele, Ferdinand Josef Maria. *The Magic Staff or Rod in Greco-Italian Antiquity.* Gent: Erasmus, 1927.

Walters, *Catalogue.*
Walters, H. B. *Catalogue of the Bronzes, Greek, Roman and Etruscan,* in the Department of Greek and Roman Antiquities, British Museum. London: British Museum, 1899.

Wessel, *Koptische Kunst.*
Wessel, Klaus. *Koptische Kunst.* Recklinghausen, Germany: Aurel Bongers, 1963.

Widengren, *Kulturbegegnung.*
Widengren, Geo. *Iranisch-semitische Kulturbegegnung in parthischer Zeit.* Köln und Opladen: Westdeutscher Verlag, 1960.

Wiegand, *Baalbek.*
Baalbek. Ed. Wiegand, Theodor.

Berlin und Leipzig: Walter de Gruyter and Co., 1921-1925. (See Bachmann.)

Winnet, *BASOR.*
Winnet, F. V. "Excavations at Dibon in Moab, 1950-51," *BASOR,* 125, February, 1952, pp. 7-20.

de Witte, Lenormant, *GA.*
de Witte, J. and Lenormant, F. *GA,* Vols. III and V, 1877 and 1879.

Woolley, Lawrence, *Zin.*
Woolley C. Leonard and Lawrence, T. E. *The Wilderness of Zin.* London: Jonathan Cape, 1936.

Wotschitzky, *Archaeology.*
Wotschitzky, Alfons. "Ephesus, Past, Present and Future of an Ancient Metropolis," *Archaeology,* XIV, 1961, pp. 205-212.

Wright, *BASOR.*
Wright, G. R. H. "The Nabataean-Roman Temple at Dhiban," *BASOR,* 163, Oct., 1961, p. 29.

_____, *PEQ.*
_____. "Structure of the Qasr Bint Far'un, A Preliminary Review," *PEQ,* XCIII, 1961, pp. 8-37.

Wright, Filson, *WHAB.*
The Westminster Historical Atlas to the Bible. Eds. Wright, George Ernest and Filson, Floyd Vivian. Philadelphia: The Westminster Press, 1945.

Yadin, *Desert Studies.*
Yadin, Yigael. *Judaean Desert Studies* (Hebrew). Jerusalem: Mosad Bialik, 1963.

_____, *Message.*
_____. *The Message of the Scrolls.* London: Weidenfeld and Nicolson, 1957.

_____, *Nabatene.*
_____. "The Nabatene, The Provincia Arabia, Petra and Engeddi in view of the Naḥal Hever Documents," pp. 149-167 in *Elath: The Eighteenth Archaeological Convention, October 1962,* Jerusalem, Israel. (Hebrew), 1963.

Zeitlin, *State.*
Zeitlin, Solomon. *The Rise and Fall of the Judaean State.* Vol. I. Philadelphia: The Jewish Publication Society of America, 1962.

Zori, "Survey."
Zori, N. "An Archaeological Survey of the Beth-Shean Valley" in *The Beth Shean Valley, The 17th Archaeological Congress,* Israel Exploration Society, Jerusalem, 1962.

NOTES*

CHAPTER I

1. Van Beek, *BA* XXIII:3, 1960, p. 93; Starcky, *BA* XVIII:4, 1955, p. 87.
2. *ANET*, pp. 298-300; cf. Robinson, *Sarcophagus*, p. 376, n. 2, pp. 474-476; Starcky, *BA*, XVIII:4, 1955, pp. 85-86, p. 85, n. 4. My colleague, Professor Ben Zion Wacholder of the Hebrew Union College, has called my attention to the following reference: Eusebius, quoting *Alexander Polyhistor* (85-40 B.C.), who cited Eupolemus, writing about 158-157 B.C., in *Praeparatio Evangelica*, IX, 30, 3, according to Jacoby, F., *Die Fragmente der griechischen Historiker*, III, C, Part 2, p. 673, lines 7-8, says: "He (King David) also led an army against the Idumaeans, Ammanites (Ammonites), Moabites, Ituraeans, Nabataeans, and the Nabdaeans, . . ." These Nabataeans and Nabdaeans may have had the same close relationship to each other as the Biblical Kenites and Kenizzites referred to in Genesis 15:19; 36:10, 11, 42; cf. Phillips, *Qataban and Sheba*, p. 104; I Kings, 11:26.
3. Diodorus, *B. h.*, XIX, 94-97.
3a. We are indebted to Mrs. Donald McClain, Atlanta, Georgia, for letting us examine, photograph and publish the pottery plaque of an enthroned Atargatis from Petra, where she purchased it in 1963.
3b. Avi-Yonah and Negev, *ILN*, Nov. 26, 1960, p. 945, Fig. 4.
3c. Lapp, *BASOR* 171, Oct. 1963; pp. 8-39; Hill, *BASOR* 171, pp. 45-55.
3d. Perrot et Chipiez, *Histoire de l'Art dans l'Antiquité, II: Chaldée et Assyrie*, p. 584, Fig. 281.
3e. I am indebted to my colleagues at the Hebrew Union College, Professors Norman Golb, William Hallo and Matitiahu Tsevat for helping to decipher various Nabataean pictograph inscriptions. In this book, however, I am publishing only the one.
4. See pp. 9-10; Starcky, *RB*, 61:2, 1954, pp. 161-181.
5. Yadin, *ILN*, Nov. 4, 1961, pp. 772-775; Nov. 11, 1961, pp. 820-822; Bar-Adon, *ILN*, Dec. 2, 1961, pp. 972-974; Yadin, *IEJ*, XII:3-4, 1962, pp. 227-257 and Pl. 48; Polotsky, *IEJ*, XII:3-4, 1962, pp. 258-262; Yadin, *Nabatene*, pp. 149-167.
6. Yadin, *ILN*, Nov. 4, 1961, p. 773.
7. Yadin, *IEJ*, XII:3-4, 1962, p. 235; *Nabatene*, p. 167.
8. Yadin, *Nabatene*, pp. 153, 154.

* Because of space restrictions it has not been possible to index the *Notes*. They refer to numerous publications and are listed in the *Bibliography* and the *Abbreviations*.

9. Yadin, *Nabatene,* p. 166.

10. Yadin, *Nabatene,* p. 167; Polotsky, *IEJ,* XII:3-4, 1962, pp. 260, 262.

11. Yadin, *Nabatene,* pp. 162-165; Polotsky, *IEJ,* XXVI:3-4, 1962, p. 260.

12. We learn from the Nahal Hever Nabataean document, number 2, dated to Dec. 2, A.D. 127, that Ain Gedi belonged to the toparchy of Jericho, as pointed out by Yadin, *Nabatene,* p. 153; cf. Mazar, *'Ein Gedi,* p. 7.

13. Mazar, *'Ein Gedi,* pp. 12, 13, 25-33.

14. Milik and Seyrig, *RN,* VI:1, 1958, pp. 11-26.

15. Cf. Starcky, *BA,* XVIII:4, 1955, p. 96, Fig. 5a.

16. Dussaud, *JA,* 1904, pp. 192, 203, 215, 216; Hill, *BMC, Arabia,* pp. xvii-xx, Pl. I:4.

17. Dussaud, *JA,* 1904, p. 207; Hill, *BMC, Arabia,* pp. xix, 5-8, 11-12, 14 and Pl. I:4; Starcky, *BA,* XVIII:4, 1955, p. 96, Fig. 5a; Milik and Seyrig, *RN,* VI:1, 1958, pp. 11-26.

18. Horsfield, G. and A., *QDAP,* VII, 1938, p. 6; Avi-Yonah and Negev, *ILN,* Nov. 26, 1960, p. 944, mention the discovery of Rhodian jar-handles and Megarian bowls belonging to the beginning of the third century B.C.; Negev, *'Avdat,* p. 23.

19. This coin was found at Abda by Mr. James Clore, formerly of the U. S. A. Embassy at Tel-Aviv. I am indebted to Professor A. R. Bellinger for determining the nature and date of this coin.

20. See n. 19.

21. Josephus, *War,* I, 4, 1-3; *Antiq.,* XIII, 14, 2; XIII, 15, 2; XIV, 1, 4; Zeitlin, *State,* pp. 329-332, 346; Negev, *'Avdat,* p. 20.

22. Josephus, *Antiq.,* XVIII, 5, 1-3.

23. Lev. 18:16; Luke 9:7-9; Matt. 14: 6-12; Mark 6:22-29.

24. Diodorus, *B.h.,* ii:48; xix:94-100.

25. Dalman, *Petra,* pp. 6, 226-229.

26. Heichelheim, *Wirtschaftsge-schichte,* I, pp. 527-528; cf. Altheim, Stiehl, *Araber,* I, p. 70, n. 3. For numerous references to the presence of Nabataeans in Egypt as priests, traders, mercenaries, and artisans, and the likelihood of their having Nabataean sanctuaries of their own, cf. Littmann, *BSOAS,* XVI, 1954, pp. 211-241; review of Littmann, *op. cit.,* by Starcky in *Syria,* XXXII, 1955, pp. 150-157; Clermont-Ganneau, *RHR,* vol. 80, 1919, pp. 1-29; *RAO,* VIII, 1924, pp. 229-257.

27. Diodorus, *B.h.,* II, p. 48; XIX, pp. 95-100; Josephus, *War,* IV, 7, 6; IV, 8, 4; Hammond, *BA,* XXII:2, 1959, pp. 40-48.

28. Zeitlin, *State,* p. 48.

29. I Kings 10:1, 2, 10.

29a. Altheim, Stiehl, *Araber,* I, pp. 72-74, 77.

30. I Macc. 5:25; 9:35; Josephus, *Antiq.,* XIII, 13, 3.

31. Josephus, *Antiq.,* XIII, 13, 5; *War,* I, 4, 4; *Antiq.,* XVII, 10, 9.

CHAPTER II

32. Josephus, *Antiq.,* I, 12, 4.

33. I Macc. 5:25; 9:35; Josephus, *Antiq.,* XIII, 15, 2.

34. See pp. 39, 40, 69, 361.

35. Savignac, *RB,* 46, 1937, p. 403.

36. Savignac, *RB,* 45, 1936, pp. 249-250; 46, 1937, p. 416.

37. Savignac, *RB,* 45, 1936, p. 349.

38. Savignac, *RB.,* 41, 1932, p. 593; *RB,* 43, 1934, p. 586.

39. Broome, *RB,* 62, 1955, pp. 246-252.
40. Glueck, *AASOR,* XVIII-XIX, 1939, p. 16, Fig. 9, from Khirbet Khaldeh; Dunand, *Soueïda,* Pl. XXX:139 and p. 68; Horsfield, *QDAP,* VII, 1938, p. 27; Parr, *PEQ,* XCII, 1960, pp. 124-135; Wright, G. R. H., *BASOR,* 163, 1961, p. 29, n. 21; Hamilton, *QDAP,* XIV, 1950, pp. 101-119; Savignac, *RB,* 44, 1935, pp. 250-258; Debevoise, *AJA,* XLV:1, 1941, pp. 55-56; Butler, *PAES,* II, A, 6, 1919, p. 398; *PA,* I, p. 166; Schmidt, *Syria,* XV, 1934, pp. 7-15.
41. Rostovtzeff, *Dura and the Problem of Parthian Art,* p. 212; Debevoise, *AJA,* XLV, 1941, pp. 45-47, 60; Goldman, *Berytus,* X, 1950-1951, pp. 13-20.
42. Hanfmann, *ILN,* March 9, 1963, pp. 340, 344, Fig. 26.
43. Dunand, *Soueïda,* p. 68 and Pl. XXX:139.
44. See pp. 144, 287, 455.
45. Wright, G. R. H., *BASOR,* 163, 1961, pp. 26-30; *PEQ,* XCIII, 1961, pp. 8-37; Avi-Yonah, *IEJ,* XII:1, 1962, pp. 75-76, in review of Bowen and Albright, *ADSA;* Avi-Yonah and Yeivin, *The Antiquities of Israel,* pp. 210-211 and Fig. 83; Rostovtzeff, *DPPA,* p. 206; *CC,* pp. 178-179, 182-183, 185; Dussaud, *MS,* p. 320; Butler, *PAES,* II, A, 6, 1919, pp. 365-390; Hopkins, *AJA,* XLVII:3, 1938, p. 334; *Berytus,* VII, 1942, pp. 1-18; Kammerer, *Petra,* pp. 436-440; Hopkins, Kraeling, *Dura,* V, 1934, pp. 73-179; Müller, *JAOS,* 60, 1940, p. 166; *SG,* p. 45, n. 10 and Fig. 6; pp. 58, 66, 69; Neugebauer, *OLZ,* 1939, p. 412; Parrot, *Syria,* XVIII, 1937, pp. 57, 58, 68; Yadin, *Nabatene,* pp. 157-164; cf. p. 56.
46. *SG,* pp. 69-70, 74.
47. Savignac, *RB,* 12, 1903, pp. 280-288; Robinson, *Sarcophagus,* p. 116; Dalman, *Petra,* pp. 157-169; Albright, *AP,* pp. 161-165; Horsfield, G. and A., *QDAP,* VII, 1938, p. 7.
48. See pp. 6, 57, 318.
49. Savignac, *RB,* 41, 1932, pp. 591-594; 42, 1933, pp. 405-422; 43, 1934, pp. 572-589; Savignac and Horsfield, *RB,* 44, 1935, pp. 245-278.
50. Savignac, *RB,* 43, 1934, pp. 572-591; Lawrence, *Pillars,* p. 355.
51. Negev, *'Avdat,* pp. 25, 34, 52.
52. See p. 464.
53. See pp. 58, 144; Savignac, *RB,* 45, 1936, p. 243 and Pl. VIII:1; *Pauly-Wissowa,* V, col. 1867.
54. See pp. 212, 213, 474.
55. See pp. 76, 212.
56. II Kings 3:27.
57. See p. 212.
58. See n. 53; *PA,* I, pp. 70-75; Musil, *AP,* I, pp. 6, 19, 22, 81-82, 367.
59. See n. 53; *PA,* I, p. 50, Fig. 28.
60. De Vaux, *RB,* 47, 1938, pp. 227-258; Musil, *AP,* I, pp. 397-399.
61. See p. 224; Schlumberger, *Syria,* XIV, 1933, p. 311, Pl. XXXVII:2; Dunand, *Soueïda,* 1934, p. 64 and Pl. XXVIII:122 (from Qanawat); Butler, *PAES,* II:A, 6, 1919, pp. 388, 389; III, 1921, pp. 336, 337.
62. Cross, *BA,* XXVI:4, Dec. 1963, pp. 110-121. I am indebted to Professor Cross for bringing these coins to my attention and for making it possible to publish one of them.
63. Cross, *BA,* XXVI:4, Dec. 1963, p. 117, Fig. 4, and p. 116.
64. I am indebted to Professor Herbert J. Muller for giving me this coin, which he purchased in Istanbul. I am also grateful to Professor Alfred R. Bellinger for the following note with regard to it: "The standard work on Sinope is still that of M. J. P. Six, *Sinope, Numismatic Chronicle,* 1885, pp. 15-65. Your coin is either Six, p. 37, no. 79 or p. 38, no. 87. The letters KA can be read under the eagle's wing; P can be assumed. . . . Both belong to his series VI B, which

he dates on reasonable grounds to 333-306 B.C. The dolphin appears first as a symbol with the eagle's head; a good example is Pl. I, 8 in the same volume of *NC*, which Six dates to about 480 B.C." I am indebted also to Dr. John C. Lilly, Communication Research Institute, for permission to publish the reverse side of a coin from Tarentum, dating to c. 302-231 B.C., showing Taras astride a dolphin and holding out a tripod(?) in his right hand (Pl. 64c); Vlasto, *The Collection of Tarentine Coins*, p. 78, Pl. XXII, 666, 8-stater.

65. See pp. 43, 44.

66. Winnett, *BASOR*, 125, 1952, pp. 16-17, 19, Fig. 6; Tushingham, *BASOR*, 133, 1954, pp. 6-26; Wright, G. R. H., *BASOR*, 163, 1961, pp. 26-30; Harding and Reed, *BA*, XVI:1, 1953, p. 6.

67. Rostovtzeff, *CC*, p. 27.

68. Albright, *BASOR*, 53, 1934, pp. 13-18.

69. Crowfoot, *PEFQS*, 1934, pp. 76-84.

70. Glueck, *AASOR*, XV, 1935, p. 64.

71. Glueck, *AASOR*, XVIII-XIX, 1939, pp. 65-67.

72. Glueck, *AASOR*, XIV, 1934, pp. 48-49.

73. Glueck, *AASOR*, XIV, 1934, p. 66.

74. Glueck, *AASOR*, XIV, 1934, p. 62; XVIII-XIX, 1939, p. 63; *PA*, I, pp. 46-52, 54-59; Musil, *AP*, I, pp. 370-375.

75. Glueck, *AASOR*, XIV, 1934, pp. 10-12.

76. Glueck, *BASOR*, 69, 1938, p. 17; *OSJ*, pp. 198-200; Horsfield, G. and A., *QDAP*, VII, 1938, pp, 1-42 and Pls. I-LXXIV; Albright, *AP*, pp. 161-165.

77. Glueck, *AASOR*, XV, 1935, pp. 54, 55; XVIII-XIX, 1939, p. 12; *BASOR*, 69, 1938, pp. 17-18; Savignac, *RB*, 41, 1932, pp. 591-594; 42, 1933, pp. 405-422; 43, 1934, pp. 572-589; Savignac and Horsfield, *RB*, 44, 1935, pp. 245-278.

78. Glueck, *AASOR*, XV, 1935, pp. 54-55; Savignac, *RB*, 43, 1934, pp. 572-591; Lawrence, *Pillars*, p. 355.

79. Glueck, *AASOR*, XV, 1935, pp. 11-17; XVIII-XIX, 1939, pp. 149-150, 152.

80. Glueck, *AASOR*, XV, 1935, pp. 35-37; XVIII-XIX, 1939, p. 14.

81. Glueck, *AASOR*, XV, 1935, pp. 32-36; XVIII-XIX, 1939, pp. 12, 38; *BASOR*, 55, 1934, pp. 8, 14; 138, 1955, p. 11, n. 12; Wright, G. R. H., *BASOR*, 163, 1961, pp. 26-30; *OSJ*, pp. 27, 50, 55, 60, 64, 68-70.

82. Glueck, *AASOR*, XV, 1935, pp. 18-19.

83. Glueck, *AASOR*, XV, 1935, p. 36, n. 86; *RITD*, pp. 231, 235.

84. Negev, *History of 'Avdat*, pp. 118-148 (Hebrew).

85. See pp. 47-61; Butler, *PAES*, II:A, 6, 1919, pp. 365-402.

86. Numbers 24:21; II Kings 14:7; Isaiah 16:1.

87. Abel, *Géographie*, I, p. 388.

88. Savignac, *RB*, 12, 1903, pp. 280-288; Robinson, *Sarcophagus*, p. 116; Dalman, *Petra*, pp. 157-169; Albright, *AP*, pp. 162-165.

89. Albright, *BASOR*, 57, 1935, pp. 18-26; *AP*, pp. 161-165; Cleveland, *AASOR*, XXXIV-XXXV, 1960, pp. 55-97.

90. Parr, *ILN*, Nov. 17, 1962, p. 789; *RB*, 69, 1962, pp. 64-79; *Scientific American*, Vol. 209:4, October 1963, pp. 94-102.

91. Kirkbride, *ILN*, Jan. 19, 1963, pp. 82-84.

92. Glueck, *AASOR*, XVIII-XIX, 1939, pp. 214-216.

93. Wright, G. R. H., *BASOR*, 163, 1961, pp. 26-30; *PEQ*, XCIII, Jan.-June, 1961, pp. 8-37; see below, n. 71.

94. Robinson, *Sarcophagus*, pp. 126, 128; Dalman, *Petra*, pp. 159, 163, 166-169.

95. See below, pp. 91-92; Morgenstern, *JBL*, LXXX:1, 1961, p. 70.

96. *SG*, pp. 69-70.

97. Strabo, XVI, 4, 18; Van Beek, *JAOS*, 78, 1958, p. 152.

97a. Dio Cassius, LXVIII, 14; *Periplus*, p. 103.

98. Strabo, XVI, 4, 21; Altheim, Stiehl, *Araber* I, pp. 66, 69, 72.

99. Negev, *'Avdat*, p. 30.

CHAPTER III

100. In 1937. See Plan H.

101. See above, p. 61; Savignac, *RB*, 45, 1936, p. 256; 46, 1937, pp. 410-412; Avi-Yonah and Negev, *ILN*, Nov. 26, 1960, p. 944.

102. Savignac, *RB*, 46, 1937, pp. 410-416.

102a. Avi-Yonah, *IEJ*, II, 2, 1951, pp. 118-124.

103. Albright, *BASOR*, 57, 1935, pp. 20-23; AP, pp. 163-165; Cleveland, *AASOR*, XXXIV-XXXV, 1960, pp. 75-83; Parr, *ILN*, Nov. 17, 1962, pp. 789-791.

104. FitzGerald, *PEQ*, 1941, p. 73, in his review of *Lachish II:* "It is noteworthy, as a proof of the essential continuity of the Temple, that each succeeding Shrine was erected on the site of the one below."

105. Savignac, *RB*, 41, 1932, pp. 595-597, Pl. XIX:2.

106. Hollis, *Temple*, pp. 132-139.

107. Avi-Yonah, ed., *IWB*, I, p. 93; Brown, *Dura*, VII-VIII, 1939, p. 137, nn. 5, 6.

CHAPTER IV

108. See pp. 7, 8, 138, 436-438.

109. Wiegand, *Petra*, p. 51, Fig. 45; *Baalbek*, I, p. 115 and Pls. 42, 133, 134.

110. Wright, G. R. H., *PEQ*, Jan.-June 1961, pp. 24-25; pp. 12, 13, Figs. 4, 5.

111. Wiegand, *Petra*, pp. 53, 54, Fig. 47; Horsfield, G. and A., *QDAP*, VII, 1938, Pl. XXX:1 and p. 10.

112. Horsfield, G. and A., *QDAP*, VII, 1938, p. 10 and Pl. XXX:1.

113. Horsfield, G. and A., *QDAP*, VII, 1938, Pls. XXV:1, LXXIII:1, LXXIV:1, 2; Butler, *PAES*, II:A, 6, 1919, p. 383, Ill. 330; Debevoise, *AJA*, XLV, 1941, p. 55.

114. Dussaud, *JA*, 1904, pp. 192, 215, 216; Savignac, *RB*, 46, 1937, pp. 405-408 and Pl. IX:1, 2; Savignac and Starcky, *RB*, 64, 1957, pp. 215-217; see pp. 101, 436-438.

114a. Van Beek, *BA*, XXIII:3, 1960, p. 89.

115. Kraeling, *Gerasa*, Pls. VIII:a, b; XXX:c.

116. Horsfield, G. and A., *QDAP*, VII, 1938, p. 7 and Pl. XV; *PA*, I, p. 170, Fig. 194.

116a. See p. 145.

117. Ingholt, *Hatra*, p. 24 and Pl. VI:2, 3.

118. Newell, *Num. Notes and Monographs*, no. 84, 1939, p. 78, coin 115; p. 95, coin 147.

118a. Ingholt, *Hatra*, pp. 33-34 and Pl. VII:2.

119. Horsfield, G. and A., *QDAP*, VII, 1938, Pls. XXV:1, LXXIII:1, LXXIV:1, 2.

120. Cook, *Zeus*, I, p. 616, Fig. 487; Abdul Hak, *AAS*, IV-V, 1954-1955, pp. 163-188 and Pls. V, VI.
121. Parr, *ADAJ*, IV-V, 1960; pp. 134-136; see p. 60; Kraeling, *Gerasa*, Pl. CXXVI:a; and p. 457.
122. Albright, *AP*, p. 165; Cleveland, *AASOR*, XXXIV-XXXV, 1960, pp. 57-78; Parr, *ILN*, Nov. 17, 1962, p. 789.
123. Savignac and Horsfield, *RB*, 44, 1935, p. 245; Butler, *PAES*, II, A, 5, 1919, pp. 4-8, 369, 441; Rowell, *Dura*, III, 1932, p. 31; Yadin, *Nabatene*, pp. 157, 160; Amy, *Syria*, XXVII, 1950, pp. 82-136.
124. Wright, G. R. H., *PEQ*, Jan.-June 1961, pp. 34-36; Schlumberger, *Syria*, XXXVII, 1960, p. 145; Rowell, *Dura*, III, 1932, pp. 31-32; see p. 249.

CHAPTER V

125. Schlumberger, *Palmyrène*, p. 105, n. 3.
126. Savignac and Horsfield, *RB*, 44, 1935, pp. 270-278 and Pls. VIII, XI.
127. Ipser, *Vatican Art*, p. 102.
128. Savignac and Horsfield, *RB*, 44, 1935, pp. 261-263.
129. Goodenough, *Symbols*, VI, p. 11; Schlumberger, *Palmyrène*, pp. 103, 105.
130. Horsfield, G. and A., *QDAP*, VII, 1938, pp. 30-42, 96; Dalman, *Petra*, pp. 60-62, 89, 110-114, 159, 162, 234, 235, 247, 291-293, 298, 329; *PA*, I, pp. 206, 240, 279, 365; Robinson, *Sarcophagus*, pp. 116, 139-140, 144, 412; Kennedy, *Petra*, pp. 25, 34, 45, 52-53, 57, 64, 73-74; Harding, *Antiquities*, pp. 131-134; Wiegand, *Petra*, pp. 89-90; Dussaud, *Arabes en Syrie*, pp. 108, 109; Strabo, XVI, 4, 26; Albright, *AP*, p. 163; Starcky, BA, XVIII:4, 1955, p. 89.
131. Horsfield, G. and A., *QDAP*, VII, 1938, Pl. LVIII:2 and p. 31, for chief triclinium of Dorotheos House.
132. Horsfield, G. and A., *QDAP*, VII, 1938, p. 39 and Pl. LXVII:1, 2; Ingholt, *Hatra*, p. 12; Dalman, *Petra*, pp. 60-62; Goodenough, *Symbols*, VI, p. 11.
133. Horsfield, G. and A., *QDAP*, VII, 1938, pp. 39-40 and Pl. LXIX:1, 2.
134. Horsfield, G. and A., *QDAP*, VII, 1938, pp. 39-40; p. 39, n. 8; Schlumberger, *Palmyrène*, p. 105; Brown, *Dura*, VII-VIII, 1939, p. 168, inscr. 871, pp. 171-172, inscr. 875.
135. Horsfield, G. and A., *QDAP*, VII, 1938, p. 39 and Pl. LXVI:2.
136. Savignac, *RB*, 12, 1903, pp. 280-288; Robinson, *Sarcophagus*, pp. 116-134; Dalman, *Petra*, pp. 157-169; Murray, *Petra*, pp. 48-50.
137. Morgenstern, *JBL*, LXXX:1, 1961, pp. 69-70, 74; Ingholt, *Hatra*, pp. 12, 13; cf. I Samuel 20:5, 24; Amos 6:4-6.
138. Campbell, *AJA*, XLII:1, 1938, pp. 205-218; Baur *et al.*, *Dura*, III, 1932, pp. 5, 19-20; Rostovtzeff, *CC*, p. 178; Ingholt, *Berytus*, V, 1938, pp. 138-139 and Pl. L; Schlumberger, *JDAI*, Arch. Anz., 50, 1935, cols. 607-610; *Palmyrène*, pp. 101-105 and Pl. IV:1-3, V:1-3; cf. Haupert, *BA*, I, Dec. 1938, p. 23 for an early prototype at Lachish.
139. Schlumberger, *Palmyrène*, pp. 59, no. 27; 60, 151, inscr. 20.
140. Lewis, *AJA*, XXXVII, 1933, p. 398; Horsfield, G. and A., *QDAP*, VII, 1938, p. 30, and also in the

temple of the Syrian gods at Delos, dated to the first half of the second century B.C., as noted in Schlumberger, *JDAI, Arch. Anz.*, 50, 1935, col. 610; Ingholt, *Hatra*, p. 20, n. 10; Roussel, *Délos*, pp. 252, 253, 259, 270.

141. Schlumberger, *Palmyrène*, pp. 103-104; Cumont, *TM*, I, pp. 63, 65.

142. Deut. 12:7; 27:7; I Samuel 9:13, 23-25; Ezekiel 46:19-24.

143. Strabo, XVI, 4, 26.

144. See pp. 12, 130-135.

145. Cumont, *TM*, I, p. 66.

146. Yadin, *ILN*, Nov. 11, 1961, pp. 820, 821, discusses Nabataean documents from Nahal Hever dealing with property deeds and rights of a Judaean woman, Babata, which were registered and confirmed by the Roman government at Petra and her claims filed there with the Roman provincial governor, on October 12, A.D. 125, against two guardians of her son, a Jew and a Nabataean. They had previously been appointed by the authorities in Petra to protect his rights, and she claims that money is owed to her son. Other Nabataean documents from there deal with the registration of her property at Rabbat Moab for a land census in A.D. 127 and of still further litigation after that in connection with her property and the income due her children by her first husband from the court appointed guardians; cf. Starcky, *RB*, 61, 1954, pp. 162-181; Robinson, *Sarcophagus*, p. 393.

147. Ingholt, *Hatra*, p. 18 and Pl. IV;

Baur, *Dura*, III, 1932, pp. 100-107 and Pl. XIV.

148. Robinson, *Sarcophagus*, p. 412; Smith, *Kinship*, p. 301.

149. Schlumberger, *JDAI, Arch. Anz.* 50, 1935, col. 610.

150. Schlumberger, *Palmyrène*, p. 104 and n. 10.

151. Schlumberger, *Palmyrène*, p. 103, nn. 1-3, pp. 104-105.

152. Schlumberger, *JDAI, Arch. Anz.* 50, 1935, col. 609; Ingholt, *Syria*, VII, 1926, pp. 128-141.

153. Schlumberger, *JDAI, Arch. Anz.* 50, 1935, col. 609, n. 1; Seyrig, *Memorial Lagrange*, pp. 51-58; Ingholt *et al.*, *Tessères*, p. 199.

154. Schlumberger, *JDAI, Arch. Anz.* 50, 1935, col. 609, n. 4.

155. Schlumberger, *Palmyrène*, p. 2, Fig. 1.

156. Schlumberger, *Palmyrène*, p. 59, no. 27, p. 60, no. 35; Ingholt *et al.*, in Schlumberger, *Palmyrène*, p. 151, no. 20.

157. Schlumberger, *JDAI, Arch. Anz.* 50, 1935, col. 604.

158. Schlumberger, *JDAI, Arch. Anz.* 50, 1935, col. 607; for use of wine in mystic ceremonies, cf. Brown, *Dura* VII-VIII, 1939, p. 156, n. 17 and references there; cf. Kennedy, *Petra*, Fig. 120.

159. Kennedy, *Petra*, Fig. 120.

160. Schlumberger, *Palmyrène*, Pl. IV: 1, 2.

161. Schlumberger, *Palmyrène*, pp. 21, 60, 151 and Pl. XXV:1, 2.

162. Schlumberger, *Palmyrène*, pp. 60, 61, 151, and Pl. XXV:3-6.

163. Schlumberger, *Palmyrène*, p. 151 and Pl. XXV:3, 4.

CHAPTER VI

164. Baur, *Dura*, III, 1932, p. 104, n. 5; Brown, *Dura*, VII-VIII, 1939, p. 165, n. 4; Hopkins, *Dura*, VII-VIII, 1939, p. 296.

165. Baur, *Dura*, III, 1932, p. 136: "Under Antiochus IV Epiphanes (175-164 B.C.) the coins of Hieropolis indicate that Hadad was

identical with Zeus"; cf. also Lucian, *De Dea Syria* §31, who in describing the cult statues of Hadad and Atargatis, which to him were "Zeus" and "Hera," says: "The effigy of Zeus recalls Zeus in all details...."; *SG*, p. 70, Fig. 7.

166. Al Asil, *ILN*, Dec. 25, 1954, p. 1160, Fig. 5.

167. Al Asil, *ILN*, Nov. 17, 1951, p. 807, Fig. 10; Ingholt, *Hatra*, p. 16, Pl. III:3.

168. Al Asil, *ILN*, Dec. 25, 1954, p. 1160, Fig. 2; Nov. 17, 1951, p. 806, Fig. 9.

169. Al Asil, *ILN*, Nov. 10, 1951, p. 765; Andrae, *Hatra*, II, p. 158, Pl. XIX; Ghirshman, *Bichapour*, II, p. 131, Fig. 37.

170. Ingholt, *Hatra*, pp. 23-24, Pl. VI:2; Al Asil, *ILN*, Dec. 18, 1954, p. 1117, Fig. 7; Nov. 17, 1951, p. 806, Fig. 8.

171. Hopkins, *Dura*, VII-VIII, 1939, pp. 293, 296.

172. Avi-Yonah and Negev, *ILN*, Nov. 26, 1960, p. 945, Fig. 3.

173. Baur, *Dura*, III, 1932, p. 104; VI, 1936, pp. 119-120 and Pl. XXVI:4, 5.

174. Baur, *Dura*, III, 1932, p. 113; Kantorowicz, *Gods in Uniform*, p. 379, Fig. 30.

175. Baur, *Dura*, III, 1932, p. 101.

176. Parr, *ADAJ*, IV-V, 1960, pp. 134-136.

177. Savignac, *RB*, 46, 1937, p. 415.

178. Albright, *ARI*, p. 74; Avi-Yonah, *IEJ*, II:2, 1952, pp. 121-122.

179. Ingholt, *Hatra*, p. 18.

180. Cook, *Zeus*, I, p. 319, Fig. 252; II:1, pp. 787, 849, 852; II:2, pp. 1051-1052, Fig. 909; Roscher, *Lexikon*, cols. 720, 748-749; Cumont, *RO*, Pl. I:1, 2; Cook, S. A., *RAPLA*, p. 157, n. 2.

181. Dussaud, *Ras Shamra et A. T.*, pp. 41-42, Figs. 15, 16; pp. 68-69; *CRAI*, 1940, p. 79; Dunand, *BMB*, IV, Dec. 1940, p. 90, n. 2; Hogarth, *Hittite Seals*, Pl. VI, n.

180; Von der Osten, *Seals*, Pl. XIX, no. 249; Delaporte, *Cyl. Or.*, nos. 230, 248-250.

182. Savignac *RB*, 46, 1937, p. 415; Joshua 11:17; 12:7; 13:5; Judges 3:3; I Chronicles 5:23; Numbers 25:3; Deut. 4:3; Ps. 106:28; Hosea 9:10.

183. Eissfeldt, *Baal Zaphon*, pp. 40-41; *OLZ*, Dec. 1937, cols. 724-725; see pp. 86, 248.

184. Judges 5:3-5; Cook, *Zeus*, I, p. 633.

185. Cook, *Zeus*, II:1, pp. 319, 787, 849, 852; II:2, pp. 1051-1052; Roscher, *Lexikon*, cols. 720, 748-749.

186. Cook, *Zeus*, II:1, p. 849.

187. Cook, *Zeus*, I, p. 633.

188. Hopkins, *Dura*, V, 1934, p. 174; Ingholt, *Hatra*, p. 9.

189. Avi-Yonah, *IEJ*, II:2, 1952, pp. 121-122; Albright, *ARI*, p. 74; du Mesnil, *TMP*, p. 205, Fig. 138; p. 222, Fig. 148; p. 458, Fig. 229.

190. Avi-Yonah, *QDAP*, XIII, 1948, pp. 143-145; *Dura*, V, 1934, Pl. XXXIII:2; du Mesnil, *TMP*, pp. 171-172, Fig. 124a:2; p. 222, Fig. 148; pp. 399-403, 458, Fig. 229.

191. Avi-Yonah and Negev, *ILN*, Nov. 26, 1960, pp. 944-947; Negev, *'Avdat*, p. 22.

192. Rostovtzeff, *CC*, pp. 186, 218, Pl. XXXII:1, Cumont, *Doura, Texte*, p. 108; Daremberg et Saglio *Dict.*, V, p. 376a.

193. Perkins, *AJA*, 55, 1951, p. 409; Hopkins, *Dura*, V, 1934, p. 108, Pl. XIII; Rostovtzeff, *CC*, pp. 186, 218, Pl. XXXII:1; Cook, *Zeus*, II:1, p. 377, Fig. 285; Cumont, *RO*, Pl. II:1, 2; *Doura, Texte*, p. 108; Ingholt, *Hatra*, Pls. III:2, VI:2.

194. Du Mesnil, *TMP*, p. 145, Fig. III:2, 3.

195. Hopkins, *Dura*, V, 1934, p. 108, Pl. XIII; Rostovtzeff, *CC*, Pl. XXXII:1 and pp. 186, 218.

196. *ILN*, April 22, 1961, p. 663.

197. Rostovtzeff, *CC*, pp. 186, 218, Pl.

XXXII:1; Hopkins, *Dura*, V, 1934, pp. 119-120.

198. Rostovtzeff, *CC*, p. 217, Pl. XXX: 2; Ingholt, *Hatra*, p. 18, Pl. IV:1; du Mesnil, *TMP*, p. 157, Fig. 118; p. 205, Fig. 138; p. 80, Fig. 38; p. 99, Fig. 53; p. 215, Figs. 143, 144; p. 368, Fig. 201.

199. Rostovtzeff, *CC*, pp. 186, 218 and Pl. XXXII:1; Hopkins, *Dura*, V, 1934, p. 108 and Pl. XIII; Al Asil, *ILN*, Nov. 17, 1951, p. 806, Fig. 8; Dec. 18, 1954, p. 1116, Figs. 3, 6; p. 1117, Fig. 9 center, Fig. 11 left side; Dec. 25, 1954, p. 1160, Fig. 3; Kantorowicz, *Gods in Uniform*, p. 377, Fig. 24 (torque on Aphlad of Dura); p. 375, Fig. 19; p. 376; Champdor, *Palmyre*, p. 48 for torques on Aglibol (moon god) and Jarhibol (sun god) of Palmyra; p. 378, Fig. 27, torque on Assur-bel of Hatra.

200. Al Asil, *ILN*, Dec. 25, 1954, p. 1160, Fig. 3.

201. Al Asil, *ILN*, Dec. 18, 1954, p. 1117, Fig. 11; Nov. 17, 1951, p. 806, Fig. 1; Dec. 25, 1954, p. 1161, Fig. 9.

202. Al Asil, *ILN*, Nov. 17, 1951, p. 806, Fig. 8; Dec. 18, 1954, p. 1116, Fig. 6; p. 1117, Fig. 9 center, Fig. 11, two reliefs at left.

203. Al Asil, *ILN*, Nov. 17, 1951, Fig. 1 at right; Dec. 18, 1954, p. 1116,

Fig. 3; Steve, *LWB*, p. 27, Ill. 14, showing a Parthian chief in bronze, wearing a fine torque from Shami, in southern Iran, now in Teheran Museum.

204. Daremberg et Saglio, *Dict.*, V, pp. 375-376; Cumont, *RO*, p. 97 and Pl. II:1, 2; Minns, *S.Gr.*, pp. 62, 197, Fig. 90; Rostovtzeff, *Iranians and Greeks*, p. 124 and Pl. XXIV: 2; Cook, *Zeus*, II: 1, p. 377, Fig. 285; Dalman, *Petra*, pp. 74-76.

205. Hopkins, *Dura*, V, 1934, p. 108.

206. Daremberg et Saglio, *Dict.*, V, p. 376; Cumont, *RO*, Pl. II:1.

207. Schlumberger, *JDAI*, Arch. Anz. 50, 1935, col. 610; Pillet, *Dura*, III, 1932, p. 12; Bellinger, *Dura*, III, 1932, p. 19; Cumont, *RO*, pp. 97-98; Picard, *Syria*, XVII, 1936, pp. 315-316; Ronzevalle, *MUSJ*, XXII, 1939, pp. 109-121.

208. Kammerer, *Pétra*, p. 450.

209. Cumont, *RO*, Pl. II:1, 2; Butler, *PAES*, II, A, 1919, Ills. 326, 338 and p. 390; Wiegand, *Baalbek*, I, Pls. 13, 60b; II, p. 8, Fig. 12; p. 11, Fig. 16; Cook, *Zeus*, II:1, p. 377 and Fig. 285; Hopkins and Rowell, *Dura*, V, 1934, pp. 229-230; Minns, *S. Gr.*, p. 62; Rostovtzeff, *Iranians and Greeks*, p. 124 and Pl. XXIV, 2; Daremberg et Saglio, *Dict.*, V, pp. 375-376; Herodotus, I, 103-106.

CHAPTER VII

210. Avi-Yonah and Negev, *ILN*, Nov. 26, 1960, pp. 944-947; Butler, *PAES*, II, A, 1919, pp. 365-390, 428, 441; Schlumberger, *Syria*, XXXVII, 1960, p. 274, nn. 2, 3.

211. For this type of headdress cf. Seyrig, *Syria*, XIII, 1932, pp. 261-264, Pl. LVII; XX, 1939, p. 179, Figs. 2, 3; XXVI, 1949, p. 29 and Pl. II; Dussaud, *Arabes en Syrie*, pp. 97-101, Figs. 18, 19, 20; More-

hart, *Berytus*, XII, 1956-1958, pp. 61-63, Figs. 11, 12; Andrae, *Hatra*, II, p. 158 and Pl. XIX:3; Avi-Yonah and Negev, *ILN*, Nov. 26, 1960, p. 945, Fig. 3; Ghirshman, *Iran*, pp. 274-275 and Fig. 81; p. 280 and Pl. 33a; Kantorowicz, *Gods in Uniform*, pp. 375-376 and Fig. 19; du Mesnil, *TMP*, p. 242, Fig. 156; p. 313, Fig. 181; p. 315, Fig. 183; p. 321, Fig. 188.

212. See pp. 224, 318; Dunand, *Soueïda*, Pl. XII, p. 31; Hopkins, *Dura*, V, 1934, p. 109 and Pl. XIII; Rostovtzeff, *DPPA*, pp. 228-232 and Fig. 38.

213. For an excellent example of the fillet of victory on a fourth-century B.C. Greek bronze, cf. Bieber, *Sculpture*, p. 11 and Fig. 9.

214. Du Mesnil, *TMP*, pp. 174-175, Fig. 127; p. 313, Fig. 181; p. 315, Fig. 183; p. 321, Fig. 188; Dussaud, *Arabes en Syrie*, p. 97, Fig. 18; p. 99, Fig. 19; Kantorowicz, *Gods in Uniform*, p. 375, n. 27 and Fig. 19; Seyrig, *Syria*, XXVI, 1949, p. 29 and Pl. II; XIII, 1932, pp. 261-264 and Pl. LVII.

215. Dussaud, *Arabes en Syrie*, pp. 100-101; Seyrig, *Syria*, XXVI, 1949, p. 29.

216. Andrae, *Hatra*, II, p. 158 and Pl. XIX, west end of south wall; Ghirshman, *Bichapour*, II, p. 131, Fig. 37.

217. Hopkins, *Dura*, V, 1934, p. 109 and Pl. XIII; Rostovtzeff, *DPPA*, pp. 228-232 and Fig. 38.

218. Numbers 21:28; II Kings 3:25-27.

219. See p. 59; Musil, *AP*, I, pp. 53-54, Fig. 18.

220. Kantorowicz, *Gods in Uniform*, pp. 376-378 and Figs. 19, 22, 24, 27; Rostovtzeff, *CC*, Pl. XXX:1, facing p. 184; Cumont, *Doura, Atlas*, Pl. LXXXIII; Dunand, *Soueïda*, pp. 37, 42, 43 and Pls. IV, VII:42, XVI:58 bis; Maricq, *Syria*, XXXV, 1958, Pl. XXIII, facing p. 354.

221. See pp. 213, 222.

222. Eisler, *Weltenmantel*, I, p. 96, Fig. 29; Exodus 28:15-21; Revelation 1:13; 15:6; 21:19-20; Seyrig, *Syria*, XVIII, 1937, pp. 24, 25, Fig. 16; see n. 239.

223. Avi-Yonah and Negev, *ILN*, Nov. 26, 1960, p. 945, Fig. 3.

224. Du Mesnil, *TMP*, p. 68, Fig. 24; pp. 174-175, Fig. 127; see p. 223.

225. I am indebted to M. Daniel Schlumberger for calling my attention to this funerary plaque from Palmyra and for placing a photograph of it at my disposal; Seyrig, *Syria*, XIV, 1933, pp. 158, 160, and Pl. XX:12; *AAS*, I, 1951, pp. 32-40. See Fig. 4 and p. 39 of this article, where Seyrig writes: "En dehors du banquet, la seule occupation où la sculpture funèbre de Palmyre représente un défunt, est celle du départ pour la chasse. De ce motif, on ne connaît qu'un seul exemple, dans le célèbre triclinium de Maqqai, où le sarcophage central (fig. 4) montre ce grand personnage, dans un costume particulièrment raffiné, au milieu des pages qui lui aménent son cheval . . ." Cf. also Ingholt, *Berytus*, III, 1936, p. 120, Pl. XXIV:2.

226. Dussaud, *Arabes en Syrie*, pp. 91, 101, and Fig. 19; Morehart, *Berytus*, XII, 1956-1958, p. 57, Fig. 3; p. 61, Fig. 10; pp. 62-63, Fig. 12; Ingholt *et al.*, *Tessères*, Pl. I:6 and p. 1, n. 6; Dunand, *Soueïda*, p. 51, Pl. XXIII:79.

227. For a similarly, frontally faced eagle from Nabataean Si'a in the Jebel Druze, cf. Butler, *PAES*, II:A, 6, 1919, p. 400, Ill. 346; du Mesnil, *TMP*, p. 137, Fig. 99:3; for the relief of a solar eagle, with head in profile, but otherwise frontally presented, surmounting the head of the deity Azizos, shown on the face of a basalt altar from Soueïda, cf. Dunand, *Soueïda*, p. 18 and Pl. IX:8; Hanfmann, *BASOR* 174, 1964, p. 36, Fig. 19.

228. Cf. Rostovtzeff in *MS*, I, p. 282 and Pl. I; *Dura*, VII-VIII, 1939, Pl. XXXIII, pp. 258-260.

229. Rostovtzeff, *CC*, pp. 193-195; *Dura*, II, 1931, pp. 194-196, 199-200 and Pls. XXIV:1-3, XXV:1, 2, XLI:2, XLIII:2; IV, 1933, pp. 219-221 and Pl. XXII:1; Hopkins, *Dura*, VI, 1936, pp. 229-234 and Pl. XXX:1-3; Ingholt, *Berytus*,

III, 1936, p. 120 and Pl. XXIV:2; Ronzevalle, *MUSJ*, XXI, 1937-1938, Pl. XVII:1 and p. 58; Seyrig and Starcky, *Syria*, XXVI, 1949, pp. 230-243 and Pls. XI and XII (between pp. 236 and 237); Virolleaud, *Syria*, V, 1924, p. 120 and Pl. XXXI:4.

230. Rostovtzeff, *Iranians and Greeks*, p. 11 and Pls. 1:1-3, XXX:2; see n. 225.

231. See n. 230.

232. Butler, *PAES*, II, A, 1919, pp. 384, 385 and Ills. 329, 334L.

233. Seyrig, *Syria*, XIV, 1933, pp. 160-161 and Pl. XX:2.

234. Hopkins, *Dura*, VI, 1936, p. 231; Morehart, *Berytus*, XII, pp. 58, 59, Fig. 7; Rostovtzeff, *Dura*, IV, 1933, p. 221.

235. Seyrig, *Syria*, XIV, 1933, pp. 161-162 and Pl. XX:1.

236. See p. 60; de Vaux, *RB*, 47, 1938, pp. 227-258.

237. Butler, *PAES*, II, A, 1919, p. 445, Ill. 388K; Oikonomides, *Archaeology*, XV:1, 1962, pp. 13-15.

238. Rostovtzeff, *CC*, Pl. XXX:1, facing p. 184; Champdor, *Palmyre*, p. 49; Seyrig, *Syria*, XVIII, 1937, pp. 10, 29.

239. Eisler, *Weltenmantel*, I, p. 96, Fig. 29; n. 222; Roscher, *Lexikon*, I, col. 2002, under "Helios"; Cumont, *TM*, II, pp. 419-420, n. 298 and Fig. 350.

239a. Baur, *Dura*, III, 1932, p. 100 and Pl. XIV; see pp. 290, 397.

240. Dunand, *Soueïda*, pp. 37, 43 and Pls. IV, VII:42, XVI:58bis; Rostovtzeff, *Dura*, IV, 1933, p. 209, Pl. XIX:1; *CC*, Pl. XXXI:1, facing p. 192; Seyrig, *Syria*, XVIII, 1937, pp. 19, 23 and Figs. 10, 14; Seyrig and Starcky, *Syria*, XXVI, 1949, pp. 230-231 and Pl. XI, facing p. 236.

241. See pp. 434-435.

242. Morehart, *Berytus*, XII:1, 1956-1957, pp. 60-62, Fig. 11; Rostovtzeff, in *MS*, I, p. 282; Seyrig and Starcky, *Syria*, XXVI, 1949, p.

230; Seyrig, *Syria*, XXVI, 1949, p. 29.

243. Seyrig, *Syria*, XVIII, 1937, p. 25 and Pl. III:2.

244. Dunand, *Soueïda*, p. 52 and Pl. XXIV:83.

245. Barnett, *ADAJ*, I, 1951, pp. 34-36, Pls. X-XIII; Pritchard, *BA*, XXIV:3, 1961, Fig. 1.

246. Dunand, *Soueïda*, p. 18 and Pl. IX:8; see n. 953.

247. Al Asil, *ILN*, Dec. 25, 1954, p. 1160, Fig. 4; Ingholt, *Hatra*, pp. 33-34 and Pl. VII:2.

248. Baur, *Dura*, III, 1932, p. 100 and Pl. XIV; Ingholt, *Hatra*, p. 18, and Pl. IV:1.

249. Josephus, *War*, I, 6, 2 describes the army of Aretas as consisting of "50,000 footmen and horsemen"; cf. I, 9, 3-4; III, 4, 2; *Antiq.*, XVII, 10, 9; XIV, 1, 4; XIV, 8, 1; IV, 2, 1; Littmann, *PAES*, IV, A, 1914, pp. 70-71 and Fig. 27, deals with a Nabataean inscription, which refers to a Nabataean cavalryman, apparently one of the mercenaries in the service of Palmyra, who were deployed along the trade route paralleling the Euphrates; *BSOAS*, XV, 1953, pp. 230, 241; Clermont-Ganneau, *RHR*, LXXX, 1919, p. 24; *RAO*, II, 1898, p. 381, n. 1; VI, pp. 214-216; Dunand, *Soueïda*, Pls. XXXIII:150, 152 and p. 71; Starcky, *BA*, XVIII:4, 1955, pp. 92, 101; see n. 225; Butler, *PAES* II, A, 1919, Ills. 329, 334, Fragment L, and p. 384.

250. *Pauly-Wissowa*, XVI:2, col. 1461.

251. Parr, *PEQ* 89, 1957, p. 10 and Pl. VIIB.

252. Rostovtzeff, *CC*, pp. 193, 195, Fig. 3; p. 211, Fig. 4; *DPPA*, Fig. 34, publishes an intaglio showing a galloping Persian or Parthian warrior, armed with two spears; *Iranians and Greeks*, pp. 29, 30, 41, 121, 161 and Pl. XXIX; *Dura*, IV, 1933, pp. 214-219, Pl. XX:1, 2; XXII:1, 2; Abdul Hak, *AAS*,

IV-V, 1954-1955, Pl. VII, after p. 186; Schlumberger, *Palmyrène,* Pls. XXII:1; XXVII:1, 3, 4; XXXI:1, 2; XXXIV: 1; XXXV:5; XXXVI:2.

253. Rostovtzeff, *CC,* p. 194, Fig. 2; *DPPA,* Figs. 40-42, 44, 57; *Dura,* II, 1931, pp. 194-196 and Pls. XLI:2; XLII:1; XLIII:2; IV, 1933, pp. 214-219, Pl. XXI:1-3; *Iranians and Greeks,* pp. 55, 160, 161; Seyrig and Starcky, *Syria,* XXVI, 1949, Pls. XI, XII; Schlumberger, *Palmyrène,* Pls. XXI:3; XXII:1; XXXVII:2.

254. Cf. relief of a mounted warrior, face in frontal position, with ends of chiton streaming backward as if he were charging into battle, in Schlumberger, *Palmyrène,* Pl. XXII:2.

255. Kitzinger, *Coptic Sculpture,* pp. 201-204; Rostovtzeff, *DPPA,* pp. 238-242; *MS,* 1, p. 282; Seyrig, *Syria,* XVIII, 1937, pp. 31-43; Hopkins, *Dura,* VII-VIII, 1939, p. 93, n. 5; pp. 295, 297; Ingholf, *Hatra,* p. 46; Avi-Yonah, *QDAP,* XIII, 1948, pp. 130-131; XIV, 1950, p. 77; Perkins in *City Invincible,* pp. 208-209; Widengren, *Kulturbegegnung,* p. 19; Hopkins, *AI,* III, 1936, pp. 187-196; *Berytus,* III:1, 1936, pp. 9-10, 34; Hopkins, *Dura* V, 1934, pp. 117-120; Morehart, *Berytus,* XII, 1956-1957, pp. 79-83.

256. Dunand, *Soueïda,* pp. 69-70 and Pl. XXXIII:145.

257. Dunand, *Soueïda,* pp. 31-32 and Pl. XIII:36; Ingholt, *Hatra,* p. 19 and Pl. V:2-3; Kantorowicz, *Gods in Uniform,* pp. 377, 379 and Figs. 22, 30; Seyrig, *Syria,* XV, 1934, p. 167, Fig. 1; see pp. 490-491.

258. Dunand, *Soueïda,* p. 64 and Pl. XXVIII:122.

259. Butler, *PAES,* II, A, 1919, p. 376, Ill. 326:1; pp. 388, 389 and Ills. 336, 337.

260. Schlumberger, *Syria,* XIV, 1933, pp. 290, 311, 315 and Pls. XXVIII:3; XXXIV:3; XXXVI:2;

XXXVII:2 (exact provenance in Hauran unknown, p. 311).

261. Schlumberger, *Syria,* XIV, 1933, p. 290 and Pl. XXVIII:2.

262. De Vaux, *RB,* 47, 1938, pp. 227-258; Musil, *AP,* I, *Moab,* pp. 397-399.

263. See p. 213.

264. Strong, *Apotheosis,* Pl. XXX, p. 226 and pp. 229-231.

265. See p. 399.

266. Contenau, *MAO,* II, p. 700, Fig. 490; p. 716, Fig. 500; III, p. 1181, Fig. 774; p. 1218, Fig. 790; Avi-Yonah, *QDAP,* X, 1944, p. 117; *ANEP,* p. 20, Figs. 65, 66; p. 71, Fig. 229; p. 180, Fig. 534; p. 182, Fig. 540; p. 190, Fig. 571; p. 200, Fig. 612.

267. Cf. p. 195.

268. *ANEP,* p. 39, Fig. 131; p. 43, Fig. 144; p. 133, Fig. 378; p. 141, Fig. 404.

269. The former Curator of the Palestine Archeological Museum, Harry J. Iliffe, thought they were masculine; cf. Avi-Yonah, *QDAP,* X, 1944, p. 117.

270. Avi-Yonah and Negev, *ILN,* Nov. 26, 1960, p. 945, Fig. 3; see pp. 20, 199.

271. Avi-Yonah and Negev, *ILN,* Nov. 26, 1960, pp. 944-948; for the protruding tongue, cf. Segall, Bowen and Albright, *ADSA,* p. 159.

272. Dalman, *Petra,* pp. 355-356 and Figs. 324-325; Wiegand, *Petra,* p. 66; *PA* I, pp. 179, 189, 319-320 and Figs. 348, 349; Kammerer, *Pétra,* p. 224, Fig. 13; Pl. 53:1; 68, Fig. 1; Hopkins, *Dura,* V, 1934, p. 106; Andrae, *Hatra,* II, p. 149, Fig. 251; Seyrig, *Syria,* XXII, 1941, pp. 31-48 and Pl. III facing p. 38; Jucker, *Blätterkelch,* Tafelband, Abb. 62-71, showing winged griffins in reliefs found from Rome to Hatra and Palmyra, with several of them in burial monuments; Gressmann, *AOB,* p. 116, Pl. CLX, Fig. 100; Avi-Yonah and Negev, *ILN,* Nov. 26, 1960, p.

945, Fig. 3; Phillips, *Qataban and Sheba,* p. 97.

273. The American School of Oriental Research expedition found the animal sculptured on a megalith of mottled red and white dolomite in October, 1962; Albright, *AP,* p. 150, Fig. 49; Lapp, *BASOR,* 171, Oct. 1963, pp. 8-39; Hill, *BASOR,* 171, Oct. 1963, pp. 45-55.

274. Leibovitch, *'Atiqot,* I, 1955, pp. 75-88.

275. Cumont, *After Life,* pp. 102, 156.

276. See p. 311.

277. Cf. Bossert, *Altsyrien,* pp. 102, 391, Fig. 1355.

278. See p. 225.

279. Avi-Yonah and Negev, *ILN,* Nov. 26, 1960, pp. 944-947.

280. Horsfield, *QDAP,* IX, 1942, pp. 113-204 and Pls. VI-XLIXB.

281. Horsfield, *QDAP,* IX, 1942, pp. 197-198 and Pl. XLVI:438.

282. See p. 222.

283. See p. 40.

284. See p. 396.

285. Dussaud, *Syria,* II, 1921, pp. 43-45.

286. For a relief on a Babylonian pottery plaque of the beginning of the second millennium B.C., showing a musician with a seven-stringed lyre, cf. Parrot, *Sumer,* 359a on p. 292; for the deity Nebo with a lyre on Palmyrenean tesserae, cf. du Mesnil, *TMP,* pp. 286-290, Fig. 176; Jucker, *Blätterkelch,* II, Abb. 106.

287. Horsfield, *QDAP,* IX, 1942, p. 197, no. 438; Broneer, *Corinth,* IV:2, 1930, Pl. VII:391; cf. Laws, *AJA,* 65:1, 1961, p. 33 and Pl. 22:5 for a comparable decoration attached to a Graeco-Scythian female figure on a gold horse frontlet.

288. Horsfield, *QDAP,* IX, 1932, Pls. XI:42, 47; XXXI:262; XLVI:437; du Mesnil, *TMP,* p. 319, Fig. 186.

289. Horsfield, *QDAP,* IX, 1942, Pls. XI:50; XXIV:174; XXVII:219; XXXI:262; XLVI:437.

290. Harding, *ADAJ,* I, 1951, p. 37 and Pl. XIV.

291. *ANEP,* pp. 186, no. 552; 187, nos. 553, 556, 557; 189, nos. 564, 567.

292. Vanden Berghe, *Iran,* pp. 90-91 and Pl. 116a.

293. *HGR,* II, 1948, p. 367b.

294. Jucker, *Blätterkelch,* p. 158 and Tafelband Abb. 41.

294a. Berenson, Bernard in Beny, *Thrones,* p. 104 and Pl. 84.

295. *OSJ,* p. 156, Fig. 86; Glueck, *AASOR,* XIV, 1934, p. 23, Fig. 6a, b.; Jucker, *Blätterkelch,* Abb. 106.

296. Harding, *ILN,* Feb. 18, 1950, p. 267, Figs. 3, 4; Barnett, *ADAJ,* I, 1951, pp. 34-36 and Pl. XI; *ANEP,* p. 20, Fig. 64; Bacon, *DFH,* p. 125 and Pl. 46b; Landes, *BA,* XXIV:3, 1961, Frontispiece, and pp. 79-80; O'Callaghan, *Orientalia,* 21, 1952, pp. 184-193.

297. *ANEP,* p. 173, Fig. 506; Kantor, *JNES,* XVI:3, 1957, p. 147, Fig. 2; Goldman, *JNES,* XX:4, 1961, p. 245, Fig. 11; Parrot, *Sumer,* pp. 124, 125, Figs. 153, 154; p. 298, Fig. 365; p. 299, Fig. 366; p. 300, Fig. 367 A, C; pp. 390-392; Gressmann, *AOB,* p. 77 and Pl. CVI: 248, 249; Akurgal, *Anatolien,* p. 39, Fig. 17; p. 40, Fig. 18; p. 41, Fig. 19; p. 44, Fig. 22; p. 45, Figs. 23, 24.

298. Parrot, *Sumer,* p. 138, Fig. 167; *ANEP,* p. 172, Fig. 505; Gressmann, *AOB,* pp. 76-77 and Pl. CVI:247.

299. *ANEP,* p. 148, Figs. 423-425; Clark, *Myth,* p. 221, Fig. 31.

300. Parrot, *Sumer,* p. 138, Fig. 167; p. 173, Fig. 208; pp. 208, 209, Figs. 257, 258; Gressmann, *AOB,* pp. 76-77 and Pl. CVI:247.

301. Parrot, *Sumer,* p. 240, Fig. 294; p. 241, Fig. 296.

301a. See p. 222; cf. Bowen and Albright, *ADSA,* p. 285, Fig. 202.

302. Harding, *ILN,* Feb. 18, 1950, p. 267, Figs. 3, 4; Barnett, *ADAJ,* I, 1951, pp. 34-36 and Pl. XI; O'Cal-

laghan, *Orientalia*, 21, 1952, pp. 184-193 and Pl. XXVI; cf. also p. 222.

303. Harding, *ILN*, Feb. 18, 1950, p. 266, Figs. 5, 6; *ADAJ*, I, 1951, p. 34, n. 1; Barnett, *ADAJ*, I, 1951, pp. 34-36 and Pls. XII, XIII.

304. *ILN*, Feb. 18, 1950, p. 266, Fig. 5; Barnett, *ADAJ*, I, 1951, p. 36 and Pl. XIII; Avi-Yonah, ed., *IWB*, II, p. 179.

305. *ILN*, Feb. 18, 1950, p. 266; Barnett, *ADAJ*, I, 1951, p. 34. There is a striking resemblance between this statuette and a statue from Zinjirli; cf. *ANEP*, p. 179, Fig. 530.

306. Bossert, *Altsyrien*, pp. 95, 360, no. 1237.

307. Cf. pp. 243, 339.

308. Toynbee, *Art*, p. 170; see pp. 353, 374, 382.

309. Goodenough, *Symbols*, VII, p. 208 and Figs. 243-247, 260-263, 266, 267, 279, 280.

310. Cumont, *Doura, Texte*, p. 240; *Atlas*, Pls. LXXXVI and LXXXVIII.

311. See p. 190.

312. *EPH-Tel*, II, p. 130; Bossert, *Altsyrien*, pp. 95, 361, Fig. 1242.

313. Parr, *PEQ*, 89, 1957, p. 13 and Pl. XIV B.

314. Kerenyi, *Dionysus u. das Tragische in der Antigone*, p. 9f., quoted by Goodenough, *Symbols*, VII, p. 207.

315. Goodenough, *Symbols*, VII, p. 209 and Fig. 245.

316. See p. 334.

317. Avigad, *IEJ*, 9:4, 1959, pp. 210-211.

318. Avigad, *IEJ*, 9:4, 1959, p. 211; Goodenough, *Symbols*, III, Figs. 84, 85.

319. Avigad, *IEJ*, 9:4, 1959, p. 211; Goodenough, *Symbols*, V, Fig. 10; cf. Lippold, *Skulpturen vat.*, III: 1, Pl. 48, Fig. 546a and p. 129.

320. Dunand, *Soueïda*, p. 37 and Pl. VII; Avi-Yonah, *Or. Art.*, p. 51.

321. Cook, *Zeus*, I, p. 565, Fig. 432; Parr, *PEQ*, 89, 1957, Pl. VIII:1

and pp. 9, 10; Segall in Bowen and Albright, *ADSA*, pp. 155-164.

322. Dunand, *Soueïda*, Pl. V:3 and pp. 14-15; also Pl. XXX:138 and p. 68; Butler, *PAES*, IIA, 6, 1919, p. 398, Ill. 343:B from Si'a.

323. Kitzinger, *Coptic Sculpture*, pp. 195-197, 200 and Pl. LXXI:2-4; Toynbee and Ward Perkins, *PBSR*, XVIII, 1950, pp. 1-43.

324. See p. 57.

325. Toynbee and Ward Perkins, *PBSR*, XVIII, 1950, p. 32; Bossert, *Altsyrien*, Fig. 1289 from Yemen.

326. Dunand, *Soueïda*, Pl. XXX:139 and p. 68; Pl. XXIX and p. 66; Kitzinger, *Coptic Sculpture*, p. 195 and Pl. LXXI:5; Breccia, *Musée*, Pl. XL:104; Minns, *S.Gr.*, p. 203, Fig. 98 top.

327. Toynbee and Ward Perkins, *PBSR*, XVIII, 1950, pp. 32, 38; for an earlier, related type of bearded head of a half-length horned ibex in squatting position at the end of a Scythian rhyton, cf. Rostovtzeff, *Iranians and Greeks*, Pl. XII A.

328. Toynbee and Ward Perkins, *PBSR*, XVIII, 1950, pp. 12, 14, 15, 18-25, 32-35, 39, 41; Toynbee, *Art*, Pls. 195, 197; Segall in Bowen and Albright, *ADSA*, pp. 158, 176, Fig. 112; Mendel, *Catalogue*, II, pp. 179-184 (from Aphrodisias).

329. Dunand, *Soueïda*, Pl. XXVIII: 156, pp. 72-73; Pl. XXIX:129 and p. 66.

330. Dussaud, *Topographie*, p. 349, no. 8; Dussaud and Macler, *Mission*, p. 20; Butler, *PAES*, II, A, 5, 1919, pp. 355-356; Toynbee and Ward Perkins, *PBSR*, XVIII, 1950, Pl. XX:2 and p. 32.

331. Dunand, *Soueïda*, Pl. XXXII:153 and p. 72.

332. Kitzinger, *Coptic Sculpture*, Pl. LXXI:2-5; Breccia, *Musée*, Pls. XXXIX:103; XL:104; XLII:109; XLV:116; Naville, *Ahnas*, Pl. XV; Petrie, *Oxyrhynkhos*, Pls. XLVI:5,

14; XLVII:6, 14; Toynbee and Ward Perkins, *PBSR,* XVIII, 1950, p. 35.

333. Kitzinger, *Coptic Sculpture,* Pl. LXXI:5; Breccia, *Musée,* Pl. XL: 104, 7.

334. Kitzinger, *Coptic Sculpture,* p. 197; Toynbee, *Art,* Pls. 195, 196 and pp. 193-194.

335. See pp. 534-535.

336. Hamilton, *QDAP,* XIV, 1950, Pls. XXXVIII:1-2; XLII:1-10; Schlumberger, *Syria,* XX, 1939, Pl. XLIV:2 and p. 328; see p. 535.

337. Butler, *PAES,* IV, A, 1914, pp. 1-2; II, A, 1919, 2, p. xviii; II, A, 1919, 4, p. 236, Ill. 211; p. 237, Ill. 212.

338. Butler, *PAES,* II, A, 1919, 2, p. xviii; III, A, 1921, 2, pp. 4-42.

339. Vanden Berghe, *Iran,* Pl. 141a,

c; Minns, *S.Gr.,* p. 260, Fig. 182[bis]; p. 207, Fig. 105.

340. Rostovtzeff, *Iranians and Greeks,* Pl. XII A, facing p. 62; Pl. XXVII:2, facing p. 138; Minns, *S.Gr.,* p. 211, Fig. 110; Ghirshman, *Iran,* Pl. 4a, after p. 192; Toynbee and Perkins, *PBSR,* XVIII, 1950, Pl. XXV:2 and p. 38.

341. Minns, *S.Gr.,* p. 274, Fig. 194; p. 197, Fig. 90:ABC.XX.2; Piggott, *Dawn,* p. 106:12; Toynbee and Ward Perkins, *PBSR,* XVIII, 1950, Pl. XXV:2 and p. 38.

342. Toynbee and Ward Perkins, *PBSR,* XVIII, 1950, pp. 4-5.

343. Toynbee and Ward Perkins, *PBSR,* XVIII, 1950, pp. 30-43.

344. Toynbee and Ward Perkins, *PBSR,* XVIII, 1950, p. 42.

CHAPTER VIII

345. Hopkins, *Dura,* V, 1934, p. 117.

346. Rostovtzeff, in *MS,* I, p. 282; Baur, *Dura,* III, 1932, p. 135; Hopkins, *AI,* III, 1936, pp. 187-196; *Berytus,* III:1, 1936, pp. 3, 9, 10; Seyrig, *Syria,* XVIII, 1937, pp. 37-40; XXII, 1941, pp. 32-33; Kitzinger, *Coptic Sculpture,* p. 203; Avi-Yonah, *QDAP,* X, 1944, pp. 130, 131; XIV, 1950, p. 77; *AJA,* XLVII:1, 1943, p. 145; Ingholt, *Hatra,* p. 46; Moortgat, *Kunst,* p. 62.

347. Hopkins, *Dura,* V, 1934, p. 117.

348. Hopkins, *Dura,* V, 1934, pp. 108, 117; Crosby, *Dura,* VI, 1936, pp. 119-120 and Pl. XXVI:4, 5.

349. Della Vida, *Clara Rhodos,* IX, pp. 139-148; Cantineau, *Nabatéen,* I, p. 21, n. 8; *CIS,* I, nos. 119, 122.

350. *CIS,* II, 1, 2, nos. 157, 158, 159; Cooke, *N-S Inscr.,* pp. 256, 259; Lidzbarski, *AT,* I, pp. 40-42, n. 52; Rostovtzeff, *CC,* p. 50; Kitz-

inger, *Coptic Sculpture,* p. 208; Picard, *RA,* X, 1937, pp. 244-249; *CRAI,* 1937, pp. 440-450; Lippold, *Skulpturen vat.,* III:1, p. 130, no. 547, Pl. 39; Kammerer, *Pétra,* p. 450, discusses the two votive figurines of camels offered to Dusares at Puteoli; Avi-Yonah, *Or. Art,* p. 55, n. 46.

351. A shrine for Hadad and Atargatis was dedicated in Delos in the year 128/7 B.C. by Achaios from Hierapolis; cf. Ingholt, *Hatra,* p. 20; Roussel, *Delos,* p. 253; Ronzevalle, *MUSJ,* XXII, 1939, pp. 109-121; Schlumberger, *JDAI Arch. Anz.* 50, 1935, col. 610; Cumont, *RO,* p. 99; Pillet, *Dura,* III, 1932, p. 12; Cook, S. A., *RAPLA,* p. 173; Picard discusses the Temple of Atargatis at Delos, A.D. 127-128, in *Collection Latomus,* II, p. 261.

352. See p. 45.

353. Rostovtzeff, *CC,* Pl. XXX:2 and

p. 217; Pl. XXXII:1 and pp. 186, 218.

354. Brown, *Dura*, VII-VIII, 1939, Pl. XXXI:1; Al Asil, *ILN*, Nov. 10, 1951, p. 765, Fig. 7; Dec. 18, 1954, p. 1117, Fig. 10.

355. Al Asil, *ILN*, Dec. 25, 1954, p. 1160, Fig. 5.

356. Al Asil, *ILN*, Dec. 18, 1954, p. 1117, Fig. 10.

357. Al Asil, *ILN*, Dec. 25, 1954, p. 1160, Fig. 5.

358. Al Asil, *ILN*, Dec. 18, 1954, p. 1117, Figs. 7, 9 center; Dec. 25, 1954, p. 1160, Fig. 2, p. 1161, Fig. 9.

359. See pp. 207-208.

360. Ingholt, *Hatra*, p. 8 and Pl. I:2; pp. 10-11, Pl. II:1, 2; pp. 23-24, Pl. VI:2, 3; p. 33, Pl. VI:1; pp. 24, 32, Pl. VII:1-3.

361. Ingholt, *Hatra*, p. 18, Pl. IV:1.

362. Ingholt *Hatra*, p. 10, Pl. I:3; p. 11, Pl. II:3.

363. Al Asil, *ILN*, Nov. 17, 1951, p. 807, Figs. 10, 11; Dec. 18, 1954, p. 1116, Fig. 4; Dec. 25, 1954, p.

1160, Fig. 1; p. 1161, Figs. 8, 9; Ingholt, *Hatra*, p. 16 and Pl. III:3; p. 52, Pl. VII:2.

364. Stève, *LWB*, Fig. 58, p. 98.

365. Hopkins, *Dura*, V, 1934, p. 117.

366. Plutarch, *Alexander*, XXXVII:2.

367. Finegan, *LfAP*, p. 208.

368. Ghirshman, *Iran*, pp. 244-245.

369. Curtius, VII, 2; Polybius, X:28.

370. Appian, *Syr.*, VI, 15; Strabo XI, 516; Polybius, X, 11, 31; *Ency. Brit.*, 1953, under "Parthia."

371. Rostovtzeff, *CC*, pp. 194-196.

372. Rostovtzeff, *CC*, pp. 98-99.

373. Rostovtzeff, *CC*, p. 101; Strabo, XI, 513; Polybius, X, 48; Justin, XI, 1, 4.

374. Gen. 11:31; Finegan, *LfAP*, pp. 55, 184.

375. Finegan, *LfAP*, p. 184.

376. Finegan, *LfAP*, p. 215; Josephus, *War*, I, 14, 1; I, 18, 3; *Antiq.* XV, 1, 2; Debevoise, *Parthia*, pp. 113, 120.

377. Rostovtzeff, *CC*, p. 110.

378. Rostovtzeff, *CC*, p. 111.

CHAPTER IX

379. *SG*, pp. 69-70.

380. Baur, *Dura*, III, 1932, pp. 100-102, 137, Pl. XIV; Hopkins, *Dura*, V, 1934, pp. 119, 143, 174; Ingholt, *Hatra*, p. 18, Pl. IV; Rostovtzeff, *CC*, pp. 178, 217.

381. Ingholt, *Hatra*, p. 18, Pl. IV:2-3.

382. Baur, *Dura*, III, 1932, pp. 100-102, 137; Hopkins, *Dura*, V, 1934, p. 143, Pl. XIV; Seyrig, *Syria*, X, 1929, p. 317, n. 7; Rotrou and Seyrig, *Syria*, XIV, 1933, Pl. V:4; Dunand, *Soueïda*, p. 83, Pl. XXXIV:169; Rostovtzeff, *CC*, pp. 78, 105, 131, 137, 151, Pl. XXI:1.

382a. Cf. Berta Segall, "The Lion-Riders from Timna" in Bowen and Albright, *ADSA*, pp. 155-172; Phillips, *Qataban and Sheba*, pp. 89-102.

383. Dunand, *Soueïda*, p. 83 and Pl. XXXIV:169; cf. du Mesnil, *TMP*, p. 215, Figs. 143, 144; p. 368, Fig. 201.

384. Dunand, *Soueïda*, p. 83, nn. 1-6, points out that the Atargatis cult existed at "Djourein" in the Hauran and possibly also at Nimre and Qarnaim there. We have previously referred to the Atargateion at the latter site, referred to in II Macc. 12:26.

385. Cook, *Zeus*, I, pp. 778-779; Baur, *Dura*, III, 1932, p. 113, n. 69, writes: "Atargatis never let Hadad feel at home in Syria as her equal." He points out further (pp. 137-139 and Pl. XIV) that in the stele bearing the relief of the two of them, Hadad is given the

poorer representation, being squeezed into about a third of the space that Atargatis occupies. Even her attendant lions are larger and more prominent than his bulls.

386. Al Asil, *ILN*, Dec. 25, 1954, p. 1160, Fig. 3; Hopkins, *Dura*, V, 1934, p. 108, Pl. XIII; Daremberg et Saglio, *Dict.*, V, pp. 375, 376; Rostovtzeff, *DPPA*, pp. 207-208, 228-230, 241; Minns, *S.Gr.*, p. 271, Fig. 187; p. 426, Fig. 317.

387. Cf. Minns, *S.Gr.*, p. 260, Fig. 182bis.

388. See p. 270; cf. Dunand, *Soueïda*, Pl. XXXIV:169 and p. 83.

389. See pp. 270, 287.

390. See p. 270; *PA*, I, p. 51, Figs. 40, 41.

391. Horsfield, *QDAP*, IX, 1940, Pl. XLIX and p. 204, no. 478; for a similarly positioned bull in relief on a sunken panel of a Nabataean altar panel originally from Qanawat in Nabataean Syria, whose frame bears a Nabataean inscription, cf. *PA*, III, p. 209, Fig. 1096; Bossert, *Altsyrien*, Fig. 1248.

392. Horsfield, *QDAP*, VII, 1938, Pl. LXXIV:2 and p. 41.

393. Dunand, *Soueïda*, Pl. XXVII:123, 124 and p. 64; Pl. XXIX:132 and p. 67; Pl. XXX:126 and p. 65; Pl. XXXIV:169 and pp. 82-83; Butler, *PAES*, II, A, 6, 1919, Ills. 326, 328.

394. Wiegand, *Baalbek*, I, Pl. 133, 60B; II, p. 8, Fig. 12; p. 11, Fig. 16.

395. Segall, in *ADSA*, pp. 155-178; Phillips, *QS*, opposite p. 96; Bossert, *Altsyrien*, p. 390, Fig. 1350.

396. Minns, *S.Gr.*, pp. 298, 299 and Fig. 11; Bossert, *Altsyrien*, pp. 35, 158 and Fig. 513; Young, *ILN*, Jan. 3, 1953, p. 23, Figs. 15, 16; Nov. 10, 1956, p. 798, Fig. 9; Avi-Yonah, *QDAP*, XIII, 1938, pp. 139-145; Richter, *Sculpture*, pp. 458-460 and Figs. 340-346; *ILN*, Dec. 22, 1951, p. 1033 for a lion's head on a Roman mosaic in cen-

tral Sicily at a site dated to about the middle of the third century A.D.

397. Segal, in Bowen, *ADSA*, p. 163; Avi-Yonah, *QDAP*, XIII, 1938, p. 145; Dussaud, *Notes Myth. Syr.*, p. 88.

398. Cf. Baur, *Dura*, III, 1932, p. 101 and Pl. XIV, showing Atargatis wearing a royal crown, decorated with zigzag lines, forming rays; also p. 122, n. 112; Genouillac, *Syria*, X, 1929, Pl. 1, Fig. 1 depicts Hadad and Atargatis, the latter wearing a polos with ascending rays; Newell, *Num. Notes & Monographs*, p. 78, coin 115.

399. Baur, *Dura*, III, 1932, pp. 110-112, Pl. XIX:2; Seyrig, *Syria*, X, 1929, pp. 317-318; Cook, *Zeus*, I, pp. 272, 558, 561, Fig. 427; III, 2, p. 1095; for the thunderbolt, ear of grain, and bull, as symbols of the god of Baalbek, cf. Avi-Yonah, *IEJ*, II, 1952, pp. 121-122; IX, 1959, p. 10; Albright, *ARI*, p. 74.

400. Baur, *Dura*, III, 1932, p. 101, Pl. XIV; Brown, *Dura*, VII-VIII, 1939, Pl. XXXIII and pp. 258-260; Hopkins, *Dura*, VII-VIII, 1939, pp. 296, 297.

401. Baur, *Dura*, III, 1932, p. 112 and Pl. XIX:2.

402. Hopkins, *Dura*, V, 1934, p. 110.

403. Rostovtzeff, in *MS* I, p. 283; cf. p. 428.

404. Cook, *Zeus*, III, p. 815.

405. Cook, *Zeus*, I, p. 583; *SG*, p. 71, art. 32; Ingholt, *Hatra*, pp. 12-13; Neumann, *The Great Mother*, p. 231.

406. Rostovtzeff, *CC*, pp. 78, 105, 131, 178, 217, Pl. XXVIII:1; see pp. 269, 270.

407. The temple of Atargatis in Ashtaroth-Qarnaim in southernmost Syria was called the Atargateion in II Macc. 12:26; Avi-Yonah, *IEJ*, 9:1, 1959, p. 9. For worship of Atargatis in Egypt, cf. Avi-Yonah, *IEJ*, 9:1, 1959, p. 9, n. 66; Vaggi, *Aegyptus*, 17, 1937, pp. 34-35.

408. For the temple of Atargatis at Delos, cf. p. 209; Ronzevalle, *MUSJ,* XXII, 1939, pp. 111-121; Avi-Yonah, *IEJ,* 9:1, 1959, p. 9; Albright, *ARI,* pp. 74-78.

409. *SG,* p. 80, art. 44.

410. *SG,* pp. 81-82, art. 47.

411. Baur, *Dura,* III, 1932, pp. 100-107 and Pl. XIV, pp. 113, 127, 138, 139; Ingholt, *Hatra,* p. 18 and Pl. IV:1; Avi-Yonah, *IEJ,* 9:1, 1959, p. 9; Cook, *Zeus,* I, p. 550; see p. 397.

412. Neumann, *The Great Mother,* Pls. 151, 153; Cook, *Zeus,* I, p. 745; Baur, *Dura,* IV, 1933, p. 44, n. 8; Goldman, *AK,* III:2, 3, 1960, p. 56.

413. Neumann, *The Great Mother,* p. 308; Cook, *Zeus,* II, 2, p. 969, n. 4; III, 1, p. 814.

414. Parr, *PEQ,* 89, 1957, p. 10 and Pl. VIII:A; Wiegand, *Petra,* p. 48, Fig. 42.

415. Cook, *Zeus,* III, 1, p. 811; Neumann, *The Great Mother,* Pls. 151, 153.

416. Cook, *Zeus,* III, 1, p. 815; see n. 419.

417. Cook, *Zeus,* I, p. 134; Elderkin, *AJA,* XLI:3, 1937, p. 429.

418. Goldman, *AK,* III:2, 3, 1960, p. 56.

419. Cook, *Zeus,* III, 1, p. 816.

419a. Horsfield, *QDAP,* VII, 1938, pp. 21-24 and Pl. L; Segall, in Bowen and Albright, pp. 157-159, and 176, Fig. 112.

420. Dunand, *Soueïda,* pp. 14-15 and Pl. V, 3.

421. See p. 244 under animal sculptures; Toynbee and Ward Perkins, *PBSR,* XVIII, 1950, pp. 31-32; Hanfmann, *ILN,* Mar. 9, 1963, pp. 341, 344 and Figs. 23, 26, 29; Wiegand, *Baalbek,* I, p. 115, Pls. 42, 133, 134.

422. Hanfmann, *ILN,* Mar. 9, 1963, p. 344, Figs. 23, 26, 29.

423. Applebaum, *ILN,* Mar. 16, 1963, p. 380, Fig. 1.

424. Parr, *ADAJ,* IV-V, 1960, pp. 134-136 and Pl. XV, 1.

425. Parr, *ADAJ,* IV-V, 1960, p. 135.

426. Lippold, *Skulpturen vat.,* III:1, Pl. 9, Fig. 520.

426a. See p. 60.

427. Picard, *RA,* X, 1937, p. 245, rejects the possibility of the veil of leaves being a mask, without going into any particulars.

427a. The Syriac inscriptions of apparently two different types under and by the side of the Hatra male Medusa have apparently not yet been published. Cf. André Caquot, *Nouvelles Inscriptions Araméennes de Hatra (V),* in *Syria,* XL, 1963, pp. 1-16.

428. Toynbee, *Art,* p. 163 and Pl. 248, no. 9; Toynbee and Perkins, *PBSR,* XVIII, 1950, p. 22 and Pl. XI:3.

429. Picard, *RA,* X, 1937, pp. 244-249; *CRAI,* 1937, pp. 440-450.

430. Hanfmann, *ILN,* March 9, 1963, pp. 340, 342 and Fig. 19; *BASOR* 174, 1964, p. 32; see p. 353 and n. 546a.

430a. See pp. 354, 360.

431. Dunand, *Soueïda,* pp. 14, 15 and Pl. V:3; Hopkins, *Dura,* VII-VIII, 1939, pp. 299-301; Kraeling, *Gerasa,* pp. 37, 385, n. 19; Robinson, *Sarcophagus,* pp. 406-408; Smith, *HGHL,* p. 628; Sourdel, *Hauran,* pp. 59-69.

Chapter X

432. Dunand, *Soueïda,* p. 12 and Pl. IV; Brown, *Dura,* VII-VIII, 1939, p. 261 and Pl. XXXIV; Newell, *Num. Notes and Monographs,* no. 84, 1939, p. 78, coin 115; p. 95, coin 147; Minns, *S.Gr.,* p. 485 and Pl. III:3; Cook, *Zeus,* I, p. 272; Dalman, *Petra,* pp. 52, 360.

433. Baur, *Dura,* III, 1932, p. 101 and Pl. XIV; pp. 111-112 and Pl. XIX:2; Brown, *Dura,* VII-VIII, 1939, p. 258 and Pl. XXXIII; Rostovtzeff, in *MS,* I, p. 283; Seyrig, *Syria,* X, 1929, pp. 317-318; Avi-Yonah, *IEJ,* 9:1, 1959, p. 10.

434. Ingholt, *Hatra,* p. 46; Hopkins, *AI,* III, 1937, pp. 187-196; *Berytus,* III:1, 1936, pp. 3, 9, 10; Seyrig, *Syria,* XVIII, 1937, pp. 31-43; XXII, 1941, pp. 31-44; Perkins in *City,* p. 208; Widengren, *Kulturbegegnung,* p. 19; Baur, *Dura,* III, 1932, p. 135; Avi-Yonah, *Or. Art.,* pp. 79-95.

435. Jucker, *Blätterkelch,* pp. 216-217.

436. Jucker, *Blätterkelch,* p. 216 and Tafelband, Abb. 73-74.

437. Reinach, *Repertoire,* V, p. 215, no. 2; de Ridder, *Bronzes du Louvre,* Tome II, *Les Instruments,* p. 43; Jucker, *Blätterkelch,* p. 197, Skizze 34; p. 203, Skizze 36; Tafelband, Abb. 41, 43, 50, 53, 64, 80, 137, 147.

438. Dunand, *Soueïda,* pp. 14-15, and Pl. V:3; Jucker, *Blätterkelch,* pp. 166-167, and Tafelband, Abb. 51.

439. Gaudin and Collignon, *CRAI,* II, 1904, p. 708; Contenau, *CP,* pp. 270-271.

440. See pp. 60, 292, 311.

441. Parr, *ADAJ,* III, 1960, p. 135 and Pl. XV:1.

442. Num. 24:21.

443. Parr, *ADAJ,* IV-V, 1960, p. 135 and Pl. XV:1.

444. Parr, *PEQ,* 89, 1957, Pl. XIV:B and p. 13.

445. Stebbins, *Dolphin,* p. 128, points out that "heads of Oceanus with dolphins escaping from his beard abound."

446. Wiegand, *Petra,* pp. 45, 48 and Fig. 38.

447. Toynbee, *Art,* p. 169.

448. Toynbee, *Art,* p. 170 and Pl. 117.

449. For the fish-tailed Capricornus in zodiacs, cf. Toynbee, *Art,* Figs. 73, 74, 245; Cumont, *TM,* II, Pl. VI facing p. 350, 389, Fig. 304; p. 395, Fig. 315; Baur, *Dura,* IV, 1933, p. 46, Pl. VII:1; Rostovtzeff, *Dura,* VI, 1936, Pl. XLVI:6, p. 386; Goodenough, *Symbols,* V, p. 13 and Fig. 13; p. 27 and Fig. 36; p. 29 and Fig. 39; Roscher, *Lexikon,* IV, col. 1459, Fig. 24; col. 1460, Fig. 29; col. 1462, Fig. 27; VI, cols. 897, 898 and Figs, 4 and 5; col. 899, Fig. 6; col. 935, Fig. 13.

450. Erim, *ILN,* Jan. 5, 1963, p. 21, Figs. 5, 8; cf. Perkins, *JRS,* XLVI, 1956, p. 12 and Pl. III:2-4 showing details of Attic sarcophagus lids with two examples of Nereids astride leaf-skirted or seaweed-skirted Sea Centaurs and accompanied, in each instance, by an Eros; Bieber, *Sculpture,* Fig. 640.

451. Yadin, *Finds from the Times of Bar-Kochba in the Cave of the Letters* (Hebrew), p. 61 and Pl. 17.

452. Pelekanides, *Benaki,* Figs. 1-6 and Pl. I, pp. 37-62.

453. Pelekanides, *Benaki,* pp. 50, 51, 56, 59, 60.

454. Erim, *ILN,* Jan. 5, 1963, p. 25, Fig. 12.

455. See pp. 136-137.

456. Toynbee, *Art,* pp. 170-171; see pp. 242, 339.

457. Avi-Yonah and Negev, *ILN,* Nov. 26, 1960, p. 945, Fig. 3; cf. Van Buren, *AJA,* 67:4, Oct. 1963, Pl. 89:3 and p. 400 for a small votive model in terra cotta of a third-second century B.C. temple from Teanum, Sidicinum, featuring a bust in relief with a dolphin on either side of it and a mask at the top of the gable containing them.

458. Avi-Yonah and Negev, *ILN,* Nov. 26, 1960, pp. 944-945, Fig. 3.

458a. Evenari, Shanan, Tadmor, *Run-off-Farming in the Negev.*

458b. According to an oral communication by Dr. A. Negev, Director of excavations at Abda (Avdat).

459. Savignac and Horsfield, *RB,* 44, 1935, p. 262, Fig. 16.

460. Ryckmans, *RB,* 43, 1934, pp. 572-

591; Savignac and Horsfield, *RB,* 44, 1935, pp. 245-278; Kirkbride, *RB,* 67, 1960, pp. 65-92.

461. Père R. de Vaux, in a letter to me dated 21 January, 1962, has suggested that the small, badly damaged and unrecognizable figure attached to the front of the garment may be a personification of a river, possibly the Orontes, assuming the possibility of the correctness of Seyrig's conjecture (as noted by Savignac and Horsfield, *RB,* 44, 1935, p. 263, n. 1) that the broken statue is that of a Tyché. In that case, the well known Tyché of Antioch with the personification of the River Orontes in front of it, comes to mind (Pl. 52a; Ipser, *Vatican Art,* p. 102). Cf. Ingholt, *Hatra,* Pl. VII:2, serpent over foot; Richter, *Sculpture,* pp. 295, 609 and Fig. 753; Bieber, *Sculpture,* p. 40 and Fig. 102.

462. Ingholt, *Hatra,* pp. 32-34 and Pl. VII:2; cf. du Mesnil, *TMP,* p. 136, Fig. 98:4.

463. See p. 144; Dunand, *Soueïda,* p. 83 and Pl. XXXIV: 169; du Mesnil, *TMP,* p. 80, Fig. 38; p. 99, Fig. 53; Baur, *Dura,* III, 1932, p. 100 and Pl. XIV.

464. Du Mesnil, *TMP,* p. 76, Fig. 37.

465. Dunand, *Soueïda,* p. 18 and Pl. IX:8; Horsfield, G. and A., *QDAP,* IX, 1942, Pl. XXXII:277-280; Musil, *AP,* II, p. 55, Fig. 17; Kammerer, *Pétra,* p. 400, Fig. 40; cf. Baur, *Dura,* III, 1932, p. 100 and Pl. XIV.

466. The horns on the forehead of the Atargatis of Hatra recall those on an earlier, bronze statuette from Syria of an Egyptianized Hadad and also bring to mind those of Dionysus-Taurus; cf. Baur, *Dura,* III, 1932, p. 134 and Pl. XX; see pp. 144, 222.

467. Du Mesnil, *TMP,* p. 136, Fig. 98:4.

468. Ingholt, *Hatra,* p. 34 and Pl. VI:1;

cf. Reinach, *Répertoire,* I, pp. 214, 215.

469. Toynbee, *Art,* p. 163 and Fig. 248; cf. Brunn, *Götterideale,* p. 37.

470. Goodenough, *Symbols,* VII, p. 239 and Fig. 285, p. 227; Toynbee, *Art,* pp. 161-164 and Pl. 96.

470a. *JRS,* XLVI, 1956, Pl. XVI:27.

471. Toynbee, *Art,* pp. 158-159 and Pl. 91.

472. Toynbee, *Art,* p. 170, Pl. 117.

473. Toynbee, *Art,* pp. 153-154 and Pl. 73.

474. See p. 352.

475. Stebbins, *Dolphin,* p. 86, points out that the dolphin and the rudder are not only connected with Isis-Tyché and, as we have emphasized, with Thalassa-Aphrodite-Atargatis, but that the dolphin and trident of Poseidon, and the eagle and thunderbolt of Zeus, are frequently associated with Serapis. Apollo, too, is sometimes associated with, or represented by, the dolphin.

476. According to I Macc. 15:23, Caria is one of the countries that received the letter of Lucius.

477. Picard, *CL,* II, pp. 257-264 and Pl. XVI; Gaudin and Collignon, *CRAI,* II, 1904, pp. 703-708 and Pl. I.

478. Virolleaud, *Syria,* V, 1924, Pl. XXXIII:1, p. 119.

479. Gaudin and Collignon, *CRAI,* II, 1904, pp. 703-711.

480. See p. 332.

481. See p. 331; Stebbins, *Dolphin,* p. 122, writes, ". . . the specialized form of the statues of Aphrodisias in Caria . . . show the goddess draped in a gown carved in imitation of heavily embroidered bands, some of which are decorated with Nereids, Tritons and dolphins . . . (which) cannot date earlier than the third century B.C. The grouping of the symbols of several aspects of the goddess into the one statue make of her a cosmic Aphrodite . . ."; cf. *Time,* Dec. 13,

1963, p. 54 for sculpture of Aphrodite of Aphrodisias with a panel clearly showing a dolphin and a Nereid seated on a sea centaur.

482. Squarciapino, *Bolletino d'Arte,* XLIV:2, April-June, 1959, Serie IV, p. 100, Fig. 2; Pelekanides, *Benaki,* p. 38, Fig. 1 and plate enlargement.

483. Du Mesnil, *TMP,* pp. 65-76.

484. Du Mesnil, *TMP,* p. 70, Fig. 27:3.

485. Du Mesnil, *TMP,* p. 76, Fig. 37; Rostovtzeff, *Dura,* IV, 1933, p. 210 and Pl. XIX:3.

486. Rostovtzeff, *DPPA,* Fig. 49, shows a stone head, with a dove(?) on each shoulder. The elaborately curled locks are covered by a veil or shawl, which we take to be the equivalent of the banderole of the heavens, and over it is a crown in the form of a turreted tower. This Dura-Europos head is much similar to that of the Zodiac-Tyché of Khirbet Tannur, except that in the latter instance the veil is placed over the turreted tower.

487. Du Mesnil, *TMP,* p. 50, Fig. 5.

488. Du Mesnil, *TMP,* p. 75, Fig. 36.

489. Du Mesnil, *TMP,* p. 72, Fig. 30.

490. Cumont, *TM,* II, p. 244, Fig. 77:F.

491. Kammerer, *Pétra,* p. 418, Fig. 42; Dussaud, *Arabes en Syrie,* p. 143; du Mesnil, *TMP,* p. 69, Fig. 26.

492. Cumont, *TM,* II, p. 236, Fig. 67; p. 239, Fig. 70; du Mesnil, *TMP,* p. 73, Fig. 32. One wonders if it is not the banderole of the heavens that envelops the rayed head and the body of Helios, seated in his chariot in the pediment of a distyle temple, shown on a bronze relief featuring Zeus Sabazios; cf. Cook, *Zeus,* I, p. 392 n. 1 and Pl. XXVII.

493. Bellinger, *Dura,* VI, 1936, Pl. XVIII:967.

494. Du Mesnil, *TMP,* p. 135, Fig. 96.

495. Du Mesnil, *TMP,* p. 71, Fig. 29.

496. For examples of the banderole signifying the arc of the heavens directly on the head of Tyché-Atargatis-Venus, cf. Dussaud, *Myth. Syr.,* p. 103, Fig. 26; Ronzevalle, *MUSJ,* XXI, 1937-38, p. 111, Fig. 14; pp. 122-126 and Pls. XXVIII:7; XXXII:3, 4; XXXIII: 1, 4-6; XXXIV:5; XXXV:3a-c; XLVII:2a-5b; Seyrig, *Syria,* X, 1929, Pls. LXXXII:2; LXXXIII:3 and p. 329; du Mesnil, *TMP,* p. 72.

497. Ronzevalle, *MUSJ,* XXI, 1937-38, Pl. XXXIII:1.

498. Du Mesnil, *TMP,* pp. 150-163; Cumont, *Danseur d'Antibes,* pp. 21-24; Virolleaud, *Syria,* V, 1924, pp. 45-49.

499. Du Mesnil, *TMP,* p. 111, Fig. 68; see pp. 242-243.

500. Minns, *S.Gr.,* pp. 484-485 and Pl. II:6-9.

501. Minns, *S.Gr.,* pp. 451-454, 483-487.

502. Minns, *S.Gr.,* Pl. II:1, 3, 4, 5.

503. Minns, *S.Gr.,* Pl. III:2, 9.

504. Minns, *S.Gr.,* Pl. VII:16.

505. See p. 136.

506. Minns, *S.Gr.,* pp. 332, 373, Fig. 277.

507. Minns, *S.Gr.,* pp. 324-328.

508. Wiegand, *Baalbek,* I, p. 115 and Pls. 111-114.

509. Wiegand, *Petra,* Fig. 38 on p. 45 and pp. 47-48.

510. Minns, *S.Gr.,* p. 426, Fig. 316.

511. Minns, *S.Gr.,* pp. 464-470.

512. See n. 499.

513. *BM,* No. 964, LV C (50); Brunn-Bruckmann, *Denkmäler,* Pl. 138; Arndt, *Register,* p. 9, no. 138.

514. *Ency. Brit.,* 1953, under "Aquileia."

515. Cumont, *RO,* pp. 98-99; *MM,* pp. 67, 73, 213 and Frontispiece; Casson, *TAPA,* LXXXI, 1950, pp. 43-56.

516. Parr, *ADAJ,* IV-V, 1960, p. 135.

517. Glueck, *AASOR,* XVIII-XIX, 1939, pp. 45, 46, Fig. 25; Parr, *ADAJ,* IV-V, 1960, pp. 134-136 and Pl. XV:1.

518. Lippold, *Skulpturen vat.*, III, Text, pp. 130-132; III:1, Pl. 39, Fig. 547; Picard, *RA*, X, 1937, pp. 244-249; *CRAI*, X, 1937, pp. 440-450.

519. Torrey, *Berytus*, IX, 1949, pp. 48-49.

520. Comfort, *BA*, II, 1939, p. 9.

521. Avi-Yonah and Negev, *ILN*, Nov. 26, 1960, p. 944.

522. Cooke, *N-S Inscr.*, pp. 256, 259; Robinson, *Sarcophagus*, p. 388.

523. Lippold, *Skulpturen vat.*, III Text, p. 131; *HGR*, II, p. 185.

524. *ILN*, Oct. 16, 1954, p. 637; Picard, *CRAI*, X, 1937, p. 449.

525. *ILN*, Oct. 16, 1954, p. 637.

526. This was suggested by Eleanor K. Vogel, Cincinnati, to Dr. Herminia Speier, Vatican Museum, who agreed the horns were added.

527. Bellido, *AA*, LVI, 1941, p. 248, Fig. 43 and p. 250; Picard, *RA*, XXVII, 1947, pp. 195-199; Chatelain, *Maroc*, pp. 60-66.

528. Dussaud, *CRAI*, 1943, p. 155.

529. Bellido, *AA*, LVI, p. 250; Picard, *RA*, XXVII, 1947, p. 195.

530. Chatelain, *Maroc*, p. 60, speaks of fishes instead of dolphins. I cannot make out, furthermore, the birds he sees in the hair of the god of Lixus. Actually, from the photograph I believe I see two more dolphins in profile than I have mentioned in the text, namely one at the top right side of the god's head and almost touching the back of the right crab's claw, and another near the top left side of his head, above and to the right of the dolphin whose beak is pointed towards the left eye of the god.

531. Ingholt, *Hatra*, p. 33 and Pl. VII:2.

532. Toynbee, *Art*, p. 163 and Fig. 248.

533. Brunn, *Götterideale*, p. 37; see p. 354.

534. Cf. Toynbee, *Art*, p. 175 and Pl. 134 for another mask of Oceanos on a bronze jug-handle from Lon-don, and pp. 196-197 and Pl. 207 for an Oceanos head on a second-century A.D. mosaic pavement from Verulamium, Hertfordshire, England.

535. Roscher, *Lexikon*, III, I, col. 818, Fig. 2; Clarac, *Musée de Sculpture*, Pl. 355, Nr. 214.

536. Picard, *RA*, XXXVII, 1951, pp. 231-233 and Fig. 11 on p. 232; Guey, *Revue Africaine*, 94, 1950, pp. 51-84 and Pl. II:2.

537. Virolleaud, *Syria*, V, 1924, p. 119 and Pl. XXXIII:1; cf. Van Buren, *AJA* 67:4, Oct. 1963, Pl. 95:6 and p. 402; see Pl. 19.

537a. Reinach, *Répertoire*, III, p. 136, no. 2.

537b. Reinach, *Répertoire*, III, p. 136, no. 1.

538. Matthews and Cook, *CS*, Pl. 81.

539. *EPH-Tel*, p. 137.

539a. *EPH-Tel*, p. 132.

540. Stebbins, *Dolphin*, pp. 84-85.

541. Lassus, in Elderkin, *Antioch*, p. 115, Fig. 1; cf. Cook, *Zeus*, 1, p. 752, Fig. 552; Kantor, *JNES*, XXI, 1962, pp. 97-99 and Fig. 7.

542. Morey, *Mosaics*, p. 34 and Pl. X.

543. Cumont, *Doura*, *Texte*, pp. 238-239; *Atlas*, Pls. LXXXVI, LXXXVIII; see p. 347.

544. Von Mercklin, *Berytus*, V, 1938, pp. 25-46 and Pls. VII-XIII.

544a. See p. 243.

545. Toynbee, *Art*, p. 170 and Pl. 117, p. 175 and Pl. 134; pp. 196-197 and Pl. 207.

546. Toynbee, *Art*, p. 163 and Pl. 248; pp. 161-164 and Pl. 96; pp. 153-154 and Pl. 73.

546a. Mellink, *AJA*, 67:2, 1963, p. 188 and Pl. 42:21.

546b. Miller, *Greek Horizons*, p. 118; Bonnard, *Les Dieux de la Grèce*, p. 47.

546c. Van Buren, *AJA*, 67:4, 1963, pp. 400, 401 and Pls. 89:3, 95:6.

546d. Berenson, Bernard in Beny, *Thrones*, p. 105 and Pl. 97.

547. Bechi, *Real Museo Borbonico*, V, Pl. XLIII, pp. 3-4; Ainé and

Barré, *HP,* pp. 155-158 and Pl. 80, facing p. 155; Reinach, *Répertoire,* V, p. 215-3; Schreiber, *Toreutik,* p. 345, Fig. 85. For the goats' heads, cf. Rostovtzeff, *Iranians and Greeks,* Pl. XII:A; Minns, *S.Gr.,* p. 211, Fig. 10; vanden Berghe, *Iran,* Pl. 141: a, c, d.

548. Rostovtzeff, *Iranians and Greeks,* p. 54 and Pl. XIV, facing p. 66; Cook, *Zeus,* I, pp. 611, 612, Fig. 480; Richter, *Sculpture,* pp. 62, 370, Fig. 76; Dussaud, *Syria,* XXIII, 1942-1943, p. 36, Fig. 11 and p. 59; Avi-Yonah, *QDAP,* XIII, 1948, p. 158, Fig. 50; Macrobius, *Saturnalia,* I, pp. 17, 66-67.

549. For examples of Medusa with head-wings and serpents, see Abdul Hak, *AAS,* IV-V, p. 176 and Pls. V, VI, from Nawa in the Hauran; Virolleaud, *Syria,* V, 1924, p. 120 and Pl. XXXI:4, facing p. 118, from the Hauran; Al Asil, *ILN,* Dec. 18, 1954, p. 1116, Fig. 5; Dec. 25, 1954, p. 1160, Fig. 2—both from Hatra.

550. See p. 465.

551. Schreiber, *Toreutik,* I, pp. 344, 345, Fig. 86 (=Nr. 69*).

552. Toynbee, *Art,* p. 163; Curb, *PSAS,* LXVI, pp. 297-298, 297, Fig. 8.

553. Picard, *RA,* XXXVII, 1951, pp. 231-232, Fig. II; Toynbee, *Art,* p. 163.

554. Toynbee, *Art,* p. 163.

555. Hinks, *Catalogue,* p. 75, Fig. 82.

556. Cook, *Zeus,* II:1, pp. 577, 787, 791, 795, 804.

557. D'Orsi, *ILN,* Nov. 6, 1954, p. 803, Fig. 6, from Rome.

558. Vermeule, *Berytus,* XIII, pp. 3-82, and Pls. II-XXVI; Goodenough, *Symbols,* VII, Figs. 56, 235, 238, 285, 287, 289, 291.

559. Toynbee, *Art,* pp. 161-164, 169-171, 199 and Pls. 96, 117, 223, 248; al Asil, *ILN,* Dec. 18, 1954, p. 1116, Fig. 5; Dec. 25, 1954, p. 1160, Fig. 2; Bacon, *DFH,* Pl. 50.

560. Abdul Hak, *AAS,* IV-V, p. 176 and Pls. V, VI.

561. Dunand, *Soueïda,* pp. 67-68 and Pl. XXXI:133-135; Butler, *PAES,* II, A, 7, 1919, pp. 442-444 and Ills. 387D, 388D.

562. A beautiful classical example of this type is represented by the Medusa Pondanini of the end of the fifth century B.C. that is in the Munich Glyptothèque, shown in *HGR,* II, 1948, p. 247.

563. Parr, *PEQ,* 89, 1957, p. 10 and Pl. VIIIB. I am indebted to Parr for making available to me this photograph and others published in his article, pp. 5-16. The capital of this relief is 0.58 m. at the base and 0.48 m. high.

564. *PA,* I, p. 164, Fig. 190, no. 452; Horsfield, *QDAP,* VII, 1938, p. 41, Pl. LXXIV:1, 2.

565. Seyrig, *Syria,* XIV, 1933, pp. 257-259, Figs. 4, 5; du Mesnil, *TMP,* pp. 50, 238-239; Drower, *JAOS,* 1950, 70, pp. 309-312; Ingholt, *Hatra,* pp. 39-42.

566. Kantorowicz, *Gods in Uniform,* p. 379, Fig. 30; Cook, *Zeus,* I, pp. 604-633 and Fig. 480 on p. 612, where not only the Medusa head is visible on the front of his breastplate but apparently also a serpent entwined around his girdle—both being symbols of immortality. Beneath the bull upon which the deity is standing is an eagle, which was possessed with the quality of eternal youth, and which, as the messenger of the sun, transported the souls of the dead to their heavenly master, the king of the planets. See also du Mesnil, *TMP,* pp. 327, 422.

567. Al Asil, *ILN,* Dec. 25, 1954, p. 1160, Fig. 2; for a Greek example of the fifth century B.C., see Van Buren, *AJA,* 66, 1962, p. 401 and Pl. 117:18.

568. Al Asil, *ILN,* Dec. 18, 1954, p. 1116, Fig. 5; Kraeling, *City,* p. 216; Bacon, *DFH,* Pl. 50; Kan-

torowicz, *Gods in Uniform,* pp. 378-379 and Fig. 27; du Mesnil, *TMP,* pp. 326-327, Fig. 190.

569. For leaves on other deities, see Reinach, S., *Repertoire,* V, p. 214:1, 5; Neugebauer, *JDAI, Arch. Anz.,* 56, 1941, pp. 180-181; Cook, *Zeus,* II, pp. 392-400 and Pls. XXII, XXIII, for two Janiform busts with leaves on their faces.

Chapter XI

570. Alpers, *Dolphins,* pp. 22, 74, 136, 241; Aristotle, *Historia Animalium,* 521b, 566b; Stebbins, *Dolphin,* p. 4.

571. Alpers, *Dolphins,* pp. 13, 241; Stebbins, *Dolphin,* pp. 4-6; Pliny, *Nat. hist.,* IX:22, 25; see Aelian, *On the Characteristics of Animals,* X, 8. We are indebted to Deputy-Director V. Loevinson-Lessing of the State Hermitage Museum, Leningrad, for the photograph and permission to publish L. Lorenzetti's "Dead Boy on a Dolphin" (Pl. 9a). Mr. James Magrish sent me an article about it from *The London Times* (Literary Supplement), Oct. 25, 1963. Dr. John C. Lilly has shown me movies of a boy actually riding a dolphin at his experimental station in the Virgin Islands; cf. Lilly, "Dolphins."

572. Cook, *Zeus,* I, pp. 582-583; Cook, S. A., *RAPLA,* pp. 170-17: *SG,* pp. 52-54; see p. 382.

573. Dunand, *Soueïda,* pp. 13-14 and Pl. V:2; Avi-Yonah, *Or. Art,* p. 51; Stebbins, *Dolphin,* p. 83; also see p. 380.

574. Matthews and Cook, *CS,* Pl. 81; Stebbins, *Dolphin,* pp. 82-83, points out that Eros figures were frequently portrayed with dolphins.

575. *EPH-Tel,* II, p. 137.

575a. Alexander, "Aphrodite," pp. 241-251.

576. *SG,* pp. 71-73; Cook, *Zeus,* I, p. 583.

577. *Ency. Brit.,* 1953, under *Aphrodite.*

578. *EPH-Tel,* p. 132.

579. Clermont-Ganneau, *RHR,* 1919, 80, pp. 1-29. We are grateful to the Antikensammlungen, Munich, for permission to publish "The Dionysos Cup" by Exekias, c. 540 B.C., (Pl. 9B).

580. *RITD,* p. 32; *AASOR,* XVIII-XIX, pp. 1-5.

581. I Kings 9:26-28.

582. Acts 23:23-33; 24:27; 25:25; 26:2; 27:1-28:14; Casson, *TAPA,* LXXXI, pp. 43-56.

583. Kammerer, *Pétra,* p. 212.

584. Kammerer, *Pétra,* pp. 212-214; Josephus, *War,* I, 29, 3; *Antiq.,* XVI, 7, 6; 9, 1-4; 10, 5, 8, 9.

585. Kammerer, *Pétra,* pp. 210-211 and Fig. 12.

586. Kawerau and Rehm, *Milt,* pp. 387-389; Sillard, *From the Gracchi to Nero,* p. 344; Stebbins, *Dolphin,* p. 4.

587. Josephus, *Antiq.,* XVI, 7:6; 9:1.

588. Stebbins, *Dolphin,* p. 81.

589. *Ency. Brit.,* 1953, II, pp. 110-111; Stebbins, *Dolphin,* pp. 77-83; Roscher, *Lexikon,* I, col. 429.

590. Roscher, *Lexikon,* I, col. 429.

591. Cook, *Zeus,* II:1, p. 205, Fig. 144.

592. Acts 20:15-16.

593. Josephus, *Antiq.,* XVI, 9:3.

594. Kammerer, *Pétra,* p. 211, n. 1.

595. Casson, *TAPA,* LXXXI, 1950, pp. 43-56.

596. See p. 347; della Vida, *Clara Rhodos,* IX, pp. 139-148; Nöldeke, *ZDMG,* XXXVIII, pp. 144, 165; *CIS,* II, 1, 2, nos. 157-159, pp. 183-187; Cumont, *RO,* p. 99; Kammerer, *Pétra,* p. 211, n. 1.

597. *CIS,* II, 1, 2, no. 157, pp. 183-

184; Kammerer, *Pétra*, p. 450; Cumont, *OR*, p. 111 and n. 17 on p. 243.

598. Cumont, *OR*, p. 111; Avi-Yonah, *Or. Art*, p. 55, n. 46.

599. Eisenberg, *ECS*, p. 11, n. 22, p. 16, Pl. XI; Cumont, *Études*, p. 70, Fig. 30: "Les vents et le dauphin rappelent le passage de l'âme à travers les airs... jusqu'à... la zone éthérée du feu, où brillent les astres"; Minns, *S.Gr.*, pp. 451-454, 483-486 and Pls. II:1-4, 7-9; III:2, 9.

600. Dunand, *Soueïda*, pp. 13-14 and Pl. V:2; Avi-Yonah, *Or. Art*, p. 51; *IEJ*, 9:1, 1959, p. 9; Vaggi, *Aegyptus*, 17, 1937, pp. 34-36; Stebbins, *Dolphin*, p. 83; see p. 360.

601. Cumont, *Études*, p. 70, Fig. 30.

602. Goodenough, *Symbols*, III, Fig. 592; Butler, *PAES*, I, A, 1930, p. 26; Avi-Yonah, *QDAP*, XIII. pp. 156-157.

603. I am indebted to Professor N. Avigad of the Hebrew University for calling this Beit She'arim sarcophagus decoration to my attention and placing a photograph at my disposal; see *IEJ*, 9, 1959, pp. 210-211, Pl. 24B; see Goodenough, *Symbols*, V, Fig. 10, for dolphins with a garland on their tails depicted on a Roman sarcophagus; III, Fig. 800, for a dolphin on a sarcophagus fragment from Catacomb Vigna Randanini, Rome; III, Figs. 84, 85, 592, for other dolphins in a mosaic floor in the courtyard of Catacomb no. 11 of Beth She'arim; see pp. 243, 352.

604. For Byzantine representations in late Hellenistic-Semitic tradition of bronzed Erotes on dolphins and of Ino and her child Melicertes on an ichthyocentaur, cf. Pelekanides, *Benaki*, pp. 37-62.

605. Stocks, *Berytus*, IV:1, 1937, pp. 33-34; Seyrig, *Syria*, XV, 1934, pp. 169-170.

606. Minns, *S.Gr.*, pp. 451-454, 483-486 and Pl. II:1-4, 7-9; Eisenberg, *ECS*, 40, p. 12, no. 22, suggests that the dolphins symbolized resurrection and salvation in Early Christian art; see pp. 242, 339.

607. Stebbins, *Dolphin*, p. 9.

608. Picard, *CL*, II, pp. 274-276.

609. Diodorus, *B.h.*, II:4; Cumont in Pauly-Wissowa, IV, under *Dea Syria*, col. 2246.

610. Lucian, *De Dea Syria*, 14; *SG*, p. 54, nn. 26-27; Cook, *Zeus*, I, pp. 582-583; Cook, S. A., *RAPLA*, pp. 170-175; Albright, *ARI*, pp. 77-78.

611. Lucian, *De Dea Syria*, §47, 48, *SG*, pp. 81-83.

612. Wotschitzky, *Archaeology*, XIV:3, 1961, pp. 206-211; Acts 19:27-28: "The great goddess Diana . . . whom all Asia and the world worshippeth... great is Diana of the Ephesians"; du Mesnil, *TMP*, p. 72, Fig. 30. The large statue in the round of Artemis of Ephesus has been found at Caesarea by the Italian Archaelogical Mission from Milan, but has not yet been published. It is on display in the Museum of the Israel Department of Antiquities.

613. Jucker, *Blätterkelch*, p. 189 and Tafelband, Abb. 147.

614. Halliday, *AAA*, XIX:1-2, March, 1932, p. 27; Wotschitzky, *Archaeology*, XIV:3, 1961, pp. 206-211 and Fig. 3; Kantor, *JNES*, VII, 1948, pp. 46-51 and Pls. IV, V, Figs. 1-3; Acts 19:27-28.

614a. Laws, G. A., *AJA*, 65:1, 1961, pp. 31-35 and Plates 21-22.

615. Goldman, *AK*, III, p. 53, Fig. 1; p. 56, Fig. 6; see du Mesnil, *TMP*, p. 72, Fig. 30.

616. Halliday, *AAA*, XIX:1-2, March, 1932, p. 23; Strabo, *Geography*, IV, 180; Pauly-Wissowa, II, 1, p. 1385.

617. Goldman, *AK*, III, p. 56, Figs. 4, 5; de Cou, *AJA*, XV, 1911, pp. 165-167 and Figs. 3-5.

618. Goldman, *AK*, III, p. 56, Figs. 4, 5.

619. Parrot, *Syria,* XXVIII, 1951, pp. 57-61; *Tello,* p. 74, Pl. III; Frankfort, *JNES,* VIII, 1949, p. 60.

620. Borovka, *SA,* p. 55 and Pl. 21A.

621. Habachi, *JNES,* XX:1, 1961, pp. 47-49.

622. Gaudin and Collignon, *CRAI,* II, 1904, pp. 709-710, Pl. V; see p. 332.

623. Seyrig, *Syria,* XV, 1934, p. 168, n. 4; de Saulcy, *Numismatique de la Terre Sainte,* p. 176, Pl. IX:3.

624. Gaudin and Collignon, *CRAI,* II, 1904, pp. 710-711; Habachi, *JNES,* XX, 1961, p. 49; Lullies and Hirmer, *Greek Sculpture,* 1957 ed.: Pls. 239, 240, 242, 243, 246; 1960 ed.: Pls. 251-259; *JDAI, Arch. Anz.,* 56, 1941, p. 846, Fig. 1.

625. Cumont in Pauly-Wissowa, under *Dea Syria,* col. 2241; *SG,* pp. 52-53, n. 25; Cook, *Zeus,* I, pp. 583-584, n. 4; Baur, *Dura,* III, 1932, p. 113, n. 70; IV, pp. 45-46; Stocks, *Berytus,* IV, 2, 1937, pp. 33-34.

626. Cumont in Pauly-Wissowa, under *Dea Syria,* col. 2241.

627. Diodorus, *B.h.,* II:4, 3; Cumont in Pauly-Wissowa, under *Dea Syria,* col. 2241; see also above, n. 625.

628. Cook, S.A., *RAPLA,* pp. 170-171 and Pl. XXXIII:20, 21; Hogarth, *Hittite Seals,* p. 35, no. 170; Eisen, *Seals,* nn. 86-88; *ANEP,* pp. 216, 329 and Fig. 665; pp. 223, 334 and Fig. 706; Albright, *ARI,* pp. 77-78; Baur, *Dura,* III, 1932, p. 113, mentions a Palmyrene tessera in private possession, on one side of which is depicted an enthroned Atargatis with a large fish in front of her; Neumann, *The Great Mother,* p. 276 and Pl. 134, which shows that the skirt of the seventh-century B.C. Boeotian "Lady of the Beasts" consists of a fish and waves; du Mesnil, *TMP,* p. 136, Fig. 98, Inman, Thomas, *Ancient Pagan and Modern Christian Symbolism,* Pl. I and p. 68, Fig. 97.

629. Cumont, *OR,* pp. 117, 245-246 and nn. 35-37; Cook, S.A., *RAPLA,* pp. 172-173; Seyrig, *Syria,* X, 1929, p. 330, n. 3; Baur, *Dura,* III, 1932, p. 108, n. 35; p. 113, n. 70; IV, 1933, p. 46.

630. Cumont in Pauly-Wissowa, under *Dea Syria,* cols. 2241-2242. In addition to Ascalon and Hierapolis, such sacred ponds existed apparently at Edessa, Smyrna, Aleppo, Doliche, Tripoli, Acco (Acre) and Memphis in Egypt; Stocks, *Berytus,* IV:2, 1938, p. 9.

631. *SG* §47, 48, pp. 81-83; Baur, *Dura,* III, 1932, p. 133, n. 163; see p. 360.

632. Diodorus, *B.h.,* II:4.

633. Evidence of such a sacred pond has been discovered at Rahle, a Druze village east of Damascus, where a Nabataean temple may have existed; see Mouterde, *MUSJ,* XXXVI:2, 1959, pp. 79-80.

634. Ingholt, *Hatra,* p. 33 and Pl. VII: 2; see p. 144.

635. Stebbins, *Dolphin,* p. 86.

Chapter XII

636. Morehart, *Berytus,* XII, 1956-1958, p. 74, Fig. 27; Ingholt, *Berytus,* III, 1936, pp. 114-115 and Pl. XXIII:1.

637. Ingholt, *Berytus,* III, 1936, pp. 114-115, Pl. XXIII; du Mesnil, *TMP,* p. 215, Figs. 143, 144; pp. 368-369 and Figs. 201, 202; Brown, *Dura,* VII-VIII, 1939, pp. 163-164.

638. Du Mesnil, *TMP,* p. 145, Fig. 111:2.

639. Cook, *Zeus* I, pp. 619-620 and Pl. XXXIV is the closest likeness; pp. 709-710; II, p. 707, Fig. 640; III, 1, p. 716, Fig. 530; Barrelet, *Syria,* XXXII, 1955, pp. 226-228, Fig. 2.

640. Cook *Zeus,* I, pp. 616-617, Fig. 488; Dussaud, *Syria,* XXIII, 1942-43, pp. 45-46, Fig. 6:1.

641. Cook, *Zeus,* I, pp. 117-186, 272, 558-559; Newell, *Num. Notes and Monographs,* no. 84, p. 78, coin 115; p. 95, coin 147; Metzger, *BA,* XI:4, 1948, p. 73, Fig. 3, and p. 75; Baur, *Dura,* III, 1932, p. 101, Pl. XIV; p. 112 and Pl. XIX:2, Brown, *Dura,* VII-VIII, 1939, pp. 258, 260, 261, 296, 297 and Pls. XXXIII, XXXIV; Hopkins, *Dura,* V, 1934, p. 110; Horsfield, *QDAP,* IX, 1942, Pls. XLIII-no. 390, XLV-no. 426; Ingholt, *Hatra,* p. 34, no. 1; Seyrig, *Syria,* X, 1929, p. 327, n. 2 and Pl. LXXXII:2; Dussaud, *Syria,* XXIII, 1942-43, pp. 45-46, 56, 57, n. 4; Ronzevalle, *MUSJ,* XXI, 1937, Pl. XXXII:4; Van Buren, *Symbols,* pp. 12-14; Avi-Yonah, *IEJ,* 9, 1959, p. 10; 2, 1952, p. 121; Neumann, *The Great Mother,* pp. 261-262; Albright, *ARI,* p. 74; Macrobius, *Saturnalia,* 1, 23, 10.

642. Ingholt, *Hatra,* pp. 33, 34 and Pl. VI:1; Baur, *Dura,* III, 1932, pp. 101, 115; Hopkins, *Dura,* V, 1934, pp. 59-60, Pl. XX:2; Cook, *Zeus,* I, p. 586; *SG,* p. 70, Fig. 7.

643. At Nabataean Soueïda, under the name of Hera, she wears a mural crown and holds two stalks of grain in her right hand and a scepter in her left; cf. Dunand, *Soueïda,* p. 12, Pl. IV, Fig. 1.

644. See n. 642.

645. De Villard, *Ahnas,* pp. 49 and 50, Pls. 31 and 32.

646. See p. 534.

647. Daremberg et Saglio, *Dict.,* p. 836a, Fig. 7452; Cook, *Zeus* II, pp. 205, Fig. 144, pp. 256, 459; du Mesnil, *TMP,* p. 287, Fig. 176.

648. On a relief from Si'a, now in the house of the Sheikh of 'Iré, part of a crescent moon appears above the right shoulder of Luna, touching the side of her torch to the right of it; cf. Pl. 138, sent me by Schlumberger, which shows reliefs of Luna and Sol, and of an eagle above them and two masks on either side of them; see p. 472.

649. Baur, *Dura,* III, 1932, pp. 116-117, 137-139, Pls. XVIII:6-8; XIX:2; Ronzevalle, *MUSJ,* XXI, 1937-1938, pp. 89-91 and Pl. XXVII:1; du Mesnil, *TMP,* p. 139, Fig. 103.

650. Baur, *Dura,* III, 1932, pp. 116, 137 and n. 184; Cook, *Zeus,* 1, pp. 616-617, Figs. 487, 488; p. 193, Fig. 142; Dussaud, *Syria* XXIII, 1942-43, p. 46, Fig. 6:1; at Sidon, too, according to Lucian, Astarte (Atargatis) appears as a moon-goddess, cf. *SG,* pp. 43-44 and art. 4; Baur, *Dura,* III, 1932, pp. 116, 135-137 and Pls. XVIII, XIX; Brown, *Dura,* VII-VIII, 1939, p. 167, Pl. XXXI:2; Ingholt, *Hatra,* p. 13; du Mesnil, *TMP,* p. 99, Fig. 54:1; p. 135, Fig. 96.

651. Ingholt, *Hatra,* pp. 10, 11, 24 and Pl. III:11; p. 11 and Pl. II:2; Dussaud, *Syria,* XXIII, 1942-1943, p. 55, Fig. 10; du Mesnil, *TMP,* p. 98, Fig. 51; p. 109, Fig. 66; p. 134, Fig. 95:5-9; p. 138, Fig. 100.

652. Ingholt, *Hatra,* p. 10, n. 15; Cumont, *Syria,* VIII, 1927, Pl. XXXVIII:3; pp. 163-167.

653. *SG,* p. 71, §32; Baur, *Dura,* III, 1932, pp. 120-121.

654. Daremberg et Saglio, *Dict.,* III, 2 under *Luna,* pp. 1386-1392.

655. Baur, *Dura,* III, 1932, pp. 120-121, Pl. XIV; pp. 117-120; Pl. XIX: 1; p. 138; Brown, *Dura,* VII-VIII, 1939, pp. 260-262 and Pl. XXXIV; Schlumberger, *JDAI, Arch. Anz.,* 50, p. 616, Fig. 50; du Mesnil, *TMP,* p. 132, Fig. 92; p. 133, Fig. 93; *SG,* frontispiece, p. 27, Fig. 5; p. 70, Fig. 7; p. 72, Fig. 8; Dunand, *Soueïda,* p. 12, Pl. IV, Fig. 1.

656. Baur, *Dura,* III, 1932, pp. 117-118 and Pl. XIX:1.

657. Du Mesnil, *TMP,* p. 132, Fig. 92; p. 133, Fig. 93; pp. 425-430; Ingholt, *Hatra,* pp. 18-23.

658. Du Mesnil, *TMP*, p. 111, Fig. 68.

659. Du Mesnil, *TMP*, p. 427, Fig. 222: H; p. 175, Fig. 127.

660. Du Mesnil, *TMP*, p. 280, Fig. 172; p. 281, Fig. 173; Schlumberger, *Palmyrène*, Pl. XXXV, 2.

661. Du Mesnil, *TMP*, p. 215, Figs. 143, 144; p. 99, Fig. 53; Rostovtzeff, *Dura Art*, frontispiece.

662. Baur, *Dura*, III, 1932, pp. 116, 137; Brown, *Dura*, VII-VIII, 1939, pp. 260-262, Pl. XXXIV; Cumont, *Doura*, p. 110 and Pl. LI; Lippold, *Skulpturen vat.*, III:1, Pl. 48, Fig. 546a.

663. Baur, *Dura*, III, 1932, p. 138; Ingholt, *Hatra*, p. 13; Fisher, in Kraeling, *Gerasa*, p. 137.

664. Baur, *Dura*, III, 1932, p. 138; Cumont, *Doura*, p. 199 and Pl. LXXXII:1.

665. Avi-Yonah and Negev, *ILN*, Nov. 26, 1960, p. 945, Fig. 3.

666. Rostovtzeff, *CC*, Pl. XXX:1, facing p. 184.

667. Gressmann, *AOB*, p. 80 and Pl. CX, Fig. 263; Cook, *Zeus* I, pp. 752-753 and Figs. 551, 552; Dussaud, *Syria* I, 1920, pp. 8-10; Lassus, in Elderkin, *Antioch* I, pp. 114, 115; Cumont, *Syria* II, 1921, pp. 44-45; Picard, *CRAI*, 1937, p. 449; Stebbins, *Dolphin*, p. 86; Reinach, *Répertoire* V, p. 492: 2-5; *HGR*, II, 1948, p. 367b; Jucker, *Blätterkelch*, p. 158 and Tafelband, Abb. 41.

668. Dalman, *Petra*, pp. 51-52; Rostovtzeff, *CC*, pp. 43, 79.

669. Ma'ayeh, *ADAJ* IV-V, 1960, p. 114 and Pl. III:1.

670. Abel, *Géographie, II*, p. 382.

671. Baur, *Dura*, III, 1932, p. 138; Kraeling, *Gerasa*, pp. 147, 490, no. 349; Bellinger, *Num. Notes and Monographs*, No. 81, p. 30, nos. 45-46; Hill, *BMC, Greek Coins*, XXXIII-XXXV, pl. V:4-6; Ma'ayeh, *ADAJ*, IV-V, 1960, p. 116.

672. Sukenik, *JPOS* II, 1922, pp. 104, 105, Figs. 1, 2; p. 108.

673. Rostovtzeff, in *MS*, I, p. 288; Daremberg et Saglio, *Dict.*, II:2, p. 1266b, Fig. 3237; Richter, *Sculpture*, p. 295 and Figs. 753-755; Bieber, *Sculpture*, Fig. 102 and p. 40; Seyffert, *Dictionary*, p. 568, Fig. 15; Cook, S.A., *RAPLA*, p. 191; Metzger, *BA* XI, Dec. 1948, p. 73, Fig. 3; p. 75, Fig. 4; Hill, *BMC, Greek Coins*, p. XCIII, Pl. XII:19-22.

674. Cook, *Zeus*, I, p. 584; *SG*, pp. 20-21, Figs. 1-8; Ingholt, *Hatra*, pp. 18-19 and Pl. IV; Baur, *Dura* III, 1932, p. 137.

675. Dunand, *Soueïda*, p. 12, Pl. IV.

676. Ingholt, *Berytus*, III, 1936, p. 114 and Pl. XXIII:1, p. 115 n. 250; it is noteworthy that in the paintings in the Temple of the Palmyrene Gods at Dura, both the Tyché of Palmyra and the Tyché of Dura are depicted side by side; cf. Baur, *Dura* III, 1932, p. 137; Cumont, *Doura*, pp. 110-111 and Pl. I; Rostovtzeff, *CC*, pp. 203-205. The Gad of Palmyra is also portrayed as Tyché with the mural crown, whose "three towers are enriched with incised pentagons, doubtless representing jewels in their settings"; cf. Brown, *Dura*, VII-VIII, 1939, pp. 260-262 and Pl. XXXIV; Ipser, *VA*, p. 102; Collart, *AAS* VII, 1957, p. 85 and Pl. VIII:3.

677. Baur, *Dura* III, 1932, p. 138: "At Dura itself was found a statuette of Fortuna . . . according to a coin-type of that place, rendering (in Greek characters) Artemis, Tyché, Gerason"; Brown, *Dura*, VII-VIII, 1939, pp. 163-165 and Pl. XXXI:1; pp. 260-262, Pl. XXXIV. Brown describes this relief on p. 164 as that of "Atargartis-Astarte, *paredros* of Adonis. In her customary character as Ba'alat, Gadda of the city, she wears the mural crown of Tyché as at Hierapolis"; Rostovtzeff, in *MS*, I, Pl. II, facing p. 284; *Dura* VII-VIII, 1939, pp. 163-165 and

Pl. XXXI:1; pp. 260-262 and Pl. XXXIV.

678. Du Mesnil, *TMP*, p. 326, Fig. 190; Kantorowicz, *Gods in Uniform*, p. 378, Fig. 27; Al Asil, *ILN*, Dec. 18, 1954, p. 1116, Fig. 6.

679. Cf. reference to the Tyché of Rome in Lieberman, *HJP*, p. 134; Lippold, *Skulpturen vat.*, III:I, *Text*, pp. 128-130; *Plates*, Pl. 48, Fig. 546a.

680. Ghirshman, *Iran*, pp. 222-232, 266-268.

681. Ghirshman, *Iran*, p. 266.

682. Du Mesnil, *TMP*, p. 326, Fig. 190; Kantorowicz, *Gods in Uniform*, pp. 378-379 and Fig. 27; Al Asil, *ILN*, Dec. 18, 1954, p. 1116, Figs. 5, 6; p. 1117, Fig. 8.

683. Al Asil, *ILN*, Dec. 18, 1954, p. 1117, Fig. 10.

684. Al Asil, *ILN*, Nov. 10, 1951, p. 765, Fig. 7; Nov. 17, 1951, p. 806, Fig. 9; Dec. 25, 1954, p. 1161, Fig. 6; Andrae, *Hatra*, II, pp. 154, 158 and Pl. XIX; Ghirshman, *Bichapour*, II, p. 131, Fig. 37 and Pl. XV:5,9.

685. Al Asil, *ILN*, Nov. 17, 1951, p. 806, Fig. 1; p. 807, Figs. 3, 7, 10, 11; Dec. 18, 1954, p. 1117, Figs. 9, 11; Dec. 25, 1954, p. 1160, Figs. 2, 3; p. 1161, Figs. 7, 8, 9; Ingholt, *Hatra*, pp. 8-9 and Pl. 1-2; p. 11 and Pl. II:2; pp. 10-11, 24 and Pl. III:1; pp. 12, 13 and Pl. III:2; p. 16 and Pl. III:3; pp. 24, 33 and Pl. VI:1; pp. 24, 29 and Pl. VI:3; pp. 24, 43 and Pl. VII:1; pp. 32-34, 43 and Pl. VII:2; pp. 35-37, 42-43 and Pl. VII:3.

686. *ILN*, Nov. 17, 1951, p. 806, Fig. 8; Kantorowicz, *Gods in Uniform*, p. 379, Fig. 28; Ingholt, *Hatra*, pp. 22-24 and Pl. VI:2.

687. Metzger, *BA*, XI, Dec. 1948, p. 73, Fig. 3.

688. Kantorowicz, *Gods in Uniform*, pp. 378-379.

689. Ma'ayeh, *ADAJ*, IV-V, 1960, p. 114 and Pl. III:1; see n. 671.

690. Kraeling, *Gerasa*, pp. 36-40; Rostovtzeff, *CC*, pp. 61-62.

691. Avi-Yonah, *IEJ*, 9:1, 1959, p. 12.

692. Glueck, *AASOR*, XVIII-XIX, p. 141; XXV-XXVIII, p. 14; *OSJ*, pp. 12, 112, 193; *RITD*, pp. 89, 196.

693. Rostovtzeff, *CC*, pp. 27, 61-62; Cook, *Zeus*, I, pp. 549-550; Avi-Yonah, *IEJ*, 9:1, 1959, pp. 5, 9; see p. 69.

694. Cook, *Zeus*, I, pp. 272, 551-552, n. 11; 709-710, 745, 752-753.

695. Cook, *Zeus* I, pp. 501-502 and Pl. XXXI, 502-503 n. 7, 598 n. 1 and Fig. 461, p. 670; Dunand, *Soueïda*, p. 37 and Pl. VII:42, pp. 34-35 and Pl. XIV:39, p. 84 and Pl. XXXVI:B.

696. Dunand, *Soueïda*, Pl. XIV:39, 40 and pp. 34-36; cf. Pl. VII:42.

697. Du Mesnil, *TMP*, p. 54, Fig. 10; p. 55, Fig. 11; pp. 80-81, Fig. 38; p. 106, Fig. 62; p. 110, Fig. 67; p. 111, Fig. 68; p. 319, Fig. 186; Ronzevalle, *MUSJ* XXI, 1937, pp. 97-140 and Pls. XXVII-XXVIII; Dussaud, *Syria*, XXIII, 1942-43, pp. 45-49, Figs. 6-8.

697a. Musil, *AP*, Edom I, Figs. 113-114, *PA* 1, p. 337, no. 468.

698. Cook, *Zeus* I, p. 756; III:2, pp. 1085-1086, Fig. 868; pp. 1158-1159; Drower, *JAOS*, 70, 1950, pp. 309-310; Cumont, *Syria*, II, 1921, pp. 43-45; de Witte and Lenormant, *GA* III, 1877, pp. 50-57 and Pls. 8, 9; V, 1879, pp. 1-6 and Pls. 1, 2; Roscher, *Lexikon*, III, under "Planeten," cols. 2538, 2539; Brown, *AJA*, XLIII, 1939, pp. 286-288; Seyrig, *Syria*, XIV, 1933, pp. 253-260; XV, 1934, pp. 155-186.

699. Cumont, *Doura*, p. 110.

700. Cook, *Zeus*, I, p. 752, Figs. 551, 552; pp. 753-754; II:2, pp. 1051-1052 and Fig. 909; III:2, pp. 1085-1086 and Fig. 868; pp. 1158-59; Cook S.A., *RAPLA*, p. 166 and Pl. XXXIII:12; Seyrig, *Syria*, XIII, 1932, p. 59; XIV, 1933, pp.

255, 258, Fig. 5; *BMC—Engraved Gems,* no. 1668, Pl. 22; Cumont, *Syria* II, 1921, pp. 40-45.

701. See p. 433.

702. Roscher, *Lexikon* III:1, col. 1468, Fig. 26.

703. Cook, *Zeus,* I, pp. 753-754.

704. Du Mesnil, *TMP,* p. 50, Fig. 5; Seyrig, *Syria,* XIV, 1933, p. 258, Fig. 5; Cumont, *RO,* p. 105, Fig. 7; see p. 435.

705. Cook, S.A., *RAPLA,* p. 207; Sukenik, *Beth Alpha,* p. 54; Avi-Yonah, *QDAP* III, 1934, pp. 124-126; V, 1936, pp. 24-25; Fitz-Gerald, *PEFQS,* 1931, pp. 62-70.

706. Hill, *London,* pp. 24-36, 47-49; Cook, *Zeus,* I, pp. 752-753; Roscher, *Lexikon,* IV, under Sterne: Tierkreis, col. 1446; Cumont, *Doura,* p. 110.

706a. See p. 465.

707. Campbell and Gute, *Dura,* VII-VIII, 1939, pp. 95-100; Cumont and Rostovtzeff, *Dura,* VII-VIII, 1939, p. 110; Cumont, *Syria,* II, 1921, pp. 44-45; *RO,* Pl. XII facing p. 140; p. 162; Brown, *AJA* XLIII:2, 1939, pp. 286-288; Seyrig, *Syria,* XIV, 1933, pp. 255-260; *BMB,* I, 1937, p. 92; Daremberg et Saglio, *Dict.,* V, p. 1049, Fig. 7588; p. 1051, Fig. 7590; p. 1052-1053, Fig. 7591; p. 1056, Fig. 7595; p. 1057, Figs. 7597, 7598; VI, p. 2123; Wotschitzky, *Archaeology,* 14, 1961, p. 207, Fig. 3 and p. 211.

708. Roscher, *Lexikon,* I, under Helios, col. 2002; Cook, *Zeus,* I, p. 516, Fig. 389; Cumont, *TM* II, Pl. VII, no. 251; *RO,* Pl. XII, facing p. 140, for zodiac in relief on a Heddernheim sculpture of Mith-ras slaying the bull. For similar zodiac on related Mithras relief at Osterburken on the Rhine, cf. Cumont, *TM,* Pl. VI, no. 246; Campbell and Gute, *Dura* VII-VIII, 1939, p. 95 and Pl. XXX; Cumont and Rostovtzeff, *Dura,* VII-VIII, 1939, p. 110 and Pl. XVIII:1, 2; Hill, *London,* fifth figure between pp. 120 and 121. For zodiac on Artemis of Ephesus, cf. Wotschitzky, *Archaeology,* 14, 1961, p. 207, Fig. 3 and p. 211.

709. Daremberg et Saglio, *Dict.,* V, p. 1049, Fig. 7588; p. 1051, Fig. 7590; pp. 1052-1053, Fig. 7591; p. 1057, Figs. 7597, 7598; Cook, *Zeus,* I, pp. 752-753, Figs. 551-553; Roscher, *Lexikon,* VI, col. 935; Dussaud, *Syria,* XXVII, 1950, p. 259, Fig. 5; Ainalov, *Art,* pp. 22-23 and Fig. 8. For a circular counter-clock-wise, second-century A.D. zodiac around a central sunken panel with a relief of Mithras slaying the bull, found in London, Eng-land, cf. the fourth figure between pp. 120 and 121, Hill, *London;* for the complex and unusual order of a circular counter-clock-wise zodiac on a second-cenutry A.D. mosaic from Sassoferrato, Italy, having the following order: Capricornus, Aquarius, Pisces, Taurus, Gemini, Cancer, Leo, Virgo, Aries, Sagittarius, Libra and Scorpio, cf. Cumont, *TM* II, p. 419, Fig. 350 and p. 420.

710. Morgenstern, *HUCA* X, 1935, pp. 3, 5, 74, 81-86; *JBL,* LXXX, 1961, p. 74; *VT,* X, 1960, p. 148; Cook, *Zeus,* I, pp. 419, 429, n. 3; Burkitt, *PGH,* p. 97; Langdon, *JRAS,* 1924, pp. 65-72; Sukenik, *Beth Alpha,* p. 38; Cumont, *RO,* p. 162; *Syria,* II, 1921, pp. 40-46; Avi-Yonah, *Or. Art,* p. 55; Brown, *AJA* XLIII, 1939, pp. 286-288; Daremberg et Saglio, *Dict.,* II, p. 831.

711. Cumont, *TM,* II, pp. 419, 420 and Fig. 350; *RO,* Pl. XII, facing p. 140; Hill, *London,* fourth and fifth figures between pp. 120-121; Cook, *Zeus,* I, p. 516, Fig. 389, pp. 752-753; Figs. 551-553; Roscher, *Lexikon,* VI, col. 935, Abb. 13; col. 970, Abb. 16; Dussaud, *Syria,* XXVII, 1950, p. 259, Fig. 5; Aina-lov, *Art,* p. 23, Fig. 8; Reinach, *Répertoire,* IV, p. 295, 1.

712. Daremberg et Saglio, *Dict.,* V, p. 1056, Fig. 7595; p. 1060; see p. 224.

713. Campbell and Gute, *Dura,* VII-VIII, 1939, p. 95; du Mesnil, *TMP,* p. 46, Fig. 3; p. 48, Fig. 4; p. 54, Fig. 8; p. 57, Fig. 13; p. 58, Figs. 14, 15.

714. Cook, *Zeus,* I, p. 616, Fig. 487.

715. Roscher, *Lexikon,* I, cols. 675-678, 690, 692; Cook, *Zeus,* I, p. 429, n. 3; Avi-Yonah, *Or. Art,* p. 55; Sourdel, *Hauran,* pp. 110-111.

716. Roscher, *Lexikon,* VI, col. 938.

717. Numbers 24:21.

718. Glueck, *AASOR,* XVIII-XIX, 1939, pp. 32, 34; *BASOR,* 69, 1938, p. 17; *OSJ,* p. 178; *RITD,* pp. 199, 224, 267; Dalman, *Petra,* pp. 57, 125, 134, 144, 147-148, 164-165, 179, 280; Sourdel, *Hauran,* pp. 62-63; see p. 86; du Mesnil, *TMP,* pp. 336-338, Fig. 194; p. 271, Fig. 169.

719. Cumont, *After Life,* pp. 203-205, 211-213.

720. Cook, *Zeus,* I, p. 616, Fig. 487.

721. Cf. Roscher, *Lexikon,* III:1, col. 158, Fig. 6.

722. Roscher, *Lexikon,* VI, col. 974.

723. Daremberg et Saglio, *Dict.,* p. 1056, mentions as a third and questionable possibility that the name of Pan may be one of those through whom Capricornus might be represented. Cf. also Roscher, *Lexikon,* III:1, col. 1348, Fig. 1; col. 1434, Figs. 13, 14; col. 1436, Fig. 15; col. 1438, Fig. 17; col. 1459, Fig. 22.

724. Roscher, *Lexikon,* VI, cols. 973-974.

725. Roscher, *Lexikon,* III:1, col. 1468, Fig. 26.

726. Roscher, *Lexikon,* VI, cols. 959-960.

727. Sarre und Herzfeld, *Iranische Felsreliefs,* pp. 84-85 and Taf. IX; see p. 211.

728. Cook, *Zeus,* I, p. 616, Fig. 487.

729. Roscher, *Lexikon,* IV, col. 1453.

730. Roscher, *Lexikon,* VI, col. 960.

731. Roscher, *Lexikon,* VI, col. 960; Cumont, *TM,* II, Pl. VII, monument 251.

732. Van de Waerdon, *AFO,* XVI, 1952-1953, p. 226 and Fig. 3.

733. Finegan, *LfAP,* pp. 259-260; Picard, *CRAI,* 1937, pp. 449-450; Lassus in Elderkin, *Antioch,* I, p. 114, n. 1 and p. 115, Fig. 1; Cook, *Zeus,* I, p. 752, Figs. 551, 552; cf. also Morey, *Mosaics,* p. 34 and Pl. X; see p. 352.

734. Cf. Dussaud, *Syria,* II, 1921, pp. 44-45; for a figurine of Isis-Tyché holding two cornucopias in her left hand and a rudder in her right hand, cf. *HGR,* II, 1948, p. 367b; cf. also Cook, *Zeus,* I, pp. 752-753 and Fig. 552; see p. 351.

735. *HGR,* II, 1948, p. 127a, bottom; see p. 288.

736. Halliday, *AAA,* XIX:1-2, 1932, pp. 23-27; cf. also Erim, *ILN,* Jan. 5, 1963, pp. 20-23.

737. Goodchild, *ILN,* Supplement, Dec. 14, 1957, p. 1034, panel no. 40; Stebbins, *Dolphin,* p. 84.

738. Contenau, *Syria,* V, 1924, Pl. XXXVI.

739. Avi-Yonah, *QDAP,* X, 1944, p. 115 and Pl. XXII:9.

740. Roscher, *Lexikon,* I, col. 429; see p. 248.

741. Rostovtzeff, *CC,* p. 178; Baur, *Dura,* III, 1932, p. 133.

742. See p. 391.

743. Roscher, *Lexikon,* VI, cols. 980-981; Baur, *Dura,* III, 1932, pp. 108, 113; cf. also above, p. 288.

744. Avi-Yonah and Negev, *ILN,* Nov. 26, 1960, p. 945, Fig. 3; see p. 332.

745. Cumont, *TM,* II, Pl. VII, no. 251.

746. Rostovtzeff, *DPPA,* p. 228, discusses the disproportion between large heads and short bodies of priest and god in the Dura stele of Aphlad.

747. Brown, *Dura,* VII-VIII, 1939, p. 261 and Pl. XXXIV; Avi-Yonah, *Or. Art,* pp. 49, 53; see p. 446. It needs to be noted that the general appearance and stance of this

Niké Caryatid of Khirbet Tannur is reflected in a graffito, not published, from Dura-Europos. It is described as showing a Niké "in front view wearing a floating dress. To right a palm branch. Her hands are lifted and support above her head a *tabula ansata* with the inscription NIKH..."; cf. Rostovtzeff, *Dura,* IV, 1933, p. 213, par. 8.

748. Grant, *The World of Rome,* Pl. 24 and pp. xi, 141.

749. Cicero, *De divinatione,* II, xlii, 89; Grant, *The World of Rome,* p. 141.

750. Dunand, *Soueïda,* p. 46 and Pl. XVII:64.

751. Dunand, *Soueïda,* p. 27 and Pl. X:d.

752. Dunand, *Soueïda,* Pl. XIX:88 and p. 54; Butler, *PAES,* II, A, 1919, pp. 130-132 for Kfer in the Southern Hauran; for Kafer, cf. Sourdel, *Hauran,* p. 36, n. 3; 70, n. 7.

753. Ingholt, *Hatra,* p. 33 and Pl. VII: 2.

754. Al-Asil, *ILN,* Dec. 25, 1954, p. 1161, Fig. 6.

755. Al-Asil, *ILN,* Dec. 18, 1954, p. 1116, Figs. 3, 4.

756. Al-Asil, *ILN,* Dec. 18, 1954, p. 1116, Fig. 4.

757. Rostovtzeff, *DPPA,* p. 234 and Fig. 46.

758. Cumont, *Doura,* p. 221 and Pl. LXXXIV:2, 4; Brown, *Dura,* VII-VIII, 1939, pp. 203-204 and Pl. XXII:5, 6; Al-Asil, *ILN,* Dec. 25, 1954, p. 1161, Fig. 6; Hinks, *Catalogue,* p. 76, no. 17a; p. 77, Fig. 83.

759. Cumont, *Doura,* pp. 101, 107.

760. Cumont, *Doura,* p. 115.

761. Brown, *Dura,* VII-VIII, 1939, p. 261 and Pl. XXXIV.

762. De Witte and Lenormant, *GA,* V, 1879, Pl. I and p. 2; see p. 413.

763. Ingholt, *Hatra,* p. 41, n. 3; De Witte, *GA,* II, 1877, pp. 83-84 and Pl. VIII:4, 5; Maass, *Tagesgötter,* p. 240 Fig. 27.

764. Johnson, *Dura,* II, 1931, pp. 78, 79, 82 and Pls. XLIV:2; XLV:1, 4; XLVI:2, 3; Nettleton, *Dura,* IV, 1933, pp. 255, 256 and Pls. XXV, XXVI.

765. Minns, *S.Gr.,* pp. 63, 167, 402.

766. Richter, *Sculpture,* pp. 59, 261 and Fig. 608.

767. Rostovtzeff, *Iranians and Greeks,* pp. 102, 142; *DPPA,* pp. 228-232; Rice, *The Scythians,* p. 144.

768. Dussaud, *Art phènicien,* p. 65 and Fig. 34.

769. Richter, *Sculpture,* Fig. 330; cf. Fig. 477.

770. Al-Asil, *ILN,* Nov. 17, 1951, p. 806, Fig. 9; Dec. 18, 1954, p. 1116, Figs. 5, 6; p. 1117, Fig. 9; Dec. 25, 1954, p. 1160, Fig. 4; p. 1161, Fig. 8; Ingholt, *Hatra,* Pls. VI:2, 3; VII:1 and p. 24.

771. Bieber, *Sculpture,* Fig. 653 and p. 153.

772. Bieber, *Sculpture,* Fig. 198 and p. 62; Richter, *Sculpture,* Fig. 737 and p. 285; Fig. 734 and p. 286.

773. Cf. Contenau, *MAO,* IV, 1947, p. 2253, Fig. 1278, for a winged bull from Susa; p. 2265, Fig. 1288, for a head of a Mede; p. 2264, Fig. 1287; Potratz, *Kunst,* Fig. 57, for an Assyrian bearded winged bull colossus; *ANEP,* p. 10, Figs. 26, 27; p. 71, Fig. 229; p. 175, Fig. 517; p. 177, Figs. 522, 526; p. 201, Figs. 614, 615; p. 202, Fig. 617; p. 212, Figs. 644, 645; p. 213, Figs. 648-651; p. 215, Fig. 659; p. 218, Fig. 667; p. 221, Fig. 694; Roscher, *Lexikon,* IV, col. 1457, Fig. 12; col. 1459, Fig. 19; col. 1489, Fig. 51; Avi-Yonah, *QDAP,* XIII, 1948, pp. 137-145, for an excellent treatment of the subject and further references.

774. Hill, *London,* pp. 21-56; Richmond, *ILN,* March 24, 1951, pp. 454-457; Grimes, *ILN,* Sept. 25, 1954, p. 495; Oct. 9, 1954, pp. 594-596; Oct. 16, 1954, pp. 636-637; Vermaseren, *ILN,* Jan. 8, 1955, pp. 60-61; Cumont, *RO,* pp.

775. Dunand, *Soueïda*, Pl. XIX:51 and p. 41.

776. Kitzinger, *Coptic Sculpture*, pp. 204-210; Avi-Yonah, *QDAP*, X, 1944, p. 114; see p. 534.

777. See p. 535.

778. Kitzinger, *Coptic Sculpture*, p. 207; Butler, *PAES*, II, A, 1919, p. XVIII.

779. Avi-Yonah, *QDAP*, XIII, 1948, p. 136; Kraeling, *BASOR*, 83, 1941, pp. 7-14; *Gerasa*, p. 147; Hill, *BMC, Greek Coins*, pp. xxxiii-xxxv and Pl. V:4-6.

780. Horsfield, *QDAP*, IX:2, 1942, p. 166 and Pl. XXXII, bottom.

781. Parr, *PEQ*, 89, 1957, Pl. IV:A and p. 8.

782. Dunand, *Soueïda*, Pl. XVI:62 and p. 45.

783. Dunand, *Soueïda*, Pl. XII:35 and and pp. 30-31.

784. Dunand, *Soueïda*, Pl. VI:19 and p. 23.

785. Dunand, *Soueïda*, Pl. IX:8 and p. 18. Dunand, following Dussaud, suggests that the equivalent of the name of Azizos in Greek letters above the eagle represents the equation of this deity with the solar god, and that the figure on the opposite side represents the person who dedicated the altar to the god.

786. Al-Asil, *ILN*, Dec. 25, 1954, p. 1160, Fig. 4.

787. I am indebted to M. Daniel Schlumberger, who in 1938 sent me a copy of this photograph, then unpublished, and who called my attention to several related funerary busts, one with a horse over the left shoulder and the other with a camel, which are from Palmyra and are found in Seyrig, *Syria*, XIV, 1933, Pl. XX: 1, 2 and pp. 158-160, and Cantineau, *IIP*, VIII, 1932, p. 31. I have pointed out the connection of the Palmyra bust with the horse over the deceased's left shoulder with the funerary bust, also with a horse over his left shoulder, which is built into the wall of the *qasr* at Kerak, and is to be identified as Nabataean; cf. Ingholt, *Berytus*, III, 1936, p. 120 and Pl. XXIV:2.

788. Dunand, *Soueïda*, Pl. XI:30 and p. 28.

789. Dunand, *Soueïda*, Pl. XIV:38bis and pp. 33-34; Butler, *PAES*, II, A, 6, 1919, Ill. 346 C and p. 401.

790. Parr, *PEQ*, 89, 1957, Pl. V:A and B and p. 9; Gressmann, *AOB*, p. 116 and Pl. CLX, Fig. 400; Dalman, *Petra*, pp. 355-356 and Figs. 324-325; Wiegand, *Petra*, pp. 66-67 and Fig. 59; *PA*, I, pp. 178, 319-320, Fig. 348; Dunand, *Soueïda*, Pl. VII:44 and p. 38; Rostovtzeff, *DPPA*, p. 229, Fig. 38, points out the Parthian-Scythian background of the torque around the neck of the god, Aphlad, which ends "in protomes of griffins or some other winged animals"; see p. 226.

790a. Lapp, *BASOR*, 171, Oct. 1963, pp. 8-39.

791. Parr, *PEQ*, 89, 1957, Pl. VI:B, p. 9.

792. Butler, *PAES*, II, A, 6, 1919, Ill. 344 R, preceding p. 385; cf. Ill. 328:12 (photographed upside down) and p. 378.

793. Dunand, *Soueïda*, Pl. XXIX:125 and p. 65; Pl. XV:119 and p. 63.

794. Sourdel, *Hauran*, pp. 29-30 and Pl. II:1, see p. 472.

795. Dunand, *Soueïda*, Pl. XIII:37 and p. 33.

796. Dunand, *Soueïda*, Pl. XII:38 and p. 33.

797. Dunand, *Soueïda*, Pl. XVI:63 and p. 45; Butler, *PAES*, II, A, 7, 1919, Ill. 355 and p. 416.

798. Butler, *PAES*, II, A, 7, 1919, p. 444, Ill. 388:G, H.

799. Avi-Yonah, *QDAP*, X, 1944, pp. 114-115; *Or. Art*, pp. 50, 51, 53.

800. *PA*, III, p. 144, Fig. 1038, from Qanawat in the Nabataean Hau-

ran; cf. Dunand, *Soueïda,* pp. 40-43 and Pls. XVIII:50, 52 and XIX:51, 57.

801. Brown, *Dura,* VII-VIII, 1939, p. 264 and Pl. XXXV:2; Kantorowicz, *Gods in Uniform,* pp. 374-375 and Fig. 16; pp. 383, 384 and Fig. 36; Ingholt, *Hatra,* p. 10 and Pl. III:1.

802. Parr, *PEQ,* 89, 1957, p. 8 and Pl. IV:A.

803. Avi-Yonah, *QDAP,* X, 1944, p. 115; Contenau, *Déesse,* p. 109; *MAO,* II, p. 678, Fig. 470.

804. Dunand, *Soueïda,* Pl. VIII:6 and p. 17.

805. Cf. Bieber, *Sculpture,* p. 28 and Fig. 68; Richter, *Sculpture,* p. 97 and Fig. 288; p. 98 and Fig. 291; p. 243 and Fig. 638.

806. Richter, *Sculpture,* p. 92.

807. Cumont, *Syria,* VIII, 1927, pp. 163-168; IX, 1928, pp. 101-113 and Pls. 38, 39; Avi-Yonah, *QDAP,* XII, 1946, p. 89 and Pl. XXVI:6.

808. Cook *Zeus,* I, p. 42, Pl. VI; III:2, pp. 1112-1113 and Fig. 882; Cumont, *Études,* 1917, pp. 35-118, and especially p. 61, Fig. 28; p. 80, Fig. 33; Seyrig, *Syria,* XXVI, 1949, pp. 34, 35 and Fig. 4; du Mesnil, *TMP,* pp. 45-52 and Fig. 4 on p. 48.

809. Dunand, *Soueïda,* p. 12 and Pl. IV; Cumont, *Doura,* pp. 100, 103, 129, 130; du Mesnil, *TMP,* p. 47.

810. Cook, *Zeus,* I, pp. 41-56; III:2, pp. 1112-1113 and Fig. 882.

811. Du Mesnil, *TMP,* pp. 47-49; *Ency. Brit.,* 1953, under "Constellation."

812. Dussaud, *Notes myth. syr.,* pp. 3-23.

813. Dussaud, *Notes myth. syr.,* p. 22, n. 3, p. 23 and Fig. 9; Cook, *Zeus,* I, pp. 603-604 and Fig. 475; III:1, p. 834 and Pl. 61; III:2, pp. 1175-1177 and Figs. 917, 918; Cumont and Rostovtzeff, *Dura,* VII-VIII, 1939, p. 106.

Chapter XIII

814. See p. 289.

815. See p. 292; Kantor, *JNES,* XXI:2, 1962, pp. 97-99 and Figs. 5, 7.

816. Jaussen et Savignac, *MA,* I, pp. 326, 347-350, 357, 370, 385, 428, 603-604, and Figs. 139, 162-165, 171, 182, 192, 218, 474, 603-604; II, Pls. XL, XLIII, XLIV, XLV:2; Cook, *Zeus,* I, p. 604, Fig. 475 on p. 603: ". . . a bronze brought from Nizib . . . shows a splendid eagle on a discoid base, which bears the name Helios . . ."; Seyrig, *Syria,* XIV, 1933, p. 256; Ingholt, *Hatra,* pp. 24, 43 and Pl. VII:1; Schlumberger, *Syria,* XXXVII, 1960, pp. 266-267 and Pl. XI:1; Dunand, *Soueïda,* p. 18 and Pl. IX:8; p. 28, Pl. XI:30; p. 33, Pl. XIII:37, 38; pp. 33-34, Pl. XIV:38bis; p. 65, Pl. XXIX:125; du Mesnil, *TMP,* p. 76, Fig.

37; p. 118, Fig. 72; p. 127, Fig. 86; p. 137, Fig. 99; p. 212, Fig. 142; p. 317, Fig. 185; p. 412, Fig. 213; cf. pp. 144-145.

817. Cf. p. 144; Kantorowicz, *Gods in Uniform,* pp. 376-379, 383-384, and Figs. 19, 20, 25, 27-29, 33, 36; Seyrig, *BMB,* I, 1937, pp. 92-95; Dussaud, *Syria,* I, 1920, pp. 12-13, Fig. 3; Cumont, *Syria,* IX, 1928, p. 101 and Pl. XXXVIII; *MM,* p. 14, Fig. 1; Gressmann, *OR,* pp. 34, 143-144; Ingholt, *Hatra,* pp. 22-24, 29, 38, 42 and Pl. VI:2, 3.

818. Kantorowicz, *Gods in Uniform,* p. 380 and Fig. 31.

819. Kantorowicz, *Gods in Uniform,* pp. 375-376 and Fig. 19; Morehart, *Berytus,* XII, 1956-1958, pp. 62-67, Figs. 11-17; du Mesnil, *TMP,* p. 242, Fig. 156.

820. Cumont, *MM,* pp. 13, 14 and Fig.

1; *RO*, p. 133, Fig. 9; Gressmann, *OR*, pp. 143-144, Abb. 53; Widengren, *Kulturbegegnung*, p. 143, Pl. 27.

821. Brown, *Dura*, VII-VIII, 1939, pp. 153, 154; Kantorowicz, *Gods in Uniform*, pp. 376, 378, 379, 384, and Figs. 20, 27, 28, 36.

822. *PA*, I, p. 50, Fig. 38; see p. 58.

823. Ingholt, *Hatra*, pp. 24, 29 and Pl. VI:3; pp. 22-24, 38 and Pl. VI:2; Kantorowicz, *Gods in Uniform*, pp. 375, 376, 378, 379 and Figs. 19, 20, 25, 28; Rostovtzeff, *CC*, Pl. XXXI:2, facing p. 196; Dussaud, *Arabes en Syrie*, p. 97, Fig. 18; Morehart, *Berytus*, XII, 1956-1958, pp. 59-61, Fig. 10; pp. 60-62, Fig. 11; pp. 62-64, Fig. 13; pp. 64, 65, 68, Fig. 18; Seyrig, *Syria*, XV, 1934, p. 179, Fig. 2; Nasrallah, *AAS*, VIII-IX, 1958-1959, pp. 66-67 and Pls. III, IV:1, from "Ma'loula," east of "Qalamoun," for reliefs of two rock cut divinities of Helios and Athena, with the head of Helios, haloed with thirteen or fourteen sun-rays, resting against a raised disc; Abdul-Hak, *AAS*, IV-V, 1954-1955, p. 173, n. 2 and Pl. IV betwen pp. 186-187, with some details on a metal helmet, showing a young beardless Helios with thirteen rays of the sun extending from his head, a winged Niké in front of him, a helmeted warrior below her, and a solar eagle on each side of him; Butler, *PAES*, II, A, 1919, pp. 384 385 and Ills. 331:G; 332; 333:G; Dunand, *Soueïda*, p. 39 and Pl. XV:46; Seyrig and Starcky, *Syria*, XXVI:3-4, 1949, p. 233, Fig. 1; Ingholt, Seyrig, Starcky, *RTP*, nos. 120, 121, 139, 141, 243, 245, 246, 335, 340.

824. *PA*, I, pp. 70-75 and Fig. 71; see p. 59.

825. See pp. 55-56.

826. Avi-Yonah and Negev, *ILN*, Nov. 26, 1960, p. 945, Fig. 3; see pp. 7, 191.

827. See p. 59.

828. Wright, G.R.H., *BASOR*, 163, 1961, pp. 26-30; Tushingham, *BASOR*, 133, 1954, pp. 6-26; Winnett, *BASOR*, 125, 1952, pp. 7-19; Murphy, *BASOR*, 125, 1952, pp. 20-23; Wright, *BA*, XXII:4, 1959, p. 99.

829. Cf. Glueck, *AJA*, XLI:3, 1937, p. 373, Fig. 11, which I wrongly designated then as a Hadad figure instead of a Helios figure. A bust in relief much similar to this one was found years ago in Amman by Littmann, who thought that "it represents a bust of Zeus Ammon, with the ram's horns . . .", according to Butler, *PAES*, II, A, 1919, p. 62, Ill. 41. The figure seems to have upswept curved, flamelike curls that characterize the Helios of Khirbet Tannur (Pl. 136). The locks of hair of this Amman bust seem to descend alongside his cheeks. His tunic and chlamys are exactly the same as those of the Khirtbet Tannur figure and of the other Helios figures from Khirbet Tannur (Pl. 137 b). The drapery is also exactly that of the figures that we identify with Hermes-Mercury (Pls. 145, 146).

830. FitzGerald, *PEFQS*, 1931, p. 63, Pl. I; Cook, *Zeus*, I, p. 193, Fig. 142; p. 617, Figs. 488, 490; Dunand, *Soueïda*, p. 33, n. 38; Dalman, *Petra*, p. 75; *PAM*, Photograph 10635, from Byzantine Beisan, showing mosaic panel of months of the zodiac surrounding circular panel of moon and sun goddess, with the moon goddess crowned with a crescent moon and holding a torch; Zori, Pl. IV: 1, after p. 136; du Mesnil, *TMP*, p. 98, Fig. 51; p. 99, Fig. 54:1; p. 109, Fig. 66; see p. 397.

831. Cumont, Rostovtzeff, *Dura*, VII-VIII, 1939, pp. 105-106, Pl. XVIII.

832. Toynbee, *Art*, p. 153 and Pl. 73.

833. Pauly-Wissowa, cols. 760, 766;

Cook, *Zeus*, II:1, p. 205, Fig. 144; pp. 256, 459; du Mesnil, *TMP*, p. 287, Fig. 176.

834. Pauly-Wissowa, col. 787; Eliot in *Life Int.*, June 18, 1962, p. 73.

835. Cook, *Zeus*, 1, p. 746, n. 1.

836. One wonders if the sculptor could have been aware of the original or perhaps of a copy of the Hermes of Praxiteles and attempted to copy its contemplative expression; cf. Richter, *Sculpture*, p. 574, Fig. 664; p. 369, Fig. 72; Eliot in *Life Int.*, June 18, 1962, pp. 70-74.

837. *AP*, p. 156; cf. n. 839.

838. Cf. Parr, *PEQ*, 89, 1957, p. 9 and Pl. VIA for the wings on the caduceus of the broken relief of a Hermes figure from Petra; also Dalman, *Petra*, p. 360, Abb. 329, for the winged caduceus over the right shoulder of yet another Hermes bas-relief from Petra.

839. Ronzevalle, *MUSJ*, XXI, pp. 118-121 and Pl. XXVIII:6; Kantorowicz, *Gods in Uniform*, pp. 377, 380 and Figs. 23, 31; Cumont, *RO*, Pl. I:1, facing p. 28, and Pl. IX:1, facing p. 102; *MM*, p. 105, Fig. 20; Ingholt, *Hatra*, p. 30, n. 10; Cook, *Zeus*, I, p. 203, Fig. 147; pp. 564-565, Fig. 432, showing "an eagle grasping a winged caduceus between garland-bearing Erotes . . ."; pp. 575, 699; II:2, p. 1043; III:2, pp. 1071-1193, n. 3; Neumann, *The Great Mother*, p. 328; Benoit, *CL*, III, pp. 1-24; de Waele, pp. 29-79 and Fig. 3, facing p. 64 and pp. 91-96; Dussaud, *Syria*, XXIII, 1942-1943, p. 55, Fig. 10; p. 77, Fig. 19; Parrot, *Sumer*, p. 236 and Fig. 289; *Tello*, p. 198 and Pl. XXI; Bacon, *AASOR*, V, 1925, pp. 8, 10 and Figs. 18, 20; Wiegand, *Baalbek*, II, Pls. 66-67; Bieber, *Sculpture*, Fig. 66. Since the writing of the part of the text with which this note deals, there has appeared Evaristus Mader's *Mambre, Die*

Ergebnisse der Ausgrabungen im heiligen Bezirk Râmat el-Halîl in südpalästina, 1926-1928, in which he publishes and comments on this relief, p. 135 and Pl. LXXIII: 137. He identifies the relief (Pl. 152C) as possibly the goddess "Iris" or as "an anonymous Hermes-Mercury with a winged staff over his left shoulder and possessing female breasts and face and ornaments" (translation mine). Prominent breasts characterize all the male sculptures of Khirbet Tannur, but none of them may be considered androgynous.

840. Parr, *PEQ*, 89, 1957, p. 8 and Pl. IVB; p. 9 and Pl. VIA.

841. Parr, *PEQ*, 89, 1957, p. 8, Pl. IVB.

842. Parr, *PEQ*, 89, 1957, p. 9, Pl. VIA.

843. Dalman, *Petra*, p. 360, Abb. 329.

844. Seyrig, *BMB*, I, 1937, Fig. 4, facing p. 92; Cook, *Zeus*, III:2, p. 1093, Figs. 872, 873; Bonner, *Amulets*, pp. 116, 148, 149, 150, 153, 282; Pl. VIII:162, 163, 164, 167, 173, 174.

845. Ingholt, *Hatra*, p. 30.

846. Kantorowicz, *Gods in Uniform*, p. 377, Fig. 23; p. 380, Fig. 31.

847. Parr, *PEQ*, 89, 1957, pp. 6-7 and Pls. I, II; Rostovtzeff in Dussaud, *MS*, I, p. 282, Pl. I; Hopkins, *Dura*, V, 1934, pp. 108, 117; VII-VIII, 1939, pp. 293-296; Avi-Yonah, *QDAP*, X, 1944, pp. 117, 120, 121; *IEJ*, 9:1, 1959, p. 10; al-Asil, *ILN*, Nov. 17, 1951, pp. 806-807 and Figs. 5, 6; Nov. 10, 1951, p. 764; *SG*, p. 74, art. 35 and n. 47.

848. Parr, *PEQ*, 89, 1957, Pls. I, II, XVB.

849. Parr, *PEQ*, 89, 1957, pp. 13-14 and Pl. XVB.

850. Seyrig, *BMB*, I, 1937, Fig. 4, facing p. 92; Cook, *Zeus*, III:2, p. 1093, Figs. 872, 873.

851. Dunand, *Soueïda*, p. 37 and Pl. VII:42; pp. 34-35 and Pl. XIV:39;

p. 84 and Pl. XXXVI B, C; Parr, *PEQ*, 89, 1957, Pl. IVA.

852. Cf. Dunand, *Soueïda*, p. 17 and Pl. VIII:6; p. 4 and Pl. XX:65, 66; p. 50 and Pl. XX:76.

853. Parr, *PEQ*, 89, 1957, p. 16.

854. Parr, *PEQ*, 89, 1957, pp. 7-8 and Pl. IIIB.

855. Andrae, *Hatra*, II, p. 157 and Pl. XIX: "Südwand, Ostlisene."

856. Horsfield, *QDAP*, IX, 1942, p. 161 and Pl. XXX:253.

857. Butler, *PAES*, II, A, 4, 1919, p. 250, Ill. 223.

858. Hopkins, *Dura*, V, 1934, p. 52 and Pl. XV:1.

859. Mallowan, *ILN*, Jan. 15, 1938, p. 95, Figs. 14, 15; *Iraq*, IX, 1947, pp. 185-186 and Pl. XL:2; Frankfort, *Art and Arch.*, p. 144, Fig. 66; p. 177 and Pl. 158c; pp. 184-185; Avi-Yonah, *IWB*, I, p. 43, showing an east Semitic ruler of Adab, ascribed to the third millennium B.C.

860. Parr, *PEQ*, 89, 1957, p. 7, n. 11.

861. Glueck, *OSJ*, p. 156, Fig. 86; *AASOR*, XIV, 1935, p. 23, Fig. 6b.

862. Harding, *ILN*, Feb. 8, 1950, p. 267, Figs. 3, 4; Barnett, *ADAJ*, I, 1951, pp. 34-36 and Pl. XI; O'Callaghan, *Orientalia*, 21, 1952, pp. 184-193 and Pl. XXVI.

863. Cumont, Rostovtzeff, *Dura*, VII-VIII, 1939, pp. 105-106 and Pl. XVIII:1-6.

864. Gandz, *Proceeding of American Association for Jewish Research*, XIII, 1943, p. 17; Ronzevalle, *MUSJ*, XXI, 1937, p. 89 and Pl. XXVII:3; Cook, S.A., *RAPLA*, pp. 66, 90, 168, 178; Daremberg et Saglio, *Dict.*, IV, p. 1088, Fig. 6121; Hill, *BMC: Palestine*, pp. 129, n. 188; 133, no. 216; 134, no. 225; Babelon, *Monnaies*, II, pp. 254, 633 under Harpé; Ghirshman, *Bichapour*, II, pp. 49, 50 and Pl. B; V:2; Cook, *Zeus*, I, p. 441, n. 1; Contenau, *ELBA*, p. 126 and Pl. XIX.

865. *ILN*, Oct. 16, 1954, p. 637.

866. Avi-Yonah, *IEJ*, IX:1, 1959, p. 10; II:2, 1952, pp. 121-122.

867. Ingholt, *Hatra*, pp. 38-42; Cumont, *RO*, p. 105, Fig. 7; Seyrig, *Syria*, XIV, 1933, p. 258, Fig. 5; du Mesnil, *TMP*, p. 50, Fig. 5; see p. 355.

868. Du Mesnil, *TMP*, pp. 50, 276, Fig. 170.

869. Dunand, *Soueïda*, p. 23 and Pl. VI:19; p. 28 and Pl. XI:30; Cumont, *RO*, Pl. I:2 facing p. 28; Pl. Xb facing p. 106; *Syria*, VIII, 1927, pp. 163-168; Cook, *Zeus*, I, pp. 188-189, Fig. 137; pp. 191-192, Fig. 138; pp. 193, 233, and Pl. XXI.

870. Baur, *Dura*, III, 1932, pp. 104, 136 and Pls. XIV, XVIII:7; Crosby, *Dura*, VI, 1936, p. 120; Dussaud, *Notes myth. syr.*, pp. 180-181.

871. Dunand, *Soueïda*, pp. 22-23 and Pl. VI:19; p. 28, n. 2; Cook, *Zeus*, I, p. 752, Fig. 551; Cumont, *Syria*, VIII, 1927, pp. 163-168; *RO*, p. 28 and Pl. I:2; du Mesnil, *TMP*, p. 137, Fig. 99:3, 4.

872. Dunand, *Soueïda*, p. 18 and Pl. IX:8; p. 23 and Pl. VI:19; p. 28 and Pl. XI:30; p. 30 and Pl. XII:35; Cumont, *Syria*, VIII, 1927, pp. 163-168.

873. Dunand, *Soueïda*, pp. 33-34 and Pls. XIII:38, XIV:38bis; Dalman, *Petra*, pp. 75, 115, 117 and Fig. 34; Rostovtzeff, *CC*, p. 187; Baur, *Dura*, III, 1932, pp. 100, 109-110 and Pl. XIV; Hopkins, *Dura*, V, 1934, pp. 153, 155, 156; Avi-Yonah, *QDAP*, XIII, 1948, p. 145; Cook, S.A., *RAPLA*, pp. 181-190, 212; Cook, *Zeus*, I, pp. 191-193, Fig. 142; II:2, p. 1185, Figs. 987-989; pp. 1193, 1224, Fig. 1022; p. 1225, Fig. 1023; Jaussen et Savignac, *MA*, pp. 400-401; Cumont, *Études*, pp. 60, 61 and Fig. 28; Seyrig, *Syria*, XIV, 1933, p. 256; Ingholt, *Hatra*, p. 29 and Pl. VI:3; Kammerer, *Pétra*, pp. 224, 225, 400, and Fig. 40; Butler, *PAES*,

II, A, 1919, p. 374, Ill. 325; p. 378, Ill. 328:12; p. 381, Ill. 329; p. 386, Ill. 335; Rostovtzeff, *DPPA*, pp. 249, 250; *Dura*, IV, 1933, pp. 210, 211 and Pl. XIX:3; Schlumberger, *Syria*, XXXVII, 1960, pp. 266-267 and Pl. XI:1, facing p. 293.

874. Ingholt, *Hatra*, pp. 22-24, 29, and Pl. VI:2, 3; Kantorowicz, *Gods in Uniform*, pp. 376, 378, Figs. 20, 27, 28; Gressmann, *OR*, pp. 143-144, Abb. 53; Seyrig, *BMB*, I, 1937, pp. 92-95; Kraeling, *Gerasa*, p. 147; cf. p. 144.

875. Seyrig, *Syria*, XIV, 1933, p. 242; Dussaud, *Notes myth. syr.*, pp. 180-181; Cook, *Zeus*, II:1, pp. 849, 852.

876. Ingholt, *Hatra*, p. 14, n. 9; p. 23 and Pl. VI:2; pp. 32-34 and Pl. VII:2; Baur, *Dura*, III, 1932, pp. 134-135 and Pl. XX; Cook, S. A., *RAPLA*, p. 221 and Pl. XXXI:1; Avi-Yonah, *IEJ*, II, 1952, pp. 120-124; du Mesnil, *TMP*, p. 172, Fig. 124a; p. 205, Fig. 138; p. 222, Fig. 148; pp. 399-403; p. 458, Fig. 229.

877. Steve, *LWB*, pp. 76, 234, Fig. 45; Dussaud, *Syria*, I, 1920, pp. 12-13, Fig. 3.

878. Cook, *Zeus*, I, pp. 188-190, 400, 599; Gressmann, *OR*, pp. 34, 143-144, Abb. 53; Kraeling, *Gerasa*, p. 147, for reference to inscription found at Gerasa in the Propylaea church, referring to "Zeus Helios Serapis"; Seyrig, *BMB*, I, 1937, pp. 92-95.

879. Butler, *PAES*, II, A, 1919, pp. 355, 365-402; *PA*, III, pp. 90-100.

880. Butler, *PAES*, II, A, 1919, pp. 398-399 and Ill. 344; Gressmann, *OR*, pp. 148-149, Abb. 56; Cook, *Zeus*, I, pp. 516-518, Fig. 389; Cumont, *MM*, p. 176, Fig. 40 and pp. 222-224, Fig. 49; du Mesnil, *TMP*, p. 134, Fig. 95; p. 135, Fig. 97; p. 140, Fig. 104; p. 145, Fig. 111.

881. Dunand, *Soueïda*, p. 28 and Pl. XI:30.

882. Cook, *Zeus*, I, p. 193, Fig. 142; pp. 616-617, Fig. 488; pp. 618-619, Fig. 490; Seyrig, *BMB*, I, 1937, pp. 91-93, Fig. 4; du Mesnil, *TMP*, p. 109, Fig. 66; p. 134, Fig. 95; p. 138, Fig. 100; p. 139, Fig. 103; p. 140, Fig. 104.

883. I am indebted to Daniel Schlumberger for the photograph and the information about the probable origin and present location of these sculptured basalt blocks. It was told to him that the provenance of the sculptures on this plate was Si'a. The lintel with the stylized vine, leaf and fruit decoration above the eagle relief could certainly have come from Si'a, to judge from closely related examples there; cf. Butler, *PAES*, II, A, 1919, pp. 376-377, Ill. 327; also Dussaud, *Topographie*, p. 356, n. 6 and Pl. II, facing p. 40; Sourdel, *Hauran*, p. 29, n. 6 and Pl. II:1.

884. See p. 472; Cumont, *MM*, p. 176, Fig. 40; Gressmann, *OR*, pp. 143-144, Abb. 53; Butler, *PAES*, II, A, p. 399, Ill. 344; Cook, *Zeus*, I, pp. 516-518, Fig. 389; Dunand, *Soueïda*, pp. 33-34 and Pls. XIII: 38, XIV; 38bis; du Mesnil, p. 109, Fig. 66.

885. Dunand, *Soueïda*, p. 18 and Pl. IX:8.

886. Seyrig, *Syria*, XIV, 1933, pp. 162-164 and Pl. XXI:1.

887. Butler, *PAES*, II, A, 1919, p. 384 and Ill. 334, L., facing p. 385; Seyrig, *Syria*, XIV, 1933, p. 160, Pl. 20; p. 157, n. 2 concerning the Nabataean cavalryman mentioned in *CIS*, II, 3973.

888. Horsfield, *QDAP*, IX, 1942, Pl. XXII:166, XXV:194, XXX:248, 252-254, XLVI:439.

889. See p. 59; Seyrig, *Syria*, XIV, 1933, p. 158 and Pl. XX:1, facing p. 160.

890. Rostovtzeff, *Iranians and Greeks*, p. 11, Pls. I, XXX:1, 2, and pp. 109, 227; *CC*, pp. 193-195; *DPPA*,

Fig. 6, p. 189; Ghirshman, *Iran,* Pl. 38a.

891. Seyrig, *Syria,* XIV, 1933, pp. 158-160 and Pl. XX:1-2; see p. 59.

892. Cumont, *Études,* pp. 35-118; Cook, *Zeus,* I, pp. 188-192; Dunand, *Soueïda,* pp. 28, 33-34 and Pls. XI:30, XIII:38, XIC:38bis; Ingholt, *Hatra,* pp. 22-24, 29 and and Pls. VI:2, 3, VII:1; Kantorowicz, *Gods in Uniform,* p. 379; Butler, *PAES,* II, A, pp. 378, 381, 400-401, Ills. 328, 329, 346C; du Mesnil, *TMP,* p. 48, Fig. 4; p. 76, Fig. 37; p. 118, Fig. 72; p. 120, Fig. 74; p. 137, Fig. 99; p. 317, Fig. 185.

893. Jaussen et Savignac, *MA,* I, pp. 400-401; 424-426; 428, Fig. 218; 431, Fig. 221; II, p. 91, Pl. XLV; Dunand, *Syria,* VII, 1926, p. 126 and Pl. XXXIII:2a, b; Avi-Yonah, *QDAP,* XIII, 1948, p. 138; Doughty, *Travels,* Pl. I, facing p. 107.

894. Dalman, *Petra,* pp. 115-117; Kennedy, *Petra,* p. 72; Horsfield, *QDAP,* IX:2-4, 1942, p. 166 and Pl. XXXII bottom; Kammerer, *Pétra,* pp. 224, 225, 400, and Fig. 40, Pl. 69.

895. Dalman, *Petra,* pp. 75, 115, 117; Rostovtzeff, *CC,* p. 187; Cook, *Zeus,* II, pp. 1185, 1193, 1224, 1225, and Figs. 987-989, 1022, 1023; Jaussen et Savignac, *MA,* I, pp. 400-401; Cumont, *RO,* Pl. Xb, facing p. 106; Cook, S.A., *RAPLA,* p. 99, n. 1, and pp. 181-190, 212; Ingholt, *Hatra,* p. 29; Kammerer, *Pétra,* pp. 224, 225, 400, and Fig. 40, Pl. 69; Cantineau, *Inscriptions Palmyreniennes,* 1930, n. 60; Seyrig, *Syria,* 36, 1959, pp. 58-60 and Pl. XI:5; Rostovtzeff, *DPPA,* pp. 248-250.

896. Du Mesnil, *TMP,* pp. 153-163, 548-556.

897. Avi-Yonah, *QDAP,* XIII, 1948, p. 136, Fig. 9.

898. Kraeling, *BASOR,* 83, 1941, pp. 7-14; *Gerasa,* p. 147.

898a. Rostovtzeff, *Dura,* IV, 1933, p. 213. We are indebted to Miss Ann Perkins for making this drawing available to us.

899. Goodenough, *Symbols,* II, p. 295.

900. Yadin, *ILN,* Nov. 11, 1961, p. 820, for Nabataean papyrus found in a cave overlooking Nahal Hever, indicating close legal and economic relationship between Nabataeans and Judaeans; see p. 266.

901. Goodenough, *Symbols,* II, pp. 244-258; III, Fig. 1083.

902. Cumont, *MM,* pp. 105-108; *RO,* p. 28 and Pl. L:1; Seyrig, *Syria,* XIII, 1932, p. 59; XIV, 1933, pp. 257-258, Fig. 4; XXXVI, 1959, pp. 58-60 and Pl. XI:5; Schlumberger, *Syria,* XXXVII, 1960, p. 300 and Pl. XI:2, facing p. 293; Cook, *Zeus,* I, p. 585.

903. Cumont, *Études,* pp. 60, 61, Fig. 28; Cook, *Zeus,* I, pp. 191-192.

904. Du Mesnil, *TMP,* pp. 326-327; Gressmann, *AOT,* p. 183, line 306 and note a.

905. Jaussen et Savignac, *MA,* I, pp. 326, 347-350, 370, 385, 428, and Figs. 139, 162-165, 171, 182, 192, 218; II, *Atlas,* Pls. XL, XLIII, XLIV, XLV:2.

906. Jaussen et Savignac, *MA,* II; *Texte,* pp. 47, 88; *Atlas,* Pl. XLIV.

906a. See p. 489.

907. Numbers 21:8-10; Kantorowicz, *Gods in Uniform,* pp. 370, 371, Figs. 5, 6; p. 373, Fig. 13; p. 380, Fig. 31, showing relief of Asklepios with serpent-entwined staff on altar fragment from the Hauran; Dunand in *Syria,* VII, 1926, p. 339 and Pl. LXX; *ANEP,* p. 218 and Fig. 669; Goodenough, *Symbols,* II, pp. 247-248, refers, as do many others, to the passage in Macrobius, *Saturnalia,* I, xx, 1-5 and xvii, 50-63, dealing with the solar serpent as the symbol of Asklepios, who symbolizes the sun, being "the healing power (like the serpent) from the substance of the

sun coming down to the souls and bodies of mortals . . . The serpent with its acutely piercing and vigilant eye imitates the nature of this star . . ."; p. 266; Hausmann, *Weihreliefs*, pp. 68-79, Abb. 38, 40, 41, 43-45; Avi-Yonah, *IEJ*, IX:1, 1959, p. 11; Bieber, *APS*, 101:1, 1957, pp. 70-92; cf. *ILN*, Sept. 25, 1954, p. 505, top.

908. Swoboda, *JOAI*, XXX:1, 1936, pp. 7-8; Albright, *BASOR*, 57, 1935, p. 57; *APB*, ed. 3, pp. 87-88; *AP*, p. 97, Fig. 20; p. 120; Gressmann, *OR*, pp. 64, 110-115, 146-149; Cook, *Zeus*, II:2, p. 1110, Fig. 946; Starcky, *Syria*, XXVI, 1949, pp. 73-74, 76; Cumont, *RO*, Pl. I:1, facing p. 28; *MM*, pp. 54-55, 117; *HGR*, II, p. 45; Dunand, *Soueïda*, p. 38 and Pl. VII:44.

909. Cook, *Zeus*, II, pp. 818, 851, 1110-1112, Figs. 782, 783, 946; Daremberg et Saglio, *Dict.*, II:1, p. 405; Gressmann, *OR*, pp. 64, Fig. 23; 110-113, Fig. 46; 114, 115, 118-120; Goodenough, *Symbols*, II, pp. 45, 48-50, 267-268; Hausmann, *Weihreliefs*, p. 81 and Pls. 47, 48, 58.

910. Seyrig, *Syria*, XIII:1, 1932, p. 59; Cook, *Zeus*, I, pp. 358-360, Fig. 275; II:2, pp. 1051-1052, Fig. 909; Hausmann, *Weihreliefs*, pp. 96-98; Gressmann, *OR*, pp. 34-41, 48-50; Goodenough, *Symbols*, II, pp. 247-248; Dussaud, *Notes Myth, Syr.*, pp. 180-181; Jaussen et Savignac, *MA*, II, Pl. LI:2, 3; Leipoldt, *Die Religionen in der Umwelt des Urchristentums*, Fig. 14; Schreiber, *Nekropole von Kom esch-Schukafa*, p. 318; von Bissing, *AO*, XXXIV, 1936, pp. 23-24, 29 and Fig. 10a.

911. Ingholt, *Hatra*, p. 16 and Pl. III:3; p. 33 and Pl. VII:2; al-Asil, *ILN*, Nov. 17, 1951, pp. 806-807 and Figs. 9-11; Rostovtzeff, *DPPA*, pp. 225, 303, and Fig. 42; Seyrig, *Syria*, XXXVI, 1959, pp. 58-60, Pl. XI:5; Swoboda, *JOAI*, XXX:

1, 1937, pp. 1-27; Cumont, *RO*, p. 28 and Pl. I:1; *MM*, pp. 105, 106, 108, 110, and Figs. 20-23.

912. Savignac, *RB*, 44, 1935, pp. 261-263 and Pl. IX.

913. In a letter of Jan. 21, 1962, Père R. de Vaux wrote me: "I see what Père Savignac meant by his 'serpent', but I am as doubtful as you are."

914. Albright, *ARI*, p. 189, n. 51; *AP*, 1960, p. 97, Fig. 20; Dunand, *Soueïda*, p. 38 and Pl. VII:44; Neumann, *The Great Mother*, Pl. 59; Parrot, *Syria*, XXVIII, 1951, pp. 57-61; Dussaud, *Syria*, VII, 1926, p. 339 and Pl. LXX, facing p. 338.

915. Al-Asil, *ILN*, Dec. 25, 1954, p. 1161, Fig. 8.

916. Cumont, *RO*, Pl. I:1, facing, p. 28; *MM*, pp. 105-112, 153, 162, 222-223, 227; *TM*, II, p. 316 and Figs. 176, 178; Gressmann, *OR*, p. 146, Fig. 54; pp. 147-148, n. 1; Ingholt, *Hatra*, p. 16 and Pl. III:3; pp. 33-34 and Pl. VII:2; Widengren, *Kulturbegegnung*, pp. 17-18, n. 57; p. 134, Fig. 8; Cook, *Zeus*, II, p. 818, Figs. 782, 783.

917. Rostovtzeff, *DPPA*, p. 303, Fig. 42; Widengren, *Kulturbegegnung*, p. 23, n. 83; p. 144, Fig. 28.

918. Gressmann, *OR*, pp. 148-149, Abb. 56; Cumont, *MM*, pp. 54-55, Figs. 14, 15; p. 117, Fig. 25; Starcky, *Syria*, XXVI, 1949, pp. 73-74, 76.

919. Seyrig, *Syria*, XXXVI, 1959, pp. 58-60 and Pl. XI:5; Schlumberger, *Syria*, XXXVII, 1960, p. 300 and Pl. XI:2, facing p. 293.

920. Kennedy, *Petra*, p. 70.

921. *PA*, I, pp. 180, 183, Figs. 207, 213; no. 303.

922. Daremberg et Saglio, *Dict.*, II:1, p. 405, point out that "le culte du Baal-Milid, adoré sous forme de serpent, a été transporté au Pirée par les matelots phéniciens et qu'il y est devenu le Zeus Milichios assis sur un trône sous lequel se dresse un serpent. Le

Zeus Sabazios, introduit d'Asie Mineure en Grèce, est caracterisé par le serpent . . ."; cf. Hausmann, *Weihreliefs,* pp. 81, 83, 95, 96, and Abb. 48, 58.

923. Dalman, *Petra,* pp. 355-356, Figs. 324, 325; Parr, *PEQ,* 89, 1937, p. 9 and Pl. V; Bachmann, Watzinger, Wiegand, *Petra,* p. 67, Fig. 59; Dunand, *Soueïda,* p. 38 and Pl. VII:44, shows a nude female figure holding a serpent parallel to her body in her raised right hand and another serpent in similar position in her lower left hand.

924. Ingholt, *Hatra,* p. 16 and Pl. III:3; Widengren, *Kulturbegegnung,* pp. 17-18, n. 57 and Fig. 8; Seyrig, *Syria,* XXIV, 1944-1945, pp. 62-80.

925. Ingholt, *Hatra,* pp. 33-34 and Pl. VII:2; Widengren, *Kulturbegegnung,* p. 23, n. 38 and Fig. 28.

926. Cf. Dunand, *Soueïda,* p. 38 and Pl. VII:44.

927. Rostovtzeff, *DPPA,* pp. 240-241.

928. Ingholt, *Hatra,* pp. 10, 11, 24, and Pls. III:1, 22-24, 29; VI:2, 3; Rostovtzeff, *DPPA,* p. 303 and Fig. 42.

929. Pauly-Wissowa, IIA, pp. 59, 509.

930. Dalman, *Petra,* pp. 74, 109-110 and Fig. 28.

931. *PA,* I, p. 180 and Fig. 207.

932. Rostovtzeff, *DPPA,* pp. 232, 236, 238-241; "Le Gad de Doura et Seleucus Nicator," in Dussaud, *MS,* I, 1939, p. 282; Hopkins, *Dura,* III, 1932, p. 135; V, 1934, pp. 113, 117-120; *Berytus,* III:1, 1936, pp. 3, 4, 9-10; *AI,* III, 1936, pp. 187-196; Seyrig, *Syria,* XVIII, 1937, pp. 31-43; Kitzinger, *Coptic Sculpture,* pp. 201-204; Kraeling and Adams, *City,* 1960, pp. 208, 222; Ingholt, *Hatra,* p. 46; Avi-Yonah, *QDAP,* X, 1944, pp. 130, 131; XIV, 1950, p. 77.

933. Butler, *PAES,* II, A, 1919, pp. 355-401; Kammerer, *Pétra,* pp. 428-444; Hopkins, *Berytus,* VII:1, 1942, p. 16; Avi-Yonah, *QDAP,* X, 1944, pp. 117, 138; XIII, 1948, pp. 136, 150, 160; XIV, 1950, pp. 49. 62.

934. Dunand, *Soueïda,* pp. 30-31 and Pl. XII:35; Avi-Yonah, *QDAP,* XIII, 1948, p. 145; Rostovtzeff, *Dura,* IV, 1933, p. 213.

935. This certainly derives from another basalt stele found at the site of the Nabataean temple of Si'a in the Jebel Druze; cf. Dunand, *Soueïda,* p. 28 and Pl. XI:30. It pictures the front of a small shrine, above whose left and right sides there are, respectively, representations of the sun and the moon. The one takes the form of a much-worn Helios mask, with twelve petals or rays extending from it, all placed on a circular, concave shield. The other is represented by a relief of a bust of the lunar goddess set in the sickle of a moon, The features of her partly damaged face can barely be discerned; her curled locks reach down to her shoulders.

Between the two is the relief of an eagle with extended wings, and its head turned in left profile to the right side of the stele. Its claws grip the edge of the architrave above the entrance to the shrine, whose façade is decorated on either side with an attached, semicircular column bearing a Corinthianized, Nabataean capital. There can be no question that this eagle stands for Ba'al-shamin or Zeus-Hadad, who is accompanied, as is so often the case, by the sun and the moon; cf. Cook, *Zeus,* I, p. 752, Fig. 551.

936. Dunand, *Soueïda,* p. 30 and Pl. XII:35; Kantorowicz, *Gods in Uniform,* p. 375, Fig. 19; Andrae, *Hatra,* II, p. 158 and Pl. XIX:3; Avi-Yonah and Negev, *ILN,* Nov. 26, 1960, p. 945, Fig. 3.

937. Dunand, *Soueïda,* p. 30. The so-called tail may indeed be just that, but it is not a part of the body

of the flute-playing figure, whose instrument, incidentally, we believe to be a single-stemmed one. The raised, curved band above the flute belongs to the continuation of the body of the serpent. It descends behind the back of the flute player, with its tail emerging beyond his right side at the waistline. The entire length of the serpent extends thus in beneficent manner from behind and beyond the flute player at one end of the stele to the side and perhaps in part originally to the rear of the spear-wielder at the other end, while its middle section rests in the claws of the eagle between them. There is a break between the left end of the part of the serpent above the flute and the outer upper edge of the right wing of the eagle. The smooth surface of the break becomes plausible when one contemplates the smooth surface of the obvious break in the top of the eagle's right wing.

938. Dunand, *Soueïda,* p. 31.
939. Cumont, *MM,* p. 113, Fig. 24; Dunand, *Soueïda,* p. 32, in connection with the interpretation of another stele from Soueïda, speaks, correctly we think, of a personage who is a "compagnon matinal du Soleil."
940. Dunand, *Soueïda,* p. 33 and Pl. XIII:38; pp. 33-34 and Pl. XIV: 38bis; Cumont, *MM,* p. 117, Fig. 25; p. 139, Fig. 35; Schlumberger, *Syria,* XXXVII, 1960, Pl. XI:1.
941. Dunand, *Soueïda,* pp. 31-32 and Pl. XIII:36; du Mesnil, *TMP,* p. 261, Fig. 164; Seyrig, *Syria,* XV, 1934, Pl. XXII, facing p. 172.
942. Bossert, *Altsyrien,* p. 99 and Fig. 1290; Rossini, *Dedalo,* VII, 1926-1927, p. 743.
943. Löwy, *Triumphbogens,* p. 2, Figs. 3, 4; pp. 4, 33.
944. Wiegand, *Petra,* p. 45, Fig. 38;

Bieber, *Sculpture,* Figs. 806-809; Yadin, *Bar-Kochba,* p. 60, Fig. 16.
945. Löwy, *Triumphbogens,* p. 2, Fig. 2.
946. Du Mesnil, *TMP,* pp. 153-163, 327, 422, 548-556; Cumont, *Danseur d'Antibes,* pp. 14-15, 24; see p. 242.
947. Dussaud in Virolleaud, *Syria,* V, 1924, pp. 45-49 and Pl. XVI; Cumont, *Danseur d'Antibes,* p. 23, Fig. 13; p. 22, Fig. 12, shows a similar arrangement, except that each ray terminates in an ivy leaf, with an ivy leaf spray betwen each of the spokes or rays; Bersu, *ILN,* March 31, 1951, p. 502, Fig. 8, shows several Roman bronze greaves from burials in Straubing, Bavaria, on one of which dolphins appear above and below reliefs of two human heads.
948. Cumont, *Danseur d'Antibes,* pp. 21-24.
949. Dunand, *Soueïda,* pp. 31-32 and Pl. XIII:36.
950. Gentili, *ILN,* March 8, 1952, p. 427, Fig. 6, from a Roman mosaic in Sicily, featuring a detail of the slaughter of giants by Hercules (Heracles) and showing a stricken anguiped with an arrow in his breast.
951. Cumont, *MM,* p. 113, Fig. 24. Bersu, *ILN,* March 31, 1951, p. 501, Fig. 4, which shows an angry anguiped about to hurl a rock, embossed on Roman horse armor found in Bavaria.
952. Seyrig, *Syria,* XV, 1934, p. 167, Fig. 1; Dunand, *Soueïda,* p. 32 and Pl. XIII:36.
953. See above, n. 246.
954. Seyrig, *Syria,* XV, 1934, pp. 165-169, and Pl. XX, facing p. 164; Bonner, *Amulets,* p. 124 and Pl. XXIII, Fig. 4.
955. Seyrig, *Syria,* XV, 1934, p. 166.
956. Cumont, *MM,* p. 113, Fig. 24; *RO,* p. 141, Fig. 11; Bersu, *ILN,* March 31, 1951, p. 501, Fig. 4.

957. Butler, *PAES*, II, A, 1919, pp. 385-390, 398-399, and Ills. 335-337, 344B.

958. Cumont, *MM*, pp. 21-24, 39, 51, 55, 117, 122, 123, 139, 151, 176, and Figs. 4-7, 10, 12, 15, 25-27, 35, 37, 40; Gressmann, *OR*, pp. 148, 152; Campbell, *Berytus*, XI, 1954, pp. 1-60 and Pls. I-IX.

959. Cumont, *MM*, Frontispiece and pp. 57, 217.

960. Cumont, *MM*, pp. 67, 73, 214.

961. Cumont, *TM*, II, p. 264, Figs. 103, 104.

962. Kramer, *MAW*, p. 126.

963. Gordon in Kramer, *MAW*, pp. 201-202; Richter, *Sculpture*, pp. 119-120 and Fig. 376.

964. Seyrig, *Syria*, XV, 1934, p. 168, n. 4.

965. Seyrig, *Syria*, XV, 1934, pp. 165-173; Bonner, *Amulets*, pp. 124-125; Bieber, *Sculpture*, p. 12.

966. Fontenrose, *AJA*, 66, 1962, p. 190; Richter, *Sculpture*, pp. 203, 539 and Fig. 563.

967. Cross, *Library*, pp. 156-162; Yadin, *Message*, pp. 128-143; Gordon in Kramer, *MAW*, p. 201.

968. Gressmann, *OR*, pp. 148, 149, Abb. 56; Cumont, *MM*, pp. 105, 108, 110, and Figs. 20-23; see p. 470.

969. Bieber, *Sculpture*, Figs. 458-468, 470; Avi-Yonah, *IWB*, V, p. 271; Dunand, *Soueïda*, p. 31; Bonner, *Amulets*, pp. 124, 125; Gentili, *ILN*, March 8, 1952, p. 427, Fig. 6; see p. 383.

970. Bieber, *Sculpture*, Figs. 530-533; Avi-Yonah, *IWB*, V, p. 227.

971. Richter, *Sculpture*, pp. 203, 539 and Fig. 563.

972. Kantorowicz, *Gods in Uniform*, pp. 374-375 and Figs. 16, 17; Bonner, *Amulets*, pp. 1-347; Goodenough, *Symbols*, II, pp. 245-258.

973. Bonner, *Amulets*, p. 125.

Chapter XIV

974. For a Nabataean inscribed altar decorated on three sides with reliefs, cf. Cumont, *Doura*, Texte, p. 69, Fig. 15; Hopkins, *Dura*, III, 1932, p. 89 and Pls. XI:2; XII:1, 2.

975. Butler, *PAES*, II, A, 1919, p. 382 and Ill. 330K; p. 385 and Ill. 334.

976. Kitzinger, *Coptic Sculpture*, p. 209 and Pl. LXXV:2.

977. For the use of figures as akroteria, cf. Bieber, *Sculpture*, pp. 9, 13, 72, 118 and Fig. 469.

978. This altar and several others, including the one bearing the Nabataean "Mati'a'el" inscription (Pl. 194) and a plain one are generically related to the *hammanim*, the altars of incense of earlier antiquity; cf. Albright, *BASOR*, 85, Feb. 1942, p. 25; *ARI*, pp. 215-216, n. 58 and references there.

979. Savignac, *RB*, 14, 1905, p. 242.

980. Dunand, *A.Or.*, XVIII:1-2, 1950, p. 145; *Soueïda*, p. 55, no. 91; p. 106, no. 218; Clermont-Ganneau, *RAO*, II, 1898, p. 21a.

981. Savignac, *RB*, XLI, 1932, p. 591, no. 1, near the Nabataean temple in the Wadi Ramm.

982. Abel, *Histoire de la Palestine*, I, p. 252, n. 2, mentions Ya'amru from Umm er-Rasas in Transjordan.

983. I Kings 16:16, 23-28, 20-34; II Kings 8:26; *ANET*, p. 285.

984. Reinach, *Répertoire*, II, p. 13: 3, 4, 5, 7.

985. Dunand, *Soueïda*, pp. 83-84 and Pl. XXXVI:A-D has published a Nabataean altar from Hebran in

Nabataean Syria, on one side of which is a relief of a male deity, whom he identifies as Dionysos-Dusares, and in whose right hand is a long staff, which may be compared to the one held by the Zeus-Hadad figure on the front side of the Khirbet Tannur Alexandros-Amrou altar. The square basalt altar from Hebran, the bottom of which is broken off, bears reliefs of deities on all four sides, each of which has been considerably damaged, with one side having been almost unrecognizably defaced. For the cornucopia held in the left hand of "Dionysos-Dusares," cf. Dunand, *Soueïda*, p. 20 and Pl. VII:37; see p. 125.

986. Hopkins, *AI*, III, 1936, p. 195, and Figs. 7a, b, 9, 10; Rostovtzeff, *DPPA*, pp. 191, 192 and Fig. 31: 1, 3, 4.

987. See p. 433.

988. Bieber, *Sculpture*, pp. 118-119 and Figs. 471-472.

989. Cook, *Zeus*, I, pp. 626-627, Fig. 492.

990. Cook, *Zeus*, I, p. 516, Fig. 389.

991. Smith, *HGHL*, pp. 187-188; Roscher, *Lexikon*, II:1, cols. 1422-1423; II:2, cols. 2379-2382; Cook, *Zeus*, I, p. 149, n. 1; I Corinthians 16:22.

992. Roscher, *Lexikon*, II:2, col. 2380.

993. Smith, *HGHL*, p. 188; Roscher, *Lexikon*, II:2, cols. 2378, 2382; Mendel, *Catalogue*, II, pp. 352-354, no. 611 (172).

994. Reinach, *Catalogue*, p. 11, no. 27; for related figures of Zeus-Hadad on the front of the Alexandros Amrou altar, cf. Reinach, *Répertoire*, II:1, p. 12:2, 3, 5, 6; p. 13:8; Mendel, *Catalogue*, p. 248, no. 535 (1132).

995. Mendel, *Catalogue*, p. 354.

996. Contenau, *Déesse*, pp. 108-110; Avi-Yonah, *QDAP*, X, 1944, p. 115.

997. Contenau, *MAO*, III, p. 1213, Fig. 786.

998. Bieber, *Sculpture*, Figs. 471, 472 and pp. 118-119.

999. Hopkins, *AI*, III, 1936, p. 194.

1000. Cf. Avi-Yonah, *QDAP*, X, 1944, p. 115.

1000a. Ingholt, *Berytus*, III, 1936, p. 98 and Pl. XIX:2; "Hatra", XII, 1954, pp. 8-10 and Pl. I:2, 3; Cumont, *Syria*, XIV, 1933, p. 385 and Pl. XIX:2; "Hatra", XII, 1932, pp. 100-107 and Pl. XIV; Al Asil, *ILN*, Dec. 18, 1954, p. 1116, Figs. 3, 4; p. 1117, Fig. 7; Dec. 25, 1954, p. 1160, Figs. 1, 2.

1001. Hopkins, *AI*, III, 1936, p. 195; Avi-Yonah, *Or. Art*, pp. 78-79; see p. 248.

1002. Savignac, *RB*, 46, 1937, pp. 405-410.

1003. Andrae, *Hatra*, II, p. 154, Fig. 262; Seyrig, *Dura*, IV, 1933, pp. 68-71 and Pl. XV:1.

1004. Parr, *ILN*, Nov. 10, 1962, p. 747, Fig. 7; Bennett, *Archaeology*, 15: 4, 1962, p. 239 top.

1005. Bowen and Albright, *ADSA*, p. 153, Fig. 96; Van Beek, *BA*, XXIII:3, 1960, p. 94, Fig. 6; *ANEP*, pp. 193, 319, Figs. 579, 581; Bossert, *Altsyrien*, p. 303, Figs. 1018 a-c and p. 80; Macalister, *Gezer*, II, pp. 442-444, Figs. 524-526; Reisner, Fisher, Lyon, *Harvard Excavations at Samaria*, II, 1924, Pl. 80 a-c; Avi-Yonah, *QDAP*, XIII, 1948, p. 132, Figs. 2, 3.

1006. Sukenik, *JPOS*, XVII, 1937, pp. 15-30 and Fig. 5; *IEJ*, VIII:2, 1958, p. 133; Perrot, *IEJ*, IX:2, 1959, pp. 266-267.

1007. Akurgal, *Anatoliens*, pp. 12-13, 301, Figs. 3-5.

1008. Lullies, *Greek Sculptures*, pp. 95-96 and Fig. 232.

1009. Cumont, *Recherches sur le Symbolisme Funéraire des Romains*, Pl. XI, facing p. 162; Pl. XVII, facing p. 218; p. 225, Fig. 46; Pl. XVIII:2, facing p. 226; Goodenough, *Symbols*, III, Figs. 106, 109, 112, 113, 139, 204, 205, 209,

237; VI, Fig. 260; VIII, Figs. 1, 16, 44, 164.

1010. The inscription was first published by Père Savignac, *RB*, 46, 1937, pp. 405-408 and Pl. IX:1, 2, and then published by Abbé Starcky, *RB*, 64, 1957, pp. 215-217, whose emended version we are employing.

1011. The translation of *r's* as "master" or "official-in-charge of" was suggested by Starcky, *RB*, 64, 1957, pp. 215-217, who was also the first to point out that the patronymic of Netir'el should be read as Zayd'el and not Zayda. It was Albright, *BASOR*, 67, 1937, p. 14, however, who was the first to point out that *'yn la'aban* was not part of a theophoric name. He translated *r's* as "source" and the entire phrase of Ras *'Ayn La'aban* as the "source of the spring of *La'aban*." Broome, too, in *RB*, 62, 1955, pp. 246-252, recognized that *'Ayn La'aban* referred to a particular locality and was not part of the name of a god.

1012. Savignac, *RB*, 46, 1937, p. 408.

1013. Savignac, *RB*, 46, 1937, p. 407.

1014. Savignac, *RB*, 46, 1937, pp. 409-410; Savignac and Starcky, *RB*, 64, 1957, pp. 215-216.

1015. Parr, *ILN*, Nov. 10, 1962, p. 747, Fig. 9; Bennett, *Archaeology*, XV:4, 1962, p. 239, for a photograph of "crude anthropomorphic idols in early levels at Petra." The one on the right has some resemblance to the Qosmilk stele.

1016. Savignac, *RB*, 46, 1937, p. 409.

1017. Albright, *BASOR*, 72, 1938, p. 12, n. 44.

1018. Savignac, *RB*, 46, 1937, p. 409; *CIS*, II, 207; Jaussen-Savignac, *MA*, I, Inscr. nabat. no. 5, pp. 151-153; *PA*, I, pp. 212, 249.

1019. Jaussen and Savignac, *MA*, II, Text, p. 520, no. 331; p. 521, no. 334.

1020. This was first called to my attention in 1939 by Professor Francis R. Walton of Haverford College, who sent me a copy of the inscription from A. Plassart, *Delos*, XI, "Sanctuaires et Cultes du M. Cynthe," p. 266.

1021. McCown, *AASOR*, XIII, 1933, pp. 155-157; Picard, *Syria*, XVII, 1936, pp. 315-316; Kraeling, *BASOR*, 83, 1941, pp. 7-14; della Vida, *BASOR*, 87, 1942, pp. 29-32; Welles in Kraeling, *Gerasa*, pp. 383-384, inscriptions 17 & 18; Vincent, *RB*, XLIX, 1940, pp. 98-129; Eissfeldt, *Tempel und Kulte syrischer Städte*, p. 25.

1022. See p. 441.

1023. Cf. Schlumberger, *Palmyrene*, Pl. XLVIII, from Kh. Semrine, no. 34.

Chapter XV

1024. Woolley and Lawrence, *Zin*, p. 117 and Pl. XXIV:4; Wiegand, *Sinai*, p. 91, Fig. 6; Avi-Yonah, *QDAP*, X, 1944, p. 138.

1025. Avi-Yonah, *QDAP*, X, 1944, p. 134 and Pl. XXVII:1.

1026. Cf. peacock on pottery lamp from Beit Nattif, Palestine, in Baramki, *QDAP*, V, 1936, p. 5, Pl. VII; Avi-Yonah, *QDAP*, XIII, 1948, p. 138 and Pl. XLII:5.

1027. Avi-Yonah, *QDAP*, XIII, 1948, p. 144 and Pl. XLII:10; Crowfoot, *Churches*, Pl. XXIXb.

1028. Avi-Yonah, *QDAP*, XIII, 1948, pp. 136, 144 and Pl. XLI:7, 10.

1028a. Avi-Yonah, *Or. Art.*, p. 63.

1029. Abel, *Géographie,* p. 54 and n. 5: "Jérôme, *Chron.,* Pl. XXVII, 618, d'où il faut corriger le *Chronicon Paschale,* PG., XCII, 618."

1030. Yadin, *ILN,* Nov. 4, 1961, pp. 772-775; Nov. 11, 1961, pp. 820-822.

1031. Negev, *History of 'Avdat,* pp. 123, 137.

1032. Kitzinger, *Coptic Sculpture,* pp. 206-210.

1033. Hammond, *BA,* XXII:2, 1959, pp. 40-48; Cantineau, *Nabatéen,* I, p. 20, nos. 2, 4.

1034. Kammerer, *Pétra,* pp. 50-52.

1035. Josephus, *War,* IV, 7, 6; 8, 4.

1036. Juvenal, *Satire,* XI, 123-127; Dussaud, *Notes myth. syr.,* p. 181.

1037. Van Beek, *BA,* XXIII:3, 1960, pp. 70-95.

1038. Negev, *History of 'Avdat,* p. 123; Starcky, *BA,* XVIII:4, 1955, p. 94; Strabo, XVI, 3, 3; 4, 18.

1039. Strabo XVI, 3, 3; 4, 18; Van Beek, *BA,* XXIII:3, 1960, p. 77; Pauly-Wissowa, under *Gerrha;* Cumont, *Doura,* pp. XXXIV-XXXVI; Schalit, *Land of Israel* (Hebrew), I, pp. 2-19.

1040. Cantineau, *Nabatéen,* frontispiece map and p. 2; Dussaud, *Arabes en Syrie,* Fig. 1; Kammerer, *Pétra,* Pl. 11, for map of Erythraean Sea; Starcky, *BA,* XVIII:4, 1955, p. 82, Fig. 2; XXIII:3, 1960, p. 90, Fig. 5, for maps of Arabian and Nabataean lands and caravan routes.

1041. Strabo, XVI, 4, 4.

1042. Strabo, XVI, 4, 24; *Periplus,* par. 19.

1043. Strabo, XVI, 4, 23; *Periplus,* par. 19; Cantineau, *Nabatéen,* pp. 2, 3; Starcky, *BA,* XVIII:4, 1955, p. 94; Van Beek, *BA,* XXIII:3, 1960, pp. 76, 80; Littmann, *BSOAS,* XVI, 1954, pp. 240, 241.

1044. Pliny, VI, 26, 102-104; Kammerer, *Pétra,* p. 43, n. 1.

1045. Strabo, XVI, 4, 24; Starcky, *BA,* XVIII:4, 1955, p. 94.

1046. Kammerer, *Pétra,* pp. 42-44, 563; Cantineau, *Nabatéen,* p. 5; Van Beek, *BA,* XXIII:3, 1960, pp. 76-82.

1047. Cantineau, *Nabatéen,* pp. 5-6; Van Beek, *BA,* XXIII:3, 1960, pp. 77-78 and map on p. 90, Fig. 5.

1048. Pliny, *Nat. hist.,* VI, 23-26; Clermont-Ganneau, *RHR,* LXXX, 1919, pp. 22-23; Starcky, *BA,* XVIII:4, 1955, pp. 55, 94; Littmann, *BSOAS,* XVI:2, 1954, pp. 239-241; Van Beek, *BA,* XXIII:3, 1960, p. 77.

1049. Starcky, *BA,* XVIII:4, 1955, p. 94; *Periplus,* par. 19 and p. 29; cf. Pliny the Elder, *Nat. hist.,* VI, 26, 101-104, who points out that transit trade charges on goods from Arabia Felix to Gaza increased the prices of items a hundredfold.

1050. Clermont - Ganneau, *RHR,* LXXX, 1919, p. 22; Kammerer, *Pétra,* pp. 195-196; Plutarch, *Anton.,* 69; Dion Cass. LI, 7; cf. Altheim-Stiehl, *Araber,* pp. 69-72.

1051. Josephus, *War,* I; XIII; V, 4, 5; *Antiq,* XV, 4, 2; 5; Diodorus, II, 48; XIX, 98; Strabo, XVI, 4, 23, Starcky, *BA,* XVIII:4, 1955, p. 93; Hammond, *BA,* XXII:2, 1955, pp. 47-48.

1052. Caesar, *Alexandrian War,* I; Starcky, *BA,* XVIII:4, 1955, p. 92.

1053. Josephus, *Antiq,* XIV, 11, 1; *War,* I, 10, 10.

1054. Cantineau, *Nabatéen,* I, pp. 5-6; Strabo, II, 5, 12; Cumont, *Doura,* pp. XXXIV, XXXV, XXXVI, n. 3; p. LI; Starcky, *BA,* XVIII:4, 1955, pp. 101-106.

1055. Nabataean cavalry was at one time in the service of Palmyra; cf. Cumont, *Doura,* p. L; Littmann, *Semitic Inscriptions,* 1904, p. 70, Fig. 27. These references deal with two altars consecrated at Palmyra by Obaidou, the son of Animu, a Nabataean, "who was a cavalryman stationed at Hirtha and in the camp of Ana." Ana or Anatha is located on an island in the Euphrates about five halting paces downstream from Dura and Hirtha (el-Hireh) is still farther down river on the west bank.

For examples of cavalrymen from Dura-Europos, whom the Nabataean cavalrymen must have resembled, cf. Cumont, *Doura,* p. 270, Fig. 59; p. 271, Fig. 60; Littmann, *BSOAS,* XVI, 1954, p. 241.

1056. Kammerer, *Pétra,* pp. 450-451; Strabo, XVI, 4, 23; Cantineau, *Nabatéen,* p. 2; Clermont-Ganneau, *RAO* II, 1898, p. 381, n. 1; VI, pp. 213-214, mentions a stele discovered in Egypt at el-Ashmunein (Hermopolis Magna, located about midway between Memphis and Thebes, which was the seat of worship of the Egyptian god Thoth, identified with Hermes), which mentions a list of foreign soldiers stationed there, including a number of unmistakable Nabataean names. He refers also to a similar list found at Memphis; cf. Littmann and Meredith, *BSOAS,* XVI, 1954, pp. 239-241; Starcky, *BA,* XVIII: 4, 1955, p. 100, n. 25; Dussaud, *Arabes en Syrie,* pp. 62-70.

1057. Littmann, *BSOAS,* XVI, 1954, pp. 239-241.

1058. Kammerer, *Pétra,* pp. 43-44; 195-196; Clermont-Ganneau, *RHR,* LXXX, 1919, pp. 23-24.

1059. Josephus, *War,* I, 6, 2; 8, 1; IX, 3; XIV, 1, 2; XIX, 1, 2.

1060. Seyrig, *Syria,* XIV, 1933, Pl. XX: 1, 2; see p. 212.

1061. Josephus, *War,* I, 6, 2; III, 4, 2; *Antiq.,* XVII, 10, 9; Horsfield, *QDAP,* IX, 1942, p. 161 and Pl. XXX:253, and p. 198 and Pl.

XLVI:439 for pottery plaques from Petra of Nabataean cavalrymen; for pottery plaques and figurines of horses alone from there, cf. Pl. XII:52, XVII:112, XX:151; XXII:166; XXV:189; XXX:248-252, 254. For small, Nabataean stone sculptures of horses from the Nabataean Hauran, cf. Butler, *PAES,* II, A, 1919, 6, p. 381, Ill. 329; p. 384, Ill. 334:L; Dunand, *Soueïda,* p. 71 and Pl. XXXIII:150, 152.

1062. For pottery figurines of camel-riders and camels from Petra, cf. Horsfield, *QDAP,* IX, 1942, Pls. XXV:188; XLVII, 448.

1063. Kammerer, *Pétra,* pp. 195-196; cf. pp. 43-45, 48-49, 59-61.

1064. For Nabataean inscriptions from Sinai, cf. Cantineau, *Nabatéen,* pp. 47-48, and bibliography, pp. 181-202; Kammerer, *Pétra,* pp. 450-468.

1065. Clermont-Ganneau, *RHR,* Vol. 80, 1919, p. 1; Kammerer, *Pétra,* p. 195.

1066. Finegan, *LfAP,* Map II; Kraeling, *Atlas,* pp. 232-233, Map V; Wright, and Filson, *WHAB,* Maps V and XIII; May, *Atlas,* maps, pp. 59, 94.

1067. Clermont-Ganneau, *RHR,* Vol. 80, 1919, pp. 1-29; Kammerer, *Pétra,* pp. 195-196.

1068. This is evidenced by the long enduring tenacity of the use of the Nabataean-Aramaic language or script for more than two centuries after Trajan had stripped the Nabataeans even of their status of political vassalage. The latest of their inscriptions in Sinai is dated to A.D. 253 (Starcky *BA,* XVIII:4, 1955, p. 106), while a bi-lingual epitaph from Meda'-in Saleh (Hejrah), written in Nabataean and in Arabic is dated to A.D. 267 (Jaussen and Savignac, *MA,* I, no. 17, pp. 172-176), and still another Nabataean one from el Ela in Arabia is dated to A.D. 307 (Jaussen and Savignac, *MA,* II, no. 386, pp. 231-233); Starcky (*BA,* XVIII:4, 1955, p. 105), also calls attention to the epitaph from en-Nemara, east of the Nabataean Jebel Druze, found by Dussaud and Macler, *Mission,* pp. 314-322, of "Imru-l-Qays, son of 'Amr, king of all the Arabs" dated to A.D. 328, the script of which is still Nabataean, but the language of which is Arabic.

1069. Drioton, *BAAAC,* III, 1937, pp. 38-40; Wessel, *Koptische Kunst,* p. 61.

1070. Drioton, *BAAAC,* III, 1937, p. 39; de Villard, *Ahnas,* pp. 81-94.

1071. Schlumberger, *Syria,* XX, 1939, p. 349; Hamilton, *QDAP,* XIV, 1950, pp. 100-119.

1071a. Bowen and Albright, *ADSA,* pp. 85-89; Rossini, *Dalle Rovine Di Ausan,* in *Dedalo,* Dec. 1926, pp. 729-734.

1072. Schlumberger, *Syria,* XX, 1939, pp. 324-373.

1073. Drioton, *BAAAC,* III, 1937, p. 39.

1074. Kitzinger, *Coptic Sculpture,* p. 207.

1075. Cumont, *RO,* pp. 4, 69-94, 236, 261-262; *MM,* pp. 91-96; Cook, *Zeus* I, pp. 188-190, 360; *ILN,* Oct. 16, 1954, p. 637.

1076. Kitzinger, *Coptic Sculpture,* p. 183; Naville, *Ahnas,* pp. 32-34; de Villard, *Ahnas,* pp. 25-50; Drioton, *BAAAC,* III, 1937, pp. 29-40.

1077. Kitzinger, *Coptic Sculpture,* p. 193.

1078. Pelekanides, *Benaki,* pp. 39, 48.

1079. Kitzinger, *Coptic Sculpture,* pp. 188, 195-196, 198-200, 214; Breccia, *Musée,* 1925-1931, pp. 60-64, Pls. 39-51; 1931-1932, pp. 36-45, Pls. XXI:70, XXVIII-XLVII;

L:132; Petrie, *Oxyrhynchos,* Pls. 45-47; Simaika Pacha, *Musée Copte,* p. 11 and Pl. XXII.

1080. Kitzinger, *Coptic Sculpture,* p. 200.

1081. Kitzinger, *Coptic Sculpture,* pp. 195, 200 and Pl. LXXI:2-5, facing p. 194.

1082. Kitzinger, *Coptic Sculpture,* p. 206 and Pl. LXXIV:2, facing p. 199.

1083. Kitzinger, *Coptic Sculpture,* p. 206 and Pl. LXXIV:7.

1084. See p. 196; Baur, *Dura,* III, 1932, p. 104, n. 5; Brown, *Dura,* VII-VIII, 1939, p. 165, n. 4; Hopkins, *AI,* III, 1936, p. 296.

1085. Kitzinger, *Coptic Sculpture,* p. 206, n. 3 and Pl. LXXIV:5.

1086. See p. 245; Hamilton *QDAP,* XIV, 1950, pp. 118-119, finds a Nabataean strain in the ingredients of the style of the stucco reliefs of Khirbet Mafjar, particularly insofar as the sculptures of human faces and of several lions are concerned. He states correctly, p. 106: "In all these heads . . . the unnatural size and protuberance of the eyes, with their drilled pupils and deeply cut corners, the small pouting mouths, the conventionalized hair and the impassive staring faces, combine to convey that blank and impersonal character which stamps comparable sculp-ture of early Palmyrene, Nabataean, Parthian and, later, Sasanian portraiture."

1087. Schlumberger, *Syria,* XX, 1939, pp. 324-373.

1088. See p. 245; Littmann, in Butler, *PAES,* IV, A, 1914, pp. 1-2.

1089. Hamilton, *QDAP,* XIV, 1950, p. 115 and Pl. XLV:5.

1090. Hamilton, *QDAP,* XIV, 1950, Pls. XLIII:1; XLV:1, 7.

PLANS

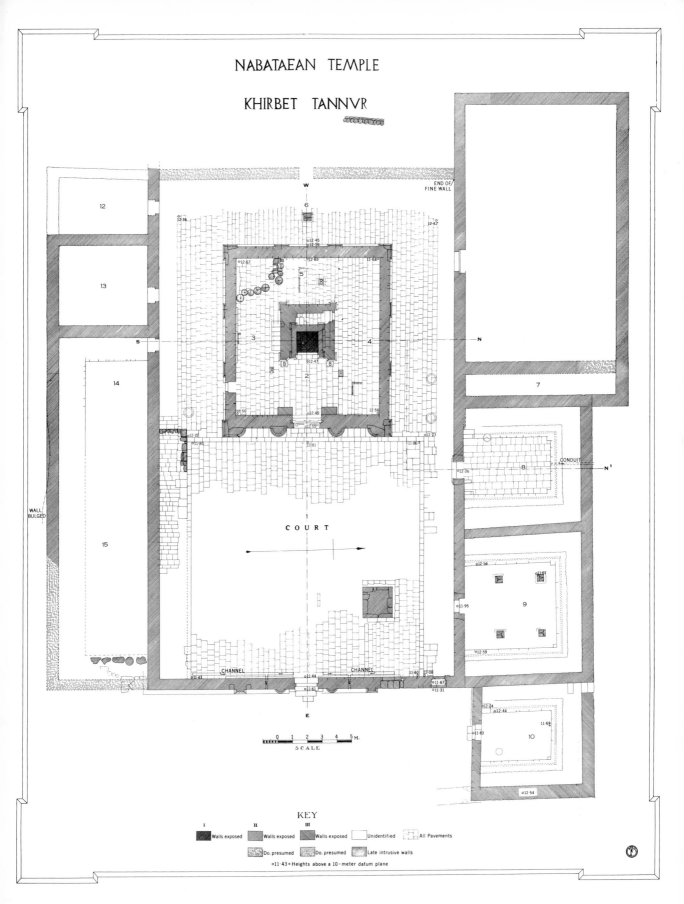

NABATAEAN TEMPLE

KHIRBET TANNVR

KEY

I		II		III				
Walls exposed		Walls exposed		Walls exposed		Unidentified		All Pavements

Do. presumed   Do. presumed   Late intrusive walls

o11·43 = Heights above a 10 - meter datum plane

PLAN A

KHIRBET TANNVR

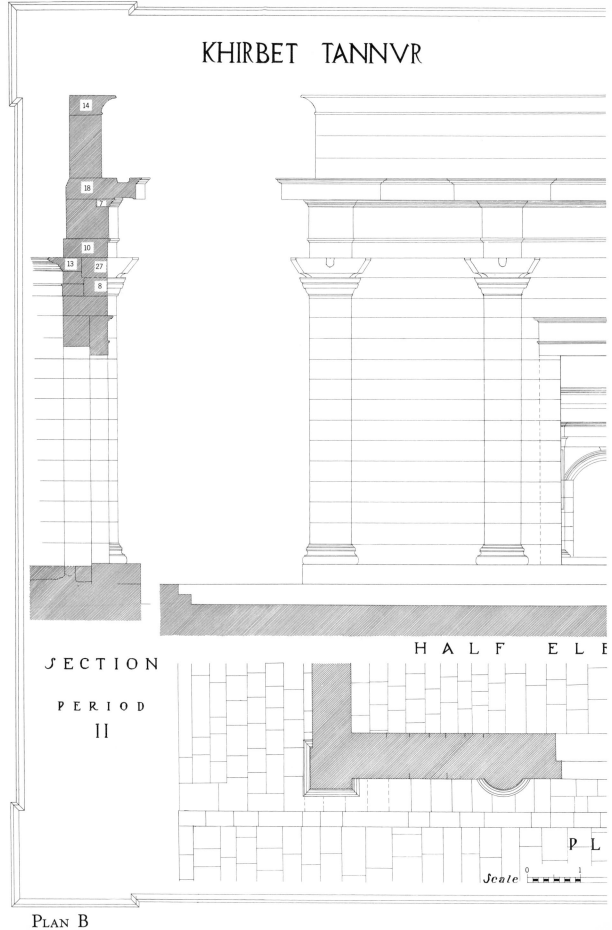

SECTION

PERIOD

II

HALF EL

PL

Scale 0 ⬛⬛⬛⬛ 1

PLAN B

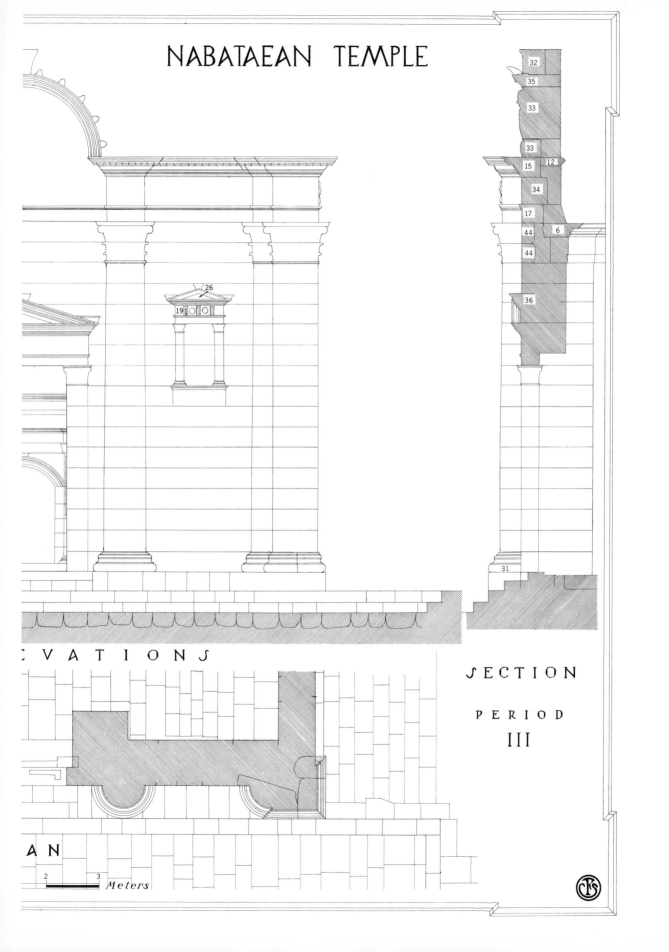

NABATAEAN TEMPLE

EVATIONS

SECTION

PERIOD

III

AN

2   3
Meters

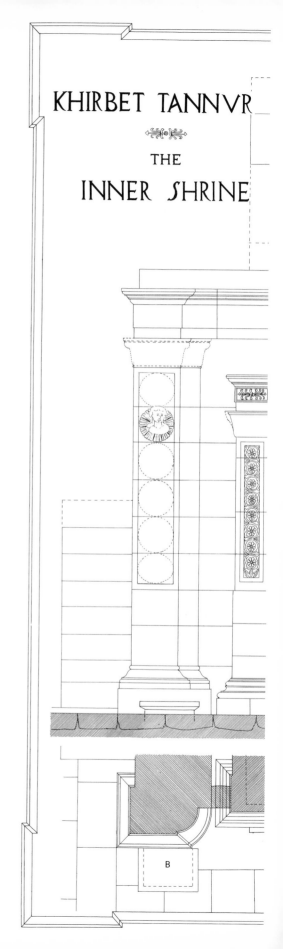

KHIRBET TANNVR

THE

INNER SHRINE

PLAN C

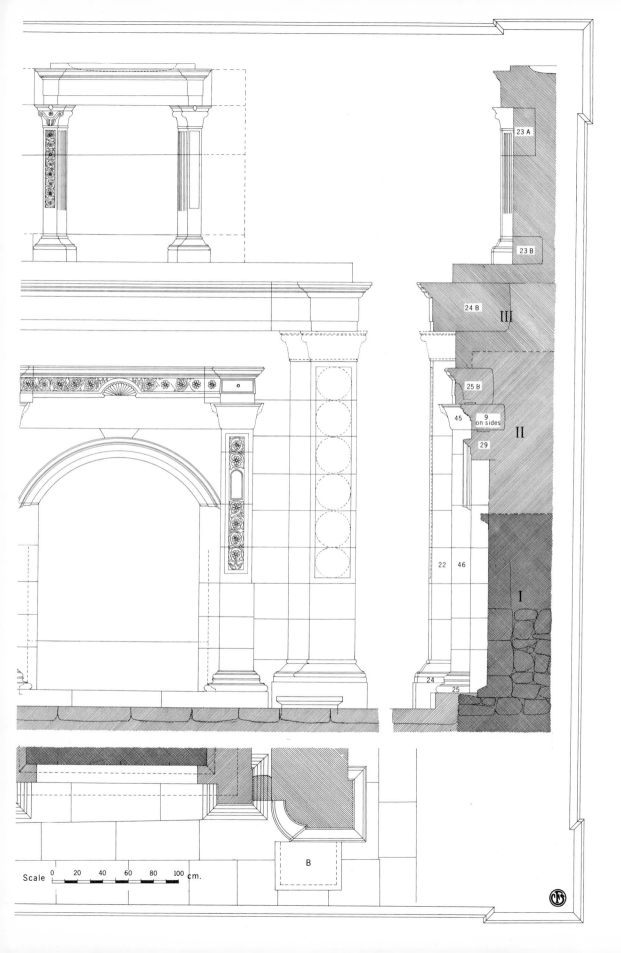

23 A

23 B

24 B III

25 B

45 9 on sides II

29

22 46 I

24 25

B

Scale 0 20 40 60 80 100 cm.

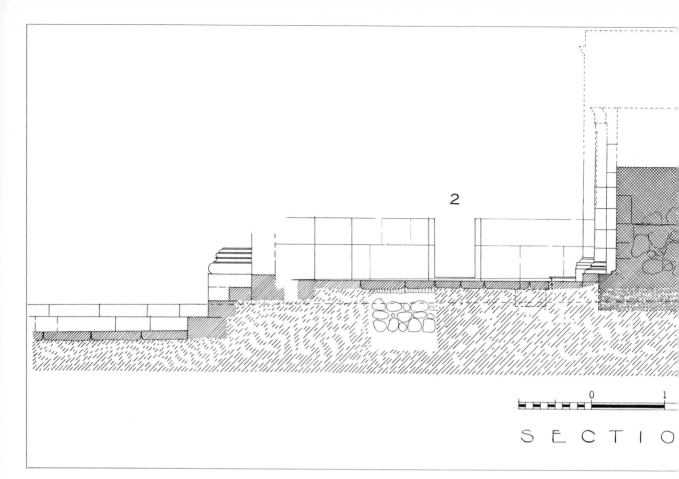

2

0   1

S E C T I O

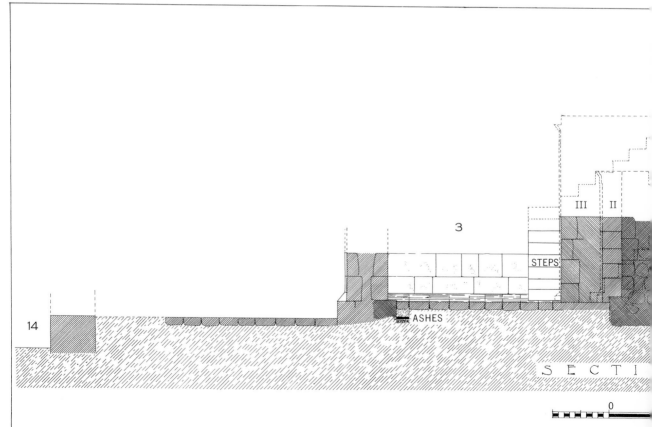

III   II

3

STEPS

14

ASHES

S E C T I

0

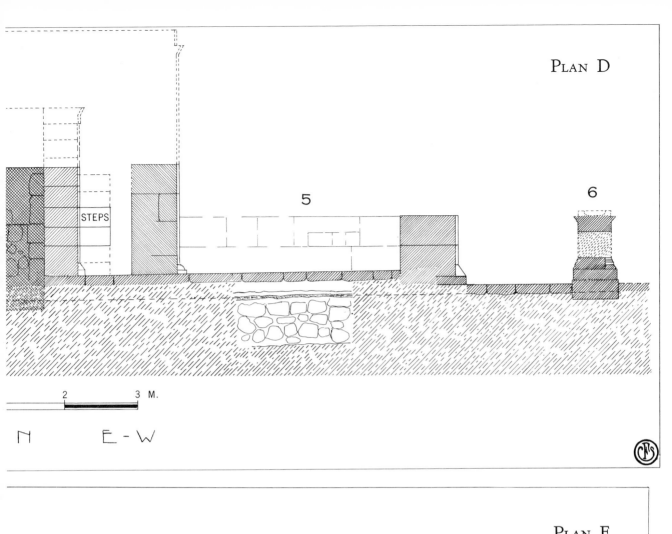

PLAN D

STEPS

5

6

2   3 M.

N   E - W

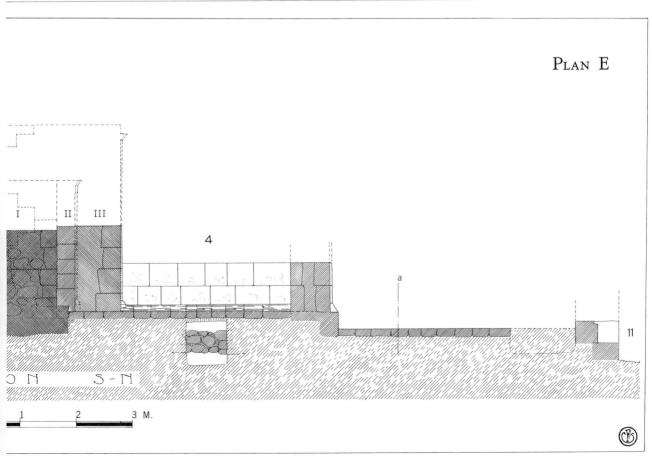

PLAN E

I   II   III

4

a

11

ᴏ N   S - N

1   2   3 M.

a

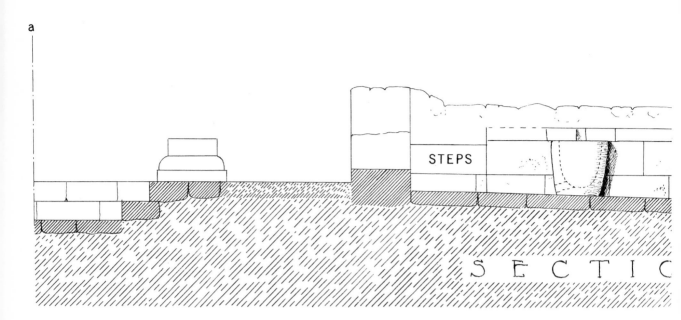

STEPS

SECTIO

8

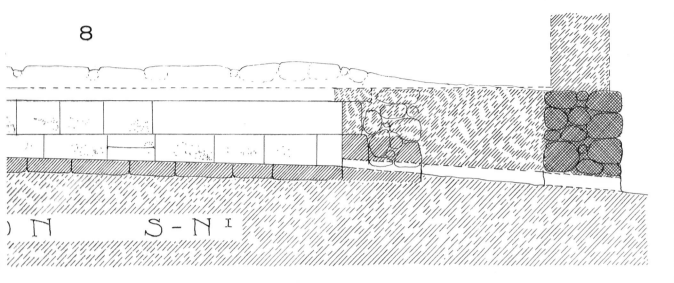

O N   S - Nᴵ

PLAN F

PLAN G

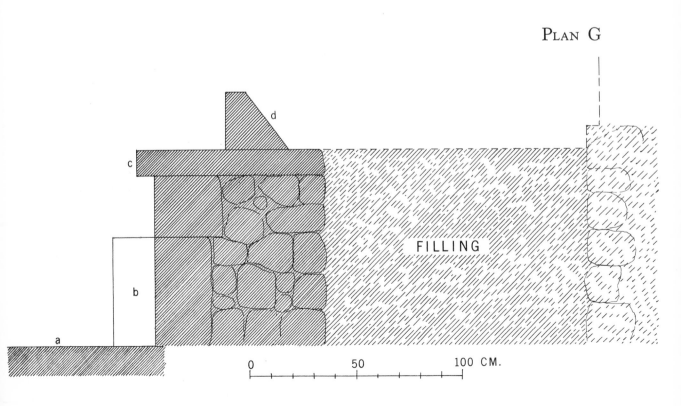

d

c

b

a

FILLING

0   50   100 CM.

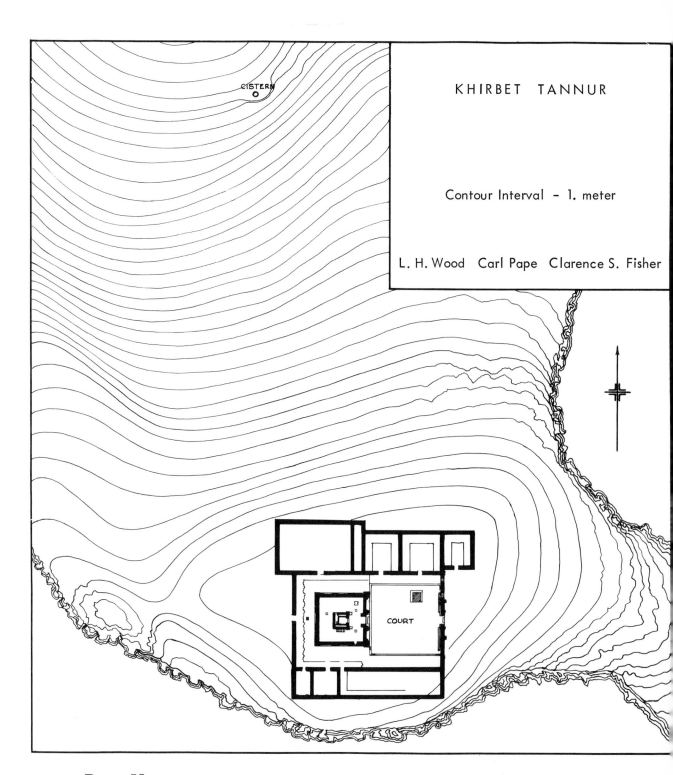

KHIRBET TANNUR

Contour Interval – 1. meter

L. H. Wood   Carl Pape   Clarence S. Fisher

CISTERN

COURT

PLAN H

MAPS

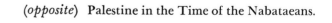
(*opposite*)   Palestine in the Time of the Nabataeans.

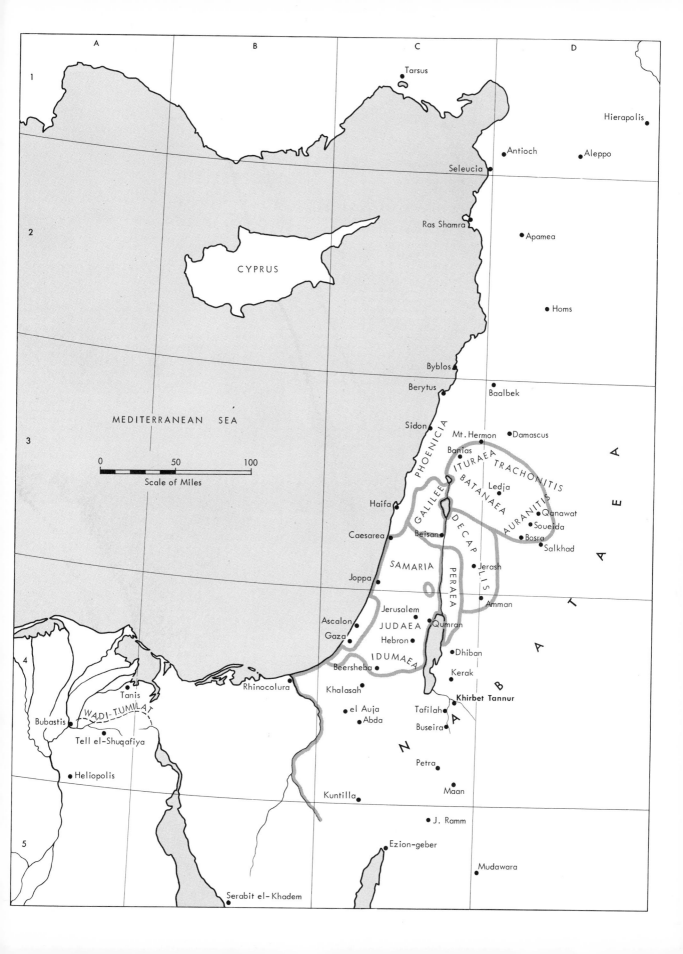

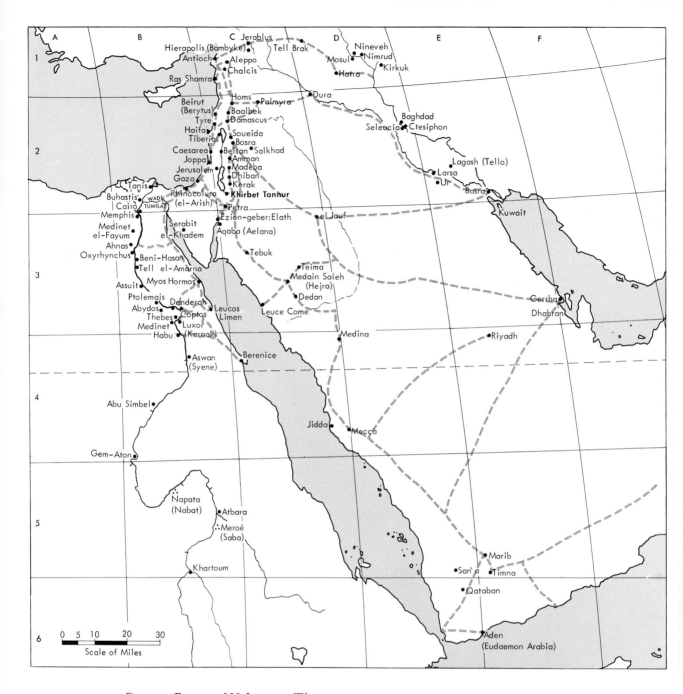

Caravan Routes of Nabataean Times.

Nabataean and Related Sites.

Contemporary World of the Nabataeans between 200 B.C. and A.D. 200.

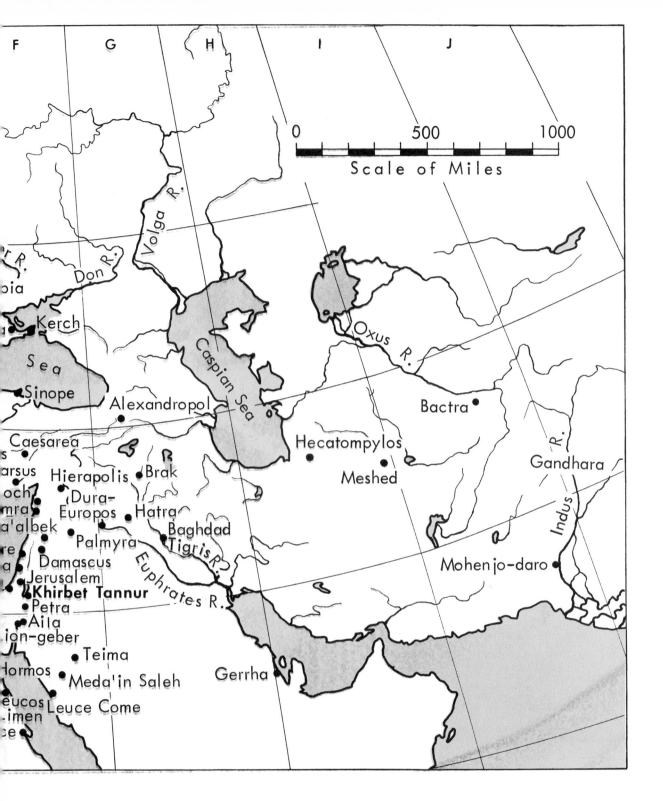

F   G   H   I   J

0   500   1000

Scale of Miles

Volga R.

Don R.

oia

Kerch

Sea

Sinope

Alexandropol

Caspian Sea

Oxus R.

Bactra

Caesarea

Hecatompylos

Gandhara

arsus

Hierapolis   Brak

Meshed

och
mra

Dura-
Europos   Hatra

Indus R.

a'albek

Baghdad

Palmyra   Tigris R.

Damascus

Jerusalem

Mohenjo-daro

Khirbet Tannur

Euphrates R.

Petra

Aila

ion-geber

Teima

Gerrha

Hormos   Meda'in Saleh

eucos   Leuce Come
imen
se

(on following page) Asia Minor and Europe in the Nabataean Period:

1. British Isles
2. Spain
3. Black Sea and Asia Minor
4. Central Europe

Wall of Antonius

Kircudbright

Hadrian's Wall

Chester

Snettisham

Mildenhall

Bath

London

Dorchester

Atlantic Ocean

0 50 100
Scale of Miles

1

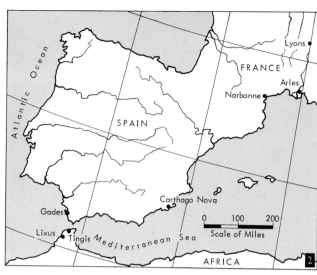

Atlantic Ocean

FRANCE

Lyons

Arles

Narbonne

SPAIN

Gades

Carthago Nova

Lixus

Tingis Mediterranean Sea

AFRICA

0 100 200
Scale of Miles

2

A   B   C   D

1

2

Weser R.   Elbe R.

Rhine R.

Vettersfelde

Oder R.

Hildesheim

Heddernheim

Trier   Mainz

Osterburken

Danube R.

Vienna

3

Hallstatt

Aquileia

Trieste

Rijeka

Pula

Corsica

Tiber R.

Rome

Ostia

Naples

Puteoli   Herculanium

Pompeii

Brundisium

Tarentum

Sardinia

4

Actium

Mycenae

0 50 100   200
Scale of Miles

5

3

A   B   C   D

Chertomlyk

Tanais

1

Olbia

Berezan Is.

Dnieper R.

Sea of Azov

Kerch   Kuban R.

Kul Oba

Great Blitznitsa
(Twin Barrows)

Constanta
(Tomi)

Chersoneus
(Sevastopol)

B L A C K   S E A

2

Sinope

Heraclea

Byzantium

Chalcedon

Halys R.

Troy

Caesarea
(Kayseri)

Pergamum

Aegean
Sea

Smyrna   Sardis

Chalcis

Ephesus   Maeander R.

Hierapolis

Athens

Miletus   Aphrodisias

Tarsus

Alexandria

3

Corinth

Lerna

Cos

Aleppo

Delos

Cnidus

Antioch

0 100 200
Scale of Miles

4

INDICES

INDEX OF BIBLICAL CITATIONS